THE
WUERTTEMBERG
EMIGRATION
INDEX

Volume Four

THE WUERTTEMBERG EMIGRATION INDEX

Volume Four

By *Trudy Schenk*
and *Ruth Froelke*

P.O. Box 476
Salt Lake City, UT 84110

Library of Congress Catalog Card Number 85-052453
ISBN Number 0-916489-26-4   (Hardbound)

First Printing 1988
10 9 8 7 6 5 4 3 2 1

Printed in the United States of America

Acknowledgements

I n compiling this book and preparing the manuscript for publication, we wish to express our appreciation to Hans Erwin Froelke for his valuable assistance.

Our appreciation is further directed to the staff of the European Reference section of the Genealogical Library of The Church of Jesus Christ of Latter-day Saints for their encouragement of our endeavor to get this volume completed and for free use of their equipment.

Finally, we express appreciation to the Wuerttemberg archive officials who made the microfilming of the Ludwigsburg Wuerttemberg emigration records possible.

Foreword

I recall a conversation which took place four or five years ago at the so-called "professional genealogists table" in the cafeteria of the LDS Church Office Building in Salt Lake City. Someone said, "Wouldn't it be nice if there were an index to the Wuerttemberg emigration registers?" We all murmured in agreement, shuddered a bit at the thought of the amount of work involved, and switched the conversation to more congenial topics.

Fortunately, at a nearby table where German was the language of luncheon conversation, three of our professional colleagues decided to do something more than indulge in wishful thinking about the Wuerttemberg registers. The initial results of their labor are in your hands.

Why have professional genealogists and others knowledgeable about German-American genealogy so eagerly awaited the publication of this index? Perhaps the best way to explain this is to cite an example. The name of Otto Walter, born in Ravensburg, Wuerttemberg, in 1832 will appear in Volume II of this work, as will that of his brother Karl, born in 1828. Otto Walter's descendants, like so many Americans of German extraction, wanted to know where he had come from in the Old World. They retained Trudy Schenk to find his exact birthplace.

The case proved to be unusually difficult. According to one family story, Otto came from Wuerttemberg. But another story said his brother Karl emigrated to California from the neighboring German state of Baden. Still another family story said the brothers were from a place called "Oldhouse." This led Mrs. Schenk to search the parish registers of every village in Baden and Wuerttemberg named Altheim, only to come up empty on all counts.

The U.S. Census returns listed only Wuerttemberg or Germany. Since Otto died before 1900, his year of emigration was not known. The naturalization papers of both brothers merely listed Wuerttemberg. All the other available American sources failed to provide the village of origin.

The key to solving the problem proved to be the Wuerttemberg emigration registers. During the preparation of this index, Mrs. Schenk found Otto Walter's name in the emigration registers of Oberamt Ravensburg. But until the publication of this volume, these registers were almost totally inaccessible to the genealogist. One faced the formidable task of reading through hundreds of reels of microfilm containing unindexed records written in difficult (for the novice virtually indecipherable) gothic script.

It should be stressed that this index does not confine itself to emigrants destined for North America. One can find names of individuals headed for the four corners of the earth, e.g. Australia, South America, and even Russia. In fact, many families left Wuerttemberg in the late eighteenth and early nineteenth centuries for a new life on the steppes of southern Russia.

But by the 1870s the threat of serving in the Czar's army caused many of them to look elsewhere for a permanent home. Tens of thousands resettled on the Great Plains of North America. With the passage of time, their descendants have become interested in the saga of the Germans from Russia. But since archives in the Soviet Union do not respond to genealogical inquiries, the quest often seemed quite hopeless. Now, with the publication of this index, many families of German-Russian descent will be able to trace their ancestral lines back to Wuerttemberg.

In summary, the publication of this index rates as a milestone in German emigrant genealogy. By using it, the family historian can avoid years of futile effort. Volume I is at hand and I eagerly await those to follow.

Richard W. Dougherty, Ph.D.

Introduction

The Wuerttemberg emigration records are a unique collection of papers and documents on applicants who filed for permission to emigrate from Wuerttemberg during the nineteenth century. These records are not alphabetized nor are the pages numbered, which makes a search through them complicated and time consuming. In many cases, as many as eight pages were written on one person, including a birth certificate or a family record, military release, and renunciation of citizenship rights. Often the handwriting in these documents is almost indecipherable for even an experienced German researcher. It is almost impossible for a layman to search through these records successfully.

Emigrants leaving without permission are, of course, not listed at the time of emigration. Yet many of these emigrants, later in life, after having arrived in the land of their destination, sent word back to the Wuerttemberg state and town officials renouncing their citizenship rights. Such repudiation is also documented in the Wuerttemberg emigration records.

There were as many as 800,000 people who emigrated to other parts of the world from Wuerttemberg since the late seventeenth century, including the period after World War II. A great number of those who emigrated to the German colonies in the Russian Empire, came to the United States in the nineteenth and early twentieth centuries. Indeed, a significant percentage of all German emigrants to North America have come from Wuerttemberg.

This volume of alphabetized names, containing such vital records as birthdate and place of origin, is a vital work for the genealogist and family historian researching their German heritage.

All information included in this volume of the *Wuerttemberg Emigration Index* has been extracted from the original Wuerttemberg emigration records filmed at Ludwigsburg and available on microfilm at the Genealogical Society of Utah in Salt Lake City. Although all of the records were handwritten by German speaking people, the spelling of names varies from one document to the other. In cases where applicants used their own signature, that spelling was used.

The user of this book should be aware of an anglicized spelling change in the United States and check out several spelling possibilities. All names listed are spelled in the most common German way. For instance a man's name "John" in America can be shown as "Johann" or even "Hans." Place names are all spelled as they will be listed in a German gazetteer or located on a German map.

One important fact should be observed when using a modern map of Germany or a map of Wuerttemberg: Within the last twenty years small villages have merged and often a new name was designated. For example, the village of Kaltenwesten in Oberamt Besigheim does not exist on any map or German gazetteer. It can only be located in conjunction with the village Neckarwestheim. Therefore, it is advisable to consult older maps in trying to locate a given area.

The original Wuerttemberg emigration records were compiled according to the Oberamt to which the applicant belonged. An Oberamt is roughly equivalent to a district town (or county seat in America).

The country of destination for each emigrant is given and regions such as Maehren (Moravia), Siebenbuergen (Transylvania), Rumaenien (Romania), Sudetenland and Czechoslovakia, which were all part of the Austrian empire, are designated as Austria. The actual emigration record gives more details on each single applicant.

Some names may be difficult to locate because of peculiarities in the German language. German surnames that carry an "Umlaut," i.e. a modified vowel (ä, ö, ü), have been changed to their English equivalents; thus ä = ae, ö = oe, ü = ue are indexed as such. Surnames composed of two or more distinct words have been alphabetized under the final word. Thus, von Vogel is found as Vogel von.

When a family or husband and wife applied jointly, the entry would be as follows: Knoedler, Johann & F, with all children listed in alphabetical order if their names were given on the application. The wife would be listed under both her married and maiden name. In a case where children may have left at an earlier time, and if such a notation is made on the application, these children will be listed with the family leaving later. In such an instance, the "Emigration" column will read "bef. 1856" (if this happens to be the date the family is making application). Occasionally the recording official will give the actual date for the early emigrants, but not their names. The reader is advised to follow every lead and check the microfilm originals for possible additional information. In case of a widow with children or a single woman with an illegitimate child, the listing will appear as follows: Widmann, Heinrike & C. A widow also may be listed as Widmann, Heinrike & F.

The date of application for emigration should not be assumed to be the date of emigration. In several cases, emigration was not granted until some time later, or the emigrant had already left secretly before that date.

ABBREVIATIONS

A-dam	= Amsterdam		Nuernb.	= Nuernberg
Augsb.	= Augsburg		Offenb.	= Offenburg
Austral	= Australia		Oldenb.	= Oldenburg
Bessar	= Bessarabien		Palest	= Palestine
D-dorf	= Dusseldorf		Pommer	= Pommerania
Darmst	= Darmstadt		Pr.-Pol	= Prussia Poland
F-burg	= Freiburg		Regb.	= Regensburg
Frankf.	= Frankfurt		Rhld.	= Rheinland
Hannov.	= Hannover		Rus-Pol	= Russia-Poland
Holst	= Holstein		S. Afri	= South Africa
Kreuzn.	= Kreuznach		S.-Amer	= South America
L-burg	= Luxemberg		S.-Russ	= South Russia
Landsb.	= Landsberg		Slovan	= Slovania
M-burg	= Mecklenburg		Switz.	= Switzerland
M-heim	= Mannheim		Thur.	= Thuringia
N.-Amer	= North America		W.-Prs	= West Prussia
Neck	= Neckarsulm		W.-Russ	= West Russia
Nuer.	= Nuertingen		Westf.	= Westphalia

ABBREVIATIONS OF OBERAEMTER = DISTRICT TOWNS

Aal	= Aalen		Herr	= Herrenberg
Bal	= Balingen		Hlbr	= Heilbronn
Bckn	= Backnang		Hll	= Hall
Bes	= Besigheim		Hor	= Horb
Bib	= Biberach		Kntl	= Knittlingen
Bib	= Blaubeuren		Krch	= Kirchheim*
Boeb	= Boeblingen		Kzs	= Kuenzelsau
Brck	= Brackenheim		Leon	= Leonberg*
Cal	= Calw		Lph	= Laupheim
Can	= Cannstatt		Ltk	= Leutkirch
Crls	= Crailsheim		Lud	= Ludwigsburg
Eh	= Ehingen		Marb	= Marbach
Ellw	= Ellwangen		Mibr	= Maulbronn
Essl	= Esslingen		Mrg	= Mergentheim
Frd	= Freudenstadt		Muens	= Muensingen
Gld	= Gaildorf		Nag	= Nagold
Gmd	= Gmuend		Nbg	= Neuenbuerg
Goep	= Goeppingen		Nds	= Neckarsulm
Grb	= Gerabronn		Ner	= Neresheim
Gsl	= Geislingen*		Nuert	= Nuertingen
Hdh	= Heidenheim		Obd	= Oberndorf

Oehr	= Oehringen		Tett	= Tettnang
Rav	= Ravensburg		Tueb	= Tuebingen
Rdl	= Riedlingen		Tutt	= Tuttlingen
Rtb	= Rottenburg		Ulm	= Ulm
Rtl	= Reutlingen*		Ur	= Urach
Rtw	= Rottweill		Vaih	= Vaihingen
Schd	= Schorndorf		Wbl	= Waiblingen
Slg	= Saulgau		Wlds	= Waldsee
Slz	= Sulz		Wng	= Wangen
Spch	= Spaichingen		Wnsb	= Weinsberg
Stu	= Stuttgart		Wlz	= Welzheim

*This indicates that the records for this Oberamt are contained in this volume. It *does not* mean that *every* record has been extracted, for new records are being added constantly. The compilers have made every effort to extract an Oberamt as completely as possible, but it cannot be assumed that it is one hundred percent complete. Check every volume of the index for the particular surname you are researching. Listed below are the Oberamts contained in previous volumes.

Volume One = Backnang; Besigheim; Biberach; Blaubeuren; Boeblingen; Brackenheim; Calw; Horb

Volume Two = Nagold; Nuertingen; Rottenburg; Rottweill; Schorndorf

Volume Three = Balingen; Calw; Freudenstadt; Herrenberg; Nagold; Sulz

Königreich ⚜ Württemberg.

Kreis. Oberamt

Bürgerrechts-Verzichts-Urkunde

zur Auswanderung.

Der Unterzeichnete *Adolph Friedrich Brauchler* geboren den *17 Apr. 1856* evangelischer Confession, *bei seinem Militär* *steht in Jahr 1876 ...* welcher nach *Nord Amerika* auszuwandern, und sich daselbst häuslich niederzulassen gesonnen ist,

bekennt durch gegenwärtige Urkunde, daß er in diesem Vorhaben auf *sein* bisheriges *Gemeindebürger* Recht zu *Aich bei Nürtingen* und auf jede Art von bürgerlichem Verband mit dem Württembergischen Staat *für sich, und seine*

willentlich und wohlbedächtig Verzicht leistet.

Zugleich verpflichtet *Adolph Friedrich Brauchler*

sich, von dem Wegzug an innerhalb Jahresfrist gegen Seine Majestät den König und das Königreich Württemberg nicht zu dienen, und eben so lange in Hinsicht auf alle nach *seinem* Wegzug etwa noch zur Sprache kommenden, vor demselben an *ihn* erwachsenen Ansprüche vor den obrigkeitlichen Behörden des Königreichs, Recht zu geben, indem *er* für die Erfüllung dieser Verbindlichkeiten den *seinen Vater...*

als Bürgen stellt, welcher zugleich für alle nachkommenden Schulden mit seinem Vermögen haftet.

Gefertigt zu *Aich* den *8 April* 18*78*

Gesehen durch das Königl.

Oberamt

den   18

T. Der Auswanderungslustige

Friedrich Brauchler

T. Der Bürge und Selbstzähler

Adam Brauchler

Example of Wuerttemberg Emigration Application

Abschrift. *Duplicat.*

N° 1/1852 der Agentur *Nagold*

Schiffs-Accord!

N°

Urkundlich, dieses verpflichtet sich der

Verein zur Beförderung deutscher Auswanderer

v o n

Dr. G. Strecker in Mainz, **Anton Joseph Klein** in Bingen und **Joseph Stöck** in Creuznach,

vertreten durch ihren bevollmächtigten und obrigkeitlich concessionirten Hauptagenten für das Königreich Würtemberg, Herrn **Louis Wölffel**, Kaufmann in Stuttgart wohnhaft,

Christian Erhard, Taglöhner von Haiterbach, Wittwer,

seine Tochter Christiana Barbara, f. 65.

[...] f. 65.

Magdalena Hufer, Wittwe, f. 65.

drei Kinder von 8, 7, 5 Jahren à f. 43. f. 129.

ein Kind von 3/4 Jahren (Säugling) f. 324

Abfahrt über den Atlantik am [...] die Reisenden müssen 50.

15 Februar 1852, in New-York [...] Person

laut Uebereinkunft von *Mannheim* nach *Antwerpen* und von da durch Vermittelung der Herren *Dr. Strecker, Klein und Stöck selbst*

auf dem in der Quittung zu benamenden Schiffe, und an dem dabei zu bestimmenden Abfahrttage unter nachstehenden Bedingungen nach *New-York in Nord-Amerika* zu befördern.

§. 1. Die Passagiere erhalten zur Fahrt von *Mannheim* bis in den Seehafen die nöthigen Billets für die Dampfschiffe und für die Eisenbahn von Cöln bis Antwerpen, wenn letztere benützt wird.

Auf dieser Fahrt haben die Passagiere freien Transport von einem Zentner Reisegepäcke pr. Person.

§. 2. Die Kosten der Visitation an den Gränzen und des Durchzugs des wirklichen Reisegepäcks hat der Verein zu tragen. Die Nachtheile unrichtiger Angabe, oder einer Verheimlichung ihrer Effekten und Waaren fallen lediglich den Eigenthümern zur Last.

§. 3. In den Städten, in welchen übernachtet wird, müssen die Passagiere auf ihre eigenen Kosten logiren; dagegen werden ihre Effekten, für sie kostenfrei, von einem Dampfschiffe auf das andere, so wie auf die Eisenbahn und in das Seeschiff gebracht. Die Eigenthümer müssen jedoch ihr Gepäck selbst überwachen, weil der Verein für Verwechselungen, Entwendungen u. s. w. nicht einzustehen hat.

§. 4. In dem Seehafen können die Passagiere spätestens am Tage vor der bestimmten Abfahrt an Bord des für ihre Ueberfahrt bestimmten Schiffes gehen, sich einrichten und wohnen, jedoch nicht kochen und rauchen, so lange dasselbe im Hafen liegt.

§. 5. Der durch gesetzliche Verfügung vorgeschriebene Seeproviant *wird den Reisenden [...]*

[...] wird ihnen verabreicht.

Die nöthigen Säcke, Gefäße und Kochgeschirre müssen die Passagiere jedenfalls selbst stellen.

Diejenigen, welchen dieser Seeproviant oder die nöthigen Mittel zu dessen Anschaffung fehlen, können nicht eingeschifft werden und müssen zurückgewiesen werden.

Example of Wuerttemberg Emigration Application

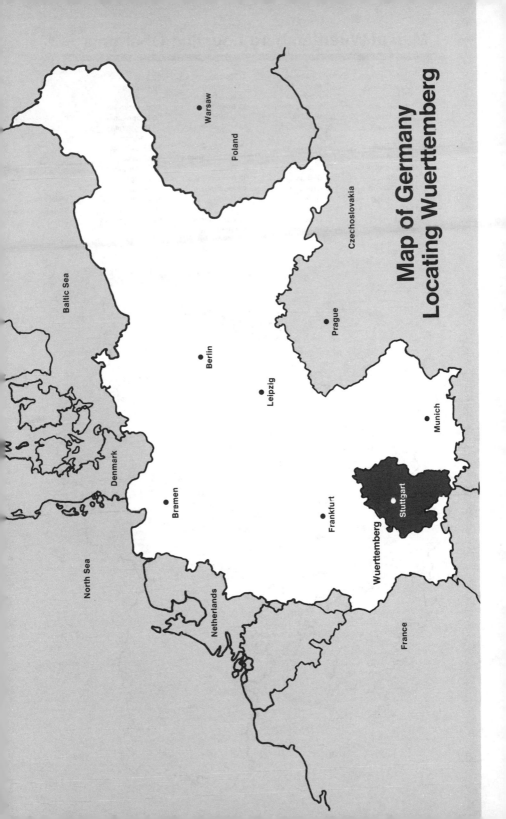

Map of Germany
Locating Wuerttemberg

Map of Wuerttemberg Locating Oberamts

1 Mergentheim
2 Kuenzelsau
3 Gerabronn
4 Oehringen
5 Neckarsulm
6 Weinsberg
7 Hall
8 Crailsheim
9 Heilbronn
10 Brackenheim
11 Knittlingen
12 Besigheim
13 Backnang
14 Gaildorf
15 Ellwangen
16 Maulbronn

17 Vaihingen
18 Marbach
19 Welzheim
20 Ludwigsburg
21 Waiblingen
22 Schorndorf
23 Aalen
24 Neresheim
25 Gmuend
26 Cannstatt
27 Stuttgart
28 Leonberg
29 Calw
30 Esslingen
31 Goeppingen
32 Heidenheim

33 Geislingen
34 Kirchheim
35 Nuertingen
36 Boeblingen
37 Neuenburg
38 Herrenberg
39 Nagold
40 Tuebingen
41 Freudenstadt
42 Horb
43 Rottenburg
44 Reutlingen
45 Urach
46 Ulm
47 Muensingen
48 Blaubeuren

49 Sulz
50 Oberndorf
51 Balingen
52 Ehingen
53 Laupheim
54 Riedlingen
55 Rottweil
56 Spaichingen
57 Biberach
58 Tuttlingen
59 Saulgau
60 Waldsee
61 Leutkirch
62 Ravensburg
63 Tettnang
64 Wangen

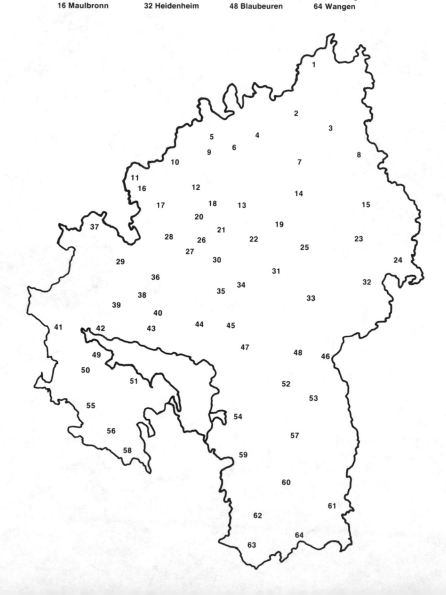

Abele, Alois	16 Apr 1850	Boehmenkirch	Gsl.	Aug 1870	N.-Amer	572047
Abele, Franz Joseph & F		Boehmenkirch	Gsl.	Jan 1854	N.-Amer	572042
Abele, Georg Jacob	29 Jun 1833	Eningen	Rtl	Oct 1868	N.-Amer	841051
Abele, Maria (wid.)		Alfdorf/Welzheim	Krch.	Sep 1866	N.-Amer	835944
Abele, Mariana	28 yrs.	Boehmenkirch	Gsl.	Mar 1850	N.-Amer	577788
Aberle, Anton	9 Sep 1830	Gosbach	Gsl.	1851	N.-Amer	572042
Aberle, Constantin	21 May 1837	Gosbach	Gsl.	Sep 1851	N.-Amer	577788
Aberle, Franz Anton	9 Sep 1830	Gosbach	Gsl.	Sep 1851	N.-Amer	577788
Aberle, Johannes	29 Mar 1836	Gosbach	Gsl.	Sep 1851	N.-Amer	577788
Aberle, Joseph	15 Jan 1839	Gosbach	Gsl.	Sep 1855	N.-Amer	572043
Abt, Andreas	11 Sep 1835	Roetenbach	Obd.	Jan 1867	France	838636
Ackerer, Mathilde	16 yrs.	Betzweiler	Obd.	Apr 1861	N.-Amer	838631
Ackerknecht, Caroline Frieder.	17 Aug 1849	Kirchheim	Krch.	Feb 1862	N.-Amer	835941
Ackerknecht, Ferdinand Gottl.	28 Apr 1833	Herrenberg	Herr.	bef 1870	N.-Amer	834629
Ackerknecht, Johann Friedrich	5 Jul 1838	Kirchheim	Krch.	Feb 1862	N.-Amer	835941
Ackerknecht, Rosine Frieder.	27 Sep 1838	Herrenberg	Herr.	bef 1870	N.-Amer	834629
Ackerle, Gregor Johannes		Weil im Dorf	Loen.	bef 1866	Russia	837967
Ackerle, Jacob Friedrich	31 Mar 1832	Weil im Dorf	Loen.	1854	N.-Amer	837967
Ackermann, Adam Friedrich	12 May 1838	Heimsheim	Leon.	Sep 1864	Holland	837955
Ackermann, Johannes	22 Aug 1837	Leonberg	Leon.	Dec 1865	N.-Amer	835787
Ade, Albert	24 Oct 1849	Oberndorf	Obd.	Dec 1869	Bavaria	838635
Ade, Ignaz		Oberndorf	Obd.	Apr 1816	Austria	838635
Ade, Peter		Oberndorf	Obd.	Jan 1816	Austria	838635
Adix, Katharina (wife)		Reutlingen	Rtl.	Mar 1862	N.-Amer	841057
Adix, Xaver & W		Reutlingen	Rtl.	Mar 1862	N.-Amer	841057
Adrian, Caroline Louise	3 Mar 1827	Alpirsbach	Obd.	Sep 1869	France	838630
Adrion, Andreas		Ehlenbogen	Obd.	bef 1869	N.-Amer	838632
Adrion, Christian		Ehlenbogen	Obd.	bef 1869	N.-Amer	838632
Adrion, Christina	29 Aug 1833	Bochingen	Obd.	Aug 1854	N.-Amer	838632
Adrion, Christina (wid.) & F		Ehlenbogen	Obd.	Apr 1861	N.-Amer	838632
Adrion, Dorothea	27 Apr 1826	Bochingen	Obd.	Aug 1854	N.-Amer	838632
Adrion, Dorothea	17 Mar 1831	Bochingen	Obd.	Aug 1852	N.-Amer	838632
Adrion, Friedrich	25 Mar 1833	Bochingen	Obd.	Jan 1852	N.-Amer	838632
Adrion, Gabriel		Ehlenbogen	Obd.	May 1866	N.-Amer	838632
Adrion, Gabriel	29 Apr 1829	Bochingen	Obd.	Aug 1852	N.-Amer	838632
Adrion, Johann Georg	27 yrs.	Peterzell	Obd.	Sep 1852	N.-Amer	838635
Adrion, Johannes		Ehlenbogen	Obd.	Apr 1861	N.-Amer	838632
Adrion, Johannes	16 Sep 1837	Bochingen	Obd.	Sep 1852	N.-Amer	838632
Adrion, Magdalena	30 Sep 1828	Bochingen	Obd.	Sep 1852	N.-Amer	838632
Ahle, Jakob	15 Apr 1830	Flacht	Leon.	bef 1860	N.-Amer	835790
Aichele, Anna Maria (wife)		Jabenhausen	Krch.	Aug 1859	N.-Amer	835946
Aichele, Johann Michael	7 Feb 1824	Bissingen	Krch.	bef 1861	N.-Amer	835943
Aichele, Michael & F	26 Sep 1811	Neidlingen	Krch.	Aug 1859	N.-Amer	835946
Aichele, Philipp Jakob	30 Mar 1824	Gaertringen	Herr.	bef 1864	N.-Amer	834630
Aichele, Wilhelmine	15 Sep 1835	Heimsheim	Leon.	Aug 1862	Switz.	837955
Aichelmann, Franz	23 Apr 1833	Harthausen	Obd.	Sep 1853	N.-Amer	838633
Aichelmann, Juliana	14 Feb 1805	Harthausen	Obd.	Oct 1845	N.-Amer	838633
Aichelmann, Katharina	14 Jan 1839	Harthausen	Obd.	Feb 1864	N.-Amer	838633
Aichelmann, Ludwika	15 Apr 1863	Harthausen	Obd.	Jun 1870	N.-Amer	838633
Aichelmann, Therese		Epfendorf	Obd.	May 1817	N.-Amer	838632

Name		Birth		Emigration			Film
Last	First	Date	Place	O'amt	Appl. Date	Dest.	Number
Aichlen, Johann Jacob			Reutlingen	Rtl.	Aug 1834	N.-Amer	841051
Aickele, Margaretha		5 Mar 1834	Reutlingen	Rtl.	Apr 1863	N.-Amer	841051
Aigeldinger, Christian		10 Dec 1845	Talhausen	Obd.	Jul 1847	N.-Amer	838632
Aigeldinger, Johannes		31 Mar 1843	Talhausen	Obd.	Jul 1847	N.-Amer	838632
Aigeldinger, Katharina		24 Nov 1837	Talhausen	Obd.	Jul 1847	N.-Amer	838632
Aigeldinger, Konrad & F		25 Oct 1806	Talhausen	Obd.	Jul 1847	N.-Amer	838632
Aigeldinger, Maria (wife)		28 Jun 1814	Talhausen	Obd.	Jul 1847	N.-Amer	838632
Aigeldinger, Moritz		23 Sep 1834	Talhausen	Obd.	Jul 1847	N.-Amer	838632
Aigeldinger, Theodora		8 Nov 1839	Talhausen	Obd.	Jul 1847	N.-Amer	838632
Aigle, Caroline		9 yrs.	Winzeln	Obd.	Oct 1852	N.-Amer	841016
Aigle, Johann & F			Winzeln	Obd.	Oct 1852	N.-Amer	841016
Aiple, Albert		8 Jun 1833	Waldmoessingen	Obd.	Mar 1853	N.-Amer	841015
Aiple, Dionisius			Epfendorf	Obd.	1852	N.-Amer	838632
Aiple, Fidel & F			Winzeln	Obd.	May 1817	N.-Amer	841016
Aiple, Gregor		20 yrs.	Epfendorf	Obd.	Sep 1853	N.-Amer	838632
Aiple, Johannes		34 yrs.	Waldmoessingen	Obd.	bef 1862	N.-Amer	841015
Aiple, Roman			Epfendorf	Obd.	bef 1852	N.-Amer	838632
Aittermann, Johannes			Leonberg	Leon.	Apr 1866	Austria	835787
Alber, Barbara		28 yrs.	Hausen a.d. Wurm	Leon.	Feb 1817	Russia	837954
Alber, Christoph Friedrich			Gerlingen	Leon.	Jul 1860	N.-Amer	837953
Alber, Johann Konrad		14 Nov 1850	Gebersheim	Leon.	Oct 1869	N.-Amer	837953
Alberle, Friedrich		5 Jun 1847	Bach-Altenberg	Obd.	Oct 1865	N.-Amer	838631
Albrecht, Angelika		1 Oct 1835	Kuchen	Gsl.	May 1852	N.-Amer	572041
Albrecht, Angelika		13 Nov 1854	Steinenkirch	Gsl.	May 1865	N.-Amer	572045
Albrecht, Anna		25 Jan 1841	Kuchen	Gsl.	Feb 1854	N.-Amer	572042
Albrecht, Anna Katharina		6 Feb 1820	Kuchen	Gsl.	Feb 1854	N.-Amer	572042
Albrecht, Anna Maria		1 Oct 1852	Steinenkirch	Gsl.	May 1865	N.-Amer	572045
Albrecht, Barbara		4 Nov 1864	Steinenkirch	Gsl.	May 1865	N.-Amer	572045
Albrecht, Barbara (wife)		23 Jun 1823	Kuchen	Gsl.	May 1865	N.-Amer	572045
Albrecht, Friedrich		19 yrs.	Hoefingen	Leon.	Sep 1854	N.-Amer	837957
Albrecht, Georg		10 Apr 1857	Steinenkirch	Gsl.	May 1865	N.-Amer	572045
Albrecht, Jakob			Kuchen	Gsl.	Feb 1853	N.-Amer	572041
Albrecht, Jakob		15 May 1832	Hoefingen	Leon.	Mar 1869	N.-Amer	837957
Albrecht, Johann Georg		30 Mar 1865	Stubersheim	Gsl.	Jul 1882	N.-Amer	572048
Albrecht, Johann Georg & F		9 Oct 1819	Steinenkirch	Gsl.	May 1865	N.-Amer	572045
Albrecht, Johann Michael & F			Steinenkirch	Gsl.	May 1865	N.-Amer	572045
Albrecht, Johannes		24 Oct 1827	Kuchen	Gsl.	Feb 1853	N.-Amer	572041
Albrecht, Johannes			Hoefingen	Leon.	Apr 1864	N.-Amer	837957
Albrecht, Katharina		8 Sep 1824	Kuchen	Gsl.	Feb 1853	N.-Amer	572041
Albrecht, Margaretha		12 Jan 1830	Kuchen	Gsl.	May 1852	N.-Amer	572041
Albrecht, Margaretha (wife)			Steinenkirch	Gsl.	May 1865	N.-Amer	572045
Albrecht, Martin			Hoefingen	Leon.	Jul 1866	N.-Amer	837957
Albrecht, Mathaeus		3 yrs	Steinenkirch	Gsl.	May 1865	N.-Amer	572045
Albrecht, Regina		24 Jun 1850	Steinenkirch	Gsl.	May 1865	N.-Amer	572045
Albrecht, Theodor			Steinenkirch	Gsl.	May 1865	N.-Amer	572045
Albrecht, Tobias		10 Feb 1861	Steinenkirch	Gsl.	May 1865	N.-Amer	572045
Albrecht, Walpurga		11 Feb 1822	Kuchen	Gsl.	Feb 1853	N.-Amer	572041
Allgaier, Anna Maria		25 Dec 1832	Schopfloch	Krch.	bef 1859	N.-Amer	835949
Allgaier, Christian		4 dec 1872	Goeppingen	Krch.	Apr 1889	N.-Amer	835949
Allgaier, Friederich		2 Oct 1869	Goeppingen	Krch.	Sep 1883	N.-Amer	548403

Allgaier, Johann Georg	27 Dec 1867	Goeppingen	Krch.	Sep 1883	N.-Amer	548403
Allgoewer, Friedrich		Geislingen	Gsl.	Apr 1853	Hamburg	572041
Allgoewer, Gustav	8 Sep 1833	Geislingen	Gsl.	Sep 1853	N.-Amer	572041
Allgoier, Dorothea		Geislingen	Gsl.	Dec 1870	N.-Amer	572047
Allgoyer, Gustav	8 Sep 1833	Geislingen	Gsl.	Sep 1853	N.-Amer	573622
Allmendinger, Albertine	9 Nov 1841	Deggingen	Gsl.	Mar 1864	N.-Amer	572045
Allmendinger, Anton	4 Aug 1832	Muehlhausen	Gsl.	Apr 1854	N.-Amer	572042
Allmendinger, Barbara	7 Nov 1854	Unterboehringen	Gsl.	Mar 1864	N.-Amer	572045
Allmendinger, Friederike (wife)	11 Jul 1817	Unterboehringen	Gsl.	Mar 1864	N.-Amer	572045
Allmendinger, Jacob Friedrich	29 Oct 1869	Schlattstall	Krch.	Jul 1883	N.-Amer	548403
Allmendinger, Jakob	13 Dec 1858	Unterboehringen	Gsl.	Mar 1864	N.-Amer	572045
Allmendinger, Jakob	29 Oct 1869	Schlattstall	Krch.	Jul 1883	N.-Amer	835949
Allmendinger, Johann Georg	14 Aug 1827	Deggingen	Gsl.	bef 1855	Holland	572043
Allmendinger, Johann Georg	9 Feb 1849	Dettingen	Krch.	May 1868	N.-Amer	835944
Allmendinger, Johann Georg & F	12 Feb 1820	Unterboehringen	Gsl.	Mar 1864	N.-Amer	572045
Allmendinger, Johann Georg Eu.	5 May 1846	Deggingen	Gsl.	Sep 1866	N.-Amer	572045
Allmendinger, Johannes	19 Sep 1845	Unterboehringen	Gsl.	Nov 1865	N.-Amer	572045
Allmendinger, Joseph	23 Jan 1834	Muehlhausen	Gsl.	Apr 1854	N.-Amer	572042
Allmendinger, Josephine	1 Oct 1844	Deggingen	Gsl.	Mar 1864	N.-Amer	572045
Allmendinger, Katharine	27 Jan 1852	Unterboehringen	Gsl.	Mar 1864	N.-Amer	572045
Allmendinger, Wilhelm	24 Dec 1840	Deggingen	Gsl.	Sep 1858	N.-Amer	572043
Alt, Catharina	36 yrs.	Korntal	Leon.	Mar 1854	N.-Amer	837957
Alt, Christina	13 Nov 1841	Oberlenningen	Krch.	Aug 1860	N.-Amer	835947
Alt, Georg Gottlieb	23 May 1840	Oberlenningen	Krch.	Mar 1860	N.-Amer	835947
Alt, Gottliebin	11 Aug 1812	Oberlenningen	Krch.	Oct 1863	Russia	835947
Alt, Jacob	25 Sep 1865	Unterlenningen	Krch.	Jan 1882	N.-Amer	835949
Alt, Jakob	5 Mar 1836	Deggingen	Gsl.	Feb 1855	N.-Amer	572043
Alt, Jakob	25 Sep 1865	Unterlenningen	Krch.	Jan 1882	N.-Amer	548403
Alt, Johannes	9 Dec 1834	Deggingen	Gsl.	Feb 1854	N.-Amer	572042
Alt, Mariana	4 Aug 1826	Deggingen	Gsl.	Feb 1854	N.-Amer	572042
Alt, Michael	30 Jun 1807	Gosbach	Gsl.	Sep 1858	N.-Amer	572043
Alt, Michael	11 May 1833	Oberlenningen	Krch.	Mar 1858	N.-Amer	835947
Alt, Wilhelm	14 Oct 1837	Deggingen	Gsl.	Feb 1857	N.-Amer	572043
Altdoerfer, Johann Christian	4 Jan 1828	Kirchheim	Krch.	bef 1867	N.-Amer	835940
Amann, Magdalena		Eltingen	Leon.	Mar 1817	N.-Amer	835789
Ambacher, Johann Bernhard	9 Nov 1846	Neidlingen	Krch.	Mar 1864	N.-Amer	835946
Ambacher, Johann Christian	14 Mar 1849	Neidlingen	Krch.	Feb 1867	N.-Amer	835946
Ambacher, Johann Michael	17 Jan 1850	Nabern	Krch.	Oct 1869	N.-Amer	835946
Ammann, Johann Christian	15 Mar 1835	Weil im Dorf	Loen.	Apr 1854	N.-Amer	837967
Ammer, Christian	6 Jul 1840	Reutlingen	Rtl.	Mar 1867	N.-Amer	841051
Ammer, Maria Salome	21 Jul 1825	Reutlingen	Rtl.	Oct 1859	Switz.	841051
Ampsler, Johann Georg	19 Dec 1865	Weilheim	Krch.	Mar 1881	N.-Amer	548403
Ampsler, Johannes	16 May 1869	Haeringen	Krch.	Jun 1885	N.-Amer	548403
Andler, Ludwig Gottfried	3 Oct 1859	Herrenberg	Herr.	bef 1883	Basel	834629
Andre, Franz Joseph & F		Oberndorf	Obd.	Mar 1849	N.-Amer	838635
Anger, Karl	19 yrs.	Wiesensteig	Gsl.	Jul 1867	N.-Amer	572046
Anger, Maria Magdalena	16 Dec 1816	Wiesensteig	Gsl.	Jul 1863	Switz.	572044
Anger, Viktoria	12 Mar 1832	Drackenstein	Gsl.	Mar 1854	N.-Amer	572042
Ankele, Anna Maria	9 Aug 1829	Unterboehringen	Gsl.	Apr 1854	N.-Amer	572042
Ankele, Christiane	27 Apr 1839	Reutlingen	Rtl.	Jul 1868	Austria	841051

4

Name		Birth		Emigration			Film
Last	First	Date	Place	O'amt	Appl. Date	Dest.	Number
Ankele, Christine Catharine		22 Apr 1839	Reutlingen	Rtl.	bef 1862	N.-Amer	841051
Ankele, Conrad		27 Jan 1838	Gomaringen	Rtl.	May 1864	A-dam	841051
Ankele, Gotthilf		10 Apr 1846	Reutlingen	Rtl.	Jul 1865	N.-Amer	841051
Ankele, Gustav		18 yrs.	Reutlingen	Rtl.	Apr 1880	N.-Amer	841051
Ankele, Joachim			Reutlingen	Rtl.	Jun 1834	N.-Amer	841051
Ankele, Johann Bernhard			Reutlingen	Rtl.	Jan 1836	N.-Amer	841051
Ankele, Johann Georg		7 Mar 1841	Gomaringen	Rtl.	Nov 1860	N.-Amer	841051
Ankele, Johannes		26 Oct 1820	Kuchen	Gsl.	Mar 1865	N.-Amer	572045
Anner, Magdalena		29 yrs.	Hochmoessingen	Obd.	Mar 1852	Austria	838633
Ansel, Catharine			Heimerdingen	Leon.	bef 1855		837954
Ansel, Johann Jakob			Heimerdingen	Leon.	bef 1855	N.-Amer	837954
Ansel, Johannes		24 Jul 1830	Heimerdingen	Leon.	bef 1870	N.-Amer	837954
Anstaett, Gottlieb		17 Dec 1839	Ditzingen	Leon.	Apr 1853	N.-Amer	835788
Anstaett, Johannes		2 Sep 1837	Ditzingen	Leon.	Mar 1854	N.-Amer	835788
Anthaler, Johann Hermann		19 Feb 1868	Jesingen	Krch.	Apr 1884	N.-Amer	548403
Anwander, Johann Christian		23 Mar 1858	Weilheim	Krch.	May 1882	N.-Amer	548403
Anwander, Johannes		13 Apr 1851	Weilheim	Krch.	Apr 1869	N.-Amer	835950
Appenzeller, Barbara (wife)		9 Oct 1826	Peterzell	Obd.	Jan 1869	N.-Amer	838635
Appenzeller, Johann Georg & F		22 Dec 1822	Peterzell	Obd.	Jan 1869	N.-Amer	838635
Appenzeller, Karolina		16 Dec 1823	Hochdorf	Krch.	Jan 1854	N.-Amer	835945
Appenzeller, Katharina		24 Jun 1867	Peterzell	Obd.	Jan 1869	N.-Amer	838635
Appenzeller, Mathias		19 Jul 1862	Peterzell	Obd.	Jan 1869	N.-Amer	838635
Appenzeller, Wilhelm		19 Mar 1866	Peterzell	Obd.	Jan 1869	N.-Amer	838635
Armbrust, Anna Maria			Perouse	Leon.	May 1856	N.-Amer	837962
Armbrust, Christian & W		16 Sep 1821	Perouse	Leon.	Jan 1852	N.-Amer	837962
Armbrust, Christine (wife)		22 Jan 1825	Perouse	Leon.	Jan 1852	N.-Amer	837962
Armbrust, Friederike		2 yrs.	Perouse	Leon.	Jun 1846	N.-Amer	837962
Armbrust, Friederike & C			Perouse	Leon.	Jun 1846	N.-Amer	837962
Armbrust, Johann Wilhelm		19 yrs.	Perouse	Leon.	Aug 1854	N.-Amer	837962
Armbruster, Abraham Gottfried			Alpirsbach	Obd.	bef 1821	France	838631
Armbruster, Carl		20 Mar 1834	Alpirsbach	Obd.	Oct 1853	N.-Amer	838630
Armbruster, Emil		29 yrs.	Beffendorf	Obd.	Nov 1861	N.-Amer	838631
Armbruster, Georg		6 Apr 1845	Stuttgart	Krch.	Mar 1857	N.-Amer	835944
Armbruster, Johann Viktor		26 Oct 1838	Bissingen	Krch.	Jul 1857	N.-Amer	835943
Armbruster, Johannes			Alpirsbach	Obd.	Oct 1825	France	838631
Armbruster, Julius		24 Jul 1838	Alpirsbach	Obd.	Jun 1870	Lippe	838630
Armbruster, Maria Magdalena			Alpirsbach	Obd.	Jun 1812	Alzey	838631
Armbruster, Matthias		13 Apr 1846	Roetenbach	Obd.	Mar 1866	N.-Amer	838636
Armbruster, Wilhelm		5 May 1838	Roetenbach	Obd.	Jul 1854	N.-Amer	838636
Arndd, Friedrich		1 Jan 1788	Alpirsbach	Obd.	Oct 1821	Bavaria	838631
Arnold, Augusta Wilhelmina		5 Jan 1836	Alpirsbach	Obd.	Nov 1864	France	838630
Arnold, Carl Otto		27 Nov 1844	Reutlingen	Rtl.	Jan 1862	N.-Amer	841051
Arnold, Caroline Margarethe		15 Mar 1831	Alpirsbach	Obd.	Nov 1854	France	838630
Arnold, Christian		6 Mar 1850	Herrenberg	Herr.	Dec 1868	N.-Amer	834629
Arnold, Christian (wid.)		11 May 1816	Peterzell	Obd.	Sep 1865	N.-Amer	838635
Arnold, Christina		1 Feb 1845	Peterzell	Obd.	Apr 1862	N.-Amer	838635
Arnold, Johann Heinrich			Alpirsbach	Obd.	Oct 1816	N.-Amer	838631
Arnold, Joseph Anton		14 Nov 1828	Weissenstein	Gsl.	Jun 1866	Austria	572045
Arzt, Andreas (wid.)		65 yrs.	Moensheim	Leon.	Mar 1844	N.-Amer	837960
Arzt, Gottlieb & F			Eltingen	Leon.	Oct 1853	N.-Amer	835789

Arzt, Julius	20 Feb 1839	Eltingen	Leon.	Oct 1853	N.-Amer	835789
Arzt, Wilhelm	30 Mar 1842	Eltingen	Leon.	Oct 1853	N.-Amer	835789
Assfahl, Gottlieb	14 Jun 1782	Friolzheim	Leon.	Mar 1831	N.-Amer	835791
Assfahl, Johannes	5 Nov 1832	Friolzheim	Leon.	bef 1867	Saxony	835791
Astfalk, Gotthold	37 yrs.	Reutlingen	Rtl.	Mar 1880	N.-Amer	841051
Astfalk, Gustav Adolf	22 Dec 1848	Reutlingen	Rtl.	Jun 1867	N.-Amer	841051
Astfalk, Johann Heinrich	29 yrs.	Reutlingen	Rtl.	Apr 1880	N.-Amer	841051
Astfalk, Johann Jacob	28 Mar 1849	Reutlingen	Rtl.	Jun 1867	N.-Amer	841051
Astfalk, Johann Wilhelm	15 Oct 1830	Eningengen	Rtl.	Mar 1863	N.-Amer	841051
Astfalk, Johannes	25 Jan 1844	Reutlingen	Rtl.	Oct 1859	N.-Amer	841051
Astfalk, Johannes Henrich	16 Jan 1846	Reutlingen	Rtl.	Jul 1865	N.-Amer	841051
Astfalk, Julius	5 Aug 1846	Reutlingen	Rtl.	Jun 1867	N.-Amer	841051
Attenweiler, Maria	2 yrs.	Epfendorf	Obd.	Mar 1858	N.-Amer	838632
Attinger, Christian	9 Jul 1871	Holzmaden	Krch.	May 1888	N.-Amer	835945
Attinger, Johann Georg	30 Nov 1868	Owen	Krch.	Jun 1883	N.-Amer	835948
Attinger, Johann Ludwig	27 Jun 1830	Brucken	Krch.	Feb 1854	N.-Amer	835944
Attinger, Philipp Friedrich	6 Dec 1834	Brucken	Krch.	Sep 1854	N.-Amer	835944
Au von, Josephine Wilhelm.H.	12 Mar 1826	Herrenberg	Herr.	Mar 1862	France	834629
Aubele, Caezilia	22 yrs.	Donzdorf	Gsl.	Mar 1854	N.-Amer	572042
Aubele, Johanna	23 yrs.	Donzdorf	Gsl.	Mar 1854	N.-Amer	572042
Auber, Christian	29 Oct 1850	Aichhalden	Obd.	Apr 1870	N.-Amer	838629
Auber, Johannes	25 yrs.	Lauterbach	Obd.	May 1854	N.-Amer	838634
Auberle, Hypolit	4 May 1844	Boehmenkirch	Gsl.	Oct 1866	N.-Amer	572045
Auer, Alexander	7 Feb 1815	Gutenberg	Krch.	Aug 1855	Prussia	835945
Auer, Catharina Barbara	27 Feb 1819	Muenchingen	Leon.	Feb 1848	N.-Amer	837961
Auer, Catharina Barbara & F		Muenchingen	Leon.	Feb 1848	N.-Amer	837961
Auer, Christine	13 May 1821	Muenchingen	Leon.	bef 1848	N.-Amer	837961
Auer, Conrad	3 Nov 1827	Muenchingen	Leon.	Feb 1848	N.-Amer	837961
Auer, Dorothea	16 Mar 1828	Gutenberg	Krch.	May 1857	N.-Amer	835945
Auer, Ezechiel & F		Gutenberg	Krch.	Apr 1804	Pr.-Pol	550804
Auer, Gottlieb	8 Feb 1835	Gingen	Gsl.	May 1852	N.-Amer	572041
Auer, Jacob	23 Jul 1829	Muenchingen	Leon.	bef 1848	N.-Amer	837961
Auer, Johann Georg	11 Jan 1834	Muenchingen	Leon.	Feb 1848	N.-Amer	837961
Auer, Johann Georg	28 Oct 1818	Gutenberg	Krch.	1858	N.-Amer	835945
Auer, Johann Michael	29 Sep 1824	Muenchingen	Leon.	Feb 1848	N.-Amer	837961
Auer, Katharina	18 Jul 1850	Gutenberg	Krch.	Feb 1868	N.-Amer	835945
Auer, Marie	15 Dec 1846	Muenchingen	Leon.	bef 1848	N.-Amer	837961
Auer, Marie & C	16 Feb 1823	Muenchingen	Leon.	bef 1848	N.-Amer	837961
Auer, Rosina	29 Sep 1826	Gutenberg	Krch.	1858	N.-Amer	835945
Autenrieth, Anna Maria	1 Mar 1831	Weilheim	Krch.	Jul 1869	N.-Amer	835950
Autenrieth, Johannes	29 Apr 1842	Weilheim	Krch.	Jan 1860	N.-Amer	835949
Authaler, Johann Hermann	19 Feb 1868	Jesingen	Krch.	Apr 1884	N.-Amer	835946
Baach, Barbara (wife)	12 Mar 1815	Hochdorf	Krch.	May 1868	N.-Amer	835945
Baach, Jakob & W	12 Jan 1809	Hochdorf	Krch.	May 1868	N.-Amer	835945
Baader, Carl Michael	22 Feb 1850	Renningen	Leon.	Sep 1866	N.-Amer	837963
Bach, Josef		Bochingen	Obd.	bef 1843	France	838632
Bach, Simon	20 Feb 1845	Winzeln	Obd.	Sep 1865	N.-Amer	841016
Bachoefer, Christian	3 Dec 1871	Weilheim	Krch.	Aug 1873	N.-Amer	548403
Bachoefer, Johann Ludwig	21 Dec 1870	Weilheim	Krch.	Aug 1873	N.-Amer	548403
Bachoefer, Johannes	17 Mar 1873	Weilheim	Krch.	Aug 1873	N.-Amer	548403

Name		Birth		Emigration			Film
Last	First	Date	Place	O'amt	Appl. Date	Dest.	Number
Bachoefer, Johannes & F		14 Dec 1845	Weilheim	Krch.	Aug 1873	N.-Amer	548403
Bachofer, Christian		19 Apr 1829	Aichelberg	Krch.	bef 1860	N.-Amer	835774
Bachofer, Friedrich		9 Jun 1893	Aichelberg	Krch.	Mar 1910	N.-Amer	835943
Bachofer, Johann Caspar		27 Jun 1850	Weilheim	Krch.	Dec 1870	N.-Amer	835950
Bachofer, Sophie Jacob. (wife)		2 Oct 1847	Weilheim	Krch.	Aug 1873	N.-Amer	835774
Bader, Adolph		26 Sep 1870	Rosswaelden	Krch.	May 1875	N.-Amer	835949
Bader, Adolph Friedrich		26 Sep 1870	Sulpach	Krch.	May 1875	N.-Amer	548403
Bader, Agnes Margaretha		11 Mar 1827	Dettingen	Krch.	bef 1865	N.-Amer	835944
Bader, Albert		26 yrs.	Oberhausen	Rtl.	Oct 1879	N.-Amer	841051
Bader, Anna		29 Jul 1846	Harthausen	Obd.	May 1869	N.-Amer	838633
Bader, Anna Elisabeth		21 Jul 1853	Oberhausen	Rtl.	Aug 1869	N.-Amer	841051
Bader, Anna Maria		17 Sep 1842	Dettingen	Krch.	Mar 1866	N.-Amer	835944
Bader, Anna Maria (wife)		54 yrs.	Gosbach	Gsl.	Feb 1853	N.-Amer	572041
Bader, August		21 Sep 1872	Rosswaelden	Krch.	May 1875	N.-Amer	835949
Bader, Bartholomaeus		31 Mar 1843	Oberhausen	Rtl.	Mar 1860	N.-Amer	841051
Bader, Catharina Bar. (wid.) & F		12 Jun 1822	Oberhausen	Rtl.	Aug 1869	N.-Amer	841051
Bader, Christian Gottlieb		23 Jan 1834	Sulpach	Krch.	May 1875	N.-Amer	548403
Bader, Elisabetha		30 Jan 1836	Gosbach	Gsl.	Feb 1853	N.-Amer	572041
Bader, Gottlob		15 Jun 1859	Oberhausen	Rtl.	Aug 1869	N.-Amer	841051
Bader, Gustav		17 Jan 1837	Harthausen	Obd.	Nov 1869	N.-Amer	838633
Bader, Gustav - twin		2 Mar 1875	Rosswaelden	Krch.	May 1875	N.-Amer	835949
Bader, J.G. Robert		31 Mar 1869	Rosswaelden	Krch.	May 1875	N.-Amer	835949
Bader, Jacob Friedrich		30 Oct 1848	Owen	Krch.	Jun 1867	N.-Amer	835948
Bader, Johann Georg		13 Mar 1829	Zell	Krch.	Apr 1855	N.-Amer	835774
Bader, Johann Georg			Betzingen	Rtl.	Mar 1867	N.-Amer	841051
Bader, Johann Martin		10 Mar 1825	Dettingen	Krch.	bef 1876	N.-Amer	835944
Bader, Johanna		4 Nov 1861	Rosswaelden	Krch.	May 1875	N.-Amer	835949
Bader, Johannes & F		51 yrs.	Gosbach	Gsl.	Feb 1853	N.-Amer	572041
Bader, Karl		28 Sep 1867	Rosswaelden	Krch.	May 1875	N.-Amer	835949
Bader, Karoline		19 Aug 1866	Rosswaelden	Krch.	May 1875	N.-Amer	835949
Bader, Katharina		15 May 1843	Harthausen	Obd.	May 1869	N.-Amer	838633
Bader, Katharina		3 Sep 1838	Rosswaelden	Krch.	May 1875	N.-Amer	835949
Bader, Ludwig Friedrich		4 Jan 1847	Owen	Krch.	Nov 1867	N.-Amer	835948
Bader, Magdalena			Oberhausen	Rtl.	Mar 1860	N.-Amer	841051
Bader, Magnus		6 Sep 1839	Gosbach	Gsl.	Feb 1853	N.-Amer	572041
Bader, Mattheus		16 Aug 1819	Unterhausen	Rtl.	bef 1861	N.-Amer	841051
Bader, Matthaeus Gottlob		3 May 1849	Unterhausen	Rtl.	May 1866	N.-Amer	841051
Bader, Theodor - twin		2 Mar 1875	Rosswaelden	Krch.	May 1875	N.-Amer	835949
Bader, Wilhelm		13 Feb 1866	Oberlenningen	Krch.	Aug 1880	N.-Amer	835947
Bader, Wilhelm Jacob		25 Nov 1846	Oberhausen	Rtl.	Oct 1866	N.-Amer	841051
Baechle, Maria		6 Oct 1844	Mariazell	Obd.	Sep 1866	Switz.	838634
Baechle, Maria Elisabeth		28 Sep 1842	Mariazell	Obd.	Mar 1864	Switz.	838634
Baechtle, Jeremias		3 Sep 1836	Tuerkheim	Gsl.	Dec 1853	N.-Amer	572041
Baeder, Friedrich August		3 Aug 1842	Haslach	Herr.	Jun 1866	Switz.	834631
Baeder, Karl Wilhelm		4 Mar 1878	Boeblingen	Herr.	Jun 1891	N.-Amer	834631
Baehser, Adam			Weil der Stadt	Leon.	Jul 1849	N.-Amer	837966
Baer, Christian & F		7 Aug 1828	Muenklingen	Leon.	bef 1859	Switz.	837962
Baer, Johann Georg		24 Oct 1856	Muenklingen	Leon.	bef 1884	Holland	837962
Baerstecher, Christian		22 Nov 1843	Bondorf	Herr.	bef 1866	N.-Amer	834630
Baertele, Margaretha		23 Apr 1832	Kuchen	Gsl.	Nov 1855	N.-Amer	572043

Name	Date	Place	Dist.	Emig.	Dest.	Film
Baerthele, Apollonia (wid.) & F		Kuchen	Gsl.	Aug 1854	N.-Amer	572042
Baerthele, Johann Georg	13 Mar 1830	Kuchen	Gsl.	Aug 1854	N.-Amer	572042
Baessler, Andreas		Fluorn	Obd.	Mar 1860	N.-Amer	838632
Baessler, Anna	11 yrs.	Fluorn	Obd.	Nov 1846	N.-Amer	838632
Baessler, Anna Maria	infant	Fluorn	Obd.	Nov 1846	N.-Amer	838632
Baessler, Anna Maria (wife)	41 yrs.	Fluorn	Obd.	Nov 1846	N.-Amer	838632
Baessler, Jakob	12 Feb 1826	Fluorn	Obd.	Mar 1860	N.-Amer	838632
Baessler, Jakob & F		Fluorn	Obd.	Nov 1846	N.-Amer	838632
Baessler, Johann Georg	4 yrs.	Fluorn	Obd.	Nov 1846	N.-Amer	838632
Baetzler, Waldburga		Alt Oberndorf	Obd.	bef 1867	N.-Amer	838631
Baeuchle, Georg	2 Apr 1848	Grosssuessen	Gsl.	Jul 1866	N.-Amer	572045
Baeuchle, Karoline	2 Sep 1845	Grosssuessen	Gsl.	Oct 1869	Switz.	572047
Baeuerle, Andreas Ciriakus	26 Dec 1872	Hepsisau	Krch.	Jan 1881	N.-Amer	835945
Baeuerle, Anna Margaretha	31 Dec 1870	Hepsisau	Krch.	Jan 1881	N.-Amer	835945
Baeuerle, Anna Maria	30 Jan 1873	Hepsisau	Krch.	Sep 1881	N.-Amer	548403
Baeuerle, Anna Maria	23 Jul 1867	Hepsisau	Krch.	Jan 1881	N.-Amer	835945
Baeuerle, Anna Maria (wife)	18 Feb 1845	Hepsisau	Krch.	Aug 1881	N.-Amer	835945
Baeuerle, Carl	19 sep 1836	Gerlingen	Leon.	Feb 1865	N.-Amer	837953
Baeuerle, Christian	31 May 1877	Hepsisau	Krch.	Jan 1881	N.-Amer	835945
Baeuerle, Christian Eduard	22 Jan 1843	Kirchheim	Krch.	Nov 1863	N.-Amer	835941
Baeuerle, Christiana		Gerlingen	Leon.	Jul 1851	N.-Amer	837953
Baeuerle, Friedrich Wilhelm	20 Nov 1846	Weil im Dorf	Loen.	Nov 1866	N.-Amer	837967
Baeuerle, Gottlieb	13 Aug 1866	Gruibingen	Krch.	Jul 1883	N.-Amer	548403
Baeuerle, Gottlob	23 Sep 1853	Weil im Dorf	Loen.	Sep 1870	Palest.	837967
Baeuerle, Johann Christian & F		Renningen	Leon.	Apr 1852	N.-Amer	837963
Baeuerle, Johann Georg		Gerlingen	Leon.	Apr 1831	N.-Amer	837953
Baeuerle, Johann Georg	24 Sep 1880	Hepsisau	Krch.	Aug 1881	N.-Amer	835945
Baeuerle, Johann Georg	10 Sep 1838	Hepsisau	Krch.	Feb 1839	N.-Amer	835945
Baeuerle, Johann Georg & F	3 Sep 1834	Hepsisau	Krch.	Jan 1881	N.-Amer	835945
Baeuerle, Johann Michael	29 Nov 1840	Renningen	Leon.	Apr 1852	N.-Amer	837963
Baeuerle, Johannes		Merklingen	Leon.	May 1855	Austral	837959
Baeuerle, Johannes	1 Feb 1875	Hepsisau	Krch.	Aug 1881	N.-Amer	835945
Baeuerle, Johannes	8 Sep 1865	Hepsisau	Krch.	Jan 1881	N.-Amer	835945
Baeuerle, Johannes	28 Mar 1835	Hepsisau	Krch.	Feb 1839	N.-Amer	835945
Baeuerle, Johannes & F	36 yrs.	Hepsisau	Krch.	Sep 1881	N.-Amer	548403
Baeuerle, Johannes & F	12 Feb 1845	Hepsisau	Krch.	Aug 1881	N.-Amer	835945
Baeuerle, Katharina (wife)	18 Jan 1841	Hepsisau	Krch.	Jan 1881	N.-Amer	835945
Baeuerle, Katharina Margar.	5 Sep 1855	Aichelberg	Krch.	Feb 1878	N.-Amer	548403
Baeuerle, Louise	25 yrs.	Gerlingen	Leon.	bef 1863	Prag	837953
Baeuerle, Magdalena	13 Oct 1874	Hepsisau	Krch.	Jan 1881	N.-Amer	835945
Baeuerle, Margaretha		Hoefingen	Leon.	Mar 1831	N.-Amer	837957
Baeuerle, Margaretha	16 May 1871	Hepsisau	Krch.	Aug 1881	N.-Amer	835945
Baeuerle, Maria Cathar. (wife)	30 Apr 1804	Hepsisau	Krch.	Feb 1839	N.-Amer	835945
Baeuerle, Maria Kath. Barbara	13 Sep 1880	Hepsisau	Krch.	Jan 1881	N.-Amer	835945
Baeuerle, Michael & F	15 Nov 1811	Hepsisau	Krch.	Feb 1839	N.-Amer	835945
Baeuerle, Rudolf	6 Jan 1850	Kirchheim	Krch.	Dec 1870	N.-Amer	835941
Baeuerle, Wilhelm	30 Jun 1858	Hepsisau	Krch.	Nov 1883	S.-Amer	835945
Baeuerle, Wilhelm Andreas	21 Feb 1864	Hepsisau	Krch.	Jan 1881	N.-Amer	835945
Baier, Christian	24 Dec 1817	Weiler	Krch.	bef 1842	Switz.	835949
Baier, Christna Elisabetha	16 Jan 1827	Weilheim	Krch.	bef 1862	N.-Amer	835950

Name		Birth		Emigration			Film
Last	First	Date	Place	O'amt	Appl. Date	Dest.	Number
Baier, Johann Georg		23 Oct 1818	Weilheim	Krch.	bef 1862	N.-Amer	835950
Baier, Johannes			Winzeln	Obd.	Sep 1860	N.-Amer	841016
Baier, Regine (wid.)		6 Feb 1799	Weilheim	Krch.	Jun 1868	N.-Amer	835950
Baisch, Anna Margar. (wife)		39 yrs.	Erpfingen	Rtl.	Jul 1880	N.-Amer	841051
Baisch, Anna Maria		5 yrs.	Erpfingen	Rtl.	Jul 1880	N.-Amer	841051
Baisch, Emma		1 yrs.	Erpfingen	Rtl.	Jul 1880	N.-Amer	841051
Baisch, Johannes		7 yrs.	Erpfingen	Rtl.	Jul 1880	N.-Amer	841051
Baisch, Katharina		20 Dec 1865	Gomaringen	Rtl.	May 1880	N.-Amer	841051
Baisch, Margaretha		11 yrs.	Erpfingen	Rtl.	Jul 1880	N.-Amer	841051
Baisch, Michael & F		45 yrs.	Erpfingen	Rtl.	Jul 1880	N.-Amer	841051
Baither, Emilie Adelheid		20 Apr 1818	Renningen	Leon.	bef 1848	Prussia	837963
Baither, Ernst		13 Feb 1846	Leonberg	Leon.	Jul 1854	N.-Amer	835786
Baither, Friederike & F			Leonberg	Leon.	Jul 1854	N.-Amer	835786
Baither, Gottlob Friedrich		16 Jan 1795	Renningen	Leon.	bef 1827	Frankf.	837963
Baither, Johannes		25 May 1824	Renningen	Leon.	bef 1855	N.-Amer	837963
Baldauf, Ottilie & C		13 Dec 1840	Epfendorf	Obd.	1870	Prussia	838632
Ballester, Johann Baptist		24 Jun 1844	Donzdorf	Gsl.	Dec 1866	N.-Amer	572045
Balz, Carl Friedrich		10 Sep 1860	Moensheim	Leon.	Oct 1881	Romania	837960
Balz, Christian Friedrich		1 Apr 1835	Moensheim	Leon.	Jan 1854	N.-Amer	837960
Balz, Ernst Wilhelm		1 Jul 1841	Moensheim	Leon.	Mar 1854	N.-Amer	837960
Balz, Karl August		14 Jul 1843	Moensheim	Leon.	Jul 1857	N.-Amer	837960
Balz, Louise Karolina		5 Jun 1848	Ditzingen	Leon.	Apr 1862	N.-Amer	835788
Balz, Ludwig Emil		25 Aug 1843	Kirchheim	Krch.	Dec 1863	N.-Amer	835941
Bames, Karl Wilhelm		17 Feb 1834	Pfullingen	Rtl.	Aug 1869	Prussia	841051
Bammesberger, Ferdinand		12 Sep 1854	Leonberg	Leon.	Jan 1871	N.-Amer	835787
Bammesberger, Louis Albrecht		15 Jul 1841	Leonberg	Leon.	Jan 1861	N.-Amer	835787
Bandle, Catharine		15 Jul 1857	Kirchheim	Krch.	Apr 1867	N.-Amer	835941
Bandle, Johann Friedrich		6 Mar 1841	Kirchheim	Krch.	Aug 1859	N.-Amer	835940
Bandle, Johanna & C		17 Jul 1815	Kirchheim	Krch.	Apr 1867	N.-Amer	835941
Bandle, Wilhelm Gottlieb		24 Sep 1844	Kirchheim	Krch.	Apr 1867	N.-Amer	835941
Bantle, Jacob Christian		18 Jun 1852	Dettingen	Krch.	bef 1871	–	835942
Bantle, Jakob		21 May 1811	Hochmoessingen	Obd.	Aug 1858	Bavaria	838633
Bantle, Wilhelm		13 Oct 1837	Kirchheim	Krch.	Feb 1855	N.-Amer	835940
Bantleon, Johann		25 Dec 1817	Kuchen	Gsl.	bef 1853	Wien	572041
Bantlin, Carl August		20 Dec 1836	Kirchheim	Krch.	Dec 1856	N.-Amer	835940
Banzhof, Johannes (wid.)			Amstetten	Gsl.	Oct 1866	N.-Amer	572045
Banzhof, Marcus		18 Nov 1835	Steinenkirch	Gsl.	Mar 1854	N.-Amer	572042
Baral, Adelheid		18 yrs.	Perouse	Leon.	Mar 1866	N.-Amer	837962
Baral, Andreas		16 yrs.	Perouse	Leon.	Mar 1866	N.-Amer	837962
Baral, Caroline		4 May 1833	Perouse	Leon.	bef 1854	N.-Amer	837962
Baral, Karl,		13 yrs.	Perouse	Leon.	Mar 1866	N.-Amer	837962
Baral, Ludwig		7 yrs.	Perouse	Leon.	Mar 1866	N.-Amer	837962
Baral, Rosina (wid.) & F			Perouse	Leon.	Mar 1866	N.-Amer	837962
Baral, Wilhelmine		6 yrs.	Perouse	Leon.	Mar 1866	N.-Amer	837962
Bardeli, Karl August Friedr.		5 Dec 1774	Peterzell	Obd.	Nov 1823	Hamburg	838635
Bardenheuer, Julius Bernhard		12 Mar 1833	Alpirsbach	Obd.	bef 1854	Prussia	838630
Bardtenschlager, Carl Ro.Imm.		25 Jul 1849	Reutlingen	Rtl.	Jun 1869	Switz.	841051
Barner, Christian Gottl. Fr.		6 Jul 1826	Owen	Krch.	Mar 1865	Prussia	835948
Barner, Georg Wendel		13 Oct 1827	Owen	Krch.	Mar 1856	N.-Amer	835948
Barner, Gottliebin		30 Mar 1830	Owen	Krch.	Mar 1865	Prussia	835948

Barner, Johann	1844	Owen	Krch.	bef 1871	N.-Amer	835948
Barner, Johann Christoph	21 Apr 1821	Owen	Krch.	Dec 1858	N.-Amer	835948
Barner, Wilhelmine Therese	28 yrs	Owen	Krch.	Jun 1868	Russia	835948
Barth, Jacob & F		Eltingen	Leon.	Jul 1830	N.-Amer	835789
Barth, Johann Jakob	11 Aug 1816	Kornwestheim	Leon.	Jan 1853	N.-Amer	837963
Barth, Kath		Reutlingen	Rtl.	May 1832	Holland	841051
Barthold, Johann Friedrich		Pfullingen	Rtl.	May 1832	N.-Amer	841051
Basler, Johann Martin		Hoefingen	Leon.	Oct 1854	Austral	837957
Batlion, Mathaeus		Kuchen	Gsl.	May 1852	N.-Amer	572041
Batzle, Anna Barbara	10 Jan 1839	Bissingen	Krch.	bef 1860	N.-Amer	835943
Batzle, Eva Catharina	27 Oct 1845	Bissingen	Krch.	Jul 1861	N.-Amer	835943
Batzle, Regina Elisabetha	2 May 1837	Bissingen	Krch.	bef 1860	N.-Amer	835943
Bauder, Carl Gottlob	27 Apr 1848	Kirchheim	Krch.	Jul 1868	N.-Amer	835941
Bauder, Maria Sophie	17 Oct 1836	Kirchheim	Krch.	Mar 1857	N.-Amer	835940
Bauder, Mathaeus (wid.)	27 Sep 1805	Pfullingen	Rtl.	Aug 1869	N.-Amer	841051
Bauer, Andreas	19 Nov 1842	Dettingen	Krch.	Jan 1867	N.-Amer	835944
Bauer, Anna Maria	31 Dec 1819	Hildrizhausen	Herr.	bef 1867	N.-Amer	834631
Bauer, Anna Maria & C	18 Mar 1823	Lindorf	Krch.	Feb 1856	N.-Amer	835946
Bauer, Anna Maria & F		Warmbronn	Leon.	Apr 1830	N.-Amer	837965
Bauer, Anna Maria (wife)		Grosssuessen	Gsl.	Aug 1867	S.-Russ	572046
Bauer, August	22 Sep 1849	Kirchheim	Krch.	Mar 1864	N.-Amer	835941
Bauer, Barbara		Wimsheim	Loen.	Mar 1852	N.-Amer	837967
Bauer, Barbara	22 Dec 1867	Holzmaden	Krch.	Feb 1867	N.-Amer	835945
Bauer, Benedikt	8 Dec 1829	Altingen	Herr.	Jan 1869	N.-Amer	834624
Bauer, Carl August	1 Feb 1847	Heimsheim	Leon.	Dec 1867	N.-Amer	837955
Bauer, Catharina	16 Mar 1851	Dettingen	Krch.	Feb 1869	N.-Amer	835944
Bauer, Christian		Gerlingen	Leon.	bef 1862	N.-Amer	837953
Bauer, Christian	14 yrs.	Holzmaden	Krch.	Apr 1879	N.-Amer	548403
Bauer, Christian	16 Sep 1850	Holzmaden	Krch.	Oct 1868	N.-Amer	835945
Bauer, Christian	3 Aug 1847	Holzmaden	Krch.	Mar 1867	N.-Amer	835945
Bauer, Christian	22 Oct 1845	Jesingen	Krch.	Mar 1865	Austral	835946
Bauer, Christian	14 Oct 1824	Weilheim	Krch.	Nov 1856	Austria	835949
Bauer, Christian Friedrich	31 Jul 1838	Dettingen	Krch.	Feb 1855	N.-Amer	835944
Bauer, Christian Gottlieb	24 Jan 1873	Dettingen	Krch.	Dec 1889	N.-Amer	835944
Bauer, Christina	26 Oct 1854	Holzmaden	Krch.	Aug 1857	N.-Amer	835945
Bauer, Christine	23 Aug 1843	Ohmden	Krch.	Jul 1862	N.-Amer	835948
Bauer, Christine Doroth. (wife)	9 Nov 1804	Bissingen	Krch.	1851	N.-Amer	835940
Bauer, Dorothea	20 yrs.	Reutlingen	Rtl.	May 1880	N.-Amer	841051
Bauer, Dorothea (wife)	7 May 1809	Ohmden	Krch.	Jul 1862	N.-Amer	835948
Bauer, Eberhard & F	24 Dec 1825	Pfullingen	Rtl.	May 1864	N.-Amer	841051
Bauer, Eberhard Ludwig	17 May 1850	Oberlenningen	Krch.	May 1869	N.-Amer	835947
Bauer, Elisabetha (wife)		Warmbronn	Leon.	Apr 1830	N.-Amer	837965
Bauer, Elisabetha Kath. (wife)	28 Apr 1836	Pfullingen	Rtl.	May 1864	N.-Amer	841051
Bauer, Eva Barbara		Heimerdingen	Leon.	May 1834	N.-Amer	837954
Bauer, Friderike	11 Apr 1811	Hildrizhausen	Herr.	bef 1867	N.-Amer	834631
Bauer, Friedrich	3 Aug 1866	Kirchheim	Krch.	Jul 1882	N.-Amer	835942
Bauer, Friedrich	11 May 1867	Bissingen	Krch.	Jun 1883	N.-Amer	835943
Bauer, Friedrich Wilhelm	7 May 1855	Heimerdingen	Leon.	Feb 1872	N.-Amer	837954
Bauer, Georg	8 Dec 1851	Reutlingen	Rtl.	Nov 1868	N.-Amer	841051
Bauer, Georg Jacob & W		Warmbronn	Leon.	Apr 1830	N.-Amer	837965

Name		Birth		Emigration			Film
Last	First	Date	Place	O'amt	Appl. Date	Dest.	Number
Bauer, Gottieb Friedrich		18 Mar 1848	Gerlingen	Leon.	bef 1868	N.-Amer	837953
Bauer, Gottlieb			Holzmaden	Krch.	bef 1866	N.-Amer	835940
Bauer, Gottlieb		24 Sep 1856	Oberlenningen	Krch.	Aug 1879	N.-Amer	835947
Bauer, Gottlieb		27 Dec 1840	Holzmaden	Krch.	Dec 1860	N.-Amer	835945
Bauer, Gottliebin		22 Sep 1838	Ohmden	Krch.	Jul 1862	N.-Amer	835948
Bauer, Immanuel		18 Aug 1866	Grosssuessen	Gsl.	Aug 1867	S.-Russ	572046
Bauer, Jacob		7 Feb 1833	Weilheim	Krch.	bef 1856	N.-Amer	835949
Bauer, Jakob		25 Sep 1865	Grosssuessen	Gsl.	Aug 1867	S.-Russ	572046
Bauer, Jakob		23 Sep 1854	Oberlenningen	Krch.	May 1869	N.-Amer	835947
Bauer, Jakob & F			Grosssuessen	Gsl.	Aug 1867	S.-Russ	572046
Bauer, Jakob Friedrich			Heimerdingen	Leon.	bef 1852	N.-Amer	837954
Bauer, Johann Christian		18 yrs.	Ruteshein	Leon.	Jun 1853	N.-Amer	837964
Bauer, Johann Christian		16 Apr 1825	Kirchheim	Krch.	Feb 1858	N.-Amer	835940
Bauer, Johann Christian		4 Jan 1865	Holzmaden	Krch.	Apr 1879	N.-Amer	835945
Bauer, Johann Christian		25 Dec 1874	Rosswaelden	Krch.	Aug 1888	N.-Amer	835949
Bauer, Johann Eberhard & F		6 Jun 1812	Reutlingen	Rtl.	Sep 1860	N.-Amer	841051
Bauer, Johann Friedrich		11 May 1867	Bissingen	Krch.	Jun 1883	N.-Amer	548403
Bauer, Johann Georg			Gerlingen	Leon.	Jun 1843	N.-Amer	837953
Bauer, Johann Jacob		13 Jun 1860	Pfullingen	Rtl.	May 1864	N.-Amer	841051
Bauer, Johann Jacob		21 Oct 1863	Dettingen	Krch.	Feb 1880	N.-Amer	548403
Bauer, Johann Martin		15 Oct 1822	Hildrizhausen	Herr.	bef 1867	N.-Amer	834631
Bauer, Johann Michael		13 Jan 1843	Holzmaden	Krch.	Aug 1864	N.-Amer	835945
Bauer, Johannes		12 Jun 1851	Pfullingen	Rtl.	Jan 1869	N.-Amer	841051
Bauer, Johannes		1 Jan 1871	Gutenberg	Krch.	Oct 1887	N.-Amer	835945
Bauer, Johannes		17 Nov 1845	Ohmden	Krch.	Jul 1860	N.-Amer	835948
Bauer, Johannes		6 Jul 1848	Jesingen	Krch.	Mar 1865	Austral	835946
Bauer, Johannes & F		18 Dec 1802	Ohmden	Krch.	Jul 1862	N.-Amer	835948
Bauer, Jonathan Christian		25 Dec 1835	Heimsheim	Leon.	Sep 1853	N.-Amer	837955
Bauer, Karl Heinrich		28 Jan 1840	Kirchheim	Krch.	Apr 1860	N.-Amer	835940
Bauer, Katharina Barb. (wife)		24 Jun 1834	Pfullingen	Rtl.	Sep 1865	N.-Amer	841051
Bauer, Ludwig		15 Mar 1842	Ohmden	Krch.	Apr 1857	N.-Amer	835948
Bauer, Ludwig & F			Bissingen	Krch.	1851	N.-Amer	835940
Bauer, Ludwig Albert		28 Oct 1849	Reutlingen	Rtl.	Sep 1860	N.-Amer	841051
Bauer, Margaretha & C		9 Oct 1820	Holzmaden	Krch.	Aug 1857	N.-Amer	835945
Bauer, Maria		20 Jan 1835	Muenchingen	Leon.	May 1866	Bavaria	837961
Bauer, Maria		7 Oct 1823	Gerlingen	Leon.	Sep 1870	N.-Amer	837953
Bauer, Maria (wid.)		63 yrs.	Reutlingen	Rtl.	Jun 1880	N.-Amer	841051
Bauer, Maria Barbara		5 Apr 1856	Ohmden	Krch.	Jul 1862	N.-Amer	835948
Bauer, Matthaeus & W		17 Dec 1833	Pfullingen	Rtl.	Sep 1865	N.-Amer	841051
Bauer, Pastor			Aichhalden	Obd.	Nov 1823	Brasil	838629
Bauer, Regina		19 Feb 1821	Bissingen	Krch.	bef 1862	N.-Amer	835943
Bauer, Sophie			Holzmaden	Krch.	1854	N.-Amer	835945
Bauer, Sophie Friederike		12 Feb 1848	Holzmaden	Krch.	Feb 1866	N.-Amer	835945
Bauer, Theresia (wife)		1824	Reutlingen	Rtl.	Sep 1860	N.-Amer	841051
Bauer, Wilhelm		24 yrs.	Reutlingen	Rtl.	Nov 1880	N.-Amer	841051
Bauer, Wilhelmine		2 Feb 1848	Kirchheim	Krch.	Apr 1866	N.-Amer	835941
Bauhof, Albert		19 Apr 1844	Kirchheim	Krch.	Nov 1863	N.-Amer	835941
Bauhof, Heinrich Albert		13 Aug 1865	Kirchheim	Krch.	May 1882	N.-Amer	548403
Bauknecht, Ferdinand		12 Oct 1832	Schramberg	Obd.	bef 1859	N.-Amer	838636
Baum, Chrysostomus		24 Nov 1847	Drackenstein	Gsl.	Apr 1867	N.-Amer	572046

Baum, Gertraut	16 Mar 1860	Drackenstein	Gsl.	Oct 1860	N.-Amer	572044
Baum, Heinrich	10 Apr 1854	Drackenstein	Gsl.	Oct 1860	N.-Amer	572044
Baum, Johann Georg	3 Nov 1863	Weilheim	Krch.	May 1878	N. Amer	835774
Baum, Johann Georg	5 Nov 1863	Weilheim	Krch.	Apr 1876	N.-Amer	548403
Baum, Johann Jacob	10 Dec 1855	Weilheim	Krch.	Oct 1869	N.-Amer	835950
Baum, Johannes	19 Aug 1862	Weilheim	Krch.	Apr 1876	N.-Amer	548403
Baum, Maria (wid.) & F	6 Nov 1822	Drackenstein	Gsl.	Oct 1860	N.-Amer	572044
Baum, Simplizius	2 Mar 1856	Drackenstein	Gsl.	Oct 1860	N.-Amer	572044
Baum, Thaddaeus	28 Feb 1849	Drackenstein	Gsl.	Oct 1860	N.-Amer	572044
Baum, Thomas	29 Jul 1844	Drackenstein	Gsl.	Oct 1860	N.-Amer	572044
Baumann, Anton		Lauterbach	Obd.	Mar 1816	Austria	838634
Baumann, Carl Friedrich	28 yrs.	Leonberg	Leon.	Oct 1856	France	835786
Baumann, Catharina	6 Dec 1832	Winzeln	Obd.	Sep 1854	N.-Amer	841016
Baumann, Eduard	18 Aug 1840	Pfullingen	Rtl.	Dec 1860	England	841051
Baumann, Johann Martin	12 Aug 1840	Pfullingen	Rtl.	Dec 1860	England	841051
Baumann, Joseph	30 Jun 1855	Dizenbach	Gsl.	Oct 1872	N.-Amer	572047
Baumann, Joseph & F		Mariazell	Obd.	May 1817	N.-Amer	838634
Baumann, Jost Friedrich		Pfullingen	Rtl.	Aug 1835	N.-Amer	841051
Baumann, Louise & C	9 Jan 1843	Mariazell	Obd.	Jun 1869	Hesse	838634
Baumann, Pius		Winzeln	Obd.	Jul 1860	N.-Amer	841016
Baumann, Wendelin	20 Oct 1852	Hohenstadt	Gsl.	Nov 1866	N.-Amer	572045
Baumeister, Andreas	25 Sep 1841	Schoeckingen	Leon.	Jul 1852	N.-Amer	837964
Baumeister, Herrmann	28 Dec 1838	Wiesensteig	Gsl.	Feb 1858	N.-Amer	572043
Baumeister, Johann Georg	8 Mar 1836	Grosssuessen	Gsl.	Mar 1856	N.-Amer	572043
Baumeister, Johann Georg		Wiesensteig	Gsl.	Aug 1870	N.-Amer	572047
Baumeister, Johann Gottlieb	13 May 1845	Schoeckingen	Leon.	Jul 1852	N.-Amer	837964
Baumeister, Johann Nikolaus F.	25 Nov 1836	Schoeckingen	Leon.	Jul 1852	N.-Amer	837964
Baumeister, Johanna Gott. (wife)	18 May 1810	Schoeckingen	Leon.	Jul 1852	N.-Amer	837964
Baumeister, Johannes	22 Feb 1834	Grosssuessen	Gsl.	Jan 1854	N.-Amer	572042
Baumeister, Josepha	30 Oct 1826	Wiesensteig	Gsl.	Apr 1855	N.-Amer	572043
Baumeister, Luise Catharine	13 Apr 1848	Schoeckingen	Leon.	Jul 1852	N.-Amer	837964
Baumeister, Michael	29 yrs.	Hausen	Gsl.	Mar 1852	N.-Amer	572041
Baumeister, Michael	15 May 1847	Kuchen	Gsl.	Jun 1867	N.-Amer	572046
Baumeister, Michael & F	20 Jan 1808	Schoeckingen	Leon.	Jul 1852	N.-Amer	837964
Baumeister, Wilhelm Carl	28 Oct 1851	Schoeckingen	Leon.	Jul 1852	N.-Amer	837964
Baur, Christian	7 Oct 1843	Kirchheim	Krch.	Dec 1869	N.-Amer	835941
Baur, Clara		Bartholomai/Gmuend	Rtl.	bef 1860	N.-Amer	841051
Baur, Friedrich		Wiesensteig	Gsl.	Mar 1852	N.-Amer	572041
Baur, Friedrich Ludwig	Jun 1828	Bartholomai/Gmuend	Rtl.	bef 1860	N.-Amer	841051
Baur, Hermann	25 Mar 1848	Dapfen	Rtl.	Jan 1867	N.-Amer	841051
Baur, Hermann	27 yrs.	Reutlingen	Rtl.	Jun 1880	N.-Amer	841051
Baur, Hermann Friedrich	6 Oct 1846	Weilheim	Krch.	Jul 1866	N.-Amer	835950
Bausch, Adolph	20 Jan 1835	Eningen	Rtl.	Apr 1860	N.-Amer	841051
Bausch, Andreas	19 yrs.	Gingen	Gsl.	Jun 1864	N.-Amer	572045
Bausch, Anna Regina	14 Feb 1834	Grosssuessen	Gsl.	Mar 1854	N.-Amer	572042
Bausch, Eustachius	18 Oct 1837	Grosssuessen	Gsl.	Feb 1854	N.-Amer	572042
Bausch, Jakob	28 Oct 1847	Weiler	Krch.	Apr 1865	N.-Amer	835949
Bauss, Catharina Barbara & C	15 Jun 1830	Renningen	Leon.	Jul 1859	N.-Amer	837963
Bauss, Catharina Gottliebin	22 Feb 1856	Renningen	Leon.	Jul 1859	N.-Amer	837963
Bauss, Johann Jakob	16 Apr 1825	Renningen	Leon.	Jul 1852	N.-Amer	837963

Name		Birth		Emigration			Film
Last	First	Date	Place	O'amt	Appl. Date	Dest.	Number
Bauss, Konrad & F			Renningen	Leon.	Jul 1859	N.-Amer	837963
Bautel, Martin		8 Dec 1819	Gingen	Gsl.	Jul 1854	N.-Amer	572042
Bautle, Franz		27 Jan 1852	Epfendorf	Obd.	Apr 1867	N.-Amer	838632
Bautlen, Gottlob & F			Kirchheim	Krch.	Jul 1857	N.-Amer	835940
Bautner, Ferdinand		15 yrs.	Schramberg	Obd.	Jun 1854	N.-Amer	838636
Baxler, Franz Xaver		17 Jan 1848	Grossengstingen	Rtl.	Apr 1868	N.-Amer	841051
Bayer, Elisabethe Margaretha		27 Nov 1834	Weilheim	Krch.	May 1868	Weimar	835950
Bayer, Friederike		13 Dec 1838	Weilheim	Krch.	Oct 1864	N.-Amer	835950
Bayer, Georg		17 yrs.	Epfendorf	Obd.	Mar 1852	–	838632
Bayer, Gottlieb		9 Jan 1849	Weilheim	Krch.	May 1867	N.-Amer	835950
Bayer, Jakob		23 Jun 1835	Rosswaelden	Krch.	Jun 1855	N.-Amer	835949
Bayer, Johann Georg			Epfendorf	Obd.	bef 1854	N.-Amer	838632
Bayer, Johann Georg		31 Oct 1863	Aichelberg	Krch.	May 1880	N.-Amer	835943
Bayer, Johann Gottlieb		23 Jun 1869	Aichelberg	Krch.	Apr 1886	N.-Amer	548403
Bayer, Johann Heinrich		27 Jul 1828	Weilheim	Krch.	bef 1870	N.-Amer	835950
Bayer, Johannes		3 Feb 1848	Zell	Krch.	Jun 1868	N.-Amer	835774
Bayer, Johannes			Kirchheim	Krch.	1854	N.-Amer	835940
Bayer, Theresia & C		25 May 1833	Oberndorf	Obd.	Jan 1865	Frankf.	838635
Bayer, Willibald			Oberndorf	Obd.	Jul 1849	N.-Amer	838635
Bazer, Conrad		27 Apr 1844	Markgroeningen	Rtl.	Mar 1866	N.-Amer	841051
Bazer, Gottlieb			Erpfingen	Rtl.	Mar 1860	N.-Amer	841051
Bazle, Barbara		28 Oct 1831	Ochsenwang	Krch.	1852	N.-Amer	835947
Bea, Daniel		19 yrs.	Lauterbach	Obd.	Apr 1854	N.-Amer	838634
Bechle, Johanna		24 Jul 1849	Harthausen	Obd.	Aug 1869	N.-Amer	838633
Bechle, Theresia		26 Aug 1846	Harthausen	Obd.	Jun 1868	N.-Amer	838633
Bechtle, Ernst Eduard		20 Sep 1851	Reutlingen	Rtl.	Sep 1859	N.-Amer	841051
Beck, Agnes (wife)		27 Aug 1828	Altenstadt-Gsl.	Gsl.	Apr 1867	N.-Amer	572046
Beck, Carl		6 May 1847	Kirchheim	Krch.	Apr 1866	N.-Amer	835941
Beck, Catharina Barbara		29 Aug 1840	Gaertringen	Herr.	bef 1864	N.-Amer	834630
Beck, Christian		12 Jun 1853	Peterzell	Obd.	Feb 1870	N.-Amer	838635
Beck, Gottlob		2 Sep 1841	Reutlingen	Rtl.	Jun 1861	N.-Amer	841051
Beck, Jacob Friedrich		28 Apr 1842	Kirchheim	Krch.	May 1857	N.-Amer	835940
Beck, Johann Georg		17 Feb 1854	Altenstadt-Gsl.	Gsl.	Apr 1867	N.-Amer	572046
Beck, Johann Georg & F		17 Jul 1831	Altenstadt-Gsl.	Gsl.	Apr 1867	N.-Amer	572046
Beck, Johann Gotthilf		31 Mar 1851	Reutlingen	Rtl.	Aug 1869	N.-Amer	841051
Beck, Johann Jakob		30 Aug 1823	Renningen	Leon.	Mar 1852	N.-Amer	837963
Beck, Johannes			Hoenweiler	Obd.	Apr 1866	N.-Amer	838635
Beck, Johannes		15 Sep 1846	Pfullingen	Rtl.	Aug 1866	N.-Amer	841051
Beck, Karl Gottlob		1 Nov 1859	Renningen	Leon.	Aug 1876	N.-Amer	837963
Beck, Mathaeus		22 Mar 1861	Altenstadt-Gsl.	Gsl.	Apr 1867	N.-Amer	572046
Beck, Regina		2 Aug 1858	Altenstadt-Gsl.	Gsl.	Apr 1867	N.-Amer	572046
Becker, Andreas		18 Sep 1835	Weilheim	Krch.	Jun 1867	N.-Amer	835950
Becker, Christine		23 May 1845	Weilheim	Krch.	bef 1868	N.-Amer	835950
Becker, Christoph Heinrich		29 Sep 1868	Weilheim	Krch.	Mar 1885	N.-Amer	548403
Becker, Johann Caspar		4 Dec 1827	Weilheim	Krch.	bef 1855	N.-Amer	835949
Beckert, Eduard		23 Oct 1854	Gosbach	Gsl.	Dec 1880	N.-Amer	572048
Beckert, Joseph		25 Oct 1819	Ditzenbach	Gsl.	1851	N.-Amer	572043
Beerstecher, Christian		15 Jul 1837	Herrenberg	Herr.	bef 1864	Oldenb.	834629
Beesch, Albert		15 Apr 1850	Waldmoessingen	Obd.	Aug 1867	N.-Amer	841015
Beesch, Anna Maria		4 yrs.	Fluorn	Obd.	Aug 1867	N.-Amer	838632

Beesch, Christina	50 yrs.	Fluorn	Obd.	Apr 1845	N.-Amer 838632
Beesch, Christina & C	25 Mar 1836	Fluorn	Obd.	Aug 1867	N.-Amer 838632
Beesch, Jakob	6 Sep 1832	Fluorn	Obd.	Aug 1852	N.-Amer 838632
Beesch, Johann Georg & F	31 Jan 1819	Fuorn	Obd.	Jun 1847	N.-Amer 838631
Beesch, Johannes	14 Feb 1845	Betzweiler	Obd.	Jun 1847	N.-Amer 838631
Beesch, Luise Auguste	14 Dec 1841	Betzweiler	Obd.	Jun 1847	N.-Amer 838631
Beesch, Maria Friederika (wife)	21 Sep 1819	Betzweiler	Obd.	Jun 1847	N.-Amer 838631
Beesch, Mathias	8 Nov 1843	Betzweiler	Obd.	Jun 1847	N.-Amer 838631
Beh, Albert	3 May 1851	Winzeln	Obd.	Sep 1867	N.-Amer 841016
Beh, Barbara	3 Dec 1832	Winzeln	Obd.	Sep 1854	N.-Amer 841016
Beh, Emilia		Winzeln	Obd.	Mar 1860	N.-Amer 841016
Beh, Helena	14 Aug 1841	Winzeln	Obd.	Aug 1868	N.-Amer 841016
Beichler, Johanna	2 Mar 1837	Kirchheim	Krch.	Aug 1862	N.-Amer 835941
Beil, Jakob		Ditzingen	Leon.	Mar 1852	S.-Amer 835788
Beilharz, – (wife)		Dornhan	Obd.	Nov 1850	N.-Amer 838638
Beilharz, Johannes	26 Dec 1830	Dornhan	Obd.	Nov 1850	N.-Amer 838638
Beilharz, Michael & F		Dornhan	Obd.	Nov 1850	N.-Amer 838638
Beilharz, Michael & W		Dornhan	Obd.	Apr 1853	N.-Amer 838638
Beiser, Catharina	16 Jul 1840	Dettingen	Krch.	May 1861	France 835944
Beiser, Jacob	16 Nov 1853	Holzmaden	Krch.	Apr 1867	N.-Amer 835945
Beisser, Friedrich	3 Mar 1849	Kirchheim	Krch.	Apr 1869	N.-Amer 835941
Beisser, Maria	19 Dec 1846	Sulgen	Obd.	Jul 1868	Switz. 838638
Beisswanger, Johannes	28 Dec 1875	Eckwaelden	Krch.	May 1891	N.-Amer 835774
Beiswanger, Jakob	15 Feb 1850	Grosssuessen	Gsl.	Dec 1866	N.-Amer 572045
Beitter, Agatha Rosina	14 Dec 1834	Tuttlingen	Leon.	bef 1863	Prussia 837961
Beitter, Hermann Gottlob & W	25 Aug 1827	Muenchingen	Leon.	bef 1863	Prussia 837961
Bek, Anton	8 Jan 1845	Waldmoessingen	Obd.	Mar 1865	N.-Amer 841015
Bek, Xaver	23 Nov 1847	Waldmoessingen	Obd.	Feb 1866	N.-Amer 841015
Belkle, Engelbert	26 yrs.	Wiesensteig	Gsl.	Oct 1852	N.-Amer 572041
Beller, Johann Andreas	4 Jun 1869	Owen	Krch.	May 1883	N.-Amer 835948
Beller, Johann Andreas	2 Nov 1850	Owen	Krch.	Sep 1867	N.-Amer 835948
Beller, Johann Georg	2 Jun 1821	Hoefingen	Leon.	bef 1867	France 837957
Beller, Katharina	7 Feb 1841	Owen	Krch.	Mar 1860	N.-Amer 835948
Beller, Peter	36 yrs.	Zell	Krch.	Oct 1879	N.-Amer 835940
Bendel, Friederich & F		Leonberg	Leon.	Mar 1851	N.-Amer 835786
Bendel, Maria	6 Mar 1850	Leonberg	Leon.	Mar 1851	N.-Amer 835786
Bendel, Maria (wife)		Leonberg	Leon.	Mar 1851	N.-Amer 835786
Bengel, Adolf	6 yrs.	Leonberg	Leon.	Jun 1852	N.-Amer 835786
Bengel, Amalie	3 yrs.	Leonberg	Leon.	Jun 1852	N.-Amer 835786
Bengel, Amalie & C	30 yrs.	Leonberg	Leon.	Jun 1852	N.-Amer 835786
Bengel, Caroline (wid.) & F		Leonberg	Leon.	Jun 1852	N.-Amer 835786
Benner, Ottilie & C		Sulgen	Obd.	Feb 1861	France 838638
Benner, Theresia	6 Jan 1858	Sulgen	Obd.	Feb 1861	France 838638
Bentel, Christian		Malmsheim	Leon.	Nov 1854	N.-Amer 837958
Bentel, Johannes	9 Jan 1847	Renningen	Leon.	May 1866	N.-Amer 837963
Benz, Albert Adolf	6 Jul 1880	Goeppingen	Krch.	Jun 1887	N.-Amer 835942
Benz, Andreas	10 Nov 1847	Alpirsbach	Obd.	Sep 1867	N.-Amer 838630
Benz, Bertha	12 Oct 1886	Kirchheim	Krch.	Jun 1887	N.-Amer 835942
Benz, Carl Friedrich	9 Mar 1873	Kirchheim	Krch.	Mar 1890	N.-Amer 835942
Benz, Christian Friedrich & F	21 Feb 1852	Kirchheim	Krch.	Jun 1887	N.-Amer 835942

14

| Name | | Birth | | Emigration | | | Film |
Last	First	Date	Place	O'amt	Appl. Date	Dest.	Number
Benz, Christina		25 Jun 1850	Alpirsbach	Obd.	Sep 1867	N.-Amer	838630
Benz, Christoph Adam		15 Nov 1832	Kirchheim	Krch.	bef 1868	N.-Amer	835941
Benz, Eugen Friedrich		2 Jul 1884	Goeppingen	Krch.	Jun 1887	N.-Amer	835942
Benz, Gottlieb			Reutlingen	Rtl.	Aug 1835	N.-Amer	841051
Benz, Gustav		27 yrs.	Reutlingen	Rtl.	Jan 1879	N.-Amer	841051
Benz, Karl		14 Aug 1885	Goeppingen	Krch.	Jun 1887	N.-Amer	835942
Benz, Karoline & C		4 Nov 1827	Beffendorf	Obd.	Mar 1864	N.-Amer	838631
Benz, Pauline Fried. (wife)		8 Mar 1861	Goeppingen	Krch.	Jun 1887	N.-Amer	835942
Benzel, Carl		15 Jul 1866	Holzmaden	Krch.	Feb 1882	N.-Amer	548403
Benzel, Carl		23 Oct 1872	Holzmaden	Krch.	Jul 1889	N.-Amer	835945
Benzel, Johann Georg		21 Jan 1845	Holzmaden	Krch.	Aug 1864	N.-Amer	835945
Benzel, Johannes		8 Jan 1839	Holzmaden	Krch.	May 1856	N.-Amer	835945
Benzel, Karl		15 Jul 1866	Holzmaden	Krch.	Feb 1882	N.-Amer	835945
Benzel, Wilhelm		36 yrs.	Leonberg	Leon.	Apr 1856	N.-Amer	835786
Benzenhoefer, Anna Barbara		31 Mar 1849	Rosswaelden	Krch.	May 1874	N.-Amer	835949
Benzenhoefer, Gottlieb		18 Oct 1851	Rosswaelden	Krch.	Aug 1881	N.-Amer	548403
Benzenhoefer, Johann Christoph		5 Jun 1857	Rosswaelden	Krch.	May 1874	N.-Amer	835949
Benzenhofer, Gottlieb		18 Oct 1851	Weiler	Krch.	Aug 1871	N.-Amer	835949
Benzenhofer, Magdalena - w.& F		30 Jun 1816	Weiler	Krch.	Aug 1871	N.-Amer	835949
Benzinger, Adolph		5 May 1842	Herrenberg	Herr.	May 1865	N.-Amer	834629
Benzinger, Andreas		20 yrs.	Friolzheim	Leon.	Oct 1853	N.-Amer	835791
Benzinger, Anna Louise		19 Aug 1858	Herrenberg	Herr.	Aug 1867	N.-Amer	834629
Benzinger, Anna Maria		30 yrs.	Wimsheim	Loen.	bef 1856	N.-Amer	837967
Benzinger, Barbara		24 yrs.	Friolzheim	Leon.	Apr 1853	N.-Amer	835791
Benzinger, Christian Friedr.			Heimsheim	Leon.	bef 1852	N.-Amer	837955
Benzinger, Elise		28 Feb 1848	Herrenberg	Herr.	Jul 1867	N.-Amer	834629
Benzinger, Friedrich		11 Jun 1851	Herrenberg	Herr.	Aug 1867	N.-Amer	834629
Benzinger, Friedrich			Heimsheim	Leon.	Dec 1866	N.-Amer	837955
Benzinger, Johann Christ. & F			Heimsheim	Leon.	Aug 1857	N.-Amer	837955
Benzinger, Johann Georg			Friolzheim	Leon.	bef 1851	N.-Amer	835791
Benzinger, Johannes			Friolzheim	Leon.	Dec 1816	France	835791
Benzinger, Maria Louisa		17 yrs.	Friolzheim	Leon.	Nov 1863	N.-Amer	835791
Berger, Christina (wife)			Bissingen	Krch.	Oct 1876	N.-Amer	835943
Berger, Friederike		7 Nov 1872	Bissingen	Krch.	Oct 1876	N.-Amer	548403
Berger, Johannes & F		26 Nov 1847	Bissingen	Krch.	Oct 1876	N.-Amer	548403
Berger, Wilhelm		7 May 1874	Esslingen	Krch.	Oct 1876	N.-Amer	835943
Berghamer, Josef		19 yrs.	Winzeln	Obd.	Sep 1852	N.-Amer	841016
Berghammer, Carl		13 Feb 1835	Winzeln	Obd.	bef 1855	N.-Amer	841016
Bergner, Johann & W		20 Apr 1820	Weil der Stadt	Leon.	Feb 1854	N.-Amer	837966
Bernauer, Johann Philipp		11 Aug 1873	Weilheim	Krch.	Feb 1890	N.-Amer	835774
Bernauer, Johannes		30 yrs.	Zell	Krch.	Mar 1880	N.-Amer	835940
Bernauer, Ludwig		17 Sep 1857	Weilheim	Krch.	May 1872	N.-Amer	835774
Bernecker, Emil		7 Jan 1851	Herrenberg	Herr.	Aug 1866	N.-Amer	834629
Bernecker, Johann Otto Reinh.		13 Aug 1858	Herrenberg	Herr.	Jul 1872	N.-Amer	834629
Berner, Jakob			Rutesheim	Leon.	May 1849	N.-Amer	837964
Bertele, Albert			Weissenstein	Gsl.	May 1873	N.-Amer	572047
Bertele, Barbara		28 Nov 1820	Weissenstein	Gsl.	Sep 1864	Austria	572045
Berteli, Constantin		15 Sep 1864	Weissenstein	Gsl.	1883	N.-Amer	572049
Bertrung, Karoline & C		29 Nov 1844	Mariazell	Obd.	Dec 1869	France	838634
Bertsch, Carl Gottlieb		24 Oct 1818	Renningen	Leon.	bef 1860	France	837963

Bertsch, Caroline	17 Jun 1853	Erligheim	Leon.	May 1859	N.-Amer	837961
Bertsch, Catharina	23 yrs.	Oberhausen	Rtl.	Mar 1860	N.-Amer	841051
Bertsch, Christiana	17 Apr 1827	Friolzheim	Leon.	Feb 1854	N.-Amer	835791
Bertsch, Christine Barbara	10 Dec 1828	Owen	Krch.	Mar 1860	N.-Amer	835948
Bertsch, Friedericke Gottl.	9 Oct 1845	Reutlingen	Rtl.	Nov 1867	France	841051
Bertsch, Friedrich Ulrich	21 Feb 1845	Unterhausen	Rtl.	Apr 1864	N.-Amer	841051
Bertsch, Johann & F		Reutlingen	Rtl.	Apr 1831	N.-Amer	841051
Bertsch, Johann Georg	16 Sep 1850	Unterhausen	Rtl.	Sep 1866	N.-Amer	841051
Bertsch, Johann Georg	23 Apr 1845	Oberhausen	Rtl.	Apr 1866	N.-Amer	841051
Bertsch, Johann Jacob	31 Aug 1843	Owen	Krch.	Mar 1860	N.-Amer	835948
Bertsch, Johanna Catharina	22 yrs.	Friolzheim	Leon.	Sep 1856	N.-Amer	835791
Bertsch, Johannes	24 May 1848	Owen	Krch.	Sep 1865	N.-Amer	835948
Besch, Christina (wife)		Peterzell	Obd.	Apr 1862	N.-Amer	838635
Besch, Johann Georg		Peterzell	Obd.	Apr 1862	N.-Amer	838635
Besch, Mathias	1834	Peterzell	Obd.	Aug 1854	N.-Amer	838635
Besserer, Caroline Louise		Leonberg	Leon.	Dec 1857	Hesse	835787
Besserer, Catharina Magd. & C		Gebersheim	Leon.	Mar 1857	N.-Amer	837953
Besserer, Christine Caroline	31 Jan 1842	Gebersheim	Leon.	Mar 1857	N.-Amer	837953
Besserer, Christine Friederike	13 Feb 1840	Gebersheim	Leon.	Mar 1857	N.-Amer	837953
Besserer, Christoph & F		Leonberg	Leon.	Apr 1833	Poland	835786
Besserer, Heinrich	8 Feb 1845	Leonberg	Leon.	Jun 1864	N.-Amer	835787
Besserer, Jakob Ludwig	8 Dec 1847	Leonberg	Leon.	Dec 1866	N.-Amer	835787
Besserer, Johann Christoph		Leonberg	Leon.	May 1857	France	835786
Besserer, Johannes	26 Sep 1845	Gebersheim	Leon.	Mar 1857	N.-Amer	837953
Besserer, Louise	10 Jun 1824	Leonberg	Leon.	Apr 1866	Austria	835787
Bessler, Rosine Barbara	8 Apr 1828	Alpirsbach	Obd.	Jan 1858	Hesse	838630
Bessmer, Anna Maria	11 Mar 1843	Neidlingen	Krch.	Aug 1860	N.-Amer	835946
Bessmer, Catharina	16 Sep 1836	Neidlingen	Krch.	1853	N.-Amer	835946
Bessmer, Catharina Marg. (wid.) & F	14 Sep 1804	Neidlingen	Krch.	Aug 1860	N.-Amer	835946
Bessmer, Christoph	24 May 1811	Nabern	Krch.	Feb 1857	N.-Amer	835946
Bessmer, Johann	27 Aug 1824	Nabern	Krch.	bef 1871	N.-Amer	835946
Bessmer, Michael	31 May 1830	Neidlingen	Krch.	1851	N.-Amer	835946
Bessmer, Michael	6 Apr 1838	Nabern	Krch.	Mar 1857	N.-Amer	835946
Betz, David	2 Feb 1816	Rosswaelden	Krch.	Mar 1867	N.-Amer	835949
Betz, Friedrich	22 Mar 1832	Kleiningstingen	Rtl.	Jul 1860	N.-Amer	841051
Betz, Georg Jakob	16 May 1880	Zell	Krch.	Sep 1896	England	835774
Betz, Gottlob	14 May 1849	Weiler	Krch.	May 1869	N.-Amer	835949
Betz, Johann Martin	9 Nov 1848	Undingen	Rtl.	Nov 1866	N.-Amer	841051
Betz, Johann Michael	27 Apr 1836	Rosswaelden	Krch.	Mar 1867	N.-Amer	835949
Betz, Johannes	9 Sep 1869	Rosswaelden	Krch.	May 1886	N.-Amer	548403
Betz, Johannes & F		Willmandingen	Rtl.	1854	N.-Amer	841051
Betz, Ludwig Friedrich	28 Mar 1877	Zell	Krch.	Feb 1894	England	835774
Betz, Ludwig Friedrich	9 Oct 1839	Pfullingen	Rtl.	1859	England	841051
Betz, Mathaeus	11 Sep 1858	Undingen	Rtl.	Jun 1880	N.-Amer	841051
Betz, Matthaeus	10 Jun 1841	Willmandingen	Rtl.	Feb 1860	N.-Amer	841051
Betz, Matthias	28 Mar 1845	Kleiningstingen	Rtl.	Jul 1865	N.-Amer	841051
Betz, Regina	11 Jun 1835	Willmandingen	Rtl.	1854	N.-Amer	841051
Betz, Rosina		Kleiningstingen	Rtl.	Sep 1867	N.-Amer	841051
Betz, Wilhelm	29 Jan 1864	Weiler	Krch.	Jan 1881	N.-Amer	835949
Betzler, Karl Eugen	16 Jul 1863	Wiesensteig	Gsl.	Mar 1880	N.-Amer	572048

Name		Birth		Emigration			Film
Last	First	Date	Place	O'amt	Appl. Date	Dest.	Number
Beutel, Anna Maria		4 Nov 1853	Pfullingen	Rtl.	Nov 1860	N.-Amer	841051
Beutel, Elisabetha Marg. (wife)		17 Feb 1809	Pfullingen	Rtl.	Nov 1860	N.-Amer	841051
Beutel, Jakob Andreas & F		21 Feb 1809	Pfullingen	Rtl.	Nov 1860	N.-Amer	841051
Beutel, Philipp Jakob		7 Jan 1843	Pfullingen	Rtl.	Nov 1860	N.-Amer	841051
Beutelschiess, Johann Adam		27 Sep 1837	Brucken	Krch.	Feb 1857	N.-Amer	835944
Beutelspacher, Adolf Heinrich		2 Apr 1853	Leonberg	Leon.	Apr 1854	N.-Amer	835786
Beutelspacher, Carl Wilhelm		3 Jun 1835	Leonberg	Leon.	Apr 1854	N.-Amer	835786
Beutelspacher, Cathar.B. (wife)			Leonberg	Leon.	Jun 1840	N.-Amer	835786
Beutelspacher, Christian Fr.		25 Nov 1821	Leonberg	Leon.	May 1856	France	835786
Beutelspacher, Christian Gott.		31 Dec 1836	Leonberg	Leon.	Apr 1854	N.-Amer	835786
Beutelspacher, Christiane M.		12 May 1846	Leonberg	Leon.	Dec 1866	Switz.	835787
Beutelspacher, Christine Lou.		4 Jan 1835	Leonberg	Leon.	Jun 1840	N.-Amer	835786
Beutelspacher, Christof E. & F			Leonberg	Leon.	Jun 1840	N.-Amer	835786
Beutelspacher, Christoph Hein.		22 yrs.	Leonberg	Leon.	Jun 1854	N.-Amer	835786
Beutelspacher, Friederike		9 yrs.	Leonberg	Leon.	May 1851	N.-Amer	835786
Beutelspacher, Friedr. Sophie		7 Jul 1814	Leonberg	Leon.	Jul 1846	France	835786
Beutelspacher, Gottlieb		14 Apr 1817	Leonberg	Leon.	bef 1860	N.-Amer	835786
Beutelspacher, Gottlieb			Leonberg	Leon.	bef 1865	N.-Amer	835787
Beutelspacher, Gottlieb Eberh.		24 Dec 1838	Leonberg	Leon.	Jun 1840	N.-Amer	835786
Beutelspacher, Gustav Gottlieb		30 Aug 1850	Leonberg	Leon.	Jun 1870	N.-Amer	835787
Beutelspacher, Heinrich		18 Feb 1865	Leonberg	Leon.	Apr 1881	N.-Amer	835787
Beutelspacher, Heinrich & F		u	Leonberg	Leon.	Apr 1854	N.-Amer	835786
Beutelspacher, Imanuel		8 yrs.	Leonberg	Leon.	May 1851	N.-Amer	835786
Beutelspacher, Imanuel & F			Leonberg	Leon.	May 1851	N.-Amer	835786
Beutelspacher, Johannes & F			Leonberg	Leon.	Jun 1840	N.-Amer	835786
Beutelspacher, Louise Fr. (wife)			Leonberg	Leon.	Jun 1840	N.-Amer	835786
Beutelspacher, Margaretha (wife)			Leonberg	Leon.	May 1851	N.-Amer	835786
Beutelspacher, Veronika			Leonberg	Leon.	Apr 1854	N.-Amer	835786
Beutelspacher, Wilhelm		14 Apr 1850	Leonberg	Leon.	Apr 1854	N.-Amer	835786
Beutelspacher, Wilhelm Joseph		25 Oct 1851	Leonberg	Leon.	Jan 1870	N.-Amer	835787
Beutenmueller, Gottlieb		8 Aug 1836	Kirchheim	Krch.	Oct 1856	N.-Amer	835940
Beuter, Johann Georg		5 Jul 1849	Stockach	Rtl.	Jul 1869	N.-Amer	841051
Beuttenmueller, Adam Christ.F.		14 Dec 1841	Kirchheim	Krch.	Oct 1859	S.-Amer	835940
Beuttenmueller, Christian Go.		24 Jul 1832	Kirchheim	Krch.	bef 1868	N.-Amer	835941
Beyer, Johann Paul		30 Jan 1811	Hochmoessingen	Obd.	Nov 1843	Switz.	838633
Beyerle, Carl & F		16 Aug 1818	Weil der Stadt	Leon.	Apr 1848	N.-Amer	837965
Beyerle, Carl Anton		3 Aug 1847	Weil der Stadt	Leon.	Apr 1848	N.-Amer	837965
Beyerle, Johanna Babette W.		12 Jul 1840	Ulm	Leon.	Nov 1859	Austria	837966
Beyerle, Paul			Weil der Stadt	Leon.	bef 1852	Prussia	837966
Beyerle, Walburga (wife)		1 May 1821	Weil der Stadt	Leon.	Apr 1848	N.-Amer	837965
Bez, Anna Elisabeth		8 Nov 1857	Maegerkingen	Rtl.	Nov 1863	N.-Amer	841051
Bez, Anna Maria		20 Apr 1841	Maegerkingen	Rtl.	Nov 1863	N.-Amer	841051
Bez, Anna Maria		11 yrs.	Brucken	Krch.	Jun 1804	Rus-Pol	550804
Bez, Anna Maria (wid.) & F		15 Nov 1808	Erpfingen	Rtl.	Mar 1866	N.-Amer	841051
Bez, Christina		9 Mar 1856	Maegerkingen	Rtl.	Nov 1863	N.-Amer	841051
Bez, Christina Barbara		21 yrs.	Brucken	Krch.	Jun 1804	Rus-Pol	550804
Bez, Christoph Adam		2 Jan 1835	Brucken	Krch.	Mar 1855	Austral	835944
Bez, Dorothea		26 Jul 1847	Maegerkingen	Rtl.	Sep 1862	S.-Russ	841051
Bez, Elisabetha Kathar. (wife)		19 Sep 1817	Maegerkingen	Rtl.	Nov 1863	N.-Amer	841051
Bez, Eva Katarina		18 yrs.	Brucken	Krch.	Jun 1804	Rus-Pol	550804

Bez, Johann Adam	8 yrs.	Brucken	Krch.	Jun 1804	Rus-Pol	550804
Bez, Johann Friedrich & W	2 Feb 1833	Owen	Krch.	Mar 1860	N.-Amer	835948
Bez, Johann Georg	18 yrs.	Erpfingen	Rtl.	Jul 1880	N.-Amer	841051
Bez, Johann Georg & F	50 yrs.	Brucken	Krch.	Jun 1804	Rus-Pol	550804
Bez, Johann Jacob	6 yrs.	Brucken	Krch.	Jun 1804	Rus-Pol	550804
Bez, Johann Michael	4 yrs.	Brucken	Krch.	Jun 1804	Rus-Pol	550804
Bez, Johannes	13 Dec 1843	Maegerkingen	Rtl.	Nov 1863	N.-Amer	841051
Bez, Johannes	13 yrs.	Brucken	Krch.	Jun 1804	Rus-Pol	550804
Bez, Johannes	26 Jun 1819	Owen	Krch.	Aug 1864	N.-Amer	835948
Bez, Johannes & F	28 Dec 1814	Maegerkingen	Rtl.	Nov 1863	N.-Amer	841051
Bez, Katharina Barbara	18 Jul 1859	Maegerkingen	Rtl.	Nov 1863	N.-Amer	841051
Bez, Ludwig	26 Jun 1848	Undingen	Rtl.	Oct 1866	N.-Amer	841051
Bez, Maria Agnes	44 yrs.	Brucken	Krch.	Jun 1804	Rus-Pol	550804
Bez, Maria Dorothea	18 mon.	Brucken	Krch.	Jun 1804	Rus-Pol	550804
Bez, Regina Margareta	16 yrs.	Brucken	Krch.	Jun 1804	Rus-Pol	550804
Bez, Rosine Catharine (wife)	11 Oct 1833	Owen	Krch.	Mar 1860	N.-Amer	835948
Bezler, Heinrich Gottlieb		Jesingen	Krch.	Dec 1863	France	835946
Bezler, Jakob Friedrich	5 May 1811	Jesingen	Krch.	Apr 1857	Hungary	835946
Bezler, Johann Friedrich	6 Aug 1874	Bissingen	Krch.	Apr 1889	N.-Amer	548323
Bezler, Johann Friedrich	6 Aug 1874	Bissingen	Krch.	Apr 1889	N.-Amer	835943
Bezler, Wilhelm	11 Jan 1826	Jesingen	Krch.	Mar 1864	France	835946
Bezold, Carl Gottlob	31 May 1838	Kirchheim	Krch.	Apr 1855	N.-Amer	835940
Bickle, Anna Catharina	8 Sep 1849	Undingen	Rtl.	Mar 1868	N.-Amer	841051
Bickle, Anna Maria	12 Dec 1863	Undingen	Rtl.	Mar 1868	N.-Amer	841051
Bickle, Anna Maria (wife)	30 Mar 1821	Undingen	Rtl.	Mar 1868	N.-Amer	841051
Bickle, Christian Gottlieb	30 Oct 1846	Undingen	Rtl.	1866	N.-Amer	841051
Bickle, Gottlieb		Undingen	Rtl.	Oct 1866	N.-Amer	841056
Bickle, Johannes	23 Aug 1845	Undingen	Rtl.	Mar 1868	N.-Amer	841051
Bickle, Mathaeus & F	20 Sep 1820	Undingen	Rtl.	Mar 1868	N.-Amer	841051
Bickle, Regina	4 Aug 1859	Undingen	Rtl.	Mar 1868	N.-Amer	841051
Biedermann, Gottlieb David	4 May 1817	Leonberg	Leon.	Mar 1844	N.-Amer	835786
Biedermann, Heinrich	2 Aug 1846	Reutlingen	Rtl.	Aug 1864	N.-Amer	841051
Biedlingmaier, Joseph & F		Wiesensteig	Gsl.	bef 1853	N.-Amer	572041
Biedlingmaier, Margaretha (wife)		Wiesensteig	Gsl.	Mar 1853	N.-Amer	572041
Biedlingmaier, Theresia	10 mon.	Wiesensteig	Gsl.	Mar 1853	N.-Amer	572041
Biegler, Michael		Oberndorf	Obd.	1829	N.-Amer	838635
Bienz, Baltas		Gerlingen	Leon.	Apr 1831	N.-Amer	837953
Bihler, Matthaeus	24 Apr 1816	Altenstadt-Gsl.	Gsl.	bef 1858	N.-Amer	572043
Bihr, Wilhelm	27 Sep 1846	Weilheim	Krch.	Mar 1867	France	835950
Bikle, Johann Georg	9 Feb 1839	Zell	Krch.	Apr 1855	N.-Amer	835774
Bilder, Valentin	2 Jul 1831	Lauterbach	Obd.	Jul 1868	N.-Amer	838634
Bindel, Christian & W		Leonberg	Leon.	Aug 1854	N.-Amer	835786
Bindel, Christiane (wife)		Leonberg	Leon.	Aug 1854	N.-Amer	835786
Binder, Agatha	20 Dec 1822	Gueltstein	Herr.	Aug 1866	N.-Amer	834631
Binder, Anna	3 Jun 1853	Altenstadt-Gsl.	Gsl.	Jul 1854	N.-Amer	572042
Binder, Anna Friederika (wife)	20 Feb 1828	Moensheim	Leon.	Jul 1854	N.-Amer	837960
Binder, Anna Maria	21 Dec 1818	Gueltstein	Herr.	Aug 1866	N.-Amer	834631
Binder, Anna Maria	9 Aug 1860	Gueltstein	Herr.	Apr 1869	N.-Amer	834631
Binder, Caroline	7 Jul 1834	Schoeckingen	Leon.	Feb 1852	N.-Amer	837964
Binder, Christian	79 yrs.	Reutlingen	Rtl.	May 1880	N.-Amer	841051

18

Name		Birth		Emigration			Film
Last	First	Date	Place	O'amt	Appl. Date	Dest.	Number
Binder, Christian Wilhelm		14 Nov 1867	Gueltstein	Herr.	Apr 1869	N.-Amer	834631
Binder, Elisabetha Cath. (wife)		7 Jan 1835	Gueltstein	Herr.	Apr 1869	N.-Amer	834631
Binder, Ferdinand			Hardt	Obd.	Apr 1854	N.-Amer	838633
Binder, Friedrich		16 Nov 1836	Schoeckingen	Leon.	Jul 1857	N.-Amer	837964
Binder, Georg & F			Rutesheim	Leon.	Mar 1830	N.-Amer	837964
Binder, Georg Gottlieb		5 Aug 1864	Gueltstein	Herr.	Apr 1869	N.-Amer	834631
Binder, Gottlieb			Renningen	Leon.	Apr 1817	N.-Amer	837963
Binder, Gottlob			Altenstadt-Gsl.	Gsl.	Feb 1853	N.-Amer	572041
Binder, Ignaz		31 Jul 1867	Boehmenkirch	Gsl.	Jan 1883	N.-Amer	572049
Binder, Ignaz		11 Nov 1850	Boehmenkirch	Gsl.	Jul 1870	N.-Amer	572047
Binder, Jakob		24 Jun 1835	Unterboehringen	Gsl.	Jul 1854	N.-Amer	572042
Binder, Jakob		29 Jul 1825	Schoeckingen	Leon.	Feb 1852	N.-Amer	837964
Binder, Jakob Friedrich & F		25 Dec 1825	Moensheim	Leon.	Jul 1854	N.-Amer	837960
Binder, Joachim			Boehmenkirch	Gsl.	Jul 1852	N.-Amer	572041
Binder, Johann Georg			Unterboehringen	Gsl.	Feb 1853	N.-Amer	572041
Binder, Johann Martin		16 Dec 1820	Rutesheim	Leon.	bef 1849	Algier	837964
Binder, Johann Martin & F		12 Mar 1832	Gueltstein	Herr.	Apr 1869	N.-Amer	834631
Binder, Johann Michael & F		24 Aug 1811	Altenstadt-Gsl.	Gsl.	Jul 1854	N.-Amer	572042
Binder, Johann Wilhelm		28 Aug 1864	Leonberg	Leon.	May 1881	N.-Amer	835787
Binder, Johanna Catharina		17 Mar 1849	Moensheim	Leon.	Jul 1854	N.-Amer	837960
Binder, Johanne Christiane		16 Jul 1797	Renningen	Leon.	Feb 1819	N.-Amer	837963
Binder, Johannes		7 Dec 1838	Boehmenkirch	Gsl.	Oct 1866	N.-Amer	572045
Binder, Johannes (wid.) & F		25 Dec 1760	Renningen	Leon.	Feb 1819	N.-Amer	837963
Binder, Josef		5 Sep 1838	Boehmenkirch	Gsl.	Jan 1867	N.-Amer	572046
Binder, Joseph		24 Aug 1831	Boehmenkirch	Gsl.	Sep 1854	N.-Amer	572042
Binder, Joseph & F			Mariazell	Obd.	May 1817	N.-Amer	838634
Binder, Karl Friedrich		18 Sep 1800	Bessigheim	Leon.	Apr 1828	N.-Amer	837963
Binder, Leonhardt			Moensheim	Leon.	Feb 1847	N.-Amer	837960
Binder, Luise		5 Aug 1832	Schoeckingen	Leon.	Feb 1852	N.-Amer	837964
Binder, Maria		27 Aug 1853	Moensheim	Leon.	Jul 1854	N.-Amer	837960
Binder, Marie Anna			Gingen	Gsl.	Mar 1853	N.-Amer	572041
Binder, Matthaeus			Altenstadt-Gsl.	Gsl.	Feb 1853	N.-Amer	572041
Binder, Ursula - (wife)		29 Sep 1809	Altenstadt-Gsl.	Gsl.	Jul 1854	N.-Amer	572042
Binder, Wilhelm Fridrich		22 Feb 1844	Herrenberg	Herr.	bef 1870	Switz.	834629
Binder, Wilhelm Michael		11 Oct 1833	Renningen	Leon.	Feb 1853	N.-Amer	837963
Bindlingmaier, Anna Katharina			Grosssuessen	Gsl.	Apr 1853	N.-Amer	572041
Bingert, Ignaz		8 Sep 1838	Boehmenkirch	Gsl.	Apr 1867	N.-Amer	572046
Binkelmann, Johann David		2 Jan 1828	Oetlingen	Krch.	1859	N.-Amer	835948
Birck, Christian		12 Sep 1863	Weiler	Krch.	Sep 1871	N.-Amer	835949
Birk, Daniel		19 Jun 1851	Hochdorf	Krch.	Mar 1867	N.-Amer	835945
Birk, Gottlieb Ferd. Edu. Her.		18 Jun 1839	Hochdorf	Krch.	Sep 1854	N.-Amer	835945
Birk, Helene		13 May 1828	Hochdorf	Krch.	bef 1865	N.-Amer	835945
Birk, Johann Georg		26 Feb 1822	Hochdorf	Krch.	Oct 1862	N.-Amer	835945
Birk, Johann Gottlieb		17 Feb 1838	Hochdorf	Krch.	Oct 1862	N.-Amer	835945
Birk, Johann Jacob		19 Jul 1840	Hochdorf	Krch.	Mar 1866	N.-Amer	835945
Birkle, Carl August		28 Sep 1865	Oberndorf	Obd.	Jul 1870	Bavaria	838635
Birkle, Ida Johanna		28 Sep 1865	Oberndorf	Obd.	Jul 1870	Bavaria	838635
Birkle, Philippine (wife)		3 Apr 1833	Oberndorf	Obd.	Jul 1870	Bavaria	838635
Birlingmeier, Johann Georg		39 yrs.	Kuchen	Gsl.	Jan 1851	N.-Amer	577788
Bischoff, Johann Georg		14 Feb 1833	Betzweiler	Obd.	Sep 1856	N.-Amer	838631

Name		Place	District	Date	Destination	No.
Bischoff, Josef & F		Weil der Stadt	Leon.	May 1833	Prussia	837965
Bischoff, Margaretha	18 yrs.	Weil der Stadt	Leon.	May 1833	Prussia	837965
Bischoff, Victoria	17 yrs.	Weil der Stadt	Leon.	May 1833	Prussia	837965
Bisswurm, Franz & F		Sulgen	Obd.	May 1817	N.-Amer	838638
Bisswurm, Jakob	3 Jul 1846	Sulgen	Obd.	Oct 1866	N.-Amer	838638
Biswurm, Johannes	1 Apr 1837	Mariazell	Obd.	Jan 1867	Bavaria	838634
Bittlinger, Katharina	22 Jun 1827	Deggingen	Gsl.	Aug 1851	N.-Amer	577788
Bittlingmeier, Marianna	29 Jul 1835	Treffelhausen	Gsl.	Oct 1853	N.-Amer	572041
Bittner, Elisabetha	14 yrs.	Westerheim	Gsl.	Mar 1852	N.-Amer	572041
Bittner, Gottfried & F		Alpirsbach	Obd.	Nov 1816	–	838631
Bittner, Johannes & F		Westerheim	Gsl.	Mar 1852	N.-Amer	572041
Bittner, Katharina (wife)		Westerheim	Gsl.	Mar 1852	N.-Amer	572041
Bittner, Maria Anna	16 yrs.	Westerheim	Gsl.	Mar 1852	N.-Amer	572041
Bittner, Michael	10 yrs.	Westerheim	Gsl.	Mar 1852	N.-Amer	572041
Bittner, Vitlein	9 yrs.	Westerheim	Gsl.	Mar 1852	N.-Amer	572041
Bitzer, Emmanuel Gotthold	25 Mar 1873	Hildrizhausen	Herr.	Jan 1892	N.-Amer	834631
Bizer, Jacob		Ditzingen	Leon.	Jan 1817	N.-Amer	835788
Blaechle, Jakob	25 Jul 1847	Fluorn	Obd.	Jul 1865	N.-Amer	838632
Blaesi, Christian Gottlieb	21 Jan 1829	Dettingen	Krch.	Feb 1854	N.-Amer	835944
Blaich, Anna Catharina	17 Mar 1834	Renningen	Leon.	bef 1857	N.-Amer	837963
Blaich, Christian Gottlieb		Renningen	Leon.	bef 1854	N.-Amer	837963
Blaich, Christiana Margaretha	16 Jun 1835	Renningen	Leon.	bef 1864	N.-Amer	837963
Blaich, Gottlieb Friedrich	6 Dec 1846	Renningen	Leon.	Sep 1865	N.-Amer	837963
Blaich, Jakob Friedrich	4 Jul 1860	Renningen	Leon.	Jun 1877	N.-Amer	837963
Blaich, Johann Jacob	7 Feb 1819	Renningen	Leon.	bef 1847	Berlin	837963
Blaich, Johann Jakob	25 Jan 1837	Renningen	Leon.	Sep 1853	N.-Amer	837963
Blaich, Wilhelm		Renningen	Leon.	bef 1870	N.-Amer	837963
Blankenhorn, Anna Maria	22 Mar 1835	Dettingen	Krch.	bef 1868	N.-Amer	835944
Blankenhorn, Christian	29 Jan 1851	Heimerdingen	Leon.	Mar 1854	N.-Amer	837954
Blankenhorn, Christian & F	26 Feb 1822	Heimerdingen	Leon.	Mar 1854	N.-Amer	837954
Blankenhorn, Christiane Carol.	30 Jul 1849	Heimerdingen	Leon.	Mar 1854	N.-Amer	837954
Blankenhorn, Christina	1 Oct 1834	Heimerdingen	Leon.	Jul 1855	N.-Amer	837954
Blankenhorn, Christine Margar.	23 Dec 1836	Dettingen	Krch.	bef 1868	N.-Amer	835944
Blankenhorn, Gottlieb	21 Mar 1841	Dettingen	Krch.	Nov 1861	N.-Amer	835944
Blankenhorn, Jakob Friedrich	7 Dec 1852	Heimerdingen	Leon.	Mar 1854	N.-Amer	837954
Blankenhorn, Johann Friedrich	31 Dec 1842	Dettingen	Krch.	Jul 1862	N.-Amer	835944
Blankenhorn, Johann Jakob	11 Oct 1863	Dettingen	Krch.	Jun 1879	N.-Amer	548403
Blankenhorn, Johann Michael	13 Jan 1857	Dettingen	Krch.	Apr 1873	N.-Amer	835944
Blankenhorn, Karl	19 Feb 1845	Kirchheim	Krch.	Jul 1865	N.-Amer	835941
Blankenhorn, Magaretha	11 Apr 1840	Dettingen	Krch.	1854	N.-Amer	835940
Blankenhorn, Maria Barbara		Dettingen	Krch.	bef 1862	N.-Amer	835944
Blanz, (daughter)	6 yrs.	Weil im Dorf	Loen.	Sep 1871	N.-Amer	837967
Blanz, Christine Magda. (wife)		Weil im Dorf	Loen.	Sep 1871	N.-Amer	837967
Blanz, Gottlieb & W		Weil im Dorf	Loen.	Mar 1853	N.-Amer	837967
Blanz, Johann Jakob & F		Weil im Dorf	Loen.	Mar 1852	N.-Amer	837967
Blanz, Johann Leonhard	11 Sep 1846	Weil im Dorf	Loen.	Mar 1852	N.-Amer	837967
Blanz, Johannes	4 Jan 1848	Weil im Dorf	Loen.	Mar 1852	N.-Amer	837967
Blanz, Johannes & F		Weil im Dorf	Loen.	Mar 1852	N.-Amer	837967
Blanz, Louise (wife)		Weil im Dorf	Loen.	Mar 1852	N.-Amer	837967
Blanz, Magdalena (wife)		Weil im Dorf	Loen.	Mar 1853	N.-Amer	837967

Name		Birth		Emigration			Film
Last	First	Date	Place	O'amt	Appl. Date	Dest.	Number
Blanz, Maria Magdalena (wife)			Weil im Dorf	Loen.	Mar 1852	N.-Amer	837967
Blanz, Philipp & F		45 yrs.	Weil im Dorf	Loen.	Sep 1871	N.-Amer	837967
Blass, Anna Maria		17 Aug 1845	Bissingen	Krch.	Mar 1864	N.-Amer	835943
Blass, Christine		7 May 1849	Bissingen	Krch.	Jul 1867	N.-Amer	835943
Blass, Jakob		18 Aug 1841	Bissingen	Krch.	Feb 1860	N.-Amer	835943
Blass, Konrad		12 Jan 1845	Bissingen	Krch.	Jun 1865	N.-Amer	835943
Blass, Maria Friederike		19 Jun 1851	Bissingen	Krch.	Oct 1871	N.-Amer	835943
Blass, Sophia Magdalena		8 Mar 1846	Bissingen	Krch.	Mar 1865	N.-Amer	835943
Bleiholder, Dorothea		17 yrs.	Moensheim	Leon.	Mar 1831	N.-Amer	837960
Bleiholder, Dorothea Frieder.		9 Jan 1847	Moensheim	Leon.	Apr 1857	N.-Amer	837960
Bleiholder, Johann Georg		24 yrs.	Moensheim	Leon.	Mar 1831	N.-Amer	837960
Bleiholder, Johanna		29 Feb 1844	Moensheim	Leon.	Apr 1857	N.-Amer	837960
Bleiholder, Johannes		26 Jun 1841	Moensheim	Leon.	Jul 1854	N.-Amer	837960
Bleiholder, Katharina Doroth.		27 Sep 1835	Moensheim	Leon.	Jul 1854	N.-Amer	837960
Bleiholder, Sibilla		23 yrs.	Moensheim	Leon.	Mar 1831	N.-Amer	837960
Blessing, Abraham		31 Oct 1822	Gebersheim	Leon.	Feb 1853	N.-Amer	837953
Blessing, Agatha (wife)		1 Sep 1826	Eybach	Gsl.	Jul 1853	N.-Amer	572041
Blessing, Aloisius		7 Mar 1851	Eybach	Gsl.	Jul 1853	N.-Amer	572041
Blessing, Christiane & C		26 Aug 1838	Jesingen	Krch.	Aug 1860	N.-Amer	835946
Blessing, Christine		10 Jan 1860	Jesingen	Krch.	Aug 1860	N.-Amer	835946
Blessing, Eberhardine (wid.)		25 Sep 1815	Jesingen	Krch.	Aug 1860	N.-Amer	835946
Blessing, Franziska		4 Jan 1850	Eybach	Gsl.	Jul 1853	N.-Amer	572041
Blessing, Gottlob		5 Dec 1839	Jesingen	Krch.	Aug 1857	N.-Amer	835946
Blessing, Johann Evangel. & F		22 Nov 1815	Eybach	Gsl.	Jul 1853	N.-Amer	572041
Blessing, Johann Georg & F			Friolzheim	Leon.	Jul 1851	N.-Amer	835791
Blessing, Johann Michael		10 Feb 1835	Jesingen	Krch.	Oct 1855	N.-Amer	835946
Blessing, Joseph			Treffelhausen	Gsl.	Mar 1850	N.-Amer	577788
Blessing, Maria Ida		5 Jan 1853	Eybach	Gsl.	Jul 1853	N.-Amer	572041
Blessing, Paul		8 Dec 1866	Boehmenkirch	Gsl.	Jul 1883	N.-Amer	572049
Bleyholder, Israel			Moensheim	Leon.	Aug 1851	N.-Amer	837960
Blickle, Christian Gottlieb		30 Oct 1846	Undingen	Rtl.	Oct 1866	N.-Amer	841051
Blind, Anna Catharina		13 Aug 1842	Owen	Krch.	bef 1873	N.-Amer	835948
Blind, Elisabetha Catharina			Holzmaden	Krch.	Aug 1870	N.-Amer	835945
Blind, Johann Konrad		26 Oct 1844	Owen	Krch.	Jul 1864	N.-Amer	835948
Blind, Johannes		29 Dec 1839	Owen	Krch.	Jun 1862	N.-Amer	835948
Blind, Veronica Sophie		16 Sep 1841	Holzmaden	Krch.	Nov 1865	N.-Amer	835945
Blind/Hausch, Maria Kath. & F		17 Oct 1797	Zell	Krch.	Apr 1855	N.-Amer	835774
Blocher, Barbara		18 Jun 1837	Roetenbach	Obd.	Jul 1869	Switz.	838636
Blocher, Jakob		10 Aug 1816	Betzweiler	Obd.	bef 1846	France	838631
Blocher, Johannes & W			Dornhan	Obd.	Apr 1850	N.-Amer	838638
Blocher, Maria (wife)			Dornhan	Obd.	Apr 1850	N.-Amer	838638
Bloechle, Andreas			Peterzell	Obd.	Nov 1865	N.-Amer	838635
Bloechle, Johann Georg		6 Jun 1849	Peterzell	Obd.	Feb 1869	N.-Amer	838635
Bloss, Conrad		14 yrs.	Hemmingen	Leon.	Apr 1860	N.-Amer	837956
Bloss, Johanna		16 yrs.	Hemmingen	Leon.	Apr 1860	N.-Amer	837956
Bloss, Maria (wid.) & F			Hemmingen	Leon.	Apr 1860	N.-Amer	837956
Blum, Catharina		15 yrs.	Schoeckingen	Leon.	May 1851	N.-Amer	837964
Blum, Catharina (wife)		45 yrs.	Schoeckingen	Leon.	May 1851	N.-Amer	837964
Blum, Friedrich			Ehlenbogen	Obd.	Apr 1861	N.-Amer	838632
Blum, Gottlieb & F			Unterschwandorf	Nag.	Jul 1852	N.-Amer	838488

Blum, Gottlieb & F		Unterschwandorf	Nag.	Jul 1852	N.-Amer	838488
Blum, Jacob		Hemmingen	Leon.	Jul 1853	N.-Amer	837956
Blum, Johann Georg	15 Nov 1850	Ehlenbogen	Obd.	Mar 1869	N.-Amer	838632
Blum, Johannes	18 Nov 1818	Ehlenbogen	Obd.	bef 1868	N.-Amer	838632
Blum, Johannes		Ehlenbogen	Obd.	Apr 1861	N.-Amer	838632
Blum, Julius Karl	5 Jun 1845	Boehmenkirch	Gsl.	Jan 1867	N.-Amer	572046
Blum, Louise	16 yrs.	Schoeckingen	Leon.	May 1851	N.-Amer	837964
Blum, Maria	18 yrs.	Schoeckingen	Leon.	May 1851	N.-Amer	837964
Blum, Michael & F	42 yrs.	Schoeckingen	Leon.	May 1851	N.-Amer	837964
Blum, Robert	3 May 1850	Kirchheim	Krch.	Mar 1869	N.-Amer	835941
Bodmer, Caroline	30 Dec 1839	Schramberg	Obd.	Jun 1868	Prussia	838636
Boebel, Johann Friedrich	4 Oct 1869	Weilheim	Krch.	Jul 1886	England	835774
Boebel, Karl August Friedrich		Reutlingen	Rtl.	May 1859	N.-Amer	841051
Boeckle, Andreas Jakob	14 Apr 1862	Bondorf	Herr.	bef 1895	Switz.	834630
Boeckle, Carl Friedrich	22 Jan 1843	Herrenberg	Herr.	bef 1870	Prussia	834629
Boeckle, Wilhelm	15 May 1879	Herrenberg	Herr.	Feb 1896	N.-Amer	834629
Boeckle, Wilhelm Philipp	9 Nov 1866	Herrenberg	Herr.	Dec 1866	N.-Amer	834629
Boehm, Robert	24 Sep 1834	Wiesensteig	Gsl.	Dec 1852	N.-Amer	572041
Boehmler, Adolph Gottlob	5 Jun 1858	Herrenberg	Herr.	Nov 1874	N.-Amer	834629
Boehmler, Bernhard	34 yrs.	Eltingen	Leon.	Feb 1817	Russia	835789
Boehmler, Bernhardt		Eltingen	Leon.	Sep 1854	N.-Amer	835789
Boehmler, Carl Friedrich	26 Oct 1835	Heimsheim	Leon.	Jul 1854	N.-Amer	837955
Boehmler, Catharina (wife)		Eltingen	Leon.	May 1853	N.-Amer	835789
Boehmler, Christian	25 Feb 1849	Eltingen	Leon.	Sep 1869	N.-Amer	835789
Boehmler, Jacob Friedrich	infant	Eltingen	Leon.	May 1853	N.-Amer	835789
Boehmler, Johann Georg	27 May 1858	Eltingen	Leon.	Jun 1880	N.-Amer	835789
Boehmler, Johann Georg	14 Dec 1861	Ohmden	Krch.	Aug 1878	N.-Amer	548403
Boehmler, Johann Gottlieb	14 Oct 1861	Ohmden	Krch.	Aug 1878	N.-Amer	835948
Boehmler, Johann Ulrich	22 Apr 1827	Eltingen	Leon.	Aug 1854	N.-Amer	835789
Boehmler, Johannes & F		Hoefingen	Leon.	Feb 1815	Hungary	837957
Boehmler, Katharina Elisabeth		Eltingen	Leon.	Aug 1867	N.-Amer	835789
Boehmler, Maria	5 yrs.	Eltingen	Leon.	May 1853	N.-Amer	835789
Boehmler, Philipp Jacob & F		Eltingen	Leon.	May 1853	N.-Amer	835789
Boehringer, Anna Cathar. (wife)	12 May 1790	Weilheim	Krch.	Apr 1867	N.-Amer	835950
Boehringer, Anna Margaretha	8 Mar 1831	Weilheim	Krch.	bef 1869	N.-Amer	835950
Boehringer, Anna Maria	2 May 1824	Weilheim	Krch.	bef 1869	N.-Amer	835950
Boehringer, Anna Maria	16 Aug 1859	Ochsenwang	Krch.	May 1861	N.-Amer	835947
Boehringer, Barbara	24 Jun 1851	Ochsenwang	Krch.	May 1861	N.-Amer	835947
Boehringer, Bernhard	27 Jan 1844	Ochsenwang	Krch.	Apr 1861	N.-Amer	835947
Boehringer, Christian	27 Dec 1821	Zell	Krch.	Oct 1858	N.-Amer	835774
Boehringer, Christoph	2 Aug 1845	Ochsenwang	Krch.	Mar 1860	N.-Amer	835947
Boehringer, Dorothea	9 Feb 1849	Ochsenwang	Krch.	May 1861	N.-Amer	835947
Boehringer, Elisabetha	6 Feb 1843	Pfullingen	Rtl.	Sep 1865	N.-Amer	841051
Boehringer, Friedrich	8 Oct 1846	Holzmaden	Krch.	May 1861	N.-Amer	835945
Boehringer, Friedrich Wilhelm	30 Jul 1841	Pfullingen	Rtl.	Sep 1865	N.-Amer	841051
Boehringer, Johann Jakob	18 Jul 1845	Pfullingen	Rtl.	Aug 1864	N.-Amer	841051
Boehringer, Johann Jakob & F	24 Dec 1815	Pfullingen	Rtl.	Sep 1865	N.-Amer	841051
Boehringer, Johanna	19 Mar 1818	Ochsenwang	Krch.	May 1861	N.-Amer	835947
Boehringer, Juliana	8 Aug 1829	Notzingen	Krch.	1858	N.-Amer	835940
Boehringer, Ludwig	14 Mar 1822	Weilheim	Krch.	Apr 1867	N.-Amer	835950

Name		Birth		Emigration			Film
Last	First	Date	Place	O'amt	Appl. Date	Dest.	Number
Boehringer, Ludwig & F		6 Aug 1791	Weilheim	Krch.	Apr 1867	N.-Amer	835950
Boehringer, Maria Kath. (wife)		22 Sep 1815	Pfullingen	Rtl.	Sep 1865	N.-Amer	841051
Boehringer, Sophie Friederike		4 May 1838	Weilheim	Krch.	bef 1869	N.-Amer	835950
Boelstler, Anna Barbara (wife)		1 May 1812	Boehmenkirch	Gsl.	Apr 1870	N.-Amer	572047
Boelstler, Johann Georg & W		6 Apr 1814	Boehmenkirch	Gsl.	Apr 1870	N.-Amer	572047
Boelstler, Joseph		8 Jan 1864	Boehmenkirch	Gsl.	Jun 1881	N.-Amer	572048
Boelstler, Joseph & W		29 Jan 1842	Boehmenkirch	Gsl.	Jan 1870	N.-Amer	572047
Boelstler, Kreszentia (wife)		7 Oct 1848	Boehmenkirch	Gsl.	Jan 1870	N.-Amer	572047
Boelstler, Sophia Kreszentia		11 Oct 1869	Boehmenkirch	Gsl.	Jan 1870	N.-Amer	572047
Boerschle, Franz Michael		14 Dec 1849	Eybach	Gsl.	Mar 1869	N.-Amer	572047
Boesch, Afra		19 yrs.	Mariazell	Obd.	Jan 1854	N.-Amer	838634
Boettiger, Andreas		49 yrs.	Fluorn	Obd.	1864	N.-Amer	838632
Boettinger, Andreas		15 May 1849	Betzweiler	Obd.	Mar 1864	N.-Amer	838631
Boetzel, Barbara		21 Feb 1811	Renningen	Leon.	1853	N.-Amer	837963
Boetzel, Christian Gottlob		22 Jan 1842	Renningen	Leon.	Apr 1852	N.-Amer	837963
Boetzel, Christian Margaretha		8 May 1847	Renningen	Leon.	Apr 1852	N.-Amer	837963
Boetzel, Christoph Friedrich		3 Oct 1838	Renningen	Leon.	Apr 1857	N.-Amer	837963
Boetzel, Ernst		27 Feb 1843	Renningen	Leon.	Apr 1852	N.-Amer	837963
Boetzel, Gottlieb Friedrich		23 Oct 1839	Renningen	Leon.	Apr 1852	N.-Amer	837963
Boetzel, Johann Andreas		11 Jan 1820	Renningen	Leon.	1853	N.-Amer	837963
Boetzel, Johann Gottfried & F			Renningen	Leon.	Apr 1852	N.-Amer	837963
Boetzel, Johannes		23 Jun 1849	Renningen	Leon.	Apr 1852	N.-Amer	837963
Boetzel, Margarethe		9 Mar 1809	Renningen	Leon.	1853	N.-Amer	837963
Boetzel, Regina (wife)			Renningen	Leon.	Apr 1852	N.-Amer	837963
Boger, Johannes		27 Jun 1849	Eybach	Gsl.	Aug 1868	N.-Amer	572046
Boger, Wilhelm		11 Mar 1855	Eybach	Gsl.	Feb 1873	N.-Amer	572047
Bohnet, Christian			Egenhausen	Nag.	Dec 1852	N.-Amer	838488
Bok, Philipp		3 May 1851	Waldmoessingen	Obd.	May 1869	N.-Amer	841015
Bokel, Wilhelmine Friederike			Pfullingen	Rtl.	Jan 1859	France	841051
Bollacher, Eduard		22 yrs.	Leonberg	Leon.	bef 1870	N.-Amer	835787
Bollacher, Gottlob Heinrich			Leonberg	Leon.	1867	N.-Amer	835787
Bomm, Alois		19 May 1837	Boehmenkirch	Gsl.	Feb 1854	N.-Amer	572042
Bomm, Michael		29 Jun 1848	Boehmenkirch	Gsl.	Jan 1867	N.-Amer	572046
Borho, Elisabeth			Mariazell	Obd.	Mar 1852	N.-Amer	838634
Borho, Karoline		6 Aug 1835	Aichhalden	Obd.	Mar 1865	France	838629
Borst, Christian Emil		20 Jan 1857	Geislingen	Gsl.	Jul 1872	N.-Amer	572047
Borst, Johannes		8 Oct 1839	Grosssuessen	Gsl.	Mar 1856	N.-Amer	572043
Borst, Wilhelmine			Geislingen	Gsl.	Oct 1865	Saxony	572045
Bosch, Anna Maria		7 Apr 1831	Notzingen	Krch.	bef 1856	N.-Amer	835947
Bosch, Anton Albert			Muehlhausen	Gsl.	bef 1860	N.-Amer	572044
Bosch, Carl		31 Jan 1851	Muenchingen	Leon.	Jun 1869	N.-Amer	837961
Bosch, Catharina		17 yrs.	Reutlingen	Rtl.	Apr 1880	N.-Amer	841051
Bosch, Johann Georg		12 May 1855	Notzingen	Krch.	Feb 1872	N.-Amer	835947
Bosch, Johannes		12 Sep 1837	Kleinsuessen	Gsl.	Feb 1854	N.-Amer	572042
Bosch, Maria Ursula		24 Oct 1808	Kitzen	Gsl.	Feb 1854	N.-Amer	572042
Bosch, Pauline		17 Dec 1835	Hochdorf	Krch.	May 1854	N.-Amer	835945
Bosch, Philipp		30 Jun 1826	Owen	Krch.	Feb 1872	N.-Amer	835948
Boser, Joseph		22 Oct 1842	Weissenstein	Gsl.	Feb 1857	N.-Amer	572043
Bossert, Andreas		54 yrs.	Wimsheim	Loen.	Feb 1855	N.-Amer	837967
Bossert, Andreas		32 yrs.	Wimsheim	Loen.	Aug 1854	N.-Amer	837967

Bossert, Jakob	26 yrs.	Dornhan	Obd.	May 1857	N.-Amer	838638
Bossert, Johannes	10 Oct 1838	Dettingen	Krch.	bef 1855	N.-Amer	835944
Bossert, Matheus & F		Mariazell	Obd.	May 1817	N.-Amer	838634
Bouc, Jean Pierre	4 Jan 1820	Perouse	Leon.	Aug 1857	N.-Amer	837962
Bozler, Elisabeth Cath. (wife)	52 yrs.	Unterlenningen	Krch.	Jun 1804	Russia	550804
Bozler, Elisabeth Catrina	19 yrs.	Unterlenningen	Krch.	Jun 1804	Russia	550804
Bozler, Elisabetha Margaretha	29 Aug 1820	Unterlenningen	Krch.	Nov 1855	N.-Amer	835949
Bozler, Johann Caspar	20 yrs.	Unterlenningen	Krch.	Jun 1804	Russia	550804
Bozler, Johannes	14 yrs.	Unterlenningen	Krch.	Jun 1804	Russia	550804
Bozler, Johannes	29 Oct 1846	Unterlenningen	Krch.	Aug 1862	N.-Amer	835949
Bozler, Johannes & F	44 yrs.	Unterlenningen	Krch.	Jun 1804	Russia	550804
Brackenhammer, Anna Mar. (wife)	21 Jan 1855	Kirchheim	Krch.	Feb 1880	N.-Amer	835942
Brackenhammer, Christian & F	9 Apr 1849	Kirchheim	Krch.	Feb 1880	N.-Amer	835942
Brackenhammer, Christian G.	9 Aug 1849	Kirchheim	Krch.	Feb 1880	N.-Amer	548403
Brackenhammer, Heinrich	3 Dec 1877	Kirchheim	Krch.	Feb 1880	N.-Amer	835942
Brackenhammer, Hermann Gottl.	12 Apr 1847	Kirchheim	Krch.	Apr 1881	N.-Amer	548403
Brackenhammer, Johann Christ.	22 Jun 1876	Kirchheim	Krch.	Feb 1880	N.-Amer	835942
Brackenhammer, Maria Emilia	6 Oct 1879	Kirchheim	Krch.	Feb 1880	N.-Amer	835942
Braeuning, Elisabetha Dor. & C		Warmbronn	Leon.	Oct 1854	N.-Amer	837965
Braeuning, Gottlieb	1 Jul 1843	Warmbronn	Leon.	Aug 1859	N.-Amer	837965
Braeuning, Johann Carl	3 mon.	Warmbronn	Leon.	Oct 1854	N.-Amer	837965
Braeuning, Johanne	2 yrs.	Warmbronn	Leon.	Oct 1854	N.-Amer	837965
Braeuning, Maria Katharina	7 Jul 1832	Merklingen	Leon.	Oct 1869	Bavaria	837959
Braeunle, Maria Katharina		Eybach	Gsl.	Aug 1860	Switz.	572044
Braeutler, Hans Jerg & F		Unterlenningen	Krch.	May 1771	Hungary	550804
Braghammer, Johannes	16 yrs.	Aichhalden	Obd.	Dec 1854	N.-Amer	838629
Braghammer, Josef	15 May 1848	Aichhalden	Obd.	Apr 1865	N.-Amer	838629
Braitmaier, Barbara (wid.)		Erpfingen	Rtl.	Jul 1880	N.-Amer	841051
Braitmaier, Johann Georg	17 yrs.	Warmbronn	Leon.	Oct 1853	N.-Amer	837965
Braitmaier, Maria Dorothea	10 Oct 1876	Herrenberg	Herr.	Jul 1896	N.-Amer	834629
Braitsch, Ahatha	28 Jan 1946	Harthausen	Obd.	Aug 1856	N.-Amer	838633
Braitsch, Andreas	20 Nov 1851	Hochmoessingen	Obd.	Mar 1867	N.-Amer	838633
Braitsch, Conrad	19 Oct 1842	Hochmoessingen	Obd.	bef 1866	N.-Amer	838633
Braitsch, Jacob	25 Jul 1841	Hochmoessingen	Obd.	bef 1866	N.-Amer	838633
Braitsch, Jacob	24 Jan 1841	Hochmoessingen	Obd.	Sep 1866	N.-Amer	838633
Braitsch, Johann & F		Aichhalden	Obd.	May 1817	N.-Amer	838629
Braitsch, Johanna & F		Harthausen	Obd.	Aug 1856	N.-Amer	838633
Braitsch, Johannes	26 Aug 1844	Hochmoessingen	Obd.	bef 1866	N.-Amer	838633
Braitsch, Johannes & F		Harthausen	Obd.	Sep 1853	N.-Amer	838633
Braitsch, Joseph	11 Dec 1848	Harthausen	Obd.	Aug 1856	N.-Amer	838633
Braitsch, Joseph & F		Aichhalden	Obd.	May 1817	N.-Amer	838629
Braitsch, Leo Fridolin	3 Mar 1834	Schramberg	Obd.	Jan 1865	Prussia	838636
Braitsch, Maria Anna	22 Oct 1841	Harthausen	Obd.	Aug 1856	N.-Amer	838633
Braitsch, Ottmar	14 Sep 1844	Harthausen	Obd.	Aug 1856	N.-Amer	838633
Braitsch, Peter		Aichhalden	Obd.	Aug 1853	N.-Amer	838629
Braitsch, Reinhard	8 May 1852	Aichhalden	Obd.	Mar 1870	N.-Amer	838629
Braitsch, Romanus	15 Jul 1849	Hochmoessingen	Obd.	Aug 1866	N.-Amer	838633
Brandeker, Adolph	30 Dec 1830	Oberndorf	Obd.	1852	N.-Amer	838635
Brandeker, Alois		Oberndorf	Obd.	Aug 1816	Austria	838635
Brandeker, Aloisa	40 yrs.	Oberndorf	Obd.	Apr 1847	N.-Amer	838635

| Name | | Birth | | Emigration | | | Film |
Last	First	Date	Place	O'amt	Appl. Date	Dest.	Number
Brandeker, Franz Anton		17 yrs.	Oberndorf	Obd.	Apr 1852	N.-Amer	838635
Brandeker, Franz Joseph			Oberndorf	Obd.	Apr 1863	Bremen	838635
Brandeker, Hieronymus			Oberndorf	Obd.	Jul 1860	N.-Amer	838635
Brandeker, Hilar & F		39 yrs.	Oberndorf	Obd.	Apr 1847	N.-Amer	838635
Brandeker, Mathilde		11 yrs.	Oberndorf	Obd.	Apr 1847	N.-Amer	838635
Brandeker, Wilhelm		30 Apr 1823	Oberndorf	Obd.	Feb 1848	N.-Amer	838635
Brander, Eva Dorothea & C			Wimsheim	Loen.	Mar 1854	N.-Amer	837967
Brander, Johann Jakob			Wimsheim	Loen.	Mar 1854	N.-Amer	837967
Brander, Michael & F			Wimsheim	Loen.	Mar 1854	N.-Amer	837967
Brander, Sophia			Wimsheim	Loen.	Mar 1854	N.-Amer	837967
Brander, Sophia (wife)			Wimsheim	Loen.	Mar 1854	N.-Amer	837967
Brandt, Anna Maria		18 Jun 1841	Bondorf	Herr.	Mar 1867	N.-Amer	834630
Brandt, Anna Maria (wid.) & F		30 Apr 1812	Bondorf	Herr.	Mar 1867	N.-Amer	834630
Brandt, Dorothea		27 Nov 1846	Bondorf	Herr.	Mar 1867	N.-Amer	834630
Brandt, Joseph		12 May 1856	Bondorf	Herr.	Mar 1867	N.-Amer	834630
Brandt, Martin		8 Jan 1845	Bondorf	Herr.	Mar 1867	N.-Amer	834630
Brasser, Dorothea			Owen	Krch.	bef 1864	N.-Amer	835940
Brasser, Eva Margaretha		23 Jul 1833	Brucken	Krch.	1857	N.-Amer	835940
Braster, Johann Konrad		24 Oct 1841	Bissingen	Krch.	Jul 1868	N.-Amer	835943
Braumueller, Johann Jacob			Jesingen	Krch.	1852	N.-Amer	835940
Braun, Andreas		22 Jul 1848	Muenklingen	Leon.	May 1880	N.-Amer	837962
Braun, Andreas		30 Jul 1869	Bissingen	Krch.	May 1885	N.-Amer	835943
Braun, Anna Maria		2 May 1832	Hepsisau	Krch.	Sep 1861	N.-Amer	835945
Braun, Anna Maria			Weilheim	Krch.	bef 1859	N.-Amer	835949
Braun, Catharina			Beffendorf	Obd.	Apr 1855	N.-Amer	838631
Braun, Catharina			Muehlhausen	Gsl.	Mar 1852	N.-Amer	572041
Braun, Christine & C			Betzingen	Rtl.	Sep 1859	N.-Amer	841051
Braun, Christine Magdalena		25 Apr 1823	Weilheim	Krch.	bef 1856	N.-Amer	835949
Braun, Elisabeth			Pfullingen	Rtl.	bef 1864	N.-Amer	841055
Braun, Elisabetha Jacob. (wife)		21 Nov 1830	Weilheim	Krch.	Dec 1863	N.-Amer	835950
Braun, Emilie			Beffendorf	Obd.	Feb 1861	N.-Amer	838631
Braun, Friedrich		27 Oct 1868	Weilheim	Krch.	May 1882	N.-Amer	548403
Braun, Georg		4 Dec 1830	Hepsisau	Krch.	May 1860	N.-Amer	835945
Braun, Georg Adam			Eltingen	Leon.	bef 1837	France	835789
Braun, Helena			Muenklingen	Leon.	Dec 1863	Switz.	837962
Braun, Jacob		23 Feb 1844	Weilheim	Krch.	Apr 1864	N.-Amer	835950
Braun, Jacob & W		25 Apr 1827	Weilheim	Krch.	Dec 1863	N.-Amer	835950
Braun, Jakob Wilhelm		21 Dec 1874	Weilheim	Krch.	May 1888	N.-Amer	835774
Braun, Johann Andreas		17 Mar 1833	Hepsisau	Krch.	May 1851	N.-Amer	835945
Braun, Johann Bernhard		19 May 1874	Hepsisau	Krch.	Apr 1890	N.-Amer	835945
Braun, Johann Carl		2 Nov 1818	Alpirsbach	Obd.	May 1846	Switz.	838630
Braun, Johann Conrad		22 Feb 1871	Bissingen	Krch.	May 1888	N.-Amer	835943
Braun, Johann Georg		23 Oct 1834	Hepsisau	Krch.	Aug 1854	N.-Amer	835945
Braun, Johann Jacob		21 Jan 1850	Weilheim	Krch.	Dec 1867	N.-Amer	835950
Braun, Johann Jakob		5 Jan 1857	Weilheim	Krch.	Mar 1873	N.-Amer	835774
Braun, Johann Michael		17 Jan 1832	Hepsisau	Krch.	Apr 1852	N.-Amer	835945
Braun, Johann Raimund		2 Sep 1868	Boehmenkirch	Gsl.	Feb 1870	N.-Amer	572047
Braun, Johannes		23 Nov 1837	Zell	Krch.	Apr 1855	N.-Amer	835940
Braun, Johannes		2 Feb 1834	Weilheim	Krch.	bef 1856	N.-Amer	835949
Braun, Joseph & F		2 May 1840	Boehmenkirch	Gsl.	Feb 1870	N.-Amer	572047

Braun, Karl	28 Jan 1857	Westerheim	Gsl.	May 1867	N.-Amer	572046
Braun, Karl Johanna	21 Sep 1846	Kirchheim	Krch.	bef 1887	N.-Amer	548323
Braun, Katharina (wife)	1 Oct 1921	Westerheim	Gsl.	May 1867	N.-Amer	572046
Braun, Leonhardt	24 Mar 1836	Aufhausen	Gsl.	Mar 1853	N.-Amer	572041
Braun, Leopoldina	15 Nov 1847	Westerheim	Gsl.	May 1867	N.-Amer	572046
Braun, Louisa	10 Sep 1870	Boehmenkirch	Gsl.	Feb 1870	N.-Amer	572047
Braun, Maria		Pfullingen	Rtl.	bef 1864	N.-Amer	841055
Braun, Maria Magdalena	11 Jul 1862	Westerheim	Gsl.	May 1867	N.-Amer	572046
Braun, Theresia	14 Nov 1866	Boehmenkirch	Gsl.	Feb 1870	N.-Amer	572047
Braun, Wendelin & F	5 Nov 1822	Westerheim	Gsl.	May 1867	N.-Amer	572046
Braun, Wilhelm	13 Jan 1836	Hepsisau	Krch.	Sep 1856	N.-Amer	835945
Braun, Wilhelm Friedrich	11 Sep 1859	Tuebingen	Herr.	1876	Switz.	834631
Braun, Wilhelm Friedrich	10 Aug 1867	Hepsisau	Krch.	Jun 1884	N.-Amer	835945
Brecher, Karl	30 Aug 1852	Grosssuessen	Gsl.	Dec 1869	N.-Amer	572047
Breimaier, Margaretha	21 yrs.	Hoefingen	Leon.	Feb 1854	N.-Amer	837957
Breining, Gottlob Israel	31 Aug 1809	Renningen	Leon.	Apr 1836	Switz.	837963
Breisch, Catharina Barbara	12 Mar 1833	Muenchingen	Leon.	Mar 1848	N.-Amer	837961
Breisch, Christine (wife)		Muenchingen	Leon.	Mar 1848	N.-Amer	837961
Breisch, Conrad	3 Oct 1823	Muenchingen	Leon.	May 1852	N.-Amer	837961
Breisch, Johann Georg & W		Muenchingen	Leon.	Mar 1848	N.-Amer	837961
Breisch, Nicolaus	18 Sep 1825	Muenchingen	Leon.	Mar 1848	N.-Amer	837961
Breitling, Christian		Renningen	Leon.	bef 1854	N.-Amer	837963
Breitling, Karl Wilhelm	26 Sep 1811	Renningen	Leon.	Apr 1839	Paris	837963
Breitmaier, Johann Georg	9 Jan 1848	Erpfingen	Rtl.	Oct 1866	N.-Amer	841051
Breitsch, Christine	29 Nov 1834	Winzeln	Obd.	Mar 1846	N.-Amer	841016
Breitsch, Georg	22 Apr 1838	Winzeln	Obd.	Mar 1846	N.-Amer	841016
Breitsch, Helena	23 Jul 1831	Winzeln	Obd.	Mar 1846	N.-Amer	841016
Breitsch, Katharina (wife)	4 Nov 1806	Winzeln	Obd.	Mar 1846	N.-Amer	841016
Breitsch, Konrad	19 Oct 1842	Hochmoessingen	Obd.	Nov 1867	N.-Amer	838633
Breitsch, Matthias & F	1799	Winzeln	Obd.	Mar 1846	N.-Amer	841016
Breitsch, Nikodemus	11 Sep 1843	Winzeln	Obd.	Mar 1846	N.-Amer	841016
Breitsch, Philippina	14 Jan 1841	Winzeln	Obd.	Mar 1846	N.-Amer	841016
Brenner, Erhard		Beffendorf	Obd.	Mar 1864	N.-Amer	838631
Brenner, Mathias & F		Sulgen	Obd.	May 1817	N.-Amer	838638
Bressmer, Anna Catharina		Ohmden	Krch.	1852	N.-Amer	835940
Bressmer, Johannes	3 Oct 1836	Ohmden	Krch.	1865	N.-Amer	835940
Breuning, Anna Maria	4 Sep 1851	Weilheim	Krch.	Nov 1869	N.-Amer	835950
Breuning, Gottlob	1 Sep 1872	Kirchheim	Krch.	Jul 1888	N.-Amer	835942
Breuninger, Eduard	17 Mar 1825	Kirchheim	Krch.	Apr 1862	Saxony	835941
Breunlin, Johann Heinrich	24 Nov 1848	Pfullingen	Rtl.	Jun 1868	N.-Amer	841051
Breuz, Heinrich	3 Jul 1839	Schopfloch	Krch.	Aug 1855	N.-Amer	835949
Breyer, Dorothea	24 Jul 1829	Rosswaelden	Krch.	bef 1859	N.-Amer	835949
Brock, Amalie	11 Jan 1846	Stuttgart	Leon.	Feb 1890	Hungary	835787
Brock, Anna	2 Jul 1877	Esslingen	Leon.	Feb 1890	Hungary	835787
Brock, Ewald & F	7 Apr 1846	Leonberg	Leon.	Feb 1890	Hungary	835787
Broghammer, Carl	14 Jan 1843	Schramberg	Obd.	Sep 1863	N.-Amer	838636
Broghammer, Josef	3 Feb 1824	Mariazell	Obd.	Jan 1849	Hesse	838634
Broghammer, Katharina		Hardt	Obd.	Mar 1854	N.-Amer	838633
Bronner, Maria Dorothea	30 Jan 1821	Heimsheim	Leon.	Jun 1846	Belgien	837955
Brost, Bernhard	12 Sep 1835	Neidlingen	Krch.	1850	N.-Amer	835940

Name		Birth		Emigration			Film
Last	First	Date	Place	O'amt	Appl. Date	Dest.	Number
Brucker, Gustav			Schramberg	Obd.	Nov 1860	N.-Amer	838636
Brucker, Johann		23 Sep 1800	Rosswaelden	Krch.	Sep 1862	N.-Amer	835949
Bruestle, Adam & F			Lauterbach	Obd.	May 1817	N.-Amer	838634
Brugger, Franziska		20 yrs.	Lauterbach	Obd.	May 1854	N.-Amer	838634
Brukmaier, Johanna Jakobina		27 Apr 1833	Eybach	Gsl.	Feb 1854	N.-Amer	572042
Brun, Anna Maria			Perouse	Leon.	Aug 1866	N.-Amer	837962
Brun, Christian		9 Sep 1843	Perouse	Leon.	Aug 1866	N.-Amer	837962
Buchel, Ursula Margaretha		27 Jan 1846	Weiler	Krch.	Jul 1869	N.-Amer	835949
Buchele, Catharina		22 Feb 1831	Weiler	Krch.	bef 1860	N.-Amer	835949
Buchele, Friederike		20 Feb 1844	Dettingen	Krch.	bef 1864	N.-Amer	835940
Buchele, Friedrich		15 Oct 1837	Dettingen	Krch.	bef 1857	N.-Amer	835944
Buchele, Johann Gottfried		10 Jan 1868	Sulpach	Krch.	Apr 1884	N.-Amer	548403
Bucher, Albert Josef & F		7 Jan 1843	Deggingen	Gsl.	Nov 1874	N.-Amer	572048
Bucher, Heinrich		9 Jul 1853	Geislingen	Gsl.	Apr 1870	N.-Amer	572047
Bucher, Johann Christian		24 Feb 1836	Deggingen	Gsl.	Jul 1855	N.-Amer	572043
Bucher, Joseph		19 Oct 1849	Deggingen	Gsl.	Nov 1869	Turkey	572047
Bucher, Magdalena (wife)		2 Sep 1840	Deggingen	Gsl.	Nov 1874	N.-Amer	572048
Bucher, Maximilian Joseph		18 Feb 1839	Deggingen	Gsl.	Oct 1859	N.-Amer	572043
Bucher, Wilhelmine		26 Dec 1870	Deggingen	Gsl.	Nov 1874	N.-Amer	572048
Bucherer, Regina			Geislingen	Gsl.	Dec 1856	Nassau	572043
Buchsteiner, Johannes		8 Sep 1837	Kuchen	Gsl.	Mar 1857	N.-Amer	572043
Buck, Agnes			Hausen a.d. Fils	Gsl.	Mar 1853	N.-Amer	572041
Buck, Emil		4 Apr 1866	Kirchheim	Krch.	Mar 1883	N.-Amer	835942
Buck, Friedrich			Reutlingen	Rtl.	bef 1867	N.-Amer	841051
Buck, Jacobina			Reutlingen	Rtl.	bef 1867	N.-Amer	841051
Buck, Jakob		14 Mar 1808	Ohmden	Krch.	Jul 1855	France	835948
Buck, Jeremias & F			Hausen a.d. Fils	Gsl.	Mar 1853	N.-Amer	572041
Buck, Johann Friedrich		22 Feb 1837	Kirchheim	Krch.	May 1857	N.-Amer	835940
Buck, Johann Jacob		10 Mar 1835	Ohmden	Krch.	Nov 1855	N.-Amer	835948
Buck, Johannes			Hausen a.d. Fils	Gsl.	Mar 1853	N.-Amer	572041
Buck, Joseph		21 Jan 1846	Reutlingen	Rtl.	Apr 1864	N.-Amer	841051
Buck, Karl		28 Jun 1866	Paris	Krch.	Sep 1882	England	835942
Buck, Maria Friederike Rosalia		6 Jul 1843	Reutlingen	Rtl.	Oct 1863	N.-Amer	841051
Buck, Michael & F			Reutlingen	Rtl.	bef 1867	N.-Amer	841051
Buck, Wilhelm Christian		10 Oct 1867	Neidlingen	Krch.	May 1882	N.-Amer	548403
Buda, Jakob		4 Feb 1826	Schopfloch	Krch.	May 1860	N.-Amer	835949
Buehler, Anna Maria (wife)		27 Nov 1808	Hofstett-Emerbuch	Gsl.	Sep 1854	N.-Amer	572042
Buehler, Apollonia		5 Nov 1831	Geislingen	Gsl.	Jun 1854	N.-Amer	572042
Buehler, August		15 Nov 1867	Treffelhausen	Gsl.	Jan 1883	N.-Amer	572049
Buehler, Barbara		19 Nov 1841	Hofstett-Emerbuch	Gsl.	Sep 1854	N.-Amer	572042
Buehler, Carl Friedrich		8 Jul 1807	Geislingen	Gsl.	May 1850	N.-Amer	577788
Buehler, Catharina		2 Jul 1837	Hofstett-Emerbuch	Gsl.	Sep 1854	N.-Amer	572042
Buehler, Catharina (wife)			Reutlingen	Rtl.	Apr 1866	N.-Amer	841051
Buehler, Christof & F			Reutlingen	Rtl.	Apr 1866	N.-Amer	841051
Buehler, David		11 May 1836	Kuchen	Gsl.	Feb 1854	N.-Amer	572042
Buehler, David		2 Dec 1817	Ohmden	Krch.	Sep 1857	N.-Amer	835948
Buehler, Ernst Josef		30 Jun 1849	Wiesensteig	Gsl.	Mar 1867	N.-Amer	572046
Buehler, Friedrich		8 yrs.	Reutlingen	Rtl.	Apr 1866	N.-Amer	841051
Buehler, Georg		18 mon.	Geislingen	Gsl.	Jan 1853	N.-Amer	572041
Buehler, Georg & F			Geislingen	Gsl.	Jan 1853	N.-Amer	572041

Buehler, Gottlieb	1 Sep 1824	Ohmden	Krch.	May 1860	N.-Amer	835948
Buehler, Jacob	10 yrs.	Reutlingen	Rtl.	Apr 1866	N.-Amer	841051
Buehler, Johann Georg	17 May 1836	Hofstett-Emerbuch	Gsl.	Sep 1854	N.-Amer	572042
Buehler, Johann Jacob	5 Sep 1840	Hofstett-Emerbuch	Gsl.	Sep 1854	N.-Amer	572042
Buehler, Johann Leonhard	7 Aug 1849	Sulpach	Krch.	Apr 1869	N.-Amer	835949
Buehler, Johannes & F	1 Apr 1804	Hofstett-Emerbuch	Gsl.	Sep 1854	N.-Amer	572042
Buehler, Johannes & F		Friolzheim	Leon.	Aug 1853	N.-Amer	835791
Buehler, Josef		Aichhalden	Obd.	Jan 1861	N.-Amer	838629
Buehler, Karoline	19 yrs.	Geislingen	Gsl.	Jul 1854	N.-Amer	572042
Buehler, Lisette	9 yrs.	Reutlingen	Rtl.	Apr 1866	N.-Amer	841051
Buehler, Magdalena (wife)		Friolzheim	Leon.	Aug 1853	N.-Amer	835791
Buehler, Margaretha	10 Sep 1823	Grosssuessen	Gsl.	Feb 1854	N.-Amer	572042
Buehler, Michael	19 yrs.	Gingen	Gsl.	Apr 1853	N.-Amer	572041
Buehler, Rosina	9 Sep 1827	Hofstett-Emerbuch	Gsl.	Sep 1854	N.-Amer	572042
Buehler, Theresia	30 yrs.	Donzdorf	Gsl.	Feb 1852	N.-Amer	572041
Buehrer, Carl Friedrich	20 Oct 1824	Herrenberg	Herr.	Mar 1870	N.-Amer	834629
Buehrer, Constantin Friedr.	13 Jun 1855	Rettersburg	Herr.	May 1881	N.-Amer	834629
Buehrle, Angelika & F	9 Jan 1799	Ueberkingen	Gsl.	Mar 1858	N.-Amer	572043
Buehrle, Johannes	50 yrs.	Aufhausen	Gsl.	Mar 1857	N.-Amer	572043
Buehrle, Katharina	19 Feb 1839	Ueberkingen	Gsl.	Mar 1858	N.-Amer	572043
Buehrle, Michael	14 Mar 1840	Ueberkingen	Gsl.	Mar 1858	N.-Amer	572043
Buehrlen, Johann Daniel	33 yrs.	Geislingen	Gsl.	Jun 1850	N.-Amer	577788
Buerck, Anna Maria	12 Jun 1835	Alpirsbach	Obd.	Jan 1859	France	838630
Buerger, Franziska	27 Nov 1831	Hohenstadt	Gsl.	Dec 1853	N.-Amer	572041
Buerger, Maria	24 Apr 1849	Westerheim	Gsl.	Mar 1854	N.-Amer	572042
Buerk, Christian	8 Apr 1862	Schwenningen	Leon.	Nov 1885	N.-Amer	841117
Buerkle, Anna Maria	7 Aug 1839	Muenchingen	Leon.	Mar 1852	N.-Amer	837961
Buerkle, Barbara	5 May 1843	Muenchingen	Leon.	Mar 1852	N.-Amer	837961
Buerkle, Christian	25 Sep 1834	Muenchingen	Leon.	Mar 1852	N.-Amer	837961
Buerkle, Christian & F		Muenchingen	Leon.	Mar 1852	N.-Amer	837961
Buerkle, Christina	11 Aug 1837	Muenchingen	Leon.	Mar 1852	N.-Amer	837961
Buerkle, Christine Marg. (wife)		Muenchingen	Leon.	Mar 1852	N.-Amer	837961
Buerkle, Johanna	8 Feb 1845	Muenchingen	Leon.	Mar 1852	N.-Amer	837961
Buerkle, Michael	28 Sep 1779	Muenchingen	Leon.	bef 1839	Russia	837961
Buerkle, Ursula	27 Dec 1857	Altenstadt-Gsl.	Gsl.	May 1873	N.-Amer	572047
Buess, Anna Katharina		Merklingen	Leon.	Apr 1853	Switz.	837959
Buess, Christian Gottlob	4 Sep 1873	Friolzheim	Leon.	Dec 1889	N.-Amer	835791
Buess, Georg Bernhardt & F	11 Apr 1820	Merklingen	Leon.	1857	N.-Amer	837959
Buess, Johann Georg		Merklingen	Leon.	bef 1867	N.-Amer	837959
Buhler, Wilhelm	15 Dec 1850	Gueltstein	Herr.	Aug 1869	N.-Amer	834631
Buhlinger, Regina Katharina	29 Jul 1839	Gueltstein	Herr.	Feb 1867	N.-Amer	834631
Buk, Johann Gottlieb & F		Reutlingen	Rtl.	May 1832	N.-Amer	841051
Bulling, Creszentia	2 Sep 1827	Treffelhausen	Gsl.	Aug 1853	N.-Amer	572041
Bundschuh, Anton		Eybach	Gsl.	Aug 1851	N.-Amer	577788
Bundschuh, Johann Georg	9 Oct 1838	Eybach	Gsl.	Mar 1866	Hannov.	572045
Bunz, Friedrich	17 Jun 1829	Geislingen	Gsl.	bef 1874	Austria	572048
Bunz, Julius	17 Jul 1828	Geislingen	Gsl.	bef 1855	N.-Amer	572043
Buob, Christian	19 yrs.	Hochdorf	Krch.	Aug 1863	N.-Amer	835945
Buob, Christian & F	49 yrs.	Hochdorf	Krch.	Aug 1863	N.-Amer	835945
Buob, Christiane Friederike	11 yrs.	Hochdorf	Krch.	Aug 1863	N.-Amer	835945

| Name | | Birth | | Emigration | | | Film |
Last	First	Date	Place	O'amt	Appl. Date	Dest.	Number
Buob,	Johann Heinrich	9 yrs.	Hochdorf	Krch.	Aug 1863	N.-Amer	835945
Buob,	Johann Jacob	17 Mar 1808	Heimsheim	Leon.	Jun 1851	N.-Amer	837955
Buob,	Maria Barbara	20 yrs.	Hochdorf	Krch.	Aug 1863	N.-Amer	835945
Buob,	Maria Barbara (wife)		Hochdorf	Krch.	Aug 1863	N.-Amer	835945
Buob,	Rosine Catharine	12 yrs.	Hochdorf	Krch.	Aug 1863	N.-Amer	835945
Buob,	Wilhelm	16 yrs.	Hochdorf	Krch.	Aug 1863	N.-Amer	835945
Buol,	Georg Friedrich		Reutlingen	Rtl.	Jun 1830	France	841051
Buost,	Wilhelm		Betzingen	Rtl.	Mar 1831	N.-Amer	841051
Burgbacher,	Johann Georg & F	8 Sep 1850	Roemlinsdorf	Obd.	Dec 1870	N.-Amer	838635
Burger,	Albert	14 Jul 1839	Leonberg	Leon.	Apr 1864	N.-Amer	835787
Burger,	Anna	25 Mar 1850	Hofstett-Emerbuch	Gsl.	Apr 1855	N.-Amer	572043
Burger,	Anna & F		Hofstett-Emerbuch	Gsl.	Apr 1855	N.-Amer	572043
Burger,	Bertha	23 Apr 1854	Wiesensteig	Gsl.	Apr 1855	N.-Amer	572043
Burger,	Carl Theodor	4 Nov 1836	Wiesensteig	Gsl.	Apr 1855	N.-Amer	572043
Burger,	Ferdinand		Wiesensteig	Gsl.	1854	N.-Amer	572043
Burger,	Friedrich	13 Dec 1852	Wiesensteig	Gsl.	Apr 1855	N.-Amer	572043
Burger,	Gottlieb		Leonberg	Leon.	bef 1860	N.-Amer	835786
Burger,	Gottlob Albrecht	28 May 1836	Leonberg	Leon.	Nov 1853	N.-Amer	835786
Burger,	Johann Friedrich	9 yrs.	Flacht	Leon.	Jul 1854	N.-Amer	835790
Burger,	Johann Friedrich & F		Flacht	Leon.	Jul 1854	N.-Amer	835790
Burger,	Johann Jacob		Wimsheim	Loen.	Mar 1849	N.-Amer	837967
Burger,	Johannes	2 yrs.	Flacht	Leon.	Jul 1854	N.-Amer	835790
Burger,	Johannes	16 yrs.	Hoefingen	Leon.	Feb 1854	N.-Amer	837957
Burger,	Josef	18 yrs.	Wiesensteig	Gsl.	Jul 1873	N.-Amer	572047
Burger,	Margaretha	11 Dec 1825	Wiesensteig	Gsl.	Apr 1855	N.-Amer	572043
Burger,	Margaretha Katharina	7 yrs.	Flacht	Leon.	Jul 1854	N.-Amer	835790
Burger,	Maria	20 yrs.	Wiesensteig	Gsl.	Jul 1873	N.-Amer	572047
Burger,	Pauline	19 Dec 1840	Leonberg	Leon.	Feb 1860	Worms	835786
Burger,	Rosina Jacobina	16 yrs.	Hoefingen	Leon.	Aug 1853	N.-Amer	837957
Burger,	Sophia	2 Sep 1831	Leonberg	Leon.	bef 1860	N.-Amer	835786
Burgmacher,	Johannes	20 Apr 1849	Roemlinsdorf	Obd.	Feb 1868	N.-Amer	838635
Burk,	Carl	2 yrs.	Leonberg	Leon.	Oct 1853	N.-Amer	835786
Burk,	Carl & F		Leonberg	Leon.	Oct 1853	N.-Amer	835786
Burk,	Michael		Reutlingen	Rtl.	bef 1865	N.-Amer	841051
Burk,	Ottilie	3 yrs.	Leonberg	Leon.	Oct 1853	N.-Amer	835786
Burk,	Ottilie (wife)		Leonberg	Leon.	Oct 1853	N.-Amer	835786
Burk,	Philipp	30 Oct 1847	Reutlingen	Rtl.	Jul 1865	N.-Amer	841051
Burkhardt,	Anna Catharina	10 Feb 1838	Unterhausen	Rtl.	Jun 1867	Switz.	841051
Burkhardt,	Friederike	20 Mar 1845	Hildrizhausen	Herr.	Mar 1865	N.-Amer	834631
Burkhardt,	Gottfried	11 Nov 1858	Unterhausen	Rtl.	Apr 1866	N.-Amer	841051
Burkhardt,	Gottlieb	16 Mar 1856	Unterhausen	Rtl.	Apr 1866	N.-Amer	841051
Burkhardt,	Johann Georg	18 Feb 1838	Unterhausen	Rtl.	Apr 1865	N.-Amer	841051
Burkhardt,	Johann Georg	11 May 1849	Neidlingen	Krch.	Feb 1868	N.-Amer	835950
Burkhardt,	Johannes	15 Mar 1849	Bissingen	Krch.	Jul 1866	N.-Amer	835943
Burkhardt,	Konrad	18 Nov 1851	Hildrizhausen	Herr.	Jul 1870	N.-Amer	834631
Burkhardt,	Louise Friederike	19 Mar 1846	Unterhausen	Rtl.	Apr 1866	N.-Amer	841051
Burkhardt,	Maria Rosina M. B.	30 Jan 1844	Unterhausen	Rtl.	1860	N.-Amer	841051
Burkhardt,	Mathias	6 Aug 1838	Unterhausen	Rtl.	1856	N.-Amer	841051
Burkhardt,	Matthaeus (wid.) & F	9 Apr 1810	Unterhausen	Rtl.	Apr 1866	N.-Amer	841051
Burkhardt,	Nikolaus	19 yrs.	Reichenbach	Gsl.	Aug 1866	N.-Amer	572045

Burr, Elisabetha	2 Jul 1847	Boehmenkirch	Gsl.	Feb 1872	N.-Amer	572047
Burr, Jakob	11 May 1854	Tuerkheim	Gsl.	Aug 1881	N.-Amer	572048
Burr, Johann Bernhard	20 Aug 1857	Boehmenkirch	Gsl.	Feb 1872	N.-Amer	572047
Burr, Joseph M.		Boehmenkirch	Gsl.	Nov 1867	N.-Amer	572046
Burr, Maria Anna	9 Feb 1845	Boehmenkirch	Gsl.	Mar 1868	N.-Amer	572046
Busch, Andreas	19 Jan 1799	Hemmingen	Leon.	Feb 1818	N.-Amer	837956
Busch, Christian	16 yrs.	Hemmingen	Leon.	Feb 1818	N.-Amer	837956
Busch, Christina	25 yrs.	Hemmingen	Leon.	Feb 1818	N.-Amer	837956
Busch, Dorothea (wife)	46 yrs.	Hemmingen	Leon.	Feb 1818	N.-Amer	837956
Busch, Gottlieb	7 yrs.	Hemmingen	Leon.	Feb 1818	N.-Amer	837956
Busch, Jakob	13 yrs.	Hemmingen	Leon.	Feb 1818	N.-Amer	837956
Busch, Johann Georg	24 Apr 1799	Hemmingen	Leon.	Feb 1818	N.-Amer	837956
Busch, Johannes	17 Feb 1797	Hemmingen	Leon.	Feb 1818	N.-Amer	837956
Busch, Johannes	26 Feb 1797	Hemmingen	Leon.	Feb 1818	N.-Amer	837956
Busch, Johannes & F	43 yrs.	Hemmingen	Leon.	Feb 1818	N.-Amer	837956
Busch, Magdalena (wife)	54 yrs.	Hemmingen	Leon.	Feb 1818	N.-Amer	837956
Busch, Milchior	15 yrs.	Hemmingen	Leon.	Feb 1818	N.-Amer	837956
Busch, Philipp Burkhardt & F	54 yrs.	Hemmingen	Leon.	Feb 1818	N.-Amer	837956
Buss, Jakob Friedrich	13 Oct 1839	Wimsheim	Loen.	Nov 1859	N.-Amer	837967
Buss, Samuel	5 Jun 1827	Moensheim	Leon.	Nov 1852	N.-Amer	837960
Butsch, Elisabet Catarina	11 yrs.	Malmsheim	Leon.	Mar 1821	N.-Amer	837958
Butsch, Friederike Charlotte	16 Sep 1802	Malmsheim	Leon.	Sep 1871	N.-Amer	837958
Butsch, Johann Jacob & F		Warmbronn	Leon.	Jan 1817	N.-Amer	837965
Butsch, Johannes	13 yrs.	Malmsheim	Leon.	Mar 1821	N.-Amer	837958
Buzer, Johann Jacob	30 Dec 1844	Gomaringen	Rtl.	Jul 1869	N.-Amer	841051
Canstetter, Friederike	13 Jan 1835	Kirchheim	Krch.	Oct 1857	N.-Amer	835940
Canstetter, Louise Carolina	23 Aug 1842	Kirchheim	Krch.	Jul 1869	Austria	835941
Charrier, Catharina	17 Jan 1793	Perouse	Leon.	Jan 1852	N.-Amer	837962
Charrier, David & W	26 Jun 1818	Perouse	Leon.	Jan 1852	N.-Amer	837962
Charrier, Susanna Fried. (wife)	17 Jan 1821	Perouse	Leon.	Jan 1852	N.-Amer	837962
Charrier, Thomasina	27 Oct 1821	Perouse	Leon.	Nov 1850	France	837962
Christmann, Maria Elisab. & C	29 yrs.	Dettingen	Krch.	Jun 1866	N.-Amer	835944
Christmann, Pauline Catharine	17 Mar 1866	Dettingen	Krch.	Jun 1866	N.-Amer	835944
Christner, Johann Friedrich		Holzelfingen	Rtl.	Mar 1831	France	841051
Class, Anna Barbara	7 Dec 1842	Bissingen	Krch.	bef 1861	N.-Amer	835943
Class, Johann Philipp	22 Feb 1846	Bissingen	Krch.	bef 1861	N.-Amer	835943
Class, Ludwig	21 Aug 1849	Bissingen	Krch.	bef 1861	N.-Amer	835943
Class, Margaretha	11 May 1823	Bissingen	Krch.	bef 1861	N.-Amer	835943
Class, Margaretha	1 Feb 1851	Bissingen	Krch.	bef 1861	N.-Amer	835943
Class, Martin	30 Sep 1818	Bissingen	Krch.	bef 1861	N.-Amer	835943
Claus, Nicolaus	32 yrs.	Hofstett-Emerbuch	Gsl.	Oct 1861	Italy	572044
Clauss, Johann Jakob		Bissingen	Krch.	Aug 1865	N.-Amer	835943
Clement, Wilhelm	22 Nov 1819	Gingen	Gsl.	Oct 1856	N.-Amer	572043
Cless, Christian	28 Jan 1828	Weilheim	Krch.	1854	N.-Amer	835949
Cless, Christoph	1 Apr 1847	Schoeckingen	Leon.	Aug 1849	N.-Amer	837964
Cless, Christoph Heinrich		Heimerdingen	Leon.	bef 1855	N.-Amer	837954
Cless, Conrad Heinrich	17 May 1826	Weilheim	Krch.	1854	N.-Amer	835949
Cless, Friederike & C	22 Aug 1818	Schoeckingen	Leon.	Aug 1849	N.-Amer	837964
Cless, Johann Gottlieb & F	18 Oct 1822	Schoeckingen	Leon.	Apr 1852	N.-Amer	837964
Cless, Johann Jakob	10 Jul 1827	Schoeckingen	Leon.	1849	N.-Amer	837964

Name		Birth		Emigration			Film
Last	First	Date	Place	O'amt	Appl. Date	Dest.	Number
Cless, Johann Konrad		17 Oct 1823	Schoeckingen	Leon.	Apr 1852	N.-Amer	837964
Cless, Pauline Caroline		17 Jun 1850	Schoeckingen	Leon.	Apr 1852	N.-Amer	837964
Cless, Pauline Christ. (wife)		10 Nov 1828	Schoeckingen	Leon.	Apr 1852	N.-Amer	837964
Cless, Wilhelm		12 Aug 1829	Schoeckingen	Leon.	Mar 1849	N.-Amer	837964
Congott, Carl Friedrich		24 yrs.	Reutlingen	Rtl.	Apr 1880	N.-Amer	841051
Congott, Robert		27 yrs.	Reutlingen	Rtl.	Nov 1880	N.-Amer	841051
Conle, Carolina Catharina		11 Mar 1845	Friolzheim	Leon.	bef 1869	Holland	835791
Counzelmann, Johann Jakob		2 Jun 1877	Herrenberg	Herr.	Apr 1891	N.-Amer	834629
Craft, Louise Margaretha			Kirchheim	Krch.	bef 1864	N.-Amer	835940
Dachtler, Friedrich Wilhelm		19 May 1850	Weil im Dorf	Loen.	Oct 1870	N.-Amer	837967
Daeuble, Andreas		4 Jan 1864	Peterzell	Obd.	Mar 1864	N.-Amer	838635
Daeuble, Andreas & F		22 Jun 1829	Peterzell	Obd.	Mar 1864	N.-Amer	838635
Daeuble, Anna Maria		21 Jun 1862	Peterzell	Obd.	Mar 1864	N.-Amer	838635
Daeuble, Anna Maria (wife)		27 Nov 1842	Peterzell	Obd.	Mar 1864	N.-Amer	838635
Daiber, Oskar Friedrich		25 Apr 1847	Herrenberg	Herr.	bef 1867	N.-Amer	834629
Damm, Carl		10 Jul 1816	Kirchheim	Krch.	Feb 1868	N.-Amer	835941
Dangel, Carl Gottlieb		29 Jul 1873	Hochdorf	Krch.	Jul 1883	N.-Amer	548403
Dangel, Christian Friedrich		13 Feb 1854	Unterlenningen	Krch.	Feb 1869	N.-Amer	835949
Dangel, Christian Jak. Fried.		22 Jan 1861	Unterlenningen	Krch.	Apr 1876	N.-Amer	835942
Dangel, Gottlieb Michael		20 Dec 1871	Unterlenningen	Krch.	Feb 1887	N.-Amer	835949
Dangel, Gustav Adolf		18 Jul 1875	Hochdorf	Krch.	Jul 1883	N.-Amer	548403
Dangel, Johann Andreas		12 Aug 1873	Owen	Krch.	Jun 1880	N.-Amer	835948
Dangel, Johann Christian		31 Oct 1865	Unterlenningen	Krch.	Jun 1882	N.-Amer	548403
Dangel, Johann David		23 Mar 1867	Hochdorf	Krch.	Jul 1883	N.-Amer	548403
Dangel, Johann David		26 Jul 1844	Hochdorf	Krch.	Apr 1882	N.-Amer	835945
Dangel, Johann Georg		19 Apr 1850	Unterlenningen	Krch.	Jul 1864	N.-Amer	835949
Dangel, Johannes		14 Sep 1838	Bissingen	Krch.	bef 1863	France	835943
Dangel, Karl Gottlieb		29 Jul 1873	Hochdorf	Krch.	Jul 1883	N.-Amer	835945
Dangel, Margaretha		16 Oct 1846	Bissingen	Krch.	Dec 1868	N.-Amer	835943
Dangel, Maria		23 Mar 1869	Hochdorf	Krch.	Jul 1883	N.-Amer	835945
Dangel, Maria Catharina		20 Jun 1828	Owen	Krch.	1866	N.-Amer	835940
Dangel, Regina Margaretha		3 Nov 1834	Owen	Krch.	1866	N.-Amer	835940
Dangel, Rosine Doro. (wid.) & F		15 Jun 1838	Owen	Krch.	Jun 1880	N.-Amer	835948
Dangel, Wilhelm Friedrich		7 Jun 1866	Unterlenningen	Krch.	May 1880	N.-Amer	835949
Dangelmaier, Johannes		16 May 1841	Boehmenkirch	Gsl.	Apr 1867	N.-Amer	572046
Dangelmayer, Johann		26 May 1833	Kleinsuessen	Gsl.	May 1852	N.-Amer	572041
Dangelmayer, Josef		18 Mar 1837	Kleinsuessen	Gsl.	May 1852	N.-Amer	572041
Dangelmayer, Maria Theresia		14 Mar 1828	Kleinsuessen	Gsl.	May 1852	N.-Amer	572041
Daniel, Emma Julie			Leonberg	Leon.	Mar 1864	Saxony	835787
Danker, Franzisca Romana		9 Mar 1842	Winzeln	Obd.	Nov 1865	N.-Amer	841016
Danker, Ofra & C		8 Aug 1816	Winzeln	Obd.	Nov 1865	N.-Amer	841016
Danker, Rosina		6 Mar 1851	Winzeln	Obd.	Nov 1865	N.-Amer	841016
Daucher, Catharina Regina		19 yrs.	Hausen a.d. Wurm	Leon.	Apr 1819	N.-Amer	837954
Daucher, Dorothea			Hausen a.d. Wurm	Leon.	1853	N.-Amer	837954
Daucher, Johannes			Hausen a.d. Wurm	Leon.	Aug 1869	N.-Amer	837954
Dauer, Eugen Chlodwig Fr. Er.		6 Feb 1848	Ueberkingen	Gsl.	Apr 1868	N.-Amer	572046
Daum, Friedrich		23 yrs.	Hoefingen	Leon.	Apr 1844	Hesse	837957
Dauner, Michael		22 Feb 1834	Stoetten	Gsl.	Oct 1853	N.-Amer	572041
Decker, Johann & F			Mariazell	Obd.	May 1817	N.-Amer	838634
Deeg, Eugenia		19 yrs.	Reutlingen	Rtl.	Apr 1880	N.-Amer	841051

Deibele, Xaver	4 Nov 1847	Donzdorf	Gsl.	Mar 1866	N.-Amer	572045
Deigendescher, Lorenz	29 Jan 1824	Eltingen	Leon.	bef 1860	N.-Amer	835789
Deininger, August Friedrich	13 Apr 1832	Weilheim	Krch.	Feb 1867	N.-Amer	835950
Deininger, Barbara & C		Hemmingen	Leon.	Mar 1852	N.-Amer	837956
Deininger, Carl Engelhardt		Hemmingen	Leon.	Mar 1852	N.-Amer	837956
Deininger, Friedrich		Sternenfels	Leon.	bef 1850	Switz.	837956
Deininger, Johann Georg	27 Nov 1828	Weilheim	Krch.	bef 1861	N.-Amer	835949
Deininger, Johann Michael	20 Dec 1873	Weilheim	Krch.	May 1888	N.-Amer	835774
Deininger, Maria Magdalena	24 Mar 1834	Weilheim	Krch.	Jun 1864	N.-Amer	835950
Deininger, Michael		Hemmingen	Leon.	Mar 1836	France	837956
Deininger, Rosine	11 Dec 1826	Weilheim	Krch.	bef 1861	N.-Amer	835949
Deininger, Ursula Margaretha	24 Jun 1822	Weilheim	Krch.	bef 1861	N.-Amer	835949
Deitter, Heinrich	17 yrs.	Willmandingen	Rtl.	Apr 1880	N.-Amer	841051
Deitter, Johann Georg	18 yrs.	Willmandingen	Rtl.	Apr 1880	N.-Amer	841051
Delkeskamp, Adolf	20 yrs.	Merklingen	Leon.	May 1851	N.-Amer	837959
Delkeskamp, Eduard	18 yrs.	Merklingen	Leon.	May 1851	N.-Amer	837959
Delkeskamp, Hermann	16 yrs.	Merklingen	Leon.	May 1851	N.-Amer	837959
Dellefant, Carl	20 Nov 1841	Boehmenkirch	Gsl.	Mar 1875	Austria	572048
Dellefant, Maxim. Bernhard	21 Aug 1840	Boehmenkirch	Gsl.	Mar 1858	N.-Amer	572043
Dellenfand, Anton	1 Feb 1833	Donzdorf	Gsl.	Mar 1850	N.-Amer	577788
Dellenfand, Theresia		Donzdorf	Gsl.	Mar 1850	N.-Amer	577788
Dentlinger, Jacob	31 yrs.	Seedorf	Obd.	Oct 1849	N.-Amer	838637
Dentlinger, Johannes	27 Nov 1850	Seedorf	Obd.	Dec 1870	N.-Amer	838637
Denzel, Gustav	22 yrs.	Reutlingen	Rtl.	Jul 1880	N.-Amer	841051
Denzel, Maria		Waldhausen	Gsl.	Feb 1870	N.-Amer	572047
Denzel, Maria	21 yrs.	Reutlingen	Rtl.	May 1880	N.-Amer	841051
Denzinger, Andreas	18 yrs.	Westerheim	Gsl.	Apr 1853	N.-Amer	572041
Denzinger, Anna Maria (wife)		Westerheim	Gsl.	May 1853	N.-Amer	572041
Denzinger, Caezilia		Westerheim	Gsl.	Oct 1851	N.-Amer	577788
Denzinger, Gertrude & C	22 yrs.	Westerheim	Gsl.	May 1853	N.-Amer	572041
Denzinger, Michael & F		Westerheim	Gsl.	Apr 1853	N.-Amer	572041
Denzinger, Rosalia	8 yrs.	Westerheim	Gsl.	May 1853	N.-Amer	572041
Denzinger, Stephan & F		Westerheim	Gsl.	May 1853	N.-Amer	572041
Deppert, Katharina (wid.) & F	31 May 1816	Scheer	Gsl.	Oct 1854	N.-Amer	572042
Deppert, Leoradie Wallpurga	4 Dec 1845	Deggingen	Gsl.	Oct 1854	N.-Amer	572042
Deppert, Turipius	26 Apr 1844	Deggingen	Gsl.	Oct 1854	N.-Amer	572042
Dersch, Ulrich	24 yrs.	Muehlhausen	Gsl.	bef 1863	N.-Amer	572044
Derscher, Jakob & F	10 Dec 1823	Gueltstein	Herr.	Feb 1866	N.-Amer	834631
Derscher, Johann Jakob	17 Jan 1861	Gueltstein	Herr.	Feb 1866	N.-Amer	834631
Derscher, Johannes	3 Jan 1865	Gueltstein	Herr.	Feb 1866	N.-Amer	834631
Derscher, Katharina	13 Sep 1863	Gueltstein	Herr.	Feb 1866	N.-Amer	834631
Derscher, Maria Susanna (wife)	10 Aug 1826	Gueltstein	Herr.	Feb 1866	N.-Amer	834631
Dertinger, Christian Wilhelm	1 Feb 1847	Malmsheim	Leon.	Apr 1867	N.-Amer	837958
Dertinger, Maria Christiane	27 Jun 1848	Malmsheim	Leon.	Jul 1867	N.-Amer	837958
Deschenski, Agatha & C	14 Mar 1820	Seedorf	Obd.	Apr 1847	N.-Amer	838637
Deschenski, Antonie	13 Jun 1829	Seedorf	Obd.	Apr 1847	N.-Amer	838637
Deschenski, Beata	19 Dec 1838	Seedorf	Obd.	Apr 1847	N.-Amer	838637
Deschenski, Carl	9 Feb 1835	Seedorf	Obd.	Apr 1847	N.-Amer	838637
Deschenski, Catharina (wife)	Jan 1794	Seedorf	Obd.	Apr 1847	N.-Amer	838637
Deschenski, Christine & C	1821	Seedorf	Obd.	Apr 1847	N.-Amer	838637

Name		Birth		Emigration			Film
Last	First	Date	Place	O'amt	Appl. Date	Dest.	Number
Deschenski, Fidel		13 May 1822	Seedorf	Obd.	Apr 1847	N.-Amer	838637
Deschenski, Fidel & F			Seedorf	Obd.	Apr 1847	N.-Amer	838637
Deschenski, Maria		26 Mar 1831	Seedorf	Obd.	Apr 1847	N.-Amer	838637
Deschler, Jacob		23 Jun 1831	Leonberg	Leon.	Jun 1840	N.-Amer	835786
Dettinger, Anna Cathar. (wife)		26 Mar 1829	Dettingen	Krch.	May 1868	N.-Amer	835944
Dettinger, Barbara		23 Nov 1864	Dettingen	Krch.	May 1868	N.-Amer	835944
Dettinger, Barbara (wife)		30 Apr 1822	Hochdorf	Krch.	May 1868	N.-Amer	835945
Dettinger, Christian		4 Oct 1867	Dettingen	Krch.	May 1868	N.-Amer	835944
Dettinger, Christiana		24 Aug 1855	Hochdorf	Krch.	May 1868	N.-Amer	835945
Dettinger, Jacob & F		22 Oct 1822	Hochdorf	Krch.	May 1868	N.-Amer	835945
Dettinger, Jakob		6 Mar 1851	Hochdorf	Krch.	May 1868	N.-Amer	835945
Dettinger, Johann Gottlieb		30 Dec 1855	Dettingen	Krch.	May 1868	N.-Amer	835944
Dettinger, Johann Gottlieb		24 Nov 1845	Dettingen	Krch.	Mar 1860	N.-Amer	835944
Dettinger, Johann Gottlieb & F		1 Nov 1822	Dettingen	Krch.	May 1868	N.-Amer	835944
Dettinger, Johann Wilhelm		16 Mar 1862	Dettingen	Krch.	May 1868	N.-Amer	835944
Dettinger, Johannes		11 Apr 1848	Dettingen	Krch.	Apr 1868	N.-Amer	835944
Dettinger, Johannes		13 May 1826	Dettingen	Krch.	May 1861	N.-Amer	835944
Dettinger, Sophie		18 Oct 1864	Hochdorf	Krch.	May 1868	N.-Amer	835945
Dettinger, Wilhelm		22 Oct 1866	Dettingen	Krch.	Jun 1882	N.-Amer	548403
Dettling, Jacob Friedrich & W			Moensheim	Leon.	Jun 1844	Russia	837960
Dettling, Wilhelmine Ch. (wife)			Moensheim	Leon.	Jun 1844	Russia	837960
Deusch, Christian Heinrich		16 Jan 1850	Alpirsbach	Obd.	Aug 1859	N.-Amer	838630
Deusch, Johann Georg & W			Fluorn	Obd.	Nov 1853	N.-Amer	838632
Deusch, Magdalena (wife)			Fluorn	Obd.	Nov 1853	N.-Amer	838632
Deusch, Margarethe Gottl. & C			Alpirsbach	Obd.	Aug 1859	N.-Amer	838630
Deusch, Matthias		24 Oct 1818	Fluorn	Obd.	Jul 1865	N.-Amer	838632
Deusch, Wilhelm		7 Feb 1845	Alpirsbach	Obd.	Aug 1859	N.-Amer	838630
Deuschle, Barbara			Jesingen	Krch.	bef 1856	N.-Amer	835946
Deuschle, Johann Jakob		10 Mar 1827	Notzingen	Krch.	bef 1869	N.-Amer	835940
Deutschle, Christoph Adam		14 Jul 1824	Notzingen	Krch.	Feb 1858	N.-Amer	835947
Deutschle, Johann Jakob		9 Sep 1836	Notzingen	Krch.	Mar 1867	N.-Amer	835947
Dick, Anna Maria		15 yrs.	Geislingen	Gsl.	Mar 1851	N.-Amer	577788
Dick, Elisabetha		18 yrs.	Geislingen	Gsl.	May 1860	N.-Amer	572044
Dick, Johannes		19 yrs.	Geislingen	Gsl.	May 1860	N.-Amer	572044
Diebold, Anton		20 yrs.	Weil der Stadt	Leon.	Apr 1867	N.-Amer	837966
Diebold, Benedict			Weil der Stadt	Leon.	bef 1822	France	837965
Diebold, Carl Wilhelm		19 yrs.	Weil der Stadt	Leon.	Jun 1853	N.-Amer	837966
Diebold, Conrad		21 Nov 1835	Heimerdingen	Leon.	Aug 1853	N.-Amer	837954
Diebold, Wilhelm Friedrich		7 Jun 1847	Heimerdingen	Leon.	Oct 1866	N.-Amer	837954
Diefenbach, Andreas		12 Feb 1827	Moensheim	Leon.	Mar 1831	N.-Amer	837960
Diefenbach, Conrad			Ditzingen	Leon.	Apr 1831	N.-Amer	835788
Diefenbach, Helena		6 Apr 1830	Moensheim	Leon.	Mar 1831	N.-Amer	837960
Diefenbach, Johann Georg & F		37 yrs.	Moensheim	Leon.	Mar 1831	N.-Amer	837960
Diefenbach, Johann Martin		13 Sep 1820	Moensheim	Leon.	Mar 1831	N.-Amer	837960
Diefenbach, Johannes		12 Jun 1823	Moensheim	Leon.	Mar 1831	N.-Amer	837960
Diefenbach, Margaretha (wife)		41 yrs.	Moensheim	Leon.	Mar 1831	N.-Amer	837960
Diefenbach, Michael & F			Ditzingen	Leon.	Feb 1829	N.-Amer	835788
Diegel, Barbara			Betzingen	Rtl.	Oct 1862	N.-Amer	841052
Diegel, Jakob		16 Nov 1847	Betzingen	Rtl.	Jul 1866	N.-Amer	841052
Diegel, Maria & C			Betzingen	Rtl.	Oct 1862	N.-Amer	841052

Diegel, Martin	15 Apr 1844	Ohmenhausen	Rtl.	Mar 1866	N.-Amer	841052
Diegel, Martin	18 Feb 1835	Betzingen	Rtl.	May 1863	N.-Amer	841052
Diemand, Anton Max	17 Feb 1858	Deggingen	Gsl.	May 1871	N.-Amer	572047
Diemand, Gottlieb	30 Mar 1847	Deggingen	Gsl.	Mar 1865	N.-Amer	572045
Diemand, Maria	30 Mar 1837	Deggingen	Gsl.	Dec 1859	N.-Amer	572047
Dierberger, Clara & F		Waldmoessingen	Obd.	Feb 1865	N.-Amer	841015
Dierberger, Georg	26 yrs.	Waldmoessingen	Obd.	Oct 1852	N.-Amer	841015
Dierberger, Jacob	24 Jul 1845	Waldmoessingen	Obd.	Mar 1861	N.-Amer	841015
Dierberger, Karl	28 Oct 1849	Waldmoessingen	Obd.	Feb 1868	N.-Amer	841015
Dierberger, Katharina		Waldmoessingen	Obd.	Feb 1864	N.-Amer	841015
Dierberger, Martina (wife)		Waldmoessingen	Obd.	Aug 1856	N.-Amer	841015
Dierberger, Mathilde	21 yrs.	Waldmoessingen	Obd.	Feb 1865	N.-Amer	841015
Dierberger, Ottomar & W	3 Sep 1829	Waldmoessingen	Obd.	Aug 1856	N.-Amer	841015
Dieterich, Catharina		Dettingen	Krch.	Sep 1859	Galicia	835944
Dieterich, Ernst	29 Aug 1864	Oberlenningen	Krch.	Apr 1881	N.-Amer	548403
Dieterich, Ernst	29 Aug 1864	Oberlenningen	Krch.	Apr 1881	N.-Amer	835947
Dieterich, Friedrich August	10 Mar 1849	Oberlenningen	Krch.	Mar 1867	Texas	835947
Dieterich, Gottlob	5 Oct 1863	Oberlenningen	Krch.	Aug 1880	N.-Amer	835947
Dieterich, Johann Adam	23 Feb 1841	Unterlenningen	Krch.	Jul 1856	N.-Amer	835949
Dieterich, Johann Conrad	31 Aug 1866	Ochsenwangen	Krch.	May 1882	N.-Amer	548403
Dieterich, Johannes	3 Oct 1829	Oberlenningen	Krch.	1848	N.-Amer	835947
Dieterich, Wilhelm David	15 Oct 1850	Oberlenningen	Krch.	Jun 1870	N.-Amer	835947
Dieterle, Anna Friederike	9 yrs.	Schoeckingen	Leon.	Nov 1852	N.-Amer	837964
Dieterle, Catharina (wife)		Schoeckingen	Leon.	Nov 1852	N.-Amer	837964
Dieterle, Georg	3 yrs.	Schoeckingen	Leon.	Nov 1852	N.-Amer	837964
Dieterle, Jakob & F	39 yrs.	Schoeckingen	Leon.	Nov 1852	N.-Amer	837964
Dieterle, Johannes	7 Nov 1891	Gueltstein	Herr.	1908	N.-Amer	834631
Dieterle, Johannes	4 yrs.	Schoeckingen	Leon.	Nov 1852	N.-Amer	837964
Dieterle, Karl	16 Oct 1843	Waldmoessingen	Obd.	Apr 1861	N.-Amer	841015
Dieterle, Rosine	8 yrs.	Schoeckingen	Leon.	Nov 1852	N.-Amer	837964
Dieterle, Wilhelm	1 yrs.	Schoeckingen	Leon.	Nov 1852	N.-Amer	837964
Dietrich, Wesley	7 Aug 1868	Weissendorf	Herr.	Jul 1885	N.-Amer	834629
Dietter, Johann Jakob	5 May 1845	Willmandingen	Rtl.	Mar 1860	N.-Amer	841052
Dietz, Karl Christian H.	20 Jul 1865	Herrenberg	Herr.	Nov 1880	N.-Amer	834629
Dietz, Katharina (wid.)	3 Apr 1824	Hepsisau	Krch.	Dec 1870	N.-Amer	835945
Dietz, Martin & F		Dettingen u. T.	Krch.	Apr 1766	Russia	550804
Dietz, Wilhelm Christian	21 Dec 1866	Herrenberg	Herr.	Jan 1883	N.-Amer	834629
Diez, Anna Maria (wife)	2 Feb 1837	Jesingen	Krch.	Apr 1865	Russia	835946
Diez, Catharina	1 Dec 1850	Dettingen	Krch.	Feb 1868	N.-Amer	835944
Diez, Christian Friedrich	5 Dec 1825	Dettingen	Krch.	bef 1867	N.-Amer	835944
Diez, Christian Friedrich	23 Aug 1853	Dettingen	Krch.	Jun 1867	N.-Amer	835944
Diez, Christine Barbara	24 Aug 1822	Dettingen	Krch.	Sep 1865	N.-Amer	835944
Diez, David	31 Aug 1871	Gutenberg	Krch.	Apr 1888	N.-Amer	835945
Diez, Dorothea	8 Jul 1841	Dettingen	Krch.	Jun 1867	N.-Amer	835944
Diez, Eva Margaretha	11 Oct 1821	Dettingen	Krch.	bef 1867	N.-Amer	835944
Diez, Franz Gottlob	17 Jun 1855	Dettingen	Krch.	Jun 1867	N.-Amer	835944
Diez, Jacob Friedrich	29 Nov 1841	Dettingen	Krch.	Jun 1860	N.-Amer	835944
Diez, Johann Albrecht	6 May 1841	Dettingen	Krch.	bef 1861	N.-Amer	835944
Diez, Johann Christian	17 Jun 1861	Dettingen	Krch.	May 1872	N.-Amer	835944
Diez, Johann Friedrich	2 Nov 1866	Dettingen	Krch.	May 1872	N.-Amer	835944

Name		Birth		Emigration			Film
Last	First	Date	Place	O'amt	Appl. Date	Dest.	Number
Diez, Johann Friedrich		16 Apr 1844	Dettingen	Krch.	Mar 1864	N.-Amer	835944
Diez, Johann Jacob		6 Jun 1821	Dettingen	Krch.	Sep 1865	N.-Amer	835944
Diez, Johann Michael		4 Jun 1860	Dettingen	Krch.	May 1872	N.-Amer	835944
Diez, Johann Michael		9 Dec 1829	Dettingen	Krch.	bef 1867	N.-Amer	835944
Diez, Johann Wilhelm		20 Oct 1827	Dettingen	Krch.	bef 1867	N.-Amer	835944
Diez, Johannes		24 Jun 1832	Dettingen	Krch.	bef 1867	N.-Amer	835944
Diez, Johannes & F		7 Oct 1837	Jesingen	Krch.	Apr 1865	Russia	835946
Diez, Magdalena (wid.) & F			Dettingen	Krch.	May 1872	N.-Amer	835944
Diez, Maria Magdalena & C		2 Sep 1832	Dettingen	Krch.	Jun 1867	N.-Amer	835944
Diez, Susanna Babara		26 Mar 1863	Dettingen	Krch.	May 1872	N.-Amer	835944
Digel, Anna Maria		24 Aug 1841	Wannweil	Rtl.	Aug 1864	N.-Amer	841052
Digel, Friedrich			Ohmenhausen	Rtl.	May 1832	N.-Amer	841051
Digel, Gottfried			Ohmenhausen	Rtl.	May 1836	N.-Amer	841051
Digel, Jakob		28 Feb 1838	Wannweil	Rtl.	Aug 1864	N.-Amer	841052
Digel, Johann Georg		26 Dec 1847	Ohmenhausen	Rtl.	Feb 1867	N.-Amer	841052
Digel, Johann Martin		28 Feb 1844	Ohmenhausen	Rtl.	May 1864	N.-Amer	841052
Digeser, Johannes		22 Dec 1853	Bochingen	Obd.	Feb 1870	N.-Amer	838632
Dinkel, Ernst		3 Jul 1832	Ditzingen	Leon.	bef 1858	N.-Amer	835788
Dirnach, Gottlobin		23 Dec 1849	Rosswaelden	Krch.	Mar 1867	N.-Amer	835949
Dirr, Friedrich		19 Apr 1831	Kirchheim	Krch.	bef 1868	N.-Amer	835941
Dittinger, Wilhelm		25 Oct 1852	Dettingen	Krch.	Jun 1868	N.-Amer	835944
Dodel, Anna		23 Feb 1837	Notzingen	Krch.	Sep 1856	N.-Amer	835947
Dodel, August Friedrich		18 Jun 1827	Notzingen	Krch.	bef 1860	N.-Amer	835947
Dodel, Carolina Friederike		15 Dec 1833	Notzingen	Krch.	Jul 1858	N.-Amer	835947
Dodel, Christoph		15 Mar 1850	Notzingen	Krch.	Feb 1869	N.-Amer	835947
Dodel, Maria		24 yrs.	Notzingen	Krch.	Aug 1865	N.-Amer	835947
Dodel, Wilhelm Friedrich		21 May 1822	Notzingen	Krch.	Jul 1858	N.-Amer	835947
Dodel, Wilhelm Gottlob		22 Apr 1865	Notzingen	Krch.	Jun 1881	N.-Amer	548403
Doenes, Jacob Friedrich & F			Reutlingen	Rtl.	May 1832	N.-Amer	841051
Doerflinger, Karl			Geislingen	Gsl.	Mar 1864	N.-Amer	572045
Doerrer, Albert		5 Dec 1848	Reutlingen	Rtl.	bef 1868	N.-Amer	841052
Doerrer, Gottlob		12 Jan 1823	Reutlingen	Rtl.	Jan 1861	N.-Amer	841052
Doerrer, Julius		2 Nov 1848	Reutlingen	Rtl.	bef 1868	N.-Amer	841052
Doerrer, Karl Jakob			Malmsheim	Leon.	Nov 1863	N.-Amer	837958
Doettling, Christina		9 May 1824	Betzweiler	Obd.	Jun 1848	N.-Amer	838631
Dold, Johann Baptist		13 Aug 1849	Schramberg	Obd.	bef 1869	N.-Amer	838636
Dolde, Karl		9 Aug 1865	Oetlingen	Krch.	Feb 1882	N.-Amer	835948
Dolde, Regine		19 Dec 1845	Oetlingen	Krch.	Nov 1866	N.-Amer	835948
Dolde, Sophia Catharina		30 Apr 1822	Oetlingen	Krch.	bef 1860	N.-Amer	835948
Dolde, Wilhelm		29 Dec 1867	Oetlingen	Krch.	Apr 1883	N.-Amer	835948
Dolfinger, Franz Paul		21 Oct 1829	Weil der Stadt	Leon.	Jul 1850	N.-Amer	837966
Dolfinger, Loreta & F		6 Jun 1797	Weil der Stadt	Leon.	Jul 1850	N.-Amer	837966
Domonell, Alvis			Harthausen	Obd.	Nov 1855	Oldenb.	838633
Domonell, Josef			Harthausen	Obd.	Jul 1854	N.-Amer	838633
Domppert, Christian		13 Mar 1872	Ditzingen	Leon.	Apr 1889	N.-Amer	835788
Domppert, Johann Jakob			Ditzingen	Leon.	Mar 1867	N.-Amer	835788
Dorfner, Wilhelm		24 Apr 1850	Kirchheim	Krch.	Aug 1869	N.-Amer	835941
Dorfschmid, Johann Georg (wid.)		28 Jun 1792	Ohmden	Krch.	Apr 1857	N.-Amer	835948
Dorn, Johann Georg			Zell	Krch.	bef 1900	Zealand	835774
Dorn, Ludwig		4 Nov 1884	Zell	Krch.	Nov 1900	Zealand	835774

Dreher, Jakob	20 Mar 1821	Gerlingen	Leon.	Jan 1854	N.-Amer	837953
Dreher, Maria	29 Jun 1859	Jesingen	Krch.	Apr 1865	Russia	835946
Dreitag, Carl Friedrich	13 May 1852	Heimerdingen	Leon.	Jun 1852	N.-Amer	837954
Dreitag, Christian	3 Apr 1846	Heimerdingen	Leon.	Jun 1852	N.-Amer	837954
Dreitag, Johann Josua	15 Oct 1843	Heimerdingen	Leon.	Jun 1852	N.-Amer	837954
Dreitag, Magdalena & C	30 Nov 1818	Heimerdingen	Leon.	Jun 1852	N.-Amer	837954
Dreitag, Margaetha Carolina	24 Sep 1839	Sinsheim	Leon.	Jun 1852	N.-Amer	837954
Dreitag, Wilhelmine	2 Jan 1842	Sinsheim	Leon.	Jun 1852	N.-Amer	837954
Dressel, Christina Marg. (wife)	37 yrs.	Hemmingen	Leon.	Mar 1827	N.-Amer	837956
Dressel, Christina Margaretha	7 yrs.	Hemmingen	Leon.	Mar 1827	N.-Amer	837956
Dressel, Gottlieb	9 yrs.	Hemmingen	Leon.	Mar 1827	N.-Amer	837956
Dressel, Jakob	12 yrs.	Hemmingen	Leon.	Mar 1827	N.-Amer	837956
Dressel, Jakob	6 yrs.	Hemmingen	Leon.	Mar 1827	N.-Amer	837956
Dressel, Johann Georg	17 yrs.	Hemmingen	Leon.	Mar 1827	N.-Amer	837956
Dressel, Johann Martin & F	46 yrs.	Hemmingen	Leon.	Mar 1827	N.-Amer	837956
Dressel, Johanna	1 yrs.	Hemmingen	Leon.	Mar 1827	N.-Amer	837956
Dressel, Johannes	20 yrs.	Hemmingen	Leon.	Mar 1827	N.-Amer	837956
Dressel, Johannes	11 yrs.	Hemmingen	Leon.	Mar 1827	N.-Amer	837956
Drexler, Bernhard	8 Mar 1832	Neidlingen	Krch.	bef 1861	N.-Amer	835946
Drexler, Johann Georg	4 Jun 1834	Neidlingen	Krch.	Apr 1866	N.-Amer	835946
Drexler, Johann Jacob	8 Dec 1826	Notzingen	Krch.	bef 1863	Austria	835947
Drexler, Johannes	18 Dec 1823	Neidlingen	Krch.	bef 1861	N.-Amer	835946
Drexler, Maria	15 Jan 1829	Neidlingen	Krch.	bef 1861	N.-Amer	835946
Drittag, Albanus & F	5 Sep 1805	Rosswaelden	Krch.	Aug 1862	N.-Amer	835949
Drittag, Caroline	18 May 1841	Rosswaelden	Krch.	Sep 1858	N.-Amer	835949
Drittag, Friedrich	16 Jul 1849	Rosswaelden	Krch.	Aug 1862	N.-Amer	835949
Drittag, Maria Barbara	3 Mar 1839	Rosswaelden	Krch.	Sep 1858	N.-Amer	835949
Drodofsky, Georg Jakob	8 Nov 1836	Heimsheim	Leon.	Aug 1853	N.-Amer	837955
Drodofsky, Israel (wid.)	48 yrs.	Moensheim	Leon.	Oct 1851	N.-Amer	837960
Drometer, Emilie	8 Apr 1850	Boehmenkirch	Gsl.	Jun 1871	N.-Amer	572047
Drometer, Johann Georg & W	31 Jan 1842	Boehmenkirch	Gsl.	Sep 1867	N.-Amer	572046
Drometer, Josefa (wife)	4 Nov 1844	Boehmenkirch	Gsl.	Sep 1867	N.-Amer	572046
Drometer, Sophia	22 Nov 1845	Boehmenkirch	Gsl.	Apr 1867	N.-Amer	572046
Duerner, Georg Adam	2 Aug 1826	Weilheim	Krch.	bef 1863	N.-Amer	835950
Duerner, Georg Adam	16 Feb 1827	Weilheim	Krch.	bef 1861	N.-Amer	835949
Duerner, Johann Christoph	3 Dec 1859	Haeringen	Krch.	Aug 1880	N.-Amer	548403
Duerner, Johann Georg	7 Feb 1835	Weilheim	Krch.	1851	N.-Amer	835949
Duerner, Johann Heinrich	26 Nov 1857	Leonberg	Leon.	Oct 1885	Holland	835787
Duerner, Johannes & F	30 May 1841	Haeringen	Krch.	Mar 1874	N.-Amer	548403
Duerner, Margaretha	25 May 1843	Weilheim	Krch.	bef 1868	N.-Amer	835950
Duerner, Maria Catharina	14 Nov 1836	Weilheim	Krch.	bef 1861	N.-Amer	835949
Duerr, Adolph	10 yrs.	Eltingen	Leon.	Oct 1853	N.-Amer	835789
Duerr, Adolph	13 Sep 1847	Eningen	Rtl.	Apr 1864	N.-Amer	841052
Duerr, August	5 yrs.	Eltingen	Leon.	Oct 1853	N.-Amer	835789
Duerr, Cardine	9 yrs.	Eltingen	Leon.	Oct 1853	N.-Amer	835789
Duerr, Catharina Regina	13 Jul 1825	Hausen a.d. Wurm	Leon.	Jul 1854	N.-Amer	837954
Duerr, Christiane (wife)		Eltingen	Leon.	Oct 1853	N.-Amer	835789
Duerr, Friedrich & F		Eltingen	Leon.	Oct 1853	N.-Amer	835789
Duerr, Georg Gottlob	24 Nov 1863	Merklingen	Leon.	Jun 1880	N.-Amer	837959
Duerr, Gottfried		Hausen a.d. Wurm	Leon.	Mar 1853	N.-Amer	837954

| Name | | Birth | | Emigration | | | Film |
Last	First	Date	Place	O'amt	Appl. Date	Dest.	Number
Duerr, Jacob Friedrich		12 Nov 1851	Owen	Krch.	Oct 1864	N.-Amer	835948
Duerr, Johann Adam		2 Jun 1839	Nabern	Krch.	Feb 1857	N.-Amer	835946
Duerr, Johann Georg		14 Mar 1848	Eningen	Rtl.	Jul 1866	N.-Amer	841052
Duerr, Johann Michael		12 Sep 1846	Nabern	Krch.	Jul 1865	N.-Amer	835946
Duerr, Johannes			Hausen a.d. Wurm	Leon.	Oct 1853	N.-Amer	837954
Duerr, Michael		3 Apr 1836	Nabern	Krch.	bef 1857	N.-Amer	835946
Duerr, Renthilde		8 yrs.	Eltingen	Leon.	Oct 1853	N.-Amer	835789
Duerr, Wilhelm		2 yrs.	Eltingen	Leon.	Oct 1853	N.-Amer	835789
Duerr, Wilhelm		29 Aug 1848	Weiler	Krch.	Jul 1866	N.-Amer	835949
Duerrschnabel, August Friedr.		27 Dec 1875	Herrenberg	Herr.	bef 1899	Switz.	834629
Dunkenberger, Hironymus		5 Jul 1845	Westerheim	Gsl.	Feb 1867	N.-Amer	572046
Duppel, Magdalena (wife)			Rutesheim	Leon.	May 1853	N.-Amer	837964
Duppel, Regina Catharina		27 Sep 1830	Rutesheim	Leon.	Feb 1851	N.-Amer	837964
Duppel, Tobias & W			Rutesheim	Leon.	May 1853	N.-Amer	837964
Durian, Johann Konrad		9 Jul 1864	Flacht	Leon.	Mar 1881	N.-Amer	835790
Durner, Lorenz		27 yrs.	Drackenstein	Gsl.	Dec 1861	N.-Amer	572044
Durrian, Michael		27 Feb 1819	Wimsheim	Loen.	Dec 1848	N.-Amer	837967
Dursch, Ulrich		1 Aug 1838	Muehlhausen	Gsl.	Feb 1854	N.-Amer	572042
Dursterwitz, Ernst Wilhelm		19 Feb 1846	Pfullingen	Rtl.	Dec 1866	England	841052
Dussling, Jakob		26 Nov 1843	Wimsheim	Loen.	Jan 1859	N.-Amer	837967
Dussling, Simon		7 Sep 1840	Wimsheim	Loen.	Jan 1859	N.-Amer	837967
Dussling, Wilhelm Heinrich		18 Feb 1863	Herrenberg	Herr.	bef 1891	Switz.	834629
Dutt, Christian & F			Flacht	Leon.	Apr 1852	N.-Amer	835790
Dutt, Christine		3 yrs.	Flacht	Leon.	Apr 1852	N.-Amer	835790
Dutt, David & F			Flacht	Leon.	May 1853	N.-Amer	835790
Dutt, Friedrike (wife)			Flacht	Leon.	Apr 1852	N.-Amer	835790
Eben, Eugen Friedrich Ludwig		26 Sep 1826	Weil im Dorf	Loen.	1847	N.-Amer	837967
Ebensperger, Anna Rosina		4 yrs.	Ditzingen	Leon.	Mar 1852	S.-Amer	835788
Ebensperger, Carl Adolf		12 yrs.	Ditzingen	Leon.	Mar 1852	S.-Amer	835788
Ebensperger, Carl Friedrich		9 yrs.	Ditzingen	Leon.	Mar 1852	S.-Amer	835788
Ebensperger, Georg Gottlob		7 yrs.	Ditzingen	Leon.	Mar 1852	S.-Amer	835788
Ebensperger, Jakob & F			Ditzingen	Leon.	Mar 1852	S.-Amer	835788
Ebensperger, Johann Jakob		16 yrs.	Ditzingen	Leon.	Mar 1852	S.-Amer	835788
Ebensperger, Paulina Mathilde		1 yrs.	Ditzingen	Leon.	Mar 1852	S.-Amer	835788
Ebensperger, Rosina (wife)			Ditzingen	Leon.	Mar 1852	S.-Amer	835788
Eberhard, Heinrich		21 Mar 1842	Kirchheim	Krch.	Feb 1866	N.-Amer	835941
Eberhard, Johannes		8 Apr 1878	Eckwaelden	Krch.	Apr 1892	N.-Amer	835774
Eberhard, Katharina		23 Nov 1846	Steinenkirch	Gsl.	May 1865	N.-Amer	572045
Eberhard, Leonhard		5 Mar 1837	Grosssuessen	Gsl.	Jan 1854	N.-Amer	572042
Eberhardt, Anna Margaretha		7 Jul 1832	Grosssuessen	Gsl.	Jan 1854	N.-Amer	572042
Eberhardt, Georg		6 Jan 1830	Grosssuessen	Gsl.	May 1851	N.-Amer	577788
Eberhart, Amalie		23 yrs.	Geislingen	Gsl.	Aug 1860	Switz.	572044
Eberhart, Gottlieb		6 May 1856	Sulpach	Krch.	Feb 1857	N.-Amer	835949
Eberhart, Gottlieb & F		14 Nov 1815	Sulpach	Krch.	Feb 1857	N.-Amer	835949
Eberhart, Johann		6 Oct 1847	Sulpach	Krch.	Feb 1857	N.-Amer	835949
Eberhart, Margaretha		14 Feb 1827	Sulpach	Krch.	Feb 1857	N.-Amer	835949
Eberle, Carl Friedr.August & F		28 Feb 1835	Rosswaelden	Krch.	Apr 1876	N.-Amer	835949
Eberle, Christian		30 Jul 1872	Rosswaelden	Krch.	Apr 1876	N.-Amer	835949
Eberle, David Friedrich		3 Aug 1845	Kirchheim	Krch.	Apr 1889	N.-Amer	835942
Eberle, Emanuel Julius		25 Dec 1886	Kirchheim	Krch.	Apr 1889	N.-Amer	835942

Eberle, Ernst Friedrich	8 Jun 1881	Kirchheim	Krch.	Apr 1889	N.-Amer	835942
Eberle, Jakob Gottlob	31 Jan 1875	Rosswaelden	Krch.	Apr 1876	N.-Amer	835949
Eberle, Joseph Hermann	18 Nov 1875	Hepsisau	Krch.	Apr 1890	N.-Amer	835945
Eberle, Ludwig	15 Jul 1869	Rosswaelden	Krch.	Apr 1876	N.-Amer	835949
Eberle, Luisa Kathar. (wife)	39 yrs.	Rosswaelder	Krch.	Apr 1876	N.-Amer	548403
Eberle, Luise Katharine	5 Nov 1837	Rosswaelden	Krch.	Apr 1876	N.-Amer	835949
Eberle, Maria Friedr. (wife)	18 Sep 1849	Kirchheim	Krch.	Apr 1889	N.-Amer	835942
Eberth, Friederich Johann. & F	12 Nov 1825	Eybach	Gsl.	Mar 1854	N.-Amer	572042
Eberth, Maria Barbara (wife)	21 Apr 1823	Eybach	Gsl.	Mar 1854	N.-Amer	572042
Eberth, Martin Friederich	10 Dec 1852	Eybach	Gsl.	Mar 1854	N.-Amer	572042
Ebinger, Andreas	9 Sep 1847	Dettingen	Krch.	Jul 1872	N.-Amer	835944
Ebinger, Johannes	26 Feb 1850	Dettingen	Krch.	Jul 1872	N.-Amer	835944
Eble, Ernst	12 Jan 1848	Weil der Stadt	Leon.	Feb 1867	N.-Amer	837966
Eble, Franziska		Weil der Stadt	Leon.	Sep 1854	N.-Amer	837966
Eble, Jean & F	1 Jan 1807	Weil der Stadt	Leon.	Jul 1853	N.-Amer	837966
Eble, Peter Paul		Weil der Stadt	Leon.	Sep 1854	N.-Amer	837966
Eble, Victor	21 Oct 1870	Ellwangen	Leon.	1885	N.-Amer	837966
Eble, Wilhelm Otto	20 Jan 1865	Weil der Stadt	Leon.	Nov 1881	N.-Amer	837966
Ebner, Barbara	1 Mar 1835	Unterboehringen	Gsl.	Feb 1854	N.-Amer	572042
Ebnerhard, Johann Tobias	16 Sep 1849	Flacht	Leon.	May 1869	N.-Amer	835790
Echle, Georg & F		Mariazell	Obd.	May 1817	N.-Amer	838634
Eck, Johannes	20 Sep 1865	Weilheim	Krch.	Apr 1882	N.-Amer	835774
Eckenfels, Catharina Barbara		Alpirsbach	Obd.	Jan 1849	N.-Amer	838630
Eckenfels, Wilhelmine & C		Alpirsbach	Obd.	Aug 1861	France	838630
Eckle, Barbara		Altenstadt-Gsl.	Gsl.	May 1864	N.-Amer	572045
Eckle, Barbara (wife)	9 Oct 1801	Kuchen	Gsl.	Feb 1856	N.-Amer	572043
Eckle, Eva	8 May 1830	Kuchen	Gsl.	Feb 1854	N.-Amer	572042
Eckle, Georg	28 Nov 1828	Kuchen	Gsl.	Feb 1856	N.-Amer	572043
Eckle, Jakob & F	18 Apr 1802	Kuchen	Gsl.	Feb 1856	N.-Amer	572043
Eckle, Leonhardt	12 Jul 1843	Kuchen	Gsl.	Feb 1857	N.-Amer	572043
Eckle, Luckrezia	26 Oct 1828	Kuchen	Gsl.	Feb 1854	N.-Amer	572042
Eckle, Margaretha	25 Jun 1850	Kuchen	Gsl.	Feb 1854	N.-Amer	572042
Eckle, Margaretha	4 Nov 1832	Kuchen	Gsl.	1853	N.-Amer	572043
Eckstein, Franziska	8 Mar 1840	Mariazell	Obd.	Jan 1864	France	838634
Eckstein, Hermann	8 May 1867	Rosswaelden	Krch.	Feb 1881	N.-Amer	835949
Edele, Friedrich	11 Apr 1844	Dettingen	Krch.	Aug 1866	N.-Amer	835944
Edelmann, Ignaz		Geislingen	Gsl.	Mar 1852	N.-Amer	572041
Edelmann, Maria (wife)	23 yrs.	Weissenstein	Gsl.	Apr 1854	N.-Amer	572042
Edelmann, Mathias & W	15 Jul 1828	Weissenstein	Gsl.	Apr 1854	N.-Amer	572042
Ederle, Christoph Gottlob	5 Aug 1872	Bissingen	Krch.	Apr 1889	N.-Amer	835943
Ege, Jacob Friedrich		Leonberg	Leon.	Apr 1866	N.-Amer	835787
Ege, Rosina		Hirschlanden	Leon.	Dec 1841	Switz.	837956
Egeler, Karl Friedrich	3 Apr 1865	Bondorf	Herr.	Feb 1881	N.-Amer	834630
Egeler, Ludwig	28 Dec 1869	Bondorf	Herr.	Jan 1886	N.-Amer	834630
Egeler, Wilhelmine Heinrike	4 Feb 1839	Boennigheim	Herr.	Dec 1869	N.-Amer	834630
Egen, August Friedrich	21 Nov 1850	Heimerdingen	Leon.	Aug 1853	N.-Amer	837954
Egen, Caroline (wife)	5 Jan 1827	Heimerdingen	Leon.	Aug 1853	N.-Amer	837954
Egen, Wilhelm Friedrich		Heimerdingen	Leon.	bef 1864	N.-Amer	837954
Egen, Wilhelm Friedrich	20 Jul 1849	Heimerdingen	Leon.	Aug 1853	N.-Amer	837954
Egen, Wilhelm Friedrich & F	9 Jul 1825	Heimerdingen	Leon.	Aug 1853	N.-Amer	837954

Name		Birth		Emigration			Film
Last	First	Date	Place	O'amt	Appl. Date	Dest.	Number
Egenriether, Gottlob		5 Feb 1866	Notzingen	Krch.	Sep 1867	N.-Amer	835947
Egenriether, Maria		22 Jun 1867	Notzingen	Krch.	Sep 1867	N.-Amer	835947
Eger, Christian & F			Alt Oberndorf	Obd.	Jul 1852	N.-Amer	838631
Eger, Genovefa (wife)			Alt Oberndorf	Obd.	Jul 1852	N.-Amer	838631
Eger, Johann David Albert		31 May 1839	Hirschlanden	Leon.	Jun 1854	N.-Amer	837956
Eger, Josef August		4 Jul 1855	Schnittlingen	Gsl.	Jun 1874	N.-Amer	572048
Egerter, Johann georg			Gerlingen	Leon.	Jan 1852	Hamburg	837953
Egerter, Maria Barbara		26 Jul 1850	Gerlingen	Leon.	Nov 1884	N.-Amer	837953
Egerter, Maria Carolina		16 May 1833	Gerlingen	Leon.	Sep 1854	N.-Amer	837953
Eggert, Matthaeus		18 Feb 1868	Zimmern	Rtw.	Jan 1885	N.-Amer	841117
Egide, Maria Magdalena			Malmsheim	Leon.	Jul 1857	N.-Amer	837958
Egle, Johannes		16 Sep 1830	Moensheim	Leon.	Jul 1850	N.-Amer	837960
Egle, Veronika		10 May 1803	Moensheim	Leon.	Mar 1854	N.-Amer	837960
Ehni, Anna Barbara (wife)		12 Feb 1836	Bissingen	Krch.	Mar 1868	N.-Amer	835943
Ehni, Anna Maria		25 Dec 1832	Esslingen	Krch.	Mar 1857	N.-Amer	835943
Ehni, Barbara		26 Mar 1876	Gutenberg	Krch.	May 1882	N.-Amer	548403
Ehni, Barbara		26 Mar 1876	Gutenberg	Krch.	Apr 1882	N.-Amer	835945
Ehni, Christoph		27 Nov 1853	Gutenberg	Krch.	Nov 1867	N.-Amer	835945
Ehni, Conrad (wid.)		4 Jul 1826	Bissingen	Krch.	Jun 1870	N.-Amer	835943
Ehni, Friedrich		30 Sep 1877	Gutenberg	Krch.	May 1882	N.-Amer	548403
Ehni, Gottfried			Bissingen	Krch.	bef 1867	N.-Amer	835943
Ehni, Gottlieb Wilhelm		21 Feb 1861	Bissingen	Krch.	Oct 1880	England	835943
Ehni, Jeremias			Gutenberg	Krch.	bef 1792	N.-Amer	550804
Ehni, Johann Adam		19 Mar 1829	Gutenberg	Krch.	bef 1874	N.-Amer	835945
Ehni, Johann Christoph		13 Jan 1872	Bissingen	Krch.	Apr 1889	N.-Amer	835943
Ehni, Johann Jakob		27 Jul 1873	Gutenberg	Krch.	May 1882	N.-Amer	548403
Ehni, Johann Michael		11 Jul 1831	Bissingen	Krch.	Jul 1856	N.-Amer	835943
Ehni, Johann Philipp & W		10 Jul 1828	Bissingen	Krch.	Mar 1868	N.-Amer	835943
Ehni, Karl		30 Apr 1839	Bissingen	Krch.	Feb 1867	N.-Amer	835943
Ehni, Magdalena		20 Sep 1865	Gutenberg	Krch.	May 1882	N.-Amer	548403
Ehni, Michael Gottlob		20 Oct 1872	Gutenberg	Krch.	May 1889	N.-Amer	835945
Ehni, Sophia		2 Apr 1868	Gutenberg	Krch.	Apr 1882	N.-Amer	835945
Ehni, Sophia (wid.) & F		26 Aug 1836	Gutenberg	Krch.	Apr 1882	N.-Amer	835945
Ehni, Wilhelm		3 May 1850	Bissingen	Krch.	Sep 1867	N.-Amer	835943
Ehninger, Friedrich		13 May 1860	Kirchheim	Krch.	Sep 1876	N.-Amer	548403
Ehninger, Rosine Wilhelmine		22 Feb 1836	Kirchheim	Krch.	Jan 1858	N.-Amer	835940
Ehninger, Wilhelm		16 Sep 1861	Kirchheim	Krch.	Aug 1878	England	548403
Ehret, Johann Michael K.		22 Nov 1840	Weil im Dorf	Loen.	Dec 1869	N.-Amer	837967
Ehrmann, Maria Louisa		21 yrs.	Geislingen	Gsl.	May 1867	Hesse	572046
Eib, Johann Martin		3 Oct 1832	Pfullingen	Rtl.	Jun 1863	N.-Amer	841052
Eibe, Carl		26 yrs.	Alpirsbach	Obd.	Jun 1851	Silesia	838630
Eiberger, Katharina			Beffendorf	Obd.	Nov 1823	Hungary	838631
Eichele, Elisabetha & C		35 yrs.	Westerheim	Gsl.	Mar 1854	N.-Amer	572042
Einsele, Carl		25 Dec 1860	Oberlenningen	Krch.	Apr 1874	N.-Amer	548403
Einsele, Friederika (wid.) & F		49 yrs.	Oberlenningen	Krch.	Apr 1874	N.-Amer	548403
Einsele, Gustav		23 Jan 1863	Oberlenningen	Krch.	Apr 1874	N.-Amer	548403
Einsele, Heinrich		20 Aug 1865	Oberlenningen	Krch.	Apr 1874	N.-Amer	548403
Einsele, Johann Friedrich		19 Sep 1869	Weilheim	Krch.	Jun 1883	Austral	548403
Einsele, Johann Friedrich		26 Aug 1844	Weilheim	Krch.	Apr 1864	N.-Amer	835950
Einsele, Johannes		1 Oct 1832	Weilheim	Krch.	bef 1858	N.-Amer	835949

Einsele, Julie	12 Sep 1852	Oberlenningen	Krch.	Apr 1874	N.-Amer	548403
Einsele, Karl Josef	7 Nov 1864	Weilheim	Krch.	Apr 1881	N.-Amer	548403
Einseler, Carl Rudolph	25 Dec 1860	Oberlenningen	Krch.	Apr 1874	N.-Amer	835947
Einseler, Ernst Wilhelm Fr.	1 Mar 1849	Oberlenningen	Krch.	Sep 1868	N.-Amer	835947
Einseler, Friederike (wid.) & F	31 Aug 1824	Oberlenningen	Krch.	Apr 1874	N.-Amer	835947
Einseler, Gustav Albert	23 Jan 1863	Oberlenningen	Krch.	Apr 1874	N.-Amer	835947
Einseler, Heinrich	20 Aug 1865	Oberlenningen	Krch.	Apr 1874	N.-Amer	835947
Einseler, Julie	17 Sep 1852	Oberlenningen	Krch.	Apr 1874	N.-Amer	835947
Einzig, Anton	23 yrs.	Schietingen	Nag.	Oct 1854	N.-Amer	838488
Eipper, Johann Jacob		Malmsheim	Leon.	bef 1820	France	837958
Eipper, Johannes	9 Jan 1847	Gueltstein	Herr.	Apr 1867	N.-Amer	834631
Eipperle, Anna Maria	26 Sep 1844	Gaertringen	Herr.	Apr 1867	N.-Amer	834630
Eipperle, Friederika	5 Apr 1826	Gaertringen	Herr.	1851	N.-Amer	834630
Eipperle, Johann Georg	22 Mar 1857	Gaertringen	Herr.	Jan 1873	N.-Amer	834630
Eisberg, Maria	9 yrs.	Beffendorf	Obd.	May 1861	N.-Amer	838631
Eisberg, Maria & C		Beffendorf	Obd.	May 1861	N.-Amer	838631
Eisberg, Paulina	10 yrs.	Beffendorf	Obd.	May 1861	N.-Amer	838631
Eisberg, Wilhelmine	14 yrs.	Beffendorf	Obd.	May 1861	N.-Amer	838631
Eisele, Adolf	1 yrs.	Gerlingen	Leon.	Jan 1853	N.-Amer	837953
Eisele, Bernhard		Donzdorf	Gsl.	Apr 1852	N.-Amer	572041
Eisele, Carl	6 yrs.	Gerlingen	Leon.	Jan 1853	N.-Amer	837953
Eisele, Christian	17 yrs.	Kirchheim	Krch.	Jul 1859	N.-Amer	835940
Eisele, Christian Friedr. & F	40 yrs.	Kirchheim	Krch.	Jul 1859	N.-Amer	835940
Eisele, Daniel	9 Mar 1827	Reutlingen	Rtl.	Oct 1861	Austria	841052
Eisele, Eleonora	11 yrs.	Donzdorf	Gsl.	Sep 1852	N.-Amer	572041
Eisele, Emma	9 yrs.	Kirchheim	Krch.	Jul 1859	N.-Amer	835940
Eisele, Gustav	8 yrs.	Gerlingen	Leon.	Jan 1853	N.-Amer	837953
Eisele, Hermann	4 Jan 1852	Reutlingen	Rtl.	May 1868	N.-Amer	841052
Eisele, Johann	12 Aug 1769	Jesingen	Krch.	bef 1806	Paris	550804
Eisele, Johann Georg	19 May 1831	Dettingen	Krch.	Mar 1869	N.-Amer	835944
Eisele, Johann Georg & F		Gerlingen	Leon.	Jan 1853	N.-Amer	837953
Eisele, Johannes		Donzdorf	Gsl.	bef 1852	N.-Amer	572041
Eisele, Johannes	5 yrs.	Donzdorf	Gsl.	Sep 1852	N.-Amer	572041
Eisele, Johannes	10 Feb 1811	Donzdorf	Gsl.	1852	N.-Amer	572043
Eisele, Joseph		Donzdorf	Gsl.	bef 1852	N.-Amer	572041
Eisele, Joseph	3 May 1848	Nenningen	Gsl.	Nov 1869	N.-Amer	572047
Eisele, Katharina	22 yrs.	Donzdorf	Gsl.	Apr 1852	N.-Amer	572041
Eisele, Louise	5 yrs.	Kirchheim	Krch.	Jul 1859	N.-Amer	835940
Eisele, Marianna	9 yrs.	Donzdorf	Gsl.	Sep 1852	N.-Amer	572041
Eisele, Regina	10 yrs.	Donzdorf	Gsl.	Sep 1852	N.-Amer	572041
Eisele, Wilhelm	36 yrs.	Gerlingen	Leon.	Jan 1853	N.-Amer	837953
Eisele, Xaver	28 Dec 1849	Nenningen	Gsl.	Feb 1869	N.-Amer	572047
Eisele, Zozilia (wife) & F		Donzdorf	Gsl.	Sep 1852	N.-Amer	572041
Eisenhard, Catharine Louise	11 Jul 1869	Malmsheim	Leon.	Mar 1884	N.-Amer	837958
Eisenhard, Christian Friedr.	1 Jul 1867	Malmsheim	Leon.	Mar 1884	N.-Amer	837958
Eisenhard, Christiane Frieder.	15 Nov 1876	Malmsheim	Leon.	Mar 1884	N.-Amer	837958
Eisenhard, Christiane Lo. (wife)		Malmsheim	Leon.	Mar 1884	N.-Amer	837958
Eisenhard, Gottlob Heinrich	23 Aug 1879	Malmsheim	Leon.	Mar 1884	N.-Amer	837958
Eisenhard, Johann Jakob	22 May 1866	Malmsheim	Leon.	Mar 1884	N.-Amer	837958
Eisenhard, Johann Jakob & F	17 Dec 1837	Malmsheim	Leon.	Mar 1884	N.-Amer	837958

Name		Birth		Emigration			Film
Last	First	Date	Place	O'amt	Appl. Date	Dest.	Number
Eisenhardt, Christian		12 Dec 1830	Bissingen	Krch.	Jul 1872	N.-Amer	835943
Eisenhardt, Gottlob		2 Apr 1840	Renningen	Leon.	Feb 1857	N.-Amer	837963
Eisenhardt, Johann Georg		9 Nov 1805	Rutesheim	Leon.	1830	N.-Amer	837964
Eisenhardt, Johann Ulrich			Rutesheim	Leon.	May 1830	N.-Amer	837964
Eisenhardt, Johannes		25 Dec 1848	Garrweiler	Leon.	Aug 1867	N.-Amer	837964
Eisenlohr, Carl		26 yrs.	Reutlingen	Rtl.	Apr 1880	N.-Amer	841051
Eisenlohr, Johann Ludwig		25 yrs.	Reutlingen	Rtl.	May 1880	N.-Amer	841051
Eisenschmid, Johann Adam		16 Sep 1819	Gutenberg	Krch.	Feb 1869	N.-Amer	835945
Eiskant, Georg		23 Apr 1808	Beffendorf	Obd.	Apr 1817	N.-Amer	838631
Eiskant, Ignatz		1 Feb 1812	Beffendorf	Obd.	Apr 1817	N.-Amer	838631
Eiskant, Johannes		28 Feb 1804	Beffendorf	Obd.	Apr 1817	N.-Amer	838631
Eiskant, Joseph		23 Mar 1798	Beffendorf	Obd.	Apr 1817	N.-Amer	838631
Eiskant, Katharina		5 Nov 1800	Beffendorf	Obd.	Apr 1817	N.-Amer	838631
Eiskant, Lugarta (wife)		14 Sep 1777	Beffendorf	Obd.	Apr 1817	N.-Amer	838631
Eiskant, Maria Eva		23 Dec 1814	Beffendorf	Obd.	Apr 1817	N.-Amer	838631
Eiskant, Rosalia		8 Sep 1809	Beffendorf	Obd.	Apr 1817	N.-Amer	838631
Eiskant, Valentin & F		14 Feb 1770	Beffendorf	Obd.	Apr 1817	N.-Amer	838631
Eiskant, Verena		1 Sep 1802	Beffendorf	Obd.	Apr 1817	N.-Amer	838631
Eiss, Dorothea			Eltingen	Leon.	Feb 1868	N.-Amer	835789
Eiss, Eva Barbara (wife)			Eltingen	Leon.	Feb 1868	N.-Amer	835789
Eiss, Gotthilf		28 Oct 1859	Eltingen	Leon.	Jul 1880	N.-Amer	835789
Eiss, Jacob & F			Eltingen	Leon.	Feb 1868	N.-Amer	835789
Eiss, Katharina		5 yrs.	Eltingen	Leon.	Feb 1868	N.-Amer	835789
Eiss, Sophie (wid.) & F			Eltingen	Leon.	Feb 1868	N.-Amer	835789
Eissinger, Heinrich & F			Willmandingen	Rtl.	Apr 1831	N.-Amer	841051
Eissler, Anna Maria		17 Nov 1835	Willmandingen	Rtl.	1854	N.-Amer	841052
Eissler, Anna Maria (wife)		29 Sep 1805	Willmandingen	Rtl.	Apr 1860	N.-Amer	841052
Eissler, Friedrich			Maegerkingen	Rtl.	Jun 1868	France	841052
Eissler, Jacob		30 Sep 1830	Willmandingen	Rtl.	bef 1869	N.-Amer	841052
Eissler, Jakob		28 Mar 1843	Willmandingen	Rtl.	Mar 1860	N.-Amer	841052
Eissler, Johann Bernhard		2 Nov 1850	Willmandingen	Rtl.	Sep 1868	N.-Amer	841052
Eissler, Johann Georg & W		6 Dec 1894	Willmandingen	Rtl.	Apr 1860	N.-Amer	841052
Eissler, Johann Martin		13 Sep 1842	Willmandingen	Rtl.	Feb 1860	N.-Amer	841052
Eissler, Johannes & W		28 Jul 1829	Holzelfingen	Rtl.	1854	N.-Amer	841052
Eissler, Juditha (wife)		27 Mar 1826	Willmandingen	Rtl.	1854	N.-Amer	841052
Eit, Johann & F			Winzeln	Obd.	May 1817	N.-Amer	841016
Eit, Maria & C			Seedorf	Obd.	May 1818	N.-Amer	841016
Eitel, Jakob Friedrich		20 Oct 1845	Moensheim	Leon.	Jan 1847	N.-Amer	837960
Eitel, Johann Michael Daniel		28 Feb 1844	Eningen	Rtl.	Aug 1864	N.-Amer	841052
Eitel, Katharina Doroth. (wife)			Moensheim	Leon.	Jan 1847	N.-Amer	837960
Eitel, Philipp & F		28 yrs.	Moensheim	Leon.	Jan 1847	N.-Amer	837960
Eitelbuss, Carolina Louisa		29 Apr 1839	Herrenberg	Herr.	Oct 1866	Austria	834629
Eitelbuss, Christ. Marth. (wife)		12 May 1844	Gueltstein	Herr.	Feb 1869	N.-Amer	834631
Eitelbuss, Gottlieb & W		3 Jan 1836	Gueltstein	Herr.	Feb 1869	N.-Amer	834631
Eith, Caezilia			Winzeln	Obd.	Apr 1866	N.-Amer	841016
Eith, Elisabeth		6 yrs.	Winzeln	Obd.	Sep 1854	N.-Amer	841016
Eith, Emmerenz & F		24 Jan 1815	Winzeln	Obd.	Oct 1847	N.-Amer	841016
Eith, Euphemia			Winzeln	Obd.	Apr 1866	N.-Amer	841016
Eith, Franziska & F			Winzeln	Obd.	Sep 1854	N.-Amer	841016
Eith, Gustav		3 yrs.	Winzeln	Obd.	Sep 1854	N.-Amer	841016

Name	Date	Place	Region	Emig.	Dest.	Film
Eith, Johann Nepomuk		Winzeln	Obd.	Apr 1866	N.-Amer	841016
Eith, Josepha & C		Winzeln	Obd.	Nov 1860	N.-Amer	841016
Eith, Karl	3 Jan 1845	Beffendorf	Obd.	Oct 1847	N.-Amer	841016
Eith, Maria	24 Nov 1837	Winzeln	Obd.	Mar 1865	N.-Amer	841016
Eith, Maria	30 Dec 1846	Winzeln	Obd.	Mar 1858	N.-Amer	841016
Eith, Paulina		Winzeln	Obd.	Nov 1860	N.-Amer	841016
Eith, Pauline	8 yrs.	Winzeln	Obd.	Sep 1854	N.-Amer	841016
Eith, Peter	14 Oct 1850	Winzeln	Obd.	Feb 1869	N.-Amer	841016
Eith, Philippina		Winzeln	Obd.	Apr 1866	N.-Amer	841016
Eith, Rosine & C	43 yrs.	Winzeln	Obd.	Sep 1853	N.-Amer	841016
Eith, Samuel		Winzeln	Obd.	bef 1854	N.-Amer	841016
Eith, Sekunda	24 Mar 1839	Winzeln	Obd.	Sep 1855	N.-Amer	841016
Elbling, Johann Anton B.	18 Aug 1833	Weil der Stadt	Leon.	bef 1859	N.-Amer	837966
Ellwanger, Wilhelm Gottlieb	18 Aug 1833	Renningen	Leon.	Feb 1853	N.-Amer	837963
Ellwein, Barbara	28 yrs.	Hemmingen	Leon.	Jul 1851	N.-Amer	837956
Ellwein, Catharina	25 yrs.	Hemmingen	Leon.	Jul 1851	N.-Amer	837956
Ellwein, Johann Andreas	4 Aug 1844	Hemmingen	Leon.	1865	-.-Amer	837956
Ellwein, Johann Georg	21 yrs.	Hemmingen	Leon.	Jul 1851	N.-Amer	837956
Ellwein, Margaretha (wid.) & F		Hemmingen	Leon.	Jul 1851	N.-Amer	837956
Ellwein, Mathias	23 Jun 1822	Hemmingen	Leon.	Mar 1848	N.-Amer	837956
Elwert, Christian August	10 Mar 1845	Reutlingen	Rtl.	Apr 1864	N.-Amer	841052
Elwert, Philipp Gottfried	7 May 1830	Reutlingen	Rtl.	Mar 1865	N.-Amer	841052
Emmerich, Maria Doroth. (wife)	3 Feb 1832	Bissingen	Krch.	1855	N.-Amer	835943
Enderle, Josef		Geislingen	Gsl.	Dec 1851	N.-Amer	577788
Endres, Carl	21 May 1857	Oberndorf	Obd.	Nov 1863	N.-Amer	838635
Endres, Ernst		Oberndorf	Obd.	Jun 1848	N.-Amer	838635
Engel, Anna Maria (wife)	9 Jul 1804	Renningen	Leon.	Apr 1852	N.-Amer	837963
Engel, Auguste Carolina	27 Aug 1827	Renningen	Leon.	Jul 1854	N.-Amer	837963
Engel, Caroline	15 Mar 1797	Renningen	Leon.	Apr 1857	N.-Amer	837963
Engel, Christina Barbara	5 Apr 1838	Renningen	Leon.	Apr 1852	N.-Amer	837963
Engel, Ernst Gottlob	13 Sep 1846	Renningen	Leon.	Apr 1852	N.-Amer	837963
Engel, Friederika	26 Mar 1845	Reutlingen	Rtl.	Jul 1863	N.-Amer	841052
Engel, Georg Karl Ernst	28 Nov 1832	Renningen	Leon.	Apr 1852	N.-Amer	837963
Engel, Georg Karl Ernst & F		Renningen	Leon.	Apr 1852	N.-Amer	837963
Engel, Johann Georg		Reutlingen	Rtl.	Nov 1835	N.-Amer	841051
Engel, Karl Theodor Friedr.	10 Jan 1823	Renningen	Leon.	bef 1857	N.-Amer	837963
Engel, Louisa Augusta	6 Mar 1836	Renningen	Leon.	Apr 1852	N.-Amer	837963
Engel, Maria Carolina	26 Feb 1831	Renningen	Leon.	Apr 1852	N.-Amer	837963
Engel, Rosina	16 May 1842	Renningen	Leon.	Apr 1852	N.-Amer	837963
Enkel, Anna Maria (wife)		Eltingen	Leon.	Sep 1854	N.-Amer	835789
Enkel, Jacob & W		Eltingen	Leon.	Sep 1854	N.-Amer	835789
Ensinger, Christiane Dor. (wife)	15 Sep 1820	Brucken	Krch.	Mar 1860	N.-Amer	835944
Ensinger, Eva Rosina	4 Mar 1851	Brucken	Krch.	Mar 1860	N.-Amer	835944
Ensinger, Joh. Adam & F	5 Apr 1826	Brucken	Krch.	Mar 1860	N.-Amer	835944
Ensinger, Johann Adam	24 Aug 1855	Brucken	Krch.	Mar 1860	N.-Amer	835944
Ensinger, Johann Friedrich	18 Apr 1857	Brucken	Krch.	Mar 1860	N.-Amer	835944
Ensinger, Johann Georg	19 Mar 1874	Brucken	Krch.	Jul 1890	N.-Amer	835942
Ensinger, Johann Jacob	2 Feb 1850	Brucken	Krch.	Mar 1860	N.-Amer	835944
Ensinger, Rosina Katharina	31 May 1859	Brucken	Krch.	Mar 1860	N.-Amer	835944
Entenmann, Christian & F		Korntal	Leon.	Mar 1854	N.-Amer	837957

Name		Birth		Emigration			Film
Last	First	Date	Place	O'amt	Appl. Date	Dest.	Number
Enz, Anna Maria		2 Feb 1831	Gosbach	Gsl.	Feb 1856	N.-Amer	572043
Enz, Anna Maria & C		31 yrs.	Eltingen	Leon.	Aug 1851	N.-Amer	835789
Enz, Carl August		28 Jan 1853	Gosbach	Gsl.	Feb 1856	N.-Amer	572043
Enz, Conrad			Heimerdingen	Leon.	bef 1852	N.-Amer	837954
Enz, Franz Anton		19 yrs.	Gosbach	Gsl.	1851	N.-Amer	577788
Enz, Franz Joseph		10 Apr 1839	Gosbach	Gsl.	bef 1859	N.-Amer	572043
Enz, Georg Adam		15 Oct 1830	Eltingen	Leon.	Dec 1850	N.-Amer	835789
Enz, Gertrud & C		5 Dec 1832	Gosbach	Gsl.	Feb 1856	N.-Amer	572043
Enz, Gottlieb		9 yrs.	Hoefingen	Leon.	Sep 1853	N.-Amer	837957
Enz, Jacob			Eltingen	Leon.	bef 1843	France	835789
Enz, Jakob		23 Oct 1845	Muenchingen	Leon.	Oct 1851	N.-Amer	837961
Enz, Johann Gottlieb		10 Feb 1846	Eltingen	Leon.	1856	N.-Amer	835789
Enz, Johanna Friederike		infant	Eltingen	Leon.	Aug 1851	N.-Amer	835789
Enz, Karl Friedrich		15 Apr 1837	Gosbach	Gsl.	Feb 1854	N.-Amer	572042
Enz, Otto			Heimerdingen	Leon.	Sep 1853	N.-Amer	837954
Enzer, Eduard		29 Apr 1848	Geislingen	Gsl.	Feb 1866	N.-Amer	572045
Enzer, Hugo		15 yrs.	Geislingen	Gsl.	Feb 1866	N.-Amer	572045
Epp, Barbara (wid.) & F		1 Sep 1823	Gomaringen	Rtl.	May 1869	N.-Amer	841052
Epp, Christiane		30 Apr 1853	Reutlingen	Rtl.	Jul 1867	N.-Amer	841052
Epp, Hermann		7 Mar 1847	Pfullingen	Rtl.	Dec 1867	England	841052
Epp, Johann Conrad			Gomaringen	Rtl.	Jun 1829	Holland	841051
Epp, Johann David		25 Jan 1852	Gomaringen	Rtl.	Apr 1869	N.-Amer	841052
Epp, Johann Friedrich		11 Feb 1852	Holzelfingen	Rtl.	Mar 1867	N.-Amer	841052
Epp, Johann Martin		9 Feb 1853	Gomaringen	Rtl.	May 1869	N.-Amer	841052
Epp, Johannes		13 Jun 1856	Gomaringen	Rtl.	May 1869	N.-Amer	841052
Epp, Magdalena		4 Apr 1850	Reutlingen	Rtl.	Jul 1867	N.-Amer	841052
Epp, Maria Barbara		19 Aug 1848	Gomaringen	Rtl.	May 1869	N.-Amer	841052
Eppinger, Anna Catharina		11 Jul 1837	Notzingen	Krch.	Jun 1867	N.-Amer	835947
Eppinger, Anna Maria (wife)		26 Jan 1828	Bissingen	Krch.	Nov 1859	N.-Amer	835943
Eppinger, Christoph		Apr 1828	Notzingen	Krch.	bef 1859	N.-Amer	835947
Eppinger, Eva Katharina & F		8 May 1836	Notzingen	Krch.	1867	N.-Amer	835947
Eppinger, Friedrich August		15 Aug 1840	Notzingen	Krch.	May 1855	N.-Amer	835947
Eppinger, Johann Georg		14 Jan 1855	Bissingen	Krch.	Nov 1859	N.-Amer	835943
Eppinger, Johann Georg & F		15 Mar 1840	Notzingen	Krch.	Apr 1867	N.-Amer	835947
Eppinger, Johannes		8 Dec 1866	Notzingen	Krch.	Oct 1885	N.-Amer	548403
Eppinger, Johannes		20 yrs.	Notzingen	Krch.	Jul 1865	N.-Amer	835947
Eppinger, Johannes & F		29 Apr 1825	Notzingen	Krch.	Nov 1859	N.-Amer	835943
Eppinger, Maria (wife)		10 May 1845	Notzingen	Krch.	Apr 1867	N.-Amer	835947
Eppinger, Maria Catharina		21 Oct 1824	Oetlingen	Krch.	Feb 1860	N.-Amer	835948
Eppinger, Maria Margaretha		18 Sep 1844	Notzingen	Krch.	Jun 1867	N.-Amer	835947
Epple, Andreas		12 yrs.	Ditzingen	Leon.	Jul 1856	Austral	835788
Epple, Anna Catharina (wife)		11 May 1841	Reisach	Leon.	May 1879	N.-Amer	837964
Epple, Anna Margaretha		20 Mar 1846	Weilheim	Krch.	Sep 1869	Leipzig	835950
Epple, Barbara		20 May 1858	Rutesheim	Leon.	Jun 1862	N.-Amer	837964
Epple, Barbara (wife)		1836	Rutesheim	Leon.	Jun 1862	N.-Amer	837964
Epple, Catharina		5 Aug 1824	Weilheim	Krch.	bef 1863	N.-Amer	835950
Epple, Catharina (wife)		23 yrs.	Rutesheim	Leon.	Apr 1818	N.-Amer	837964
Epple, Catharina Friedrich		4 yrs.	Rutesheim	Leon.	Apr 1818	N.-Amer	837964
Epple, Christian		21 Dec 1832	Weilheim	Krch.	Mar 1863	N.-Amer	835950
Epple, Christian & F		6 Dec 1833	Rutesheim	Leon.	May 1879	N.-Amer	837964

Epple, Christian Friedrich	27 Nov 1873	Rutesheim	Leon.	May 1879	N.-Amer	837964
Epple, Christian Karl	8 Feb 1856	Rutesheim	Leon.	Apr 1882	N.-Amer	837964
Epple, Christiane	infant	Ditzingen	Leon.	Jul 1856	Austral	835788
Epple, Conrad	infant	Ditzingen	Leon.	Mar 1852	S.-Amer	835788
Epple, Conrad & F		Ditzingen	Leon.	Mar 1852	S.-Amer	835788
Epple, Conrad Gottlob	27 Nov 1878	Rutesheim	Leon.	May 1879	N.-Amer	837964
Epple, David	4 yrs.	Ditzingen	Leon.	Jul 1856	Austral	835788
Epple, Eberhard	4 yrs.	Ditzingen	Leon.	Mar 1852	S.-Amer	835788
Epple, Elisabetha	6 Mar 1835	Weilheim	Krch.	bef 1863	N.-Amer	835950
Epple, Friederike	10 yrs.	Ditzingen	Leon.	Jul 1856	Austral	835788
Epple, Friederike (wife)	39 yrs.	Ditzingen	Leon.	Jul 1856	Austral	835788
Epple, Friedrich	16 yrs.	Ditzingen	Leon.	Jul 1856	Austral	835788
Epple, Friedrich & F	40 yrs.	Ditzingen	Leon.	Jul 1856	Austral	835788
Epple, Georg & F		Ditzingen	Leon.	Mar 1852	S.-Amer	835788
Epple, Jakob	20 Nov 1819	Ditzingen	Leon.	May 1852	N.-Amer	835788
Epple, Jakob Friedrich	7 Mar 1869	Rutesheim	Leon.	May 1879	N.-Amer	837964
Epple, Johann Georg	5 yrs.	Ditzingen	Leon.	Mar 1852	S.-Amer	835788
Epple, Johann Georg & F	26 yrs.	Rutesheim	Leon.	Apr 1818	N.-Amer	837964
Epple, Johann Gottlieb	15 Mar 1831	Rutesheim	Leon.	Jan 1851	N.-Amer	837964
Epple, Johann Jacob	20 Mar 1860	Rutesheim	Leon.	Jun 1862	N.-Amer	837964
Epple, Johann Jacob	20 Jul 1874	Owen	Krch.	Jul 1889	N.-Amer	835948
Epple, Johannes	14 yrs.	Ditzingen	Leon.	Jul 1856	Austral	835788
Epple, Johannes & F	19 Mar 1823	Rutesheim	Leon.	Jun 1862	N.-Amer	837964
Epple, Katharina	1 yrs.	Ditzingen	Leon.	Mar 1852	S.-Amer	835788
Epple, Katharina	3 yrs.	Ditzingen	Leon.	Mar 1852	S.-Amer	835788
Epple, Katharina (wife)	28 yrs.	Ditzingen	Leon.	Mar 1852	S.-Amer	835788
Epple, Leonhardt		Rutesheim	Leon.	Jun 1857	N.-Amer	837964
Epple, Ludwig	6 yrs.	Ditzingen	Leon.	Jul 1856	Austral	835788
Epple, Magdalena	24 Aug 1855	Rutesheim	Leon.	Jun 1862	N.-Amer	837964
Epple, Philippine (wife)		Ditzingen	Leon.	Mar 1852	S.-Amer	835788
Epple, Regina Magdalena	29 Sep 1875	Rutesheim	Leon.	May 1879	N.-Amer	837964
Eppler, Caroline Math.	6 yrs.	Rutesheim	Leon.	Feb 1852	N.-Amer	837964
Eppler, Christiane Heinrike	11 yrs.	Rutesheim	Leon.	Feb 1852	N.-Amer	837964
Eppler, Jacob Friedrich	1 yrs.	Rutesheim	Leon.	Feb 1852	N.-Amer	837964
Eppler, Johannes		Rutesheim	Leon.	Feb 1852	N.-Amer	837964
Eppler, Johannes	12 yrs.	Rutesheim	Leon.	Feb 1852	N.-Amer	837964
Eppler, Maria Catharina	15 yrs.	Rutesheim	Leon.	Feb 1852	N.-Amer	837964
Erath, Amalia	2 Oct 1844	Seedorf	Obd.	May 1867	N.-Amer	838637
Erath, Rupert	26 Mar 1843	Waldmoessingen	Obd.	Mar 1859	N.-Amer	841015
Erbe, Christian Heinrich	17 Oct 1805	Alpirsbach	Obd.	Mar 1844	Berlin	838630
Erbe, Georg Jakob	29 Sep 1837	Oberndorf	Obd.	Feb 1868	Prussia	838635
Erbe, Johann Georg	5 Jul 1817	Pfullingen	Rtl.	Nov 1862	England	841052
Erbele, Christine Kathar. & C	12 Oct 1847	Sulz	Herr.	Mar 1888	N.-Amer	834630
Erbele, Gottlob	13 Dec 1873	Sulz	Herr.	Mar 1888	N.-Amer	834630
Erbele, Maria Katharina	8 Oct 1876	Oberjesingen	Herr.	Mar 1888	N.-Amer	834630
Ergenzinger, Cathar. B. (wid.) & F	28 Jan 1800	Eltingen	Leon.	Apr 1850	N.-Amer	835789
Ergenzinger, Catharina Johanna	8 Apr 1844	Eltingen	Leon.	Apr 1850	N.-Amer	835789
Ergenzinger, Christian August	15 Mar 1830	Eltingen	Leon.	Apr 1850	N.-Amer	835789
Ergenzinger, Gotthold		Eltingen	Leon.	bef 1861	N.-Amer	835789
Ergenzinger, Kardine Frieder.	29 Jul 1844	Eltingen	Leon.	Apr 1850	N.-Amer	835789

Name		Birth		Emigration			Film
Last	First	Date	Place	O'amt	Appl. Date	Dest.	Number
Erhard, Friederika			Flacht	Leon.	Feb 1853	N.-Amer	835790
Erhard, Michael		21 Aug 1898	Flacht	Leon.	1824	France	835790
Erkel, Anna Maria			Friolzheim	Leon.	Mar 1830	N.-Amer	835791
Erlemaier, Carl		25 yrs.	Soehnstetten	Leon.	Mar 1861	N.-Amer	837960
Erlemaier, Jakobina Maria		29 Jan 1840	Moensheim	Leon.	1865	Austria	837960
Erlemaier, Karoline Maria		4 Oct 1838	Moensheim	Leon.	Apr 1864	Switz.	837960
Erlenmaier, Albrecht		31 Oct 1826	Moensheim	Leon.	Feb 1852	N.-Amer	837960
Ernst, Johann Gottlob		26 Jul 1872	Holzmaden	Krch.	Apr 1889	N.-Amer	835945
Ernster, Ferdinand Richard		21 Jun 1852	Zarenhausen	Rtl.	May 1870	N.-Amer	841052
Eschele, Johann		8 May 1811	Schramberg	Obd.	Mar 1840	Bavaria	838637
Esel, Lazarus & F			Beffendorf	Obd.	Apr 1817	N.-Amer	838631
Esenwein, Johann Georg		20 Sep 1871	Holzmaden	Krch.	Aug 1888	N.-Amer	835945
Essich, Catharina (wid.) & F			Bissingen	Krch.	Jul 1860	N.-Amer	835943
Essich, Johann Georg		32 yrs.	Bissingen	Krch.	Jul 1860	N.-Amer	835943
Essig, Catharina		13 Mar 1818	Flacht	Leon.	Apr 1848	N.-Amer	835790
Essig, Catharina Dor. (wid.) & F			Flacht	Leon.	Jul 1851	N.-Amer	835790
Essig, Catharina Dorothea		8 Apr 1822	Flacht	Leon.	Aug 1847	N.-Amer	835790
Essig, Christian			Leonberg	Leon.	bef 1847	E.India	835786
Essig, Christian Friedrich		17 Apr 1868	Flacht	Leon.	Mar 1884	N.-Amer	835790
Essig, Christina (wife)			Wimsheim	Loen.	Jun 1855	N.-Amer	837967
Essig, Christina Dorothea		22 yrs.	Flacht	Leon.	Mar 1845	N.-Amer	835790
Essig, Christof Friedrich		23 Mar 1823	Flacht	Leon.	1852	N.-Amer	835790
Essig, Eberhardine Wilhelmine		24 Jan 1849	Leonberg	Leon.	Apr 1869	Austria	835787
Essig, Elise Catharine			Flacht	Leon.	May 1854	N.-Amer	835790
Essig, Ernst Gottlob		1 Jul 1843	Renningen	Leon.	Jun 1862	N.-Amer	837963
Essig, Friederike		24 yrs.	Flacht	Leon.	Mar 1845	N.-Amer	835790
Essig, Georg Adam		1 Sep 1843	Heimsheim	Leon.	Jun 1851	N.-Amer	837955
Essig, Georg Jacob			Renningen	Leon.	Jan 1854	N.-Amer	837963
Essig, Gottlieb		16 Nov 1851	Renningen	Leon.	Apr 1869	N.-Amer	837963
Essig, Gottlieb Wilhelm		9 Jul 1851	Leonberg	Leon.	Jan 1870	N.-Amer	835787
Essig, Gustav Adolph		12 Nov 1866	Leonberg	Leon.	May 1880	N.-Amer	835787
Essig, Johann Friedrich			Flacht	Leon.	Apr 1852	N.-Amer	835790
Essig, Johann Georg		2 Feb 1848	Maegerkingen	Rtl.	Jun 1868	N.-Amer	841052
Essig, Johann Georg & F			Wimsheim	Loen.	Jun 1855	N.-Amer	837967
Essig, Johann Heinrich			Leonberg	Leon.	Jun 1827	Hesse	835786
Essig, Johann Jakob		19 Jul 1818	Flacht	Leon.	Aug 1847	N.-Amer	835790
Essig, Johann Philipp Jakob			Flacht	Leon.	Jul 1851	N.-Amer	835790
Essig, Johanna Dorothea		3 Oct 1825	Flacht	Leon.	Apr 1848	N.-Amer	835790
Essig, Johannes			Wimsheim	Loen.	Jun 1855	N.-Amer	837967
Essig, Johannes		13 Oct 1836	Renningen	Leon.	Apr 1865	N.-Amer	837963
Essig, Johannes			Flacht	Leon.	Jul 1851	N.-Amer	835790
Essig, Kristian Friedrich			Flacht	Leon.	May 1854	N.-Amer	835790
Essig, Maria Magdalena			Wimsheim	Loen.	Jun 1855	N.-Amer	837967
Essig, Philipp		12 Oct 1846	Maegerkingen	Rtl.	Feb 1866	N.-Amer	841052
Essig, Rosine Katharine			Moensheim	Leon.	Apr 1857	N.-Amer	837960
Esslinger, Lucia			Peterzell	Obd.	Feb 1861	N.-Amer	838635
Etzel, Carl Friedrich		19 Nov 1849	Hochdorf	Krch.	May 1867	N.-Amer	835945
Etzel, Carl Ludwig			Hoefingen	Leon.	Apr 1867	N.-Amer	837957
Etzel, Catharina Magdalena		20 yrs.	Hoefingen	Leon.	Feb 1854	N.-Amer	837957
Etzel, Christian		10 Nov 1865	Weiler	Krch.	Apr 1866	N.-Amer	835949

Etzel, Christian Wilhelm	- Nov 1846	Hoefingen	Leon.	Apr 1867	N.-Amer	837957
Etzel, Ludwig	15 Apr 1852	Hochdorf	Krch.	May 1868	N.-Amer	835945
Etzel, Maria Friederike	28 Nov 1866	Hochdorf	Krch.	Jul 1871	N.-Amer	835945
Euchner, Carl & F	12 Jan 1840	Holzmaden	Krch.	Oct 1865	N.-Amer	835945
Euchner, Christina	30 Aug 1840	Dettingen	Krch.	bef 1867	N.-Amer	835944
Euchner, Friederike & C	13 Dec 1828	Hochdorf	Krch.	May 1868	N.-Amer	835945
Euchner, Friederike (wife)	5 Dec 1839	Holzmaden	Krch.	Oct 1865	N.-Amer	835945
Euchner, Jakob & F	25 Feb 1844	Hochdorf	Krch.	May 1880	N.-Amer	548403
Euchner, Johann Adolph	20 Apr 1845	Bissingen	Krch.	Mar 1867	N.-Amer	835943
Euchner, Johann Carl Wilhelm	15 Aug 1863	Holzmaden	Krch.	Oct 1865	N.-Amer	835945
Euchner, Johann Jakob	5 Oct 1877	Hochdorf	Krch.	May 1880	N.-Amer	548403
Euchner, Johannes	17 Jun 1839	Hochdorf	Krch.	Apr 1867	N.-Amer	835945
Euchner, Johannes	25 Jun 1842	Bissingen	Krch.	Nov 1867	N.-Amer	835943
Euchner, Maria	9 Jun 1865	Holzmaden	Krch.	Oct 1865	N.-Amer	835945
Euchner, Maria Barbara	25 Feb 1827	Dettingen	Krch.	bef 1867	N.-Amer	835944
Euchner, Maria Dorothea (wife)	6 Jan 1839	Hochdorf	Krch.	May 1880	N.-Amer	548403
Euchner, Rosina	29 May 1858	Hochdorf	Krch.	May 1868	N.-Amer	835945
Eusinger, Barbara	17 Jul 1835	Unterlenningen	Krch.	1851	N.-Amer	835949
Eusinger, Michael	4 May 1838	Unterlenningen	Krch.	1851	N.-Amer	835949
Evers, Heinrich		Leonberg	Leon.	Apr 1853	N.-Amer	835786
Eyb, Johann Georg		Pfullingen	Rtl.	Apr 1832	N.-Amer	841051
Eyth, Clara	25 Dec 1831	Alpirsbach	Obd.	Jun 1858	Switz.	838630
Eyth, Ludwig Friedrich	15 Apr 1808	Alpirsbach	Obd.	Mar 1846	Austria	838630
Faber, Christian	30 May 1846	Unterlenningen	Krch.	Apr 1866	N.-Amer	835941
Faber, Karl Otto	18 Nov 1863	Goeppingen	Krch.	bef 1888	N.-Amer	548323
Fader, Andreas		Sulgau	Leon.	Dec 1846	N.-Amer	838637
Fader, Bartholomae & F	40 yrs.	Schramberg	Obd.	Mar 1848	N.-Amer	838637
Fader, Christina (wife)		Sulgau	Obd.	Apr 1854	N.-Amer	838637
Fader, Ludwig	5 yrs.	Schramberg	Obd.	Mar 1848	N.-Amer	838637
Fader, Magdalena	3 yrs.	Schramberg	Obd.	Mar 1848	N.-Amer	838637
Fader, Mathias & F	58 yrs.	Sulgau	Obd.	Apr 1854	N.-Amer	838637
Fader, Salomea		Sulgau	Obd.	Apr 1854	N.-Amer	838637
Fader, Ursula (wife)		Schramberg	Obd.	Mar 1848	N.-Amer	838637
Faerber, Alois		Boehmenkirch	Gsl.	Jan 1853	N.-Amer	572041
Faerber, Franz Anton		Boehmenkirch	Gsl.	Feb 1853	N.-Amer	572041
Faerber, Georg & F	20 Nov 1816	Boehmenkirch	Gsl.	Mar 1854	N.-Amer	572042
Faerber, Joseph	21 Nov 1837	Boehmenkirch	Gsl.	Apr 1853	N.-Amer	572041
Faerber, Joseph	7 Dec 1851	Boehmenkirch	Gsl.	Sep 1870	N.-Amer	572047
Faerber, Josepha	10 May 1852	Boehmenkirch	Gsl.	Mar 1854	N.-Amer	572042
Faerber, Katharina	7 Mar 1833	Boehmenkirch	Gsl.	Feb 1854	N.-Amer	572042
Faerber, Maria (wife)	9 Aug 1826	Boehmenkirch	Gsl.	Mar 1854	N.-Amer	572042
Faerber, Maria Anna	11 Dec 1847	Boehmenkirch	Gsl.	Sep 1870	N.-Amer	572047
Faerber, Marianna	7 Mar 1845	Boehmenkirch	Gsl.	Mar 1854	N.-Amer	572042
Fahr, Barbara (wid.)	35 yrs.	Geislingen	Gsl.	Nov 1860	Austria	572044
Fahr, Carl Julius	28 Apr 1843	Geislingen	Gsl.	bef 1867	N.-Amer	572046
Fahrion, Conrad	16 Apr 1836	Hoefingen	Leon.	bef 1857	N.-Amer	837957
Fahrion, Johann Georg	7 Feb 1855	Hoefingen	Leon.	Jan 1880	N.-Amer	837957
Fahrion, Karl	19 yrs.	Hoefingen	Leon.	Sep 1853	N.-Amer	837957
Fahrion, Wilhelm	19 yrs.	Hoefingen	Leon.	Apr 1852	N.-Amer	837957
Fahrner, Johann & F		Reutin	Obd.	Apr 1817	N.-Amer	838635

Name		Birth		Emigration			Film
Last	First	Date	Place	O'amt	Appl. Date	Dest.	Number
Faiss, Jacob Friedrich			Betzingen	Rtl.	Apr 1831	N.-Amer	841051
Fakler, Carl		4 yrs.	Sternenfels	Leon.	Feb 1851	N.-Amer	837956
Falch, Carl Ferdinand		23 Jun 1836	Oberlenningen	Krch.	Dec 1856	Texas	835947
Falkenstein, Adolf Friedrich		19 Apr 1847	Kirchheim	Krch.	bef 1884	Wien	835942
Falkenstein, Gottfried Fr. & W		8 Oct 1848	Kirchheim	Krch.	bef 1878	Wien	835942
Falkenstein, Johannes		13 Sep 1873	Owen	Krch.	Jun 1890	N.-Amer	835948
Falkenstein, Maria		15 Dec 1848	Hall	Krch.	bef 1878	Wien	835942
Faller, Barbara		1 Jun 1834	Hohenstadt	Gsl.	Jul 1856	N.-Amer	572043
Faller, Johann Georg		10 Feb 1842	Hohenstadt	Gsl.	Jul 1856	N.-Amer	572043
Faller, Johannes			Schramberg	Obd.	Oct 1853	N.-Amer	838636
Faller, Magdalena		22 Jul 1836	Hohenstadt	Gsl.	Jul 1856	N.-Amer	572043
Fassnacht, Alfred		22 yrs.	Reutlingen	Rtl.	Nov 1880	N.-Amer	841051
Fassnacht, Barbara			Reutlingen	Rtl.	May 1828	N.-Amer	841051
Fassnacht, Carl Heinrich		12 Nov 1857	Gaertringen	Herr.	Nov 1865	France	834630
Fassnacht, Johann Michael		1 Jan 1824	Reutlingen	Rtl.	Jan 1861	Switz.	841052
Faul, August Friedrich		8 May 1842	Kirchheim	Krch.	Aug 1856	N.-Amer	835940
Fausel, Kaspar		17 yrs.	Eningen	Rtl.	Mar 1863	N.-Amer	841052
Fauser, Anna Dorothea		29 Jul 1840	Gomaringen	Rtl.	Sep 1859	N.-Amer	841052
Fauser, Georg Friedrich			Perouse	Leon.	Jul 1854	N.-Amer	837962
Fauser, Maria Barbara		5 Dec 1849	Gomaringen	Rtl.	Sep 1859	N.-Amer	841052
Fauser, Maria Katharina		1 Mar 1844	Gomaringen	Rtl.	Sep 1859	N.-Amer	841052
Fausser, Gottlieb Friedrich			Heimsheim	Leon.	1817	Prussia	837955
Fauth, Barbara & C		24 yrs.	Geislingen	Gsl.	Mar 1854	N.-Amer	572042
Feber, Heinrich		10 Apr 1842	Kirchheim	Krch.	Oct 1868	N.-Amer	835941
Feeser, Johannes			Friolzheim	Leon.	bef 1859	N.-Amer	835791
Feger, Franz		14 Oct 1846	Winzeln	Obd.	Mar 1865	N.-Amer	841016
Feger, Georg		21 yrs.	Winzeln	Obd.	Oct 1853	N.-Amer	841016
Feger, Johannes		24 Aug 1849	Winzeln	Obd.	Mar 1865	N.-Amer	841016
Feger, Magdalena		20 yrs.	Winzeln	Obd.	Oct 1853	N.-Amer	841016
Fehrenbacher, Agatha			Lauterbach	Obd.	Oct 1852	N.-Amer	838634
Fehrenbacher, Jakob			Hochmoessingen	Obd.	bef 1859	N.-Amer	838633
Fehrenbacher, Johann			Lauterbach	Obd.	bef 1864	N.-Amer	838634
Fehrenbacher, Joseph		22 yrs.	Lauterbach	Obd.	Oct 1853	N.-Amer	838634
Fehrenbacher, Joseph & F			Waldmoessingen	Obd.	bef 1859	N.-Amer	841015
Feigel, Friedrich		1 Feb 1849	Reutlingen	Rtl.	Nov 1869	N.-Amer	841052
Feigele, Maria		5 Dec 1844	Rosswaelden	Krch.	Feb 1863	N.-Amer	835949
Feil, – Dr.			Rotfelden	Nag.	Aug 1852	N.-Amer	838488
Feil, Ernestine Karoline		12 Mar 1830	Deggingen	Gsl.	Jun 1867	Austria	572046
Feil, Gustav Wilhelm		24 Aug 1837	Lauchheim	Gsl.	Feb 1854	N.-Amer	572042
Feil, Julius Ottmar		1 Jan 1841	Bissingen	Krch.	bef 1866	London	835943
Feil, Maria Theodolinde Wilh.		26 Jan 1844	Bissingen	Krch.	Nov 1866	Nassau	835943
Feil, Mathaeus Xaverus		7 Sep 1836	Eybach	Gsl.	Feb 1855	N.-Amer	572043
Feil, Wilhelm Eugen August		17 Jan 1847	Grossengstingen	Krch.	1865	N.-Amer	835943
Feiler, Gottfried Michael		28 Sep 1867	Flacht	Leon.	Aug 1883	N.-Amer	835790
Feiler, Karl Friedrich		20 Apr 1867	Friolzheim	Leon.	Apr 1884	N.-Amer	835791
Feiler, Regina Catharina			Wimsheim	Loen.	Apr 1854	N.-Amer	837967
Felder, Johannes			Hildrizhausen	Herr.	1849	N.-Amer	834631
Felger, Johann Michael		22 yrs.	Hoefingen	Leon.	Jul 1851	N.-Amer	837957
Feller, Anna Barbara (wife)			Oberlenningen	Krch.	Apr 1872	N.-Amer	835947
Feller, Carl		28 Jun 1857	Oberlenningen	Krch.	Apr 1874	N.-Amer	548403

Feller, Carl Friedr. Wilh. & F	1 Aug 1842	Oberlenningen	Krch.	1872	N.-Amer	835947
Feller, Carl Gottlieb	12 Sep 1857	Oberlenningen	Krch.	Apr 1872	N.-Amer	835947
Feller, Christian Friedrich	4 Mar 1867	Oberlenningen	Krch.	1878	N.-Amer	835947
Feller, Christian Friedrich	16 Apr 1868	Oberlenningen	Krch.	Apr 1872	N.-Amer	835947
Feller, Christiane Margaretha	1 Aug 1842	Oberlenningen	Krch.	bef 1881	N.-Amer	548403
Feller, Christine	22 Jan 1841	Oberlenningen	Krch.	May 1860	N.-Amer	835947
Feller, Christine Margar. & F	30 Jan 1842	Oberlenningen	Krch.	1878	N.-Amer	835947
Feller, David & F		Oberlenningen	Krch.	Apr 1872	N.-Amer	835947
Feller, Gottlieb	18 Jun 1870	Oberlenningen	Krch.	1878	N.-Amer	835947
Feller, Gottlob	26 Feb 1850	Unterlenningen	Krch.	Aug 1867	N.-Amer	835949
Feller, Johann Georg	20 Jul 1855	Oberlenningen	Krch.	Apr 1872	N.-Amer	835947
Feller, Karl	26 Jun 1857	Oberlenningen	Krch.	May 1874	N.-Amer	835947
Feller, Maria	27 Dec 1844	Oberlenningen	Krch.	Aug 1860	N.-Amer	835947
Feller, Marie Catharine	2 Mar 1864	Oberlenningen	Krch.	Apr 1872	N.-Amer	835947
Feller, Regine	6 Mar 1859	Oberlenningen	Krch.	Apr 1872	N.-Amer	835947
Fenzel, Margaretha	4 Feb 1832	Geislingen	Gsl.	Jul 1854	N.-Amer	572042
Ferber, Ernst	1 Dec 1839	Kirchheim	Krch.	Jul 1876	London	548403
Ferber, Felix		Oberndorf	Obd.	Jul 1849	N.-Amer	838635
Ferber, Franz Joseph	17 yrs.	Oberndorf	Obd.	Jul 1856	N.-Amer	838635
Ferber, Friederike		Oberndorf	Obd.	bef 1854	N.-Amer	838635
Ferber, Johannes	29 Dec 1791	Oberndorf	Obd.	bef 1851	Switz.	838635
Ferber, Joseph	16 yrs.	Oberndorf	Obd.	Dec 1854	N.-Amer	838635
Ferber, Karl	25 Nov 1852	Oberndorf	Obd.	Nov 1869	N.-Amer	838635
Ferber, Therese		Oberndorf	Obd.	Nov 1838	Austria	838635
Fetzer, Anna	20 yrs.	Gingen	Gsl.	Apr 1853	N.-Amer	572041
Fetzer, Anna Maria (wife)	22 Nov 1816	Gingen	Gsl.	Apr 1854	N.-Amer	572042
Fetzer, Georg	23 yrs.	Gingen	Gsl.	May 1853	N.-Amer	572041
Fetzer, Jakob	13 Oct 1833	Gingen	Gsl.	Jun 1854	N.-Amer	572042
Fetzer, Katharina	1 Aug 1842	Gingen	Gsl.	Apr 1854	N.-Amer	572042
Fetzer, Leonhard & F	18 Apr 1813	Gingen	Gsl.	Apr 1854	N.-Amer	572042
Fetzer, Sophia Magdalena	2 Jun 1846	Bissingen	Krch.	Feb 1861	N.-Amer	835943
Fetzer, Valentin	27 Jun 1835	Dettingen	Krch.	Nov 1855	N.-Amer	835944
Feucht, Adam		Eltingen	Leon.	bef 1865	N.-Amer	835789
Feucht, Christiane Wilhelmine	14 yrs.	Ditzingen	Leon.	May 1851	N.-Amer	835788
Feucht, Elisabetha Cath. (wife)		Hoefingen	Leon.	May 1853	N.-Amer	837957
Feucht, Johann Georg & W		Hoefingen	Leon.	May 1853	N.-Amer	837957
Feucht, Magdalena		Wimsheim	Loen.	Apr 1854	N.-Amer	837967
Feucht, Magdalena		Eltingen	Leon.	bef 1865	N.-Amer	835789
Feucht, Magdalena & F		Wimsheim	Loen.	Apr 1854	N.-Amer	837967
Feucht, Maria		Wimsheim	Loen.	Apr 1854	N.-Amer	837967
Feuchtenbeiner, Andreas		Altenstadt-Gsl.	Gsl.	Nov 1867	N.-Amer	572046
Feyler, Johann Andreas	18 yrs.	Flacht	Leon.	Oct 1866	N.-Amer	835790
Fezer, Anna Maria	5 Oct 1838	Unterhausen	Rtl.	Apr 1864	N.-Amer	841052
Fezer, Jakob	16 Mar 1829	Ohmenhausen	Rtl.	Jun 1862	N.-Amer	841052
Fezer, Johann Jakob	2 Dec 1872	Bissingen	Krch.	Mar 1889	N.-Amer	835943
Fichtler, Heinrich	10 Jul 1827	Schramberg	Obd.	Sep 1863	N.-Amer	838636
Fimpel, Carl Friedrich	1 Oct 1845	Notzingen	Krch.	Feb 1872	N.-Amer	835947
Finck, Gottlob	18 Jan 1849	Reutlingen	Rtl.	Oct 1869	N.-Amer	841052
Find, Christian Friedrich	22 Apr 1850	Dettingen	Krch.	Jul 1868	N.-Amer	835944
Findling, Philipp		Perouse	Leon.	Oct 1856	N.-Amer	837962

Name		Birth		Emigration			Film
Last	First	Date	Place	O'amt	Appl. Date	Dest.	Number
Fineise, Friederike		12 Mar 1814	Leonberg	Leon.	Nov 1854	N.-Amer	835786
Fineise, Johann Matthaeus & W			Leonberg	Leon.	Oct 1852	N.-Amer	835786
Fineise, Margaretha			Leonberg	Leon.	Oct 1852	N.-Amer	835786
Fink, Barbara Katharina		22 Jan 1825	Wiesenbach	Gsl.	bef 1855	Hesse	572043
Fink, David			Oppingen	Gsl.	Feb 1852	N.-Amer	572041
Fischaess, Anna Maria & C		28 Mar 1807	Oberlenningen	Krch.	Sep 1856	Texas	835947
Fischaess, Friedrich			Oberlenningen	Krch.	bef 1867	Texas	835947
Fischaess, Gottlieb		30 Jan 1847	Oberlenningen	Krch.	Apr 1866	N.-Amer	835947
Fischaess, Maria		2 May 1840	Oberlenningen	Krch.	Sep 1856	Texas	835947
Fischer, Agatha & F			Oberndorf	Obd.	Jul 1849	N.-Amer	838635
Fischer, Alois		12 Sep 1850	Kleinsuessen	Gsl.	Jul 1870	N.-Amer	572047
Fischer, Anna Barbara			Hepsisau	Krch.	bef 1866	N.-Amer	835940
Fischer, Anna Maria		16 Aug 1829	Weilheim	Krch.	bef 1856	N.-Amer	835949
Fischer, Anna Maria		18 Mar 1830	Hildrizhausen	Herr.	1853	N.-Amer	834631
Fischer, Anton & F			Beffendorf	Obd.	Aug 1817	N.-Amer	838631
Fischer, Barbara			Hepsisau	Krch.	1848	N.-Amer	835945
Fischer, Barbara		9 Mar 1817	Hepsisau	Krch.	Apr 1847	N.-Amer	835945
Fischer, Barbara		18 Jun 1843	Schopfloch	Krch.	Oct 1860	N.-Amer	835949
Fischer, Carl August		25 Feb 1846	Unterlenningen	Krch.	Sep 1866	N.-Amer	835949
Fischer, Carl Edwin		10 Jun 1861	Ludwigsburg	Gsl.	May 1878	N.-Amer	572048
Fischer, Carl Ignaz			Oberndorf	Obd.	Feb 1864	Hesse	838635
Fischer, Catharina (wid.)		8 Aug 1832	Hildrizhausen	Herr.	May 1865	N.-Amer	834631
Fischer, Christian		25 Feb 1835	Hepsisau	Krch.	May 1854	N.-Amer	835945
Fischer, Christian David		18 Jul 1850	Kirchheim	Krch.	Feb 1867	N.-Amer	835941
Fischer, Christian Friedrich		19 Apr 1820	Dettingen	Krch.	bef 1856	France	835944
Fischer, Christoph		22 Oct 1827	Weilheim	Krch.	bef 1859	N.-Amer	835949
Fischer, Dorothea & C		18 Oct 1833	Hochdorf	Krch.	May 1868	N.-Amer	835945
Fischer, Felix			Aichhalden	Obd.	Dec 1850	N.-Amer	838629
Fischer, Ferdinand		9 Feb 1866	Oetlingen	Krch.	Jan 1883	N.-Amer	835948
Fischer, Florian			Oberndorf	Obd.	Dec 1850	N.-Amer	838635
Fischer, Florian			Oberndorf	Obd.	bef 1849	N.-Amer	838635
Fischer, Georg		15 May 1829	Kleinsuessen	Gsl.	Jan 1856	N.-Amer	572043
Fischer, Georg & F			Friolzheim	Leon.	Jul 1851	N.-Amer	835791
Fischer, Gottlieb		27 yrs.	Friolzheim	Leon.	Jul 1851	N.-Amer	835791
Fischer, Gottlieb Erhard			Reutlingen	Rtl.	bef 1865	Bremen	841052
Fischer, Gottlob		17 yrs.	Reutlingen	Rtl.	Nov 1880	N.-Amer	841051
Fischer, Gottlob August		1 Nov 1848	Herrenberg	Herr.	Nov 1868	N.-Amer	834629
Fischer, Jacob			Geislingen	Gsl.	Feb 1851	N.-Amer	577788
Fischer, Jacob Friedrich		25 Sep 1834	Hochdorf	Krch.	Aug 1854	N.-Amer	835945
Fischer, Jakob Friedrich		20 Aug 1822	Hildrizhausen	Herr.	1852	N.-Amer	834631
Fischer, Johann Conrad		22 May 1844	Ochsenwang	Krch.	Jul 1862	N.-Amer	835947
Fischer, Johann Georg		31 Aug 1833	Weilheim	Krch.	bef 1856	N.-Amer	835949
Fischer, Johann Georg			Hoefingen	Leon.	Mar 1827	N.-Amer	837957
Fischer, Johann Georg		3 Jan 1846	Ochsenwang	Krch.	Mar 1864	N.-Amer	835947
Fischer, Johann Michael		18 May 1848	Hildrizhausen	Herr.	Mar 1867	N.-Amer	834631
Fischer, Johannes			Fluorn	Obd.	bef 1843	France	838632
Fischer, Johannes		24 May 1853	Friolzheim	Leon.	Jul 1881	N.-Amer	835791
Fischer, Johannes		22 Jan 1832	Hochdorf	Krch.	Jan 1854	N.-Amer	835945
Fischer, Josef		1 Jan 1866	Treffelhausen	Gsl.	Feb 1883	N.-Amer	572049
Fischer, Josua		2 Nov 1837	Hochdorf	Krch.	Jan 1854	N.-Amer	835945

Fischer, Karl Ferdinand	9 Feb 1866	Oetlingen	Krch.	Jan 1883	N.-Amer	548403
Fischer, Karl Ludwig	2 May 1846	Herrenberg	Herr.	Aug 1872	N.-Amer	834629
Fischer, Katharina (wife)		Friolzheim	Leon.	Jul 1851	N.-Amer	835791
Fischer, Maria	28 Feb 1846	Eybach	Gsl.	May 1852	N.-Amer	572041
Fischer, Maria	28 Jan 1858	Hochdorf	Krch.	May 1868	N.-Amer	835945
Fischer, Maria Barbara (wife)		Eybach	Gsl.	May 1852	N.-Amer	572041
Fischer, Maria Rosina	21 Aug 1834	Malmsheim	Leon.	Aug 1856	N.-Amer	837958
Fischer, Matthias		Aichhalden	Obd.	Dec 1850	N.-Amer	838629
Fischer, Michael & F		Eybach	Gsl.	May 1852	N.-Amer	572041
Fischer, Michael & F		Gutenberg	Krch.	Apr 1804	Pr.-Pol	550804
Fischer, Otto	9 yrs.	Oberndorf	Obd.	Jul 1849	N.-Amer	838635
Fischer, Rosina	28 yrs.	Friolzheim	Leon.	Feb 1859	N.-Amer	835791
Fischer, Ursula Catharina	7 Jan 1831	Willmandingen	Rtl.	bef 1861	N.-Amer	841056
Fischer, Wilhelm	11 yrs.	Oberndorf	Obd.	Jul 1849	N.-Amer	838635
Fischer, Wilhelmine	18 Aug 1846	Hochdorf	Krch.	Mar 1866	N.-Amer	835945
Fischinger, Anna		Beffendorf	Obd.	Sep 1857	Bavaria	838631
Fischinger, Dominikus		Beffendorf	Obd.	Oct 1863	N.-Amer	838631
Fisel, August Anton	3 Aug 1827	Hochdorf	Krch.	Jul 1861	Hamburg	835945
Fix, Agatha	5 Jan 1841	Oberndorf	Obd.	Feb 1869	W.Pruss	838635
Fix, Andreas		Schramberg	Obd.	Sep 1846	N.-Amer	838637
Fix, Constantin & F		Oberndorf	Obd.	Oct 1846	N.-Amer	838635
Fix, Heinrich	19 Jan 1855	Oberndorf	Obd.	May 1870	N.-Amer	838635
Fix, Johann Evangelist	infant	Oberndorf	Obd.	Oct 1846	N.-Amer	838635
Fix, Karl Anton	2 yrs.	Oberndorf	Obd.	Oct 1846	N.-Amer	838635
Fix, Theresia (wife)		Oberndorf	Obd.	Oct 1846	N.-Amer	838635
Flad, Carl Hermann	8 Oct 1868	Metzingen	Krch.	Oct 1871	N.-Amer	835944
Flad, Gottlieb Friedrich	1 Oct 1865	Metzingen	Krch.	Oct 1871	N.-Amer	835944
Flad, Gustav Robert	4 May 1859	Metzingen	Krch.	Oct 1871	N.-Amer	835944
Flad, Johann Georg	17 May 1840	Undingen	Rtl.	Jun 1867	N.-Amer	841052
Flad, Philipp		Metzingen	Krch.	bef 1871	N.-Amer	835944
Flad, Rosine Catharine & F	15 Jul 1825	Metzingen	Krch.	Oct 1871	N.-Amer	835944
Flaig, Agatha	30 Mar 1809	Seedorf	Obd.	Apr 1847	N.-Amer	838637
Flaig, Albertine		Schramberg	Obd.	Mar 1863	N.-Amer	838636
Flaig, Alois	21 Jun 1850	Aichhalden	Obd.	Oct 1867	N.-Amer	838629
Flaig, Andreas & F		Sulgen	Obd.	May 1817	N.-Amer	838638
Flaig, Augustin	30 yrs.	Sulgen	Obd.	Dec 1859	N.-Amer	838638
Flaig, Crecentia	24 Aug 1814	Sulgen	Obd.	Jul 1857	N.-Amer	838638
Flaig, Dorothea (wid.) & F	51 yrs.	Winzeln	Obd.	Nov 1866	N.-Amer	841016
Flaig, Ferdinand	7 Oct 1845	Aichhalden	Obd.	Mar 1865	N.-Amer	838629
Flaig, Fridolin	20 Feb 1839	Winzeln	Obd.	Aug 1858	N.-Amer	841016
Flaig, Gregor	12 Jan 1830	Sulgen	Obd.	Jan 1849	N.-Amer	838638
Flaig, Gustav	10 Jul 1831	Schramberg	Obd.	bef 1857	N.-Amer	838636
Flaig, Jakob & F		Sulgen	Obd.	May 1817	N.-Amer	838638
Flaig, Johann Georg		Schramberg	Obd.	Feb 1854	N.-Amer	838636
Flaig, Johann Georg & F		Sulgen	Obd.	May 1817	N.-Amer	838638
Flaig, Johannes	24 Jul 1817	Sulgen	Obd.	Oct 1851	N.-Amer	838638
Flaig, Joseph	20 yrs.	Mariazell	Obd.	Aug 1852	N.-Amer	838634
Flaig, Konstantin	27 Mar 1816	Mariazell	Obd.	bef 1853	Switz.	838634
Flaig, Lorenz	1820	Schramberg	Obd.	Feb 1854	N.-Amer	838636
Flaig, Maria	19 yrs.	Winzeln	Obd.	Nov 1866	N.-Amer	841016

Name		Birth		Emigration			Film
Last	First	Date	Place	O'amt	Appl. Date	Dest.	Number
Flaig, Mathaeus			Winzeln	Obd.	Nov 1860	N.-Amer	841016
Flaig, Xaver		17 yrs.	Schramberg	Obd.	Mar 1855	N.-Amer	838636
Flaig, Xaver		18 Jan 1806	Sulgen	Obd.	Jul 1857	N.-Amer	838638
Flaith, Johannes		23 Dec 1848	Seedorf	Obd.	Jun 1866	N.-Amer	838637
Fleischhauer, Johanne Auguste		30 Jul 1840	Reutlingen	Rtl.	bef 1863	Switz.	841052
Fleischmann, Pauline		29 Mar 1829	Stuttgart	Gsl.	bef 1853	France	572041
Flick, Karl		5 Jul 1867	Gerlingen	Leon.	Apr 1884	N.-Amer	837953
Flogaus, Johann		21 Jun 1822	Weiler	Krch.	Mar 1863	N.-Amer	835949
Flogaus, Johann Georg		18 Oct 1873	Rosswaelden	Krch.	Apr 1889	N.-Amer	835949
Flogaus, Leonhard & F			Westerheim	Gsl.	Mar 1852	N.-Amer	572041
Flogaus, Maria Agnes		16 yrs.	Westerheim	Gsl.	Mar 1852	N.-Amer	572041
Flogaus, Theresia (wife)			Westerheim	Gsl.	Mar 1852	N.-Amer	572041
Flogaus, Wilhelm Leonhard		8 yrs.	Westerheim	Gsl.	Mar 1852	N.-Amer	572041
Foehrenbacher, Carl			Schramberg	Obd.	bef 1839	Austria	838637
Foell, Adam Friedrich		22 Mar 1841	Gomaringen	Rtl.	Oct 1863	N.-Amer	841052
Foell, Gottliebin		infant	Owen	Krch.	Aug 1864	N.-Amer	835948
Foell, Johann Georg		5 May 1848	Gomaringen	Rtl.	Jul 1867	N.-Amer	841052
Forstner, Reinhold		15 Feb 1840	Eningen	Rtl.	Apr 1860	N.-Amer	841052
Frank, Anna Margaretha		4 Oct 1877	Pliensbach	Krch.	May 1883	N.-Amer	548403
Frank, Barbara (wife)		22 Sep 1824	Grosssuessen	Gsl.	May 1854	N.-Amer	572042
Frank, Carl August		13 Feb 1876	Pliensbach	Krch.	May 1883	N.-Amer	548403
Frank, Christine (wife)		13 Jun 1850	Pliensbach	Krch.	May 1883	N.-Amer	548403
Frank, Christoph		6 Mar 1842	Geislingen	Gsl.	Mar 1861	N.-Amer	572044
Frank, Conrad		14 Sep 1824	Hemmingen	Leon.	1848	N.-Amer	837956
Frank, Gottlieb & F		11 Aug 1848	Pliensbach	Krch.	May 1883	N.-Amer	548403
Frank, Heinrich		4 Apr 1854	Aufhausen	Gsl.	May 1854	N.-Amer	572042
Frank, Jacob Gottlob		2 Feb 1837	Weilheim	Krch.	1853	N.-Amer	835949
Frank, Johann Georg			Kirchheim	Krch.	bef 1866	N.-Amer	835940
Frank, Johannes		20 Jan 1824	Weilheim	Krch.	Dec 1859	N.-Amer	835949
Frank, Johannes		26 Oct 1841	Neidlingen	Krch.	Oct 1860	N.-Amer	835946
Frank, Karl		21 yrs.	Geislingen	Gsl.	Feb 1866	N.-Amer	572045
Frank, Leonhard		18 Apr 1856	Grosssuessen	Gsl.	Apr 1881	N.-Amer	572048
Frank, Margaretha		26 Oct 1851	Grosssuessen	Gsl.	May 1854	N.-Amer	572042
Frank, Maria		9 Dec 1839	Geislingen	Gsl.	Mar 1861	N.-Amer	572044
Frank, Michael & F		10 Apr 1821	Temmenhausen	Gsl.	May 1854	N.-Amer	572042
Frank, Michael Friedrich		5 Jun 1867	Weilheim	Krch.	Apr 1883	N.-Amer	548403
Frank, Regine Elisabetha		27 Oct 1826	Weilheim	Krch.	1853	N.-Amer	835949
Frank, Rosine		18 Oct 1841	Weilheim	Krch.	1853	N.-Amer	835949
Franz, Christian		24 Sep 1845	Roetenbach	Obd.	Aug 1865	N.-Amer	838636
Franz, Christiane & C		9 Mar 1841	Alpirsbach	Obd.	Apr 1866	N.-Amer	838630
Franz, Dorothea		24 yrs.	Roetenbach	Obd.	Apr 1857	N.-Amer	838636
Franz, Johannes		11 Jun 1838	Roetenbach	Obd.	Jul 1854	N.-Amer	838636
Franz, Joseph		21 Feb 1863	Alpirsbach	Obd.	Apr 1866	N.-Amer	838630
Frasch, Anna Barbara		11 Jun 1830	Hepsisau	Krch.	Feb 1862	N.-Amer	835945
Frasch, Catharina		22 Jan 1853	Bissingen	Krch.	Apr 1870	N.-Amer	835943
Frasch, Catharina		28 Oct 1828	Bissingen	Krch.	Jul 1862	N.-Amer	835943
Frasch, Georg Bernhard		5 Nov 1805	Hepsisau	Krch.	bef 1846	N.-Amer	835945
Frasch, Karl Gustav		28 Oct 1829	Hessigheim/Bes.	Krch.	May 1853	N.-Amer	835948
Frasch, Karl Robert		28 Apr 1836	Hessigheim/Bes.	Krch.	May 1853	N.-Amer	835948
Frasch, Marie Sophie		19 Oct 1849	Kirchheim	Krch.	Oct 1870	N.-Amer	835941

Frech, Christian	7 yrs.	Gingen	Gsl.	Aug 1851	N.-Amer	577788
Frech, Jakob	6 yrs.	Gingen	Gsl.	Aug 1851	N.-Amer	577788
Frech, Jenaeus Germanus	6 mon.	Gingen	Gsl.	Aug 1851	N.-Amer	577788
Frech, Jenaeus Germanus & F		Gingen	Gsl.	Aug 1851	N.-Amer	577788
Frech, Johann Andreas		Hausen a.d. Wurm	Leon.	Jan 1833	Switz.	837954
Frech, Johannes	3 yrs.	Gingen	Gsl.	Aug 1851	N.-Amer	577788
Frech, Karl Wilhelm	23 Feb 1865	Eltingen	Leon.	Jun 1881	N.-Amer	835789
Frech, Rosina (wife)		Gingen	Gsl.	Aug 1851	N.-Amer	577788
Frech, Wilhelm	1 Dec 1834	Merklingen	Leon.	May 1854	N.-Amer	837959
Frei, Caroline Christiane		Eltingen	Leon.	May 1869	Bavaria	835789
Frei, Johannes		Pfullingen	Rtl.	Mar 1834	N.-Amer	841051
Frei, Josef Anton	8 Feb 1836	Waldmoessingen	Obd.	Feb 1854	N.-Amer	841015
Freiberger, Friedrich	6 Nov 1860	Gueltstein	Herr.	bef 1896	Switz.	834631
Freiberger, Gottlieb Friedrich	11 Sep 1864	Gueltstein	Herr.	1894	Switz.	834631
Freiberger, Johann Georg	12 Jun 1884	Gueltstein	Herr.	1893	Switz.	834631
Freiberger, Johann Jakob	30 Mar 1856	Gueltstein	Herr.	bef 1886	Switz.	834631
Freitag, Magdalena	10 Feb 1831	Bissingen	Krch.	bef 1864	France	835943
Fretz, Christina Rosina	4 yrs.	Rutesheim	Leon.	Feb 1852	N.-Amer	837964
Fretz, Johann Georg & F	41 yrs.	Rutesheim	Leon.	Feb 1852	N.-Amer	837964
Fretz, Maria Cathar. (wife)	35 yrs.	Rutesheim	Leon.	Feb 1852	N.-Amer	837964
Fretz, Maria Catharina	8 yrs.	Rutesheim	Leon.	Feb 1852	N.-Amer	837964
Fretz, Maria Rosine Frieder.	7 yrs.	Rutesheim	Leon.	Feb 1852	N.-Amer	837964
Fretz, Marie Barbara	34 yrs.	Rutesheim	Leon.	Feb 1852	N.-Amer	837964
Fretz, Marie Magdalena	1 yrs.	Rutesheim	Leon.	Feb 1852	N.-Amer	837964
Freudenweiler, Johann Christ.		Reutlingen	Rtl.	1866	N.-Amer	841052
Freundle, Jakob & F		Muenklingen	Leon.	Mar 1854	N.-Amer	837962
Frey, Andreas	23 May 1844	Ueberkingen	Gsl.	Jun 1856	N.-Amer	572043
Frey, Andreas & F		Ueberkingen	Gsl.	Jun 1856	N.-Amer	572043
Frey, Anna		Waldmoessingen	Obd.	1847	N.-Amer	841015
Frey, Anna (wid.)	1 Apr 1806	Altenstadt-Gsl.	Gsl.	Apr 1867	N.-Amer	572046
Frey, Anna Margaretha (wife)		Ueberkingen	Gsl.	Jun 1856	N.-Amer	572043
Frey, Anna Maria	8 Mar 1838	Eybach	Gsl.	Jun 1867	N.-Amer	572046
Frey, Anton & F		Alt Oberndorf	Obd.	Feb 1857	N.-Amer	838631
Frey, Barbara		Altenstadt-Gsl.	Gsl.	Feb 1860	N.-Amer	572044
Frey, Bonavent	2 Jul 1848	Hochmoessingen	Obd.	Dec 1868	N.-Amer	838633
Frey, Bonifazius	6 May 1816	Hochmoessingen	Obd.	bef 1866	N.-Amer	838633
Frey, Caroline	19 Jul 1845	Heimerdingen	Leon.	Mar 1854	N.-Amer	837954
Frey, Christian David	11 Feb 1872	Zell	Krch.	Apr 1886	N.-Amer	548403
Frey, Christian David	19 Mar 1871	Rosswaelden	Krch.	Jul 1887	N.-Amer	835949
Frey, Christiana	21 Sep 1830	Heimerdingen	Leon.	Mar 1853	N.-Amer	837954
Frey, Christina	12 Jul 1835	Gingen	Gsl.	May 1854	N.-Amer	572042
Frey, Daniel	4 Dec 1834	Ueberkingen	Gsl.	bef 1854	N.-Amer	572042
Frey, Elisabetha	7 Nov 1834	Altenstadt-Gsl.	Gsl.	Feb 1854	N.-Amer	572042
Frey, Franz Joseph	14 Sep 1842	Hochmoessingen	Obd.	Oct 1868	Prussia	838633
Frey, Georg	12 Jul 1829	Kuchen	Gsl.	Dec 1854	N.-Amer	572042
Frey, German	11 Oct 1839	Waldmoessingen	Obd.	Aug 1856	N.-Amer	841015
Frey, Gottlieb Heinrich	11 Mar 1825	Kirchheim	Krch.	Oct 1859	N.-Amer	835940
Frey, Jacob & F	29 Jan 1825	Heimerdingen	Leon.	Mar 1854	N.-Amer	837954
Frey, Johann Baptist		Donzdorf	Gsl.	Nov 1859	N.-Amer	572043
Frey, Johann Georg	26 Sep 1844	Kuchen	Gsl.	Apr 1865	N.-Amer	572045

| Name | | Birth | | Emigration | | | Film |
Last	First	Date	Place	O'amt	Appl. Date	Dest.	Number
Frey,	Johann Georg	21 Dec 1871	Rosswaelden	Krch.	Jun 1887	N.-Amer	835949
Frey,	Johann Michael	9 Sep 1859	Eybach	Gsl.	Jun 1876	N.-Amer	572048
Frey,	Johannes	17 Dec 1848	Ueberkingen	Gsl.	Jun 1856	N.-Amer	572043
Frey,	Johannes	18 Feb 1845	Pfullingen	Rtl.	Aug 1861	England	841052
Frey,	Karl Eugen	22 Feb 1874	Kirchheim	Krch.	Oct 1890	N.-Amer	835942
Frey,	Karl Wilhelm	4 Mar 1874	Zell	Krch.	Jan 1890	N.-Amer	835774
Frey,	Konrad	21 Nov 1807	Hochmoessingen	Obd.	1841	N.-Amer	838633
Frey,	Leonhardt	11 May 1833	Altenstadt-Gsl.	Gsl.	Mar 1856	N.-Amer	572043
Frey,	Maria Anna (wife)		Alt Oberndorf	Obd.	Feb 1857	N.-Amer	838631
Frey,	Marianne	10 yrs.	Alt Oberndorf	Obd.	Feb 1857	N.-Amer	838631
Frey,	Marzell	20 Jun 1801	Eybach	Gsl.	Jun 1867	N.-Amer	572046
Frey,	Michael		Hochmoessingen	Obd.	Aug 1851	France	838633
Frey,	Rosa	9 yrs.	Alt Oberndorf	Obd.	Feb 1857	N.-Amer	838631
Frey,	Sophia	14 May 1848	Altenstadt-Gsl.	Gsl.	Dec 1866	N.-Amer	572045
Frey,	Tekla		Hochmoessingen	Obd.	Sep 1860	France	838633
Frey,	Wilhelm		Eltingen	Leon.	bef 1869	N.-Amer	835789
Frey,	Wilhelm Friedrich	7 Jul 1852	Heimerdingen	Leon.	Mar 1854	N.-Amer	837954
Frick,	Andreas	27 Sep 1826	Bochingen	Obd.	Jul 1853	N.-Amer	838632
Frick,	Andreas Wilhelm	27 May 1835	Alpirsbach	Obd.	Mar 1854	N.-Amer	838630
Frick,	Anna Maria	4 Sep 1828	Alpirsbach	Obd.	Jun 1856	France	838630
Frick,	Anna Maria	10 Sep 1814	Bochingen	Obd.	Apr 1852	N.-Amer	838632
Frick,	Anna Maria	3 May 1838	Muenklingen	Leon.	Feb 1847	Hungary	837962
Frick,	Anna Maria (wife)		Muenklingen	Leon.	Feb 1847	Hungary	837962
Frick,	Anna Pauline (wife)	6 Mar 1843	Undingen	Rtl.	Dec 1865	Bremen	841052
Frick,	Anna Rosina (wife)		Erpfingen	Rtl.	Sep 1859	N.-Amer	841052
Frick,	Carolina (wife)		Leonberg	Leon.	Feb 1852	N.-Amer	835786
Frick,	Caroline	4 yrs.	Leonberg	Leon.	Feb 1852	N.-Amer	835786
Frick,	Christian & F		Leonberg	Leon.	Feb 1852	N.-Amer	835786
Frick,	Christiane	19 Feb 1821	Alpirsbach	Obd.	Oct 1855	Switz.	838630
Frick,	Christina		Alpirsbach	Obd.	May 1809	Hesse	838631
Frick,	Christine	7 yrs.	Leonberg	Leon.	Feb 1852	N.-Amer	835786
Frick,	Friederich	16 yrs.	Leonberg	Leon.	Feb 1852	N.-Amer	835786
Frick,	Friederike		Alpirsbach	Obd.	May 1862	France	838630
Frick,	Friederike	18 yrs.	Leonberg	Leon.	Feb 1852	N.-Amer	835786
Frick,	Friedrich	14 Jul 1849	Roetenbach	Obd.	Aug 1867	N.-Amer	838636
Frick,	Friedrich & F	56 yrs.	Muenklingen	Leon.	Feb 1847	Hungary	837962
Frick,	Friedrich Wilhelm & W	11 Aug 1835	Undingen	Rtl.	Dec 1865	Bremen	841052
Frick,	Jacob Franz	2 May 1837	Alpirsbach	Obd.	Aug 1856	N.-Amer	838630
Frick,	Johann Ludwig	13 Oct 1835	Muenklingen	Leon.	Feb 1847	Hungary	837962
Frick,	Johannes	12 Mar 1856	Schopfloch	Krch.	Feb 1868	N.-Amer	835949
Frick,	Karl Friedrich	11 Jun 1833	Muenklingen	Leon.	Feb 1847	Hungary	837962
Frick,	Karl Friedrich	25 Mar 1871	Weilheim	Krch.	Feb 1888	N.-Amer	835774
Frick,	Ludwig	30 Aug 1843	Erpfingen	Rtl.	Apr 1861	N.-Amer	841052
Frick,	Ludwig		Erpfingen	Rtl.	Oct 1859	N.-Amer	841052
Frick,	Maria Juliana	23 Oct 1838	Erpfingen	Rtl.	Nov 1863	N.-Amer	841052
Frick,	Philipp Jakob & W		Erpfingen	Rtl.	Sep 1859	N.-Amer	841052
Frick,	Rosina	14 Aug 1833	Alpirsbach	Obd.	Jun 1858	Switz.	838630
Frick,	Rosina	27 Apr 1843	Muenklingen	Leon.	Feb 1847	Hungary	837962
Frick,	Wilhelm	27 Sep 1841	Muenklingen	Leon.	Feb 1847	Hungary	837962
Frick,	Wilhelm	14 yrs.	Leonberg	Leon.	Feb 1852	N.-Amer	835786

Friedel, Adolf Friedrich	8 Jan 1860	Geislingen	Gsl.	Aug 1876	N.-Amer	572048
Friedel, Franz Anton	12 Sep 1831	Donzdorf	Gsl.	bef 1856	N.-Amer	572049
Friedel, Franz Anton & F		Donzdorf	Gsl.	Apr 1857	N.-Amer	572043
Friedel, Georg	11 Mar 1827	Treffelhausen	Gsl.	Dec 1855	Switz.	572045
Friedel, Johann Daniel	26 Jul 1852	Geislingen	Gsl.	Aug 1869	England	572047
Friedel, Johannes Baptist	12 Dec 1856	Donzdorf	Gsl.	Apr 1857	N.-Amer	572043
Friedel, Karl	25 Apr 1843	Geislingen	Gsl.	Jun 1870	Palest.	572047
Friedel, Katharina		Treffelhausen	Gsl.	1853	N.-Amer	572041
Friedel, Ursula (wife)		Donzdorf	Gsl.	Apr 1857	N.-Amer	572043
Friedle, Alphons	9 Jan 1853	Bochingen	Obd.	Feb 1870	N.-Amer	838632
Friedrich, Emil	16 yrs.	Reutlingen	Rtl.	May 1880	N.-Amer	841051
Friedrich, Johann Jacob	5 Aug 1846	Kirchheim	Krch.	Dec 1866	N.-Amer	835941
Friegel, David	22 Jan 1840	Kuchen	Gsl.	Mar 1857	N.-Amer	572043
Friegel, Jakob	24 Jan 1843	Kuchen	Gsl.	Feb 1870	Berlin	572047
Friegel, Juliana (wid.)		Kuchen	Gsl.	Jan 1868	N.-Amer	572046
Friegel, Konrad		Kuchen	Gsl.	Feb 1853	N.-Amer	572041
Fries, Leonhard	28 Oct 1826	Ohmden	Krch.	Jul 1858	N.-Amer	835948
Friesinger, Heinrich & F		Oetlingen	Krch.	Mar 1804	Russia	550804
Friesinger, Susanna	27 Aug 1824	Grossengstingen	Rtl.	Apr 1866	N.-Amer	841052
Friess, Andreas, Jr. & F		Renningen	Leon.	Apr 1852	N.-Amer	837963
Friess, Anna Maria	28 Nov 1844	Renningen	Leon.	Apr 1852	N.-Amer	837963
Friess, Barbara	13 Jan 1786	Merklingen	Leon.	Apr 1830	N.-Amer	837963
Friess, Christian	1 Oct 1846	Renningen	Leon.	Apr 1852	N.-Amer	837963
Friess, Christine	14 Aug 1851	Renningen	Leon.	Feb 1870	N.-Amer	837963
Friess, Ernst Gottlob	31 Mar 1843	Renningen	Leon.	Apr 1852	N.-Amer	837963
Friess, Friederika (wife)		Renningen	Leon.	Apr 1852	N.-Amer	837963
Friess, Gottfried Leonhardt	14 Feb 1848	Renningen	Leon.	Apr 1852	N.-Amer	837963
Friess, Gottlob Jakob	23 Apr 1842	Renningen	Leon.	Apr 1852	N.-Amer	837963
Friess, Johann Georg	15 Sep 1838	Renningen	Leon.	Apr 1852	N.-Amer	837963
Friess, Johann Jakob	23 Apr 1850	Renningen	Leon.	Apr 1852	N.-Amer	837963
Friess, Johann Michael & F		Renningen	Leon.	Apr 1852	N.-Amer	837963
Friess, Johanne Leontine		Renningen	Leon.	bef 1857	Prussia	837963
Friess, Johannes	16 Aug 1840	Renningen	Leon.	Apr 1852	N.-Amer	837963
Friess, Michael, Sr. & F		Renningen	Leon.	May 1853	N.-Amer	837963
Friess, Regina Dorothea	3 Dec 1849	Renningen	Leon.	Apr 1852	N.-Amer	837963
Friess, Rosina Katharina (wife)		Renningen	Leon.	Apr 1852	N.-Amer	837963
Friess, Traugott Christian	6 Jun 1840	Renningen	Leon.	Apr 1852	N.-Amer	837963
Friessinger, Albert	9 Jan 1877	Friolzheim	Leon.	Feb 1881	N.-Amer	835791
Friessinger, Bertha	29 Jun 1872	Friolzheim	Leon.	Feb 1881	N.-Amer	835791
Friessinger, Carl Robert	13 May 1866	Friolzheim	Leon.	Oct 1885	N.-Amer	835791
Friessinger, Caroline	13 Nov 1873	Friolzheim	Leon.	Feb 1881	N.-Amer	835791
Friessinger, Caroline (wife)	13 May 1841	Friolzheim	Leon.	Feb 1881	N.-Amer	835791
Friessinger, Christian Fr. & F	29 Oct 1834	Friolzheim	Leon.	Feb 1881	N.-Amer	835791
Friessinger, Emilie	30 Aug 1869	Friolzheim	Leon.	Feb 1881	N.-Amer	835791
Friessinger, Gustav	3 Aug 1875	Friolzheim	Leon.	Feb 1881	N.-Amer	835791
Friessinger, Otto	23 Feb 1880	Friolzheim	Leon.	Feb 1881	N.-Amer	835791
Fritz, Andreas	26 Aug 1787	Schoeckingen	Leon.	1804	Russia	837964
Fritz, Carl Friedrich	29 Oct 1878	Kirchheim	Krch.	Aug 1884	N.-Amer	835942
Fritz, Carl Friedrich & F	1 Nov 1847	Kirchheim	Krch.	Aug 1884	N.-Amer	835942
Fritz, Carl Gottlieb	1 Jul 1876	Kirchheim	Krch.	Aug 1884	N.-Amer	835942

Name		Birth		Emigration			Film
Last	First	Date	Place	O'amt	Appl. Date	Dest.	Number
Fritz, Christina		20 yrs.	Hoefingen	Leon.	Sep 1853	N.-Amer	837957
Fritz, Dorothea (wife)			Schoeckingen	Leon.	1804	Russia	837964
Fritz, Eva Margaretha (wife)		18 Sep 1848	Kirchheim	Krch.	Aug 1884	N.-Amer	835942
Fritz, Gottfried		12 Jun 1785	Schoeckingen	Leon.	1804	Russia	837964
Fritz, Hermann		12 Aug 1882	Kirchheim	Krch.	Aug 1884	N.-Amer	835942
Fritz, Jacob			Hoefingen	Leon.	May 1853	N.-Amer	837957
Fritz, Jakob & F			Schoeckingen	Leon.	1804	Russia	837964
Fritz, Maria Margaretha		17 Feb 1790	Schoeckingen	Leon.	1804	Russia	837964
Fritz, Max		17 Jul 1850	Donzdorf	Gsl.	Dec 1869	N.-Amer	572047
Fritz, Pauline Regine		6 Jan 1884	Kirchheim	Krch.	Aug 1884	N.-Amer	835942
Friz, Caroline		22 Oct 1844	Kirchheim	Krch.	1866	N.-Amer	835940
Friz, Christina			Hemmingen	Leon.	Feb 1853	N.-Amer	837956
Friz, Friedrich			Hemmingen	Leon.	Apr 1839	N.-Amer	837956
Froehle, Crescenz		28 Oct 1826	Deggingen	Gsl.	Feb 1854	N.-Amer	572042
Froehlich, Andreas		15 yrs.	Weil der Stadt	Leon.	Sep 1851	N.-Amer	837966
Froehlich, Andreas			Weil der Stadt	Leon.	bef 1851	N.-Amer	837966
Froehlich, Ida		11 yrs.	Weil der Stadt	Leon.	Sep 1851	N.-Amer	837966
Froehlich, Karl		9 yrs.	Weil der Stadt	Leon.	Sep 1851	N.-Amer	837966
Froehlich, Louise		3 yrs.	Weil der Stadt	Leon.	Sep 1851	N.-Amer	837966
Froehlich, Magdalena		18 yrs.	Weil der Stadt	Leon.	Sep 1851	N.-Amer	837966
Froehlich, Magdalena & F			Weil der Stadt	Leon.	Sep 1851	N.-Amer	837966
Froehlich, Mathilde		14 yrs.	Weil der Stadt	Leon.	Sep 1851	N.-Amer	837966
Froeschle, – (wife)		17 Sep 1824	Eltingen	Leon.	Mar 1851	N.-Amer	835789
Froeschle, Brigitta (wife)		33 yrs.	Leonberg	Leon.	Dec 1816	Russia	835789
Froeschle, Christian Adam		2 yrs.	Leonberg	Leon.	Dec 1816	Russia	835789
Froeschle, Emma Pauline		1 yrs.	Leonberg	Leon.	Sep 1853	N.-Amer	835786
Froeschle, Friederike H. (wife)		17 Dec 1828	Eltingen	Leon.	Feb 1870	Palest.	835789
Froeschle, Georg Friedrich		20 Nov 1846	Eltingen	Leon.	Mar 1851	N.-Amer	835789
Froeschle, Georg Michael		4 May 1825	Eltingen	Leon.	Feb 1870	Palest.	835789
Froeschle, Gustav Otto		3 yrs.	Leonberg	Leon.	Sep 1853	N.-Amer	835786
Froeschle, Jakob Friedrich		10 Aug 1853	Eltingen	Leon.	Feb 1870	Palest.	835789
Froeschle, Johann Georg		29 Nov 1851	Eltingen	Leon.	1869	Palest.	835789
Froeschle, Johanna		21 Aug 1869	Eltingen	Leon.	Feb 1870	Palest.	835789
Froeschle, Johannes		17 Dec 1848	Eltingen	Leon.	Mar 1851	N.-Amer	835789
Froeschle, Johannes & F			Leonberg	Leon.	Sep 1853	N.-Amer	835786
Froeschle, Johannes & F		15 Jul 1822	Eltingen	Leon.	Mar 1851	N.-Amer	835789
Froeschle, Lorenz & F			Eltingen	Leon.	Apr 1830	N.-Amer	835789
Froeschle, Lorenz & F		37 yrs.	Leonberg	Leon.	Dec 1816	Russia	835789
Froeschle, Ottilie Amalie		5 yrs.	Leonberg	Leon.	Sep 1853	N.-Amer	835786
Froeschle, Wilhelmine (wife)			Leonberg	Leon.	Sep 1853	N.-Amer	835786
Frosch, Catharina Barbara		3 Aug 1824	Owen	Krch.	Aug 1862	France	835948
Frosch, Johann Jacob		9 Nov 1874	Oberlenningen	Krch.	Jun 1890	N.-Amer	835947
Frucht, Friedrich		22 Jun 1823	Hemmingen	Leon.	Aug 1845	N.-Amer	837956
Frucht, Johannes		20 Mar 1802	Heimerdingen	Leon.	Jan 1854	N.-Amer	837954
Frucht, Johannes		18 Oct 1827	Heimerdingen	Leon.	Mar 1851	N.-Amer	837954
Frueh, Jacob			Betzingen	Rtl.	May 1831	N.-Amer	841051
Frueh, Jakob		15 Dec 1856	Undingen	Rtl.	Jun 1880	N.-Amer	841051
Frueh, Johann Georg			Wannweil	Rtl.	1832	N.-Amer	841052
Frueh, Johannes		6 Oct 1837	Undingen	Rtl.	bef 1864	N.-Amer	841052
Frueth, Josefa		21 Oct 1823	Oberndorf	Obd.	Sep 1867	France	838635

Fuchs, Alois	31 Aug 1830	Boehmenkirch	Gsl.	Jan 1862	N.-Amer	572044
Fuchs, Alois	27 Sep 1849	Boehmenkirch	Gsl.	Apr 1867	N.-Amer	572046
Fuchs, Anna Maria	15 Jan 1816	Rosswaelden	Krch.	May 1855	N.-Amer	835949
Fuchs, Anna Maria & F		Hemmingen	Leon.	bef 1856	N.-Amer	837956
Fuchs, Bernhard	3 Feb 1847	Boehmenkirch	Gsl.	May 1867	N.-Amer	572046
Fuchs, Carl		Boehmenkirch	Gsl.	Mar 1852	N.-Amer	572041
Fuchs, Carl & F		Flacht	Leon.	Jul 1853	N.-Amer	835790
Fuchs, Carolina		Flacht	Leon.	Jul 1853	N.-Amer	835790
Fuchs, Christiana & F	15 Apr 1815	Schierbach	Krch.	Mar 1857	N.-Amer	835949
Fuchs, Christiane Heinrike	24 Sep 1844	Rosswaelden	Krch.	Mar 1857	N.-Amer	835949
Fuchs, Christoph Friedrich	1 Aug 1845	Oberlenningen	Krch.	Oct 1866	N.-Amer	835947
Fuchs, Elisabeth		Harthausen	Obd.	Oct 1845	N.-Amer	838633
Fuchs, Friederike	1849	Rosswaelden	Krch.	Mar 1857	N.-Amer	835949
Fuchs, Genofeva & C	27 Dec 1807	Harthausen	Obd.	Oct 1845	N.-Amer	838633
Fuchs, Georg		Hemmingen	Leon.	bef 1856	N.-Amer	837956
Fuchs, Gottfried	7 Mar 1850	Alt Oberndorf	Obd.	May 1869	N.-Amer	838631
Fuchs, Gottlob Ulrich	25 Aug 1847	Reutlingen	Rtl.	Jul 1865	N.-Amer	841052
Fuchs, Jakob Friedrich	25 Oct 1840	Unterlenningen	Krch.	Apr 1855	N.-Amer	835949
Fuchs, Johann	30 Mar 1842	Rosswaelden	Krch.	Mar 1857	N.-Amer	835949
Fuchs, Johann Balthasar & F		Reutlingen	Rtl.	May 1832	N.-Amer	841051
Fuchs, Johann Michael	1 Jul 1845	Oberlenningen	Krch.	Jun 1864	N.-Amer	835947
Fuchs, Johann Michael		Rosswaelden	Krch.	bef 1857	N.-Amer	835949
Fuchs, Johann Michael (wid.)	9 Apr 1787	Rosswaelden	Krch.	Mar 1857	N.-Amer	835949
Fuchs, Johanna	14 Apr 1851	Rosswaelden	Krch.	Mar 1857	N.-Amer	835949
Fuchs, Johannes	20 Feb 1840	Boehmenkirch	Gsl.	Apr 1867	N.-Amer	572046
Fuchs, Johannes	15 Jul 1845	Treffelhausen	Gsl.	Oct 1866	N.-Amer	572045
Fuchs, Josefa (wife)		Boehmenkirch	Gsl.	Mar 1852	N.-Amer	572041
Fuchs, Joseph	29 Apr 1837	Boehmenkirch	Gsl.	Feb 1854	N.-Amer	572042
Fuchs, Josepha	4 Nov 1844	Boehmenkirch	Gsl.	Jan 1862	N.-Amer	572044
Fuchs, Juliana	14 Feb 1805	Harthausen	Obd.	Oct 1845	N.-Amer	838633
Fuchs, Karl & W		Boehmenkirch	Gsl.	Mar 1852	N.-Amer	572041
Fuchs, Leonhard		Harthausen	Obd.	Oct 1845	N.-Amer	838633
Fuchs, Maria	11 Aug 1849	Boehmenkirch	Gsl.	Sep 1867	N.-Amer	572046
Fuchs, Rosine	13 May 1843	Rosswaelden	Krch.	Mar 1857	N.-Amer	835949
Fuchs, Sebastian	28 Mar 1826	Reutlingen	Rtl.	Nov 1860	N.-Amer	841052
Fuchs, Wilhelmine	26 Feb 1836	Unterlenningen	Krch.	Apr 1855	N.-Amer	835949
Fuchs, Wilhelmine Jakobine	30 Oct 1840	Rosswaelden	Krch.	May 1855	N.-Amer	835949
Fueller, Franz Xaver	2 Dec 1850	Westerheim	Gsl.	May 1868	N.-Amer	572046
Fueller, Michael	10 Feb 1849	Westerheim	Gsl.	May 1868	N.-Amer	572046
Fuessel, Johann Georg & F		Merklingen	Leon.	May 1853	N.-Amer	837959
Funk, Johann Jacob	8 Nov 1838	Oberjesingen	Herr.	bef 1864	Switz.	834630
Fuoss, Johannes	26 yrs.	Butschhof	Obd.	May 1854	N.-Amer	838632
Fus, Catharina (wife)	14 Feb 1801	Seedorf	Obd.	Apr 1847	N.-Amer	838637
Fus, Jakob & F	16 Apr 1797	Seedorf	Obd.	Apr 1847	N.-Amer	838637
Fus, Josepha	15 Dec 1824	Seedorf	Obd.	Apr 1847	N.-Amer	838637
Fus, Katharina	1 Nov 1835	Seedorf	Obd.	Apr 1847	N.-Amer	838637
Fus, Magdalena	16 May 1833	Seedorf	Obd.	Apr 1847	N.-Amer	838637
Fus, Theresia	15 Oct 1828	Seedorf	Obd.	Apr 1847	N.-Amer	838637
Fus, Zachaeus	20 Nov 1837	Seedorf	Obd.	Apr 1847	N.-Amer	838637
Fuss, Carl		Weil im Dorf	Loen.	1860	Basel	837967

Name		Birth		Emigration			Film
Last	First	Date	Place	O'amt	Appl. Date	Dest.	Number
Gabler, Anna Maria (wife)		33 yrs.	Oberlenningen	Krch.	Jul 1873	N.-Amer	548403
Gabler, Catharina (wife)		5 Oct 1827	Oberlenningen	Krch.	Feb 1867	N.-Amer	835947
Gabler, Christian		4 yrs.	Oberlenningen	Krch.	Jul 1873	N.-Amer	548403
Gabler, Christian		15 Jan 1869	Oberlenningen	Krch.	Jul 1873	N.-Amer	835947
Gabler, Christoph		11 May 1849	Oberlenningen	Krch.	Feb 1867	N.-Amer	835947
Gabler, Eva		infant	Oberlenningen	Krch.	Jul 1873	N.-Amer	548403
Gabler, Eva Katharina		20 Jun 1873	Oberlenningen	Krch.	Jul 1873	N.-Amer	835947
Gabler, Eva Maria Sophia		4 Apr 1866	Oberlenningen	Krch.	Feb 1867	N.-Amer	835947
Gabler, Gottlieb Adam		8 Dec 1857	Oberlenningen	Krch.	Feb 1867	N.-Amer	835947
Gabler, Isak Jacob		6 Feb 1861	Oberlenningen	Krch.	Feb 1867	N.-Amer	835947
Gabler, Jakob		14 Jan 1844	Oberlenningen	Krch.	Jan 1870	N.-Amer	835947
Gabler, Jakob (wid.)			Oberlenningen	Krch.	Aug 1873	N.-Amer	548403
Gabler, Jakob (wid.)		18 Feb 1797	Oberlenningen	Krch.	Aug 1873	N.-Amer	835947
Gabler, Johann Gottlieb & F		1 Mar 1825	Oberlenningen	Krch.	Feb 1867	N.-Amer	835947
Gabler, Johann Michael & F		33 yrs.	Oberlenningen	Krch.	Jul 1873	N.-Amer	548403
Gaehr, Christian Gottlieb		10 Nov 1842	Kirchheim	Krch.	Apr 1866	N.-Amer	835941
Gaehr, Gottlob		9 Oct 1849	Kirchheim	Krch.	Jul 1865	N.-Amer	835941
Gaehr, Wilhelm		27 Feb 1846	Kirchheim	Krch.	Jul 1865	N.-Amer	835941
Gaensle, Johann Christoph			Gerlingen	Leon.	Apr 1831	N.-Amer	837953
Gaenzle, Georg Friedrich		4 Dec 1858	Ohmden	Krch.	Oct 1865	N.-Amer	835948
Gaenzle, Johann Georg & F		19 Feb 1831	Ohmden	Krch.	Oct 1865	N.-Amer	835948
Gaenzle, Johann Michael		4 Jun 1850	Ohmden	Krch.	Feb 1870	N.-Amer	835948
Gaenzle, Johannes		29 Jul 1860	Ohmden	Krch.	Oct 1865	N.-Amer	835948
Gaenzle, Katharina		28 Jun 1861	Ohmden	Krch.	Oct 1865	N.-Amer	835948
Gaenzle, Margaretha Ros. (wife)		27 May 1838	Ohmden	Krch.	Oct 1865	N.-Amer	835948
Gaenzle, Maria		22 Dec 1862	Ohmden	Krch.	Oct 1865	N.-Amer	835948
Gaertner, Johann Friedrich			Gerlingen	Leon.	Apr 1840	France	837953
Gaertner, Johann Georg		26 Jun 1829	Oberjesingen	Herr.	bef 1865	N.-Amer	834630
Gaertner, Johann Georg		8 Jan 1822	Gerlingen	Leon.	May 1864	N.-Amer	837953
Gaertner, Johannes		5 Dec 1819	Gerlingen	Leon.	Aug 1848	N.-Amer	837953
Gaier, Johann Georg & F			Gebersheim	Leon.	Mar 1852	N.-Amer	837953
Gaier, Johannes			Gebersheim	Leon.	Jun 1853	N.-Amer	837953
Gaier, Wilhelm		2 Aug 1839	Roemlinsdorf	Obd.	Nov 1859	England	838635
Gairing, Anna		10 Dec 1834	Kuchen	Gsl.	Dec 1853	N.-Amer	572041
Gairing, Anna Maria Ursula		27 May 1830	Hausen	Gsl.	Oct 1854	N.-Amer	572042
Gairing, David		29 Jun 1849	Unterboehringen	Gsl.	Jun 1874	N.-Amer	572048
Gairing, Johann Georg		3 Apr 1839	Kuchen	Gsl.	Feb 1854	N.-Amer	572042
Gairing, Johann Ulrich		20 Feb 1834	Unterboehringen	Gsl.	May 1854	N.-Amer	572042
Gaiser, Anna Maria & F			Hozelfingen	Rtl.	Oct 1868	N.-Amer	841052
Gaiser, Barbara		31 Dec 1832	Dettingen	Krch.	1854	N.-Amer	835944
Gaiser, Carl			Hozelfingen	Rtl.	bef 1868	N.-Amer	841052
Gaiser, Christian		13 Oct 1849	Wannweil	Rtl.	May 1867	N.-Amer	841052
Gaiser, Christiana		25 Jun 1837	Dettingen	Krch.	1854	N.-Amer	835944
Gaiser, Ludwig		13 yrs.	Merklingen	Leon.	Feb 1846	N.-Amer	837959
Gall, Adolph			Weil der Stadt	Leon.	Jul 1847	N.-Amer	837965
Gall, Anna Rosina		28 Feb 1839	Weil der Stadt	Leon.	Sep 1842	N.-Amer	837965
Gall, Carl Friedrich		15 Dec 1866	Weiheim	Krch.	Apr 1882	N.-Amer	548403
Gall, Carl Theodor & F			Weil der Stadt	Leon.	Jul 1847	N.-Amer	837965
Gall, Catharina			Weil der Stadt	Leon.	Jul 1847	N.-Amer	837965
Gall, Jakob			Weil der Stadt	Leon.	Aug 1859	France	837966

Name	Date	Place	Region	Emig. Date	Destination	Film
Gall, Josephine	24 Aug 1843	Weil der Stadt	Leon.	Jul 1847	N.-Amer	837965
Gall, Josephine & C		Weil der Stadt	Leon.	Jul 1847	N.-Amer	837965
Gall, Magdalena		Weil der Stadt	Leon.	Jul 1847	N.-Amer	837965
Gall, Maria Anna (wife)		Weil der Stadt	Leon.	Jul 1847	N.-Amer	837965
Gall, Maria Theresia		Weil der Stadt	Leon.	Jul 1847	N.-Amer	837965
Gall, Maria Victoria		Weil der Stadt	Leon.	Jul 1847	N.-Amer	837965
Gall, Sophie & C	28 Oct 1815	Weil der Stadt	Leon.	Sep 1842	N.-Amer	837965
Gall, Victoria		Weil der Stadt	Leon.	Jul 1847	N.-Amer	837965
Gall, Xaver		Weil der Stadt	Leon.	Jun 1853	N.-Amer	837966
Gallus, Christian August	14 Jun 1823	Weilheim	Krch.	bef 1860	N.-Amer	835949
Gams, Maria Johanna		Grossengstingen	Rtl.	Aug 1827	N.-Amer	841051
Gann, Johann Leonhard		Heimsheim	Leon.	Dec 1833	Austria	837955
Gansloser, Pius & F	25 Sep 1819	Deggingen	Gsl.	Feb 1863	Bavaria	572044
Garg, Johann & F		Seedorf	Obd.	May 1817	N.-Amer	841016
Gartich, Lorenz	6 Aug 1811	Ohmden	Krch.	Aug 1862	France	835948
Gasteyger, Carl Wilhelm		Renningen	Leon.	bef 1846	Prussia	837963
Gau, Anna Maria	6 Jul 1833	Ohmden	Krch.	May 1856	N.-Amer	835948
Gaugler, August		Weil der Stadt	Leon.	bef 1856	Prussia	837966
Gaus, Felix		Winzeln	Obd.	Jul 1862	N.-Amer	841016
Gaus, Florentin	18 Oct 1848	Winzeln	Obd.	Aug 1867	N.-Amer	841016
Gaus, Franz	24 Mar 1853	Winzeln	Obd.	Feb 1869	N.-Amer	841016
Gaus, Johannes	25 Dec 1838	Beffendorf	Obd.	Oct 1847	N.-Amer	841016
Gaus, Lorenz	2 Aug 1832	Winzeln	Obd.	May 1854	N.-Amer	841016
Gaus, Maria	14 Sep 1838	Winzeln	Obd.	Apr 1868	N.-Amer	841016
Gaus, Mathias	22 Feb 1850	Winzeln	Obd.	Oct 1866	N.-Amer	841016
Gaus, Mathilda	14 Mar 1847	Winzeln	Obd.	Feb 1869	N.-Amer	841016
Gaus, Moriz & F		Winzeln	Obd.	May 1817	N.-Amer	841016
Gaus, Nikolaus	5 Dec 1839	Winzeln	Obd.	Sep 1855	N.-Amer	841016
Gaus, Rosine (wid.) & F	26 Aug 1806	Winzeln	Obd.	Apr 1868	N.-Amer	841016
Gauss, Anna Maria	10 Mar 1864	Dettingen	Krch.	Feb 1869	N.-Amer	835944
Gauss, Anna Maria	29 Dec 1830	Weilheim	Krch.	bef 1857	N.-Amer	835949
Gauss, Balbina & F	29 Mar 1814	Winzeln	Obd.	Oct 1847	N.-Amer	841016
Gauss, Catharina	15 May 1868	Dettingen	Krch.	Feb 1869	N.-Amer	835944
Gauss, Catharina (wife)	16 Dec 1846	Dettingen	Krch.	Feb 1869	N.-Amer	835944
Gauss, Christian Gottlieb	3 Sep 1866	Dettingen	Krch.	Feb 1869	N.-Amer	835944
Gauss, Jakob	10 Jan 1838	Oberjesingen	Herr.	Sep 1863	N.-Amer	834630
Gauss, Jakob Daniel & F	26 Aug 1843	Dettingen	Krch.	Feb 1869	N.-Amer	835944
Gauss, Michael	6 Feb 1844	Hildrizhausen	Herr.	Mar 1869	N.-Amer	834631
Gauss, Pauline		Winzeln	Obd.	Sep 1854	N.-Amer	841016
Gayde, Gottlieb	20 Aug 1839	Perouse	Leon.	bef 1867	France	837962
Gayring, Michael		Kuchen	Gsl.	Feb 1853	N.-Amer	572041
Gayring, Theodor		Kuchen	Gsl.	Feb 1853	N.-Amer	572041
Gebert, Lucas	1834	Winzeln	Obd.	Aug 1853	N.-Amer	841016
Geckeler, Bertha Catharina	23 Dec 1865	Unterhausen	Rtl.	Nov 1867	N.-Amer	841052
Geckeler, Catharina Barb. (wife)	22 Jun 1835	Unterhausen	Rtl.	Nov 1867	N.-Amer	841052
Geckeler, Clara	16 Nov 1858	Unterhausen	Rtl.	Nov 1867	N.-Amer	841052
Geckeler, Friedrich	23 Jan 1823	Holzelfingen	Rtl.	1833	N.-Amer	841052
Geckeler, Georg		Honau	Rtl.	May 1860	N.-Amer	841052
Geckeler, Jacob Michael	6 May 1845	Reutlingen	Rtl.	Sep 1863	N.-Amer	841052
Geckeler, Johann Heinrich	8 Dec 1860	Unterhausen	Rtl.	Nov 1867	N.-Amer	841052

Name		Birth		Emigration			Film
Last	First	Date	Place	O'amt	Appl. Date	Dest.	Number
Geckeler, Johann Stefan & F		9 Sep 1833	Unterhausen	Rtl.	Nov 1867	N.-Amer	841052
Geckeler, Ludwig		22 Dec 1828	Holzelfingen	Rtl.	1850	N.-Amer	841052
Geckeler, Maria Magdalena		28 Jul 1861	Reutlingen	Rtl.	May 1869	N.-Amer	841052
Geiger, Agatha			Treffelhausen	Loen.	May 1852	N.-Amer	572041
Geiger, Anna Catharina		21 Jun 1865	Owen	Krch.	Feb 1868	N.-Amer	835948
Geiger, Anna Maria			Aichelberg	Krch.	bef 1865	N.-Amer	835940
Geiger, Anna Maria		1 Feb 1860	Owen	Krch.	Feb 1868	N.-Amer	835948
Geiger, Anton		17 Feb 1833	Nenningen	Gsl.	Jan 1856	N.-Amer	572043
Geiger, Anton		7 Jan 1829	Treffelhausen	Gsl.	bef 1861	N.-Amer	572044
Geiger, Augustine Rosina		29 Aug 1850	Owen	Krch.	Feb 1868	N.-Amer	835948
Geiger, Bertha Kathar. Vero.		4 Dec 1881	Weil im Dorf	Loen.	Mar 1884	N.-Amer	837967
Geiger, Carl		23 May 1850	Kirchheim	Krch.	Apr 1865	N.-Amer	835941
Geiger, Catharina		18 Feb 1826	Lindorf	Krch.	Aug 1856	N.-Amer	835946
Geiger, Christian		5 Feb 1843	Dettingen	Krch.	Aug 1866	N.-Amer	835944
Geiger, Christiane Friederike		26 Jul 1861	Owen	Krch.	Feb 1868	N.-Amer	835948
Geiger, Dorothea		14 Sep 1841	Lindorf	Krch.	Oct 1867	Hannov.	835946
Geiger, Elisabetha		11 Feb 1833	Steinenkirch	Gsl.	Aug 1860	Austria	572044
Geiger, Florian		13 Aug 1847	Treffelhausen	Gsl.	Feb 1867	N.-Amer	572046
Geiger, Friedrich August		21 Nov 1842	Kirchheim	Krch.	Feb 1870	N.-Amer	835941
Geiger, Georg		20 Aug 1832	Lindorf	Krch.	Aug 1856	N.-Amer	835946
Geiger, Georg & F			Nenningen	Gsl.	Dec 1851	N.-Amer	577788
Geiger, Helena			Oberlenningen	Krch.	1854	N.-Amer	835940
Geiger, Johann Andreas		5 Feb 1853	Owen	Krch.	Feb 1868	N.-Amer	835948
Geiger, Johann Baptist & F			Alt Oberndorf	Obd.	Apr 1817	N.-Amer	838631
Geiger, Johann Friedrich		15 Mar 1864	Owen	Krch.	Feb 1868	N.-Amer	835948
Geiger, Johann Georg		22 Aug 1841	Aichelberg	Krch.	Jun 1855	N.-Amer	835774
Geiger, Johann Jacob		3 Jul 1852	Owen	Krch.	Feb 1868	N.-Amer	835948
Geiger, Johann Jacob & F		15 Dec 1826	Owen	Krch.	Feb 1868	N.-Amer	835948
Geiger, Johannes		24 Mar 1854	Owen	Krch.	Feb 1868	N.-Amer	835948
Geiger, Joseph		19 yrs.	Donzdorf	Gsl.	Mar 1852	N.-Amer	572041
Geiger, Joseph		19 yrs.	Boehmenkirch	Gsl.	Mar 1850	N.-Amer	577788
Geiger, Joseph		14 Jan 1847	Treffelhausen	Gsl.	Oct 1866	N.-Amer	572045
Geiger, Joseph & F			Treffelhausen	Loen.	May 1852	N.-Amer	572041
Geiger, Katharina & C		6 Oct 1860	Weil im Dorf	Loen.	Mar 1884	N.-Amer	837967
Geiger, Ludwig Wilhelm		2 Oct 1876	Eckwaelden	Krch.	Apr 1892	N.-Amer	835774
Geiger, Maria (wife)			Nenningen	Gsl.	Dec 1851	N.-Amer	577788
Geiger, Maria Dorothea (wife)		10 Oct 1828	Owen	Krch.	Feb 1868	N.-Amer	835948
Geiger, Theresia			Schramberg	Obd.	Oct 1853	N.-Amer	838636
Geiger, Wendelin		19 Oct 1836	Nenningen	Gsl.	Jan 1856	N.-Amer	572043
Geiger, Wendelin		27 Jun 1844	Treffelhausen	Gsl.	Sep 1869	N.-Amer	572047
Geiger, Wilhelm		27 Dec 1832	Betzweiler	Obd.	Sep 1852	N.-Amer	838631
Geiger, Wilhelm		27 May 1888	Zell	Krch.	Nov 1904	N.-Amer	835774
Geiger, Wilhelm Christian		19 Nov 1835	Kirchheim	Krch.	May 1859	N.-Amer	835940
Geigis, Hermann		20 Apr 1849	Schramberg	Obd.	Sep 1869	N.-Amer	838636
Geisel, Johann Jacob		28 Feb 1841	Pfullingen	Rtl.	Feb 1861	England	841052
Geisel, Maria Margaretha		29 Dec 1820	Pfullingen	Rtl.	bef 1861	N.-Amer	841052
Geiselhart, Katharina Barbara		30 Jul 1847	Oberhausen	Rtl.	Jul 1865	N.-Amer	841052
Geisert, Johann Gottfried		21 Feb 1849	Hoefingen	Leon.	Aug 1868	N.-Amer	837957
Geisler, Carl		26 yrs.	Reutlingen	Rtl.	Jun 1880	N.-Amer	841051
Geissel, Caroline		30 yrs.	Reutlingen	Rtl.	Jun 1880	N.-Amer	841051

Geissel, Michael	19 yrs.	Hemmingen	Leon.	Jul 1853	N.-Amer	837956
Geisselbrecht, Emil Lud. Fr.	4 Aug 1841	Pfullingen	Rtl.	bef 1868	N.-Amer	841052
Geissele, Carl Friedrich		Weil im Dorf	Loen.	bef 1854	Wien	837967
Geissele, Johann Georg	25 Feb 1864	Hoefingen	Leon.	May 1880	N.-Amer	837957
Geisselhardt, Katharina		Wimsheim	Loen.	Mar 1854	N.-Amer	837967
Geissler, Simon & F		Ditzingen	Leon.	Feb 1827	N.-Amer	835788
Geiwitz, Agnes		Kuchen	Gsl.	Jul 1858	France	572043
Geiwitz, Anna Katharina	14 Feb 1802	Kuchen	Gsl.	Feb 1854	N.-Amer	572042
Geiwitz, Anna Katharina	22 Jul 1847	Kuchen	Gsl.	Feb 1854	N.-Amer	572042
Geiwitz, Anna Maria	14 Jun 1845	Kuchen	Gsl.	Feb 1854	N.-Amer	572042
Geiwitz, Georg		Altenstadt-Gsl.	Gsl.	May 1854	N.-Amer	572042
Geiwitz, Georg & F	5 Feb 1817	Kuchen	Gsl.	Feb 1854	N.-Amer	572042
Geiwitz, Jakob	1 Jul 1843	Kuchen	Gsl.	Feb 1854	N.-Amer	572042
Geiwitz, Johann Georg	1 Apr 1842	Kuchen	Gsl.	Feb 1854	N.-Amer	572042
Geiwitz, Walburga (wife)	11 Oct 1819	Kuchen	Gsl.	Feb 1854	N.-Amer	572042
Geiwiz, Anna Barbara (wife)		Kuchen	Gsl.	Apr 1858	N.-Amer	572043
Geiwiz, Michael	45 yrs.	Kuchen	Gsl.	Mar 1857	N.-Amer	572043
Gengenbach, Catharina Elisab.	26 Oct 1826	Kuppingen	Herr.	Jun 1864	N.-Amer	834630
Gengenbach, Johannes	13 Jul 1807	Bondorf	Herr.	bef 1865	N.-Amer	834630
Genter, Christian Gottlob	19 Mar 1857	Leonberg	Leon.	Jul 1873	N.-Amer	835787
Genthner, Jonathan		Friolzheim	Leon.	Jan 1852	Hungary	835791
Gentner, Amalie	20 Nov 1828	Leonberg	Leon.	May 1852	N.-Amer	835786
Gentner, Carl David	2 Jun 1823	Leonberg	Leon.	bef 1855	N.-Amer	835786
Gentner, Carl Max	9 Jan 1861	Kirchheim	Krch.	Dec 1877	N.-Amer	548403
Gentner, Catharina Dorothea		Leonberg	Leon.	Jun 1857	Switz.	835786
Gentner, Christian Carl	19 Jul 1836	Kirchheim	Krch.	Mar 1855	N.-Amer	835940
Gentner, Christiane	17 yrs.	Hoefingen	Leon.	Mar 1849	N.-Amer	837957
Gentner, Christiane (wife)		Hoefingen	Leon.	Mar 1849	N.-Amer	837957
Gentner, Eberhardine (wife)		Leonberg	Leon.	Apr 1855	N.-Amer	835786
Gentner, Ernst	16 Apr 1865	Kirchheim	Krch.	May 1882	N.-Amer	548403
Gentner, Ernst Friedrich	15 May 1844	Leonberg	Leon.	Apr 1855	N.-Amer	835786
Gentner, Friedrich	infant	Hoefingen	Leon.	Mar 1849	N.-Amer	837957
Gentner, Friedrich & F		Leonberg	Leon.	Apr 1855	N.-Amer	835786
Gentner, Friedrich David	27 Oct 1850	Leonberg	Leon.	Jan 1870	N.-Amer	835787
Gentner, Friedrich Heinrich	19 yrs.	Leonberg	Leon.	May 1853	N.-Amer	835786
Gentner, Gottfried Eberhard	10 Mar 1847	Leonberg	Leon.	Apr 1855	N.-Amer	835786
Gentner, Gotthilf	10 Oct 1857	Leonberg	Leon.	Apr 1872	N.-Amer	835787
Gentner, Gottlieb		Leonberg	Leon.	Jul 1857	N.-Amer	835786
Gentner, Gottlieb	11 yrs.	Hoefingen	Leon.	Mar 1849	N.-Amer	837957
Gentner, Gottlob		Malmsheim	Leon.	May 1827	Prussia	837958
Gentner, Heinrich David	10 Mar 1851	Leonberg	Leon.	Mar 1870	N.-Amer	835787
Gentner, Immanuel Friedrich	30 Jan 1827	Herrenberg	Herr.	bef 1865	Berlin	834629
Gentner, Jakob Heinrich	11 Jun 1842	Leonberg	Leon.	Apr 1855	N.-Amer	835786
Gentner, Johann Christian	14 yrs.	Hoefingen	Leon.	Mar 1849	N.-Amer	837957
Gentner, Johannes	27 Nov 1846	Leonberg	Leon.	May 1869	N.-Amer	835787
Gentner, Johannes & F		Hoefingen	Leon.	Mar 1849	N.-Amer	837957
Gentner, Johannes Carl	8 yrs.	Hoefingen	Leon.	Mar 1849	N.-Amer	837957
Gentner, Louise	14 yrs.	Leonberg	Leon.	Sep 1853	N.-Amer	835786
Gentner, Maria Catharina	24 May 1837	Weilheim	Krch.	bef 1855	N.-Amer	835940
Gentner, Samuel Gotthilf	27 Feb 1855	Leonberg	Leon.	Apr 1855	N.-Amer	835786

Name		Birth		Emigration			Film
Last	First	Date	Place	O'amt	Appl. Date	Dest.	Number
Gentner, Wilhelm		infant	Hoefingen	Leon.	Mar 1849	N.-Amer	837957
Gerber, Otto Carl		13 Jan 1860	Rottweil	Krch.	bef 1889	Hamburg	835949
Gerlach, Barbara			Betzingen	Rtl.	Mar 1834	N.-Amer	841051
Gerlach, Christian		22 Jun 1836	Herrenberg	Herr.	May 1865	N.-Amer	834629
Gerlach, Christian		17 Jan 1844	Grosssuessen	Gsl.	Apr 1864	N.-Amer	572045
Gerlach, Dorothea Friederike		11 Mar 1851	Grosssuessen	Gsl.	Feb 1854	N.-Amer	572042
Gerlach, Jakob Heinrich & F		18 Jan 1817	Grosssuessen	Gsl.	Feb 1854	N.-Amer	572042
Gerlach, Maria Ursula (wife)		24 Oct 1808	Grosssuessen	Gsl.	Feb 1854	N.-Amer	572042
Gerst, Johannes		2 Oct 1846	Alpirsbach	Obd.	Apr 1866	N.-Amer	838630
Gerst, Wilhelm		28 Jun 1847	Alpirsbach	Obd.	Sep 1866	N.-Amer	838630
Gerster, Bernhardt		20 Jul 1828	Schramberg	Obd.	Apr 1858	Prussia	838636
Gerstmann, Jacobine			Kirchheim	Krch.	Apr 1866	N.-Amer	835941
Gerstner, Friedrich		15 May 1843	Kirchheim	Krch.	Jan 1865	N.-Amer	835941
Gerstner, Valentin		9 Dec 1836	Winzeln	Obd.	Sep 1854	N.-Amer	841016
Gertmann, Magdalena		28 Jan 1833	Deggingen	Gsl.	Sep 1857	N.-Amer	572043
Gessler, Anna Maria		25 Jul 1824	Ehlenbogen	Obd.	Sep 1854	N.-Amer	838632
Gessler, Johann Friedrich		10 Jun 1827	Bochingen	Obd.	Sep 1852	N.-Amer	838632
Gesswein, Albert Friedrich		9 Oct 1851	Leonberg	Leon.	Jan 1870	N.-Amer	835787
Gesswein, Gottlob Christoph		14 Mar 1856	Leonberg	Leon.	Sep 1874	N.-Amer	835787
Geyer, Gottlieb		10 Aug 1851	Oetlingen	Krch.	Apr 1870	N.-Amer	835948
Geywitz, Johannes		3 Oct 1845	Altenstadt-Gsl.	Gsl.	Feb 1864	N.-Amer	572045
Geywitz, Magdalena		23 Dec 1833	Kuchen	Gsl.	Mar 1864	France	572045
Geywitz, Ursula			Kuchen	Gsl.	Sep 1866	N.-Amer	572045
Gicken, Christina Catharina			Schoeckingen	Leon.	bef 1839	N.-Amer	837964
Gieck, Christiane			Hemmingen	Leon.	Aug 1853	N.-Amer	837956
Gieck, Johannes		23 yrs.	Hemmingen	Leon.	Jan 1852	N.-Amer	837956
Gienger, Christian		2 Jan 1868	Weilheim	Krch.	Jun 1883	Austral	548403
Gienger, Elisabetha		28 Jul 1829	Weilheim	Krch.	Apr 1857	N.-Amer	835949
Gienger, Friedrich		16 Apr 1868	Weilheim	Krch.	Jan 1884	N.-Amer	548403
Gienger, Johann Georg		18 Aug 1865	Weilheim	Krch.	Jan 1882	N.-Amer	548403
Gienger, Johann Jakob		16 Jan 1843	Neidlingen	Krch.	Jan 1860	N.-Amer	835946
Gienger, Johann Jakob		25 Oct 1838	Neidlingen	Krch.	May 1857	N.-Amer	835946
Gienger, Johannes		6 Nov 1869	Weilheim	Krch.	Aug 1886	N.-Amer	835774
Gienger, Johannes Bernhard		9 Feb 1845	Neidlingen	Krch.	Sep 1866	N.-Amer	835946
Giesser, Johann Heinrich		2 Nov 1827	Reutlingen	Rtl.	bef 1869	N.-Amer	841052
Ginger, Andreas		17 Nov 1833	Hepsisau	Krch.	Aug 1849	N.-Amer	835945
Ginger, Anna Margar. (wife)		9 Aug 1799	Hepsisau	Krch.	Aug 1849	N.-Amer	835945
Ginger, Catharina		27 Dec 1828	Hepsisau	Krch.	Dec 1853	N.-Amer	835945
Ginger, Georg		6 May 1825	Hepsisau	Krch.	Aug 1849	N.-Amer	835945
Ginger, Georg & F		4 Mar 1798	Hepsisau	Krch.	Aug 1949	N.-Amer	835945
Ginger, Jakob		11 Dec 1826	Hepsisau	Krch.	Aug 1849	N.-Amer	835945
Ginter, Hermann		24 Oct 1841	Hochmoessingen	Obd.	Jul 1870	Prussia	838634
Ginter, Michael & F			Sulgen	Obd.	May 1817	N.-Amer	838638
Girbach, Michael & F		40 yrs.	Enztal	Nag.	Dec 1850	N.-Amer	838488
Girk, Katharina			Gebersheim	Leon.	May 1805	Russia	837953
Glaathaar, Wendelin			Waldmoessingen	Obd.	Apr 1862	N.-Amer	841015
Glaser, Andreas			Weil im Dorf	Loen.	1854	N.-Amer	837967
Glaser, Andreas		12 Jul 1849	Weil im Dorf	Loen.	Mar 1853	N.-Amer	837967
Glaser, Carl Gottlob		14 Jun 1862	Weil im Dorf	Loen.	May 1864	N.-Amer	837967
Glaser, Caroline Barbara (wife)		20 Jun 1842	Weil im Dorf	Loen.	May 1864	N.-Amer	837967

Glaser, Catharina	4 yrs.	Weil im Dorf	Loen.	Aug 1853	N.-Amer	837967
Glaser, Christian & W		Weil im Dorf	Loen.	Mar 1853	N.-Amer	837967
Glaser, Dorothea (wife)		Weil im Dorf	Loen.	Mar 1853	N.-Amer	837967
Glaser, Eberhard Ferdinand & F	30 Dec 1832	Weil im Dorf	Loen.	May 1864	N.-Amer	837967
Glaser, Emilie	2 yrs.	Weil im Dorf	Loen.	Aug 1853	N.-Amer	837967
Glaser, Gottlieb		Weil im Dorf	Loen.	1853	N.-Amer	837967
Glaser, Johann Jacob & F		Weil im Dorf	Loen.	Aug 1853	N.-Amer	837967
Glaser, Louise & C	25 yrs.	Weil im Dorf	Loen.	Mar 1853	N.-Amer	837967
Glaser, Marie Christiane	2 Jan 1864	Weil im Dorf	Loen.	May 1864	N.-Amer	837967
Glatthaar, Franz Joseph	19 yrs.	Beffendorf	Obd.	May 1853	N.-Amer	838631
Glatthaar, Johannes	13 May 1824	Beffendorf	Obd.	Apr 1857	N.-Amer	838631
Glatthaar, Johannes	28 Dec 1849	Seedorf	Obd.	Nov 1866	N.-Amer	838637
Glatthaar, Joseph	5 Aug 1847	Hochmoessingen	Obd.	Mar 1869	N.-Amer	838633
Glatthaar, Lorenz		Waldmoessingen	Obd.	May 1846	N.-Amer	841015
Glatthaar, Lorenz & F		Beffendorf	Obd.	Aug 1817	N.-Amer	838631
Glatthaar, Ludwig		Beffendorf	Obd.	Aug 1817	N.-Amer	838631
Glatz, Johannes	31 Mar 1837	Hardt	Obd.	Jan 1859	N.-Amer	838633
Glatz, Magdalena	5 Mar 1834	Hardt	Obd.	Jan 1859	N.-Amer	838633
Glatz, Magdalena (wid.) & F	6 Jun 1812	Hardt	Obd.	Jan 1859	N.-Amer	838633
Glatz, Michael	3 Jun 1848	Hardt	Obd.	Jan 1859	N.-Amer	838633
Glatzle, Joseph Imanuel	6 Jul 1854	Warmbronn	Leon.	bef 1888	N.-Amer	837965
Gleisner, Johann August		Merklingen	Leon.	Jul 1841	N.-Amer	837959
Glenz, Ferdinand	3 Oct 1846	Schramberg	Obd.	Sep 1863	N.-Amer	838636
Glenz, Johannes	34 yrs.	Schramberg	Obd.	Apr 1840	Austria	838637
Gloekle, Johann Georg	14 yrs.	Unterboehringen	Gsl.	Nov 1866	N.-Amer	572045
Gloekle, Johannes	16 yrs.	Unterboehringen	Gsl.	Aug 1868	N.-Amer	572046
Glos, Adam	19 Jun 1830	Moensheim	Leon.	Apr 1850	N.-Amer	837960
Glos, Anna Maria (wife)		Moensheim	Leon.	Apr 1856	N.-Amer	837960
Glos, Christian	3 Jul 1834	Moensheim	Leon.	Mar 1854	N.-Amer	837960
Glos, Dorothea	16 Sep 1846	Moensheim	Leon.	Apr 1856	N.-Amer	837960
Glos, Johann Georg & F		Moensheim	Leon.	Apr 1856	N.-Amer	837960
Glos, Johannes	19 Apr 1849	Moensheim	Leon.	Apr 1856	N.-Amer	837960
Gloss, Johann Georg	8 Feb 1828	Weil im Dorf	Loen.	1850	N.-Amer	837967
Glueck, Johann Christian	1 Mar 1854	Oetlingen	Krch.	Oct 1871	N.-Amer	835948
Glueck, Johann Georg	30 Sep 1844	Holzelfingen	Rtl.	Oct 1866	N.-Amer	841052
Glueck, Karl Friedrich	25 Nov 1850	Oetlingen	Krch.	Oct 1866	N.-Amer	835948
Gluek, Maria Regina	10 yrs.	Merklingen	Leon.	Apr 1852	N.-Amer	837959
Gluek, Regina & F		Merklingen	Leon.	Apr 1852	N.-Amer	837959
Glunk, Alois	17 Jun 1833	Winzeln	Obd.	Sep 1853	N.-Amer	841016
Glunk, Balthasar	6 Jan 1852	Seedorf	Obd.	Apr 1870	N.-Amer	838637
Gmaehle, Jakob Friedrich & W	20 Dec 1824	Perouse	Leon.	Jan 1852	N.-Amer	837962
Gmaehle, Lorenz	19 Aug 1832	Perouse	Leon.	Jan 1852	N.-Amer	837962
Gmaehle, Susanna (wife)	23 Jan 1825	Perouse	Leon.	Jan 1852	N.-Amer	837962
Gmelin, Adolf Gustav Wilh.	1 Nov 1849	Pfullingen	Rtl.	Apr 1867	N.-Amer	841052
Gminder, Carl Wilhelm	8 Nov 1836	Reutlingen	Rtl.	bef 1862	N.-Amer	841052
Gminder, Gotthilf Heinrich	16 Dec 1834	Reutlingen	Rtl.	bef 1861	N.-Amer	841052
Gminder, Johann Jacob	24 Apr 1831	Reutlingen	Rtl.	Feb 1864	N.-Amer	841052
Gminder, Karl		Reutlingen	Rtl.	bef 1868	N.-Amer	841052
Gneiding, Karl	15 Jun 1871	Esslingen	Krch.	Jul 1888	N.-Amer	835944
Gochner, Anna	31 yrs.	Reutlingen	Rtl.	Apr 1880	N.-Amer	841051

Name		Birth		Emigration			Film
Last	First	Date	Place	O'amt	Appl. Date	Dest.	Number
Gockele, Johann Georg		9 Mar 1867	Dettingen	Krch.	Jun 1881	N.-Amer	548403
Gockeler, Christian		24 Oct 1864	Boehmenkirch	Gsl.	Apr 1881	N.-Amer	572048
Gockeler, Christian Gottlieb		5 Sep 1834	Renningen	Leon.	Mar 1854	N.-Amer	837963
Gockeler, Georg Jakob		2 May 1832	Renningen	Leon.	Jan 1852	N.-Amer	837963
Godel, Catharina Margaretha		23 Apr 1841	Weil im Dorf	Loen.	1855	N.-Amer	837967
Godel, Georg			Weil im Dorf	Loen.	bef 1855	N.-Amer	837967
Godel, Gottlieb Andreas		26 Jun 1822	Weil im Dorf	Loen.	Jan 1848	N.-Amer	837967
Godel, Louise Margaretha		22 Nov 1847	Weil im Dorf	Loen.	1855	N.-Amer	837967
Godel, Ludwig		27 yrs.	Weil im Dorf	Loen.	bef 1856	N.-Amer	837967
Godel, Maria Rosine		30 Jun 1844	Weil im Dorf	Loen.	1855	N.-Amer	837967
Godel, Rosine (wife) & F			Weil im Dorf	Loen.	1855	N.-Amer	837967
Goebel, Gottlob			Reutlingen	Rtl.	May 1860	N.-Amer	841052
Goebel, Gustav Adolf		19 yrs.	Reutlingen	Rtl.	Jun 1880	N.-Amer	841051
Goebel, Paul Anton		30 Jun 1853	Reutlingen	Rtl.	Aug 1867	N.-Amer	841052
Goeckeler, Anna Maria		52 yrs.	Dettingen	Krch.	Jul 1858	N.-Amer	835944
Goefer, Barbara		6 yrs.	Wiesensteig	Gsl.	Aug 1851	N.-Amer	577788
Goefer, Josefa & C			Wiesensteig	Gsl.	Aug 1851	N.-Amer	577788
Goefer, Wilhelm		6 mon.	Wiesensteig	Gsl.	Aug 1851	N.-Amer	577788
Goeft, Joseph Friedrich		20 Feb 1843	Kirchheim	Krch.	Aug 1869	Hamburg	835941
Goeggelmann, Johann Thomas		17 Mar 1823	Eybach	Gsl.	May 1853	N.-Amer	572041
Goehring, Carl Heinr. Lud. W.		24 Dec 1840	Leonberg	Leon.	Jul 1860	N.-Amer	835786
Goehring, Christiana Dorothea		15 Aug 1846	Owen	Krch.	bef 1873	N.-Amer	835948
Goehring, Friedrich		15 Jul 1854	Leonberg	Leon.	Jun 1871	N.-Amer	835787
Goehring, Johann Andreas		25 Aug 1835	Owen	Krch.	Mar 1860	N.-Amer	835948
Goehring, Johann Samuel		27 Sep 1842	Owen	Krch.	Mar 1860	N.-Amer	835948
Goekeler, Augustina Cath. (wife)		24 Mar 1828	Brucken	Krch.	May 1869	N.-Amer	835944
Goekeler, Augustina Catharina		24 Feb 1861	Brucken	Krch.	May 1869	N.-Amer	835944
Goekeler, Christine Frieder.		16 Aug 1862	Brucken	Krch.	May 1869	N.-Amer	835944
Goekeler, Friedrich		26 Jul 1867	Brucken	Krch.	May 1869	N.-Amer	835944
Goekeler, Johannes & F		13 Jun 1837	Brucken	Krch.	May 1869	N.-Amer	835944
Goelz, Anna Margaretha		27 Dec 1827	Weilheim	Krch.	bef 1868	N.-Amer	835950
Goelz, Barbara		15 May 1831	Bissingen	Krch.	bef 1862	N.-Amer	835943
Goelz, Catharina			Gingen	Gsl.	bef 1863	N.-Amer	572044
Goelz, Christian Gottlieb		24 Jan 1867	Bissingen	Krch.	Oct 1881	N.-Amer	835943
Goelz, Friedrich		27 Apr 1875	Pliensbach	Krch.	May 1891	N.-Amer	835774
Goelz, Johann Christoph		20 Jan 1822	Weilheim	Krch.	Jun 1868	N.-Amer	835950
Goelz, Johann Georg		23 Jul 1876	Eckwaelden	Krch.	Apr 1892	N.-Amer	835774
Goelz, Johann Jacob		13 Mar 1851	Nabern	Krch.	bef 1888	N.-Amer	835946
Goelz, Johann Kaspar & F		29 May 1840	Bissingen	Krch.	1883	N.-Amer	835943
Goelz, Johann Konrad		27 May 1830	Unterboehringen	Gsl.	May 1854	N.-Amer	572042
Goelz, Johanna Friederika		29 Jan 1866	Bissingen	Krch.	1883	N.-Amer	835943
Goelz, Johannes		1 Jan 1822	Gingen	Gsl.	bef 1863	N.-Amer	572044
Goelz, Johannes		17 Dec 1864	Bissingen	Krch.	Oct 1881	N.-Amer	835943
Goelz, Johannes		11 Dec 1870	Bissingen	Krch.	1883	N.-Amer	835943
Goelz, Michael		18 Jun 1828	Gingen	Gsl.	bef 1863	N.-Amer	572044
Goelz, Regina (wife)		2 Sep 1842	Bissingen	Krch.	1883	N.-Amer	835943
Goeppinger, Johann Gottfried		21 Jul 1800	Reutlingen	Rtl.	bef 1861	N.-Amer	841052
Goerlach, Daniel		23 Oct 1846	Betzingen	Rtl.	Jun 1866	N.-Amer	841052
Goerner, Sebastian Bernhard		20 Aug 1805	Muehlhausen	Gsl.	Feb 1854	N.-Amer	572042
Goeser, Otto		27 May 1849	Schnittling	Gsl.	Feb 1869	N.-Amer	572047

Goesser, Joseph	37 yrs.	Drackenstein	Gsl.	Feb 1853	N.-Amer	572041
Goetz, – (wid.)	2 Mar 1808	Lindorf	Krch.	Aug 1856	N.-Amer	835946
Goetz, Anna	22 Aug 1835	Pfullingen	Rtl.	Jan 1867	N.-Amer	841052
Goetz, August Alfred	5 Aug 1868	Lindorf	Krch.	Apr 1884	N.-Amer	548403
Goetz, Carl Heinrich	2 Sep 1866	Lindorf	Krch.	Mar 1883	N.-Amer	548403
Goetz, Christian	8 Mar 1850	Pfullingen	Rtl.	Apr 1867	N.-Amer	841052
Goetz, Christian	2 Jun 1825	Jesingen	Krch.	Aug 1857	N.-Amer	835946
Goetz, Friedericka	16 Oct 1829	Pfullingen	Rtl.	May 1860	N.-Amer	841052
Goetz, Friedrich	9 Dec 1850	Lindorf	Krch.	Apr 1870	N.-Amer	835946
Goetz, Johann David	13 Jan 1837	Lindorf	Krch.	Aug 1856	N.-Amer	835946
Goetz, Johann Georg	18 Jul 1849	Nabern	Krch.	Jul 1869	N.-Amer	835946
Goetz, Karl Heinrich	3 Sep 1866	Lindorf	Krch.	Feb 1883	N.-Amer	835946
Goetz, Magdalena	11 May 1832	Pfullingen	Rtl.	bef 1859	N.-Amer	841052
Goetz, Maria		Pfullingen	Rtl.	Feb 1862	Switz.	841052
Goetz, Martin		Betzingen	Rtl.	bef 1867	N.-Amer	841052
Goetz, Pauline	9 Apr 1863	Lindorf	Krch.	Apr 1881	N.-Amer	835946
Goez, Christian Rudolf (wid.)	12 Feb 1812	Nabern	Krch.	Feb 1866	N.-Amer	835946
Goez, Eva	13 Jun 1832	Dettingen	Krch.	bef 1855	N.-Amer	835944
Goez, Jacob		Betzingen	Rtl.	Sep 1830	Austria	841051
Goez, Johann Georg	19 yrs.	Hemmingen	Leon.	Jul 1853	N.-Amer	837956
Goll, Carl	12 Oct 1859	Weilheim	Krch.	Aug 1873	N.-Amer	548403
Goll, Christiane Auguste	10 Dec 1858	Weilheim	Krch.	Feb 1870	N.-Amer	835950
Goll, Cordula	8 Dec 1820	Weilheim	Krch.	bef 1858	N.-Amer	835949
Goll, Elisabetha	24 Dec 1849	Bissingen	Krch.	May 1867	N.-Amer	835943
Goll, Elisabetha Friederika	14 Mar 1849	Alpirsbach	Obd.	Sep 1869	Bavaria	838630
Goll, Friedrich	15 Dec 1866	Weilheim	Krch.	Apr 1882	N.-Amer	835774
Goll, Heinrich	12 Sep 1857	Weilheim	Krch.	Aug 1873	N. Amer	548403
Goll, Jakob	9 Sep 1867	Kuchen	Gsl.	May 1883	N.-Amer	572049
Goll, Johann Christian	20 May 1849	Weilheim	Krch.	Sep 1866	N.-Amer	835950
Goll, Johann Cunrad	7 Feb 1834	Bissingen	Krch.	Apr 1858	N.-Amer	835943
Goll, Johann Georg	16 Nov 1825	Weilheim	Krch.	May 1864	N.-Amer	835950
Goll, Karl Joh. Heinrich	28 Oct 1871	Weilheim	Krch.	Feb 1888	N.-Amer	835774
Goll, Magdalena		Kuchen	Gsl.	Mar 1867	Switz.	572046
Goll, Magdalena	31 Aug 1848	Bissingen	Krch.	bef 1869	Switz.	835943
Goll, Tobias	20 Nov 1834	Kuchen	Gsl.	Jan 1854	N.-Amer	572042
Goll, Tobias	23 Jul 1865	Kuchen	Gsl.	May 1883	N.-Amer	572049
Gollmer, Christian Hugo	25 May 1811	Kirchheim	Krch.	Mar 1860	N.-Amer	835940
Gollmer, Gebhard & F	30 yrs.	Unterlenningen	Krch.	Jun 1804	Russia	550804
Gollmer, Gottlieb	15 Oct 1844	Oberlenningen	Krch.	Jun 1864	N.-Amer	835947
Gollmer, Johann Albrecht	5 yrs.	Unterlenningen	Krch.	Jun 1804	Russia	550804
Gollmer, Johann Jakob	24 Jan 1844	Oberlenningen	Krch.	Oct 1866	N.-Amer	835947
Gollmer, Johanna Dorothea	2 yrs.	Unterlenningen	Krch.	Jun 1804	Russia	550804
Gollmer, Maria Catrina (wife)	32 yrs.	Unterlenningen	Krch.	Jun 1804	Russia	550804
Gols, Johann Georg	1 Apr 1843	Moensheim	Leon.	Apr 1856	N.-Amer	837960
Gommel, Caroline Friederike	8 Jul 1866	Flacht	Leon.	Dec 1872	N.-Amer	835790
Gommel, Christian Friedrich	17 yrs.	Flacht	Leon.	Aug 1852	N.-Amer	835790
Gommel, Eugen Heinrich	31 Jul 1873	Leonberg	Leon.	Jul 1889	N.-Amer	835787
Gommel, Friedrich August	25 May 1850	Leonberg	Leon.	Dec 1870	N.-Amer	835787
Gommels, Carl		Schoeckingen	Leon.	Mar 1821	France	837964
Gommer, Wilhelm	17 yrs.	Reutlingen	Rtl.	Jun 1880	N.-Amer	841051

Name		Birth		Emigration			Film
Last	First	Date	Place	O'amt	Appl. Date	Dest.	Number
Gotl, Katharina		26 Jul 1824	Bissingen	Krch.	Oct 1866	Switz.	835943
Gottschalk, Georg Julius		19 Oct 1858	Heimsheim	Leon.	Aug 1881	N.-Amer	837955
Graeter, Anna		26 Nov 1884	Brucken	Krch.	Aug 1889	N.-Amer	835944
Graeter, Carl		15 Jul 1846	Oberlenningen	Krch.	Jan 1870	N.-Amer	835947
Graeter, Christian		2 May 1873	Oberlenningen	Krch.	Aug 1889	N.-Amer	835947
Graeter, Ernst Gottlob		11 Sep 1880	Brucken	Krch.	Aug 1889	N.-Amer	835944
Graeter, Gottlieb		5 Apr 1851	Oberlenningen	Krch.	Jan 1870	N.-Amer	835947
Graeter, Gottlieb		27 Jun 1839	Oberlenningen	Krch.	Jun 1866	N.-Amer	835947
Graeter, Gottlieb Eberhardt		18 Sep 1866	Oberlenningen	Krch.	Aug 1883	N.-Amer	548403
Graeter, Gottlieb Friedrich		9 Oct 1877	Oberlenningen	Krch.	Aug 1889	N.-Amer	835947
Graeter, Gottlob Friedrich & F		25 Jan 1854	Brucken	Krch.	Aug 1889	N.-Amer	835944
Graeter, Johann Georg		31 Dec 1816	Oberlenningen	Krch.	Jan 1867	N.-Amer	835947
Graeter, Johanna		19 Jun 1882	Brucken	Krch.	Aug 1889	N.-Amer	835944
Graeter, Johanna Doroth. (wife)		9 Jun 1856	Brucken	Krch.	Aug 1889	N.-Amer	835944
Graeter, Johannes & F		5 Sep 1841	Oberlenningen	Krch.	Aug 1889	N.-Amer	835947
Graeter, Karl		19 May 1847	Oberlenningen	Krch.	Oct 1866	N.-Amer	835947
Graeter, Karl Friedrich		19 May 1879	Brucken	Krch.	Aug 1889	N.-Amer	835944
Graeter, Karl Gottlieb		15 Jan 1875	Oberlenningen	Krch.	Aug 1889	N.-Amer	835947
Graeter, Karoline (wife)		25 May 1848	Oberlenningen	Krch.	Aug 1889	N.-Amer	835947
Graeter, Maria Sophie		4 Sep 1887	Brucken	Krch.	Aug 1889	N.-Amer	835944
Graeter, Paulina		2 Nov 1837	Oberlenningen	Krch.	May 1860	N.-Amer	835947
Graeter, Regina Katharina		19 Oct 1867	Oberlenningen	Krch.	Apr 1881	N.-Amer	835947
Graeter, Wilhelmine Karoline		17 Jun 1885	Oberlenningen	Krch.	Aug 1889	N.-Amer	835947
Graf, Andreas			Betzweiler	Obd.	Mar 1849	N.-Amer	838631
Graf, Andreas		21 Sep 1849	Peterzell	Obd.	bef 1856	N.-Amer	838635
Graf, Anna Maria (wife)		19 Feb 1808	Dottenweiler	Obd.	May 1847	N.-Amer	838631
Graf, Christina		15 Jul 1831	Dottenweiler	Obd.	May 1847	N.-Amer	838631
Graf, Gottlieb		30 Jan 1842	Betzweiler	Obd.	Apr 1856	N.-Amer	838631
Graf, Jacob			Winzeln	Obd.	1847	N.-Amer	841016
Graf, Johannes			Harthausen	Obd.	Jul 1854	N.-Amer	838633
Graf, Johannes		18 yrs.	Merklingen	Leon.	Feb 1854	N.-Amer	837959
Graf, Josef		17 Mar 1832	Seedorf	Obd.	Feb 1852	N.-Amer	838637
Graf, Konstantin		17 May 1833	Harthausen	Obd.	Sep 1853	N.-Amer	838633
Graf, Matthias		1 Mar 1847	Peterzell	Obd.	May 1862	N.-Amer	838635
Graf, Sophie			Aichhalden	Obd.	Aug 1853	N.-Amer	838629
Grall, Christian Friedrich			Malmsheim	Leon.	bef 1862	N.-Amer	837958
Grall, Friedrich Wilhelm		27 Oct 1863	Malmsheim	Leon.	Oct 1880	N.-Amer	837958
Grall, Gabriel		27 Oct 1863	Malmsheim	Leon.	Oct 1880	N.-Amer	837958
Grall, Jacob F.			Malmsheim	Leon.	Feb 1865	N.-Amer	837958
Grall, Johann Jakob		20 Jan 1854	Malmsheim	Leon.	Dec 1882	N.-Amer	837958
Grall, Karl Friedrich		8 Apr 1833	Malmsheim	Leon.	Apr 1867	N.-Amer	837958
Gramann, Conrad			Weiler	Krch.	May 1862	N.-Amer	835949
Gramer, Georg Friedrich			Gerlingen	Leon.	Oct 1845	Switz.	837953
Graner, Carl		1 Sep 1865	Oberlenningen	Krch.	Mar 1882	N.-Amer	548403
Graner, Christian		15 Jul 1874	Oberlenningen	Krch.	Jun 1890	N.-Amer	835947
Graner, Jakob Friedrich		18 Jul 1867	Notzingen	Krch.	Jun 1881	N.-Amer	548403
Graner, Johann Michael		18 Jul 1867	Notzingen	Krch.	Jun 1881	N.-Amer	835947
Graner, Karl		1 Sep 1865	Oberlenningen	Krch.	Feb 1882	N.-Amer	835947
Graninger, Margaretha		14 Dec 1844	Kuchen	Gsl.	Sep 1866	N.-Amer	572045
Grathwohl, Andreas		20 yrs.	Roemlinsdorf	Obd.	Apr 1849	N.-Amer	838635

Grathwohl, Martin		Roemlinsdorf	Obd.	Sep 1860	N.-Amer	838635
Gratwohl, Julie		Reutlingen	Rtl.	Jan 1862	Switz.	841052
Grau, Christian Ludwig	30 Apr 1857	Ohmden	Krch.	Jun 1873	N.-Amer	835948
Grau, Maria Catharina	15 Sep 1849	Ohmden	Krch.	May 1869	N.-Amer	835948
Graze, Carolina Barbara (wife)		Heimsheim	Leon.	Sep 1853	N.-Amer	837955
Graze, Christian		Weil der Stadt	Leon.	Jul 1854	N.-Amer	837966
Graze, Georg Heinrich & F		Heimsheim	Leon.	Sep 1853	N.-Amer	837955
Graze, Paul Friedrich	18 yrs.	Heimsheim	Leon.	Sep 1853	N.-Amer	837955
Greb, Andreas		Friolzheim	Leon.	Oct 1845	Switz.	835791
Greb, Andreas		Friolzheim	Leon.	bef 1844	Switz.	835791
Greb, Catharina	27 Dec 1824	Friolzheim	Leon.	Apr 1848	Switz.	835791
Greb, Tobias		Friolzheim	Leon.	Mar 1845	Switz.	835791
Greb, Wilhelm	31 Jan 1818	Friolzheim	Leon.	Feb 1842	Switz.	835791
Greb, Wilhelm	31 Jan 1818	Friolzheim	Leon.	Apr 1844	Switz.	835791
Greiner, Albert	16 Oct 1849	Oberndorf	Obd.	Jan 1868	N.-Amer	838635
Greiner, Christian	May 1835	Oberndorf	Obd.	Apr 1854	N.-Amer	838635
Greiner, Christiana Fr. (wife)		Flacht	Leon.	bef 1865	N.-Amer	835790
Greiner, Gustav	8 Jul 1844	Kirchheim	Krch.	Jan 1864	N.-Amer	835941
Greiner, Jakob & F		Flacht	Leon.	bef 1865	N.-Amer	835790
Greiner, Johann Andreas	3 Nov 1844	Owen	Krch.	Jul 1868	N.-Amer	835948
Greiner, Johannes	7 Dec 1836	Oberndorf	Obd.	Apr 1854	N.-Amer	838635
Greiner, Johannes	19 Jan 1878	Zell	Krch.	May 1891	N.-Amer	835774
Greiner, Johannes	23 Aug 1870	Bissingen	Krch.	Jul 1887	N.-Amer	835943
Greiner, Karl Adolf	18 Apr 1867	Hepsisau	Krch.	Jul 1883	N.-Amer	548403
Greiner, Mathaeus	20 Nov 1824	Ohmden	Krch.	May 1860	N.-Amer	835948
Grieser, Anton	26 Jun 1850	Boehmenkirch	Gsl.	Mar 1868	N.-Amer	572046
Grieser, Johann Ignaz	18 Apr 1850	Boehmenkirch	Gsl.	Feb 1867	N.-Amer	572046
Grieshaber, Johann Ludwig	16 Oct 1842	Hemmingen	Leon.	bef 1866	N.-Amer	837956
Grieshaber, Severin		Lauterbach	Obd.	Aug 1849	N.-Amer	838634
Grimm, Franz	4 Oct 1827	Epfendorf	Obd.	Dec 1866	N.-Amer	838632
Grob, Johann Jakob		Warmbronn	Leon.	bef 1860	Austria	837965
Groeder, Franziska	9 Dec 1827	Weil der Stadt	Leon.	Mar 1848	N.-Amer	837965
Groetzinger, Catharina	2 Oct 1836	Muenchingen	Leon.	Jan 1857	N.-Amer	837961
Groetzinger, Ernst Gottlob	10 Oct 1869	Renningen	Leon.	May 1887	N.-Amer	837963
Groezinger, Andreas	1 yr.	Betzweiler	Obd.	Jun 1848	N.-Amer	838631
Groezinger, Anna Maria & C	17 Apr 1816	Betzweiler	Obd.	Jun 1848	N.-Amer	838631
Groezinger, Barbara	6 yrs.	Betzweiler	Obd.	Jun 1848	N.-Amer	838631
Groezinger, Conrad	75 yrs.	Owen	Krch.	Mar 1804	Holland	550804
Groezinger, Creszentia V. (wife)		Freiburg/Baden	Leon.	May 1830	N.-Amer	837963
Groezinger, Friedrich	18 Jun 1826	Reutlingen	Rtl.	Sep 1860	N.-Amer	841052
Groezinger, Gottlob Friedr.	1831	Malmsheim	Leon.	1853	N.-Amer	837958
Groezinger, Jakob Friedrich		Ditzingen	Leon.	Feb 1819	Prussia	835788
Groezinger, Jakob Michael	27 Apr 1827	Ohmenhausen	Rtl.	Mar 1867	N.-Amer	841052
Groezinger, Johann Conrad	14 Apr 1847	Pfullingen	Rtl.	bef 1866	N.-Amer	841052
Groezinger, Johann Georg		Hoefingen	Leon.	bef 1869	N.-Amer	837957
Groezinger, Johann Gottlob	6 Aug 1807	Malmsheim	Leon.	Apr 1832	Saxony	837958
Groezinger, Johann Jakob	26 Aug 1831	Muenchingen	Leon.	bef 1860	N.-Amer	837961
Groezinger, Johannes & W		Renningen	Leon.	May 1830	N.-Amer	837963
Groezinger, Karl Friedrich	22 yrs.	Ditzingen	Leon.	Jan 1870	N.-Amer	835788
Groezinger, Margaretha B. (wid.)	19 Nov 1822	Hoefingen	Leon.	Jun 1873	N.-Amer	837957

Name		Birth		Emigration			Film
Last	First	Date	Place	O'amt	Appl. Date	Dest.	Number
Groll, Johann Christian		16 May 1844	Weil im Dorf	Loen.	Nov 1871	N.-Amer	837967
Groninger, Anna		30 Jun 1852	Kuchen	Gsl.	Jun 1856	N.-Amer	572043
Groninger, Dorothea (wife) & F		19 Sep 1818	Kuchen	Gsl.	May 1855	N.-Amer	572043
Groninger, Johann Jakob		9 Feb 1822	Kuchen	Gsl.	bef 1856	N.-Amer	572043
Groninger, Katharina		16 Jun 1833	Kuchen	Gsl.	Feb 1857	N.-Amer	572043
Groninger, Magdalena (wife) & F		1 Feb 1825	Kuchen	Gsl.	Jun 1856	N.-Amer	572043
Groninger, Matthaeus		17 Jun 1848	Kuchen	Gsl.	Jun 1856	N.-Amer	572043
Groninger, Michael		5 Feb 1850	Kuchen	Gsl.	May 1855	N.-Amer	572043
Groninger, Michael			Kuchen	Gsl.	bef 1855	N.-Amer	572043
Gronninger, Johann Georg			Kuchen	Gsl.	Feb 1853	N.-Amer	572041
Gros, Carl Hermann		22 Nov 1846	Hirschlanden	Leon.	Jan 1866	N.-Amer	837956
Gros, Robert Heinrich		5 Aug 1850	Hirschlanden	Leon.	bef 1869	N.-Amer	837956
Gross, Anna		18 May 1864	Kirchheim	Krch.	Mar 1876	N.-Amer	835942
Gross, Anton		10 May 1835	Epfendorf	Obd.	May 1847	N.-Amer	838632
Gross, Arnold			Kirchheim	Krch.	1876	N.-Amer	835942
Gross, Barbara		5 Jan 1840	Bissingen	Krch.	Mar 1865	N.-Amer	835943
Gross, Catharina			Weil im Dorf	Loen.	Mar 1853	N.-Amer	837967
Gross, Catharina (wife)			Weil im Dorf	Loen.	Mar 1852	N.-Amer	837967
Gross, Clara		20 Oct 1869	Kirchheim	Krch.	Mar 1876	N.-Amer	835942
Gross, Conrad		23 yrs.	Weil im Dorf	Loen.	1852	N.-Amer	837967
Gross, Franziska		5 Mar 1833	Epfendorf	Obd.	May 1847	N.-Amer	838632
Gross, Friederike Luise & F		23 Sep 1839	Kirchheim	Krch.	Mar 1885	N.-Amer	835942
Gross, Gottlieb Friedrich		28 Nov 1822	Kirchheim	Krch.	Dec 1855	N.-Amer	835940
Gross, Ida		31 Oct 1874	Kirchheim	Krch.	Mar 1876	N.-Amer	835942
Gross, Johann Georg & F			Weil im Dorf	Loen.	Mar 1852	N.-Amer	837967
Gross, Johanna		24 May 1840	Epfendorf	Obd.	May 1847	N.-Amer	838632
Gross, Joseph & F		5 Sep 1801	Epfendorf	Obd.	May 1847	N.-Amer	838632
Gross, Karl		31 Oct 1830	Epfendorf	Obd.	May 1847	N.-Amer	838632
Gross, Louise Pauline		8 Nov 1834	Kirchheim	Krch.	Dec 1855	N.-Amer	835940
Gross, Magdalena Elis. Fried.		18 Sep 1824	Eningen	Rtl.	bef 1861	N.-Amer	841052
Gross, Ottilia		10 Dec 1836	Epfendorf	Obd.	May 1847	N.-Amer	838632
Gross, Otto		29 Jan 1871	Kirchheim	Krch.	Feb 1876	N.-Amer	835942
Gross, Rosalia (wife)		29 Aug 1807	Beffendorf	Obd.	May 1847	N.-Amer	838632
Gross, Theresia		28 Sep 1844	Epfendorf	Obd.	May 1847	N.-Amer	838632
Grosshans, Ulrich			Berneck	Nag.	Aug 1852	N.-Amer	838488
Grosshaupt, Christine (wife)		12 Aug 1838	Hemmingen	Leon.	Oct 1864	N.-Amer	837956
Grosshaupt, Friederike		23 yrs.	Hemmingen	Leon.	Apr 1869	N.-Amer	837956
Grosshaupt, Jacob Friedr. & F		19 Sep 1830	Hemmingen	Leon.	bef 1868	N.-Amer	837956
Grossmann, Carl Conrad		1 Aug 1866	Hoefingen	Leon.	Jul 1868	N.-Amer	837957
Grossmann, Conrad		41 yrs.	Hoefingen	Leon.	Dec 1867	N.-Amer	837957
Grossmann, Gottlieb		20 yrs.	Hirschlanden	Leon.	May 1853	N.-Amer	837956
Gruber, Andreas		3 Feb 1846	Roemlinsdorf	Obd.	Feb 1870	N.-Amer	838635
Gruber, Philipp		5 Feb 1847	Waldmoessingen	Obd.	May 1867	N.-Amer	841015
Grueb, Theodor Heinr. Eduard		3 Nov 1846	Owen	Krch.	Mar 1864	N.-Amer	835948
Gruel, Augustine Rosine		15 Jan 1835	Owen	Krch.	May 1860	N.-Amer	835948
Gruel, Emilie Auguste		13 Apr 1837	Owen	Krch.	Aug 1857	N.-Amer	835948
Gruel, Emma Bertha		15 Apr 1842	Owen	Krch.	May 1859	N.-Amer	835948
Gruel, Johann Andreas		28 Nov 1847	Owen	Krch.	Sep 1867	N.-Amer	835948
Gruel, Maria Mathilde		12 Jun 1830	Owen	Krch.	Apr 1857	N.-Amer	835948
Gruel, Samuel		17 Aug 1851	Owen	Krch.	Oct 1869	N.-Amer	835948

Gruendler, Friederike	4 Mar 1839	Kirchheim	Krch.	Jun 1868	N.-Amer	835941
Gruener, Engelbert	10 Sep 1846	Schramberg	Obd.	Jul 1865	N.-Amer	838636
Gruener, Franz	20 Mar 1835	Weil der Stadt	Leon.	Jan 1854	N.-Amer	837966
Grueninger, Adolph	20 Nov 1842	Reutlingen	Rtl.	Aug 1860	N.-Amer	841052
Grueninger, Carl	24 yrs.	Reutlingen	Rtl.	Jul 1880	N.-Amer	841051
Grueninger, Elisabeth Maria	14 Jun 1832	Reutlingen	Rtl.	Apr 1864	N.-Amer	841052
Grueninger, Friedrich Wilhelm	22 Apr 1835	Reutlingen	Rtl.	bef 1861	N.-Amer	841052
Grueninger, Wilhelmine Carl.	19 Mar 1838	Reutlingen	Rtl.	bef 1863	France	841052
Gruner, Matthaeus	21 Sep 1831	Ohmenhausen	Rtl.	May 1861	N.-Amer	841052
Gruoner, Christine Magdalena		Ohmenhausen	Rtl.	May 1836	N.-Amer	841051
Gruoner, Dorothea	21 yrs.	Reutlingen	Rtl.	Dec 1880	N.-Amer	841051
Gruoner, Georg	9 Dec 1846	Reutlingen	Rtl.	Nov 1866	N.-Amer	841052
Gruoner, Gottliebin Math.	25 yrs.	Reutlingen	Rtl.	Jun 1860	N.-Amer	841052
Gruoner, Gottlob	22 Nov 1848	Reutlingen	Rtl.	Nov 1866	N.-Amer	841052
Gruoner, Jacob & F		Ohmenhausen	Rtl.	May 1836	N.-Amer	841051
Gruoner, Ulrike	30 yrs.	Reutlingen	Rtl.	Jun 1860	N.-Amer	841052
Grupp, Genofeva	24 yrs.	Boehmenkirch	Gsl.	Mar 1852	N.-Amer	572041
Grupp, Johannes	4 Jan 1850	Boehmenkirch	Gsl.	Mar 1868	N.-Amer	572046
Gruss, Johann Konrad	15 yrs.	Geislingen	Gsl.	May 1852	N.-Amer	572041
Gscheidle, Johannes	28 Sep 1840	Notzingen	Krch.	Feb 1858	N.-Amer	835947
Gubler, Andreas	8 Feb 1807	Fluorn	Obd.	Aug 1817	N.-Amer	838629
Gubler, Christian	20 Jul 1810	Fluorn	Obd.	Aug 1817	N.-Amer	838629
Gubler, Christina (wife)	19 Mar 1777	Fluorn	Obd.	Aug 1817	N.-Amer	838629
Gubler, Friederich	19 Apr 1813	Fluorn	Obd.	Aug 1817	N.-Amer	838629
Gubler, Friedrich	27 Aug 1846	Fluorn	Obd.	Apr 1866	N.-Amer	838632
Gubler, Johann Georg	29 Jun 1778	Fluorn	Obd.	Aug 1817	N.-Amer	838629
Gubler, Johann Georg	16 Jul 1816	Fluorn	Obd.	Aug 1817	N.-Amer	838629
Gubler, Maria Catharina	9 Apr 1804	Fluorn	Obd.	Aug 1817	N.-Amer	838629
Guellet, Johannes	45 yrs.	Alt Oberndorf	Obd.	Nov 1853	N.-Amer	838632
Guenter, Carolina		Oberndorf	Obd.	bef 1858	N.-Amer	838635
Guenter, Eduard	6 Sep 1848	Aichhalden	Obd.	Jul 1865	N.-Amer	838629
Guenter, Joseph	3 Feb 1854	Sulgen	Obd.	May 1869	France	838638
Guenter, Joseph	24 Mar 1827	Sulgen	Obd.	Oct 1866	France	838638
Guenter, Paulina	32 yrs.	Sulgau	Obd.	May 1857	France	838629
Guenter, Paulina & C	23 Jun 1833	Sulgen	Obd.	May 1869	France	838638
Guenther, Anton	24 Feb 1849	Hochmoessingen	Obd.	Mar 1867	N.-Amer	838633
Guenther, Carl Friedrich	8 Sep 1837	Friolzheim	Leon.	Feb 1863	N.-Amer	835791
Guenther, Johannes	15 Apr 1852	Peterzell	Obd.	Apr 1862	N.-Amer	838635
Guenther, Marie Louise	9 Aug 1833	Alpirsbach	Obd.	May 1852	N.-Amer	838630
Guenther, Mathias & F	6 Feb 1817	Betzweiler	Obd.	May 1847	N.-Amer	838631
Guenthner, Gottlieb Eberhard	11 May 1868	Weilheim	Krch.	May 1882	N.-Amer	548403
Guentner, Jakob Johannes		Simmersfeld	Nag.	Jul 1852	N.-Amer	838488
Guethlein, Anna Barbara	18 mon.	Geislingen	Gsl.	Aug 1852	N.-Amer	572041
Guethlein, Johann & F		Geislingen	Gsl.	Aug 1852	N.-Amer	572041
Guethler, Christian Ernst	24 May 1822	Renningen	Leon.	Nov 1846	Prussia	837963
Guethler, Michael	10 Aug 1831	Grosssuessen	Gsl.	Jan 1858	N.-Amer	572043
Gummel, Catharina & C	27 yrs.	Ditzingen	Leon.	Jan 1854	N.-Amer	835788
Gummel, Maria Catharina	7 Apr 1851	Ditzingen	Leon.	Jan 1854	N.-Amer	835788
Gumper, Anna Maria	25 Sep 1869	Oberlenningen	Krch.	Apr 1884	N.-Amer	835947
Gumper, Anna Maria (wife)	59 yrs.	Oberlenningen	Krch.	Jul 1873	N.-Amer	548403

Name		Birth		Emigration			Film
Last	First	Date	Place	O'amt	Appl. Date	Dest.	Number
Gumper, Barbara		1 Feb 1882	Oberlenningen	Krch.	Apr 1884	N.-Amer	835947
Gumper, Christian		16 Feb 1859	Oberlenningen	Krch.	Jul 1873	N.-Amer	835947
Gumper, David & F		22 Nov 1810	Oberlenningen	Krch.	Jul 1873	N.-Amer	548403
Gumper, Gottlieb		25 Nov 1875	Oberlenningen	Krch.	Apr 1884	N.-Amer	835947
Gumper, Gottlieb		6 Sep 1849	Oberlenningen	Krch.	Aug 1867	N.-Amer	835947
Gumper, Gottlieb David (wid.) & F		28 Jan 1844	Oberlenningen	Krch.	Apr 1884	N.-Amer	835947
Gumper, Katharina		4 Jun 1852	Oberlenningen	Krch.	Jul 1873	N.-Amer	548403
Gumper, Louise		8 Oct 1879	Oberlenningen	Krch.	Apr 1884	N.-Amer	835947
Gumper, Sophie Christine		8 Feb 1868	Oberlenningen	Krch.	Apr 1884	N.-Amer	835947
Gumper, Wilhelm		21 May 1871	Oberlenningen	Krch.	Apr 1884	N.-Amer	835947
Gumpper, Christoph Friedrich		28 Mar 1847	Pfullingen	Rtl.	Sep 1866	N.-Amer	841052
Gumpper, Jacob			Pfullingen	Rtl.	Apr 1830	N.-Amer	841051
Gunser, Eva Catharina & C			Gerlingen	Leon.	Apr 1837	N.-Amer	837953
Guntzenhauser, Johann Georg		22 Jul 1843	Altenstadt-Gsl.	Gsl.	Feb 1859	N.-Amer	572043
Guntzenhauser, Peter		17 Oct 1834	Altenstadt-Gsl.	Gsl.	Feb 1854	N.-Amer	572042
Gunzenhauser, Anna		7 Aug 1831	Grosssuessen	Gsl.	Mar 1852	N.-Amer	572041
Gunzenhauser, Babette (wife)			Geislingen	Gsl.	Apr 1866	N.-Amer	572045
Gunzenhauser, Christian		9 Jan 1866	Altenstadt-Gsl.	Gsl.	1884	N.-Amer	572049
Gunzenhauser, Franz		30 Dec 1868	Boehmenkirch	Gsl.	May 1884	N.-Amer	572049
Gunzenhauser, Friederike		1 yrs.	Geislingen	Gsl.	Apr 1866	N.-Amer	572045
Gunzenhauser, Friedrich & F			Geislingen	Gsl.	Apr 1866	N.-Amer	572045
Gunzenhauser, Jakob		19 Apr 1835	Altenstadt-Gsl.	Gsl.	Feb 1854	N.-Amer	572042
Gunzenhauser, Josias			Boehmenkirch	Gsl.	Mar 1852	N.-Amer	572041
Gunzenhauser, Kaspar		16 Nov 1823	Kuchen	Gsl.	Jul 1863	N.-Amer	572044
Gurr, Robert Friedrich		5 May 1849	Reutlingen	Rtl.	Dec 1869	N.-Amer	841052
Gutbrecht, Barbara		15 yrs.	Hemmingen	Leon.	May 1821	N.-Amer	837956
Gutbrecht, Barbara (wife)		42 yrs.	Hemmingen	Leon.	May 1821	N.-Amer	837956
Gutbrecht, Catarina		10 yrs.	Hemmingen	Leon.	May 1821	N.-Amer	837956
Gutbrecht, Christian		13 yrs.	Hemmingen	Leon.	May 1821	N.-Amer	837956
Gutbrecht, Christiana Dorothea		2 yrs.	Hemmingen	Leon.	May 1821	N.-Amer	837956
Gutbrecht, Elisabetha Sibyla		7 yrs.	Hemmingen	Leon.	May 1821	N.-Amer	837956
Gutbrecht, Johann Christof		5 yrs.	Hemmingen	Leon.	May 1821	N.-Amer	837956
Gutbrecht, Johann Konrad		14 yrs.	Hemmingen	Leon.	May 1821	N.-Amer	837956
Gutbrecht, Johannes & F		40 yrs.	Hemmingen	Leon.	May 1821	N.-Amer	837956
Gutbrod, Johann Georg		16 Jan 1850	Gebersheim	Leon.	Aug 1868	N.-Amer	837953
Gutbrod, Johann Jacob & F			Reutlingen	Rtl.	May 1832	N.-Amer	841051
Gutekunst, Anna Maria (wife)			Heimsheim	Leon.	Jul 1851	N.-Amer	837955
Gutekunst, Catrina		16 yrs.	Heimsheim	Leon.	Jul 1851	N.-Amer	837955
Gutekunst, Christof Fried. & F			Heimsheim	Leon.	Jul 1851	N.-Amer	837955
Gutekunst, Christof Friedr.		9 yrs.	Heimsheim	Leon.	Jul 1851	N.-Amer	837955
Gutekunst, Friederika		28 May 1840	Heimerdingen	Leon.	Sep 1867	N.-Amer	837954
Gutekunst, Gottlieb Friedrich		1 Jun 1832	Heimsheim	Leon.	bef 1857	N.-Amer	837955
Gutekunst, Margaretha		10 Aug 1830	Heimerdingen	Leon.	1853	N.-Amer	837954
Gutekunst, Sophie		5 yrs.	Heimsheim	Leon.	Jul 1851	N.-Amer	837955
Gutheinz, Carl Sebastian		29 yrs.	Oberndorf	Obd.	bef 1858	N.-Amer	838635
Gutjahr, Christian Ludwig		14 Feb 1844	Renningen	Leon.	Apr 1852	N.-Amer	837963
Gutjahr, Immanuel		3 Jul 1821	Renningen	Leon.	Aug 1851	N.-Amer	837963
Gutjahr, Justina Dor. (wife)		10 Mar 1815	Renningen	Leon.	Apr 1852	N.-Amer	837963
Gutjahr, Louise Friederike		27 Jan 1846	Renningen	Leon.	Apr 1852	N.-Amer	837963
Gutjahr, Ludwig & F			Renningen	Leon.	Apr 1852	N.-Amer	837963

Name	Date	Place	Region	Date	Destination	Film
Gutjahr, Michael Gottlob	9 Jan 1848	Renningen	Leon.	Apr 1852	N.-Amer	837963
Gutjahr, Regina Sara	19 Aug 1850	Renningen	Leon.	Apr 1852	N.-Amer	837963
Gutmann, Johann Andreas	15 May 1848	Affstaett	Herr.	Apr 1867	N.-Amer	834630
Gutmann, Johanna	22 Feb 1834	Oberjesingen	Herr.	Apr 1864	N.-Amer	834630
Gutscher, Balthasar & F	39 yrs.	Hemmingen	Leon.	Feb 1827	N.-Amer	837956
Gutscher, Barbara (wife)	32 yrs.	Hemmingen	Leon.	Feb 1827	N.-Amer	837956
Gutscher, Catarina	infant	Hemmingen	Leon.	Feb 1827	N.-Amer	837956
Gutscher, Christiana	6 yrs.	Hemmingen	Leon.	Feb 1827	N.-Amer	837956
Gutscher, Gottlob	13 Sep 1858	Flacht	Leon.	Sep 1874	Russia	835790
Gutscher, Johann Georg	3 yrs.	Hemmingen	Leon.	Feb 1827	N.-Amer	837956
Gutscher, Johannes	5 yrs.	Hemmingen	Leon.	Feb 1827	N.-Amer	837956
Gwinner, Christian Friedrich		Malmsheim	Leon.	1854	N.-Amer	837958
Gwinner, Dorothea	29 Jun 1838	Malmsheim	Leon.	May 1852	N.-Amer	837958
Gwinner, Dorothea (wife)	28 May 1806	Malmsheim	Leon.	May 1852	N.-Amer	837958
Gwinner, Georg	18 Feb 1842	Malmsheim	Leon.	May 1852	N.-Amer	837958
Gwinner, Jacob	14 Feb 1835	Malmsheim	Leon.	May 1852	N.-Amer	837958
Gwinner, Johann Georg & F	18 Dec 1808	Malmsheim	Leon.	May 1852	N.-Amer	837958
Gwinner, Johann Michael	2 Sep 1838	Malmsheim	Leon.	Jun 1870	N.-Amer	837958
Gwinner, Johannes	20 Aug 1845	Malmsheim	Leon.	May 1852	N.-Amer	837958
Gwinner, Magdalena	4 Jul 1843	Malmsheim	Leon.	May 1852	N.-Amer	837958
Haag, Anton	24 Oct 1806	Seedorf	Obd.	bef 1817	Austria	838637
Haag, Augustin		Bochingen	Obd.	Jun 1860	Hungary	838632
Haag, Franziskus	4 Oct 1843	Seedorf	Obd.	May 1870	N.-Amer	838637
Haag, Johannes & F	27 Dec 1760	Seedorf	Obd.	bef 1817	Austria	838637
Haag, Maria (wife)	23 Aug 1762	Seedorf	Obd.	bef 1817	Austria	838637
Haag, Mathaeus	12 Aug 1789	Seedorf	Obd.	bef 1817	Austria	838637
Haag, Regina	6 Sep 1788	Seedorf	Obd.	bef 1817	Austria	838637
Haag, Scholastika	18 Feb 1803	Seedorf	Obd.	bef 1817	Austria	838637
Haag, Wendelin	18 Sep 1794	Seedorf	Obd.	bef 1817	Austria	838637
Haaga, Andreas		Beffendorf	Obd.	Feb 1861	N.-Amer	838631
Haaga, August Friedrich	5 Feb 1829	Beffendorf	Obd.	Jul 1847	N.-Amer	838631
Haaga, Catharina	24 Oct 1826	Beffendorf	Obd.	bef 1852	N.-Amer	838631
Haaga, Gregor - twin	5 Feb 1847	Beffendorf	Obd.	Jul 1847	N.-Amer	838631
Haaga, Johannes	11 Jul 1851	Hochmoessingen	Obd.	Mar 1869	N.-Amer	838633
Haaga, Johannes - twin	5 Feb 1847	Beffendorf	Obd.	Jul 1847	N.-Amer	838631
Haaga, Joseph		Beffendorf	Obd.	Dec 1857	N.-Amer	838631
Haaga, Josepha (wife)	19 Mar 1812	Beffendorf	Obd.	Jul 1847	N.-Amer	838631
Haaga, Karl	26 Apr 1853	Hochmoessingen	Obd.	Apr 1869	N.-Amer	838633
Haaga, Karl	20 yrs.	Hochmoessingen	Obd.	Nov 1868	N.-Amer	838633
Haaga, Lukas	16 Oct 1843	Beffendorf	Obd.	Jul 1847	N.-Amer	838631
Haaga, Maria	8 Sep 1842	Beffendorf	Obd.	Jul 1847	N.-Amer	838631
Haaga, Petronilla		Beffendorf	Obd.	Oct 1856	France	838631
Haaga, Raimund & F	31 Aug 1808	Beffendorf	Obd.	Jul 1847	N.-Amer	838631
Haaga, Salome	26 yrs.	Beffendorf	Obd.	Aug 1854	N.-Amer	838631
Haager, Dominikus	4 Aug 1850	Bach-Altenberg	Obd.	Jun 1867	N.-Amer	838631
Haakh, Wilhelm Julius	22 Apr 1856	Renningen	Leon.	Nov 1872	N.-Amer	837963
Haar, Jakob	28 Mar 1848	Moensheim	Leon.	bef 1873	Palest	837960
Haas, Adam		Weil der Stadt	Leon.	Jan 1854	N.-Amer	837966
Haas, Agatha	1 Sep 1853	Schramberg	Obd.	May 1859	N.-Amer	838636
Haas, Agnes	6 Jun 1864	Aichhalden	Obd.	Apr 1865	N.-Amer	838629

Name		Birth		Emigration			Film
Last	First	Date	Place	O'amt	Appl. Date	Dest.	Number
Haas,	Albert	20 May 1862	Aichhalden	Obd.	Apr 1865	N.-Amer	838629
Haas,	Albertina	25 yrs.	Beffendorf	Obd.	Sep 1854	N.-Amer	838631
Haas,	Amalie	7 Oct 1825	Lauterbach	Obd.	Jul 1864	Belgium	838634
Haas,	Andreas	22 yrs.	Lauterbach	Obd.	Apr 1854	N.-Amer	838634
Haas,	August	27 May 1865	Kirchheim	Krch.	Feb 1882	N.-Amer	835942
Haas,	Barbara	10 Apr 1854	Kirchheim	Krch.	Apr 1870	N.-Amer	835941
Haas,	Beata	3 May 1860	Aichhalden	Obd.	Apr 1865	N.-Amer	838629
Haas,	Christian Friedrich	8 yrs.	Brucken	Krch.	Jun 1804	Russia	550804
Haas,	Christiana Dorotea	5 yrs.	Brucken	Krch.	Jun 1804	Russia	550804
Haas,	Christina	29 yrs.	Sulgau	Obd.	Mar 1855	Switz.	838637
Haas,	Christine		Gomaringen	Rtl.	bef 1862	N.-Amer	841053
Haas,	Christof Adam	4 yrs.	Brucken	Krch.	Jun 1804	Russia	550804
Haas,	Christof Adam & F	32 yrs.	Brucken	Krch.	Jun 1804	Russia	550804
Haas,	Dorothea & C	12 Sep 1811	Kirchheim	Krch.	Apr 1870	N.-Amer	835941
Haas,	Elisabetha	12 Jun 1855	Schramberg	Obd.	May 1859	N.-Amer	838636
Haas,	Eva Margaretha (wife)	26 yrs.	Goeppingen	Krch.	Jun 1804	Russia	550804
Haas,	Ferdinand & F		Lauterbach	Obd.	May 1846	France	838634
Haas,	Fridolin		Winzeln	Obd.	Mar 1860	N.-Amer	841016
Haas,	Friedrich	4 Sep 1857	Aichhalden	Obd.	Apr 1865	N.-Amer	838629
Haas,	Friedrich	15 Dec 1849	Kirchheim	Krch.	May 1866	N.-Amer	835941
Haas,	Gebhard		Aichhalden	Obd.	May 1817	N.-Amer	838629
Haas,	Germann	16 Nov 1857	Schramberg	Obd.	May 1859	N.-Amer	838636
Haas,	Hugo	30 May 1860	Gammertingen	Rtl.	Apr 1862	N.-Amer	841057
Haas,	Jacob	16 Jul 1845	Winzeln	Obd.	Dec 1867	N.-Amer	841016
Haas,	Johann & F		Peterzell	Obd.	Jun 1817	N.-Amer	838635
Haas,	Johann Adam	18 mon.	Brucken	Krch.	Jun 1804	Russia	550804
Haas,	Johann Evangelist	7 Dec 1849	Schramberg	Obd.	May 1859	N.-Amer	838636
Haas,	Johann Friedrich	infant	Brucken	Krch.	Jun 1804	Russia	550804
Haas,	Johanna Friederike	28 Feb 1846	Kirchheim	Krch.	Apr 1870	N.-Amer	835941
Haas,	Johannes	13 yrs.	Waldmoessingen	Obd.	Mar 1865	N.-Amer	841015
Haas,	Johannes		Weil der Stadt	Leon.	Jun 1853	N.-Amer	837966
Haas,	Johannes	31 yrs.	Muehlhausen	Gsl.	Jun 1856	N.-Amer	572043
Haas,	Johannes Evangelist	27 Dec 1851	Bach-Altenberg	Obd.	Aug 1869	N.-Amer	838631
Haas,	Josef & F	8 Jul 1824	Schramberg	Obd.	May 1859	N.-Amer	838636
Haas,	Joseph		Beffendorf	Obd.	Feb 1857	N.-Amer	838631
Haas,	Joseph	20 yrs.	Beffendorf	Obd.	Oct 1853	N.-Amer	838631
Haas,	Joseph	2 Dec 1850	Mariazell	Obd.	Dec 1870	N.-Amer	838634
Haas,	Joseph		Schramberg	Obd.	Mar 1841	N.-Amer	838637
Haas,	Karl		Winzeln	Obd.	Apr 1866	N.-Amer	841016
Haas,	Karoline	23 Jan 1857	Kirchheim	Krch.	Apr 1870	N.-Amer	835941
Haas,	Ludwig	30 Nov 1851	Schramberg	Obd.	May 1859	N.-Amer	838636
Haas,	Ludwig		Schramberg	Obd.	May 1817	A.-Amer	838637
Haas,	Luzia & C	9 Dec 1834	Bronnen	Rtl.	Apr 1862	N.-Amer	841057
Haas,	Luzia & F		Aichhalden	Obd.	Aug 1859	N.-Amer	838629
Haas,	Maria		Aichhalden	Obd.	Aug 1859	N.-Amer	838629
Haas,	Maria	11 Aug 1842	Winzeln	Obd.	Apr 1868	N.-Amer	841016
Haas,	Maria Agnes		Gomaringen	Rtl.	bef 1862	N.-Amer	841053
Haas,	Maria Louisa		Aichhalden	Obd.	Aug 1859	N.-Amer	838629
Haas,	Markus		Sulgen	Obd.	bef 1863	France	838638
Haas,	Michael	22 yrs.	Lauterbach	Obd.	Sep 1860	N.-Amer	838634

Haas, Michael	18 yrs.	Lauterbach	Obd.	Mar 1857	N.-Amer	838634
Haas, Nothburga & C		Aichhalden	Obd.	May 1848	N.-Amer	838629
Haas, Robert	11 Dec 1848	Sulgen	Obd.	Mar 1868	N.-Amer	838638
Haas, Rosa		Aichhalden	Obd.	Aug 1859	N.-Amer	838629
Haas, Sabina & C		Aichhalden	Obd.	Aug 1859	N.-Amer	838629
Haas, Salome		Sulgau	Obd.	bef 1841	Switz.	838637
Haas, Sebastian & F		Lauterbach	Obd.	May 1817	N.-Amer	838634
Haas, Severin		Schramberg	Obd.	bef 1860	N.-Amer	838636
Haas, Siegfried		Aichhalden	Obd.	Mar 1863	N.-Amer	838629
Haas, Teresia & F		Beffendorf	Obd.	Sep 1854	N.-Amer	838631
Haas, Thomas	18 yrs.	Beffendorf	Obd.	Sep 1854	N.-Amer	838631
Haas, Veronica (wife)	27 Dec 1822	Schramberg	Obd.	May 1859	N.-Amer	838636
Haas, Vincenz & F	4 Apr 1830	Aichhalden	Obd.	Apr 1865	N.-Amer	838629
Haas, Wendelin		Aichhalden	Obd.	bef 1847	N.-Amer	838629
Haas, Wendelin	19 Oct 1849	Bach-Altenberg	Obd.	Aug 1869	N.-Amer	838631
Haberer, Andreas	25 Nov 1849	Bach-Altenberg	Obd.	Dec 1869	N.-Amer	838631
Haberer, Andreas	28 Apr 1840	Peterzell	Obd.	bef 1865	N.-Amer	838635
Haberer, Andreas	17 yrs.	Peterzell	Obd.	Sep 1857	N.-Amer	838635
Haberer, Anna Maria	27 Mar 1842	Peterzell	Obd.	bef 1865	N.-Amer	838635
Haberer, Christina	11 Nov 1837	Peterzell	Obd.	May 1865	N.-Amer	838635
Haberer, Jakob	8 Jun 1850	Peterzell	Obd.	May 1865	N.-Amer	838635
Haberer, Johann Georg	23 May 1846	Peterzell	Obd.	May 1865	N.-Amer	838635
Haberer, Johannes	30 Mar 1848	Peterzell	Obd.	May 1865	N.-Amer	838635
Haberer, Katharina	1 Jul 1855	Peterzell	Obd.	May 1865	N.-Amer	838635
Haberer, Louise	1842	Oberndorf	Obd.	Jul 1863	Switz.	838635
Haberer, Pius	20 Jun 1847	Oberndorf	Obd.	Jul 1867	N.-Amer	838635
Haberer, Salome	25 yrs.	Bach-Altenberg	Obd.	Feb 1854	N.-Amer	838631
Haberer, Salome - wid & F	22 Apr 1811	Peterzell	Obd.	May 1865	N.-Amer	838635
Haberer, Theresia	10 Jun 1841	Oberndorf	Obd.	Jul 1863	Switz.	838635
Habler, Gottlieb	23 Nov 1868	Oberlenningen	Krch.	Apr 1884	N.-Amer	548403
Hack, Adolf	14 Oct 1835	Reutlingen	Rtl.	May 1861	Austria	841053
Hack, Anna Maria (wife) & F	5 May 1832	Ohmenhausen	Rtl.	Apr 1868	N.-Amer	841058
Hack, Jakob		Ohmenhausen	Rtl.	bef 1868	N.-Amer	841058
Hack, Johann Georg		Lindorf	Krch.	May 1861	N.-Amer	835946
Hack, Johann Wilhelm	6 Dec 1851	Dettingen	Krch.	Dec 1867	N.-Amer	835944
Hack, Johannes	16 Aug 1822	Dettingen	Krch.	Jun 1860	N.-Amer	835944
Hack, Johannes	18 Dec 1828	Bissingen	Krch.	bef 1869	France	835943
Hack, Maria	21 Jul 1863	Ohmenhausen	Rtl.	Apr 1868	N.-Amer	841058
Hackh, Christina Rosina	27 Mar 1836	Bissingen	Krch.	Aug 1865	Switz.	835943
Hackius, Christian Wilhelm		Renningen	Leon.	Jun 1858	Saxony	837963
Hackius, Gottlieb		Schoeckingen	Leon.	bef 1853	N.-Amer	837964
Hackius, Jakob Friedrich	8 Aug 1835	Schoeckingen	Leon.	Sep 1855	N.-Amer	837964
Hackius, Johann Jacob	2 Aug 1869	Heimerdingen	Leon.	May 1885	N.-Amer	837954
Hadelmaier, Anna Maria (wife)		Owen	Krch.	May 1858	N.-Amer	835948
Hadelmaier, Friedrich & F	12 Mar 1801	Hagenlohe	Krch.	May 1858	N.-Amer	835948
Haebe, Heinrich	5 Feb 1841	Unterhausen	Rtl.	Apr 1860	N.-Amer	841053
Haebe, Johann Christoph	12 Feb 1846	Unterhausen	Rtl.	Sep 1866	N.-Amer	841053
Haebe, Ludwig	11 Feb 1838	Unterhausen	Rtl.	Sep 1865	N.-Amer	841053
Haeberle, Jakob	5 Feb 1869	Magstadt	Leon.	Jan 1886	N.-Amer	837963
Haeberle, Paul Friedrich	1 Sep 1860	Deggingen	Gsl.	Feb 1877	N.-Amer	572048

Name		Birth		Emigration			Film
Last	First	Date	Place	O'amt	Appl. Date	Dest.	Number
Haebich, Christian Friedrich			Heimerdingen	Leon.	bef 1864	N.-Amer	837954
Haebich, Christiane (wife)		19 Oct 1821	Heimerdingen	Leon.	Mar 1853	N.-Amer	837954
Haebich, Eva Christiane		20 Jun 1830	Heimerdingen	Leon.	Mar 1853	N.-Amer	837954
Haebich, Johannes		7 May 1851	Heimerdingen	Leon.	Mar 1853	N.-Amer	837954
Haebich, Johannes & F		4 Dec 1824	Heimerdingen	Leon.	Mar 1853	N.-Amer	837954
Haeckel, Johann Wilhelm		13 Apr 1846	Kirchheim	Krch.	Nov 1867	N.-Amer	835941
Haefele, Anna Maria		25 Mar 1805	Grosssuessen	Gsl.	Sep 1854	N.-Amer	572042
Haefele, Franz Wilhelm		6 Jul 1845	Ulm	Gsl.	Jan 1854	N.-Amer	572042
Haefele, Georg		22 Jul 1841	Grosssuessen	Gsl.	Sep 1854	N.-Amer	572042
Haefele, Jacob		11 Feb 1805	Grosssuessen	Gsl.	Sep 1854	N.-Amer	572042
Haefele, Jacob		23 May 1834	Grosssuessen	Gsl.	Jan 1854	N.-Amer	572042
Haefele, Johannes		24 yrs.	Gingen	Gsl.	Dec 1864	N.-Amer	572045
Haefele, Johannes & F		37 yrs.	Geislingen	Gsl.	Jan 1854	N.-Amer	572042
Haefele, Konrad		16 Aug 1837	Grosssuessen	Gsl.	Sep 1854	N.-Amer	572042
Haefele, Ursula		8 Jul 1832	Grosssuessen	Gsl.	Apr 1857	N.-Amer	572043
Haefele, Ursula			Grosssuessen	Gsl.	Sep 1862	Switz.	572044
Haefner, Anna Friederike		14 Aug 1848	Eltingen	Leon.	Mar 1852	N.-Amer	835789
Haefner, Carl Christian		3 Oct 1847	Renningen	Leon.	bef 1872	Basel	837963
Haefner, Christian Ernst		24 Jan 1833	Dettingen	Krch.	bef 1858	N.-Amer	835944
Haefner, Christian Gottlob		19 Dec 1831	Eltingen	Leon.	Mar 1852	N.-Amer	835789
Haefner, Christian Gottlob & F		20 Dec 1805	Eltingen	Leon.	Mar 1852	N.-Amer	835789
Haefner, Christiane Fr. (wife)		28 Aug 1808	Eltingen	Leon.	Mar 1852	N.-Amer	835789
Haefner, Johannes		12 Oct 1842	Eltingen	Leon.	Mar 1852	N.-Amer	835789
Haefner, Louise Catharine		9 Dec 1850	Eltingen	Leon.	Mar 1852	N.-Amer	835789
Haefner, Mathilde		28 Aug 1832	Leonberg	Leon.	Mar 1852	N.-Amer	835786
Haefner, Rosine		20 yrs.	Leonberg	Leon.	Aug 1854	N.-Amer	835786
Haegele, – (wid.) & F			Goeppingen	Krch.	1888	N.-Amer	835942
Haegele, Gottlieb & F			Leonberg	Leon.	May 1827	N.-Amer	835786
Haegele, Gustav Adolf		24 Jan 1881	Goeppingen	Krch.	1888	N.-Amer	835942
Haegele, Jakob Heinrich		17 Mar 1865	Hemmingen	Leon.	Mar 1882	N.-Amer	837956
Haegele, Johann Gottfried			Walddorf	Nag.	Jul 1852	N.-Amer	838488
Haegele, Maria Konstantina			Leonberg	Leon.	Apr 1842	N.-Amer	835786
Haehnle, Barbara (wife)		5 Mar 1831	Boehmenkirch	Gsl.	Mar 1855	N.-Amer	572043
Haehnle, Christine Barbara		5 Aug 1842	Altenstadt-Gsl.	Gsl.	Mar 1855	N.-Amer	572043
Haehnle, Georg		7 Sep 1843	Altenstadt-Gsl.	Gsl.	Mar 1855	N.-Amer	572043
Haehnle, Jakob		11 Apr 1838	Altenstadt-Gsl.	Gsl.	bef 1855	N.-Amer	572043
Haehnle, Johann Georg & F		24 May 1800	Gerstetten	Gsl.	Mar 1855	N.-Amer	572043
Haehnle, Johannes		17 Mar 1834	Altenstadt-Gsl.	Gsl.	bef 1855	N.-Amer	572043
Haehnle, Johannes		11 Mar 1872	Gutenberg	Krch.	Jan 1887	N.-Amer	835945
Haeker, Johann Jakob			Merklingen	Leon.	Apr 1854	N.-Amer	837959
Haeker, Maria Catharina			Merklingen	Leon.	Mar 1853	N.-Amer	837959
Haemmerle, August		21 Dec 1809	Weilheim	Krch.	Jan 1866	N.-Amer	835950
Haemmerle, August Friderike		5 Jan 1843	Weilheim	Krch.	Aug 1864	N.-Amer	835950
Haenger, Johannes		12 Jun 1848	Geislingen	Gsl.	May 1871	N.-Amer	572047
Haer, Barbara & C			Enztal	Nag.	Dec 1850	N.-Amer	838488
Haer, Georg & F		45 yrs.	Enztal	Nag.	Dec 1850	N.-Amer	838488
Haering, Alexander			Gebersheim	Leon.	May 1851	N.-Amer	837953
Haering, Gottfried		3 May 1848	Eltingen	Leon.	Feb 1867	N.-Amer	835789
Haerlin, Anna Maria		27 Feb 1847	Renningen	Leon.	Apr 1849	N.-Amer	837963
Haerlin, Christian Friedrich		31 Jan 1839	Renningen	Leon.	Apr 1849	N.-Amer	837963

Haerlin, Christiana Martha	5 Jan 1844	Renningen	Leon.	Apr 1849	N.-Amer	837963
Haerlin, Christoph Chr. Fr.& F		Renningen	Leon.	Apr 1849	N.-Amer	837963
Haerlin, Friederika Dorothea	28 Apr 1845	Renningen	Leon.	Apr 1849	N.-Amer	837963
Haerlin, Katharina (wife)		Renningen	Leon.	Apr 1849	N.-Amer	837963
Haerter, Johann Valentin		Merklingen	Leon.	bef 1821	France	837959
Haertter, Andreas & F		Hemmingen	Leon.	Apr 1833	N.-Amer	837956
Haertter, Anna Maria	5 Jul 1813	Renningen	Leon.	Apr 1834	N.-Amer	837963
Haertter, Christian Friedrich	14 May 1817	Renningen	Leon.	Apr 1834	N.-Amer	837963
Haertter, Christian Johannes	10 yrs.	Heimsheim	Leon.	Aug 1853	N.-Amer	837955
Haertter, Christina Cath. (wife)		Heimsheim	Leon.	Aug 1853	N.-Amer	837955
Haertter, Christina Catharina	21 yrs.	Heimsheim	Leon.	Aug 1853	N.-Amer	837955
Haertter, Christina Maria	15 yrs.	Heimsheim	Leon.	Aug 1853	N.-Amer	837955
Haertter, Eva Barbara W & F	28 Jun 1781	Renningen	Leon.	Apr 1834	N.-Amer	837963
Haertter, Johannes & F		Heimsheim	Leon.	Aug 1853	N.-Amer	837955
Haertter, Maria (wife)		Hemmingen	Leon.	Apr 1833	N.-Amer	837956
Haettich, Ferdinand	8 Aug 1841	Hardt	Obd.	Feb 1860	N.-Amer	838633
Haeusler, Karl	4 May 1864	Gutenberg	Krch.	Mar 1881	N.-Amer	835945
Haeusler, Matthaeus	5 Oct 1827	Owen	Krch.	Jan 1859	N.-Amer	835948
Haeussler, Carl	5 Jan 1835	Leonberg	Leon.	Feb 1853	N.-Amer	835786
Haeussler, Christian	30 Oct 1848	Kirchheim	Krch.	Aug 1864	N.-Amer	835941
Haeussler, Christian Gottlieb	5 Oct 1847	Kirchheim	Krch.	Jul 1866	N.-Amer	835941
Haeussler, Friedrich	1 Apr 1837	Kirchheim	Krch.	Aug 1862	Austral	835941
Haeussler, Karl	4 May 1864	Gutenberg	Krch.	Mar 1881	N.-Amer	548403
Haeussler, Marcus		Hochmoessingen	Obd.	bef 1843	Austria	838633
Haeussler, Simon		Hochmoessingen	Obd.	bef 1843	Austria	838633
Hafa, Apollonia	5 Oct 1833	Seedorf	Obd.	Apr 1847	N.-Amer	838637
Hafa, Clara	3 Jul 1841	Seedorf	Obd.	Apr 1847	N.-Amer	838637
Hafa, Joseph	25 Jul 1845	Seedorf	Obd.	Apr 1847	N.-Amer	838637
Hafa, Joseph & F	4 Jun 1799	Seedorf	Obd.	Apr 1847	N.-Amer	838637
Hafa, Kumerana (wife)	16 Nov 1809	Seedorf	Obd.	Apr 1847	N.-Amer	838637
Hafa, Maria Anna	22 Oct 1827	Seedorf	Obd.	Apr 1847	N.-Amer	838637
Hafele, Johannes	15 Apr 1826	Grosssuessen	Gsl.	Jan 1852	N.-Amer	572041
Hafenbrack, Carl	2 Jul 1817	Kirchheim	Krch.	Oct 1855	N.-Amer	835940
Hafenbrack, Gottlieb Wilhelm	30 Jul 1819	Kirchheim	Krch.	Oct 1855	N.-Amer	835940
Hafenbrack, Johann Gottlieb	1 Mar 1870	Dettingen	Krch.	May 1887	N.-Amer	835944
Hafenbrak, Hermann Gottlieb	7 Jun 1849	Kirchheim	Krch.	Mar 1869	N.-Amer	835941
Haffner, Anna Maria (wife)	20 Dec 1830	Nussdorf	Leon.	Mar 1881	N.-Amer	837964
Haffner, Friedrich & F	4 Sep 1824	Rutesheim	Leon.	Mar 1881	N.-Amer	837964
Haffner, Gottlob Friedrich	24 Dec 1874	Rutesheim	Leon.	Feb 1879	N.-Amer	837964
Haffner, Johann Gottlieb	5 Sep 1865	Rutesheim	Leon.	Mar 1881	N.-Amer	837964
Haffner, Martin & F	13 Sep 1851	Rutesheim	Leon.	Feb 1879	N.-Amer	837964
Haffner, Max Ulrich	14 Jan 1876	Rutesheim	Leon.	Feb 1879	N.-Amer	837964
Haffner, Pauline Marie	26 Aug 1878	Rutesheim	Leon.	Feb 1879	N.-Amer	837964
Haffner, Regina (wife)	24 Nov 1850	Oberrot	Leon.	Feb 1879	N.-Amer	837964
Haffner, Wilhelm Karl	8 Mar 1877	Rutesheim	Leon.	Feb 1879	N.-Amer	837964
Hafner, Anna Katharina	50 yrs.	Grosssuessen	Gsl.	Feb 1853	N.-Amer	572041
Hafner, Anna Maria	19 Dec 1828	Grosssuessen	Gsl.	Mar 1852	N.-Amer	572041
Hafner, Barbara	13 yrs.	Ditzingen	Leon.	Jul 1856	Austral	835788
Hafner, Barbara (wife)	42 yrs.	Ditzingen	Leon.	Jul 1856	Austral	835788
Hafner, Christian	13 Apr 1831	Neidlingen	Krch.	Oct 1859	N.-Amer	835946

Name		Birth		Emigration			Film
Last	First	Date	Place	O'amt	Appl. Date	Dest.	Number
Hafner,	Jacob	12 yrs.	Ditzingen	Leon.	Jul 1856	Austral	835788
Hafner,	Jacob & F	42 yrs.	Ditzingen	Leon.	Jul 1856	Austral	835788
Hafner,	Johann Georg & W		Muenchingen	Leon.	Mar 1848	N.-Amer	837961
Hafner,	Johannes	6 yrs.	Ditzingen	Leon.	Jul 1856	Austral	835788
Hafner,	Margaretha	8 Jan 1826	Grosssuessen	Gsl.	Jan 1852	N.-Amer	572041
Hafner,	Maria Catharina	4 Nov 1843	Muenchingen	Leon.	Aug 1867	N.-Amer	837961
Hafner,	Robert	17 Jul 1863	Geislingen	Gsl.	Nov 1881	N.-Amer	572048
Hafner,	Wilhelmine (wife)		Muenchingen	Leon.	Mar 1848	N.-Amer	837961
Hagelstein,	Louise (wid.) & F	30 Jun 1822	Weilheim	Krch.	Mar 1870	N.-Amer	835940
Hagelstein,	Philipp Ludwig	9 Apr 1850	Weilheim	Krch.	Mar 1870	N.-Amer	835940
Hagenloch,	Johann Georg	23 Apr 1851	Pfullingen	Rtl.	Jan 1869	England	841053
Hagenloch,	Maria Katharina	1 Jun 1837	Pfullingen	Rtl.	Aug 1859	N.-Amer	841053
Hagenloch,	Maria Ursula	7 Jul 1840	Pfullingen	Rtl.	Mar 1869	N.-Amer	841053
Hagenlocher,	Johann Christian	30 Aug 1863	Renningen	Leon.	Dec 1879	N.-Amer	837963
Hagenlocher,	Reinhold	12 May 1850	Renningen	Leon.	Nov 1870	N.-Amer	837963
Hagenmaier,	Gebhard		Deggingen	Gsl.	Oct 1851	N.-Amer	577788
Hagenmayer,	Gebhard		Deggingen	Gsl.	May 1852	N.-Amer	572041
Hagenmayer,	Johann Georg	1 Sep 1827	Degginen	Gsl.	1848	N.-Amer	572045
Hagenmayer,	Magdalena		Deggingen	Gsl.	May 1852	N.-Amer	572041
Hagenmayer,	Monika		Deggingen	Gsl.	Mar 1852	N.-Amer	572041
Hagenmeier,	Barbara (wife)		Deggingen	Gsl.	Jul 1851	N.-Amer	577788
Hagenmeier,	Erna	11 May 1851	Deggingen	Gsl.	Jul 1851	N.-Amer	577788
Hagenmeier,	Idda	4 Feb 1850	Deggingen	Gsl.	Jul 1851	N.-Amer	577788
Hagenmeier,	Sebastian & F		Deggingen	Gsl.	Jul 1851	N.-Amer	577788
Hagenmeyer,	Engelbert Th.	7 Nov 1842	Deggingen	Gsl.	Apr 1855	N.-Amer	572043
Hagenmeyer,	Gebhard	1 Sep 1831	Deggingen	Gsl.	bef 1864	N.-Amer	572045
Hagenmeyer,	Louise	15 Jan 1835	Deggingen	Gsl.	Apr 1855	N.-Amer	572043
Hagenmeyer,	Magdalena	11 Jun 1833	Deggingen	Gsl.	bef 1864	N.-Amer	572045
Hagenmeyer,	Maria Anna		Ditzenbach	Gsl.	Mar 1850	N.-Amer	577788
Hagenmeyer,	Theresia	11 Apr 1836	Deggingen	Gsl.	Apr 1855	N.-Amer	572043
Hagenmeyer,	Theresia Stephane		Deggingen	Gsl.	bef 1864	N.-Amer	572045
Hagmaier,	Carl Friedrich	14 Jan 1864	Pfullingen	Rtl.	Jan 1866	N.-Amer	841053
Hagmaier,	Johann Georg	8 Mar 1865	Pfullingen	Rtl.	Jan 1866	N.-Amer	841053
Hagmaier,	Johann Georg	5 Nov 1845	Pfullingen	Rtl.	Apr 1864	N.-Amer	841053
Hagmaier,	Johann Georg & F	4 Feb 1825	Pfullingen	Rtl.	Jan 1866	N.-Amer	841053
Hagmaier,	Marta Elis. (wife)	27 Sep 1836	Pfullingen	Rtl.	Jan 1866	N.-Amer	841053
Hagmaier,	Philipp Friedrich	20 May 1849	Pfullingen	Rtl.	Sep 1866	N.-Amer	841053
Hagmann,	Andreas	27 Nov 1875	Eckwaelden	Krch.	May 1891	N.-Amer	835774
Hagmann,	Christian	27 Feb 1854	Zell	Krch.	Nov 1879	N.-Amer	835940
Hagmann,	Christian Gottfried	27 Feb 1868	Weilheim	Krch.	Feb 1884	N.-Amer	835942
Hagmann,	Jacob	25 Dec 1828	Zell	Krch.	1847	N.-Amer	835940
Hagmann,	Johann Georg	10 Sep 1877	Zell	Krch.	Apr 1894	N.-Amer	835774
Hagmann,	Johannes	6 Sep 1854	Kuchen	Gsl.	Aug 1872	N.-Amer	572047
Hagmann,	Johannes	18 Jan 1849	Kuchen	Gsl.	Aug 1867	N.-Amer	572046
Hahl,	Johann Friederike	6 Sep 1845	Muenchingen	Leon.	Jul 1869	S.-Amer	837961
Hahl,	Johann Jakob	19 Nov 1833	Muenchingen	Leon.	bef 1863	Bavaria	837961
Hahn,	Anna Catharina	30 May 1841	Gueltstein	Herr.	Apr 1869	N.-Amer	834631
Hahn,	Caroline Magdalene		Hildrizhausen	Herr.	1852	N.-Amer	834631
Hahn,	Ernst Gottlob	2 Jun 1873	Kusterdingen	Herr.	May 1890	N.-Amer	834631
Hahn,	Georg Wilhelm	28 Oct 1874	Kusterdingen	Herr.	May 1890	N.-Amer	834631

Hahn, Jacob Adam		Gomaringen	Rtl.	May 1832	N.-Amer	841051
Hahn, Johann Georg	25 yrs.	Willmandingen	Rtl.	Apr 1880	N.-Amer	841051
Hahn, Johann Gottlieb	4 Aug 1846	Gueltstein	Herr.	Nov 1867	N.-Amer	834631
Hahn, Johann Jakob	11 Jun 1843	Gueltstein	Herr.	Apr 1869	N.-Amer	834631
Hahn, Johann Jakob	31 Jan 1850	Gomaringen	Rtl.	Apr 1866	N.-Amer	841053
Hahn, Johannes	9 Jun 1838	Gueltstein	Herr.	Apr 1869	N.-Amer	834631
Hahn, Karl		Eningen	Rtl.	May 1861	N.-Amer	841053
Hahn, Max Louis Eugen	24 May 1851	Stuttgart	Herr.	bef 1887	Wien	834629
Hahn, Wilhelm	18 Sep 1855	Kleinaspach	Herr.	Apr 1872	N.-Amer	834630
Haid, Carolina	2 Feb 1840	Honau	Rtl.	May 1859	N.-Amer	841053
Haid, Christiana & F		Honau	Rtl.	May 1859	N.-Amer	841053
Haid, Elisabeth & F	23 Mar 1824	Unterhausen	Rtl.	1853	N.-Amer	841053
Haid, Ernst	2 Nov 1844	Honau	Rtl.	May 1859	N.-Amer	841053
Haid, Jakob Friedrich	21 Jun 1850	Unterhausen	Rtl.	1853	N.-Amer	841053
Haid, Jakob Friedrich		Honau	Rtl.	bef 1859	N.-Amer	841053
Haid, Jesias		Honau	Rtl.	May 1833	N.-Amer	841051
Haid, Johannes	25 Nov 1848	Oberndorf	Obd.	Oct 1867	N.-Amer	838635
Haid, Ludwig		Honau	Rtl.	May 1833	N.-Amer	841051
Haid, Maria	25 Dec 1851	Honau	Rtl.	May 1859	N.-Amer	841053
Haid, Maria Magdalena (wid.)		Honau	Rtl.	May 1832	N.-Amer	841051
Haid, Matthaeus	31 Mar 1847	Oberndorf	Obd.	Oct 1867	N.-Amer	838635
Haidt, Karl Friedrich	20 Apr 1832	Weil im Dorf	Loen.	Jul 1869	France	837967
Haier, Christian Friedrich	21 Nov 1824	Kirchheim	Krch.	bef 1860	N.-Amer	835940
Haier, Jacob Heinrich	15 Dec 1822	Kirchheim	Krch.	bef 1860	N.-Amer	835940
Haier, Johann Gottlieb	21 Jun 1826	Kirchheim	Krch.	bef 1860	N.-Amer	835940
Hailer, Joseph		Alt Oberndorf	Obd.	May 1870	N.-Amer	838631
Hailfinger, Anna Catharina	1 Dec 1796	Undingen	Rtl.	Mar 1868	N.-Amer	841053
Hainz, Andreas Carl	20 Feb 1861	Honau	Rtl.	Jun 1880	N.-Amer	841051
Haisch, Bernhard & W		Kleinsuessen	Gsl.	Apr 1860	N.-Amer	572044
Haisch, Maria Anna (wife)		Weissenstein	Gsl.	Apr 1860	N.-Amer	572044
Haizmann, Georg	23 Apr 1824	Bochingen	Obd.	Jan 1858	Prussia	838632
Hak, Georg		Ohmenhausen	Rtl.	May 1832	N.-Amer	841051
Hak, Martin (wid.)		Ohmenhausen	Rtl.	May 1832	N.-Amer	841051
Hakius, Andreas	9 Nov 1829	Heimerdingen	Leon.	bef 1870	N.-Amer	837954
Hakius, Conrad	23 Jan 1824	Heimerdingen	Leon.	1853	N.-Amer	837954
Hakius, Georg Adam	6 Nov 1828	Heimerdingen	Leon.	bef 1862	N.-Amer	837954
Hakius, Konrad	24 Feb 1857	Heimerdingen	Leon.	Apr 1880	N.-Amer	837954
Haller, Anton	18 May 1821	Schramberg	Obd.	Jun 1859	Bavaria	838636
Haller, Barbara	8 yrs.	Hemmingen	Leon.	Mar 1832	N.-Amer	837956
Haller, Caroline	5 yrs.	Hemmingen	Leon.	Mar 1832	N.-Amer	837956
Haller, Catarina	7 yrs.	Hemmingen	Leon.	Mar 1832	N.-Amer	837956
Haller, Christian	16 Dec 1839	Bondorf	Herr.	Oct 1866	N.-Amer	834630
Haller, Christiana	10 yrs.	Hemmingen	Leon.	Mar 1832	N.-Amer	837956
Haller, Georg	1 Mar 1829	Weiler	Gsl.	Feb 1854	N.-Amer	572042
Haller, Gottlieb	4 yrs.	Hemmingen	Leon.	Mar 1832	N.-Amer	837956
Haller, Jakob	13 yrs.	Hemmingen	Leon.	Mar 1832	N.-Amer	837956
Haller, Jakob & F	42 yrs.	Hemmingen	Leon.	Mar 1832	N.-Amer	837956
Haller, Johann Georg	1 yrs.	Hemmingen	Leon.	Mar 1832	N.-Amer	837956
Haller, Johann Georg & W	24 Mar 1822	Bondorf	Herr.	Apr 1869	N.-Amer	834630
Haller, Karl August	21 Nov 1861	Enzweihingen	Leon.	bef 1883	N.-Amer	837954

Name		Birth		Emigration			Film
Last	First	Date	Place	O'amt	Appl. Date	Dest.	Number
Haller, Maria & W		39 yrs.	Hemmingen	Leon.	Mar 1832	N.-Amer	837956
Haller, Maria Catharina (wife)		24 Mar 1811	Bondorf	Herr.	Apr 1869	N.-Amer	834630
Haller, Mathilde Wilhelmine		6 Mar 1847	Leonberg	Leon.	Feb 1869	N.-Amer	835787
Haller, Wilhelm		6 Aug 1856	Hoefingen	Leon.	Jan 1881	N.-Amer	837957
Hamann, – (wid.) & F		26 Dec 1809	Hepsisau	Krch.	Aug 1854	N.-Amer	835945
Hamann, Anna Barbara		18 yrs.	Hepsisau	Krch.	Aug 1854	N.-Amer	835945
Hamann, Anna Barbara		2 Jun 1816	Hepsisau	Krch.	Feb 1839	N.-Amer	835945
Hamann, Anna Barbara (wife)		14 Jul 1808	Hepsisau	Krch.	Feb 1839	N.-Amer	835945
Hamann, Anna Katharina		7 yrs.	Hepsisau	Krch.	Aug 1854	N.-Amer	835945
Hamann, Anna Margaretha		14 yrs.	Hepsisau	Krch.	Aug 1854	N.-Amer	835945
Hamann, Anna Margaretha		25 Nov 1837	Hepsisau	Krch.	Feb 1839	N.-Amer	835945
Hamann, Anna Maria		16 yrs.	Hepsisau	Krch.	Aug 1854	N.-Amer	835945
Hamann, Elisabeth (wife)		19 Jan 1775	Hepsisau	Krch.	Feb 1839	N.-Amer	835945
Hamann, Jacob & F		22 Mar 1775	Hepsisau	Krch.	Feb 1839	N.-Amer	835945
Hamann, Johannes		4 Jul 1832	Hepsisau	Krch.	May 1851	N.-Amer	835945
Hamann, Johannes & F		24 Feb 1807	Hepsisau	Krch.	Feb 1839	N.-Amer	835945
Hamann, Magdalena		11 yrs.	Hepsisau	Krch.	Aug 1854	N.-Amer	835945
Hamann, Michael		29 Dec 1831	Hepsisau	Krch.	May 1851	N.-Amer	835945
Hamann, Michael		6 Jan 1833	Hepsisau	Krch.	Feb 1839	N.-Amer	835945
Hambuch, Karl			Herrenberg	Herr.	Apr 1874	N.-Amer	834629
Hammann, Anna Barbara & C		8 Sep 1836	Bissingen	Krch.	Apr 1869	N.-Amer	835943
Hammeley, Ernst Jakob		13 Dec 1835	Weissach	Leon.	Mar 1851	N.-Amer	837963
Hammeley, Theophil			Reutlingen	Rtl.	Apr 1865	Algier	841053
Hammer, Bernhard Georg			Merklingen	Leon.	May 1855	Austral	837959
Hammer, Michael			Egenhausen	Nag.	Oct 1852	Austral	838488
Hammer, Victoria		18 yrs.	Reutlingen	Rtl.	Apr 1880	N.-Amer	841051
Hammerle, Johann Georg		3 Mar 1834	Oberjesingen	Herr.	May 1862	N.-Amer	834630
Handel, Cardine		20 Mar 1830	Leonberg	Leon.	Mar 1853	N.-Amer	835786
Handel, Carl		15 Mar 1853	Leonberg	Leon.	Aug 1854	N.-Amer	835786
Handel, Christian Gottlob		20 Apr 1833	Leonberg	Leon.	Mar 1853	N.-Amer	835786
Handel, Elisabetha Magdalena		21 Sep 1828	Leonberg	Leon.	Mar 1853	N.-Amer	835786
Handel, Friederika & C		22 Dec 1825	Leonberg	Leon.	Aug 1854	N.-Amer	835786
Handel, Friedrich		6 May 1824	Leonberg	Leon.	Aug 1854	N.-Amer	835786
Hanne, Johann Christoph		5 Jul 1806	Ohmden	Krch.	Jun 1855	N.-Amer	835948
Hanselmann, Johann Georg		26 May 1814	Renningen	Leon.	Mar 1848	Hesse	837963
Harllaub, Christiane Philipp.			Leonberg	Leon.	Jun 1869	Saxony	835787
Harr, Jacob Friedrich		18 Jul 1826	Oberjesingen	Herr.	bef 1863	N.-Amer	834630
Harter, Ferdinand		28 Sep 1827	Mariazell	Obd.	Jun 1870	N.-Amer	838634
Harter, Wendelin		20 Apr 1836	Mariazell	Obd.	Jun 1870	N.-Amer	838634
Hartlieb, Catharina Doro. & C		14 Feb 1830	Notzingen	Krch.	Sep 1867	N.-Amer	835947
Hartlieb, Wilhelm Friedrich		1 Nov 1850	Notzingen	Krch.	Feb 1869	N.-Amer	835947
Hartmann, Catharina		17 May 1824	Moensheim	Leon.	Mar 1830	N.-Amer	837960
Hartmann, Christina Soph.Marg.		30 Sep 1812	Moensheim	Leon.	Mar 1830	N.-Amer	837960
Hartmann, Dorothea		26 Aug 1828	Moensheim	Leon.	Mar 1830	N.-Amer	837960
Hartmann, Jacob		22 Apr 1830	Eltingen	Leon.	Dec 1850	N.-Amer	835789
Hartmann, Johann Michael		31 Dec 1817	Moensheim	Leon.	Mar 1830	N.-Amer	837960
Hartmann, Johannes		18 Nov 1820	Moensheim	Leon.	Mar 1830	N.-Amer	837960
Hartmann, Johannes Jakob		22 Feb 1842	Ditzingen	Leon.	Jun 1864	N.-Amer	835788
Hartmann, Katharina		26 Aug 1866	Ditzingen	Leon.	Feb 1870	N.-Amer	835788
Hartmann, Michael & F		46 yrs.	Moensheim	Leon.	Mar 1830	N.-Amer	837960

Hartmann, Nicolaus	27 Feb 1843	Geislingen	Gsl.	May 1863	N.-Amer	572044
Hartmann, Regina	26 Apr 1823	Moensheim	Leon.	Mar 1830	N.-Amer	837960
Hartmann, Regina (wife)	36 yrs.	Moensheim	Leon.	Mar 1830	N.-Amer	837960
Hartmann, Reinhold	16 Apr 1836	Wiesensteig	Gsl.	Mar 1854	N.-Amer	572042
Hartmann, Wilhelmine Phil.		Pfullingen	Rtl.	Oct 1828	N.-Amer	841051
Hartorn, Gottlieb		Heimerdingen	Leon.	bef 1834	N.-Amer	837954
Hartorn, Maria Catharina	10 yrs.	Heimerdingen	Leon.	Jul 1834	N.-Amer	837954
Hartstein, Andreas	15 Jul 1858	Reutlingen	Rtl.	May 1879	N.-Amer	841051
Hartstein, Johann Jakob	9 Aug 1829	Unterhausen	Rtl.	bef 1865	N.-Amer	841053
Hartstein, Matthaeus	21 Oct 1837	Unterhausen	Rtl.	Apr 1865	N.-Amer	841053
Hartter, Johannes		Hemmingen	Leon.	Nov 1853	N.-Amer	837956
Harttmann, Anna Maria	2 yrs.	Leonberg	Leon.	Dec 1816	Russia	835789
Harttmann, Georg Adam & F	30 yrs.	Leonberg	Leon.	Dec 1816	Russia	835789
Harttmann, Gottlieb		Warmbronn	Leon.	Apr 1830	N.-Amer	837965
Harttmann, Johannes & F		Warmbronn	Leon.	Apr 1830	N.-Amer	837965
Harttmann, Katharina	3 yrs.	Leonberg	Leon.	Dec 1816	Russia	835789
Harttmann, Margaretha	infant	Leonberg	Leon.	Dec 1816	Russia	835789
Harttmann, Margaretha (wife)	25 yrs.	Leonberg	Leon.	Dec 1816	Russia	835789
Harttmann, Sophia	15 Apr 1841	Oberndorf	Obd.	Mar 1869	Switz.	838635
Hasenmaier, Carolina	infant	Heimsheim	Leon.	Jul 1851	N.-Amer	837955
Hasenmaier, Carolina Barb. & C	22 yrs.	Heimsheim	Leon.	Jul 1851	N.-Amer	837955
Hasenmaier, Catrina Barbara	24 yrs.	Heimsheim	Leon.	Jul 1851	N.-Amer	837955
Hasenmaier, Christoph Friedr.		Heimsheim	Leon.	Jun 1822	France	837955
Hasenmaier, Georg Friedrich		Heimsheim	Leon.	bef 1820	France	837955
Hasenmaier, Gottlieb Friedr.		Renningen	Leon.	Apr 1852	N.-Amer	837963
Hasenmaier, Johann Georg		Heimsheim	Leon.	Jan 1819	France	837955
Hasenmaier, Philipp Adam	17 Apr 1833	Heimsheim	Leon.	May 1853	N.-Amer	837955
Hasenmayer, Christoph Friedr.		Leonberg	Leon.	Dec 1821	France	835786
Haspel, Christiana	11 Dec 1833	Gebersheim	Leon.	Feb 1853	N.-Amer	837953
Haspel, Gottfried		Ditzingen	Leon.	Jul 1846	France	835788
Haspel, Michael		Ditzingen	Leon.	Dec 1841	Prussia	835788
Haspel, Wilhelm		Ditzingen	Leon.	bef 1871	N.-Amer	835788
Hass, Louise Friederike	25 Dec 1839	Kirchheim	Krch.	May 1860	N.-Amer	835940
Hass, Maria Wilhelmine	14 Dec 1838	Kirchheim	Krch.	May 1860	N.-Amer	835940
Hass, Marie	14 Mar 1847	Kirchheim	Krch.	Apr 1862	N.-Amer	835941
Hassler, Andreas	30 Apr 1842	Ueberkingen	Gsl.	Dec 1853	N.-Amer	572041
Hassler, Anna & C	21 Dec 1835	Ueberkingen	Gsl.	May 1861	N.-Amer	572044
Hassler, Anna Maria	22 Dec 1857	Ueberkingen	Gsl.	May 1861	N.-Amer	572044
Hassler, Daniel	29 Oct 1834	Ueberkingen	Gsl.	May 1861	N.-Amer	572044
Hassler, Johannes		Ueberkingen	Gsl.	Apr 1852	N.-Amer	572041
Hassler, Johannes & F		Ueberkingen	Gsl.	Dec 1853	N.-Amer	572041
Hassler, Maria	4 Oct 1833	Ueberkingen	Gsl.	Jun 1861	N.-Amer	572044
Hassler, Wilhelm Friedrich	3 Mar 1839	Leonberg	Leon.	May 1857	N.-Amer	835786
Hauch, Johann Jakob	4 Sep 1847	Zell	Krch.	May 1856	N.-Amer	835774
Haueisen, Paul Eugen	24 Apr 1845	Leonberg	Leon.	Aug 1866	N.-Amer	835787
Hauer, Lorenz	14 yrs.	Aichhalden	Obd.	Dec 1854	N.-Amer	838629
Hauer, Wendelin	13 Aug 1851	Aichhalden	Obd.	May 1869	N.-Amer	838629
Haug, Anna Maria	14 Feb 1833	Gingen	Gsl.	Sep 1853	N.-Amer	572041
Haug, Anna Maria	3 Apr 1838	Gingen	Gsl.	Jul 1864	N.-Amer	572045
Haug, Christoph Friedrich	20 Nov 1851	Notzingen	Krch.	Mar 1868	N.-Amer	835947

Name		Birth		Emigration			Film
Last	First	Date	Place	O'amt	Appl. Date	Dest.	Number
Haug, Jacob		29 Mar 1848	Schoeckingen	Leon.	Nov 1872	N.-Amer	837964
Haug, Jakob Thomas & F		18 Dec 1841	Hoefingen	Leon.	Aug 1887	N.-Amer	837957
Haug, Johann Jakob		18 Dec 1825	Schoeckingen	Leon.	Apr 1852	N.-Amer	837964
Haug, Karl Ludwig		14 Aug 1881	Hoefingen	Leon.	Aug 1887	N.-Amer	837957
Haug, Lukas (wid.) & F			Gingen	Gsl.	Sep 1853	N.-Amer	572041
Haug, Maria Katharina		28 Dec 1868	Wellingen	Krch.	Apr 1884	N.-Amer	835947
Haug, Marie Emilie (wife)		23 Sep 1837	Wengen	Leon.	Aug 1887	N.-Amer	837957
Haug, Marie Katharine		28 Dec 1868	Wellingen	Krch.	Apr 1884	N.-Amer	548403
Haug, Michael		15 Nov 1836	Gingen	Gsl.	Mar 1856	N.-Amer	572043
Haug, Philipp		20 yrs.	Gingen	Gsl.	Mar 1853	N.-Amer	572041
Haupp, Waldburga			Alt Oberndorf	Obd.	bef 1867	N.-Amer	838631
Hausch, Anna Magdalena		8 Jul 1832	Zell	Krch.	Apr 1855	N.-Amer	835774
Hausch, Elisabetha		28 Sep 1835	Zell	Krch.	Apr 1855	N.-Amer	835774
Hausch, Johann Georg		14 May 1868	Pliensbach	Krch.	Dec 1884	N.-Amer	548403
Hausch, Sophie & F		25 Oct 1805	Zell	Krch.	May 1856	N.-Amer	835774
Hausch, Wilhelm		11 Oct 1801	Zell	Krch.	Jun 1856	N.-Amer	835774
Hausch, Wilhelm		4 Oct 1833	Zell	Krch.	Apr 1855	N.-Amer	835774
Hausel, Katharina		25 Feb 1830	Brucken	Krch.	Aug 1867	N.-Amer	835944
Hauser, Anna Barbara & C			Merklingen	Leon.	Feb 1846	N.-Amer	837959
Hauser, Carl Friedrich		12 Jun 1841	Herrenberg	Herr.	bef 1870	Bavaria	834629
Hauser, Catharina Magdal. & C			Merklingen	Leon.	Jul 1841	N.-Amer	837959
Hauser, Johannes		30 Mar 1859	Genkingen	Rtl.	Apr 1880	N.-Amer	841051
Hauser, Regina			Merklingen	Leon.	Feb 1846	N.-Amer	837959
Hauser, Sophie Christina			Renningen	Leon.	Apr 1852	N.-Amer	837963
Hauser, Wilhelm		7 Apr 1877	Herrenberg	Herr.	Apr 1892	N.-Amer	834629
Hausler, Carl		27 May 1797	Kirchheim	Krch.	Sep 1867	N.-Amer	835941
Hausmann, Jacob		25 Apr 1807	Dettingen	Krch.	Mar 1858	N.-Amer	835944
Hausmann, Johannes		31 Dec 1841	Bissingen	Krch.	bef 1867	N.-Amer	835940
Hausmann, Johannes		31 Dec 1845	Bissingen	Krch.	dec 1865	N.-Amer	835943
Hausmann, Ludwig		14 Jul 1838	Oetlingen	Krch.	Jun 1866	N.-Amer	835948
Hausmann, Maria Agnes		31 Aug 1844	Bissingen	Krch.	bef 1867	N.-Amer	835940
Hausmann, Maria Agnes		31 Aug 1844	Reudern/Nuert.	Krch.	Nov 1867	N.-Amer	835943
Hausmann, Michael			Bissingen	Krch.	bef 1867	N.-Amer	835940
Haussmann, Ernst		12 Apr 1848	Kirchheim	Krch.	Jul 1867	N.-Amer	835941
Haussmann, Johann Georg		22 Jun 1872	Oetlingen	Krch.	Jan 1889	N.-Amer	835948
Haussmann, Johannes		21 Sep 1848	Lindorf	Krch.	Oct 1868	N.-Amer	835946
Haussmann, Louise		3 Feb 1825	Reutlingen	Rtl.	Jan 1861	Switz.	841053
Haux, Hans		8 Aug 1863	Kirchheim	Krch.	Apr 1881	N.-Amer	548403
Haux, Hans		8 Aug 1863	Stuttgart	Krch.	Apr 1881	N.-Amer	835942
Haux, Jacob		3 Dec 1846	Honau	Rtl.	Oct 1866	N.-Amer	841053
Hayer, Adolph		26 Feb 1847	Kirchheim	Krch.	Jul 1866	N.-Amer	835941
Hayer, Carl Gottlob		12 Nov 1842	Kirchheim	Krch.	Jul 1866	N.-Amer	835941
Hayer, Christian Friedr.		20 Mar 1849	Moensheim	Leon.	May 1849	N.-Amer	837960
Hayer, Christian Friedr. & F			Moensheim	Leon.	May 1849	N.-Amer	837960
Hayer, Franz Ludwig			Moensheim	Leon.	bef 1851	N.-Amer	837960
Hayer, Friederika (wife)			Moensheim	Leon.	May 1849	N.-Amer	837960
Hayer, Friederike		15 Dec 1840	Kirchheim	Krch.	Feb 1866	N.-Amer	835941
Hayer, Gottlieb Gottlob		12 Mar 1845	Kirchheim	Krch.	Sep 1866	N.-Amer	835941
Hayer, Johann Georg		18 Nov 1784	Schoeckingen	Leon.	bef 1820	France	837964
Hebsacker, Emil		30 Mar 1849	Reutlingen	Rtl.	Jan 1869	N.-Amer	841053

Name	Date/Age	Place	Region	Date	Destination	Film
Hecht, Anna Maria		Gueltstein	Herr.	1863	Leipzig	834631
Hecht, Ernst	17 yrs.	Reutlingen	Rtl.	Apr 1880	N.-Amer	841051
Hecht, Johannes	12 Apr 1841	Reutlingen	Rtl.	Aug 1860	N.-Amer	841053
Hecht, Maria Agnes	8 May 1843	Gueltstein	Leon.	Dec 1862	Leipzig	834624
Heck, Christine	9 yrs.	Gerlingen	Leon.	Aug 1860	N.-Amer	837953
Heck, Dorothea (wife)	39 yrs.	Gerlingen	Leon.	Aug 1860	N.-Amer	837953
Heck, Friedrich & F	9 Aug 1817	Gerlingen	Leon.	Aug 1860	N.-Amer	837953
Heck, Georg	24 yrs.	Muenchingen	Leon.	Jan 1855	N.-Amer	837961
Heck, Johann Georg	29 yrs.	Gerlingen	Leon.	Mar 1852	S.-Amer	837953
Heckeler, Catharina	12 Dec 1828	Schoeckingen	Leon.	Jul 1852	N.-Amer	837964
Heckeler, Christoph Ludwig	26 Feb 1832	Schoeckingen	Leon.	Aug 1853	N.-Amer	837964
Heckeler, Johann Peter & F		Schoeckingen	Leon.	Aug 1853	N.-Amer	837964
Heckeler, Margaretha		Jesingen	Krch.	Apr 1860	N.-Amer	835946
Heer, Christina Wilhelmina	14 Jan 1859	Conweiler/Neuenburg	Leon.	Dec 1888	N.-Amer	837959
Heerbrandt, Gottlob Albrecht	17 Aug 1846	Reutlingen	Rtl.	Jun 1865	N.-Amer	841053
Heerbrandt, Pauline	29 Mar 1832	Reutlingen	Rtl.	bef 1860	N.-Amer	841053
Hees, – (wife) & F		Oberndorf	Obd.	May 1854	N.-Amer	838635
Hees, Ignaz		Oberndorf	Obd.	bef 1854	N.-Amer	838635
Heetzel, Andreas	23 Jan 1806	Alpirsbach	Obd.	bef 1869	Switz.	838630
Hegele, Cardine Pauline	11 Dec 1849	Leonberg	Leon.	Nov 1852	N.-Amer	835786
Hegele, Carl Wilhelm	19 yrs.	Sulz	Leon.	Jun 1854	N.-Amer	837956
Hegele, Catharina & F		Leonberg	Leon.	Nov 1852	N.-Amer	835786
Hegele, Christian	8 Mar 1850	Leonberg	Leon.	Jul 1869	N.-Amer	835787
Hegele, Christina Catharina	33 yrs.	Leonberg	Leon.	Apr 1843	N.-Amer	835786
Hegele, Gottlieb		Leonberg	Leon.	bef 1853	N.-Amer	835786
Hegele, Gustav Adolph	28 Apr 1845	Sulz	Leon.	Oct 1860	N.-Amer	837956
Hegele, Louise Ottilie	9 Sep 1848	Leonberg	Leon.	Nov 1852	N.-Amer	835786
Hegele, Marie Catharine	9 Sep 1845	Leonberg	Leon.	Nov 1852	N.-Amer	835786
Hegele, Sophie Mathilde	17 Nov 1843	Leonberg	Leon.	Nov 1852	N.-Amer	835786
Hegele, Wilhelm Gustav	13 Oct 1863	Hirschlanden	Leon.	Oct 1880	N.-Amer	837956
Hegele, Wilhelmine Pauline	22 Nov 1851	Leonberg	Leon.	Nov 1852	N.-Amer	835786
Heid, Bertha (wife)	8 Sep 1842	Eifa/Hesse	Rtl.	Apr 1869	N.-Amer	841053
Heid, Carl Alex & W	5 Dec 1842	Honau	Rtl.	Apr 1869	N.-Amer	841053
Heid, Carl Jakob	10 Jan 1866	Honau	Rtl.	Apr 1867	N.-Amer	841053
Heid, Christian & F	2 Oct 1837	Honau	Rtl.	Apr 1867	N.-Amer	841053
Heid, Johann Georg	19 Mar 1843	Pfullingen	Rtl.	Oct 1862	N.-Amer	841053
Heid, Johannes	26 Nov 1846	Unterhausen	Rtl.	Apr 1864	N.-Amer	841053
Heid, Philippina (wife)	26 Oct 1842	Honau	Rtl.	Apr 1867	N.-Amer	841053
Heidle, Conrad	27 yrs.	Hoefingen	Leon.	May 1857	N.-Amer	837957
Heidle, Margaretha	20 yrs.	Hoefingen	Leon.	May 1857	N.-Amer	837957
Heilemann, – (wife)	61 yrs.	Dettingen	Krch.	Jan 1874	N.-Amer	548403
Heilemann, Anna	27 Aug 1846	Ochsenwang	Krch.	Feb 1868	N.-Amer	835947
Heilemann, Anna Maria (wife)	21 May 1832	Ochsenwang	Krch.	Feb 1868	N.-Amer	835947
Heilemann, August	1 Aug 1846	Neidlingen	Krch.	Dec 1865	England	835946
Heilemann, Christian	11 May 1855	Ochsenwang	Krch.	Feb 1868	N.-Amer	835947
Heilemann, Christian & F	21 Dec 1816	Dettingen	Krch.	Dec 1873	N.-Amer	835944
Heilemann, Eberhard	6 Sep 1848	Notzingen	Krch.	Apr 1866	N.-Amer	835947
Heilemann, Friederike	17 Dec 1850	Dettingen	Krch.	Dec 1873	N.-Amer	835944
Heilemann, Heinrich	25 Dec 1850	Ochsenwang	Krch.	Feb 1868	N.-Amer	835947
Heilemann, Johann Christian	20 Mar 1868	Dettingen	Krch.	Dec 1873	N.-Amer	835944

Name		Birth		Emigration			Film
Last	First	Date	Place	O'amt	Appl. Date	Dest.	Number
Heilemann, Johann David		21 Jan 1836	Notzingen	Krch.	May 1855	N.-Amer	835947
Heilemann, Johann Georg		13 Jun 1862	Ochsenwang	Krch.	Feb 1868	N.-Amer	835947
Heilemann, Johann Georg		14 Jun 1842	Weiler	Krch.	Jul 1868	N.-Amer	835949
Heilemann, Johannes			Neidlingen	Krch.	bef 1866	N.-Amer	835940
Heilemann, Johannes		4 Dec 1871	Ochsenwang	Krch.	Feb 1888	N.-Amer	835947
Heilemann, Johannes		30 Jan 1860	Ochsenwang	Krch.	Feb 1868	N.-Amer	835947
Heilemann, Johannes		9 Jan 1830	Neidlingen	Krch.	Sep 1866	N.-Amer	835946
Heilemann, Johannes Gottlieb		12 Jun 1845	Neidlingen	Krch.	Oct 1860	N.-Amer	835946
Heilemann, Karoline		9 Aug 1836	Ochsenwang	Krch.	May 1860	N.-Amer	835947
Heilemann, Katharina		29 May 1844	Ochsenwang	Rtl.	Oct 1866	N.-Amer	841057
Heilemann, Michael		25 Oct 1863	Ochsenwang	Krch.	Feb 1868	N.-Amer	835947
Heilemann, Michael & F		7 Jul 1821	Ochsenwang	Krch.	Feb 1868	N.-Amer	835947
Heilemann, Rosina (wife)		13 Mar 1813	Dettingen	Krch.	Dec 1873	N.-Amer	835944
Heilemann, Rosine		25 Dec 1848	Ochsenwang	Krch.	Feb 1868	N.-Amer	835947
Heilig, Franz			Treffelhausen	Gsl.	Mar 1850	N.-Amer	577788
Heiligmann, Christiane		19 yrs.	Gueltstein	Herr.	1873	N.-Amer	834631
Heiligmann, Joh.Georg (wid.) & F		53 yrs.	Gueltstein	Herr.	1873	N.-Amer	834631
Heiligmann, Johann Martin		5 yrs.	Gueltstein	Herr.	1873	N.-Amer	834631
Heiligmann, Johannes		14 yrs.	Gueltstein	Herr.	1873	N.-Amer	834631
Heim, Christian		16 Aug 1838	Zell	Krch.	Mar 1855	N.-Amer	835774
Heim, Christian Friedrich			Kirchheim	Krch.	bef 1867	A-dam	835940
Heim, Christian Friedrich		18 Jan 1876	Aichelberg	Krch.	Apr 1892	N.-Amer	835943
Heim, Christiane Friederike		23 Oct 1836	Owen	Krch.	Sep 1860	N.-Amer	835948
Heim, Georg			Oberlenningen	Krch.	1817	N.-Amer	835940
Heim, Jacob Gottlieb			Kirchheim	Krch.	bef 1867	A-dam	835940
Heim, Johann Georg		7 Sep 1872	Aichelberg	Krch.	Apr 1888	N.-Amer	835943
Heim, Johannes		14 Mar 1874	Zell	Krch.	Jan 1890	N.-Amer	835774
Heim, Johannes		21 Sep 1873	Aichelberg	Krch.	Apr 1888	N.-Amer	835943
Heim, Leo Alexander			Oberndorf	Obd.	Mar 1849	N.-Amer	838635
Heim, Maria		16 Jan 1844	Winzeln	Obd.	Sep 1863	N.-Amer	841016
Heim, Maria Theresia			Oberndorf	Obd.	Mar 1849	N.-Amer	838635
Heim, Monika & C			Oberndorf	Obd.	Mar 1849	N.-Amer	838635
Heim, Pauline Louise		20 Jan 1835	Owen	Krch.	Nov 1856	France	835948
Heim, Sebastian			Oberndorf	Obd.	Mar 1849	N.-Amer	838635
Heim, Wilhelm		26 May 1847	Winzeln	Obd.	Sep 1863	N.-Amer	841016
Heimerdinger, Christian Gottl.			Hausen/Brackenheim	Leon.	bef 1856	N.-Amer	837963
Heine, Mathias		17 Feb 1811	Schramberg	Obd.	May 1839	Austria	838637
Heinkel, Caroline		24 Mar 1844	Kirchheim	Krch.	Feb 1866	N.-Amer	835941
Heinkel, Johannes		29 Jan 1881	Herrenberg	Herr.	Oct 1896	N.-Amer	834629
Heinkel, Johannes Friedrich		22 Nov 1879	Tuebingen	Herr.	Oct 1896	N.-Amer	834629
Heinkel, Karl Wilhelm		1 Apr 1868	Kirchheim	Krch.	May 1884	N.-Amer	548403
Heinle, Catharina Brigitta & F		23 Sep 1810	Pfullingen	Rtl.	Mar 1864	N.-Amer	841053
Heinle, Elisabetha Christina		27 Jan 1837	Pfullingen	Rtl.	Mar 1864	N.-Amer	841053
Heinle, Imanuel Gottlieb		25 Feb 1847	Pfullingen	Rtl.	Mar 1864	N.-Amer	841053
Heinle, Johann Ludwig			Pfullingen	Rtl.	Aug 1835	N.-Amer	841051
Heinle, Ludwig			Pfullingen	Rtl.	May 1832	N.-Amer	841051
Heinle, Maria Louisa		15 Mar 1845	Pfullingen	Rtl.	Mar 1864	N.-Amer	841053
Heinle, Wilhelm Jacob		3 Aug 1830	Pfullingen	Rtl.	bef 1864	N.-Amer	841053
Heinlin, Johann Friedrich		2 Aug 1850	Pfullingen	Rtl.	May 1867	N.-Amer	841053
Heinrich, Margaretha		1 Apr 1837	Oetlingen	Krch.	bef 1860	N.-Amer	835948

Heinz, Anna Maria	12 Oct 1839	Willmandingen	Rtl.	bef 1868	N.-Amer	841053
Heinz, Anna Maria (wife)		Perouse	Leon.	Mar 1831	N.-Amer	837962
Heinz, Catharina	11 yrs.	Perouse	Leon.	Mar 1831	N.-Amer	837962
Heinz, Catharina	11 Feb 1844	Willmandingen	Rtl.	Apr 1861	N.-Amer	841053
Heinz, David	27 Oct 1849	Willmandingen	Rtl.	Dec 1867	N.-Amer	841053
Heinz, Friedrich	9 yrs.	Perouse	Leon.	Mar 1831	N.-Amer	837962
Heinz, Georg Friedrich & F		Perouse	Leon.	Mar 1831	N.-Amer	837962
Heinz, Jakob	20 yrs.	Perouse	Leon.	Mar 1831	N.-Amer	837962
Heinz, Johann Georg	25 May 1849	Willmandingen	Rtl.	Feb 1867	N.-Amer	841053
Heinz, Johannes	6 mon.	Perouse	Leon.	Mar 1831	N.-Amer	837962
Heinz, Johannes	19 Jun 1852	Willmandingen	Rtl.	Feb 1867	N.-Amer	841053
Heinz, Katharina (wid.) & F	27 Aug 1811	Willmandingen	Rtl.	Apr 1861	N.-Amer	841053
Heinz, Ludwig	21 Aug 1846	Willmandingen	Rtl.	Apr 1860	N.-Amer	841053
Heinz, Maria Barbara	1 Jan 1849	Willmandingen	Rtl.	Apr 1861	N.-Amer	841053
Heinz, Wilhelm	7 yrs.	Perouse	Leon.	Mar 1831	N.-Amer	837962
Heinzelmann, Andreas		Harthausen	Obd.	Dec 1853	N.-Amer	838633
Heinzelmann, Andreas	2 Aug 1848	Roetenbach	Obd.	Oct 1867	N.-Amer	838636
Heinzelmann, Andreas	16 Oct 1834	Roetenbach	Obd.	Nov 1853	N.-Amer	838636
Heinzelmann, Barbara	11 yrs.	Fluorn	Obd.	Apr 1860	N.-Amer	838632
Heinzelmann, Carl Georg	19 Oct 1834	Alpirsbach	Obd.	Mar 1854	N.-Amer	838630
Heinzelmann, Christina	11 yrs.	Fluorn	Obd.	Apr 1860	N.-Amer	838632
Heinzelmann, Friederike	3 Jul 1845	Alpirsbach	Obd.	Jul 1868	France	838630
Heinzelmann, Gottfried & C	6 Dec 1841	Alpirsbach	Obd.	Apr 1867	N.-Amer	838630
Heinzelmann, Gottlieb	29 Jun 1823	Hemmingen	Leon.	bef 1859	N.-Amer	837956
Heinzelmann, Heinrich	15 Dec 1865	Alpirsbach	Obd.	Apr 1867	N.-Amer	838630
Heinzelmann, Jacob		Alpirsbach	Obd.	Sep 1816	Hesse	838631
Heinzelmann, Johann	4 Jun 1850	Fluorn	Obd.	Aug 1864	N.-Amer	838632
Heinzelmann, Johann Christoph		Alpirsbach	Obd.	Jan 1838	France	838631
Heinzelmann, Johann Georg & F		Beffendorf	Obd.	Apr 1817	N.-Amer	838631
Heinzelmann, Johannes	23 Dec 1849	Peterzell	Obd.	Sep 1869	N.-Amer	838635
Heinzelmann, Margaretha Fried.		Alpirsbach	Obd.	Apr 1863	France	838630
Heinzelmann, Maria Barb. (wife)		Alpirsbach	Obd.	Apr 1867	France	838630
Heinzelmann, Sophie	4 Jun 1841	Alpirsbach	Obd.	Aug 1868	France	838630
Heinzler, Rosina	11 Apr 1826	Alpirsbach	Obd.	Jul 1856	Switz.	838630
Heinzmann, Alois	11 Feb 1853	Donzdorf	Gsl.	May 1870	N.-Amer	572047
Heinzmann, Anton	6 Oct 1822	Boehmenkirch	Gsl.	Apr 1857	N.-Amer	572043
Heinzmann, August	1 Jul 1851	Schramberg	Obd.	Oct 1868	N.-Amer	838636
Heinzmann, Bernhard		Boehmenkirch	Gsl.	Mar 1852	N.-Amer	572041
Heinzmann, Bernhard	28 Dec 1825	Boehmenkirch	Gsl.	Jan 1867	N.-Amer	572046
Heinzmann, Bernhardina		Boehmenkirch	Gsl.	May 1852	N.-Amer	572041
Heinzmann, Carl		Boehmenkirch	Gsl.	Mar 1852	N.-Amer	572041
Heinzmann, Genovefa		Boehmenkirch	Gsl.	Mar 1852	N.-Amer	572041
Heinzmann, Ignaz	18 yrs.	Boehmenkirch	Gsl.	Jun 1867	N.-Amer	572046
Heinzmann, Johann Georg		Lauterbach	Obd.	Apr 1854	N.-Amer	838634
Heinzmann, Johannes		Boehmenkirch	Gsl.	Jun 1867	N.-Amer	572046
Heinzmann, Josef	20 Feb 1845	Boehmenkirch	Gsl.	Jan 1867	N.-Amer	572046
Heinzmann, Katharina	9 Dec 1831	Boehmenkirch	Gsl.	May 1852	N.-Amer	572041
Heinzmann, Katharina		Boehmenkirch	Gsl.	Sep 1853	N.-Amer	572041
Heinzmann, Lorenz		Boehmenkirch	Gsl.	May 1852	N.-Amer	572041
Heinzmann, Lorenz		Boehmenkirch	Gsl.	Mar 1852	N.-Amer	572041

Name		Birth		Emigration			Film
Last	First	Date	Place	O'amt	Appl. Date	Dest.	Number
Heinzmann, Lorenz (wid.) & F			Donzdorf	Gsl.	Mar 1852	N.-Amer	572041
Heinzmann, Maria		22 May 1841	Boehmenkirch	Gsl.	Sep 1867	N.-Amer	572046
Hek, Johann Georg		21 yrs.	Muenchingen	Leon.	1837	Russia	837961
Hekeler, Johann Georg		26 Sep 1829	Jesingen	Krch.	Sep 1870	N.-Amer	835946
Helb, Johann Eberhard		22 Mar 1839	Reutlingen	Rtl.	Aug 1864	N.-Amer	841053
Helb, Johannes		21 Feb 1842	Pfullingen	Rtl.	1861	N.-Amer	841053
Held, Anna Maria		8 Sep 1854	Moensheim	Leon.	Sep 1856	N.-Amer	837960
Held, Christian Friedrich		27 Jul 1852	Moensheim	Leon.	Sep 1856	N.-Amer	837960
Held, Christina (wife)			Moensheim	Leon.	Sep 1856	N.-Amer	837960
Held, Friedrich		22 yrs.	Reutlingen	Rtl.	Nov 1880	N.-Amer	841051
Held, Jakob Friedrich		11 Sep 1847	Moensheim	Leon.	Sep 1856	N.-Amer	837960
Held, Johann Daniel		13 Dec 1849	Moensheim	Leon.	Sep 1856	N.-Amer	837960
Held, Johann David & F			Moensheim	Leon.	Sep 1856	N.-Amer	837960
Held, Johann Georg		8 May 1845	Moensheim	Leon.	Sep 1856	N.-Amer	837960
Held, Regina		24 Feb 1844	Moensheim	Leon.	Sep 1856	N.-Amer	837960
Heldele, Veit		30 Dec 1829	Treffelhausen	Gsl.	Oct 1866	N.-Amer	572045
Helferich, Alexander		10 Mar 1843	Kirchheim	Krch.	1863	N.-Amer	835940
Helferich, Mina		11 Nov 1844	Kirchheim	Krch.	Aug 1866	N.-Amer	835941
Helfferich, Alexander		10 Mar 1843	Kirchheim	Krch.	Aug 1863	N.-Amer	835941
Heller, Anna Maria (wife)			Renningen	Leon.	Apr 1852	N.-Amer	837963
Heller, Christoph Friedr. & F			Renningen	Leon.	Apr 1852	N.-Amer	837963
Heller, Johannes		19 May 1864	Geislingen	Gsl.	Jun 1879	N.-Amer	572048
Heller, Rosina		25 May 1845	Renningen	Leon.	Apr 1852	N.-Amer	837963
Hengstler, Heinrich		45 yrs.	Leonberg	Leon.	May 1842	Austria	835786
Hengstler, Jacob Friedrich		15 Oct 1812	Leonberg	Leon.	Sep 1835	Austria	835786
Hengstler, Johannes		17 Jun 1818	Leonberg	Leon.	Jul 1853	Austria	835786
Henig, Johann Bernhard		22 yrs.	Willmandingen	Rtl.	Jan 1880	N.-Amer	841051
Henne, Anna (wife)			Wimsheim	Loen.	Oct 1870	Austria	837967
Henne, Bertha		18 mon.	Wimsheim	Loen.	Oct 1870	Austria	837967
Henne, Friedrich Ludwig		1 Dec 1830	Ellwangen	Loen.	Oct 1870	Austria	837967
Henne, Johann Bernhard		21 Feb 1841	Hoefingen	Leon.	Jul 1873	N.-Amer	837957
Henne, Johannes		5 Oct 1823	Hausen a.d. Wurm	Leon.	1850	N.-Amer	837954
Henne, Wilhelm		3 yrs.	Wimsheim	Loen.	Oct 1870	Austria	837967
Henninger, Louis Heinrich		10 Sep 1815	Alpirsbach	Obd.	Jan 1858	N.-Amer	838630
Hepperle, Johann David		21 Feb 1819	Weilheim	Krch.	bef 1857	N.-Amer	835949
Hepperle, Johann Georg			Neidlingen	Krch.	bef 1866	N.-Amer	835940
Hepperle, Johann Georg		12 Mar 1824	Neidlingen	Krch.	Jun 1866	N.-Amer	835946
Hepperle, Johann Jakob		3 May 1823	Neidlingen	Krch.	Sep 1866	N.-Amer	835946
Hepperle, Karl		27 Mar 1873	Weilheim	Krch.	Sep 1887	N.-Amer	835774
Hepperle, Wilhelm		23 Nov 1872	Neidlingen	Krch.	Apr 1889	N.-Amer	835946
Herbster, Albert Leopold		29 Oct 1863	Wiesensteig	Gsl.	Sep 1866	N.-Amer	572045
Herbster, Franz		28 Jul 1852	Wiesensteig	Gsl.	Apr 1857	N.-Amer	572043
Herbster, Josef		10 May 1866	Wiesensteig	Gsl.	Sep 1866	N.-Amer	572045
Herbster, Maria Barbara		5 Dec 1864	Wiesensteig	Gsl.	Sep 1866	N.-Amer	572045
Herbster, Pauline (wife)		27 Oct 1840	Wiesensteig	Gsl.	Sep 1866	N.-Amer	572045
Herbster, Sebastian & F		19 Jan 1839	Wiesensteig	Gsl.	Sep 1866	N.-Amer	572045
Herbster, Zezilia & C		22 Aug 1829	Wiesensteig	Gsl.	Apr 1857	N.-Amer	572043
Herbstreut, Matthias		17 Jun 1826	Betzweiler	Obd.	Mar 1851	N.-Amer	838631
Hering, Andreas & F			Warmbronn	Leon.	Apr 1830	N.-Amer	837965
Hering, Catharina		21 yrs.	Warmbronn	Leon.	Apr 1830	N.-Amer	837965

Heritier, Friederika & F	5 Nov 1790	Perouse	Leon.	Jan 1852	N.-Amer	837962
Heritier, Friederike		Perouse	Leon.	Sep 1857	N.-Amer	837962
Heritier, Marie Catharine	22 Nov 1828	Perouse	Leon.	Jan 1852	N.-Amer	837962
Herlikofer, Carl	17 yrs.	Schramberg	Obd.	Jun 1855	N.-Amer	838636
Herlinger, Anna Katharina		Altenstadt-Gsl.	Gsl.	Jan 1854	N.-Amer	572042
Hermann, Catharina Elisabetha		Reutlingen	Rtl.	Jul 1860	N.-Amer	841053
Hermann, Christian		Friolzheim	Leon.	Apr 1855	N.-Amer	835791
Hermann, Christian Gottlob	13 Apr 1834	Friolzheim	Leon.	May 1851	N.-Amer	835791
Hermann, Eberhard	22 yrs.	Weil im Dorf	Loen.	Feb 1852	N.-Amer	837967
Hermann, Elisabetha	28 yrs.	Friolzheim	Leon.	Apr 1852	N.-Amer	835791
Hermann, Georg		Friolzheim	Leon.	Apr 1855	Switz.	835791
Hermann, Georg	6 Oct 1842	Reutlingen	Rtl.	Mar 1860	N.-Amer	841053
Hermann, Georg Lorenz		Friolzheim	Leon.	Nov 1818	France	835791
Hermann, Gottlieb	16 yrs.	Weil im Dorf	Loen.	Feb 1853	N.-Amer	837967
Hermann, Johann Georg	30 Nov 1841	Ohmenhausen	Rtl.	Mar 1865	N.-Amer	841053
Hermann, Johanna (wid.)		Eltingen	Leon.	Jul 1853	N.-Amer	835789
Hermann, Johannes	24 yrs.	Friolzheim	Leon.	Apr 1864	N.-Amer	835791
Hermann, Karl Friedrich	13 May 1867	Friolzheim	Leon.	Mar 1884	N.-Amer	835791
Hermann, Lorenz	18 May 1865	Kuchen	Gsl.	Aug 1882	N.-Amer	572048
Hermann, Marx		Friolzheim	Leon.	bef 1867	France	835791
Hermann, Michael	27 yrs.	Weil im Dorf	Loen.	Feb 1852	N.-Amer	837967
Herr, Johann Georg		Warmbronn	Leon.	Apr 1853	N.-Amer	837965
Herr, Joseph	32 yrs.	Warmbronn	Leon.	May 1853	N.-Amer	837965
Herr, Joseph	20 Dec 1843	Donzdorf	Gsl.	Sep 1866	N.-Amer	572045
Herre, Andreas & W		Ludwigsburg	Obd.	Jul 1863	N.-Amer	838636
Herre, Christine (wife)		Roetenbach	Obd.	Jul 1863	N.-Amer	838636
Herrlinger, Andreas	16 May 1840	Altenstadt-Gsl.	Gsl.	Aug 1853	N.-Amer	572041
Herrlinger, Anna	1 Aug 1839	Gosbach	Gsl.	Feb 1856	N.-Amer	572043
Herrlinger, Anna Maria	13 Apr 1836	Kuchen	Gsl.	bef 1854	N.-Amer	572042
Herrlinger, Anna Maria	27 Nov 1830	Kuchen	Gsl.	Feb 1854	N.-Amer	572042
Herrlinger, Apollonia	16 Aug 1805	Kuchen	Gsl.	Feb 1854	N.-Amer	572042
Herrlinger, David	26 Apr 1805	Kuchen	Gsl.	Feb 1854	N.-Amer	572042
Herrlinger, Eva	29 Aug 1832	Kuchen	Gsl.	bef 1854	N.-Amer	572042
Herrlinger, Jakob	18 yrs.	Ueberkingen	Gsl.	May 1864	N.-Amer	572045
Herrlinger, Johann Georg	14 Sep 1828	Altenstadt-Gsl.	Gsl.	Aug 1853	N.-Amer	572041
Herrlinger, Johanna Elis. (wife)	27 Nov 1804	Altenstadt-Gsl.	Gsl.	Aug 1853	N.-Amer	572041
Herrlinger, Juliana	12 Dec 1839	Kuchen	Gsl.	Feb 1854	N.-Amer	572042
Herrlinger, Leonhard		Geislingen	Gsl.	bef 1852	N.-Amer	572041
Herrlinger, Leonhardt	27 Mar 1823	Altenstadt-Gsl.	Gsl.	Aug 1853	N.-Amer	572041
Herrlinger, Leonhardt & F	5 Jul 1798	Altenstadt-Gsl.	Gsl.	Aug 1853	N.-Amer	572041
Herrlinger, Margaretha	21 Aug 1830	Kuchen	Gsl.	bef 1854	N.-Amer	572042
Herrlinger, Matthaeus	26 Jul 1831	Altenstadt-Gsl.	Gsl.	Aug 1853	N.-Amer	572041
Herrlinger, Michael	28 Apr 1834	Kuchen	Gsl.	bef 1854	N.-Amer	572042
Herrmann, Andreas & F	6 May 1818	Weil der Stadt	Leon.	Jun 1854	N.-Amer	837966
Herrmann, Anna	6 Apr 1827	Gingen	Gsl.	bef 1855	N.-Amer	572043
Herrmann, Anna Maria (wife)	42 yrs.	Hausen a. d. Wurm	Leon.	Aug 1819	N.-Amer	837955
Herrmann, Anna Walpurga	1 May 1845	Donzdorf	Gsl.	Jul 1854	N.-Amer	572042
Herrmann, Anson	20 Oct 1849	Donzdorf	Gsl.	Jul 1854	N.-Amer	572042
Herrmann, Catrine Barbara	13 yrs.	Heimsheim	Leon.	Aug 1819	N.-Amer	837955
Herrmann, Christian	37 yrs.	Weil der Stadt	Leon.	Oct 1870	Holland	837966

Name		Birth		Emigration			Film
Last	First	Date	Place	O'amt	Appl. Date	Dest.	Number
Herrmann, Christoph & F		10 Aug 1833	Genkingen	Rtl.	Jun 1880	N.-Amer	841051
Herrmann, Christoph Friedr.& F		40 yrs.	Heimsheim	Leon.	Aug 1819	N.-Amer	837955
Herrmann, Christoph Friedrich		7 yrs.	Heimsheim	Leon.	Aug 1819	N.-Amer	837955
Herrmann, David		26 yrs.	Kuchen	Gsl.	Jan 1868	N.-Amer	572046
Herrmann, Franz Josef & W		4 Oct 1803	Weil der Stadt	Leon.	Apr 1848	N.-Amer	837965
Herrmann, Gottlieb Friedrich		11 yrs.	Heimsheim	Leon.	Aug 1819	N.-Amer	837955
Herrmann, Jacob Friedrich		2 yrs.	Heimsheim	Leon.	Aug 1819	N.-Amer	837955
Herrmann, Johann		16 Jan 1862	Genkingen	Rtl.	Jun 1880	N.-Amer	841051
Herrmann, Johann Baptist & F		1 Nov 1815	Donzdorf	Gsl.	Jul 1854	N.-Amer	572042
Herrmann, Johann Georg			Donzdorf	Gsl.	Dec 1851	N.-Amer	577788
Herrmann, Johann Georg & F		23 Nov 1823	Unterhausen	Rtl.	Apr 1864	N.-Amer	841053
Herrmann, Johann Jacob Emil		20 Oct 1858	Unterhausen	Rtl.	Apr 1864	N.-Amer	841053
Herrmann, Johann Nepomuk			Donzdorf	Gsl.	Dec 1851	N.-Amer	577788
Herrmann, Johannes		28 Feb 1836	Hohenstadt	Gsl.	Mar 1854	N.-Amer	572042
Herrmann, Johannes		26 Jan 1852	Donzdorf	Gsl.	Jul 1854	N.-Amer	572042
Herrmann, Josefa			Donzdorf	Gsl.	Dec 1851	N.-Amer	577788
Herrmann, Josefa (wife)			Donzdorf	Gsl.	Dec 1851	N.-Amer	577788
Herrmann, Joseph Thomas & F			Donzdorf	Gsl.	Dec 1851	N.-Amer	577788
Herrmann, Karolina			Donzdorf	Gsl.	Dec 1851	N.-Amer	577788
Herrmann, Katharina (wife)		9 Jul 1819	Donzdorf	Gsl.	Jul 1854	N.-Amer	572042
Herrmann, Magdalena		19 Jun 1838	Hohenstadt	Gsl.	Mar 1854	N.-Amer	572042
Herrmann, Magdalena (wife)		12 Dec 1823	Weil der Stadt	Leon.	Jun 1854	N.-Amer	837966
Herrmann, Maria Barbara		29 Apr 1821	Renningen	Leon.	Sep 1843	Bavaria	837963
Herrmann, Marianna			Donzdorf	Gsl.	Dec 1851	N.-Amer	577788
Herrmann, Mathaeus & F			Gomaringen	Rtl.	May 1832	N.-Amer	841051
Herrmann, Philipp & F			Sulgen	Obd.	Apr 1817	N.-Amer	838638
Herrmann, Sibilla Aga. (wife)		30 Mar 1817	Unterhausen	Rtl.	Apr 1864	N.-Amer	841053
Herrmann, Sophie		6 Jun 1847	Donzdorf	Gsl.	Jul 1854	N.-Amer	572042
Herrmann, Theresia		2 Sep 1853	Weil der Stadt	Leon.	Mar 1854	N.-Amer	837966
Herrmann, Theresia (wife)		15 Jan 1810	Weil der Stadt	Leon.	Apr 1848	N.-Amer	837965
Herrmann, Valentin		27 Sep 1850	Hohenstadt	Gsl.	Aug 1868	N.-Amer	572046
Herrmann, Wendelin		15 Oct 1851	Sulgen	Obd.	Oct 1866	N.-Amer	838638
Herrmann, Wilhelm		17 Jun 1848	Undingen	Rtl.	May 1867	Russia	841053
Hertner, Johannes		14 Jun 1847	Pfullingen	Rtl.	Dec 1867	England	841053
Herzer, Alois		17 Aug 1844	Weissenstein	Gsl.	1869	N.-Amer	572047
Herzer, Johannes		16 Nov 1840	Weissenstein	Gsl.	Jul 1882	Austria	572048
Herzer, Maria Anna & C		1 Nov 1830	Weissenstein	Gsl.	1869	N.-Amer	572047
Herzer, Theresia			Weissenstein	Gsl.	Mar 1866	N.-Amer	572045
Herzog, Johann Nepomuk		27 Jul 1816	Schramberg	Obd.	Nov 1846	N.-Amer	838637
Hess, Anna Maria (wid.) & F		7 Aug 1812	Reutlingen	Rtl.	Oct 1867	N.-Amer	841053
Hess, Carl August		1 Mar 1868	Esslingen	Krch.	May 1885	N.-Amer	835948
Hess, Christian & F			Roemlinsdorf	Obd.	Mar 1852	N.-Amer	838635
Hess, Christian Friedrich		6 Feb 1866	Friolzheim	Leon.	Mar 1881	N.-Amer	835791
Hess, Christiane Louise		6 yrs.	Rutesheim	Leon.	Feb 1852	N.-Amer	837964
Hess, Christina		14 yrs.	Rutesheim	Leon.	Feb 1852	N.-Amer	837964
Hess, Elisabetha		4 Dec 1842	Reutlingen	Rtl.	May 1865	N.-Amer	841053
Hess, Georg Balthas		16 yrs.	Rutesheim	Leon.	Feb 1852	N.-Amer	837964
Hess, Georg Friedrich		2 yrs.	Rutesheim	Leon.	Feb 1852	N.-Amer	837964
Hess, Heinrike		10 yrs.	Rutesheim	Leon.	Feb 1852	N.-Amer	837964
Hess, Johann Georg & F			Rutesheim	Leon.	Feb 1852	N.-Amer	837964

Hess, Johann Jacob	20 Nov 1841	Owen	Krch.	Mar 1860	N.-Amer 835948
Hess, Johann Jakob	16 Jul 1845	Pfullingen	Rtl.	Oct 1865	N.-Amer 841053
Hess, Johann Peter	11 Nov 1847	Reutlingen	Rtl.	Oct 1867	N.-Amer 841053
Hess, Johannes	27 Apr 1855	Friolzheim	Leon.	May 1871	N.-Amer 835791
Hess, Johannes	18 Oct 1845	Owen	Krch.	Mar 1860	N.-Amer 835948
Hess, Karl August	14 Mar 1868	Esslingen	Krch.	Jun 1885	N.-Amer 548403
Hess, Maria Magdalena	23 Jul 1844	Reutlingen	Rtl.	Oct 1867	N.-Amer 841053
Hess, Matthias	16 Jan 1848	Peterzell	Obd.	Jan 1868	N.-Amer 838635
Hess, Robert	1 Jun 1849	Waldmoessingen	Obd.	May 1869	N.-Amer 841015
Hettich, Christiane		Perouse	Leon.	Nov 1853	N.-Amer 837962
Hettich, Friedrich Lorenz		Leonberg	Leon.	Apr 1832	Hesse 835786
Hetzler, Gustav	17 Jun 1851	Altenstadt-Gsl.	Gsl.	Feb 1870	N.-Amer 572047
Hetzler, Johannes	28 Dec 1858	Ehrenstein	Gsl.	Feb 1877	N.-Amer 572048
Hetzler, Johannes	18 Aug 1843	Altenstadt-Gsl.	Gsl.	Mar 1864	N.-Amer 572045
Heuberger, Jakob	17 yrs.	Gingen	Gsl.	Feb 1853	N.-Amer 572041
Heueisen, Christian	4 Oct 1836	Leonberg	Leon.	Apr 1854	N.-Amer 835786
Heusel, Gottlieb	16 Jul 1875	Gerlingen	Leon.	Sep 1889	N.-Amer 837953
Heusel, Maria Margaretha	19 yrs.	Gerlingen	Leon.	Jan 1852	N.-Amer 837953
Heusel, Rosine Pauline	24 Oct 1830	Eningen	Rtl.	Sep 1861	Bavaria 841053
Heyd, Katharina		Peterzell	Obd.	Apr 1856	N.-Amer 838635
Heydlauf, Hedwig Christine	15 Oct 1845	Gueltstein	Herr.	Apr 1866	N.-Amer 834631
Heydlauf, Wilhelm Andreas	5 Jun 1848	Gueltstein	Herr.	Apr 1864	N.-Amer 834631
Hezel, Andreas	1 Mar 1822	Kleinsuessen	Gsl.	1848	N.-Amer 572043
Hezel, Carl	29 Jan 1847	Winzeln	Obd.	Mar 1867	N.-Amer 841016
Hezel, Christiane Susanne	19 Feb 1827	Alpirsbach	Obd.	Aug 1848	N.-Amer 838630
Hezel, Franziska		Winzeln	Obd.	1850	N.-Amer 841016
Hezel, Georg	25 yrs.	Winzeln	Obd.	bef 1857	N.-Amer 841016
Hezel, Johann Georg		Alpirsbach	Obd.	Jun 1843	Saxony 838631
Hezel, Johannes	15 Nov 1795	Alpirsbach	Obd.	Jan 1838	Switz. 838631
Hezel, Johannes		Seedorf	Obd.	bef 1862	Austria 838637
Hezel, Josepha		Winzeln	Obd.	1850	N.-Amer 841016
Hezel, Maria Cleopha	4 Apr 1828	Winzeln	Obd.	bef 1850	N.-Amer 841016
Hezel, Michael	4 Sep 1826	Winzeln	Obd.	Nov 1867	N.-Amer 841016
Hezele, Carl Christian Friedr.	22 Jul 1852	Leonberg	Leon.	Mar 1854	N.-Amer 835786
Hezler, Angelika	6 Apr 1832	Stoetten	Gsl.	Apr 1854	N.-Amer 572042
Hieldinger, Caroline Kathar.	22 Jul 1858	Muenchingen	Leon.	Jun 1874	N.-Amer 837961
Hieldinger, Christian Gottl.	23 Jan 1857	Muenchingen	Leon.	Jun 1874	N.-Amer 837961
Hieldinger, Christiane L. (wife)	11 Aug 1830	Bissingen	Leon.	Jun 1874	N.-Amer 837961
Hieldinger, Christina	7 Oct 1868	Muenchingen	Leon.	Jun 1874	N.-Amer 837961
Hieldinger, Franz	10 Sep 1861	Muenchingen	Leon.	Jun 1874	N.-Amer 837961
Hieldinger, Gotthilfe	4 Dec 1873	Muenchingen	Leon.	Jun 1874	N.-Amer 837961
Hieldinger, Gottlieb & F	6 Jan 1828	Muenchingen	Leon.	Jun 1874	N.-Amer 837961
Hieldinger, Regina	14 Dec 1862	Muenchingen	Leon.	Jun 1874	N.-Amer 837961
Hilber, Johann Baptist		Lauterbach	Obd.	Apr 1850	France 838634
Hildenbrand, Julius Heinrich	6 Aug 1844	Genkingen	Rtl.	Mar 1864	N.-Amer 841053
Hildinger, Anna Maria	1 Apr 1828	Muenchingen	Leon.	bef 1855	N.-Amer 837961
Hildinger, Anna Maria	43 yrs.	Muenchingen	Leon.	May 1852	N.-Amer 837961
Hildinger, Anna Maria (wife)		Muenchingen	Leon.	Nov 1861	N.-Amer 837961
Hildinger, Anna Maria (wife)		Muenchingen	Leon.	Oct 1851	N.-Amer 837961
Hildinger, Caspar & F	41 yrs.	Weil im Dorf	Loen.	Apr 1858	N.-Amer 837967

Name		Birth		Emigration			Film
Last	First	Date	Place	O'amt	Appl. Date	Dest.	Number
Hildinger, Catharina Maria		28 Dec 1850	Muenchingen	Leon.	Oct 1851	N.-Amer	837961
Hildinger, Christina (wife)			Muenchingen	Leon.	Oct 1851	N.-Amer	837961
Hildinger, Conrad		1 Jan 1818	Muenchingen	Leon.	1847	N.-Amer	837961
Hildinger, Georg Gottlieb			Muenchingen	Leon.	Oct 1851	N.-Amer	837961
Hildinger, Jakob		5 Aug 1822	Muenchingen	Leon.	1848	N.-Amer	837961
Hildinger, Jakob		1 Oct 1845	Weil im Dorf	Loen.	Apr 1858	N.-Amer	837967
Hildinger, Johann Georg		31 May 1819	Muenchingen	Leon.	1848	N.-Amer	837961
Hildinger, Johann Georg & F			Muenchingen	Leon.	Oct 1851	N.-Amer	837961
Hildinger, Johann Gottlieb		31 Dec 1848	Weil im Dorf	Loen.	Apr 1858	N.-Amer	837967
Hildinger, Johann Jakob		3 Jan 1842	Muenchingen	Leon.	Nov 1861	N.-Amer	837961
Hildinger, Johann Jakob & F		1 Jan 1811	Muenchingen	Leon.	Nov 1861	N.-Amer	837961
Hildinger, Johanna		10 Apr 1839	Muenchingen	Leon.	Nov 1861	N.-Amer	837961
Hildinger, Johannes		26 Dec 1845	Muenchingen	Leon.	Nov 1861	N.-Amer	837961
Hildinger, Johannes		30 Jul 1843	Weil im Dorf	Loen.	Apr 1858	N.-Amer	837967
Hildinger, Michael & F			Muenchingen	Leon.	Oct 1851	N.-Amer	837961
Hildinger, Tobias		3 Sep 1830	Weil im Dorf	Loen.	Jan 1854	N.-Amer	837967
Hildinger, Veit		5 Feb 1844	Muenchingen	Leon.	Nov 1861	N.-Amer	837961
Hillenbrand, Apollonia		7 Feb 1854	Boehmenkirch	Gsl.	Jul 1857	N.-Amer	572043
Hillenbrand, Christina		17 yrs.	Boehmenkirch	Gsl.	Dec 1850	N.-Amer	577788
Hillenbrand, Josef		7 Mar 1833	Boehmenkirch	Gsl.	May 1884	Austria	572049
Hillenbrand, Josepha		23 yrs.	Treffelhausen	Gsl.	May 1852	N.-Amer	572041
Hillenbrand, Karolina		15 Jul 1837	Boehmenkirch	Gsl.	Jan 1854	N.-Amer	572042
Hillenbrand, Konrad		7 Dec 1835	Boehmenkirch	Gsl.	Jan 1854	N.-Amer	572042
Hillenbrand, Kreszenz		4 May 1841	Boehmenkirch	Gsl.	Nov 1857	N.-Amer	572043
Hillenbrand, Theresia & C		29 Sep 1830	Boehmenkirch	Gsl.	Jul 1857	N.-Amer	572043
Hiller, Catharina		9 Jul 1844	Schopfloch	Krch.	May 1867	N.-Amer	835949
Hiller, David		16 yrs.	Nabern	Krch.	Aug 1873	N.-Amer	548403
Hiller, David		26 Feb 1857	Nabern	Krch.	Aug 1873	N.-Amer	835946
Hiller, Friederike			Haiterbach	Nag.	Aug 1852	N.-Amer	838488
Hiller, Gottlieb		9 mon.	Warmbronn	Leon.	Apr 1854	N.-Amer	837965
Hiller, Helene & C			Warmbronn	Leon.	Apr 1854	N.-Amer	837965
Hiller, Isaak		4 Sep 1832	Gutenberg	Krch.	May 1862	N.-Amer	835945
Hiller, Johann Georg		5 Apr 1850	Nabern	Krch.	Feb 1866	N.-Amer	835946
Hiller, Johannes		6 Oct 1878	Zell	Krch.	May 1895	N.-Amer	835774
Hiller, Magdalena			Kirchheim	Krch.	bef 1870	N.-Amer	835940
Hiller, Otto		25 Mar 1849	Kirchheim	Krch.	Feb 1868	N.-Amer	835941
Hiller, Wilhelm		26 Jan 1875	Aichelberg	Krch.	Jan 1892	N.-Amer	835943
Hils, Andreas		20 Apr 1850	Seedorf	Obd.	Mar 1867	N.-Amer	838637
Hils, Christian		16 Sep 1847	Seedorf	Obd.	Mar 1867	N.-Amer	838637
Hils, Johann & F			Mariazell	Obd.	May 1817	N.-Amer	838634
Hils, Johannes		16 Jun 1849	Hardt	Obd.	Aug 1869	Bavaria	838633
Hinger, Albert		4 Jul 1859	Reutlingen	Rtl.	Mar 1880	N.-Amer	841051
Hinger, Andreas		21 Sep 1834	Unterhausen	Rtl.	Apr 1862	N.-Amer	841053
Hinger, Anna Maria		20 Jul 1833	Unterhausen	Rtl.	bef 1868	N.-Amer	841053
Hinger, Anna Rosine		16 Feb 1865	Reutlingen	Rtl.	May 1880	N.-Amer	841051
Hinger, Christine Regine		16 Dec 1869	Reutlingen	Rtl.	May 1880	N.-Amer	841051
Hinger, Gottfried		6 Nov 1872	Reutlingen	Rtl.	May 1880	N.-Amer	841051
Hinger, Gottfried Hermann		2 Apr 1860	Reutlingen	Rtl.	May 1880	N.-Amer	841051
Hinger, Jakob & W		17 Nov 1828	Unterhausen	Rtl.	bef 1868	N.-Amer	841053
Hinger, Johann Georg		8 Aug 1847	Unterhausen	Rtl.	Apr 1862	N.-Amer	841053

Hinger, Matthes & F	54 yrs.	Reutlingen	Rtl.	May 1880	N.-Amer	841051
Hinh, Johannes	19 Dec 1872	Gutenberg	Krch.	May 1878	N.-Amer	548403
Hink, Barbara (wid.) & F	19 Mar 1842	Gutenberg	Krch.	May 1878	N.-Amer	548403
Hink, Christina Barbara	5 Apr 1869	Gutenberg	Krch.	May 1878	N.-Amer	835945
Hink, Johannes	19 Dec 1872	Gutenberg	Krch.	May 1878	N.-Amer	835945
Hink, Katharina	3 Apr 1867	Gutenberg	Krch.	May 1878	N.-Amer	548403
Hink, Margaretha	23 Jun 1874	Gutenberg	Krch.	May 1878	N.-Amer	835945
Hintrager, Robert	21 Jan 1828	Heimsheim	Leon.	Nov 1859	Bavaria	837955
Hipp, Anna Maria		Betzingen	Rtl.	bef 1835	N.-Amer	841051
Hipp, Christina	28 Jun 1828	Wannweil	Rtl.	May 1867	N.-Amer	841053
Hipp, Johann Georg		Wannweil	Rtl.	May 1832	N.-Amer	841051
Hipp, Johannes	17 Jun 1839	Betzingen	Rtl.	Mar 1864	N.-Amer	841053
Hipp, Johannes & F		Leonberg	Leon.	Apr 1831	N.-Amer	835786
Hipp, Johannes (wid.)		Leonberg	Leon.	Apr 1831	N.-Amer	835786
Hipp, Karl Theodor		Reutlingen	Rtl.	bef 1870	Switz.	841053
Hirdtle, Johannes	24 Sep 1832	Hochdorf	Krch.	May 1857	N.-Amer	835945
Hirning, Barbara	29 Mar 1842	Gutenberg	Krch.	Jun 1865	N.-Amer	835945
Hirrlinger, Christine	22 Aug 1844	Reutlingen	Rtl.	May 1865	N.-Amer	841053
Hirsch, Eva Katharina	5 Jun 1832	Brucken	Krch.	Mar 1855	N.-Amer	835944
Hirsch, Johann Gottfried	20 Apr 1840	Brucken	Krch.	Sep 1860	N.-Amer	835944
Hirschburger, Elisabetha	20 Jul 1836	Reutlingen	Rtl.	May 1869	Switz.	841053
Hirschburger, Johannes	2 Apr 1837	Reutlingen	Rtl.	May 1869	France	841053
Hirschburger, Max	30 yrs.	Reutlingen	Rtl.	Apr 1880	N.-Amer	841051
Hirschmann, Johann Paulus	18 Jun 1846	Holzmaden	Krch.	Sep 1865	N.-Amer	835945
Hirt, Franz Xaver	30 Jul 1812	Oberndorf	Obd.	bef 1848	Hungary	838635
Hirth, Karoline		Reutlingen	Rtl.	Sep 1866	Switz.	841053
Hirzel, Rudolf	9 Oct 1845	Kirchheim	Krch.	Jul 1865	N.-Amer	835941
Hoch, Christiana (wife)	23 Feb 1835	Pfullingen	Rtl.	May 1864	N.-Amer	841053
Hoch, David		Renningen	Leon.	bef 1856	Hungary	837963
Hoch, Jakob & F		Enzweihingen	Leon.	Dec 1872	N.-Amer	835790
Hoch, Johann Georg		Wannweil	Rtl.	Oct 1859	N.-Amer	841053
Hoch, Johann Jakob	3 Mar 1833	Renningen	Leon.	May 1853	N.-Amer	837963
Hoch, Philipp Jakob	11 Jul 1863	Pfullingen	Rtl.	May 1864	N.-Amer	841053
Hoch, Stephan	29 Feb 1848	Ohmenhausen	Rtl.	Dec 1868	N.-Amer	841053
Hoch, Wilhelm & F	18 Jun 1837	Pfullingen	Rtl.	May 1864	N.-Amer	841053
Hoch, Wilhelmine Christiane	6 Jul 1860	Pfullingen	Rtl.	May 1864	N.-Amer	841053
Hochberger, Anna Maria & C	16 Sep 1824	Stuttgart	Krch.	Mar 1857	N.-Amer	835944
Hochberger, Barbara		Dettingen	Krch.	bef 1864	N.-Amer	835944
Hochberger, Georg & W	24 Jan 1804	Dettingen	Krch.	Aug 1866	N.-Amer	835944
Hochberger, Magdalena (wife)		Dettingen	Krch.	Aug 1866	N.-Amer	835944
Hock, Margaretha (wife)		Flacht	Leon.	Dec 1872	N.-Amer	835790
Hoefel, Anna Magdalena	5 Mar 1834	Gaertringen	Herr.	bef 1867	N.-Amer	834630
Hoefele, Bernhard		Donzdorf	Gsl.	Aug 1851	N.-Amer	577788
Hoefele, Mathias		Donzdorf	Gsl.	Aug 1851	N.-Amer	577788
Hoefele, Regina	26 Aug 1823	Grosssuessen	Gsl.	Apr 1852	N.-Amer	572041
Hoefle, Wilhelm	1 May 1864	Altenstadt-Gsl.	Gsl.	Apr 1883	N.-Amer	572049
Hoeflinger, Christian	22 Oct 1843	Neidlingen	Krch.	Nov 1868	N.-Amer	835946
Hoeflinger, Johann Georg	21 Mar 1833	Neidlingen	Krch.	Jan 1865	N.-Amer	835946
Hoeflinger, Johanna & C	21 Aug 1835	Kirchheim	Krch.	Oct 1866	N.-Amer	835941
Hoeflinger, Karl Friedrich	19 Mar 1872	Kirchheim	Krch.	Apr 1888	N.-Amer	835942

Name		Birth		Emigration			Film
Last	First	Date	Place	O'amt	Appl. Date	Dest.	Number
Hoeflinger, Maria		4 Feb 1857	Kirchheim	Krch.	Oct 1866	N.-Amer	835941
Hoeger, CHristina Barbara		31 Mar 1833	Renningen	Leon.	Apr 1852	N.-Amer	837963
Hoeger, Johann Georg			Eltingen	Leon.	Feb 1830	N.-Amer	835789
Hoehn, Donisius		18 yrs.	Bochingen	Obd.	Sep 1856	N.-Amer	838632
Hoehn, Elisabetha (wife)			Bochingen	Obd.	Sep 1846	N.-Amer	838632
Hoehn, Georg		19 Apr 1844	Harthausen	Obd.	Feb 1868	N.-Amer	838633
Hoehn, Jakob & F			Bochingen	Obd.	Sep 1846	N.-Amer	838632
Hoehn, Jakobina		10 Jul 1842	Bochingen	Obd.	Sep 1846	N.-Amer	838632
Hoehn, Johannes		25 Sep 1848	Harthausen	Obd.	Mar 1867	N.-Amer	838633
Hoehn, Joseph		3 Jan 1848	Bochingen	Obd.	May 1867	N.-Amer	838632
Hoehn, Moritz			Bochingen	Obd.	bef 1844	N.-Amer	838632
Hoehn, Wilhelm		28 May 1834	Bochingen	Obd.	Sep 1846	N.-Amer	838632
Hoehni, Andreas		8 yrs.	Fluorn	Obd.	Nov 1846	N.-Amer	838632
Hoehni, Anna Maria		21 yrs.	Fluorn	Obd.	Nov 1846	N.-Amer	838632
Hoehni, Barbara		4 yrs.	Fluorn	Obd.	Nov 1846	N.-Amer	838632
Hoehni, Elisabeth (wife)		46 yrs.	Fluorn	Obd.	Nov 1846	N.-Amer	838632
Hoehni, Jakob		15 yrs.	Fluorn	Obd.	Nov 1846	N.-Amer	838632
Hoehni, Johann Georg		23 yrs.	Fluorn	Obd.	Nov 1846	N.-Amer	838632
Hoehni, Johann Georg & F			Fluorn	Obd.	Nov 1846	N.-Amer	838632
Hoehni, Johannes		16 yrs.	Fluorn	Obd.	Sep 1853	N.-Amer	838632
Hoehni, Johannes		12 yrs.	Fluorn	Obd.	Nov 1846	N.-Amer	838632
Hoehnle, Fidelis		19 Apr 1836	Epfendorf	Obd.	May 1854	N.-Amer	838632
Hoeler, Carl Friedrich		12 Jul 1852	Kirchheim	Krch.	Jul 1870	N.-Amer	835941
Hoell, Anna		- 1863	Bissingen	Krch.	Oct 1867	N.-Amer	835943
Hoell, Friedrich & F		24 Nov 1842	Bissingen	Krch.	Oct 1867	N.-Amer	835943
Hoell, Maria		1 Dec 1861	Bissingen	Krch.	Oct 1867	N.-Amer	835943
Hoell, Regina (wife)		14 Apr 1838	Bissingen	Krch.	Oct 1867	N.-Amer	835943
Hoellriegel, Thomas			Altenstadt-Gsl.	Gsl.	Feb 1853	N.-Amer	572041
Hoenes, Anna Catharina		7 May 1831	Muenchingen	Leon.	Mar 1852	N.-Amer	837961
Hoenes, Anna Maria		26 Dec 1833	Muenchingen	Leon.	Mar 1852	N.-Amer	837961
Hoenes, Barbara		23 Jun 1827	Muenchingen	Leon.	Mar 1852	N.-Amer	837961
Hoenes, Barbara (wife)			Muenchingen	Leon.	Mar 1844	Rus-Pol	837961
Hoenes, Catharina			Muenchingen	Leon.	Mar 1852	N.-Amer	837961
Hoenes, Catharina Barbara			Muenchingen	Leon.	1849	N.-Amer	837961
Hoenes, Christiane		24 Dec 1838	Muenchingen	Leon.	Mar 1852	N.-Amer	837961
Hoenes, Christina Margar. & C		13 Sep 1841	Muenchingen	Leon.	Mar 1844	Rus-Pol	837961
Hoenes, Conrad		6 Jan 1824	Muenchingen	Leon.	Mar 1852	N.-Amer	837961
Hoenes, Conrad & F			Muenchingen	Leon.	Mar 1852	N.-Amer	837961
Hoenes, Friedrich (wid.)		29 Jun 1811	Muenchingen	Leon.	May 1855	N.-Amer	837961
Hoenes, Jakob		9 Aug 1837	Muenchingen	Leon.	Mar 1844	Rus-Pol	837961
Hoenes, Jakob Friedrich		9 May 1832	Muenchingen	Leon.	Jun 1853	N.-Amer	837961
Hoenes, Johann Georg		25 Oct 1825	Muenchingen	Leon.	bef 1870	N.-Amer	837961
Hoenes, Johanna		26 Sep 1840	Muenchingen	Leon.	Mar 1852	N.-Amer	837961
Hoenes, Katharina		19 Dec 1839	Muenchingen	Leon.	Mar 1844	Rus-Pol	837961
Hoenes, Konrad & F			Muenchingen	Leon.	Mar 1844	Rus-Pol	837961
Hoenes, Maria Magdalena		23 Dec 1842	Muenchingen	Leon.	Mar 1844	Rus-Pol	837961
Hoenes, Michael			Muenchingen	Leon.	bef 1853	N.-Amer	837961
Hoenes, Philipp Jakob		13 Feb 1843	Muenchingen	Leon.	1863	N.-Amer	837961
Hoeness, Christoph		22 yrs.	Erpfingen	Rtl.	Jul 1880	N.-Amer	841051
Hoeni, Anna Maria		32 yrs.	Fluorn	Obd.	Nov 1853	N.-Amer	838632

Hoeni, Hermann	22 Mar 1847	Fluorn	Obd.	Feb 1864	N.-Amer	838632
Hoeni, Johannes	9 Jan 1850	Fluorn	Obd.	May 1869	N.-Amer	838632
Hoeni, Karl Friedrich	17 Dec 1850	Fluorn	Obd.	Oct 1868	N.-Amer	838632
Hoermann, Johann	8 Nov 1847	Oberndorf	Obd.	Mar 1865	N.-Amer	838635
Hoernle, Anna Maria	15 Dec 1846	Moensheim	Leon.	May 1866	N.-Amer	837960
Hoernle, Johann Michael	13 Jan 1838	Moensheim	Leon.	Jul 1864	N.-Amer	837960
Hoernle, Johannes		Moensheim	Leon.	bef 1852	N.-Amer	837960
Hoernle, Rosina Katharina	8 Dec 1844	Moensheim	Leon.	Jul 1864	N.-Amer	837960
Hoerrmann, Carl		Oberndorf	Obd.	Sep 1860	N.-Amer	838635
Hoerter, Louise Rosine	26 Apr 1850	Leonberg	Leon.	Oct 1870	Austria	835787
Hoeschele, Christina	Infant	Nordheim	Leon.	May 1826	N.-Amer	837953
Hoeschele, Christina (wife)	24 yrs.	Nordheim	Leon.	May 1826	N.-Amer	837953
Hoeschele, Christof	2 yrs.	Nordheim	Leon.	May 1826	N.-Amer	837953
Hoeschele, Christoph		Gerlingen	Leon.	Apr 1831	N.-Amer	837953
Hoeschele, David		Gerlingen	Leon.	bef 1837	N.-Amer	837953
Hoeschele, David	6 yrs.	Nordheim	Leon.	May 1826	N.-Amer	837953
Hoeschele, Dorothea (wid.)	2 Nov 1822	Gerlingen	Leon.	Jul 1872	Palest.	837953
Hoeschele, Friederike	7 Nov 1843	Gerlingen	Leon.	Jul 1872	Palast.	837953
Hoeschele, Jacob	4 yrs.	Nordheim	Leon.	May 1826	N.-Amer	837953
Hoeschele, Johann Georg & F		Gerlingen	Leon.	May 1826	N.-Amer	837953
Hoetzel, Franz Hubert	16 Oct 1846	Deggingen	Gsl.	Sep 1866	N.-Amer	572045
Hoetzel, Joseph	8 Jul 1832	Deggingen	Gsl.	Mar 1852	N.-Amer	572041
Hoetzel, Joseph	9 Nov 1835	Deggingen	Gsl.	May 1855	N.-Amer	572043
Hoetzel, Joseph	2 Aug 1831	Deggingen	Gsl.	Apr 1855	N.-Amer	572043
Hoetzel, Maria Anna	24 Dec 1833	Deggingen	Gsl.	May 1855	N.-Amer	572043
Hoetzel, Reinold	10 Apr 1848	Deggingen	Gsl.	May 1868	N.-Amer	572046
Hofele, Alois	18 mon.	Donzdorf	Gsl.	Sep 1852	N.-Amer	572041
Hofele, Ambrosius	5 Nov 1828	Deggingen	Gsl.	Jan 1858	Holland	572043
Hofele, Bernhard	3 yrs.	Donzdorf	Gsl.	Sep 1852	N.-Amer	572041
Hofele, Joseph & F		Donzdorf	Gsl.	Sep 1852	N.-Amer	572041
Hofele, Lorenz	1 mon.	Donzdorf	Gsl.	Sep 1852	N.-Amer	572041
Hofele, Matthias	30 Sep 1830	Donzdorf	Gsl.	bef 1854	N.-Amer	572042
Hofele, Theresia (wife)		Donzdorf	Gsl.	Sep 1852	N.-Amer	572041
Hofelich, Johanna Chr. (wife)		Sternenfels	Leon.	Feb 1851	N.-Amer	837956
Hofelich, Joseph & F		Sternenfels	Leon.	Feb 1851	N.-Amer	837956
Hofer, Amalie		Oberndorf	Obd.	Sep 1837	N.-Amer	838635
Hofer, Carl		Oberndorf	Obd.	bef 1837	N.-Amer	838635
Hofer, Catharina		Oberndorf	Obd.	Sep 1837	N.-Amer	838635
Hofer, Johann Martin & F		Ohmenhausen	Rtl.	May 1831	N.-Amer	841051
Hofer, Josefa		Oberndorf	Obd.	Sep 1837	N.-Amer	838635
Hofer, Marianne & F		Oberndorf	Obd.	Sep 1837	N.-Amer	838635
Hofer, Theresia	20 yrs.	Oberndorf	Obd.	Mar 1855	Switz.	838635
Hoffacker, Jacobine Sib.		Merklingen	Leon.	1834	Wien	837959
Hoffacker, Wilhelmina Fried.		Merklingen	Leon.	May 1868	Wien	837959
Hoffaker, Louise Friederike	18 Apr 1821	Merklingen	Leon.	bef 1847	Wien	837959
Hoffaker, Sophie Sib.	7 Nov 1809	Merklingen	Leon.	Apr 1845	Wien	837959
Hoffmann, Anna Maria (wid.) & F		Ditzingen	Leon.	Apr 1854	N.-Amer	835788
Hoffmann, Beate Frieder. Paul.	17 Apr 1845	Leonberg	Leon.	May 1868	Palest.	835787
Hoffmann, Carl August	9 Sep 1847	Ditzingen	Leon.	Sep 1867	N.-Amer	835788
Hoffmann, Christoph	9 Dec 1842	Leonberg	Leon.	Nov 1867	Turkey	835787

Name		Birth		Emigration			Film
Last	First	Date	Place	O'amt	Appl. Date	Dest.	Number
Hoffmann, Friederike			Ditzingen	Leon.	Apr 1854	N.-Amer	835788
Hoffmann, Georg Friedrich			Heimsheim	Leon.	Oct 1844	France	837955
Hoffmann, Georg Jacob		23 May 1864	Heimsheim	Leon.	Mar 1881	N.-Amer	837955
Hoffmann, Kaspar Adelbert			Eningen	Rtl.	Jul 1866	N.-Amer	841053
Hoffmann, Ludwig Fried. Jona.		12 Jan 1852	Kornwestheim	Leon.	Aug 1871	Israel	835787
Hoffmann, Paul			Weil im Dorf	Loen.	bef 1869	N.-Amer	837967
Hoffmann, Paul			Leonberg	Leon.	May 1867	Prussia	835787
Hoffmann, Samuel		26 Jun 1849	Leonberg	Leon.	Jul 1869	Turky	835787
Hoffmann, Seth		23 Sep 1863	Leonberg	Leon.	1868	Palest.	835787
Hoffmann, Wilhelm		15 Feb 1830	Ditzingen	Leon.	Apr 1854	N.-Amer	835788
Hofmaier, Wilhelm		2 May 1828	Warmbronn	Leon.	bef 1855	N.-Amer	837965
Hofmann, Jacob		30 Jan 1842	Reusten	Krch.	Aug 1870	Palast	835940
Hofmann, Johann Adam		3 Feb 1840	Eningen	Rtl.	Aug 1866	N.-Amer	841053
Hofmann, Johann Martin		29 Sep 1844	Unterboehringen	Gsl.	Jul 1869	N.-Amer	572047
Hofmann, Johannes		25 Apr 1835	Unterboehringen	Gsl.	May 1854	N.-Amer	572042
Hofmann, Wilhelm		26 Jul 1858	Dettingen	Krch.	Jun 1887	N.-Amer	835944
Hofmayer, Christian Gottlob		18 yrs.	Warmbronn	Leon.	Feb 1854	N.-Amer	837965
Hogenpoz, Johann		4 yrs.	Wimsheim	Loen.	Feb 1849	N.-Amer	837967
Hogenpoz, Johannes & F		30 yrs.	Wimsheim	Loen.	Feb 1849	N.-Amer	837967
Hogenpoz, Juditha (wife)			Wimsheim	Loen.	Feb 1849	N.-Amer	837967
Hogenpoz, Katharina		2 yrs.	Wimsheim	Loen.	Feb 1849	N.-Amer	837967
Hohenstein, Caroline (wife)			Weil der Stadt	Leon.	Apr 1848	N.-Amer	837965
Hohenstein, Ensilius		16 Oct 1845	Weil der Stadt	Leon.	Apr 1848	N.-Amer	837965
Hohenstein, Fidel & F			Weil der Stadt	Leon.	Apr 1848	N.-Amer	837965
Hohenstein, Juliane		28 Dec 1838	Weil der Stadt	Leon.	Apr 1848	N.-Amer	837965
Hohenstein, Karl August		13 Apr 1833	Weil der Stadt	Leon.	Dec 1861	Hamburg	837966
Hohenstein, Thomas		11 Dec 1846	Weil der Stadt	Leon.	Apr 1848	N.-Amer	837965
Hohl, Anna Maria			Sulpach	Krch.	bef 1857	N.-Amer	835949
Hohl, Johann Jacob		18 Dec 1847	Ebersbach	Krch.	Mar 1857	N.-Amer	835949
Hohlach, Anna Maria		10 Mar 1841	Reutlingen	Rtl.	Apr 1864	Austria	841053
Hohlin, Christina Margaretha			Renningen	Leon.	Apr 1852	N.-Amer	837963
Hohlin, Rosina Catharina		21 Jun 1846	Renningen	Leon.	Apr 1852	N.-Amer	837963
Hohloch, Friedrich		18 Feb 1833	Reutlingen	Rtl.	Jan 1861	N.-Amer	841053
Hohloch, Maria Katharina Marg.			Reutlingen	Rtl.	Jul 1862	Switz.	841053
Hohnacker, Johann		3 Apr 1830	Weilheim	Krch.	bef 1867	N.-Amer	835940
Hohnecker, Johannes		3 Apr 1830	Weilheim	Krch.	Mar 1867	N.-Amer	835950
Hohner, Johannes		8 Nov 1868	Deisslingen	Rtw.	May 1885	N.-Amer	841117
Hoiler, Ernst Friedrich		15 Jan 1863	Kirchheim	Krch.	Jun 1880	N.-Amer	548403
Hoiler, Richard Alfred		18 Mar 1863	Kirchheim	Krch.	Apr 1880	N.-Amer	835942
Holder, Christian August		13 Jul 1881	Neidlingen	Krch.	Aug 1890	N.-Amer	548323
Holder, Gottlieb		25 Jun 1839	Oberlenningen	Krch.	Apr 1864	N.-Amer	835947
Holder, Jakob Friedrich		1 Sep 1846	Neidlingen	Krch.	Aug 1890	N.-Amer	835946
Holder, Johann Friedrich		2 Nov 1876	Neidlingen	Krch.	Jan 1890	N.-Amer	835946
Holder, Johann Jakob		20 Apr 1878	Neidlingen	Krch.	Aug 1890	N.-Amer	548323
Holder, Johannes		29 Dec 1879	Neidlingen	Krch.	Aug 1890	N.-Amer	548323
Holder, Johannes		12 Nov 1833	Neidlingen	Krch.	Feb 1860	N.-Amer	835946
Holder, Luise (wife)		31 Jan 1862	Neidlingen	Krch.	Aug 1890	N.-Amer	548323
Holderer, − (wid.) & F			Weil im Dorf	Loen.	Apr 1852	N.-Amer	837967
Holderer, Andreas		3 Oct 1833	Weil im Dorf	Loen.	Apr 1852	N.-Amer	837967
Holl, Bernhard		12 Sep 1827	Donzdorf	Gsl.	Aug 1859	N.-Amer	572043

Holl, Caroline Christiane	18 Dec 1858	Jesingen	Krch.	Jan 1871	N.-Amer	835946
Holl, Christian	7 Nov 1874	Weilheim	Krch.	May 1890	England	835774
Holl, Dorothea Margaretha & C	8 Apr 1838	Jesingen	Krch.	Jan 1871	N.-Amer	835946
Holl, Johann Georg	21 Nov 1873	Rosswaelden	Krch.	Apr 1887	N.-Amer	835949
Holl, Johann Gottlob	9 Mar 1843	Jesingen	Krch.	Mar 1866	N.-Amer	835946
Holl, Johann Heinrich	30 Jan 1873	Weilheim	Krch.	Jun 1889	England	835774
Holl, Johann Jakob	2 Jun 1849	Jesingen	Krch.	Jun 1867	N.-Amer	835946
Holl, Josepha	28 yrs.	Donzdorf	Gsl.	Apr 1852	N.-Amer	572041
Holl, Tobias	22 Feb 1840	Donzdorf	Gsl.	Feb 1855	N.-Amer	572043
Holl, Tobias	14 Jul 1830	Donzdorf	Gsl.	bef 1867	N.-Amer	572046
Holl, Tobias & F		Donzdorf	Gsl.	Feb 1855	N.-Amer	572043
Holl, Wilhelm	2 Jun 1849	Jesingen	Krch.	Mar 1866	N.-Amer	835946
Holl, Wilhelmine	11 Jul 1846	Jesingen	Krch.	Aug 1866	N.-Amer	835946
Holpp, Johann Conrad	5 Sep 1846	Bissingen	Krch.	Sep 1866	N.-Amer	835943
Holz, Wilhelm Friedrich	18 Nov 1845	Stuttgart	Herr.	Nov 1864	N.-Amer	834631
Holzapfel, Wilhelm Friedrich	17 Nov 1867	Kirchheim	Krch.	May 1882	N.-Amer	835942
Holzer, Konstantin	16 Feb 1834	Beffendorf	Obd.	Mar 1854	N.-Amer	838631
Holzhauer, Gottlob	21 yrs.	Pfullingen	Rtl.	Jun 1880	N.-Amer	841051
Holzinger, Andreas	17 yrs.	Merklingen	Leon.	Feb 1854	N.-Amer	837959
Holzinger, Gottlieb	2 Jun 1842	Merklingen	Leon.	Jun 1870	France	837959
Holzinger, Johann Georg		Merklingen	Leon.	May 1868	N.-Amer	837959
Holzinger, Johann Melchior	28 Nov 1854	Merklingen	Leon.	1882	N.-Amer	837959
Holzinger, Johannes		Merklingen	Leon.	May 1868	N.-Amer	837959
Holzwarth, Carl Ferdinand	30 Nov 1822	Schoeckingen	Leon.	Jul 1854	Austral	837964
Hommel, Anna & C		Altenstadt-Gsl.	Gsl.	Feb 1853	N.-Amer	572041
Hommel, David	8 Jun 1846	Gingen	Gsl.	May 1867	N.-Amer	572046
Hommel, Jakob	23 Apr 1818	Kuchen	Gsl.	Feb 1854	N.-Amer	572042
Hommel, Johannes		Geislingen	Gsl.	Mar 1863	N.-Amer	572044
Hommel, Katharina	18 yrs.	Gingen	Gsl.	Aug 1853	N.-Amer	572041
Hommel, Martin		Altenstadt-Gsl.	Gsl.	Aug 1853	N.-Amer	572041
Honold, Ernst Baltas		Renningen	Leon.	Apr 1852	N.-Amer	837963
Honold, Michael	2 Jul 1842	Kuchen	Gsl.	bef 1868	Austria	572048
Hopff, Carl Theodor	8 Nov 1844	Owen	Krch.	Nov 1864	Hamburg	835948
Hopff, Emilie	26 Dec 1836	Owen	Krch.	Apr 1863	Hamburg	835948
Hopff, Hermann Theodor		Owen	Krch.	Oct 1858	N.-Amer	835948
Horber, Anna	24 Jul 1858	Gerlingen	Leon.	Jul 1872	N.-Amer	837953
Horber, Dorothea Fr. (wid.) & F	5 Sep 1828	Gerlingen	Leon.	Jul 1872	N.-Amer	837953
Horber, Karl Rainmund	6 Nov 1860	Gerlingen	Leon.	Jul 1872	N.-Amer	837953
Hornberger, Andreas	9 Oct 1844	Fluorn	Obd.	Feb 1864	N.-Amer	838632
Hornung, Anna Maria	3 Oct 1831	Muenchingen	Leon.	bef 1867	N.-Amer	837961
Hornung, Anna Maria		Ohmenhausen	Rtl.	May 1832	N.-Amer	841051
Hornung, Barbara		Ohmenhausen	Rtl.	1853	N.-Amer	841053
Hornung, Carl	6 Jul 1855	Heimsheim	Leon.	Sep 1869	N.-Amer	837955
Hornung, Johann Georg	7 Jan 1844	Gomaringen	Rtl.	Nov 1863	N.-Amer	841053
Hornung, Johann Georg	18 Jul 1831	Ohmenhausen	Rtl.	1854	N.-Amer	841053
Hornung, Johann Jacob	12 Nov 1839	Gomaringen	Rtl.	Oct 1859	N.-Amer	841053
Hornung, Johannes	31 Jan 1811	Ohmenhausen	Rtl.	1853	N.-Amer	841053
Hornung, Katharina Frieder.	28 Nov 1846	Gomaringen	Rtl.	Nov 1863	N.-Amer	841053
Hornung, Maria & F	12 Oct 1815	Gomaringen	Rtl.	Nov 1863	N.-Amer	841053
Hornung, Maria Barbara	10 Feb 1843	Gomaringen	Rtl.	Nov 1863	N.-Amer	841053

Name		Birth		Emigration			Film
Last	First	Date	Place	O'amt	Appl. Date	Dest.	Number
Horsch, Wilhelmine L. M.		18 Apr 1849	Herrenberg	Herr.	Jul 1865	N.-Amer	834629
Hoyer, Johannes		15 Aug 1841	Oetlingen	Krch.	Jun 1866	N.-Amer	835948
Hoyler, Anna Maria		30 Apr 1832	Hochdorf	Krch.	Jul 1864	N.-Amer	835945
Hoyler, Anna Maria		3 Aug 1862	Rosswaelden	Krch.	Mar 1867	N.-Amer	835949
Hoyler, Anna Maria (wife)		27 May 1829	Rosswaelden	Krch.	Mar 1867	N.-Amer	835949
Hoyler, Barbara (wife)		15 May 1831	Bissingen	Krch.	bef 1862	N.-Amer	835943
Hoyler, Carl Ernst		12 Sep 1864	Kirchheim	Krch.	Feb 1870	N.-Amer	835941
Hoyler, Carl Heinrich		- Sep 1845	Kirchheim	Krch.	Jan 1865	N.-Amer	835941
Hoyler, Carl Hermann		8 Oct 1867	Kirchheim	Krch.	Aug 1884	N.-Amer	548403
Hoyler, Catharina		28 Jan 1843	Kirchheim	Krch.	Jan 1865	N.-Amer	835941
Hoyler, Christiana		20 Jun 1838	Weiler	Krch.	Dec 1859	Italy	835949
Hoyler, Christiane & F		28 Aug 1841	Kirchheim	Krch.	Feb 1870	N.-Amer	835941
Hoyler, Christiane Wilhelmine		8 Sep 1865	Kirchheim	Krch.	Feb 1870	N.-Amer	835941
Hoyler, Elisabetha		27 Mar 1857	Rosswaelden	Krch.	Mar 1867	N.-Amer	835949
Hoyler, Ernst		2 Feb 1870	Kirchheim	Krch.	Mar 1883	N.-Amer	548403
Hoyler, Friedrich		4 Mar 1829	Hochdorf	Krch.	Jul 1864	N.-Amer	835945
Hoyler, Friedrich Wilhelm		7 May 1860	Rosswaelden	Krch.	Mar 1867	N.-Amer	835949
Hoyler, Gottlieb		12 Apr 1843	Kirchheim	Krch.	bef 1867	N.-Amer	835941
Hoyler, Gottlob			Kirchheim	Krch.	bef 1870	N.-Amer	835941
Hoyler, Hermann		5 Jan 1871	Kirchheim	Krch.	Dec 1887	N.-Amer	835942
Hoyler, Jacob Michael			Ochsenwang	Krch.	bef 1855	N.-Amer	835940
Hoyler, Johann Georg & F		19 Dec 1809	Rosswaelden	Krch.	Mar 1867	N.-Amer	835949
Hoyler, Johann Michael		7 Feb 1858	Rosswaelden	Krch.	Mar 1867	N.-Amer	835949
Hoyler, Karl Christian		14 Nov 1865	Kirchheim	Krch.	Jul 1882	N.-Amer	548403
Hoyler, Michael		21 Dec 1828	Ochsenwang	Krch.	1854	N.-Amer	835947
Hoyler, Pauline		10 Dec 1840	Kirchheim	Krch.	Mar 1866	N.-Amer	835941
Hoyler, Richard Alfred			Kirchheim	Krch.	Apr 1880	N.-Amer	548403
Hoyler, Wilhelm Heinrich		12 Dec 1867	Kirchheim	Krch.	Feb 1870	N.-Amer	835941
Huber, Anna (wid.) & F		15 May 1805	Gerlingen	Leon.	Jul 1871	Palest.	837953
Huber, Anna Maria			Oberlenningen	Krch.	Aug 1875	N.-Amer	548403
Huber, Anna Maria		19 Apr 1851	Oberlenningen	Krch.	Aug 1875	N.-Amer	835947
Huber, Anna Maria (wife)		9 Nov 1832	Bissingen	Krch.	Aug 1870	N.-Amer	835943
Huber, August		2 yrs.	Oberlenningen	Krch.	Apr 1874	N.-Amer	548403
Huber, August & F		31 yrs.	Oberlenningen	Krch.	Apr 1874	N.-Amer	548403
Huber, August Christoph		10 Apr 1873	Oberlenningen	Krch.	Apr 1874	N.-Amer	835947
Huber, August Friedrich & F		31 yrs.	Oberlenningen	Krch.	Apr 1874	N.-Amer	835947
Huber, Barbara (wife)			Oberlenningen	Krch.	Apr 1874	N.-Amer	835947
Huber, Carl Albert		11 Jul 1846	Kirchheim	Krch.	Jul 1865	N.-Amer	835941
Huber, Carl Christoph		1 Feb 1870	Oberlenningen	Krch.	May 1877	N.-Amer	548403
Huber, Catharina		5 Jun 1869	Bissingen	Krch.	Aug 1870	N.-Amer	835943
Huber, Catharina (wife)		28 Aug 1852	Oberlenningen	Krch.	Sep 1872	N.-Amer	835947
Huber, Christian & F			Oberlenningen	Krch.	Sep 1872	N.-Amer	835947
Huber, Christian Friedrich		3 Jan 1867	Owen	Krch.	Dec 1883	N.-Amer	835948
Huber, Christina		13 Jan 1841	Oberlenningen	Krch.	Mar 1867	Texas	835947
Huber, Christoph & F		4 Mar 1841	Oberlenningen	Krch.	May 1877	N.-Amer	548403
Huber, Christoph Ludwig & F		4 Jul 1829	Bissingen	Krch.	Aug 1870	N.-Amer	835943
Huber, Conrad		11 Aug 1856	Bissingen	Krch.	Aug 1870	N.-Amer	835943
Huber, Eva Friederikeich		22 Apr 1877	Oberlenningen	Krch.	May 1877	N.-Amer	548403
Huber, Friederike		25 Dec 1862	Oberlenningmen	Krch.	Jul 1873	N.-Amer	548403
Huber, Friedrich		22 Nov 1864	Bissingen	Krch.	Aug 1870	N.-Amer	835943

Huber, Gottlieb	5 Dec 1867	Oberlenningen	Krch.	Aug 1873	N.-Amer	835947
Huber, Gottlieb Heinrich	25 Jan 1869	Oberlenningen	Krch.	May 1877	N.-Amer	548403
Huber, Jacob	15 Apr 1837	Gerlingen	Leon.	Jul 1871	Palest.	837953
Huber, Jerg		Oberlenningen	Krch.	May 1771	Hungary	550804
Huber, Johann	10 Jan 1866	Oberlenningem	Krch.	Jul 1873	N.-Amer	548403
Huber, Johann Georg	4 Mar 1856	Oberlenningen	Krch.	Apr 1872	N.-Amer	835947
Huber, Johann Georg & F	30 Jun 1831	Oberlenningen	Krch.	Jul 1873	N.-Amer	548403
Huber, Johann Heinrich Carl	12 Oct 1864	Basel/Switz.	Krch.	Jul 1881	N.-Amer	548403
Huber, Johann Jakob & F	9 Feb 1832	Oberlenningen	Krch.	Jul 1873	N.-Amer	548403
Huber, Johanna	14 Nov 1841	Gerlingen	Leon.	Apr 1862	N.-Amer	837953
Huber, Johannes	20 Aug 1863	Oberlenningen	Krch.	Jul 1873	N.-Amer	548403
Huber, Johannes	10 Jan 1866	Oberlenningen	Krch.	Aug 1873	N.-Amer	835947
Huber, Johannes	17 Dec 1863	Oberlenningen	Krch.	Sep 1872	N.-Amer	835947
Huber, Johannes	18 Feb 1848	Oberlenningen	Krch.	Mar 1868	N.-Amer	835947
Huber, Johannes	28 Oct 1833	Owen	Krch.	Nov 1867	N.-Amer	835948
Huber, Karl Christoph	11 May 1867	Oberlenningen	Krch.	Sep 1872	N.-Amer	835947
Huber, Katharina	25 Feb 1870	Oberlenningen	Krch.	Jul 1873	N.-Amer	548403
Huber, Katharina Sophie (wife)	29 Aug 1844	Oberlenningen	Krch.	May 1877	N.-Amer	548403
Huber, Katharine Regine	25 Feb 1870	Oberlenningen	Krch.	Aug 1873	N.-Amer	835947
Huber, Ludwig	24 Aug 1847	Schramberg	Obd.	Feb 1867	N.-Amer	838636
Huber, Maria	40 yrs.	Oberlenningen	Krch.	Jul 1873	N.-Amer	548403
Huber, Maria Christine	25 Aug 1871	Oberlenningen	Krch.	Aug 1873	N.-Amer	835947
Huber, Maria Regina (wife)		Oberlenningen	Krch.	Aug 1873	N.-Amer	835947
Huber, Michael	17 Oct 1840	Hemmingen	Leon.	Mar 1861	France	837956
Huber, Peter	19 yrs.	Hemmingen	Leon.	Oct 1858	N.-Amer	837956
Huber, Philipp		Owen	Krch.	bef 1867	N.-Amer	835948
Huber, Regina	2 yrs.	Oberlenningen	Krch.	Apr 1874	N.-Amer	548403
Huber, Regina Marie	4 Mar 1872	Oberlenningen	Krch.	Apr 1874	N.-Amer	835947
Huber, Regine (wife)	45 yrs.	Oberlenningen	Krch.	Aug 1873	N.-Amer	835947
Huber, Wilhelm	21 Sep 1856	Kirchheim	Krch.	May 1873	N.-Amer	548403
Huber, Wilhelm Friedrich	6 Apr 1876	Oberlenningen	Krch.	May 1877	N.-Amer	548403
Hueberle, Johannes	25 Dec 1846	Sulgen	Obd.	Mar 1868	N.-Amer	838638
Huenle, Marianna		Weissenstein	Gsl.	Oct 1868	Hesse	572046
Hug, Andreas		Lauterbach	Obd.	bef 1848	Austria	838634
Hug, Apolonia	16 Apr 1824	Lauterbach	Obd.	Jun 1854	N.-Amer	838634
Hug, Ferdinand	28 yrs.	Lauterbach	Obd.	Oct 1853	N.-Amer	838634
Hug, Jacob & F		Mariazell	Obd.	May 1817	N.-Amer	838634
Hug, Jahannes	15 Dec 1858	Lauterbach	Obd.	Nov 1868	Italy	838634
Hug, Katharina	26 Oct 1827	Lauterbach	Obd.	Jun 1854	N.-Amer	838634
Hug, Sophia	29 yrs.	Lauterbach	Obd.	Sep 1862	France	838634
Hug, Theresia	23 Sep 1839	Lauterbach	Obd.	Nov 1868	Italy	838634
Hummel, Albert	16 Dec 1864	Kirchheim	Krch.	Apr 1873	N.-Amer	548403
Hummel, Amalie Mathilde	20 Dec 1848	Reutlingen	Rtl.	Aug 1859	N.-Amer	841053
Hummel, August	23 Jan 1863	Kirchheim	Krch.	Apr 1873	N.-Amer	548403
Hummel, Bertha	26 Jan 1858	Kirchheim	Krch.	Apr 1873	N.-Amer	835942
Hummel, Carl	1 Jan 1853	Kirchheim	Krch.	Jul 1870	N.-Amer	835941
Hummel, Catharina - twin	5 Apr 1855	Oberlenningen	Krch.	Apr 1868	N. Amer	835947
Hummel, Catharina Margar. (wife)		Weil im Dorf	Loen.	Mar 1854	N.-Amer	837967
Hummel, Christian	6 Sep 1856	Kirchheim	Krch.	Apr 1873	N.-Amer	548403
Hummel, Christian Philipp	15 Dec 1849	Eningen	Rtl.	Nov 1869	N.-Amer	841053

Name		Birth		Emigration			Film
Last	First	Date	Place	O'amt	Appl. Date	Dest.	Number
Hummel, Christiana		27 May 1849	Oberlenningen	Krch.	Apr 1868	N.-Amer	835947
Hummel, Christiana (wife)		8 Apr 1812	Oberlenningen	Krch.	Apr 1868	N.-Amer	835947
Hummel, Christiane		29 Jun 1830	Heimerdingen	Leon.	Mar 1853	N.-Amer	837954
Hummel, Coecilia		29 Mar 1830	Donzdorf	Gsl.	Apr 1858	Prussia	572043
Hummel, Eberhardt Carl		14 Dec 1850	Oberlenningen	Krch.	Apr 1867	N.-Amer	835947
Hummel, Ernst Wilhelm			Reutlingen	Rtl.	bef 1866	France	841053
Hummel, Friederike		15 Aug 1866	Kirchheim	Krch.	Apr 1873	N.-Amer	548403
Hummel, Georg Michael		5 Aug 1874	Oetlingen	Krch.	Mar 1889	N.-Amer	835948
Hummel, Gotthard Friedrich		31 Jun 1840	Oberlenningen	Krch.	Sep 1857	N.-Amer	835947
Hummel, Gustav		1 Apr 1847	Oberlenningen	Krch.	Apr 1866	N.-Amer	835947
Hummel, Gustav Adolf		22 Sep 1850	Reutlingen	Rtl.	Jun 1868	N.-Amer	841053
Hummel, Gustav Adolph		19 Jul 1852	Reutlingen	Rtl.	Aug 1859	N.-Amer	841053
Hummel, Jacob & W			Weil im Dorf	Loen.	Mar 1854	N.-Amer	837967
Hummel, Jakob		18 Aug 1827	Tuerkheim	Gsl.	Mar 1853	N.-Amer	572041
Hummel, Jakob - twin		5 Apr 1855	Oberlenningen	Krch.	Apr 1868	N.-Amer	835947
Hummel, Jochem		27 Jun 1855	Kirchheim	Krch.	Apr 1873	N.-Amer	548403
Hummel, Johann			Kirchheim	Krch.	bef 1873	N.-Amer	548403
Hummel, Johann Christian		27 May 1838	Oberlenningen	Krch.	Sep 1857	N.-Amer	835947
Hummel, Johann David		2 Dec 1846	Oetlingen	Krch.	Jun 1866	N.-Amer	835948
Hummel, Johann Ernst		9 Jan 1871	Oetlingen	Krch.	Feb 1887	N.-Amer	835948
Hummel, Johann Georg Gottlob		18 Oct 1841	Eningen	Rtl.	Aug 1864	N.-Amer	841053
Hummel, Johanna Marie Luise		20 Jan 1851	Kirchheim	Krch.	Apr 1873	N.-Amer	835942
Hummel, Johannes Baptist		29 Aug 1862	Donzdorf	Gsl.	Sep 1880	N.-Amer	572048
Hummel, Joseph Anton		17 Oct 1851	Weissenstein	Gsl.	May 1869	N.-Amer	572047
Hummel, Kunigunde (wid.) & F		1822	Notzingen	Krch.	Dec 1859	Prussia	835947
Hummel, Lorenz			Weissenstein	Gsl.	May 1866	N.-Amer	572045
Hummel, Louise		20 Jan 1851	Kirchheim	Krch.	Apr 1873	N.-Amer	548403
Hummel, Ludwig & F		3 Jan 1815	Oberlenningen	Krch.	Apr 1868	N.-Amer	835947
Hummel, Otto		44 yrs.	Reutlingen	Rtl.	Mar 1880	N.-Amer	841051
Hummel, Pauline		16 May 1826	Reutlingen	Rtl.	Aug 1860	N.-Amer	841053
Hummel, Philipp Michael & W			Weil im Dorf	Loen.	Sep 1854	N.-Amer	837967
Hummel, Sophie Wilh.Jakob		27 Jun 1855	Kirchheim	Krch.	Apr 1873	N.-Amer	835942
Hummel, Wilhelm		13 Jan 1838	Owen	Krch.	Feb 1863	N.-Amer	835948
Hummel, Wilhelm Albert		16 Dec 1864	Kirchheim	Krch.	Apr 1873	N.-Amer	835942
Hummel, Wilhelm August		23 Jan 1862	Kirchheim	Krch.	Apr 1873	N.-Amer	835942
Hummel, Wilhelme Friedrike		25 Aug 1866	Kirchheim	Krch.	Apr 1873	N.-Amer	835942
Hummel, Wilhelmine		14 Mar 1844	Oberlenningen	Krch.	Apr 1866	N.-Amer	835947
Hummel, Wilhelmine & F		4 Apr 1828	Kirchheim	Krch.	Apr 1873	N.-Amer	548403
Humper, Anna Maria		25 Sep 1869	Oberlenningen	Krch.	Apr 1884	N.-Amer	548403
Humper, Barbara		1 Feb 1882	Oberlenningen	Krch.	Apr 1884	N.-Amer	548403
Humper, Gottlieb		25 Nov 1875	Oberlenningen	Krch.	Apr 1884	N.-Amer	548403
Humper, Gottlieb Dav. (wid.) & F		28 Jan 1844	Oberlenningen	Krch.	Apr 1884	N.-Amer	548403
Humper, Louise		8 Oct 1879	Oberlenningen	Krch.	Apr 1884	N.-Amer	548403
Humper, Sofie Christine		8 Feb 1868	Oberlenningen	Krch.	Apr 1884	N.-Amer	548403
Humper, Wilhelmine		21 May 1871	Oberlenningen	Krch.	Apr 1884	N.-Amer	548403
Huober, Johann Conrad		8 Jan 1848	Bissingen	Krch.	Jul 1866	N.-Amer	835943
Hurr, Jakob		27 May 1839	Betzingen	Rtl.	Mar 1860	N.-Amer	841053
Hurr, Rosine			Betzingen	Rtl.	Feb 1830	Russia	841051
Husel, Christoph Karl & F		38 yrs.	Unterboehringen	Gsl.	May 1851	N.-Amer	577788
Hutzmann, Jacob Friedrich		34 yrs.	Friolzheim	Leon.	Aug 1853	N.-Amer	835791

Huzelau, Johann Jakob	18 Mar 1821	Lindorf	Krch.	Jul 1867	N.-Amer	835946
Ilg, Johannes	6 Nov 1831	Altenstadt-Gsl.	Gsl.	Feb 1854	N.-Amer	572042
Ilg, Wilhelmina Magdalena	27 Sep 1858	Notzingen	Krch.	Jul 1880	N.-Amer	835940
Illingen, Johann Michael		Rutesheim	Leon.	bef 1834	London	837964
Imhof, Conrad	26 Nov 1800	Epfendorf	Obd.	Aug 1817	N.-Amer	838629
Imhof, Francisca	10 Apr 1814	Epfendorf	Obd.	Aug 1817	N.-Amer	838629
Imhof, Franziska & C	10 Apr 1814	Epfendorf	Obd.	May 1847	N.-Amer	838632
Imhof, Ignaz		Epfendorf	Obd.	Apr 1817	Russia	838632
Imhof, Joseph & F		Epfendorf	Obd.	Aug 1817	N.-Amer	838629
Imhof, Joseph & F		Epfendorf	Obd.	May 1817	N.-Amer	838632
Imhof, Katharina	19 Apr 1845	Epfendorf	Obd.	May 1847	N.-Amer	838632
Imhof, Maria	3 Apr 1810	Epfendorf	Obd.	Aug 1817	N.-Amer	838629
Imhof, Michael	14 Sep 1827	Harthausen	Obd.	Dec 1853	N.-Amer	838633
Imhof, Sebastian	17 Jul 1807	Epfendorf	Obd.	Aug 1817	N.-Amer	838629
Imhof, Theodora	31 Mar 1836	Epfendorf	Obd.	May 1847	N.-Amer	838632
Imhof, Victoria (wife)		Epfendorf	Obd.	Aug 1817	N.-Amer	838629
Irion, Barbara	23 Apr 1825	Alpirsbach	Obd.	bef 1852	Hesse	838630
Irion, Carl	16 yrs.	Alpirsbach	Obd.	Aug 1854	N.-Amer	838630
Irion, Christian	30 Nov 1846	Alpirsbach	Obd.	Apr 1866	N.-Amer	838630
Irion, Johann Friedrich	1 Dec 1826	Alpirsbach	Obd.	bef 1856	N.-Amer	838630
Irion, Magdalena	7 Sep 1853	Alpirsbach	Obd.	Jun 1867	Switz.	838630
Isler, Gottlieb Friedrich		Gerlingen	Leon.	Aug 1832	Russia	837953
Issler, Barbara & F		Gebersheim	Leon.	May 1850	N.-Amer	837953
Issler, Beata Friederike	11 Sep 1826	Korntal	Leon.	Aug 1854	N.-Amer	837957
Issler, Friedrich	14 Sep 1851	Gebersheim	Leon.	Apr 1867	N.-Amer	837953
Issler, Immanuel Gottlieb	6 Aug 1832	Korntal	Leon.	Sep 1857	Bavaria	837957
Issler, Johann Michael & F		Gebersheim	Leon.	Aug 1822	Russia	837953
Issler, Maria Magdalena & C		Gebersheim	Leon.	May 1850	N.-Amer	837953
Issler, Pauline Friderike		Korntal	Leon.	Jan 1852	N.-Amer	837957
Issler, Rudolf	2 Nov 1857	Gebersheim	Leon.	bef 1874	N.-Amer	837953
Jacker, Franz	25 Jun 1840	Ellwangen	Gsl.	Jul 1859	N.-Amer	572043
Jacker, Joseph Theodor	19 Jul 1834	Donzdorf	Gsl.	Apr 1854	N.-Amer	572042
Jacober, Rosine Catharine	21 May 1848	Unterlenningen	Krch.	Oct 1865	N.-Amer	835949
Jacobus, Friedrich		Holzmaden	Krch.	Oct 1870	N.-Amer	835945
Jaeckh, Christian & F		Ditzingen	Leon.	Oct 1854	N.-Amer	835788
Jaeckle, Christian	31 Oct 1817	Betzweiler	Obd.	Jun 1846	France	838631
Jaeckle, Christian	28 Sep 1846	Heimerdingen	Leon.	May 1866	N.-Amer	837954
Jaeckle, Mathias	22 Jul 1820	Betzweiler	Obd.	Jul 1847	France	838631
Jaeger, Carl	17 Oct 1863	Ulm	Krch.	1881	N.-Amer	548403
Jaeger, Caroline (wife)	1805	Heimerdingen	Leon.	Jun 1832	N.-Amer	837954
Jaeger, Caspar & F		Hoefingen	Leon.	May 1832	N.-Amer	837957
Jaeger, Charlotte		Eningen	Rtl.	Aug 1864	N.-Amer	841055
Jaeger, Emil Alfred	10 May 1860	Weil im Dorf	Loen.	Apr 1883	N.-Amer	837967
Jaeger, Johann Georg	24 Nov 1831	Weissach	Leon.	Oct 1850	N.-Amer	837963
Jaeger, Johannes	18 Apr 1848	Oberjesingen	Herr.	1874	N.-Amer	834630
Jaeger, Johannes		Eningen	Rtl.	Nov 1853	Switz.	841053
Jaeger, Johannes Wilhelm	15 Sep 1846	Eningen	Rtl.	Aug 1866	N.-Amer	841053
Jaeger, Karl	17 Oct 1863	Kirchheim	Krch.	May 1881	N.-Amer	835942
Jaeger, Kaspar & F	7 Dec 1805	Heimerdingen	Leon.	Jun 1832	N.-Amer	837954
Jaeger, Robert Ulrich	15 Aug 1855	Weil im Dorf	Loen.	Mar 1881	N.-Amer	837967

Name		Birth		Emigration			Film
Last	First	Date	Place	O'amt	Appl. Date	Dest.	Number
Jaegerin, Christoph		6 Dec 1818	Schoeckingen	Leon.	Mar 1831	N.-Amer	837964
Jaegerin, Gottlieb Friedrich		3 Sep 1822	Schoeckingen	Leon.	Mar 1831	N.-Amer	837964
Jaegerin, Katharine & C		25 Jul 1796	Schoeckingen	Leon.	Mar 1831	N.-Amer	837964
Jaekh, Johannes		3 Apr 1822	Weil im Dorf	Loen.	Jun 1852	N.-Amer	837967
Jaekle, Anna Catharina & F		11 Jan 1778	Heimerdingen	Leon.	Apr 1838	Russia	837954
Jaekle, Bernhardt		23 Jun 1863	Heimerdingen	Leon.	Jan 1864	Westf.	837954
Jaekle, Caroline		23 Nov 1848	Heimerdingen	Leon.	Aug 1853	N.-Amer	837954
Jaekle, Christian		25 Oct 1832	Heimerdingen	Leon.	Aug 1853	N.-Amer	837954
Jaekle, Christian & F		2 Sep 1812	Heimerdingen	Leon.	Aug 1853	N.-Amer	837954
Jaekle, Christina Barbara		23 Feb 1783	Heimerdingen	Leon.	bef 1818	N.-Amer	837954
Jaekle, Christina Margaretha		20 Nov 1793	Heimerdingen	Leon.	bef 1818	N.-Amer	837954
Jaekle, Christine (wife)		24 Oct 1812	Heimerdingen	Leon.	Aug 1853	N.-Amer	837954
Jaekle, Christine Doro. S. & C		14 Feb 1824	Heimerdingen	Leon.	Jan 1864	Westf.	837954
Jaekle, Conrad		13 Aug 1835	Heimerdingen	Leon.	Aug 1853	N.-Amer	837954
Jaekle, Conrad		75 yrs.	Heimerdingen	Leon.	bef 1818	N.-Amer	837954
Jaekle, Eberhard Ludwig		24 yrs.	Heimerdingen	Leon.	May 1831	N.-Amer	837954
Jaekle, Elias		23 yrs.	Heimerdingen	Leon.	bef 1818	N.-Amer	837954
Jaekle, Friedrich			Peterzell	Obd.	Nov 1846	Austria	838635
Jaekle, Gottlieb Friedrich		17 Nov 1845	Heimerdingen	Leon.	Aug 1853	N.-Amer	837954
Jaekle, Gustav August		2 Aug 1838	Heimerdingen	Leon.	Aug 1857	N.-Amer	837954
Jaekle, Jacob Friedrich		11 Feb 1817	Heimerdingen	Leon.	Apr 1838	Russia	837954
Jaekle, Johann Conrad		31 May 1842	Heimerdingen	Leon.	Aug 1857	N.-Amer	837954
Jaekle, Johann Georg			Heimerdingen	Leon.	1817	N.-Amer	837954
Jaekle, Johann Georg		18 yrs.	Heimerdingen	Leon.	bef 1818	N.-Amer	837954
Jaekle, Johann Jacob Friedr.			Heimerdingen	Leon.	Oct 1852	N.-Amer	837954
Jaekle, Johannes		15 yrs.	Heimerdingen	Leon.	bef 1818	N.-Amer	837954
Jaekle, Katharina		28 Sep 1838	Peterzell	Obd.	Jan 1869	N.-Amer	838635
Jaekle, Maria Barbara & C		11 Aug 1776	Heimerdingen	Leon.	bef 1818	N.-Amer	837954
Jaekle, Maria Christiana		5 Jun 1828	Heimerdingen	Leon.	Aug 1853	N.-Amer	837954
Jaekle, Maria Friederike		13 Nov 1852	Heimerdingen	Leon.	Aug 1853	N.-Amer	837954
Jaerkh, Johanna Barb. Cathar.		20 Mar 1829	Weil im Dorf	Loen.	1851	N.-Amer	837967
Jaimel, Caroline (wife)			Heimsheim	Leon.	Jul 1854	N.-Amer	837955
Jaimel, Louis & F			Heimsheim	Leon.	Jul 1854	N.-Amer	837955
Jaimet, Charles & F			Perouse	Leon.	Mar 1830	N.-Amer	837962
Jauch, Andreas		18 yrs.	Oberndorf	Obd.	Oct 1854	N.-Amer	838635
Jauch, Johann Babtist		18 Jul 1853	Beffendorf	Obd.	Mar 1864	N.-Amer	838631
Jauch, Johann Georg		27 May 1859	Ditzingen	Leon.	bef 1883	N.-Amer	835788
Jauch, Johann Nepomuk		20 May 1830	Winzeln	Obd.	1846	N.-Amer	841016
Jauch, Joseph			Oberndorf	Obd.	bef 1854	N.-Amer	838635
Jauch, Kaspar			Waldmoessingen	Obd.	Feb 1861	N.-Amer	841015
Jauch, Katharina & C		8 Apr 1830	Waldmoessingen	Obd.	Nov 1863	Switz.	841015
Jauch, Konrad		19 Jul 1817	Alt Oberndorf	Obd.	Sep 1848	France	838631
Jauch, Konrad		25 Nov 1823	Waldmoessingen	Obd.	Mar 1865	N.-Amer	841015
Jauch, Maria & C			Waldmoessingen	Obd.	Mar 1864	N.-Amer	841015
Jauch, Maria Anna			Oberndorf	Obd.	Mar 1849	N.-Amer	838635
Jauch, Rudolf		15 yrs.	Waldmoessingen	Obd.	Mar 1864	N.-Amer	841015
Jauch, Sabina		27 Oct 1832	Winzeln	Obd.	1846	N.-Amer	841016
Jauss, David		6 Jan 1840	Haslach	Herr.	Sep 1864	N.-Amer	834631
Jauss, Kardine		1 Jul 1845	Leonberg	Leon.	Aug 1866	Switz.	835787
Jauss, Maria		7 Mar 1848	Gerlingen	Leon.	Sep 1868	N.-Amer	837953

Jauss, Maria	25 yrs.	Eltingen	Leon.	Dec 1851	N.-Amer	835789
Jeggle, Michael	29 Sep 1827	Schramberg	Obd.	Feb 1854	N.-Amer	838636
Jeggle, Wilhelm	4 May 1843	Schramberg	Obd.	May 1870	Prussia	838636
Jehle, Catharina	38 yrs.	Aichhalden	Obd.	1855	France	838629
Jehle, Jacob	6 Aug 1837	Gutenberg	Krch.	Jul 1856	N.-Amer	835945
Jehle, Maria Agnes (wid.)	25 Nov 1797	Gutenberg	Krch.	Jul 1856	N.-Amer	835945
Jenthner, Jonathan	16 Sep 1803	Friolzheim	Leon.	Jan 1848	France	835791
Jentner, Barbara		Wimsheim	Loen.	Aug 1854	N.-Amer	837967
Jentner, Barbara (wid.) & F		Wimsheim	Loen.	May 1852	N.-Amer	837967
Jentner, Georg & F		Wimsheim	Loen.	Aug 1854	N.-Amer	837967
Jentner, Johann Georg		Wimsheim	Loen.	Aug 1854	N.-Amer	837967
Jentner, Johann Michael	15 Jul 1838	Wimsheim	Loen.	Nov 1853	N.-Amer	837967
Jentner, Rosina		Wimsheim	Loen.	Aug 1854	N.-Amer	837967
Jentner, Rosina (wife)		Wimsheim	Loen.	Aug 1854	N.-Amer	837967
Jocher, Christiane		Perouse	Leon.	bef 1857	France	837962
Jocher, Conrad		Heimerdingen	Leon.	1852	N.-Amer	837954
Jocher, Johann David		Heimerdingen	Leon.	Mar 1854	N.-Amer	837954
Jocher, Karl August	21 Jun 1861	Heimerdingen	Leon.	bef 1887	N.-Amer	837954
Jocher, Leonhardt	17 Nov 1836	Heimerdingen	Leon.	Mar 1854	N.-Amer	837954
Joerg, Barbara	infant	Ditzingen	Leon.	Jun 1817	Hungary	835788
Joerg, Barbara (wife)	24 yrs.	Ditzingen	Leon.	Jun 1817	Hungary	835788
Joerg, Christian Friedrich		Ditzingen	Leon.	bef 1859	Switz.	835788
Joerg, Christiana		Ditzingen	Leon.	Mar 1852	N.-Amer	835788
Joerg, Conrad	15 Aug 1818	Ditzingen	Leon.	Mar 1860	France	835788
Joerg, Conrad	2 yrs.	Ditzingen	Leon.	Jun 1817	Hungary	835788
Joerg, Conrad & F		Ditzingen	Leon.	Aug 1820	Russia	835788
Joerg, Conrad & F	25 yrs.	Ditzingen	Leon.	Jun 1817	Hungary	835788
Joerg, Conrad Friedrich	17 Oct 1834	Ditzingen	Leon.	Mar 1855	N.-Amer	835788
Joos, Heinrich	23 Feb 1859	Owen	Krch.	Jun 1862	N.-Amer	835948
Josenhannes, Christiane Ros.S.	20 yrs.	Leonberg	Leon.	Apr 1831	N.-Amer	835786
Josenhans , Carl	2 yrs.	Eltingen	Leon.	Mar 1852	N.-Amer	835789
Josenhans , Louis	infant	Eltingen	Leon.	Mar 1852	N.-Amer	835789
Josenhans , Louise	1 yrs.	Eltingen	Leon.	Mar 1852	N.-Amer	835789
Josenhans, Agatha	20 Jul 1850	Leonberg	Leon.	Sep 1855	N.-Amer	835786
Josenhans, Carl	22 Jun 1837	Leonberg	Leon.	Feb 1854	N.-Amer	835786
Josenhans, Carl Friedrich	27 Nov 1836	Leonberg	Leon.	Jun 1853	N.-Amer	835786
Josenhans, Caroline	3 Apr 1843	Leonberg	Leon.	Sep 1855	N.-Amer	835786
Josenhans, Charlotta (wife)		Leonberg	Leon.	Sep 1855	N.-Amer	835786
Josenhans, Christian	8 Apr 1825	Leonberg	Leon.	Feb 1854	N.-Amer	835786
Josenhans, Christian & F		Leonberg	Leon.	Feb 1854	N.-Amer	835786
Josenhans, Christian Gottfr.	24 Jul 1835	Leonberg	Leon.	Jun 1853	N.-Amer	835786
Josenhans, Christian Josef & F		Eltingen	Leon.	Mar 1852	N.-Amer	835789
Josenhans, Elisabetha Frieder.	4 May 1861	Leonberg	Leon.	Mar 1875	N.-Amer	835787
Josenhans, Emma Aug. Eli. Ber.	11 May 1859	Leonberg	Leon.	Mar 1875	N.-Amer	835787
Josenhans, Friederich	28 Aug 1851	Leonberg	Leon.	Sep 1855	N.-Amer	835786
Josenhans, Gerhard	5 Jan 1855	Leonberg	Leon.	Sep 1855	N.-Amer	835786
Josenhans, Gotthold	17 Aug 1846	Leonberg	Leon.	Sep 1855	N.-Amer	835786
Josenhans, Johann Friedrich	20 Oct 1848	Rutesheim	Leon.	May 1867	N.-Amer	837964
Josenhans, Johanna	2 Mar 1842	Leonberg	Leon.	Sep 1855	N.-Amer	835786
Josenhans, Johannes	25 Jun 1836	Leonberg	Leon.	Apr 1853	N.-Amer	835786

| Name | | Birth | | Emigration | | | Film |
Last	First	Date	Place	O'amt	Appl. Date	Dest.	Number
Josenhans,	Johannes Karl Rei.	27 Sep 1857	Leonberg	Leon.	Mar 1875	N.-Amer	835787
Josenhans,	Jonathan & F	40 yrs.	Leonberg	Leon.	Sep 1855	N.-Amer	835786
Josenhans,	Leonhard	11 Aug 1844	Leonberg	Leon.	Sep 1855	N.-Amer	835786
Josenhans,	Nathanael Jerem & F	26 Jun 1822	Leonberg	Leon.	Mar 1875	N.-Amer	835787
Josenhans,	Reinhold	20 Sep 1869	Leonberg	Leon.	Mar 1875	N.-Amer	835787
Josenhans,	Samuel	25 Nov 1847	Leonberg	Leon.	Sep 1855	N.-Amer	835786
Josenhans,	Theodor	27 Sep 1852	Leonberg	Leon.	Sep 1855	N.-Amer	835786
Josenhans,	Thimothee	11 Oct 1853	Leonberg	Leon.	Sep 1855	N.-Amer	835786
Josenhans,	Wilhelmine (wife)		Eltingen	Leon.	Mar 1852	N.-Amer	835789
Juengling,	Adam Ulrich	23 Dec 1875	Rutesheim	Leon.	Apr 1881	N.-Amer	837964
Juengling,	Anna Maria (wife)	3 Apr 1852	Rutesheim	Leon.	Apr 1881	N.-Amer	837964
Juengling,	Caroline (wife)		Gebersheim	Leon.	Jun 1854	N.-Amer	837953
Juengling,	Catharina		Hirschlanden	Leon.	1853	N.-Amer	837956
Juengling,	Christian Gottlieb	1849	Rutesheim	Leon.	Jan 1869	N.-Amer	837964
Juengling,	Christian Wilhelm	14 Sep 1859	Gebersheim	Leon.	Mar 1884	N.-Amer	837953
Juengling,	Christine Emil. & F		Gebersheim	Leon.	May 1855	N.-Amer	837953
Juengling,	Ferdinand	30 Mar 1868	Marktlustenau	Leon.	1884	N.-Amer	837964
Juengling,	Friedrich		Rutesheim	Leon.	bef 1861	N.-Amer	837964
Juengling,	Friedrich		Gebersheim	Leon.	1853	N.-Amer	837953
Juengling,	Georg Gottlieb	17 Oct 1873	Rutesheim	Leon.	Apr 1881	N.-Amer	837964
Juengling,	Jacob	11 Nov 1816	Rutesheim	Leon.	bef 1857	N.-Amer	837964
Juengling,	Jacob & F		Gebersheim	Leon.	Jun 1854	N.-Amer	837953
Juengling,	Johann Georg		Gebersheim	Leon.	Sep 1854	Austria	837953
Juengling,	Johann Jakob		Rutesheim	Leon.	Oct 1856	N.-Amer	837964
Juengling,	Johannes & F	16 Oct 1850	Rutesheim	Leon.	Apr 1881	N.-Amer	837964
Juengling,	Lukas & F		Ruetesheim	Leon.	1853	N.-Amer	837956
Juengling,	Margaretha		Rutesheim	Leon.	1852	N.-Amer	837964
Juengling,	Maria Barbara		Rutesheim	Leon.	1860	N.-Amer	837964
Juengling,	Maria Margaretha	17 yrs.	Rutesheim	Leon.	Feb 1852	N.-Amer	837964
Juengling,	Maria Rosina	12 Dec 1876	Rutesheim	Leon.	Apr 1881	N.-Amer	837964
Juengling,	Rosina		Rutesheim	Leon.	1853	N.-Amer	837964
Jung,	Anna Maria		Wannweil	Rtl.	Apr 1833	N.-Amer	841051
Jung,	Elisabeth		Wannweil	Rtl.	Apr 1833	N.-Amer	841051
Jung,	Johann Georg		Wannweil	Rtl.	Apr 1833	N.-Amer	841051
Jung,	Johann Gottlieb	23 Sep 1813	Heimsheim	Leon.	Oct 1844	Holland	837955
Junger,	Crescenz (wife)		Gomaringen	Rtl.	Jun 1866	N.-Amer	841053
Junger,	Jacob	8 Mar 1840	Gomaringen	Rtl.	Oct 1866	N.-Amer	841053
Junger,	Jacob		Gomaringen	Rtl.	Jul 1865	N.-Amer	841053
Junger,	Johann Jacob	28 Jun 1850	Gomaringen	Rtl.	Apr 1858	N.-Amer	841053
Junger,	Joseph & W		Gomaringen	Rtl.	Jun 1866	N.-Amer	841053
Junginger,	Karl	27 Feb 1851	Geislingen	Gsl.	Jul 1869	N.-Amer	572047
Junt,	Jacob	24 Mar 1851	Ehlenbogen	Obd.	Mar 1869	N.-Amer	838632
Kaag,	Anna Maria	25 Nov 1837	Oberlenningen	Krch.	bef 1865	Prussia	835947
Kaag,	Johann Christoph	24 Oct 1857	Oberlenningen	Krch.	Jun 1874	N.-Amer	835947
Kaag,	Johannes	28 Mar 1857	Oberlenningen	Krch.	Jan 1872	N.-Amer	835947
Kaag,	Karl Gottlieb	1 Dec 1863	Oberlenningen	Krch.	Nov 1880	N.-Amer	835947
Kachler,	Karl Martin	11 Nov 1843	Leonberg	Leon.	bef 1868	N.-Amer	835787
Kaechele,	Anna Maria (wid.)	14 Aug 1805	Owen	Krch.	May 1871	N.-Amer	835948
Kaechele,	Anna Maria (wife)	21 Dec 1833	Bissingen	Krch.	Oct 1867	N.-Amer	835943
Kaechele,	Catharina	15 May 1864	Bissingen	Krch.	Oct 1867	N.-Amer	835943

Kaechele, Christian Friedrich	10 Nov 1840	Owen	Krch.	Jul 1860	N.-Amer	835948
Kaechele, Conrad	2 Jun 1866	Bissingen	Krch.	Oct 1867	N.-Amer	835943
Kaechele, Dorothea	21 Sep 1867	Bissingen	Krch.	Oct 1867	N.-Amer	835943
Kaechele, Johann Friedrich	7 Oct 1866	Owen	Krch.	May 1882	N.-Amer	835948
Kaechele, Johann Georg & F	17 Aug 1836	Bissingen	Krch.	Oct 1867	N.-Amer	835943
Kaefer, Anna Catharine	20 Sep 1850	Heimerdingen	Leon.	May 1853	N.-Amer	837954
Kaefer, Catharina Margar. (wife)	4 Oct 1828	Heimerdingen	Leon.	Feb 1852	N.-Amer	837954
Kaefer, Christian & F	25 Dec 1825	Heimerdingen	Leon.	Feb 1852	N.-Amer	837954
Kaefer, Christiane	14 Jun 1843	Heimerdingen	Leon.	May 1853	N.-Amer	837954
Kaefer, Jakob Christian	12 Jul 1848	Warmbronn	Leon.	Nov 1865	N.-Amer	837965
Kaefer, Jakob Martin & F	26 Oct 1817	Heimerdingen	Leon.	May 1853	N.-Amer	837954
Kaefer, Jakobine Christi. (wife)	16 Sep 1822	Heimerdingen	Leon.	May 1853	N.-Amer	837954
Kaefer, Johann Christof	18 yrs.	Heimerdingen	Leon.	May 1831	N.-Amer	837954
Kaefer, Marie Catharine	23 Feb 1846	Heimerdingen	Leon.	May 1853	N.-Amer	837954
Kaefer, Wilhelm Friedrich	infant	Heimerdingen	Leon.	Feb 1852	N.-Amer	837954
Kaelberer, Jacob	60 yrs.	Jesingen	Krch.	Jul 1804	Hungary	550804
Kaelberer, Jacob Wilhelm	20 Mar 1842	Notzingen	Krch.	Apr 1864	Hesse	835947
Kaelberer, Johann Friedrich	23 Mar 1852	Ohmden	Krch.	Aug 1870	N.-Amer	835948
Kaelberer, Johann Georg	23 Feb 1840	Notzingen	Krch.	Apr 1864	Hesse	835947
Kaelberer, Tobias	29 May 1833	Ohmden	Krch.	bef 1870	N.-Amer	835948
Kaemmerle, Johann Gottfried	4 Jan 1835	Leonberg	Leon.	Apr 1853	N.-Amer	835786
Kaercher, Alexander	25 Nov 1842	Moensheim	Leon.	Apr 1854	N.-Amer	837960
Kaercher, Alexander & W		Moensheim	Leon.	Apr 1857	N.-Amer	837960
Kaercher, Andreas		Moensheim	Leon.	Apr 1857	N.-Amer	837960
Kaercher, Barbara (wife)		Moensheim	Leon.	Aug 1851	N.-Amer	837960
Kaercher, Caroline	1 yrs.	Moensheim	Leon.	Aug 1851	N.-Amer	837960
Kaercher, Catharina	7 yrs.	Moensheim	Leon.	Aug 1851	N.-Amer	837960
Kaercher, Georg Friedrich		Leonberg	Leon.	Jan 1817	Russia	835785
Kaercher, Gottlieb	18 Jan 1844	Moensheim	Leon.	bef 1853	Hungary	837960
Kaercher, Gottlieb & F		Moensheim	Leon.	Apr 1854	N.-Amer	837960
Kaercher, Helena	5 yrs.	Moensheim	Leon.	Aug 1851	N.-Amer	837960
Kaercher, Jakob Friedrich	25 Jan 1847	Moensheim	Leon.	bef 1853	Hungary	837960
Kaercher, Johann Friedrich		Rutesheim	Leon.	bef 1870	N.-Amer	837964
Kaercher, Johann Georg	1 Dec 1844	Moensheim	Leon.	Apr 1854	N.-Amer	837960
Kaercher, Johann Georg & F		Wimsheim	Loen.	Jul 1851	N.-Amer	837967
Kaercher, Johann Mattheus	2 May 1852	Moensheim	Leon.	bef 1853	Hungary	837960
Kaercher, Johann Mattheus & F		Moensheim	Leon.	bef 1853	Hungary	837960
Kaercher, Johann Michael	25 Mar 1839	Moensheim	Leon.	Apr 1854	N.-Amer	837960
Kaercher, Johanna (wife)		Moensheim	Leon.	Apr 1857	N.-Amer	837960
Kaercher, Johannes	5 Jul 1847	Moensheim	Leon.	Apr 1854	N.-Amer	837960
Kaercher, Johannes & F		Moensheim	Leon.	Aug 1851	N.-Amer	837960
Kaercher, Margaretha	15 Mar 1850	Moensheim	Leon.	bef 1853	Hungary	837960
Kaercher, Margaretha (wife)		Moensheim	Leon.	bef 1853	Hungary	837960
Kaercher, Michael	10 yrs.	Moensheim	Leon.	Aug 1851	N.-Amer	837960
Kaercher, Regina	3 yrs.	Moensheim	Leon.	Aug 1851	N.-Amer	837960
Kaercher, Rosina Catharina	7 Mar 1841	Moensheim	Leon.	Apr 1854	N.-Amer	837960
Kaercher, Salome	10 Sep 1845	Moensheim	Leon.	bef 1853	Hungary	837960
Kag, Anna Maria	16 Jun 1835	Oberlenningen	Krch.	Mar 1858	N.-Amer	835947
Kag, Johannes	23 Sep 1840	Oberlenningen	Krch.	Feb 1857	N.-Amer	835947
Kaiser, Elisabetha		Sulgen	Obd.	bef 1861	N.-Amer	838638

| Name | | Birth | | Emigration | | | Film |
Last	First	Date	Place	O'amt	Appl. Date	Dest.	Number
Kaiser, Franz Seraph		27 Sep 1832	Schnittlingen	Gsl.	Jul 1866	N.-Amer	572045
Kaiser, Johann Georg		6 Mar 1835	Treffelhausen	Gsl.	Feb 1854	N.-Amer	572042
Kaiser, Joseph			Sulgen	Obd.	bef 1860	Switz.	838638
Kaiser, Joseph		2 Feb 1826	Schnittlingen	Gsl.	Mar 1850	N.-Amer	577788
Kaiser, Maria Catharina		30 Apr 1822	Kirchheim	Krch.	Dec 1859	N.-Amer	835940
Kaiser, Wilhelm		23 Dec 1846	Oetlingen	Krch.	Oct 1866	N.-Amer	835948
Kalb, Anton		13 Jun 1833	Boehmenkirch	Gsl.	Sep 1853	N.-Amer	572041
Kalbfell, Johann Martin		28 Apr 1847	Reutlingen	Rtl.	Oct 1866	N.-Amer	841054
Kalbfell, Judith Salome			Reutlingen	Rtl.	Jul 1836	N.-Amer	841051
Kalmbach, Christiana			Enztal	Nag.	Apr 1851	N.-Amer	838488
Kalmbach, Georg Jacob & F			Alpirsbach	Obd.	Apr 1817	Russia	838631
Kaltenbacher, Dominicus		12 Jun 1843	Lauterbach	Obd.	Sep 1859	N.-Amer	838634
Kaltenbacher, Elisabeth		17 Oct 1836	Lauterbach	Obd.	Sep 1859	N.-Amer	838634
Kaltenbacher, Genovefa (wife)		6 Jan 1807	Lauterbach	Obd.	Sep 1859	N.-Amer	838634
Kaltenbacher, Johannes		15 Jun 1838	Lauterbach	Obd.	Sep 1859	N.-Amer	838634
Kaltenbacher, Joseph		17 Feb 1841	Lauterbach	Obd.	Sep 1859	N.-Amer	838634
Kaltenbacher, Leopold		19 yrs.	Schramberg	Obd.	Aug 1853	N.-Amer	838636
Kaltenbacher, Louis			Schramberg	Obd.	Jun 1856	Paris	838636
Kaltenbacher, Sebastian		8 Jan 1845	Lauterbach	Obd.	Sep 1859	N.-Amer	838634
Kaltenbacher, Stephan & F		6 Jul 1796	Lauterbach	Obd.	Sep 1859	N.-Amer	838634
Kamm, Anna Maria			Wimsheim	Loen.	Aug 1854	N.-Amer	837967
Kamm, Christian			Wimsheim	Loen.	Aug 1854	N.-Amer	837967
Kamm, Dorothea Charlotte		30 Nov 1842	Reutlingen	Rtl.	Dec 1868	Oldenb.	841054
Kamm, Johann			Reutlingen	Rtl.	May 1835	N.-Amer	841051
Kamm, Margaretha & C			Wimsheim	Loen.	Aug 1854	N.-Amer	837967
Kamm, Marie Agnes		30 Mar 1840	Reutlingen	Rtl.	Dec 1868	Bohemia	841054
Kamm, Nanette		2 Jan 1844	Reutlingen	Rtl.	Jun 1865	N.-Amer	841054
Kamm, Salomon			Wimsheim	Loen.	Aug 1854	N.-Amer	837967
Kammerer, Anna - (wid.) & F		54 yrs.	Epfendorf	Obd.	Apr 1867	N.-Amer	838632
Kammerer, Ferdinand		19 Feb 1846	Epfendorf	Obd.	Jul 1865	N.-Amer	838632
Kammerer, Johannes		9 yrs.	Epfendorf	Obd.	Apr 1867	N.-Amer	838632
Kammerer, Markus		15 yrs.	Epfendorf	Obd.	Apr 1867	N.-Amer	838632
Kapp, Anna Maria		26 Apr 1831	Gueltstein	Herr.	Feb 1866	N.-Amer	834631
Kapp, August Friedrich			Gerlingen	Leon.	Jul 1854	N.-Amer	837953
Kapp, Barbara		23 yrs.	Betzweiler	Obd.	Apr 1852	N.-Amer	838631
Kapp, Christian Franz		19 Feb 1842	Gueltstein	Herr.	Feb 1866	N.-Amer	834631
Kapp, Christine Barbara		6 Jan 1838	Gueltstein	Herr.	Feb 1866	N.-Amer	834631
Kapp, Franz		25 Nov 1810	Gueltstein	Herr.	Mar 1861	N.-Amer	834631
Kapp, Johann Jakob		9 Nov 1826	Gueltstein	Herr.	Feb 1866	N.-Amer	834631
Kapp, Johann Ulrich		13 May 1871	Gueltstein	Herr.	bef 1896	Switz.	834631
Kapp, Kristina		19 yrs.	Betzweiler	Obd.	Apr 1852	N.-Amer	838631
Kapp, Maria Katharina		24 Mar 1861	Gueltstein	Herr.	Feb 1866	N.-Amer	834631
Kapp, Maria Katharina & C		12 Jul 1839	Gueltstein	Herr.	Feb 1866	N.-Amer	834631
Kapp, Wilhelm Friedrich & F			Gomaringen	Rtl.	May 1832	N.-Amer	841051
Kappes, Johann Andreas		18 yrs.	Flacht	Leon.	Oct 1866	N.-Amer	835790
Kappler, Dorothea		27 Oct 1822	Hausen a.d. Wurm	Leon.	Jul 1851	N.-Amer	837954
Kappler, Gottfried		28 yrs.	Heimsheim	Leon.	Sep 1854	N.-Amer	837955
Kappler, Johann Wilhelm		21 Mar 1858	Reutlingen	Rtl.	Apr 1879	N.-Amer	841051
Kappler, Katharina			Weil der Stadt	Leon.	1854	N.-Amer	837966
Kappler, Konstantin		6 Apr 1825	Weil der Stadt	Leon.	Oct 1850	N.-Amer	837966

Kappus, Jacob Friedrich	13 Jan 1833	Gerlingen	Leon.	Jul 1853	N.-Amer	837953
Karmarzin, Simon	7 Jun 1847	Gueltstein	Herr.	Aug 1872	N.-Amer	834631
Katz, Isaak		Unterschwandorf	Nag.	Nov 1849	N.-Amer	838488
Katz, Moses		Unterschwandorf	Nag.	Nov 1849	N.-Amer	838488
Kauber, Jakob Friedrich	14 Aug 1873	Dettingen	Krch.	Mar 1887	N.-Amer	548323
Kauber, Johann Georg	18 May 1866	Dettingen	Krch.	Mar 1883	N.-Amer	548403
Kauderer, Elisabetha	27 Nov 1833	Weilheim	Krch.	Dec 1861	France	835949
Kauderer, Gottlieb	24 yrs.	Weiler	Krch.	Aug 1873	N.-Amer	548403
Kauderer, Gottlieb	30 Jun 1849	Rosswaelden	Krch.	Aug 1873	N.-Amer	835949
Kaufmann, Adolph	30 Sep 1831	Renningen	Leon.	bef 1859	N.-Amer	837963
Kaufmann, Andreas	28 yrs.	Fluorn	Obd.	May 1853	N.-Amer	838632
Kaufmann, Anna Barbara	3 Jul 1829	Bissingen	Krch.	1855	N.-Amer	835943
Kaufmann, Elisabeth		Fluorn	Obd.	bef 1859	N.-Amer	838632
Kaufmann, Emilie Luise	18 May 1866	Geislingen	Gsl.	Apr 1880	N.-Amer	572048
Kaufmann, Ernst	10 Jan 1874	Bissingen	Krch.	Mar 1890	N.-Amer	835943
Kaufmann, Georg Jakob	29 Sep 1869	Renningen	Leon.	May 1885	N.-Amer	837963
Kaufmann, Gottlob	25 Feb 1871	Bissingen	Krch.	Aug 1887	N.-Amer	835943
Kaufmann, Jakob	19 yrs.	Fluorn	Obd.	Mar 1857	N.-Amer	838632
Kaufmann, Johann Jacob	5 Sep 1868	Bissingen	Krch.	Aug 1884	N.-Amer	548403
Kaufmann, Johannes	8 Mar 1841	Bissingen	Krch.	Apr 1857	N.-Amer	835943
Kaufmann, Margaretha	10 Sep 1845	Bissingen	Krch.	Sep 1866	N.-Amer	835943
Kaufmann, Margarethe	7 yrs.	Eltingen	Leon.	Apr 1856	N.-Amer	835789
Kaufmann, Maria	13 yrs.	Eltingen	Leon.	Apr 1856	N.-Amer	835789
Kaufmann, Maria Dorothea	3 Feb 1832	Bissingen	Krch.	1855	N.-Amer	835943
Kaufmann, Maria Katharina	34 yrs.	Rutesheim	Leon.	Jun 1853	N.-Amer	837964
Kaufmann, Mathaeus & F		Eltingen	Leon.	Apr 1856	N.-Amer	835789
Kaufmann, Wilhelm	17 yrs.	Fluorn	Obd.	Feb 1861	N.-Amer	838632
Kaus, Augustin	19 Aug 1831	Beffendorf	Obd.	Mar 1854	N.-Amer	838631
Kaus, Magda	8 May 1840	Beffendorf	Obd.	Mar 1854	N.-Amer	838631
Kautter, Eberhard Friedrich	8 Oct 1829	Weilheim	Krch.	Jul 1862	N.-Amer	835950
Kautter, Johann David	30 Jun 1851	Bissingen	Krch.	Aug 1869	N.-Amer	835943
Kautter, Johann Georg (wife) & F	19 Oct 1816	Bissingen	Krch.	Mar 1862	N.-Amer	835943
Kautter, Johann Michael	12 Nov 1871	Bissingen	Krch.	Mar 1888	N.-Amer	835943
Kautter, Johannes	1 Mar 1845	Bissingen	Krch.	Mar 1862	N.-Amer	835943
Kautter, Kaspar	23 Nov 1850	Bissingen	Krch.	May 1867	N.-Amer	835943
Kauzmann, Wilhelm. Karoline		Geislingen	Gsl.	Jul 1858	Prussia	572043
Kayser, Catharina	29 Jan 1830	Muenchingen	Leon.	Jul 1864	N.-Amer	837961
Kayser, Konrad	26 Jan 1826	Muenchingen	Leon.	Jul 1864	N.-Amer	837961
Kaz, Karl Andreas	25 May 1866	Erdmannshausen	Herr.	May 1883	N.-Amer	834629
Kazmeier, Gottlieb	6 Apr 1830	Honau	Rtl.	May 1860	France	841054
Keck, Anna Maria	26 yrs.	Betzweiler	Obd.	Apr 1857	N.-Amer	838631
Keck, Christina	15 Nov 1830	Fluorn	Obd.	Feb 1854	N.-Amer	838632
Keck, Immanuel Friedrich	3 Aug 1839	Malmsheim	Leon.	Jun 1869	N.-Amer	837958
Keck, Justina	4 Jul 1828	Fluorn	Obd.	Apr 1859	N.-Amer	838632
Kegel, Elisabetha Friederike	4 Mar 1828	Kirchheim	Krch.	Nov 1859	N.-Amer	835940
Kehrer, Andreas	1 yrs.	Boehmenkirch	Gsl.	Sep 1854	N.-Amer	572042
Kehrer, Anna Margaretha		Betzingen	Rtl.	May 1829	Switz.	841051
Kehrer, Anna Maria		Betzingen	Rtl.	Jun 1831	N.-Amer	841051
Kehrer, Barbara & F	47 yrs.	Boehmenkirch	Gsl.	Sep 1854	N.-Amer	572042
Kehrer, Franziska	11 yrs.	Boehmenkirch	Gsl.	Sep 1854	N.-Amer	572042

Name		Birth		Emigration			Film
Last	First	Date	Place	O'amt	Appl. Date	Dest.	Number
Kehrer, Franziska		9 Jul 1848	Boehmenkirch	Gsl.	Feb 1872	N.-Amer	572047
Kehrer, Gotthilf		22 Nov 1827	Reutlingen	Rtl.	bef 1863	N.-Amer	841054
Kehrer, Ignaz		29 May 1851	Boehmenkirch	Gsl.	Feb 1870	N.-Amer	572047
Kehrer, Jacob			Betzingen	Rtl.	May 1831	N.-Amer	841051
Kehrer, Johann Baptist		24 Nov 1834	Boehmenkirch	Gsl.	Mar 1861	N.-Amer	572044
Kehrer, Johann Evangelist		14 yrs.	Boehmenkirch	Gsl.	Sep 1854	N.-Amer	572042
Kehrer, Johann Georg		8 yrs.	Boehmenkirch	Gsl.	Sep 1854	N.-Amer	572042
Kehrer, Johann Georg			Betzingen	Rtl.	May 1832	N.-Amer	841051
Kehrer, Johann Georg		20 Aug 1835	Betzingen	Rtl.	May 1863	N.-Amer	841054
Kehrer, Johann Georg & F			Betzingen	Rtl.	Apr 1836	N.-Amer	841051
Kehrer, Johannes		3 Jan 1821	Boehmenkirch	Gsl.	Mar 1854	N.-Amer	572042
Kehrer, Leonhard		12 Apr 1833	Boehmenkirch	Gsl.	Jan 1862	N.-Amer	572044
Kehrer, Marianna		5 yrs.	Boehmenkirch	Gsl.	Sep 1854	N.-Amer	572042
Kehrer, Martin			Betzingen	Rtl.	May 1832	N.-Amer	841051
Kehrer, Michael			Boehmenkirch	Gsl.	bef 1854	N.-Amer	572042
Kehrer, Theresia		28 Jun 1854	Boehmenkirch	Gsl.	Feb 1872	N.-Amer	572047
Keidel, Anna Maria		8 Nov 1845	Grosssuessen	Gsl.	Oct 1853	N.-Amer	572041
Keidel, Anna Ursula (wife)			Grosssuessen	Gsl.	Oct 1853	N.-Amer	572041
Keidel, Johann Georg & F			Grosssuessen	Gsl.	Oct 1853	N.-Amer	572041
Keidel, Karl		13 Jan 1850	Grosssuessen	Gsl.	Oct 1853	N.-Amer	572041
Keidel, Karoline		19 Mar 1853	Grosssuessen	Gsl.	Oct 1853	N.-Amer	572041
Keil, , Gottlieb		9 mon.	Warmbronn	Leon.	Apr 1854	N.-Amer	837965
Keil, Anna Maria & C		22 yrs.	Gerlingen	Leon.	Apr 1857	N.-Amer	837953
Keil, Christine		11 Oct 1847	Gerlingen	Leon.	Aug 1870	Palest.	837953
Keil, Johann Georg		25 Apr 1830	Gerlingen	Leon.	Apr 1854	N.-Amer	837953
Kek, Jakob		21 Feb 1812	Malmsheim	Leon.	May 1852	N.-Amer	837958
Keller, Carl			Altenstaig	Nag.	Jul 1852	N.-Amer	838488
Keller, Catharina Dorothea		9 Mar 1862	Hochdorf	Krch.	Jun 1871	N.-Amer	835945
Keller, Christine Kathar. & F		24 Sep 1824	Hochdorf	Krch.	Jun 1871	N.-Amer	835945
Keller, Ezechiel		3 Nov 1839	Harthausen	Obd.	May 1867	N.-Amer	838633
Keller, Gottlieb Immanuel		28 Mar 1865	Hochdorf	Krch.	Jun 1871	N.-Amer	835945
Keller, Gustav Adolf			Rutesheim	Leon.	Jun 1852	N.-Amer	837964
Keller, Gustav Adolph		12 Dec 1859	Hochdorf	Krch.	Jun 1871	N.-Amer	835945
Keller, Jacob		27 Feb 1826	Hochdorf	Krch.	bef 1871	N.-Amer	835945
Keller, Johann Christian		25 Jun 1849	Bondorf	Herr.	Oct 1866	N.-Amer	834630
Keller, Johann Christian		2 May 1858	Hochdorf	Krch.	Jun 1871	N.-Amer	835945
Keller, Johann Friedrich		30 Dec 1856	Hochdorf	Krch.	Jun 1871	N.-Amer	835945
Keller, Johannes			Hemmingen	Leon.	May 1855	N.-Amer	837956
Keller, Johannes & F			Rutesheim	Leon.	Feb 1849	N.-Amer	837964
Keller, Karl		19 yrs.	Harthausen	Obd.	Apr 1857	N.-Amer	838633
Keller, Karl August		8 Feb 1861	Hochdorf	Krch.	Jun 1871	N.-Amer	835945
Keller, Karl Friedrich		25 May 1871	Gutenberg	Krch.	Oct 1887	N.-Amer	835945
Keller, Maria			Harthausen	Obd.	Jul 1854	N.-Amer	838633
Keller, Michael		28 Oct 1822	Muenchingen	Leon.	1851	N.-Amer	837961
Keller, Pauline			Seedorf	Obd.	bef 1862	N.-Amer	838637
Keller, Rosine		26 yrs.	Seedorf	Obd.	Mar 1854	N.-Amer	838637
Kellinger, Johannes			Korntal	Leon.	May 1853	N.-Amer	837957
Kemmel, Friedrich		7 Feb 1831	Ueberkingen	Gsl.	Mar 1854	N.-Amer	572042
Kemmeler, Gottlieb Adam		10 Jun 1848	Gebersheim	Leon.	bef 1873	N.-Amer	837953
Kemmerle, Martin		8 Nov 1853	Ohmenhausen	Rtl.	Oct 1869	N.-Amer	841054

Kemmler, Adam	20 Jan 1862	Betzingen	Rtl.	Apr 1866	N.-Amer	841054
Kemmler, Barbara	18 Apr 1842	Betzingen	Rtl.	Oct 1864	N.-Amer	841054
Kemmler, Barbara (wife)	17 Jun 1819	Betzingen	Rtl.	Apr 1866	N.-Amer	841054
Kemmler, Christine	14 Sep 1857	Betzingen	Rtl.	Apr 1866	N.-Amer	841054
Kemmler, Christine Magdalene	31 Oct 1825	Ohmenhausen	Rtl.	bef 1861	N.-Amer	841054
Kemmler, Christof	29 Jan 1850	Betzingen	Rtl.	Aug 1866	N.-Amer	841054
Kemmler, Georg	1 Feb 1847	Betzingen	Rtl.	Oct 1864	N.-Amer	841054
Kemmler, Jacob	18 Jun 1855	Betzingen	Rtl.	Apr 1866	N.-Amer	841054
Kemmler, Jacob Friedrich & F		Gomaringen	Rtl.	May 1832	N.-Amer	841051
Kemmler, Jobst Friedrich	29 Sep 1846	Pfullingen	Rtl.	Jun 1865	N.-Amer	841054
Kemmler, Martin	10 Mar 1844	Betzingen	Rtl.	Oct 1864	N.-Amer	841054
Kemmler, Martin & F	5 May 1816	Betzingen	Rtl.	Apr 1866	N.-Amer	841054
Kenngott, Catharina & C	30 Apr 1834	Kirchheim	Krch.	Jul 1860	N.-Amer	835940
Kenngott, Ernst Christoph	3 Oct 1851	Kirchheim	Krch.	Jul 1866	N.-Amer	835941
Kenngott, Georg Gottlieb	18 Nov 1862	Kirchheim	Krch.	Jan 1874	N.-Amer	835942
Kenngott, Gottlieb	2 Jul 1848	Kirchheim	Krch.	Apr 1866	N.-Amer	835941
Kenngott, Gottlieb Heinrich	10 Feb 1839	Kirchheim	Krch.	Dec 1859	N.-Amer	835940
Kenngott, Johannes	17 Mar 1857	Kirchheim	Krch.	Jan 1874	N.-Amer	835942
Kenngott, Louise	5 Feb 1846	Kirchheim	Krch.	Jul 1860	N.-Amer	835940
Kenngott, Marie Barbara	7 Oct 1818	Kirchheim	Krch.	bef 1883	N.-Amer	548403
Kenngott, Sophie Sib. (wid.) & F	1 Jul 1824	Waldenbuch/Stutt.	Krch.	Jan 1874	N.-Amer	835942
Kenngott, Wilhelm	11 Apr 1859	Kirchheim	Krch.	Jul 1860	N.-Amer	835940
Keppeler, Georg Friedrich	11 Jul 1849	Pfullingen	Rtl.	Oct 1866	N.-Amer	841054
Keppeler, Johann Georg Ludw.	25 May 1846	Unterhausen	Rtl.	May 1866	N.-Amer	841054
Keppeler, Johann Ludwig	22 Mar 1848	Unterhausen	Rtl.	Mar 1867	N.-Amer	841054
Keppeler, Johannes	30 May 1838	Oberhausen	Rtl.	Mar 1860	N.-Amer	841054
Keppler, – (wid.)	54 yrs.	Pfullingen	Rtl.	Aug 1879	N.-Amer	841051
Keppler, Abraham	1 Dec 1844	Pfullingen	Rtl.	Apr 1864	N.-Amer	841054
Keppler, Anna Ernest.C. (wife)		Heimsheim	Leon.	Mar 1854	N.-Amer	837955
Keppler, Anna Maria		Pfullingen	Rtl.	Aug 1829	Austria	841051
Keppler, Caroline Barbara		Heimsheim	Leon.	Mar 1854	N.-Amer	837955
Keppler, Christian Ludwig	7 Nov 1847	Leonberg	Leon.	Nov 1867	N.-Amer	835787
Keppler, Georg Friedrich		Pfullingen	Rtl.	Apr 1830	N.-Amer	841051
Keppler, Heinrich	21 yrs.	Pfullingen	Rtl.	Apr 1880	N.-Amer	841051
Keppler, Jacob Friedrich	5 Apr 1849	Pfullingen	Rtl.	Jul 1866	N.-Amer	841054
Keppler, Johann Martin	25 Feb 1830	Pfullingen	Rtl.	May 1860	N.-Amer	841054
Keppler, Johann Robert		Heimsheim	Leon.	Mar 1854	N.-Amer	837955
Keppler, Johannes	9 Jun 1842	Pfullingen	Rtl.	Nov 1862	England	841054
Keppler, Johannes & F		Heimsheim	Leon.	Mar 1854	N.-Amer	837955
Keppler, Simon Friedrich	4 Aug 1849	Pfullingen	Rtl.	Sep 1865	N.-Amer	841054
Keppler, Wilhelm	28 Mar 1853	Pfullingen	Rtl.	Aug 1869	N.-Amer	841054
Kern, Adam	27 Dec 1803	Gomaringen	Rtl.	Mar 1863	N.-Amer	841054
Kern, Adolph	3 Aug 1864	Wannweil	Rtl.	Apr 1867	N.-Amer	841054
Kern, Bertha	14 Sep 1846	Winzeln	Obd.	Aug 1868	N.-Amer	841016
Kern, Christoph August	30 Aug 1836	Geislingen	Gsl.	Apr 1854	N.-Amer	572042
Kern, Emilie	27 Jan 1846	Wannweil	Rtl.	Apr 1867	N.-Amer	841054
Kern, Franz Xaver		Schramberg	Obd.	bef 1870	N.-Amer	838636
Kern, Friederike	12 Oct 1851	Wannweil	Rtl.	Apr 1867	N.-Amer	841054
Kern, Johann Baptist	26 Apr 1783	Mariazell	Obd.	May 1816	-	838634
Kern, Johann Baptist	21 Jun 1852	Schramberg	Obd.	Mar 1869	N.-Amer	838636

Name		Birth		Emigration			Film
Last	First	Date	Place	O'amt	Appl. Date	Dest.	Number
Kern, Johann Georg		3 Feb 1851	Gomaringen	Rtl.	Mar 1869	N.-Amer	841054
Kern, Johannes			Winzeln	Obd.	Mar 1860	N.-Amer	841016
Kern, Johannes (wid.) & F			Wannweil	Rtl.	Apr 1867	N.-Amer	841054
Kern, Louise & C		25 Dec 1844	Wannweil	Rtl.	Apr 1867	N.-Amer	841054
Kern, Paulina			Winzeln	Obd.	Apr 1866	N.-Amer	841016
Kern, Udo		7 Aug 1850	Wannweil	Rtl.	Apr 1867	N.-Amer	841054
Kern, Waldburga			Schramberg	Obd.	Jun 1813	France	838637
Kern, Wilhelmina		25 Oct 1842	Winzeln	Obd.	Sep 1863	N.-Amer	841016
Kerner, Anna Maria Frieder.		24 Aug 1839	Oberlenningen	Krch.	Sep 1856	Texas	835947
Kerner, Anton		19 yrs.	Weil der Stadt	Leon.	Mar 1854	N.-Amer	837966
Kerner, Carl		9 Apr 1855	Oberlenningen	Krch.	Mar 1867	N.-Amer	835947
Kerner, Carl Albert		24 Jan 1846	Kirchheim	Krch.	bef 1869	N.-Amer	835941
Kerner, Carl Gottlieb & F			Kirchheim	Krch.	bef 1869	N.-Amer	835941
Kerner, Elisabetha Loise		9 Feb 1837	Oberlenningen	Krch.	Sep 1856	Texas	835947
Kerner, Ferdinand Wilhelm		13 Jul 1838	Kirchheim	Krch.	bef 1869	N.-Amer	835941
Kerner, Friedrich		5 May 1846	Owen	Krch.	Jun 1865	N.-Amer	835948
Kerner, Gottliebin (wife)		9 Jan 1813	Oberlenningen	Krch.	Apr 1867	N.-Amer	835947
Kerner, Heinrich Wilhelm			Kirchheim	Krch.	bef 1869	N.-Amer	835941
Kerner, Jacob & F		15 Oct 1809	Oberlenningen	Krch.	Apr 1867	N.-Amer	835947
Kerner, Jacob Friedrich			Kirchheim	Krch.	bef 1869	N.-Amer	835941
Kerner, Johann Christian		23 Jan 1831	Kirchheim	Krch.	Jan 1856	N.-Amer	835940
Kerner, Johann Gottlieb		5 Feb 1822	Kirchheim	Krch.	bef 1861	Wien	835942
Kerner, Johann Gottlob		16 Nov 1842	Kirchheim	Krch.	May 1869	Saxony	835941
Kerner, Maria			Kirchheim	Krch.	bef 1869	N.-Amer	835941
Kerner, Maria Friederike		13 Jul 1848	Kirchheim	Krch.	bef 1869	N.-Amer	835941
Kerner, Matthaeus		11 Oct 1822	Owen	Krch.	Apr 1874	N.-Amer	548403
Kessler, Adolf		19 yrs.	Geislingen	Gsl.	Sep 1869	N.-Amer	572047
Kessler, David		15 Oct 1848	Oetlingen	Krch.	Feb 1867	N.-Amer	835948
Kessler, Emil		6 yrs.	Geislingen	Gsl.	Nov 1864	Berlin	572045
Kessler, Eugen		4 Feb 1867	Geislingen	Gsl.	Nov 1883	N.-Amer	572049
Kessler, Johannes Veit & F			Geislingen	Gsl.	Nov 1864	Berlin	572045
Kessler, Karl Elias		4 Oct 1847	Geislingen	Gsl.	May 1867	N.-Amer	572046
Keuber, Georg		9 Dec 1838	Dettingen	Krch.	Mar 1857	N.-Amer	835944
Keuerleber, Anna Maria		17 Jan 1869	Jesingen	Krch.	May 1867	France	835946
Keuerleber, Johann Georg		30 Oct 1810	Jesingen	Krch.	Jul 1862	France	835946
Khoenle, Friederich		9 Nov 1859	Herrenberg	Herr.	Dec 1876	N.-Amer	834629
Khoenle, Julius		7 Jan 1847	Herrenberg	Herr.	Dec 1867	N.-Amer	834629
Kibler, Karl Friedrich		19 Feb 1865	Kirchheim	Krch.	Apr 1881	N.-Amer	835942
Kicherer, Eugen		4 Sep 1883	Kirchheim	Krch.	Apr 1888	N.-Amer	835942
Kicherer, Karl Friedr. Gottl.			Kirchheim	Krch.	bef 1888	N.-Amer	835942
Kicherer, Karl Georg		23 Jul 1877	Kirchheim	Krch.	Apr 1888	N.-Amer	835942
Kicherer, Marie Pauline		25 Feb 1851	Oberlenningen	Krch.	May 1871	N.-Amer	835947
Kicherer, Paul		25 Feb 1881	Kirchheim	Krch.	Apr 1888	N.-Amer	835942
Kick, Anna Maria (wid.)		13 Feb 1809	Rosswaelden	Krch.	Aug 1855	N.-Amer	835949
Kiedaisch, Christian Friedr.		2 Jul 1840	Owen	Krch.	Jun 1859	N.-Amer	835948
Kiedaisch, Johann Andreas		20 Dec 1867	Owen	Krch.	May 1883	N.-Amer	548403
Kiedaisch, Johann Georg		20 May 1856	Dettingen	Krch.	Mar 1872	N.-Amer	835944
Kiedaisch, Johann Georg		12 Mar 1831	Owen	Krch.	Mar 1859	N.-Amer	835948
Kiedaisch, Johannes		7 Jan 1828	Owen	Krch.	Mar 1860	N.-Amer	835948
Kiedaisch, Wilhelm		1 Jun 1866	Owen	Krch.	May 1883	N.-Amer	548403

Kiefer, Gottlob Julius	22 yrs.	Reutlingen	Rtl.	Sep 1879	N.-Amer	841051
Kiefer, Maria Agnes	20 yrs.	Willmandingen	Rtl.	Jun 1880	N.-Amer	841051
Kieferle, Johann Conrad	28 Mar 1830	Bissingen	Krch.	Nov 1864	N.-Amer	835943
Klelenker, Johannes	26 Jun 1830	Brucken	Krch.	1865	N.-Amer	835944
Kienhoefer, Anton	1 Nov 1830	Reichenbach	Gsl.	Feb 1852	N.-Amer	572041
Kienle, Jacob Friedrich	2 Jun 1864	Moensheim	Leon.	Apr 1881	N.-Amer	837960
Kienle, Johann Gottlieb	25 yrs.	Moensheim	Leon.	Apr 1851	N.-Amer	837960
Kienle, Johann Jakob	7 Sep 1813	Moensheim	Leon.	Mar 1844	N.-Amer	837960
Kienle, Johannes	15 Nov 1850	Heimsheim	Leon.	Feb 1869	N.-Amer	837955
Kienle/Kuenle, Johann & F		Gerlingen	Leon.	Jun 1818	Hungary	837953
Kienler, Johannes		Gerlingen	Leon.	Apr 1831	N.-Amer	837953
Kienzle, Anna Maria	28 Oct 1862	Effringen	Herr.	Feb 1881	N.-Amer	834630
Kienzle, Anna Maria	infant	Eltingen	Leon.	1852	N.-Amer	835789
Kienzle, Dorothea	18 yrs.	Eltingen	Leon.	1852	N.-Amer	835789
Kienzle, Friederike	12 Oct 1820	Leonberg	Leon.	bef 1860	N.-Amer	835786
Kienzle, Friederike	4 yrs.	Eltingen	Leon.	1852	N.-Amer	835789
Kienzle, Gottlieb	6 yrs.	Eltingen	Leon.	1852	N.-Amer	835789
Kienzle, Johann Jacob	6 Feb 1864	Effringen	Herr.	Feb 1881	N.-Amer	834630
Kienzle, Johannes	1 Jul 1840	Eltingen	Leon.	1852	N.-Amer	835789
Kienzle, Johannes & F		Eltingen	Leon.	1852	N.-Amer	835789
Kienzle, Margarethe	7 yrs.	Eltingen	Leon.	1852	N.-Amer	835789
Kienzle, Rosine (wife)		Eltingen	Leon.	1852	N.-Amer	835789
Kienzle, Sebastian	7 Sep 1825	Eltingen	Leon.	Dec 1862	Bavaria	835789
Kieser, Gottfried Heinrich	17 Aug 1853	Geislingen	Gsl.	Mar 1871	N.-Amer	572047
Kieser, Heinrich		Geislingen	Gsl.	Sep 1851	Switz.	577788
Kilgus, Anna Barbara	27 Jun 1850	Roetenbach	Obd.	Mar 1864	France	838636
Kilgus, Anna Maria & C	17 May 1814	Roetenbach	Obd.	Mar 1864	France	838636
Kilgus, Christian		Roetenbach	Obd.	Aug 1860	N.-Amer	838636
Kilgus, Friedrich		Roemlinsdorf	Obd.	Mar 1861	N.-Amer	838635
Kilgus, Friedrich		Roetenbach	Obd.	bef 1859	N.-Amer	838636
Kilgus, Johann Georg			Obd.	Sep 1816	France	838636
Kilgus, Johann Jakob	2 Nov 1847	Roetenbach	Obd.	Apr 1869	N.-Amer	838636
Kilgus, Matthias	12 Apr 1850	Roetenbach	Obd.	May 1870	N.-Amer	838636
Kill, August Wilhelm	23 Dec 1857	Zell	Krch.	May 1880	N.-Amer	835940
Kill, Friedrich	21 Sep 1877	Pliensbach	Krch.	May 1891	N.-Amer	835774
Killinger, Anna Maria		Muenchingen	Leon.	bef 1855	N.-Amer	837961
Killinger, Anna Maria (wife)	3 Oct 1831	Muenchingen	Leon.	1855	N.-Amer	837961
Killinger, Johann Georg	20 Mar 1834	Muenchingen	Leon.	1857	N.-Amer	837961
Killinger, Johann Jacob		Muenchingen	Leon.	1855	N.-Amer	837961
Killinger, Johann Jakob	6 Apr 1828	Muenchingen	Leon.	May 1855	N.-Amer	837961
Killinger, Johannes	10 Jul 1820	Muenchingen	Leon.	1853	N.-Amer	837961
Killinger, Josephine	4 Jan 1837	Muenchingen	Leon.	Aug 1863	N.-Amer	837961
Killinger, Regine	28 yrs.	Muenchingen	Leon.	May 1859	N.-Amer	837961
Kilper, Balthasar	5 Dec 1831	Rutesheim	Leon.	bef 1860	N.-Amer	837964
Kilper, Barbara	20 yrs.	Rutesheim	Leon.	May 1857	N.-Amer	837964
Kilper, Johanna	22 Mar 1823	Rutesheim	Leon.	Apr 1853	N.-Amer	837964
Kilper. Johann Georg	27 Apr 1829	Rutesheim	Leon.	Mar 1857	N.-Amer	837964
Kimich, Severin	30 Sep 1842	Sulgen	Obd.	Jan 1867	France	838638
Kimmel, Johannes	9 Feb 1866	Treffelhausen	Gsl.	Jan 1883	N.-Amer	572049
Kimmel, Joseph	2 May 1835	Treffelhausen	Gsl.	Jan 1867	N.-Amer	572046

Name		Birth		Emigration			Film
Last	First	Date	Place	O'amt	Appl. Date	Dest.	Number
Kimmerle, Christian		18 Feb 1879	Oberjesingen	Herr.	Jan 1896	N.-Amer	834630
Kimmich, Adelgunde		14 Jan 1844	Sulgen	Obd.	Sep 1857	N.-Amer	838638
Kimmich, Adolphe		15 yrs.	Sulgen	Obd.	Oct 1855	N.-Amer	838638
Kimmich, Agatha (wife)			Aichhalden	Obd.	May 1854	N.-Amer	838629
Kimmich, Alois & W		42 yrs.	Aichhalden	Obd.	Sep 1847	N.-Amer	838629
Kimmich, Anton & F			Aichhalden	Obd.	May 1817	N.-Amer	838629
Kimmich, Barbara		6 Sep 1831	Aichhalden	Obd.	Mar 1870	France	838629
Kimmich, Beata		21 Dec 1827	Aichhalden	Obd.	Jan 1865	France	838629
Kimmich, Carl		3 Nov 1849	Schramberg	Obd.	May 1869	N.-Amer	838636
Kimmich, Eberhard		18 Jan 1847	Schramberg	Obd.	Oct 1865	N.-Amer	838636
Kimmich, Felix		11 May 1849	Aichhalden	Obd.	Sep 1865	N.-Amer	838629
Kimmich, Genovefa & F			Sulgen	Obd.	Sep 1857	N.-Amer	838638
Kimmich, Helena		20 yrs.	Aichhalden	Obd.	Sep 1854	N.-Amer	838629
Kimmich, Jacob		10 Jul 1814	Aichhalden	Obd.	Nov 1842	France	838629
Kimmich, Johannes		9 Dec 1843	Aichhalden	Obd.	Mar 1854	Africa	838629
Kimmich, Johannes		22 Dec 1846	Waldmoessingen	Obd.	Apr 1866	N.-Amer	841015
Kimmich, Josef		30 Jan 1838	Aichhalden	Obd.	Dec 1854	N.-Amer	838629
Kimmich, Josef & F		29 Jan 1817	Aichhalden	Obd.	Mar 1854	Africa	838629
Kimmich, Joseph & W		35 yrs.	Aichhalden	Obd.	May 1854	N.-Amer	838629
Kimmich, Josepha		12 Mar 1849	Sulgen	Obd.	Sep 1857	N.-Amer	838638
Kimmich, Leonhardt		5 Nov 1846	Sulgen	Obd.	Sep 1857	N.-Amer	838638
Kimmich, Maria Luisa		3 Oct 1843	Aichhalden	Obd.	Mar 1854	Africa	838629
Kimmich, Mechtilde (wife)		28 Mar 1824	Aichhalden	Obd.	Mar 1854	Africa	838629
Kimmich, Michael		19 yrs.	Aichhalden	Obd.	Oct 1852	N.-Amer	838629
Kimmich, Nikolaus			Sulgen	Obd.	1853	N.-Amer	838638
Kimmich, Pauline		25 Apr 1851	Sulgen	Obd.	Sep 1857	N.-Amer	838638
Kimmich, Regina		51 yrs.	Sulgen	Obd.	Sep 1857	N.-Amer	838638
Kimmich, Rudolph		10 yrs.	Sulgen	Obd.	Oct 1855	N.-Amer	838638
Kimmich, Wilhelm		26 Sep 1845	Sulgen	Obd.	Sep 1857	N.-Amer	838638
Kinavik, Reinhold		2 Dec 1844	Eningen	Rtl.	Dec 1863	Austral	841054
King, Andreas		8 Nov 1844	Mariazell	Obd.	Jun 1864	N.-Amer	838634
King, Augustin			Hochmoessingen	Obd.	Jun 1869	N.-Amer	838633
King, Christina		infant	Lauterbach	Obd.	Apr 1853	N.-Amer	838634
King, Emilie			Schramberg	Obd.	bef 1860	N.-Amer	838636
King, Gabriel			Hochmoessingen	Obd.	Nov 1859	Hungary	838633
King, Hubert & F			Mariazell	Obd.	May 1817	N.-Amer	838634
King, Johannes			Aichhalden	Obd.	Jun 1815	-	838629
King, Johannes			Mariazell	Obd.	Jan 1860	Hesse	838634
King, Josepha		24 Apr 1835	Aichhalden	Obd.	Apr 1856	France	838629
King, Karolina			Aichhalden	Obd.	Jan 1861	France	838629
King, Katharina & C		26 yrs.	Lauterbach	Obd.	Apr 1853	N.-Amer	838634
King, Maria		11 Nov 1838	Mariazell	Obd.	May 1865	France	838634
King, Maria Magdalena		31 Jul 1837	Schramberg	Obd.	Nov 1863	France	838636
King, Priska			Mariazell	Obd.	May 1817	N.-Amer	838634
King, Rosalie		31 Aug 1839	Schramberg	Obd.	May 1864	France	838636
King, Rosina		2 Mar 1837	Aichhalden	Obd.	Jun 1858	France	838629
King, Ursula			Mariazell	Obd.	Feb 1854	N.-Amer	838634
King, Vinzenz		25 yrs.	Lauterbach	Obd.	Apr 1854	N.-Amer	838634
King, Walburga			Mariazell	Obd.	Apr 1860	N.-Amer	838634
King, Wendelin		18 yrs	Lauterbach	Obd.	Apr 1854	N.-Amer	838634

King, Wilhelm	13 May 1852	Schramberg	Obd.	Jun 1869	N.-Amer	838636
Kinkele, Christof Philipp	17 Dec 1847	Pfullingen	Rtl.	Apr 1859	N.-Amer	841054
Kinkele, Jakob Friedrich	8 Oct 1843	Pfullingen	Rtl.	Jul 1863	England	841054
Kinkele, Philipp Jacob		Reutlingen	Rtl.	May 1831	N.-Amer	841051
Kinkelin, Elisabetha	28 yrs.	Pfullingen	Rtl.	Aug 1879	N.-Amer	841051
Kinkelin, Ferdinand	3 May 1846	Pfullingen	Rtl.	Jul 1866	England	841054
Kinkelin, Johannes	24 Jun 1821	Pfullingen	Rtl.	Jun 1865	N.-Amer	841054
Kinkelin, Maria Catharina	18 Jul 1831	Pfullingen	Rtl.	Jun 1865	N.-Amer	841054
Kinninger, Emilie	12 Oct 1847	Diggingen	Gsl.	bef 1868	Switz.	572046
Kinninger, Joseph	10 Apr 1850	Deggingen	Gsl.	Mar 1868	N.-Amer	572046
Kinninger, Karl	30 Sep 1848	Deggingen	Gsl.	Dec 1868	N.-Amer	572046
Kirchner, Heinrich	27 Aug 1848	Owen	Krch.	Feb 1868	N.-Amer	835948
Kirchner, Johann Georg	5 Feb 1802	Hemmingen	Leon.	bef 1832	France	837956
Kirchner, Johann Michael		Gerlingen	Leon.	Apr 1831	N.-Amer	837953
Kirchner, Louise	18 Oct 1848	Gerlingen	Leon.	Nov 1861	N.-Amer	837953
Kirchner, Theodor	2 Oct 1852	Owen	Krch.	Apr 1869	N.-Amer	835948
Kirgis, Anna	8 Mar 1838	Roetenbach	Obd.	May 1855	N.-Amer	838636
Kirgis, Anna Catharina	10 Jan 1834	Roetenbach	Obd.	May 1855	N.-Amer	838636
Kirgis, Christina	20 Oct 1844	Roetenbach	Obd.	May 1855	N.-Amer	838636
Kirgis, Johann Georg & F	1 Sep 1805	Reichenbaechle	Obd.	May 1855	N.-Amer	838636
Kirgiss, Johann Fiedrich		Betzweiler	Obd.	Apr 1861	N.-Amer	838631
Kirgiss, Johannes	29 Apr 1853	Betzweiler	Obd.	Mar 1869	N.-Amer	838631
Kirner, Carl Paul	9 Jul 1851	Weil der Stadt	Leon.	Jun 1852	N.-Amer	837966
Kirner, Christiane Lea	19 Sep 1865	Schoeckingen	Leon.	May 1881	N.-Amer	837964
Kirner, Maria	8 Mar 1818	Weil der Stadt	Leon.	Mar 1848	N.-Amer	837965
Kirner, Maria Magdalena	25 May 1840	Weil der Stadt	Leon.	Jun 1852	N.-Amer	837966
Kirner, Maria Walburga	10 Jan 1836	Weil der Stadt	Leon.	Jun 1852	N.-Amer	837966
Kirner, Melchior & F		Weil der Stadt	Leon.	Jun 1852	N.-Amer	837966
Kirner, Theodor & F		Weil der Stadt	Leon.	Mar 1852	N.-Amer	837966
Kirschinger, Matthias		Weil der Stadt	Leon.	Jul 1851	N.-Amer	837966
Kirschmann, Jacob		Holzmaden	Krch.	May 1771	-	550804
Kistenfeger, Johann Georg	14 Oct 1829	Ditzbach	Gsl.	Aug 1854	N.-Amer	572042
Kittelberger, Johann Georg		Betzweiler	Obd.	Nov 1854	N.-Amer	838631
Klaiber, Ewald Friedrich	3 May 1835	Kirchheim	Krch.	bef 1867	N.-Amer	835940
Klass, Johann Michael	3 Apr 1841	Brucken	Krch.	Mar 1859	N.-Amer	835944
Klaus, Augustin	15 Sep 1850	Weissenstein	Gsl.	Mar 1854	N.-Amer	572042
Klaus, Creszencia	31 Oct 1846	Weissenstein	Gsl.	Mar 1854	N.-Amer	572042
Klaus, Johannes & F	19 Feb 1821	Weissenstein	Gsl.	Mar 1854	N.-Amer	572042
Klaus, Josef		Treffelhausen	Gsl.	Oct 1865	N.-Amer	572045
Klaus, Joseph	18 yrs.	Donzdorf	Gsl.	Mar 1852	N.-Amer	572041
Klaus, Karolina	23 Apr 1852	Weissenstein	Gsl.	Mar 1854	N.-Amer	572042
Klaus, Marianna (wife)	16 Aug 1821	Weissenstein	Gsl.	Mar 1854	N.-Amer	572042
Klaus, Theresia		Donzdorf	Gsl.	May 1863	Switz.	572044
Klausner, Fridolin	18 yrs.	Schramberg	Obd.	Sep 1854	N.-Amer	838636
Klausner, Joseph	40 yrs.	Schramberg	Obd.	Jul 1838	Austria	838637
Klauss, Josepha	30 Jun 1798	Kleinsuessen	Gsl.	May 1852	N.-Amer	572041
Klaussner, Blandine	3 Nov 1846	Mariazell	Obd.	Mar 1859	N.-Amer	838634
Klaussner, Engelbert	19 Jun 1839	Mariazell	Obd.	Apr 1858	N.-Amer	838634
Klaussner, Josef & F	18 Jan 1804	Mariazell	Obd.	Mar 1859	N.-Amer	838634
Klaussner, Magdalena	24 Jul 1830	Mariazell	Obd.	Nov 1856	N.-Amer	838634

Name		Birth		Emigration			Film
Last	First	Date	Place	O'amt	Appl. Date	Dest.	Number
Klaussner, Maria Ursula (wife)		29 Sep 1808	Mariazell	Obd.	Mar 1859	N.-Amer	838634
Klaussner, Meinhard		24 Jun 1856	Mariazell	Obd.	Mar 1859	N.-Amer	838634
Klaussner, Monika		26 yrs.	Mariazell	Obd.	Dec 1854	N.-Amer	838634
Klaussner, Walpurga		26 Feb 1831	Mariazell	Obd.	Nov 1856	N.-Amer	838634
Kleiber, Heinrich		15 Oct 1865	Kirchheim	Krch.	Apr 1882	N.-Amer	548403
Klein, Agnes Margaretha		22 Jan 1863	Dettingen	Krch.	May 1872	N.-Amer	835944
Klein, Carl August Friedrich		7 Aug 1847	Owen	Krch.	Apr 1867	N.-Amer	835948
Klein, Christian David		17 Jun 1850	Dettingen	Krch.	Jun 1867	N.-Amer	835944
Klein, Christian Wilhelm		13 Oct 1867	Dettingen	Krch.	May 1872	N.-Amer	835944
Klein, Eva Rosine		23 Jun 1837	Owen	Krch.	Mar 1860	N.-Amer	835948
Klein, Friedrich Wilhelm		15 Oct 1814	Dettingen	Krch.	bef 1869	N.-Amer	835944
Klein, Georg		24 Apr 1842	Reutlingen	Rtl.	bef 1867	N.-Amer	841054
Klein, Georg Friedrich		29 Oct 1843	Owen	Krch.	Feb 1862	N.-Amer	835948
Klein, Gustav Adolf		30 Jan 1848	Dettingen	Krch.	Sep 1866	N.-Amer	835944
Klein, Gustav Adolph		2 Jul 1849	Reutlingen	Rtl.	Dec 1869	N.-Amer	841054
Klein, Johann Georg		29 Apr 1834	Dettingen	Krch.	bef 1871	N.-Amer	835944
Klein, Johann Georg		1 Apr 1850	Holzmaden	Krch.	Apr 1867	N.-Amer	835945
Klein, Johann Georg & F		26 Feb 1834	Dettingen	Krch.	May 1872	N.-Amer	835944
Klein, Johann Jacob		1 Nov 1814	Dettingen	Krch.	bef 1862	N.-Amer	835944
Klein, Johann Jacob		26 Feb 1836	Dettingen	Krch.	bef 1859	N.-Amer	835944
Klein, Johann Jacob		27 Mar 1843	Owen	Krch.	Sep 1860	N.-Amer	835948
Klein, Johann Jakob		8 Aug 1851	Dettingen	Krch.	May 1868	N.-Amer	835944
Klein, Josef		22 Sep 1855	Dettingen	Krch.	Jul 1872	N.-Amer	835944
Klein, Maria Dorothea		2 Sep 1865	Dettingen	Krch.	May 1872	N.-Amer	835944
Klein, Maria Dorothea (wife)		24 Aug 1837	Dettingen	Krch.	May 1872	N.-Amer	835944
Klein, Michael		7 Sep 1822	Weilheim	Krch.	1854	N.-Amer	835949
Klein, Robert		4 Jun 1849	Reutlingen	Rtl.	Feb 1869	England	841054
Klein, Wilhelm		11 Dec 1855	Hildrizhausen	Herr.	bef 1889	Switz.	834631
Klein, Wilhelmine		9 Mar 1869	Dettingen	Krch.	May 1872	N.-Amer	835944
Kleinbach, Andreas		21 Dec 1870	Weilheim	Krch.	Sep 1887	N.-Amer	835774
Kleiner, Jakob Friedrich		5 Nov 1841	Moensheim	Leon.	Jan 1867	N.-Amer	837960
Kleinfelder, Imanuel Gottl.		16 Apr 1821	Leonberg	Leon.	Feb 1842	Saxony	835786
Kleinfelder, Johann Michael			Muenklingen	Leon.	Oct 1854	N.-Amer	837962
Kleinfelder, Josef		19 Sep 1864	Muenklingen	Leon.	bef 1883	N.-Amer	837962
Kleinheim, Philipp			Weissenstein	Gsl.	Apr 1853	N.-Amer	572041
Klement, Georg		21 May 1837	Kuchen	Gsl.	Feb 1854	N.-Amer	572042
Klement, Jakob		56 yrs.	Kuchen	Gsl.	Feb 1852	N.-Amer	572041
Klemm, Anna Maria		29 Jan 1829	Weilheim	Krch.	bef 1861	N.-Amer	835949
Klemm, Johann Georg		29 Nov 1831	Weilheim	Krch.	Jan 1861	N.-Amer	835949
Klenk, Christian Conradt		19 Apr 1850	Lindorf	Krch.	Feb 1868	N.-Amer	835946
Klenk, Juditha (wid.) & F		22 Jul 1820	Lindorf	Krch.	Feb 1868	N.-Amer	835946
Klesattel, Ambros			Weissenstein	Gsl.	bef 1854	N.-Amer	572042
Klesattel, Karl		9 Nov 1853	Weissenstein	Gsl.	Feb 1854	N.-Amer	572042
Klesattel, Katharina (wife)		30 yrs.	Weissenstein	Gsl.	Feb 1854	N.-Amer	572042
Klett, Eugen		16 Apr 1849	Dettingen	Krch.	Sep 1866	N.-Amer	835944
Klett, Irene		22 Jan 1848	Dettingen	Krch.	Sep 1866	N.-Amer	835944
Kling, Christian		11 yrs.	Flacht	Leon.	Jul 1854	N.-Amer	835790
Kling, Christian Friedrich		22 yrs.	Flacht	Leon.	Jul 1854	N.-Amer	835790
Kling, Christoph		9 yrs.	Flacht	Leon.	Jul 1854	N.-Amer	835790
Kling, Friedrich		20 Sep 1824	Flacht	Leon.	Apr 1850	France	835790

Kling, Georg Adam & F		Flacht	Leon.	Jul 1854	N.-Amer	835790
Kling, Jakob Friedrich	5 Jul 1833	Malmsheim	Leon.	May 1856	N.-Amer	837958
Kling, Johann Friedrich	19 Oct 1841	Flacht	Leon.	Jun 1864	N.-Amer	835790
Kling, Johann Heinrich	1825	Malmsheim	Leon.	bef 1862	N.-Amer	837958
Kling, Johann Jakob	16 yrs.	Flacht	Leon.	Jul 1854	N.-Amer	835790
Kling, Johann Jakob & F		Muenklingen	Leon.	Apr 1854	N.-Amer	837962
Kling, Johann Konrad	7 Oct 1820	Malmsheim	Leon.	bef 1862	N.-Amer	837958
Kling, Johannes		Flacht	Leon.	Jun 1857	N.-Amer	835790
Kling, Karoline	13 yrs.	Flacht	Leon.	Jul 1854	N.-Amer	835790
Kling, Katharina Dorothea	20 yrs.	Flacht	Leon.	Jul 1854	N.-Amer	835790
Kling, Wilhelmine	7 yrs.	Flacht	Leon.	Jul 1854	N.-Amer	835790
Klingel, Adam Friedrich	30 Nov 1845	Heimsheim	Leon.	bef 1870	N.-Amer	837955
Klingel, Anna Maria	8 yrs.	Wimsheim	Loen.	Jun 1855	N.-Amer	837967
Klingel, Anna Maria (wife)		Wimsheim	Loen.	Mar 1854	N.-Amer	837967
Klingel, Catharina	8 yrs.	Wimsheim	Loen.	Feb 1852	N.-Amer	837967
Klingel, Christian	5 yrs.	Wimsheim	Loen.	Feb 1852	N.-Amer	837967
Klingel, Christina (wife)		Wimsheim	Loen.	Apr 1852	Hungary	837967
Klingel, Dorothea	31 yrs.	Wimsheim	Loen.	Feb 1853	France	837967
Klingel, Friedrich	12 yrs.	Wimsheim	Loen.	Feb 1852	N.-Amer	837967
Klingel, Georg & F		Wimsheim	Loen.	Mar 1854	N.-Amer	837967
Klingel, Gottlieb Jakob	3 Jun 1851	Heimsheim	Leon.	Apr 1869	N.-Amer	837955
Klingel, Heinrich		Heimsheim	Leon.	Apr 1830	N.-Amer	837955
Klingel, Johann Adam	25 Jul 1838	Heimsheim	Leon.	Jul 1854	N.-Amer	837955
Klingel, Johann Georg & F		Wimsheim	Loen.	Apr 1852	Hungary	837967
Klingel, Johannes	10 yrs.	Wimsheim	Loen.	Jul 1858	N.-Amer	837967
Klingel, Johannes & F		Wimsheim	Loen.	Jul 1858	N.-Amer	837967
Klingel, Johannes & F		Wimsheim	Loen	1847	N. Amer	837967
Klingel, Josef	18 mon.	Wimsheim	Loen.	Feb 1852	N.-Amer	837967
Klingel, Louise	10 yrs.	Wimsheim	Loen.	Feb 1852	N.-Amer	837967
Klingel, Margaretha Eva & C		Wimsheim	Loen.	Jun 1855	N.-Amer	837967
Klingel, Maria		Wimsheim	Loen.	1847	N.-Amer	837967
Klingel, Maria (wife)		Wimsheim	Loen.	Feb 1852	N.-Amer	837967
Klingel, Mathias & F		Wimsheim	Loen.	Feb 1852	Hungary	837967
Klingel, Michael	19 Aug 1825	Wimsheim	Loen.	Nov 1860	N.-Amer	837967
Klingel, Regina	74 yrs.	Wimsheim	Loen.	Apr 1852	Hungary	837967
Klingel, Regina Dorothea	28 Jan 1842	Wimsheim	Loen.	Nov 1868	N.-Amer	837967
Klingel, Regina Friederika		Wimsheim	Loen.	Aug 1852	S.-Amer	837967
Klingenstein, Jakob Friedrich	24 Oct 1866	Hildrizhausen	Herr.	Feb 1892	N.-Amer	834631
Klingler, Elisabetha	28 May 1848	Geislingen	Gsl.	Apr 1874	N.-Amer	572048
Klingler, Gottfried	7 Jun 1832	Boehmenkirch	Gsl.	bef 1854	N.-Amer	572042
Klingler, Hippolit	24 yrs.	Boehmenkirch	Gsl.	Feb 1853	N.-Amer	572041
Klingler, Joseph		Gingen	Gsl.	Mar 1853	N.-Amer	572041
Klotz, Christina	28 Mar 1846	Weilheim	Krch.	Apr 1867	N.-Amer	835950
Knaeble, Catharine		Oberndorf	Obd.	bef 1856	N.-Amer	838635
Knaeble, Therese		Oberndorf	Obd.	Jul 1849	N.-Amer	838635
Knapp, Anna Maria	21 Jan 1830	Flacht	Leon.	1852	N.-Amer	835790
Knapp, Anna Maria	24 yrs.	Hoefingen	Leon.	Feb 1854	N.-Amer	837957
Knapp, Dorothea	8 May 1871	Moensheim	Leon.	Jul 1882	N.-Amer	837960
Knapp, Dorothea Elisabetha	9 Jun 1824	Moensheim	Leon.	Feb 1854	N.-Amer	837960
Knapp, Friederika	18 Nov 1881	Moensheim	Leon.	Jul 1882	N.-Amer	837960

Name		Birth		Emigration			Film
Last	First	Date	Place	O'amt	Appl. Date	Dest.	Number
Knapp, Friedrich		4 Sep 1875	Moensheim	Leon.	Jul 1882	N.-Amer	837960
Knapp, Georg Adam			Flacht	Leon.	Apr 1857	N.-Amer	835790
Knapp, Hermann			Kirchheim	Krch.	bef 1870	N.-Amer	835940
Knapp, Jacob Heinrich			Reutlingen	Rtl.	Jan 1836	N.-Amer	841051
Knapp, Johann Andreas		29 Aug 1823	Flacht	Leon.	May 1862	N.-Amer	835790
Knapp, Johann Georg		10 Apr 1845	Wannweil	Rtl.	Oct 1868	N.-Amer	841054
Knapp, Julius		1841	Pfullingen	Rtl.	1861	N.-Amer	841054
Knapp, Maria			Kirchheim	Krch.	bef 1870	N.-Amer	835940
Knapp, Rosine Katharine		4 Oct 1878	Moensheim	Leon.	Jul 1882	N.-Amer	837960
Knapp, Sophia Kathar. (wid.) & F		3 Jan 1851	Moensheim	Leon.	Jul 1882	N.-Amer	837960
Knapp, Tobias			Flacht	Leon.	1844	N.-Amer	835790
Knaub, Genovefa		23 Aug 1836	Deggingen	Gsl.	Feb 1857	N.-Amer	572043
Knaupp, Christiana		10 Sep 1839	Weiler	Krch.	Sep 1862	N.-Amer	835949
Knaupp, Johann Heinrich		2 Mar 1855	Holzmaden	Krch.	Jan 1872	N.-Amer	835945
Knaus, Johann Peter		13 Jan 1843	Hochdorf	Krch.	Dec 1863	N.-Amer	835945
Knauss, Franz Ludwig & W		14 Apr 1807	Dettingen	Krch.	bef 1850	N.-Amer	835944
Knauss, Friederike Wilh. (wife)		16 May 1810	Stuttgart	Krch.	bef 1850	N.-Amer	835944
Knauss, Karoline Dorothea		20 Mar 1831	Hochdorf	Krch.	Jul 1854	N.-Amer	835945
Knayer, Anna Maria		28 Jan 1839	Weilheim	Krch.	Dec 1866	N.-Amer	835950
Knayer, Jacob Heinrich		30 Apr 1842	Weilheim	Krch.	Dec 1866	N.-Amer	835950
Knecht, Carl Leopold			Geislingen	Gsl.	bef 1861	N.-Amer	572044
Knecht, Regine		1 Nov 1825	Gerlingen	Leon.	Apr 1854	N.-Amer	837953
Kneer, Maria Barbara		20 Feb 1825	Westerheim	Gsl.	Aug 1859	N.-Amer	572043
Kneile, Johann Georg		12 Mar 1842	Holzmaden	Krch.	Sep 1865	N.-Amer	835945
Knies, August Richard Otto		20 Jul 1844	Eningen	Rtl.	Aug 1864	N.-Amer	841054
Knisel, Andreas		6 May 1828	Heimerdingen	Leon.	Apr 1833	N.-Amer	837954
Knisel, Andreas & F		26 Nov 1794	Heimerdingen	Leon.	Apr 1833	N.-Amer	837954
Knisel, Christina		3 May 1810	Heimerdingen	Leon.	Apr 1833	N.-Amer	837954
Knisel, Eva Barbara		5 Aug 1821	Heimerdingen	Leon.	Apr 1833	N.-Amer	837954
Knisel, Eva Catharina		24 Oct 1822	Heimerdingen	Leon.	Apr 1833	N.-Amer	837954
Knisel, Eva Catharina (wife)		17 Oct 1796	Heimerdingen	Leon.	Apr 1833	N.-Amer	837954
Knisel, Johann Georg		8 Jul 1792	Heimerdingen	Leon.	bef 1844	N.-Amer	837954
Knisel, Johann Georg		5 Apr 1825	Heimerdingen	Leon.	Apr 1833	N.-Amer	837954
Knisel, Johann Georg		24 yrs.	Heimerdingen	Leon.	bef 1818	N.-Amer	837954
Knoblauch, Barbara		7 Nov 1866	Boehmenkirch	Gsl.	Apr 1867	N.-Amer	572046
Knoblauch, Bernhard			Boehmenkirch	Gsl.	Jun 1852	N.-Amer	572041
Knoblauch, Bernhard		25 Oct 1867	Boehmenkirch	Gsl.	Feb 1884	N.-Amer	572049
Knoblauch, David		9 Jul 1855	Boehmenkirch	Gsl.	Feb 1857	N.-Amer	572043
Knoblauch, Elisabeth			Boehmenkirch	Gsl.	Jun 1852	N.-Amer	572041
Knoblauch, Elisabeth		20 Oct 1845	Boehmenkirch	Gsl.	Feb 1857	N.-Amer	572043
Knoblauch, Genovefa		26 Sep 1863	Boehmenkirch	Gsl.	Sep 1871	N.-Amer	572047
Knoblauch, Genovefa & C		28 Aug 1843	Boehmenkirch	Gsl.	Apr 1867	N.-Amer	572046
Knoblauch, Gertrud		10 Feb 1852	Boehmenkirch	Gsl.	Feb 1857	N.-Amer	572043
Knoblauch, Ignaz			Boehmenkirch	Gsl.	Jun 1852	N.-Amer	572041
Knoblauch, Johann Baptist		1 Aug 1855	Boehmenkirch	Gsl.	Sep 1871	N.-Amer	572047
Knoblauch, Johann Baptist & F		14 Sep 1825	Boehmenkirch	Gsl.	Sep 1871	N.-Amer	572047
Knoblauch, Johann Georg		22 Aug 1832	Boehmenkirch	Gsl.	Jan 1852	N.-Amer	572041
Knoblauch, Johannes			Boehmenkirch	Loen.	Jun 1852	N.-Amer	572041
Knoblauch, Johannes		14 Oct 1841	Eybach	Gsl.	Jun 1856	N.-Amer	572043
Knoblauch, Johannes		7 Aug 1847	Boehmenkirch	Gsl.	Feb 1857	N.-Amer	572043

Knoblauch, Johannes	8 Apr 1858	Unterboehringen	Gsl.	Jul 1874	N.-Amer	572048
Knoblauch, Johannes & F	22 May 1814	Boehmenkirch	Gsl.	Feb 1857	N.-Amer	572043
Knoblauch, Josef		Boehmenkirch	Loen.	Jun 1852	N.-Amer	572041
Knoblauch, Josef	18 Apr 1845	Boehmenkirch	Gsl.	Jan 1867	N.-Amer	572046
Knoblauch, Joseph	16 Oct 1841	Boehmkirchen	Gsl.	Feb 1854	N.-Amer	572042
Knoblauch, Joseph	26 Nov 1829	Boehmenkirch	Gsl.	Feb 1854	N.-Amer	572042
Knoblauch, Joseph	2 May 1867	Boehmenkirch	Gsl.	Apr 1883	N.-Amer	572049
Knoblauch, Joseph	13 Jan 1854	Boehmenkirch	Gsl.	Sep 1871	N.-Amer	572047
Knoblauch, Josepha (wife)	30 Sep 1828	Boehmenkirch	Gsl.	Sep 1871	N.-Amer	572047
Knoblauch, Katharina		Boehmenkirch	Loen.	Jun 1852	N.-Amer	572041
Knoblauch, Katharina	24 May 1838	Boehmenkirch	Gsl.	Feb 1854	N.-Amer	572042
Knoblauch, Katharina	13 Dec 1836	Boehmenkirch	Gsl.	Feb 1854	N.-Amer	572042
Knoblauch, Katharina (wife)	14 Mar 1815	Boehmenkirch	Gsl.	Feb 1857	N.-Amer	572043
Knoblauch, Kreszenz	29 Sep 1843	Boehmenkirch	Gsl.	Feb 1857	N.-Amer	572043
Knoblauch, Maria	18 yrs.	Boehmenkirch	Gsl.	Sep 1854	N.-Amer	572042
Knoblauch, Marianna	30 Jan 1850	Boehmenkirch	Gsl.	Feb 1857	N.-Amer	572043
Knoblauch, Michael	2 Jun 1853	Boehmenkirch	Gsl.	Feb 1871	N.-Amer	572047
Knoblauch, Philomina	30 Dec 1858	Boehmenkirch	Gsl.	Sep 1871	N.-Amer	572047
Knoblauch, Theresia	24 Jun 1857	Boehmenkirch	Gsl.	Sep 1871	N.-Amer	572047
Knoblauch, Ursula	23 Apr 1846	Boehmenkirch	Gsl.	Jun 1868	N.-Amer	572046
Knoblauch, Wilhelm		Boehmenkirch	Gsl.	Jun 1852	N.-Amer	572041
Knoblauch, Xaver		Boehmenkirch	Gsl.	Jun 1852	N.-Amer	572041
Knoblauch, Xaver & F		Boehmenkirch	Loen.	Jun 1852	N.-Amer	572041
Knobloch, Gottlob	36 yrs.	Reutlingen	Rtl.	May 1880	N.-Amer	841051
Knoebel, Christian	25 Jul 1849	Owen	Krch.	Jul 1866	N.-Amer	835948
Knoebel, Johannes	25 Aug 1840	Owen	Krch.	Feb 1859	N.-Amer	835948
Knoepfle, Anna Maria	21 yrs.	Fluorn	Obd.	Nov 1846	N.-Amer	838632
Knoepfle, Anna Maria (wife)	18 Mar 1780	Fluorn	Obd.	Aug 1817	N.-Amer	838629
Knoepfle, Barbara	15 Jun 1810	Fluorn	Obd.	Aug 1817	N.-Amer	838629
Knoepfle, Catharina	21 Jan 1815	Fluorn	Obd.	Aug 1817	N.-Amer	838629
Knoepfle, Christina	1 Dec 1795	Fluorn	Obd.	Aug 1817	N.-Amer	838629
Knoepfle, Jacob	13 Oct 1792	Fluorn	Obd.	Aug 1817	N.-Amer	838629
Knoepfle, Jakob	11 Jan 1808	Fluorn	Obd.	Aug 1817	N.-Amer	838629
Knoepfle, Johann Georg	23 yrs.	Fluorn	Obd.	Nov 1846	N.-Amer	838632
Knoepfle, Johannes	11 Jul 1804	Fluorn	Obd.	Aug 1817	N.-Amer	838629
Knoepfle, Mathias & F	31 Mar 1767	Fluorn	Obd.	Aug 1817	N.-Amer	838629
Knorr, Carl		Stubersheim	Gsl.	May 1864	Russia	572045
Knorr, Paul		Stubersheim	Gsl.	May 1864	Russia	572045
Knorr, Wilhelm & F		Stubersheim	Gsl.	May 1864	Russia	572045
Kober, Emil	13 Sep 1868	Aalen	Herr.	bef 1891	N.-Amer	834629
Kober, Friedrich	18 yrs.	Pfullingen	Rtl.	May 1880	N.-Amer	841051
Kober, Gottlob Friedrich	26 May 1823	Kirchheim	Krch.	Oct 1857	N.-Amer	835940
Koch, Adolf	17 yrs.	Waldmoessingen	Obd.	Oct 1852	N.-Amer	841015
Koch, Barbara	10 Sep 1839	Boehmenkirch	Gsl.	Jul 1865	N.-Amer	572045
Koch, Christina	28 yrs.	Hoefingen	Leon.	Jan 1854	N.-Amer	837957
Koch, Christine Catharine	30 yrs.	Hoefingen	Leon.	Aug 1865	N.-Amer	837957
Koch, Eugen	16 yrs.	Reutlingen	Rtl.	Apr 1880	N.-Amer	841051
Koch, Friedrich	19 yrs.	Hoefingen	Leon.	Jan 1854	N.-Amer	837957
Koch, Friedrich Philipp	22 Feb 1846	Eningen	Rtl.	Jul 1865	N.-Amer	841054
Koch, Gottlieb	25 Oct 1849	Hoefingen	Leon.	Feb 1867	N.-Amer	837957

Name		Birth		Emigration			Film
Last	First	Date	Place	O'amt	Appl. Date	Dest.	Number
Koch, Gottlieb		8 Mar 1841	Oetlingen	Krch.	Mar 1867	N.-Amer	835948
Koch, Johann & F			Waldmoessingen	Obd.	1817	N.-Amer	841015
Koch, Johann Georg		7 Sep 1829	Hoefingen	Leon.	Jan 1854	N.-Amer	837957
Koch, Johann Mathaeus & W			Malmsheim	Leon.	Oct 1870	N.-Amer	837958
Koch, Johannes		27 Jul 1839	Oetlingen	Krch.	Mar 1867	N.-Amer	835948
Koch, Karolina (wife)			Malmsheim	Leon.	Oct 1870	N.-Amer	837958
Koch, Luise			Eningen	Rtl.	bef 1863	N.-Amer	841054
Koch, Margaretha		4 Mar 1830	Oetlingen	Krch.	Dec 1855	N.-Amer	835948
Koch, Reinhold		9 Jan 1842	Waldmoessingen	Obd.	Mar 1859	N.-Amer	841015
Kocher, Christian Gottfried		4 Jul 1844	Ditzingen	Leon.	Jun 1872	N.-Amer	835788
Kocher, Christine Frieder. J.		3 Feb 1834	Leonberg	Leon.	Mar 1868	Prussia	835787
Kocher, Daniel Friedrich		7 Jan 1832	Ditzingen	Leon.	Apr 1852	N.-Amer	835788
Kocher, Johann Christian		17 Apr 1845	Ditzingen	Leon.	Jul 1865	N.-Amer	835788
Kocher, Johannes		9 Jul 1819	Ditzingen	Leon.	1847	N.-Amer	835788
Kocher, Johannes & F			Ditzingen	Leon.	Jul 1854	N.-Amer	835788
Kocher, Michael		17 Dec 1821	Ditzingen	Leon.	Feb 1853	N.-Amer	835788
Kocher, Wilhelm Friedrich		30 Jan 1832	Ditzingen	Leon.	Feb 1852	N.-Amer	835788
Koebele, Christine Friedrike		24 Aug 1821	Alpirsbach	Obd.	May 1846	Switz.	838630
Koebele, Karl Heinrich		22 May 1851	Alpirsbach	Obd.	Oct 1869	N.-Amer	838630
Koeber, Gottlob Friedrich		29 Nov 1863	Kirchheim	Krch.	Jun 1880	N.-Amer	548403
Koegel, Andreas & F		41 yrs.	Hemmingen	Leon.	Feb 1818	N.-Amer	837956
Koegel, Barbara		2 yrs.	Hemmingen	Leon.	Feb 1818	N.-Amer	837956
Koegel, Barbara (wife)			Hemmingen	Leon.	Apr 1833	N.-Amer	837956
Koegel, Christiana		8 yrs.	Hemmingen	Leon.	Feb 1818	N.-Amer	837956
Koegel, Gottlieb		3 yrs.	Hemmingen	Leon.	Feb 1818	N.-Amer	837956
Koegel, Johann Andreas		13 yrs.	Hemmingen	Leon.	Feb 1818	N.-Amer	837956
Koegel, Maria Catarina (wife)		41 yrs.	Hemmingen	Leon.	Feb 1818	N.-Amer	837956
Koegel, Michael & W			Hemmingen	Leon.	Apr 1833	N.-Amer	837956
Koehler, Friedrich			Kirchheim	Krch.	bef 1850	N.-Amer	835940
Koehler, Maria Catharina		26 Jul 1846	Gutenberg	Krch.	Aug 1865	N.-Amer	835945
Koelle, Georg		12 Jul 1849	Aufhausen	Gsl.	Jul 1869	N.-Amer	572047
Koellreutter, Karl August		15 yrs.	Warmbronn	Leon.	Jul 1854	N.-Amer	837965
Koellreutter, Maria Amalia		30 Apr 1843	Warmbronn	Leon.	May 1864	N.-Amer	837965
Koenig, Adam		18 Jan 1849	Dettingen	Krch.	Aug 1866	N.-Amer	835944
Koenig, Anton & F			Mariazell	Obd.	May 1817	N.-Amer	838634
Koenig, Daniel & F		53 yrs.	Hemmingen	Leon.	Jan 1854	N.-Amer	837956
Koenig, Jakob Friedrich		18 May 1855	Notzingen	Krch.	May 1870	N.-Amer	835947
Koenig, Johann Gottlieb		29 Aug 1840	Dettingen	Krch.	Mar 1869	N.-Amer	835944
Koenig, Johann Gottlieb		13 Nov 1831	Dettingen	Krch.	Nov 1868	N.-Amer	835944
Koenig, Johann Jakob		10 Nov 1830	Dettingen	Krch.	bef 1866	N.-Amer	835944
Koenig, Johann Jakob		18 Jun 1843	Dettingen	Krch.	Feb 1861	N.-Amer	835944
Koenig, Joseph			Hemmingen	Leon.	Aug 1853	N.-Amer	837956
Koenig, Maria Dorothea		9 Sep 1826	Dettingen	Krch.	Nov 1868	N.-Amer	835944
Koenig, Ursula Margaretha		17 Nov 1827	Dettingen	Krch.	Nov 1868	N.-Amer	835944
Koepf, Anna Catharina			Kuchen	Gsl.	Jul 1868	N.-Amer	572046
Koepf, Johannes		17 Apr 1858	Unterboehringen	Gsl.	Jan 1884	N.-Amer	572049
Koffler, Anna Barbara			Ditzingen	Leon.	bef 1820	Prussia	835788
Kogel, Christina Magdalena			Friolzheim	Leon.	Oct 1838	Switz.	835791
Kogel, Friederike			Rutesheim	Leon.	Mar 1862	N.-Amer	837964
Kogel, Friedrich			Rutesheim	Leon.	Apr 1849	N.-Amer	837964

Kogel, Gottlieb Friedrich	22 Mar 1853	Friolzheim	Leon.	Jul 1880	N.-Amer	835791
Kogel, Johann Conrad		Rutesheim	Leon.	Jun 1857	N.-Amer	837964
Kogel, Wilhelm Heinrich	26 Oct 1855	Rutesheim	Leon.	Mar 1881	N.-Amer	837964
Kohler, Andreas Philipp	31 Oct 1813	Weil im Dorf	Loen.	Feb 1854	N.-Amer	837967
Kohler, Anna & C	12 Oct 1844	Fluorn	Obd.	Mar 1870	N.-Amer	838632
Kohler, Carl	11 Nov 1851	Herrenberg	Herr.	1865	N.-Amer	834629
Kohler, Carl Gottlob	23 Mar 1847	Malmsheim	Leon.	May 1852	N.-Amer	837958
Kohler, Christina	18 yrs.	Fluorn	Obd.	Apr 1857	N.-Amer	838632
Kohler, Dorothea	21 yrs.	Malmsheim	Leon.	Sep 1853	N.-Amer	837958
Kohler, Ernst Jakob	17 Oct 1845	Malmsheim	Leon.	May 1852	N.-Amer	837958
Kohler, Georg Friedrich & W		Malmsheim	Leon.	Feb 1817	N.-Amer	837958
Kohler, Gottlieb	22 yrs.	Hoefingen	Leon.	Feb 1854	N.-Amer	837957
Kohler, Gottlieb Friedrich	7 Jun 1820	Leonberg	Leon.	bef 1857	N.-Amer	835786
Kohler, Jacob		Hirschlanden	Leon.	bef 1848	Hungary	837956
Kohler, Johann Andreas	26 Feb 1836	Malmsheim	Leon.	Aug 1856	N.-Amer	837958
Kohler, Johann Jakob	12 Mar 1835	Malmsheim	Leon.	Aug 1854	N.-Amer	837958
Kohler, Johann Jakob	15 Mar 1834	Malmsheim	Leon.	Aug 1854	N.-Amer	837958
Kohler, Johanna Dorothea	27 May 1841	Malmsheim	Leon.	May 1852	N.-Amer	837958
Kohler, Johannes	24 Jun 1840	Malmsheim	Leon.	May 1852	N.-Amer	837958
Kohler, Johannes & F	19 Jun 1811	Malmsheim	Leon.	May 1852	N.-Amer	837958
Kohler, Karl Friedrich	8 Jan 1856	Malmsheim	Leon.	Aug 1866	N.-Amer	837958
Kohler, Katharina Friederika	23 Mar 1860	Malmsheim	Leon.	Aug 1866	N.-Amer	837958
Kohler, Konrad & F	3 Dec 1809	Hirschlanden	Leon.	Apr 1854	N.-Amer	837956
Kohler, Ludwig	6 Apr 1853	Herrenberg	Herr.	Aug 1868	N.-Amer	834629
Kohler, Maria Barbara (wife)	3 Sep 1813	Malmsheim	Leon.	May 1852	N.-Amer	837958
Kohler, Maria Catharina	14 Oct 1841	Fluorn	Obd.	Feb 1864	N.-Amer	838632
Kohler, Maria Catharina	6 Jan 1848	Malmsheim	Leon.	May 1852	N.-Amer	837958
Kohler, Maria Katharina & C		Malmsheim	Leon.	Aug 1866	N.-Amer	837958
Kohler, Matthias	15 Aug 1866	Fluorn	Obd.	Mar 1870	N.-Amer	838632
Kohler, Salome	17 Mar 1846	Fluorn	Obd.	Feb 1864	N.-Amer	838632
Kohler, Sara (wife)		Hirschlanden	Leon.	Apr 1854	N.-Amer	837956
Kohler, Wilhelm Friedrich	24 Dec 1848	Herrenberg	Herr.	Dec 1868	N.-Amer	834629
Kohler, Wilhelm Heinrich		Malmsheim	Leon.	Aug 1866	N.-Amer	837958
Kohn, Anna Maria	2 Dec 1815	Geislingen	Gsl.	Jan 1854	N.-Amer	572042
Kohn, Elisabetha	6 Jan 1837	Geislingen	Gsl.	Mar 1854	N.-Amer	572042
Kohn, Johann Jacob	26 Jul 1849	Geislingen	Gsl.	Jan 1854	N.-Amer	572042
Kohn, Karl	28 Sep 1850	Geislingen	Gsl.	Jan 1854	N.-Amer	572042
Kohn, Maria		Unterschwandorf	Nag.	Jul 1852	N.-Amer	838488
Kohn, Sixtus & F	5 Mar 1812	Geislingen	Gsl.	Jan 1854	N.-Amer	572042
Kohn, Ursula	19 Apr 1838	Altenstadt-Gsl.	Gsl.	Jul 1866	N.-Amer	572045
Kok, Adrian	18 yrs.	Waldmoessingen	Obd.	Apr 1860	N.-Amer	841015
Kolb, Alois & F	16 Jan 1856	Boehmenkirch	Gsl.	Apr 1883	N.-Amer	572049
Kolb, Carl Christian	14 Dec 1863	Schorndorf	Krch.	Jun 1881	N.-Amer	548403
Kolb, Carl Christian	14 Dec 1863	Erolzheim/Bib.	Krch.	Jun 1881	N.-Amer	835942
Kolb, Gustav Albert	29 Jan 1847	Kirchheim	Krch.	Oct 1865	N.-Amer	835941
Kolb, Johann	15 yrs.	Boehmenkirch	Gsl.	Mar 1852	N.-Amer	572041
Kolb, Johann Georg		Malmsheim	Leon.	bef 1806	Prussia	837958
Kolb, Josef	21 Mar 1882	Boehmenkirch	Gsl.	Apr 1883	N.-Amer	572049
Kolb, Joseph	11 Mar 1846	Boehmenkirch	Gsl.	Mar 1868	N.-Amer	572046
Kolb, Kreszenz (wife)	7 Jun 1857	Boehmenkirch	Gsl.	Apr 1883	N.-Amer	572049

Name		Birth		Emigration			Film
Last	First	Date	Place	O'amt	Appl. Date	Dest.	Number
Kolb, Leonhard		8 Jun 1832	Weil im Dorf	Loen.	Sep 1852	N.-Amer	837967
Kolb, Theresia		1 Sep 1880	Boehmenkirch	Gsl.	Apr 1883	N.-Amer	572049
Kollmer, Christian Heinrich		12 Jul 1830	Malmsheim	Leon.	Mar 1857	N.-Amer	837958
Kommerer, Nikolaus		6 Dec 1842	Seedorf	Obd.	Mar 1861	N.-Amer	838637
Konz, Jakob			Flacht	Leon.	Aug 1854	N.-Amer	835790
Konzelmann, Johannes		4 Sep 1842	Zell	Krch.	May 1856	N.-Amer	835774
Kopf, Anna Maria & C		26 yrs.	Peterzell	Obd.	Mar 1861	N.-Amer	838635
Kopf, Christian		infant	Peterzell	Obd.	Mar 1861	N.-Amer	838635
Kopf, Gottlieb		19 yrs.	Peterzell	Obd.	Jul 1854	N.-Amer	838635
Kopp, Amalia			Aichhalden	Obd.	bef 1858	N.-Amer	838629
Kopp, Andreas		30 Nov 1835	Muehlhausen/Elsass	Obd.	May 1847	N.-Amer	838631
Kopp, Andreas		20 Oct 1845	Betzweiler	Obd.	May 1847	N.-Amer	838631
Kopp, Andreas		22 Mar 1836	Roemlinsdorf	Obd.	Apr 1866	N.-Amer	838635
Kopp, Andreas		19 May 1843	Waldmoessingen	Obd.	Sep 1856	N.-Amer	841015
Kopp, Andreas		20 Oct 1858	Moensheim	Leon.	Jul 1873	N.-Amer	837960
Kopp, Andreas		7 Sep 1836	Moensheim	Leon.	Apr 1854	N.-Amer	837960
Kopp, Andreas		2 Jul 1840	Moensheim	Leon.	Feb 1854	N.-Amer	837960
Kopp, Anna		15 Aug 1841	Betzweiler	Obd.	Jun 1847	N.-Amer	838631
Kopp, Anna Friederika		24 Nov 1842	Moensheim	Leon.	Apr 1854	N.-Amer	837960
Kopp, Anna Maria			Betzweiler	Obd.	Apr 1861	N.-Amer	838631
Kopp, Anna Maria			Betzweiler	Obd.	Oct 1854	N.-Amer	838631
Kopp, Anna Maria		5 May 1842	Betzweiler	Obd.	May 1847	N.-Amer	838631
Kopp, Anna Maria		23 yrs.	Roemlinsdorf	Obd.	Apr 1853	N.-Amer	838635
Kopp, Anna Maria		16 Apr 1851	Gueltstein	Herr.	Apr 1869	N.-Amer	834631
Kopp, Anna Maria		11 Dec 1841	Moensheim	Leon.	Feb 1854	N.-Amer	837960
Kopp, Anna Maria & C		19 Sep 1827	Moensheim	Leon.	Apr 1854	N.-Amer	837960
Kopp, Anna Maria (wife)			Moensheim	Leon.	Feb 1854	N.-Amer	837960
Kopp, Barbara		20 Aug 1843	Betzweiler	Obd.	Jun 1847	N.-Amer	838631
Kopp, Barbara		2 Dec 1836	Roemlinsdorf	Obd.	Apr 1866	N.-Amer	838635
Kopp, Barbara		3 Apr 1844	Dornhan	Obd.	bef 1866	France	838638
Kopp, Carl		26 Nov 1849	Winzeln	Obd.	Dec 1867	N.-Amer	841016
Kopp, Catharina		7 Feb 1839	Betzweiler	Obd.	May 1847	N.-Amer	838631
Kopp, Christian			Betzweiler	Obd.	Jul 1854	N.-Amer	838631
Kopp, Christina			Roemlinsdorf	Obd.	Apr 1857	N.-Amer	838635
Kopp, Christina		3 Dec 1846	Moensheim	Leon.	Jul 1864	N.-Amer	837960
Kopp, Christine (wife)		23 Mar 1817	Geroldweiler	Obd.	Jun 1847	N.-Amer	838631
Kopp, Christine (wife)		26 May 1819	Betzweiler	Obd.	May 1847	N.-Amer	838631
Kopp, Friedrich		19 Sep 1845	Betzweiler	Obd.	May 1847	N.-Amer	838631
Kopp, Friedrich		20 Apr 1847	Betzweiler	Obd.	May 1847	N.-Amer	838631
Kopp, Friedrich			Peterzell	Obd.	May 1864	N.-Amer	838635
Kopp, Friedrich & F			Kirchheim	Krch.	May 1855	N.-Amer	835940
Kopp, Georg Friedrich (wid.) & F			Moensheim	Leon.	Apr 1854	N.-Amer	837960
Kopp, Helena		13 Jun 1852	Moensheim	Leon.	Feb 1854	N.-Amer	837960
Kopp, Jacob		2 Dec 1834	Muehlhausen/Elsass	Obd.	May 1847	N.-Amer	838631
Kopp, Jakob		10 Aug 1850	Betzweiler	Obd.	Dec 1870	N.-Amer	838631
Kopp, Jakob		17 yrs.	Betzweiler	Obd.	Apr 1861	N.-Amer	838631
Kopp, Johann Georg		8 Jul 1819	Aichhalden	Obd.	Dec 1844	N.-Amer	838629
Kopp, Johann Georg		31 Oct 1837	Betzweiler	Obd.	May 1847	N.-Amer	838631
Kopp, Johann Georg		19 Jul 1844	Betzweiler	Obd.	May 1847	N.-Amer	838631
Kopp, Johann Georg		5 Nov 1852	Gueltstein	Herr.	Apr 1869	N.-Amer	834631

Kopp, Johann Georg & F	2 Mar 1806	Betzweiler	Obd.	May 1847	N.-Amer	838631
Kopp, Johann Georg & F	26 Aug 1816	Gueltstein	Herr.	Apr 1869	N.-Amer	834631
Kopp, Johann Simon	22 Sep 1856	Gueltstein	Herr.	Apr 1869	N.-Amer	834631
Kopp, Johannes		Aichhalden	Obd.	Jun 1860	Prussia	838629
Kopp, Johannes	27 Dec 1837	Aichhalden	Obd.	Sep 1858	N.-Amer	838629
Kopp, Johannes	19 yrs.	Betzweiler	Obd.	Apr 1861	N.-Amer	838631
Kopp, Johannes	27 Apr 1840	Betzweiler	Obd.	May 1847	N.-Amer	838631
Kopp, Johannes	20 Apr 1847	Betzweiler	Obd.	May 1847	N.-Amer	838631
Kopp, Johannes	4 Apr 1786	Peterzell	Obd.	Oct 1847	N.-Amer	838635
Kopp, Johannes	13 Sep 1854	Gueltstein	Herr.	Apr 1869	N.-Amer	834631
Kopp, Johannes	17 Jul 1849	Moensheim	Leon.	Feb 1854	N.-Amer	837960
Kopp, Johannes	1836	Aichhalden	Obd.	Jan 1869	Bavaria	838629
Kopp, Johannes & F	1829	Aichhalden	Obd.	Mar 1865	N.-Amer	838629
Kopp, Johannes & F	6 Jun 1814	Betzweiler	Obd.	Jun 1847	N.-Amer	838631
Kopp, Johannes & F		Moensheim	Leon.	Feb 1854	N.-Amer	837960
Kopp, Karl	20 yrs.	Waldmoessingen	Obd.	Aug 1854	N.-Amer	841015
Kopp, Katharina	25 Jun 1851	Moensheim	Leon.	Apr 1854	N.-Amer	837960
Kopp, Katharina Dorothea	27 Nov 1839	Moensheim	Leon.	Apr 1854	N.-Amer	837960
Kopp, Katharina Dorothea	20 Jul 1847	Moensheim	Leon.	Feb 1854	N.-Amer	837960
Kopp, Leonhard	11 Mar 1847	Moensheim	Leon.	1873	N.-Amer	837960
Kopp, Magdalena	3 Jul 1845	Moensheim	Leon.	Feb 1854	N.-Amer	837960
Kopp, Maria Agatha		Hardt	Obd.	Jul 1864	N.-Amer	838633
Kopp, Maria Catharina	10 Aug 1846	Gueltstein	Herr.	Apr 1869	N.-Amer	834631
Kopp, Maria Dorothea (wife)	14 Mar 1823	Gueltstein	Herr.	Apr 1869	N.-Amer	834631
Kopp, Mathias	10 Jan 1842	Betzweiler	Obd.	May 1847	N.-Amer	838631
Kopp, Michael		Aichhalden	Obd.	May 1817	N.-Amer	838629
Kopp, Otto	13 Nov 1847	Schramberg	Obd.	Feb 1867	N.-Amer	838636
Kopp, Philipp Jakob	1 May 1848	Gueltstein	Herr.	Aug 1868	N.-Amer	834631
Kopp, Rosina	18 yrs.	Betzweiler	Obd.	Feb 1858	Paris	838631
Kopp, Rosina		Betzweiler	Obd.	Oct 1854	N.-Amer	838631
Kopp, Rosina Friederika	26 Nov 1832	Moensheim	Leon.	Apr 1854	N.-Amer	837960
Kopp, Sabina	27 Oct 1861	Gueltstein	Herr.	Apr 1869	N.-Amer	834631
Kopp, Salome (wife)		Kirchheim	Krch.	May 1855	N.-Amer	835940
Kopp, Valentin		Winzeln	Obd.	Jul 1860	N.-Amer	841016
Kopp, Wilhelm	19 Nov 1845	Schramberg	Obd.	Jun 1864	N.-Amer	838636
Kopp, Xaver	5 Feb 1840	Waldmoessingen	Obd.	Sep 1856	N.-Amer	841015
Kordon, Fridolin		Weissenstein	Gsl.	Jan 1868	Austria	572046
Korneli, Theresia	23 Oct 1833	Schramberg	Obd.	Feb 1867	Austria	838636
Koser, Johann Friedrich	16 Jan 1867	Kirchheim	Krch.	Apr 1883	N.-Amer	548403
Koser, Karl Christian	31 Dec 1846	Kirchheim	Krch.	Dec 1868	N.-Amer	835941
Kost, Maria Barbara	21 Jun 1841	Hausen a.d.Lauchert	Rtl.	May 1865	France	841054
Kostenbader, Johannes	31 Jan 1848	Pfullingen	Rtl.	Nov 1867	N.-Amer	841054
Kostenbader, Ulrich	12 Apr 1849	Pfullingen	Rtl.	May 1864	N.-Amer	841054
Kottmann, Anna Barbara	3 May 1834	Geislingen	Gsl.	Sep 1861	Switz.	572044
Kraecher, Gottlieb	24 Jun 1843	Weil im Dorf	Loen.	1864	N.-Amer	837967
Kraecher, Johannes	31 Aug 1840	Weil im Dorf	Loen.	May 1867	N.-Amer	837967
Kraehmer, Magdalena Carolina	5 Dec 1832	Ueberkingen	Gsl.	Sep 1857	Switz.	572043
Kraehmer, Wilhelm		Ueberkingen	Gsl.	bef 1859	Switz.	573622
Kraemer, Agnes Margar. (wife)		Malmsheim	Leon.	Mar 1830	N.-Amer	837958
Kraemer, Anna Maria	5 yrs.	Malmsheim	Leon.	Mar 1830	N.-Amer	837958

Name		Birth		Emigration			Film
Last	First	Date	Place	O'amt	Appl. Date	Dest.	Number
Kraemer, Barbara			Eltingen	Leon.	Apr 1830	N.-Amer	835789
Kraemer, Catharina Margaretha		7 yrs.	Malmsheim	Leon.	Mar 1830	N.-Amer	837958
Kraemer, Christian Friedrich		2 yrs.	Malmsheim	Leon.	Mar 1830	N.-Amer	837958
Kraemer, Christina		3 yrs.	Malmsheim	Leon.	Mar 1830	N.-Amer	837958
Kraemer, Christina (wid.)		77 yrs.	Leonberg	Leon.	Dec 1816	Russia	835789
Kraemer, Gottliebin			Eltingen	Leon.	Apr 1830	N.-Amer	835789
Kraemer, Gustav		7 yrs.	Hemmingen	Leon.	Dec 1864	France	837956
Kraemer, Jakob Friedrich & F			Malmsheim	Leon.	Mar 1830	N.-Amer	837958
Kraemer, Johann Georg		30 yrs.	Hemmingen	Leon.	Feb 1818	N.-Amer	837956
Kraemer, Johannes			Hemmingen	Leon.	Dec 1830	Hesse	837956
Kraemer, Johannes		7 Mar 1853	Malmsheim	Leon.	May 1882	N.-Amer	837958
Kraemer, Johannes		22 Dec 1856	Malmsheim	Leon.	May 1870	N.-Amer	837958
Kraemer, Johannes & F			Hemmingen	Leon.	Dec 1864	France	837956
Kraemer, Karl Jakob		9 Jun 1853	Malmsheim	Leon.	Jun 1869	N.-Amer	837958
Kraemer, Lorentz & F			Eltingen	Leon.	Apr 1830	N.-Amer	835789
Kraemer, Maria			Hausen a.d. Wurm	Leon.	bef 1864	N.-Amer	837954
Kraemer, Maria Catharina		17 Feb 1858	Malmsheim	Leon.	Sep 1871	N.-Amer	837958
Kraemer, Wilhelm Friedrich & F			Malmsheim	Leon.	Mar 1830	N.-Amer	837958
Krafft, Barbara (wife)			Hoefingen	Leon.	Feb 1853	N.-Amer	837957
Krafft, Christian & F			Hoefingen	Leon.	Feb 1853	N.-Amer	837957
Krafft, Ernst Julius		11 Nov 1855	Leonberg	Leon.	Sep 1872	N.-Amer	835787
Kraft, Christoph			Altenstadt-Gsl.	Gsl.	Mar 1853	N.-Amer	572041
Kraft, Georg		8 Mar 1833	Schopfloch	Krch.	Mar 1862	Hamburg	835949
Kraft, Gottlieb		10 May 1857	Hoefingen	Leon.	Nov 1881	N.-Amer	837957
Kraft, Johann Evangelist		2 Jan 1831	Winzeln	Obd.	Sep 1854	N.-Amer	841016
Kraft, Johann Georg & F			Roemlinsdorf	Obd.	Jun 1854	N.-Amer	838635
Kraft, Johann Jakob		6 Aug 1866	Lindorf	Krch.	Apr 1883	N.-Amer	548403
Kraft, Sabine Catharina		18 Nov 1820	Muenchingen	Leon.	Apr 1848	N.-Amer	837961
Kramer, Eleonore			Oberndorf	Obd.	Jan 1843	France	838635
Kramer, Vinzenz			Seedorf	Obd.	Dec 1860	N.-Amer	838637
Kramer, Xaver			Oberndorf	Obd.	Jul 1851	N.-Amer	838635
Kranich, Barbara (wife)			Hemmingen	Leon.	Apr 1833	N.-Amer	837956
Kranich, Christian		28 yrs.	Hemmingen	Leon.	Jun 1865	N.-Amer	837956
Kranich, Christiane		20 yrs.	Hemmingen	Leon.	Jun 1865	N.-Amer	837956
Kranich, Jacob			Hemmingen	Leon.	Jul 1864	N.-Amer	837956
Kranich, Johann Georg & F			Hemmingen	Leon.	Apr 1833	N.-Amer	837956
Kranich, Johannes			Hemmingen	Leon.	Jan 1867	N.-Amer	837956
Kranz, Ludwig Wilhelm Fried.			Geislingen	Gsl.	bef 1852	Prussia	572041
Kratt, Christian		20 Jul 1841	Hardt	Obd.	Feb 1860	N.-Amer	838633
Kratt, Dorothea (wid.)		11 Jan 1803	Hardt	Obd.	Sep 1866	N.-Amer	838633
Kratt, Gottfried			Hardt	Obd.	Mar 1861	N.-Amer	838633
Kratt, Johannes			Hardt	Obd.	Mar 1861	N.-Amer	838633
Kratt, Mathias			Hardt	Obd.	Mar 1861	N.-Amer	838633
Krauch, Eugenie Jul. Frieder.		24 Oct 1868	Weil im Dorf	Loen.	Jul 1881	N.-Amer	837967
Krauch, Friedrich Jonathan & F		26 Feb 1838	Cleebronn	Loen.	bef 1881	N.-Amer	837967
Krauch, Karl Adolf Ludwig		24 Jun 1867	Weil im Dorf	Loen.	Jul 1881	N.-Amer	837967
Krauch, Oskar Wilhelm Ludw.		16 May 1871	Weil im Dorf	Loen.	Jul 1881	N.-Amer	837967
Krauch, Pauline Henriette (wife)		21 May 1839	Gossenzugen	Loen.	Jul 1881	N.-Amer	837967
Krauch, Rudolf Adolf		3 Jun 1866	Weil im Dorf	Loen.	Jul 1881	N.-Amer	837967
Kraus, Anna Ursula		14 Oct 1837	Steinenkirch	Gsl.	Feb 1854	N.-Amer	572042

Kraus, Jakob	22 May 1834	Steinenkirch	Gsl.	Feb 1854	N.-Amer	572042
Kraus, Jakob	18 yrs.	Boehmenkirch	Gsl.	Mar 1869	N.-Amer	572047
Kraus, Johannes	6 Aug 1832	Steinenkirch	Gsl.	Feb 1854	N.-Amer	572042
Krausbek, Adolf	19 Dec 1868	Dunningen	Rtw.	Aug 1885	N.-Amer	841117
Krauss, Anna Barbara (wife)	15 Mar 1796	Renningen	Leon.	Apr 1852	N.-Amer	837963
Krauss, Anna Ursula	22 yrs.	Gingen	Gsl.	Jun 1853	N.-Amer	572041
Krauss, Bernhard	12 Jan 1858	Boehmenkirch	Gsl.	Jun 1874	N.-Amer	572048
Krauss, Christian	20 Nov 1811	Ditzingen	Leon.	Aug 1848	Switz.	835788
Krauss, Christina Magdalena	11 Jul 1828	Renningen	Leon.	Apr 1852	N.-Amer	837963
Krauss, Gottfried & F	44 yrs.	Hausen a.d. Wurm	Leon.	Aug 1869	N.-Amer	837954
Krauss, Gottlob Ludwig	11 Jun 1872	Merklingen	Leon.	bef 1889	N.-Amer	837959
Krauss, Heinrich	28 Aug 1831	Geislingen	Gsl.	1859	Switz.	573622
Krauss, Jakob August	7 Sep 1840	Renningen	Leon.	Apr 1852	N.-Amer	837963
Krauss, Johann Friedrich	45 yrs.	Weil im Dorf	Loen.	Mar 1852	N.-Amer	837967
Krauss, Johann Georg	6 Apr 1849	Gueltstein	Herr.	Apr 1869	N.-Amer	834631
Krauss, Johann Georg & W		Gerlingen	Leon.	Apr 1854	N.-Amer	837953
Krauss, Johann Michael	8 Jan 1836	Renningen	Leon.	Apr 1852	N.-Amer	837963
Krauss, Johannes	2 Aug 1838	Renningen	Leon.	Apr 1852	N.-Amer	837963
Krauss, Johannes & F		Renningen	Leon.	Apr 1852	N.-Amer	837963
Krauss, Louise (wife)		Gerlingen	Leon.	Apr 1854	N.-Amer	837953
Krauss, Ludwig Friedrich	14 Sep 1873	Merklingen	Leon.	bef 1889	N.-Amer	837959
Krauss, Pauline	19 yrs.	Hausen a.d. Wurm	Leon.	Aug 1869	N.-Amer	837954
Krauss, Sophie		Ditzingen	Leon.	Aug 1832	Switz.	835788
Krautter, August	6 Aug 1837	Pfullingen	Rtl.	Aug 1864	Belgien	841054
Krautwasser, Charlotte Chr.		Reutlingen	Rtl.	bef 1862	England	841054
Krautwasser, Christine		Reutlingen	Rtl.	1858	N.-Amer	841057
Krazeisen, Johannes	7 Sep 1843	Ditzingen	Leon.	May 1871	N.-Amer	835788
Krechler, Agatha & C	5 Feb 1804	Hochmoessingen	Obd.	Aug 1843	France	838633
Krechler, Kreszentia	13 Sep 1835	Hochmoessingen	Obd.	Aug 1843	France	838633
Krechler, Theresia	20 Nov 1823	Hochmoessingen	Obd.	Aug 1843	France	838633
Krederer, Agatha		Oberndorf	Obd.	Mar 1849	N.-Amer	838635
Kreiser, Johann Georg	17 May 1826	Waldhausen	Gsl.	Nov 1861	Hungary	572044
Kreiser, Johannes	41 yrs.	Gingen	Gsl.	Jun 1854	N.-Amer	572042
Kreiser, Johannes	7 Apr 1840	Gingen	Gsl.	Aug 1856	N.-Amer	572043
Kreiser, Julius	7 Jul 1848	Gingen	Gsl.	Apr 1857	N.-Amer	572043
Kreiser, Maria	27 Mar 1842	Gingen	Gsl.	Aug 1856	N.-Amer	572043
Kreisser, Johann Georg	3 Feb 1821	Geislingen	Gsl.	bef 1852	France	572041
Kreppel, Carl	19 Jan 1830	Leonberg	Leon.	Dec 1855	N.-Amer	835786
Kreppel, Christian Heinrich	14 Apr 1835	Leonberg	Leon.	May 1863	N.-Amer	835787
Kreppel, Maria	2 May 1835	Leonberg	Leon.	bef 1856	N.-Amer	835786
Kretz, Friedrike Caroline	15 Nov 1824	Alpirsbach	Obd.	Mar 1849	France	838630
Kreusser, Christiane Karoline		Kirchheim	Krch.	Sep 1867	N.-Amer	835941
Kreuzbacher, Valentin	12 Feb 1833	Hochmoessingen	Obd.	Apr 1851	N.-Amer	838633
Kreuzberger, Emilie	9 Oct 1846	Winzeln	Obd.	Sep 1868	N.-Amer	841016
Kreuzberger, Fridolin	26 Feb 1849	Winzeln	Obd.	Nov 1867	N.-Amer	841016
Kreuzberger, Marx & F		Winzeln	Obd.	May 1817	N.-Amer	841016
Kreuzberger, Michel	20 yrs.	Winzeln	Obd.	Sep 1857	N.-Amer	841016
Kreuzberger, Rosina	5 Jul 1842	Winzeln	Obd.	Sep 1869	N.-Amer	841016
Kreuzberger, Rupert		Winzeln	Obd.	Sep 1863	N.-Amer	841016
Kreuzberger, Sophia		Winzeln	Obd.	Oct 1863	N.-Amer	841016

Name		Birth		Emigration			Film
Last	First	Date	Place	O'amt	Appl. Date	Dest.	Number
Krieg, Georg		23 Sep 1832	Tuerkheim	Gsl.	Mar 1855	N.-Amer	572043
Krieg, Jakob		6 Mar 1823	Tuerkheim	Gsl.	Apr 1857	N.-Amer	572043
Krieg, Johannes		13 Sep 1840	Tuerkheim	Gsl.	Mar 1857	N.-Amer	572043
Krieg, Johannes		29 Sep 1874	Owen	Krch.	Jun 1890	N.-Amer	548323
Krieg, Maria Elisabeth			Honau	Rtl.	May 1862	Switz.	841054
Krimmel, August		14 May 1849	Reutlingen	Rtl.	Aug 1867	N.-Amer	841054
Krissler, Friederike		8 Feb 1867	Weilheim	Krch.	bef 1870	N.-Amer	835950
Krissler, Johannes		8 Dec 1865	Weilheim	Krch.	bef 1870	N.-Amer	835950
Krissler, Karl		13 Nov 1873	Weilheim	Krch.	Jan 1890	N.-Amer	835774
Krissler, Luise & F		19 Mar 1836	Weilheim	Krch.	bef 1870	N.-Amer	835950
Kroener, Sophie Maria		25 Oct 1846	Geislingen	Gsl.	Mar 1870	Austria	572047
Kroetz, Georg Jakob		10 Oct 1852	Roetenbach	Obd.	Apr 1869	N.-Amer	838636
Kromer, Andreas			Ditzingen	Leon.	Apr 1841	Hungary	835788
Kromer, Jakob Friedrich		21 Feb 1846	Oetlingen	Krch.	Jul 1866	N.-Amer	835948
Kromer, Johann Stephan		18 Mar 1850	Unterhausen	Rtl.	Sep 1866	N.-Amer	841054
Kruck, Johann Michael		21 Mar 1827	Gerlingen	Leon.	Mar 1861	Prussia	837953
Kruegler, Johannes		14 Jul 1863	Moensheim	Leon.	1870	Palest.	837960
Kruk, Johanna			Gerlingen	Leon.	bef 1818	Poland	837953
Krumm, Johann Georg			Ohmenhausen	Rtl.	May 1831	N.-Amer	841051
Krumm, Martin			Bronnweiler	Rtl.	May 1832	N.-Amer	841051
Krumm, Michael			Bronnweiler	Rtl.	May 1832	N.-Amer	841051
Kuch, Johann Georg		21 Sep 1875	Neidlingen	Krch.	Apr 1889	N.-Amer	835946
Kuch, Karl Friedrich		28 Jun 1865	Kirchheim	Krch.	Jul 1882	N.-Amer	548403
Kuch, Karl Georg		2 Apr 1871	Neidlingen	Krch.	Mar 1887	N.-Amer	835946
Kuch, Pauline Maria		24 Jun 1842	Kirchheim	Krch.	Aug 1868	Italy	835941
Kuch, Wilhelm Georg		10 Aug 1858	Kirchheim	Krch.	Aug 1875	N.-Amer	548403
Kuebler, Anna Maria		17 Apr 1852	Moensheim	Leon.	Jul 1853	N.-Amer	837960
Kuebler, Anna Maria & C		38 yrs.	Peterzell	Obd.	Sep 1857	N.-Amer	838635
Kuebler, Elisabetha Christine		2 Mar 1839	Weilheim	Krch.	Apr 1859	N.-Amer	835949
Kuebler, Eva Kathar. (wid.) & F		27 Aug 1798	Weilheim	Krch.	Apr 1859	N.-Amer	835949
Kuebler, Friedrike (wife)			Hoefingen	Leon.	Feb 1851	N.-Amer	837957
Kuebler, Georg Friedrich		9 Mar 1845	Weilheim	Krch.	Aug 1864	N.-Amer	835950
Kuebler, Hermann		28 Sep 1849	Weilheim	Krch.	Dec 1867	N.-Amer	835950
Kuebler, Johann Christian		10 Jan 1849	Weilheim	Krch.	Nov 1865	N.-Amer	835950
Kuebler, Johann Georg			Peterzell	Obd.	Sep 1857	N.-Amer	838635
Kuebler, Johann Georg		21 Oct 1841	Weilheim	Krch.	Aug 1856	N.-Amer	835949
Kuebler, Johann Georg & F			Moensheim	Leon.	Jul 1853	N.-Amer	837960
Kuebler, Johann Georg & W			Hoefingen	Leon.	Feb 1851	N.-Amer	837957
Kuebler, Johann Michael		23 Mar 1833	Moensheim	Leon.	Mar 1853	N.-Amer	837960
Kuebler, Johannes			Altensteig	Nag.	Jul 1852	N.-Amer	838488
Kuebler, Johannes		4 Jul 1844	Wellingen	Krch.	May 1862	N.-Amer	835947
Kuebler, Maria Friederike		29 Oct 1844	Weilheim	Krch.	Mar 1866	N.-Amer	835950
Kuebler, Maria Katharina		15 Nov 1850	Moensheim	Leon.	Jul 1853	N.-Amer	837960
Kuebler, Maria Katharina (wife)			Moensheim	Leon.	Jul 1853	N.-Amer	837960
Kuebler, Philipp		20 Feb 1846	Weilheim	Krch.	Dec 1866	N.-Amer	835950
Kuebler, Richard		4 Dec 1873	Gerlingen	Leon.	Nov 1888	N.-Amer	837953
Kuebler, Wilhelm Gottfried		16 Feb 1863	Gerlingen	Leon.	Sep 1878	Brasil.	837953
Kuechle, Christine		9 Nov 1829	Muenchingen	Leon.	Nov 1866	Prussia	837961
Kuechle, Christine			Muenchingen	Leon.	Jan 1855	N.-Amer	837961
Kuechle, Johann Georg		29 Dec 1831	Muenchingen	Leon.	Nov 1855	N.-Amer	837961

Kuechle, Johann Jakob	25 Jun 1847	Muenchingen	Leon.	Aug 1867	N.-Amer	837961
Kuechle, Johann Jakob	22 Aug 1823	Muenchingen	Leon.	May 1859	N.-Amer	837961
Kuechle, Johanna Marg. & F		Muenchingen	Leon.	Jul 1860	N.-Amer	837961
Kuechle, Katharina	21 yrs.	Treffelhausen	Gsl.	Jun 1869	N.-Amer	572047
Kuechle, Margaretha		Muenchingen	Leon.	Jul 1860	N.-Amer	837961
Kuechle, Maria		Muenchingen	Leon.	Jul 1860	N.-Amer	837961
Kuechle, Maria Magdalena (wife)	7 Sep 1820	Muenchingen	Leon.	May 1859	N.-Amer	837961
Kuechle, Philipp & F	25 Jun 1814	Muenchingen	Leon.	May 1859	N.-Amer	837961
Kuehbauch, Johann Georg	26 Nov 1839	Gomaringen	Rtl.	bef 1860	N.-Amer	841054
Kuehlwein, Apollonia	20 yrs.	Geislingen	Gsl.	Apr 1866	N.-Amer	572045
Kuehn, Johann Georg	12 Feb 1847	Muenchingen	Leon.	Apr 1866	N.-Amer	837961
Kuehnle, Christian	27 Mar 1838	Heimsheim	Leon.	Feb 1865	N.-Amer	837955
Kuehnle, Georg Friedrich	7 Oct 1777	Heimsheim	Leon.	Feb 1820	Switz.	837955
Kuehnle, Johann Georg	27 Jul 1845	Warmbronn	Leon.	Nov 1865	N.-Amer	837965
Kuehnle, Johanna Christina	19 yrs.	Heimsheim	Leon.	Jun 1851	N.-Amer	837955
Kuehnle, Johannes	28 yrs.	Heimsheim	Leon.	Jun 1861	N.-Amer	837955
Kuehnle, Justine Catrine	22 yrs.	Heimsheim	Leon.	Jun 1851	N.-Amer	837955
Kuehnle, Marie Christine	30 Mar 1831	Heimsheim	Leon.	Sep 1864	Bavaria	837955
Kuemmele, Theodor	2 Nov 1842	Oberlenningen	Krch.	May 1864	N.-Amer	835947
Kuemmerle, Anna Maria	13 Jan 1849	Renningen	Leon.	Aug 1854	N.-Amer	837963
Kuemmerle, Auguste Marie Lou.	2 Jul 1850	Renningen	Leon.	Jul 1853	N.-Amer	837963
Kuemmerle, Catharina Margar.	16 Jan 1835	Renningen	Leon.	Apr 1852	N.-Amer	837963
Kuemmerle, Christian Gottlieb	31 Dec 1841	Renningen	Leon.	Apr 1852	N.-Amer	837963
Kuemmerle, Gottlieb & F		Renningen	Leon.	Jul 1853	N.-Amer	837963
Kuemmerle, Johann Friedrich	11 Aug 1833	Renningen	Leon.	Apr 1852	N.-Amer	837963
Kuemmerle, Johanna Kath. Fr.	12 Dec 1817	Malmsheim	Leon.	Jul 1851	Hesse	837958
Kuemmerle, Johannes & F		Renningen	Leon.	Apr 1852	N.-Amer	837963
Kuemmerle, Maria Rosina	13 Apr 1839	Renningen	Leon.	Apr 1852	N.-Amer	837963
Kuemmerle, Maria Rosina & C	7 Dec 1826	Renningen	Leon.	Aug 1854	N.-Amer	837963
Kuemmerle, S. Catharina (wife)		Renningen	Leon.	Jul 1853	N.-Amer	837963
Kuemmerle, Sophie (wife)		Renningen	Leon.	Apr 1852	N.-Amer	837963
Kuester, Franz & F		Oberndorf	Obd.	Apr 1849	N.-Amer	838635
Kugler, Johann Georg		Mariazell	Obd.	May 1817	N.-Amer	838634
Kugler, Johann Wilhelm	10 Oct 1830	Kirchheim	Krch.	bef 1867	N.-Amer	835941
Kugler, Marie	10 Mar 1828	Kirchheim	Krch.	Jan 1855	N.-Amer	835940
Kuhn, Anna Maria (wife)	12 Aug 1823	Friolzheim	Leon.	Jul 1851	N.-Amer	835791
Kuhn, Barbara (wife)		Friolzheim	Leon.	Jul 1851	N.-Amer	835791
Kuhn, Basill		Weil der Stadt	Leon.	Sep 1852	N.-Amer	837966
Kuhn, Christoph Heinrich	1 Feb 1823	Owen	Krch.	Dec 1868	N.-Amer	835948
Kuhn, Erhard		Talhausen	Obd.	Apr 1881	N.-Amer	838632
Kuhn, Gottlieb & W		Friolzheim	Leon.	Jul 1851	N.-Amer	835791
Kuhn, Gottlieb Fried. Christ.	22 Dec 1852	Unterlenningen	Krch.	Jan 1867	N.-Amer	835949
Kuhn, Johann Gottlob	10 Sep 1850	Friolzheim	Leon.	Jul 1851	N.-Amer	835791
Kuhn, Louise Catharina	19 Mar 1844	Friolzheim	Leon.	Jul 1851	N.-Amer	835791
Kuhn, Maria	28 yrs.	Alt Oberndorf	Obd.	Mar 1853	N.-Amer	838631
Kuhn, Maria Barbara	23 Aug 1848	Friolzheim	Leon.	Jul 1851	N.-Amer	835791
Kuhn, Nikolaus	19 Jun 1850	Unterlenningen	Krch.	Jul 1864	N.-Amer	835949
Kummer, Maria Agatha	29 Apr 1810	Eybach	Gsl.	Jan 1852	N.-Amer	572041
Kunkele, Ursula Margaretha	15 Jun 1825	Weilheim	Krch.	bef 1859	N.-Amer	835949
Kunz, Johannes		Bochingen	Obd.	Apr 1860	N.-Amer	838632

Name		Birth		Emigration			Film
Last	First	Date	Place	O'amt	Appl. Date	Dest.	Number
Kunz, Maria		32 yrs.	Lauterbach	Obd.	Oct 1853	N.-Amer	838634
Kunzmann, Anna Barbara (wife)		6 Nov 1842	Dettingen	Krch.	Feb 1887	N.-Amer	835944
Kunzmann, Anna Maria		21 Sep 1882	Dettingen	Krch.	Feb 1887	N.-Amer	835944
Kunzmann, Christian & F		15 Dec 1840	Dettingen	Krch.	Feb 1887	N.-Amer	835944
Kunzmann, Christian Friedrich		30 Aug 1873	Dettingen	Krch.	Feb 1887	N.-Amer	835944
Kunzmann, Christine Magdalena		18 Aug 1869	Dettingen	Krch.	Feb 1887	N.-Amer	835944
Kunzmann, Georg Friedrich		8 Jun 1879	Dettingen	Krch.	Feb 1887	N.-Amer	835944
Kunzmann, Johann Wilhelm		1 Jan 1872	Dettingen	Krch.	Feb 1887	N.-Amer	835944
Kunzmann, Karl		20 Sep 1876	Dettingen	Krch.	Feb 1887	N.-Amer	835944
Kunzmann, Maria Barbara		6 Oct 1870	Dettingen	Krch.	Feb 1887	N.-Amer	835944
Kunzmann, Maria Magdalena		18 Feb 1875	Dettingen	Krch.	Feb 1887	N.-Amer	835944
Kuoh, Karl Friedrich		28 Jun 1865	Kirchheim	Krch.	Jul 1882	N.-Amer	835942
Kuohn, Johannes		30 May 1841	Eningen	Rtl.	Aug 1861	N.-Amer	841054
Kuom, Christian Friedrich			Heimerdingen	Leon.	Jan 1859	Egypt	837954
Kuppinger, Gottlieb Friedrich		8 Sep 1837	Kirchheim	Krch.	Mar 1857	N.-Amer	835940
Kurfuess, Carl Friedrich & F			Friolzheim	Leon.	Jun 1851	N.-Amer	835791
Kurfuess, Eva Barbara			Wimsheim	Leon.	Jun 1851	N.-Amer	835791
Kurfuess, Sophie		3 yrs.	Friolzheim	Leon.	Jun 1851	N.-Amer	835791
Kurr, Xaver		7 Apr 1849	Westerheim	Gsl.	May 1868	N.-Amer	572046
Kurz, Anna Barbara			Reutlingen	Rtl.	Jul 1830	E.-Prs.	841051
Kurz, Anna Barbara & F		16 May 1821	Betzingen	Rtl.	bef 1865	N.-Amer	841054
Kurz, Anna Barbara (wid.) & F		27 Aug 1795	Hausen a.d. Wurm	Leon.	1853	N.-Amer	837954
Kurz, Barbara		9 Oct 1844	Betzingen	Rtl.	bef 1865	N.-Amer	841054
Kurz, Catharina		12 Oct 1823	Heimerdingen	Leon.	May 1854	N.-Amer	837954
Kurz, Christian		7 Feb 1842	Heimerdingen	Leon.	Aug 1881	N.-Amer	837954
Kurz, Christian Friedrich		17 Feb 1866	Kirchheim	Krch.	Mar 1881	N.-Amer	548403
Kurz, Conrad & F			Nabern	Krch.	May 1866	N.-Amer	835946
Kurz, Dorothea		28 Nov 1833	Heimerdingen	Leon.	Feb 1852	N.-Amer	837954
Kurz, Elisabetha Catharina		8 Aug 1843	Nabern	Krch.	May 1866	N.-Amer	835946
Kurz, Fanny		19 Jun 1843	Reutlingen	Rtl.	bef 1866	N.-Amer	841054
Kurz, Georg		15 Sep 1842	Betzingen	Rtl.	bef 1865	N.-Amer	841054
Kurz, Georg Adam		22 Sep 1827	Brucken	Krch.	Mar 1854	N.-Amer	835944
Kurz, Gottlob		17 Sep 1842	Betzingen	Rtl.	Apr 1862	N.-Amer	841054
Kurz, Jacob		9 Nov 1849	Betzingen	Rtl.	bef 1865	N.-Amer	841054
Kurz, Jacob			Betzingen	Rtl.	bef 1864	N.-Amer	841054
Kurz, Jacob Friedrich		23 May 1781	Heimsheim	Leon.	Jan 1821	France	837955
Kurz, Jakob		1 Apr 1825	Heimerdingen	Leon.	Feb 1855	N.-Amer	837954
Kurz, Johann Chr. Mich. & F			Reutlingen	Rtl.	May 1832	N.-Amer	841051
Kurz, Johann Georg		18 Oct 1835	Hausen a.d. Wurm	Leon.	1853	N.-Amer	837954
Kurz, Johann Georg		27 Dec 1838	Heimerdingen	Leon.	Aug 1881	N.-Amer	837954
Kurz, Johann Georg & F		9 Jan 1841	Betzingen	Rtl.	bef 1869	N.-Amer	841054
Kurz, Johann Georg & F		5 Apr 1815	Betzingen	Rtl.	bef 1865	N.-Amer	841054
Kurz, Johannes		19 Jun 1852	Betzingen	Rtl.	bef 1865	N.-Amer	841054
Kurz, Johannes		27 Jun 1871	Brucken	Krch.	Mar 1888	N.-Amer	835944
Kurz, Leonhard Heinrich		5 Mar 1823	Moensheim	Leon.	bef 1857	Russia	837960
Kurz, Maria		7 Jan 1835	Betzingen	Rtl.	bef 1869	N.-Amer	841054
Kurz, Maria Barbara		14 Aug 1822	Hausen a.d. Wurm	Leon.	1853	N.-Amer	837954
Kurz, Martin		24 Jan 1845	Betzingen	Rtl.	Oct 1865	N.-Amer	841054
Kurz, Martin		9 Apr 1840	Betzingen	Rtl.	Sep 1860	N.-Amer	841054
Kurz, Robert Julius		30 Nov 1846	Reutlingen	Rtl.	Apr 1864	N.-Amer	841054

Kurz, Wilhelm	30 Dec 1823	Kirchheim	Krch.	Jul 1857	N.-Amer	835940
Kurz, Wilhelm Friedrich	8 Apr 1866	Hoefingen	Leon.	Jul 1882	N.-Amer	837957
Kusterer, Carl Gottlieb	14 Jan 1838	Leonberg	Leon.	Jun 1853	N.-Amer	835786
Kusterer, Caroline (wife)	29 Jan 1829	Heimerdingen	Leon.	Aug 1853	N.-Amer	837954
Kusterer, Caroline Christiane	14 Jan 1833	Heimerdingen	Leon.	Aug 1853	N.-Amer	837954
Kusterer, Conrad & F	20 Mar 1829	Heimerdingen	Leon.	Aug 1853	N.-Amer	837954
Kusterer, Elias Johannes	13 Jan 1793	Heimerdingen	Leon.	Apr 1836	N.-Amer	837954
Kusterer, Johann Gottlob	3 Jul 1830	Heimerdingen	Leon.	bef 1854	N.-Amer	837954
Kusterer, Johannes		Leonberg	Leon.	bef 1853	N.-Amer	835786
Kusterer, Louise	10 yrs.	Leonberg	Leon.	Aug 1854	N.-Amer	835786
Kusterer, Wilhelmine Frieder.	20 Sep 1851	Heimerdingen	Leon.	Aug 1853	N.-Amer	837954
Lachenmaier, Maria Friederike	22 Jan 1832	Gerlingen	Leon.	Aug 1854	N.-Amer	837953
Lachenmann, Anna Barbara	31 Mar 1828	Reutlingen	Rtl.	bef 1866	N.-Amer	841055
Lachenmann, Barbara	19 Dec 1845	Reutlingen	Rtl.	Mar 1863	N.-Amer	841055
Lachenmann, Rosine (wife)		Reutlingen	Rtl.	Mar 1863	N.-Amer	841055
Lachenmann, Sophie	8 Mar 1861	Reutlingen	Rtl.	Mar 1863	N.-Amer	841055
Lachenmann, Wilhelm & F		Reutlingen	Rtl.	Mar 1863	N.-Amer	841055
Laderer, Christian	24 Oct 1867	Ochsenwang	Krch.	May 1888	N.-Amer	835947
Laderer, Johannes	7 Jul 1866	Ochsenwang	Krch.	May 1882	N.-Amer	548403
Laderer, Johannes	7 Jul 1866	Ochsenwang	Krch.	May 1888	N.-Amer	835947
Laechler, Anna Maria	11 Jan 1826	Muenklingen	Leon.	Aug 1851	N.-Amer	837962
Laechler, Johannes	7 Apr 1825	Rutesheim	Leon.	Mar 1850	N.-Amer	837964
Laechler, Katharina Margar.	6 Jan 1823	Muenklingen	Leon.	Aug 1851	N.-Amer	837962
Laender, David	22 Apr 1859	Flacht	Leon.	Mar 1880	N.-Amer	835790
Laengerer, Christian Gottlieb	26 Nov 1836	Leonberg	Leon.	Apr 1854	N.-Amer	835786
Laepple, Conrad Wilhelm	7 Jan 1838	Flacht	Leon.	May 1862	Prussia	835790
Laepple, Georg Friedrich		Muenklingen	Leon.	May 1869	S.-Amer	837962
Laepple, Johann Jacob	22 Apr 1819	Merklingen	Leon.	bef 1847	Frankf.	837959
Laepple, Johann Michael		Merklingen	Leon.	Feb 1852	N.-Amer	837959
Laepple, Maria Barbara		Merklingen	Leon.	Dec 1835	Hesse	837959
Laepple, Maria Catharina		Merklingen	Leon.	Aug 1845	N.-Amer	837959
Laessing, Christian Gottlieb	15 Mar 1842	Kirchheim	Krch.	Apr 1859	N.-Amer	835940
Laessing, Christiane Frieder.	27 Apr 1825	Kirchheim	Krch.	Jul 1856	N.-Amer	835940
Laessing, Johanna Wilhelmine	5 Oct 1843	Kirchheim	Krch.	Feb 1867	N.-Amer	835941
Laessing, Johannes Ludwig	15 Dec 1840	Kirchheim	Krch.	May 1857	N.-Amer	835940
Laessing, Luise	19 Sep 1837	Kirchheim	Krch.	Sep 1870	N.-Amer	835941
Lambrecht, Benedikt		Sulgen	Obd.	May 1817	N.-Amer	838638
Lambrecht, Bernhard	7 Aug 1847	Aichhalden	Obd.	Apr 1865	N.-Amer	838629
Lambrecht, Magdalena	17 yrs.	Aichhalden	Obd.	Aug 1859	N.-Amer	838629
Lambrecht, Maximilian	11 Oct 1824	Aichhalden	Obd.	Mar 1856	Austria	838629
Lamparter, Babette (wid.) & F	35 yrs	Reutlingen	Rtl.	Oct 1879	N.-Amer	841051
Lamparter, Christoph Peter		Reutlingen	Rtl.	Jan 1829	France	841051
Lamparter, Emilie	8 yrs.	Reutlingen	Rtl.	Oct 1879	N.-Amer	841051
Lamparter, Eugen	7 Apr 1847	Reutlingen	Rtl.	Aug 1866	N.-Amer	841055
Lamparter, Georg	26 May 1847	Reutlingen	Rtl.	Feb 1867	N.-Amer	841055
Lamparter, Heinrich		Reutlingen	Rtl.	May 1832	N.-Amer	841051
Lamparter, Johann Jacob		Reutlingen	Rtl.	Jun 1833	Austria	841051
Lamparter, Johanna	5 yrs.	Reutlingen	Rtl.	Oct 1879	N.-Amer	841051
Lamparter, Julie	9 yrs.	Reutlingen	Rtl.	Oct 1879	N.-Amer	841051
Lamparter, Wilhelm		Reutlingen	Rtl.	Apr 1829	France	841051

Name		Birth		Emigration			Film
Last	First	Date	Place	O'amt	Appl. Date	Dest.	Number
Lamprecht, Constantin		21 May 1849	Sulgen	Obd.	May 1869	N.-Amer	838638
Lamprecht, Joseph		7 Jan 1850	Aichhalden	Obd.	Dec 1870	N.-Amer	838629
Lamprecht, Peter Paul		37 yrs.	Sulgen	Obd.	Jul 1860	N.-Amer	838638
Lamprecht, Walburga		16 Jan 1801	Waldmoessingen	Obd.	Feb 1854	Africa	841015
Lamprecht, Wendelin		37 yrs.	Winzeln	Obd.	Mar 1850	N.-Amer	841016
Landauer, Christian		6 Aug 1849	Kirchheim	Krch.	Nov 1864	N.-Amer	835941
Landauer, Ernst		7 Jan 1835	Kirchheim	Krch.	May 1865	N.-Amer	835941
Landenberger, Johannes		17 Nov 1806	Pfullingen	Rtl.	May 1864	England	841055
Landmesser, Catharina (wife)			Muenchingen	Leon.	Mar 1852	N.-Amer	837961
Landmesser, Johannes & W			Muenchingen	Leon.	Mar 1852	N.-Amer	837961
Lang, Andreas		27 yrs.	Roetenbach	Obd.	Aug 1858	N.-Amer	838636
Lang, Anton		3 Aug 1849	Boehmenkirch	Gsl.	Mar 1868	N.-Amer	572046
Lang, Barbara		23 Jul 1842	Boehmenkirch	Gsl.	Aug 1867	N.-Amer	572046
Lang, Carl		8 May 1833	Kirchheim	Krch.	Oct 1862	Hungary	835941
Lang, Christiane Marie & C		24 Nov 1837	Leonberg	Leon.	Mar 1867	Hesse	835787
Lang, Christoph Friedrich		29 Jan 1821	Ohmden	Krch.	Jan 1855	N.-Amer	835948
Lang, Creszenz		25 Dec 1846	Boehmenkirch	Gsl.	May 1866	N.-Amer	572045
Lang, Elisabetha (wife)			Boehmenkirch	Gsl.	Mar 1852	N.-Amer	572041
Lang, Franziska		22 yrs.	Boehmenkirch	Gsl.	May 1852	N.-Amer	572041
Lang, Johannes		18 Jan 1850	Boehmenkirch	Gsl.	Sep 1870	N.-Amer	572047
Lang, Lorenz		35 yrs.	Boehmenkirch	Gsl.	Apr 1857	N.-Amer	572043
Lang, Lorenz		14 Dec 1866	Boehmenkirch	Gsl.	Jul 1883	N.-Amer	572049
Lang, Lorenz		22 Aug 1849	Boehmenkirch	Gsl.	May 1867	N.-Amer	572046
Lang, Ludwig			Hemmingen	Leon.	bef 1858	N.-Amer	837956
Lang, Michael & F			Boehmenkirch	Gsl.	Mar 1852	N.-Amer	572041
Lang, Richard Johann		17 May 1846	Boehmenkirch	Gsl.	may 1871	N.-Amer	572047
Lang, Ursula			Boehmenkirch	Gsl.	Mar 1852	N.-Amer	572041
Lang, Wilhelm		16 Nov 1842	Stockach	Rtl.	Aug 1869	France	841055
Lang, Xaver			Boehmenkirch	Gsl.	Mar 1852	N.-Amer	572041
Langbein, Adolf Tobias		18 Jun 1863	Pforzheim	Leon.	May 1880	N.-Amer	835791
Langbein, Christian		16 Sep 1832	Friolzheim	Leon.	May 1872	N.-Amer	835791
Langbein, Ferdinand & F			Friolzheim	Leon.	Aug 1852	N.-Amer	835791
Langbein, Johann Andreas		21 yrs.	Friolzheim	Leon.	Oct 1865	N.-Amer	835791
Langbein, Johann Michael		17 Oct 1837	Friolzheim	Leon.	Oct 1853	N.-Amer	835791
Langbein, Wilhelm Friedrich		8 Jul 1843	Friolzheim	Leon.	Jan 1869	N.-Amer	835791
Langenbacher, Anna		20 Jul 1846	Waldmoessingen	Obd.	Mar 1865	N.-Amer	841015
Langenbacher, Cyprian		11 yrs.	Waldmoessingen	Obd.	Jun 1861	N.-Amer	841015
Langenbacher, Franz Xaver		8 yrs.	Waldmoessingen	Obd.	Jun 1861	N.-Amer	841015
Langenbacher, Jakob		8 Jul 1829	Schramberg	Obd.	bef 1858	N.-Amer	838636
Langenbacher, Johannes			Waldmoessingen	Obd.	Apr 1862	N.-Amer	841015
Langenbacher, Josef			Mariazell	Obd.	Mar 1859	N.-Amer	838634
Langenbacher, Josef		33 yrs.	Waldmoessingen	Obd.	Sep 1858	France	841015
Langenbacher, Josefa		17 Mar 1844	Mariazell	Obd.	Jan 1868	France	838634
Langenbacher, Joseph		27 Jul 1842	Schramberg	Obd.	Feb 1864	N.-Amer	838636
Langenbacher, Joseph		16 yrs.	Waldmoessingen	Obd.	Jun 1861	N.-Amer	841015
Langenbacher, Joseph (wid.) & F			Waldmoessingen	Obd.	Jun 1861	N.-Amer	841015
Langenbacher, Matthias		20 Feb 1835	Waldmoessingen	Obd.	Feb 1854	N.-Amer	841015
Langenbacher, Viktoria		23 Dec 1813	Waldmoessingen	Obd.	Apr 1849	France	841015
Langenbacher, Wendelin		5 yrs.	Waldmoessingen	Obd.	Jun 1861	N.-Amer	841015
Lassner, Ursula			Geislingen	Gsl.	Aug 1857	Mainz	572043

Lauer, Anton & F	27 Aug 1823	Oberndorf	Obd.	May 1868	N.-Amer	838635
Lauer, Ferdinand Josef	2 Mar 1862	Oberndorf	Obd.	May 1868	N.-Amer	838635
Lauer, Gustav	21 Dec 1853	Oberndorf	Obd.	May 1868	N.-Amer	838635
Lauer, Johann Michael	6 Sep 1829	Ditzingen	Leon.	Apr 1851	N.-Amer	835788
Lauer, Johanna	2 Mar 1858	Oberndorf	Obd.	May 1868	N.-Amer	838635
Lauer, Johanna (wife)	22 Mar 1826	Oberndorf	Obd.	May 1868	N.-Amer	838635
Lauer, Maria Anna	18 Aug 1827	Oberndorf	Obd.	Oct 1845	France	838635
Lauer, Melchior		Merklingen	Leon.	bef 1816	Poland	837959
Lauer, Michael		Merklingen	Leon.	1803	Poland	837959
Lauer, Otto Carl	19 Dec 1859	Oberndorf	Obd.	May 1868	N.-Amer	838635
Lauer, Viktor	10 Jan 1868	Oberndorf	Obd.	May 1868	N.-Amer	838635
Laufer, Christiane	1 yrs.	Malmsheim	Leon.	Aug 1839	N.-Amer	837958
Laufer, Jacob		Malmsheim	Leon.	Jun 1848	N.-Amer	837958
Laufer, Johann Martin	10 yrs.	Malmsheim	Leon.	Aug 1839	N.-Amer	837958
Laufer, Johannes & F		Malmsheim	Leon.	Aug 1839	N.-Amer	837958
Laufer, Louise Frieder. (wife)		Malmsheim	Leon.	Aug 1839	N.-Amer	837958
Laufer, Louise Friederike	9 yrs.	Malmsheim	Leon.	Aug 1839	N.-Amer	837958
Laufer, Maria Catharina	6 yrs.	Malmsheim	Leon.	Aug 1839	N.-Amer	837958
Laufer, Philipp Friedrich	5 yrs.	Malmsheim	Leon.	Aug 1839	N.-Amer	837958
Laufer, Regine Magdalene	3 yrs.	Malmsheim	Leon.	Aug 1839	N.-Amer	837958
Lauffer, Bernhardt	17 Aug 1823	Winzeln	Obd.	Sep 1854	N.-Amer	841016
Lauffer, Friedrich	10 Mar 1832	Leonberg	Leon.	Apr 1852	N.-Amer	835786
Lauser, Gottlob	19 Oct 1853	Malmsheim	Leon.	Apr 1881	N.-Amer	837958
Lauser, Gottlob Friedrich	6 Apr 1867	Malmsheim	Leon.	Jul 1883	N.-Amer	837958
Lauser, Johann Georg	5 Apr 1824	Gaertringen	Herr.	bef 1858	France	834630
Lauser, Johann Jakob	3 Oct 1847	Malmsheim	Leon.	Aug 1867	N.-Amer	837958
Lautenschlaeger, Anna Barbara	27 yrs.	Flacht	Leon.	bef 1817	N.-Amer	835790
Lautenschlaeger, Anna Maria		Renningen	Leon.	Apr 1831	N.-Amer	837963
Lautenschlaeger, Christoph & F	62 yrs.	Flacht	Leon.	Sep 1817	N.-Amer	835790
Lautenschlaeger, Christoph H.	16 yrs.	Flacht	Leon.	Jan 1817	N.-Amer	835790
Lautenschlaeger, Elisab.D.wife	56 yrs.	Iptingen	Leon.	Sep 1817	N.-Amer	835790
Lautenschlaeger, Eva Dorothea	19 yrs.	Flacht	Leon.	Jan 1817	N.-Amer	835790
Lautenschlaeger, Friederika		Renningen	Leon.	Apr 1831	N.-Amer	837963
Lautenschlaeger, Georg Adam		Flacht	Leon.	bef 1855	N.-Amer	835790
Lautenschlaeger, Georg Adam	21 yrs.	Flacht	Leon.	bef 1817	N.-Amer	835790
Lautenschlaeger, Georg Jakob		Renningen	Leon.	Apr 1831	N.-Amer	837963
Lautenschlaeger, Gottlob	16 Apr 1859	Flacht	Leon.	Apr 1882	N.-Amer	835790
Lautenschlaeger, Johann Fried.		Renningen	Leon.	Apr 1831	N.-Amer	837963
Lautenschlaeger, Johann Jakob		Flacht	Leon.	bef 1817	N.-Amer	835790
Lautenschlaeger, Johannes		Malmsheim	Leon.	1839	N.-Amer	837958
Lautenschlaeger, Maria Rosina		Renningen	Leon.	Apr 1831	N.-Amer	837963
Lautenschlaeger, Martin- w.& F		Renningen	Leon.	Apr 1831	N.-Amer	837963
Lautenschlaeger, Regina Barb.		Renningen	Leon.	Apr 1831	N.-Amer	837963
Lautenschlaeger, Sara		Renningen	Leon.	Apr 1831	N.-Amer	837963
Lautenschlager, Albrecht & F		Malmsheim	Leon.	Apr 1831	N.-Amer	837958
Lautenschlager, Albrecht Fr.	17 Feb 1818	Malmsheim	Leon.	Apr 1831	N.-Amer	837958
Lautenschlager, Anna Mar. (wife)	45 yrs.	Malmsheim	Leon.	Mar 1830	N.-Amer	837958
Lautenschlager, Anna Maria	16 yrs.	Malmsheim	Leon.	Mar 1830	N.-Amer	837958
Lautenschlager, Christina Ca.		Malmsheim	Leon.	Apr 1831	N.-Amer	837958
Lautenschlager, Christina Dor.	30 Aug 1826	Malmsheim	Leon.	Apr 1831	N.-Amer	837958

Name		Birth		Emigration			Film
Last	First	Date	Place	O'amt	Appl. Date	Dest.	Number
Lautenschlager, Gottlob Fr.& F		46 yrs.	Malmsheim	Leon.	Mar 1830	N.-Amer	837958
Lautenschlager, Gottlob Fried.		19 yrs.	Malmsheim	Leon.	Mar 1830	N.-Amer	837958
Lautenschlager, Jakob Friedr.		23 Apr 1820	Malmsheim	Leon.	Apr 1831	N.-Amer	837958
Lautenschlager, Johann Georg		2 Jun 1824	Malmsheim	Leon.	Apr 1831	N.-Amer	837958
Lautenschlager, Johanna Chr.		12 yrs.	Malmsheim	Leon.	Mar 1830	N.-Amer	837958
Lautenschlager, Maria Cathar.		17 yrs.	Malmsheim	Leon.	Mar 1830	N.-Amer	837958
Lautenschlager, Maria Jud.wife			Malmsheim	Leon.	Apr 1831	N.-Amer	837958
Lautenschlager, Philipp J. & F			Malmsheim	Leon.	May 1827	Rus-Pol	837958
Lautenschlager, Philipp Jakob			Malmsheim	Leon.	bef 1822	France	837958
Lay, Jakob Friedrich		4 Apr 1834	Moensheim	Leon.	Apr 1854	N.-Amer	837960
Lebhard, Sophia Mathilde			Kuchen	Gsl.	Aug 1850	N.-Amer	577788
Lebhardt, Caroline Albertine			Kuchen	Gsl.	Feb 1853	N.-Amer	572041
Lecher, Eberhard		9 Jun 1856	Leonberg	Leon.	Mar 1860	N.-Amer	835787
Lechler, Anna Maria			Muenklingen	Leon.	Aug 1851	N.-Amer	837962
Lechler, Catharina Magdalena			Muenklingen	Leon.	Aug 1851	N.-Amer	837962
Lechler, Christian & F			Muenklingen	Leon.	Aug 1851	N.-Amer	837962
Lechler, Michael		12 Sep 1835	Muenklingen	Leon.	Aug 1851	N.-Amer	837962
Lehle, Jakob		7 Dec 1832	Altenstadt-Gsl.	Gsl.	May 1854	N.-Amer	572042
Lehle, Johann Michael		20 Apr 1846	Altenstadt-Gsl.	Gsl.	Oct 1866	N.-Amer	572045
Lehle, Johannes		27 Oct 1863	Altenstadt-Gsl.	Gsl.	Apr 1880	N.-Amer	572048
Lehle, Katharina		26 Apr 1821	Altenstadt-Gsl.	Gsl.	Apr 1854	N.-Amer	572042
Lehle, Ludwig		26 Nov 1839	Altenstadt-Gsl.	Gsl.	May 1854	N.-Amer	572042
Lehmann, Andreas		33 yrs.	Winzeln	Obd.	Oct 1847	N.-Amer	841016
Lehmann, Andreas & F		14 Oct 1814	Beffendorf	Obd.	Oct 1847	N.-Amer	841016
Lehmann, Anna Barbara (wife)		43 yrs.	Fluorn	Obd.	Nov 1846	N.-Amer	838632
Lehmann, Anna Maria		3 yrs.	Fluorn	Obd.	Nov 1846	N.-Amer	838632
Lehmann, Antonia		27 Aug 1867	Harthausen	Obd.	Nov 1869	N.-Amer	838633
Lehmann, Balbine (wife)			Offenburg/Baden	Obd.	Feb 1854	Africa	838631
Lehmann, Dorothea			Alpirsbach	Obd.	Dec 1858	France	838630
Lehmann, Franz		12 Oct 1835	Harthausen	Obd.	Sep 1853	N.-Amer	838633
Lehmann, Franz		10 Sep 1848	Winzeln	Obd.	Apr 1867	N.-Amer	841016
Lehmann, Friedrich		6 Jul 1828	Peterzell	Obd.	Aug 1848	N.-Amer	838635
Lehmann, Jakob		5 yrs.	Fluorn	Obd.	Nov 1846	N.-Amer	838632
Lehmann, Johann Friedrich		23 Sep 1857	Notzingen	Krch.	Dec 1859	Prussia	835947
Lehmann, Johann Georg		6 Jul 1832	Peterzell	Obd.	Aug 1848	N.-Amer	838635
Lehmann, Johann Jakob Wilhelm		19 yrs.	Fluorn	Obd.	Nov 1846	N.-Amer	838632
Lehmann, Johannes		16 yrs.	Fluorn	Obd.	Nov 1846	N.-Amer	838632
Lehmann, Johannes		7 Mar 1845	Winzeln	Obd.	Oct 1847	N.-Amer	841016
Lehmann, Josepha & C		26 Mar 1843	Harthausen	Obd.	Nov 1869	N.-Amer	838633
Lehmann, Matheus		7 yrs.	Fluorn	Obd.	Nov 1846	N.-Amer	838632
Lehmann, Matheus & F		26 Feb 1793	Fluorn	Obd.	Nov 1846	N.-Amer	838632
Lehmann, Mathias & W		24 Feb 1816	Alt Oberndorf	Obd.	Feb 1854	Africa	838631
Lehmann, Matthias		27 Jan 1839	Peterzell	Obd.	Sep 1865	N.-Amer	838635
Lehmann, Salome (wife)		2 Oct 1811	Beffendorf	Obd.	Oct 1847	N.-Amer	841016
Lehner, Jakob		14 Aug 1825	Ueberkingen	Gsl.	Feb 1852	N.-Amer	572041
Lehrer, Anna Maria & C			Roetenbach	Obd.	May 1860	N.-Amer	838636
Lehrer, Thomas		10 yrs.	Roetenbach	Obd.	May 1860	N.-Amer	838636
Lehrmann, Christoph		28 Jan 1834	Kuchen	Gsl.	Feb 1857	N.-Amer	572043
Leibbrand, David August Fried.		8 Jun 1854	Gerlingen	Leon.	Aug 1880	N.-Amer	837953
Leibbrand, Johann Georg		9 Mar 1855	Hemmingen	Leon.	Jul 1880	N.-Amer	837956

Leibbrand, Wilhelm	7 May 1872	Grossbottwar	Leon.	Sep 1888	N.-Amer	837956
Leibfarth, Christian	4 Feb 1851	Oberlenningen	Krch.	Mar 1868	N.-Amer	835947
Leibforth, Jakob & F	5 Apr 1833	Oberlenningen	Krch.	Jul 1866	N.-Amer	835947
Leibforth, Johann Jakob	9 Oct 1863	Oberlenningen	Krch.	Jul 1866	N.-Amer	835947
Leibforth, Maria El.Soph.wife	4 Dec 1833	Oberlenningen	Krch.	Jul 1866	N.-Amer	835947
Leibforth, Marie Sophie	29 Sep 1861	Oberlenningen	Krch.	Jul 1866	N.-Amer	835947
Leibforth, Wilhelmine Fried.	18 Sep 1865	Oberlenningen	Krch.	Jul 1866	N.-Amer	835947
Leibfriz, Christof	17 Nov 1840	Ditzingen	Leon.	Apr 1851	N.-Amer	835788
Leibfriz, Conrad	7 Sep 1834	Ditzingen	Leon.	Apr 1851	N.-Amer	835788
Leibfriz, Friedrich	25 Aug 1833	Ditzingen	Leon.	Apr 1851	N.-Amer	835788
Leibfriz, Gottlieb	1 Apr 1846	Ditzingen	Leon.	Apr 1851	N.-Amer	835788
Leibfriz, Jacob	15 Oct 1831	Ditzingen	Leon.	Apr 1851	N.-Amer	835788
Leibfriz, Jakob Fried. (wid.) & F		Ditzingen	Leon.	Apr 1851	N.-Amer	835788
Leibiger, Friederike	18 May 1827	Alpirsbach	Obd.	Feb 1864	France	838630
Leibiger, Ludwig	1 Jul 1834	Alpirsbach	Obd.	Mar 1854	N.-Amer	838630
Leibsle, Anna Barbara		Betzingen	Rtl.	May 1832	N.-Amer	841051
Leibsle, Jacob	9 Feb 1854	Betzingen	Rtl.	Jan 1869	N.-Amer	841055
Leibsle, Michael		Betzingen	Rtl.	Mar 1831	N.-Amer	841051
Leicht, David		Bissingen	Krch.	bef 1860	N.-Amer	835943
Leicht, Johann Georg	3 Oct 1849	Bissingen	Krch.	Sep 1860	N.-Amer	835943
Leichtle, Alexius	8 yrs.	Westerheim	Gsl.	May 1853	N.-Amer	572041
Leichtle, Franziska	13 yrs.	Westerheim	Gsl.	May 1853	N.-Amer	572041
Leichtle, Johann Carl	12 yrs.	Westerheim	Gsl.	May 1853	N.-Amer	572041
Leichtle, Johannes & F		Westerheim	Gsl.	May 1853	N.-Amer	572041
Leichtle, Theresia (wife)		Westerheim	Gsl.	May 1853	N.-Amer	572041
Leichtle, Wilhelm	11 yrs.	Westerheim	Gsl.	May 1853	N.-Amer	572041
Leipert, Barbara		Bronnen	Rtl.	Jan 1836	N.-Amer	841051
Leiz, Andreas		Wart	Nag.	Aug 1852	N.-Amer	838488
Leiz, Georg Adam		Wart	Nag.	Aug 1852	N.-Amer	838488
Leiz, Johannes		Wart	Nag.	Aug 1852	N.-Amer	838488
Lemperle, Philipp	26 Feb 1852	Oberndorf	Obd.	Aug 1867	N.-Amer	838635
Lemperle, Rosa	29 Aug 1827	Beffendorf	Obd.	May 1847	N.-Amer	838632
Lenz, Andreas	20 Jan 1847	Gingen	Gsl.	Jun 1854	N.-Amer	572042
Lenz, Anna Agatha	7 Apr 1839	Gingen	Gsl.	Jun 1854	N.-Amer	572042
Lenz, Barbara	9 Jul 1834	Gingen	Gsl.	Jun 1854	N.-Amer	572042
Lenz, Christoph	1 Jan 1808	Ueberkingen	Gsl.	Feb 1854	N.-Amer	572042
Lenz, Friedrich	16 Jan 1834	Ueberkingen	Gsl.	Feb 1854	N.-Amer	572042
Lenz, Georg	22 yrs.	Gingen	Gsl.	May 1853	N.-Amer	572041
Lenz, Jakob	13 Apr 1835	Ueberkingen	Gsl.	Feb 1855	N.-Amer	572043
Lenz, Johann Michael		Ueberkingen	Gsl.	Jul 1863	Bremen	572044
Lenz, Johannes	17 yrs.	Gingen	Gsl.	May 1853	N.-Amer	572041
Lenz, Louisa	20 yrs.	Geislingen	Gsl.	Apr 1862	Bremen	572044
Lenz, Lukas		Gingen	Gsl.	bef 1868	N.-Amer	572047
Lenz, Margaretha	24 Sep 1837	Gingen	Gsl.	Jun 1854	N.-Amer	572042
Lenz, Melchior	9 Jun 1840	Gingen	Gsl.	Jun 1854	N.-Amer	572042
Lenz, Melchior		Gingen	Gsl.	bef 1858	N.-Amer	573622
Lenz, Melchior (wid.) & F	20 Mar 1808	Gingen	Gsl.	Jun 1854	N.-Amer	572042
Lenz, Nikolaus	22 May 1840	Altenstadt-Gsl.	Gsl.	Feb 1859	N.-Amer	572043
Lenz, Rebekka	13 Feb 1845	Gingen	Gsl.	Jun 1854	N.-Amer	572042
Lenz, Ursula		Altenstadt-Gsl.	Gsl.	Feb 1860	N.-Amer	572044

Name		Birth		Emigration			Film
Last	First	Date	Place	O'amt	Appl. Date	Dest.	Number
Leopold, Andreas			Leonberg	Leon.	Oct 1821	France	835786
Leopold, Elisabetha (wife)			Leonberg	Leon.	Sep 1853	N.-Amer	835786
Leopold, Emilie		3 yrs.	Leonberg	Leon.	Sep 1853	N.-Amer	835786
Leopold, Friedrich Lorenz & F			Leonberg	Leon.	Sep 1853	N.-Amer	835786
Leopold, Gustav		2 yrs.	Leonberg	Leon.	Sep 1853	N.-Amer	835786
Leopold, Karl		10 Aug 1838	Leonberg	Leon.	Sep 1854	N.-Amer	835786
Leopold, Sophie Friederike		26 Jul 1827	Leonberg	Leon	Feb 1854	N.-Amer	835786
Leopold, Theodor		3 May 1859	Leonberg	Leon.	Dec 1882	Switz.	835787
Lercher, Karl Friedrich & F		9 Jan 1809	Geislingen	Gsl.	Mar 1854	N.-Amer	572042
Lesch, Friedrich			Pfullingen	Rtl.	Apr 1830	N.-Amer	841051
Lessing, Catharina Amalie		10 Aug 1835	Owen	Krch.	Mar 1861	England	835948
Letsch, Elisabetha Barnb. (wife)		31 May 1835	Undingen	Rtl.	Sep 1866	N.-Amer	841055
Letsch, Johannes		6 Oct 1864	Undingen	Rtl.	Sep 1866	N.-Amer	841055
Letsche, Christof & F		15 Jul 1838	Undingen	Rtl.	Sep 1866	N.-Amer	841055
Leuerle, Katharina Margaretha		5 Sep 1855	Aichelberg	Krch.	Feb 1878	N.-Amer	835943
Leurle, Karl		10 May 1893	Schalkstetten	Krch.	1908	N.-Amer	835943
Leuther, Friedrich		20 yrs.	Weil der Stadt	Leon.	Sep 1851	N.-Amer	837966
Leuther, Thekla			Weil der Stadt	Leon.	Oct 1854	N.-Amer	837966
Leypoldt, Albert		3 Apr 1864	Kirchheim	Krch.	Jan 1881	N.-Amer	835942
Liebermann, Severin & F			Oberndorf	Obd.	Oct 1854	N.-Amer	838635
Limberger, Adolf		16 yrs.	Reutlingen	Rtl.	Jun 1880	N.-Amer	841051
Link, Maria Katharina		2 Feb 1853	Tuebingen	Rtl.	Mar 1861	N.-Amer	841055
Link, Rosine		19 yrs.	Malmsheim	Leon.	Aug 1829	N.-Amer	837958
Linsemann, Andreas		21 Nov 1807	Epfendorf	Obd.	Aug 1817	N.-Amer	838629
Linsemann, Catharina (wife)			Epfendorf	Obd.	Aug 1817	N.-Amer	838629
Linsemann, Johannes		25 Jun 1802	Epfendorf	Obd.	Aug 1817	N.-Amer	838629
Linsemann, Lazarus		17 Dec 1805	Epfendorf	Obd.	Aug 1817	N.-Amer	838629
Linsemann, Maria		14 Aug 1815	Epfendorf	Obd.	Aug 1817	N.-Amer	838629
Linsemann, Valentin & F			Epfendorf	Obd.	Aug 1817	N.-Amer	838629
Linsenmann, Andreas		21 Nov 1807	Epfendorf	Obd.	May 1847	N.-Amer	838632
Linsenmann, Galle		15 Oct 1818	Epfendorf	Obd.	May 1847	N.-Amer	838632
Linsenmann, Johannes & F		25 Jun 1802	Epfendorf	Obd.	May 1847	N.-Amer	838632
Linsenmann, Kaspar		6 Jan 1841	Epfendorf	Obd.	May 1847	N.-Amer	838632
Linsenmann, Konrad		26 Nov 1842	Epfendorf	Obd.	May 1847	N.-Amer	838632
Linsenmann, Maria (wife)		4 Nov 1803	Seedorf	Obd.	May 1847	N.-Amer	838632
Linsenmann, Martin		9 Nov 1838	Epfendorf	Obd.	May 1847	N.-Amer	838632
Linsenmann, Mathias		17 Feb 1850	Epfendorf	Obd.	May 1866	N.-Amer	838632
Linsenmann, Valentin & F			Epfendorf	Obd.	May 1817	N.-Amer	838632
Linsenmayer, Johannes			Holzmaden	Krch.	May 1771	-	550804
Lips, Eberhardt Ulrich			Warmbronn	Leon.	Mar 1843	N.-Amer	837965
Lips, Johann Friedrich			Warmbronn	Leon.	bef 1843	N.-Amer	837965
Lips, Johann Georg & F			Warmbronn	Leon.	Mar 1843	N.-Amer	837965
Lips, Johannes			Warmbronn	Leon.	bef 1843	N.-Amer	837965
Lipss, Wilhelmine Katharine			Warmbronn	Leon.	bef 1864	N.-Amer	837965
List, Georg Friedrich			Pfullingen	Rtl.	Jul 1836	N.-Amer	841051
List, Jacob Friedrich		11 Jan 1846	Pfullingen	Rtl.	Aug 1866	N.-Amer	841055
List, Jeremias		12 Mar 1847	Pfullingen	Rtl.	May 1867	N.-Amer	841055
List, Johannes		21 Oct 1848	Unterhausen	Rtl.	Nov 1867	N.-Amer	841055
List, Ludwig			Pfullingen	Rtl.	Jul 1836	N.-Amer	841051
List, Philipp Friedrich		27 Jan 1845	Pfullingen	Rtl.	Feb 1864	England	841055

Loeffler, Albert	3 Oct 1843	Renningen	Leon.	bef 1869	Russia	837963
Loeffler, August Gottlieb	9 Feb 1877	Leonberg	Leon.	Jul 1882	N.-Amer	835787
Loeffler, Gottlob Christian	22 Jan 1875	Leonberg	Leon.	Jul 1882	N.-Amer	835787
Loeffler, Jakob		Warmbronn	Leon.	bef 1849	Basel	837965
Loeffler, Johann	17 yrs.	Ulm	Leon.	Mar 1859	N.-Amer	835786
Loeffler, Johann Georg		Gerlingen	Leon.	bef 1847	N.-Amer	837953
Loeffler, Johannes		Korntal	Leon.	May 1853	N.-Amer	837957
Loeffler, Louise (wid.) & F	4 Jun 1838	Leonberg	Leon.	Jul 1882	N.-Amer	835787
Loeffler, Louise Christiane	23 Nov 1868	Leonberg	Leon.	Jul 1882	N.-Amer	835787
Loeffler, Marie Caroline Fr.	4 Jun 1871	Leonberg	Leon.	Jul 1882	N.-Amer	835787
Loehner, Andreas	3 Jul 1813	Geislingen	Gsl.	bef 1841	Bavaria	572043
Loercher, Anna	25 May 1843	Geislingen	Gsl.	Mar 1854	N.-Amer	572042
Loercher, Anna (wife)	3 Sep 1816	Geislingen	Gsl.	Mar 1854	N.-Amer	572042
Loercher, Christiane	8 Nov 1843	Herrenberg	Herr.	Nov 1867	N.-Amer	834629
Loercher, Friedrich Karl	8 Jul 1842	Geislingen	Gsl.	Mar 1854	N.-Amer	572042
Loercher, Friedrich Karl & F	9 Jan 1809	Geislingen	Gsl.	Mar 1854	N.-Amer	572042
Loercher, Johannes	13 Nov 1844	Geislingen	Gsl.	Mar 1854	N.-Amer	572042
Loew, Anna Catharina & C	13 Aug 1842	Owen	Krch.	Jul 1868	N.-Amer	835948
Loew, Catharina		Dettingen	Krch.	bef 1866	N.-Amer	835940
Loew, Catharina	17 Sep 1829	Dettingen	Krch.	bef 1866	N.-Amer	835944
Loew, Christian Gottlieb	18 Jan 1830	Leonberg	Leon.	Feb 1852	N.-Amer	835786
Loew, Gottfried	20 Jun 1834	Leonberg	Leon.	Mar 1852	N.-Amer	835786
Loew, Jacob (wid.)	30 Jul 1810	Owen	Krch.	Nov 1861	N.-Amer	835948
Loew, Jakob	25 Aug 1837	Owen	Krch.	bef 1871	N.-Amer	835948
Loew, Jakob Friedrich & W	16 Oct 1827	Leonberg	Leon.	Jun 1877	Switz.	835787
Loew, Johann Andreas	27 Sep 1840	Owen	Krch.	Feb 1867	N.-Amer	835948
Loew, Johann Christian		Leonberg	Leon.	1817	N.-Amer	835786
Loew, Johann Georg	13 Aug 1865	Owen	Krch.	Jul 1868	N.-Amer	835948
Loew, Karl Wilhelm	26 Jun 1869	Stuttgart	Krch.	Mar 1888	N.-Amer	835944
Loew, Louise		Leonberg	Leon.	Mar 1852	N.-Amer	835786
Loew, Mathilde Joseph. (wife)	23 Feb 1834	Boeblingen	Leon.	Jun 1877	Switz.	835787
Loew, Wilhelmine		Leonberg	Leon.	Mar 1855	Switz.	835786
Lohmann, Rosa	26 Dec 1846	Oberndorf	Obd.	Apr 1869	Nuernbg	838635
Lohrmann, Friederike	6 Oct 1788	Leonberg	Leon.	bef 1832	Odessa	835786
Lohrmann, Friederike		Hoefingen	Leon.	May 1832	Russia	837957
Lohrmann, Johann Friedrich	30 Dec 1825	Ueberkingen	Gsl.	Mar 1852	N.-Amer	572041
Lohrmann, Joseph	9 Jan 1832	Kleinsuessen	Gsl.	Feb 1854	N.-Amer	572042
Lohrmann, Kaspar	2 Oct 1829	Ueberkingen	Gsl.	Mar 1852	N.-Amer	572041
Lohrmann, Michael	22 Mar 1866	Ueberkingen	Gsl.	May 1884	N.-Amer	572049
Lorch, Bernhard	30 Jun 1849	Hausen a.d.Lauchert	Rtl.	bef 1867	N.-Amer	841055
Lorch, Ernst	21 yrs.	Hausen a.d.Lauchert	Rtl.	Mar 1880	N.-Amer	841051
Lorentz, Karl Heinrich	17 Sep 1835	Leonberg	Leon.	Jun 1853	N.-Amer	835786
Lorenz, Gottlob	19 Sep 1866	Leonberg	Leon.	Jul 1880	N.-Amer	835787
Lorenz, Jakob Gottlieb	9 Dec 1864	Leonberg	Leon.	Jul 1880	N.-Amer	835787
Losch, Johann Georg	16 Jan 1849	Pfullingen	Rtl.	Nov 1868	N.-Amer	841055
Losch, Johannes	17 Feb 1846	Pfullingen	Rtl.	Oct 1866	N.-Amer	841055
Lotterer, Albert Friedrich	18 Feb 1849	Eningen	Rtl.	Aug 1869	N.-Amer	841055
Lotterer, Flora	9 mon.	Eningen	Rtl.	Sep 1865	N.-Amer	841055
Lotterer, Gottlieb Kasp. Chr.	4 yrs.	Eningen	Rtl.	Sep 1865	N.-Amer	841055
Lotterer, Kaspar Christ. & F	17 Mar 1829	Eningen	Rtl.	Sep 1865	N.-Amer	841055

Name		Birth		Emigration			Film
Last	First	Date	Place	O'amt	Appl. Date	Dest.	Number
Lotterer, Katarina Paul. (wife)		25 May 1841	Eningen	Rtl.	Sep 1865	N.-Amer	841055
Ludmann, Johann Kaspar & F		27 yrs.	Hoefingen	Leon.	Feb 1819	Russia	837957
Ludwig, Carl August			Geislingen	Gsl.	bef 1869	N.-Amer	572047
Ludwig, Christoph		17 Apr 1813	Weilheim	Krch.	Nov 1860	Rom	835949
Ludwig, Juditha & C		24 Jun 1825	Kleinengstingen	Rtl.	Mar 1861	N.-Amer	841055
Ludwig, Oscar		16 Sep 1847	Geislingen	Gsl.	Aug 1873	N.-Amer	572047
Luekart, Johann Jacob		24 Nov 1832	Brucken	Krch.	bef 1859	N.-Amer	835944
Luekart, Johannes & F		30 Jul 1824	Brucken	Krch.	Feb 1854	N.-Amer	835944
Luekart, Maria Cathar. (wife)		25 Jul 1827	Brucken	Krch.	Feb 1854	N.-Amer	835944
Luekart, Philipp Friedrich		9 Oct 1853	Brucken	Krch.	Feb 1854	N.-Amer	835944
Luik, Daniel		22 Jun 1825	Aichelberg	Krch.	Aug 1855	N.-Amer	835774
Luikart, Gottlieb August		12 Oct 1852	Unterlenningen	Krch.	Mar 1870	N.-Amer	835949
Luikart, Maria Caroline		31 Jan 1846	Unterlenningen	Krch.	Mar 1870	N.-Amer	835949
Luikhardt, Wilhelm Christian		10 Oct 1867	Neidlingen	Krch.	May 1882	N.-Amer	835946
Luipold, Gottlieb		12 Dec 1836	Pfullingen	Rtl.	Mar 1864	England	841055
Lumpp, Anna Maria			Ohmenhausen	Rtl.	May 1831	N.-Amer	841051
Lumpp, Friederike		24 Apr 1845	Ohmenhausen	Rtl.	Apr 1866	N.-Amer	841055
Lumpp, Ludwig		30 Nov 1838	Ohmenhausen	Rtl.	Sep 1865	N.-Amer	841055
Luppold, Anna		25 Mar 1850	Fluorn	Obd.	Aug 1868	N.-Amer	838632
Luppold, Katharina		19 Sep 1846	Fluorn	Obd.	Aug 1868	N.-Amer	838632
Luppold, Matthias		6 Aug 1847	Fluorn	Obd.	Sep 1867	N.-Amer	838632
Lus, Eleonora		20 Feb 1846	Epfendorf	Obd.	Mar 1867	Austria	838632
Lus, Wendelin		27 Oct 1847	Epfendorf	Obd.	Apr 1867	N.-Amer	838632
Lutz, Anna Maria			Ueberberg	Nag.	1846	N.-Amer	838488
Lutz, Anna Maria		1 May 1824	Ueberberg	Nag.	1843	N.-Amer	838488
Lutz, Christian		18 Feb 1878	Zell	Krch.	Mar 1894	N.-Amer	835774
Lutz, Christoph Friedrich		17 Jan 1821	Heimsheim	Leon.	Apr 1870	N.-Amer	837955
Lutz, Elisabetha Barbara & C		21 Mar 1840	Oberjesingen	Herr.	May 1868	N.-Amer	834630
Lutz, Georg		28 Sep 1848	Pfullingen	Rtl.	Sep 1865	N.-Amer	841055
Lutz, Georg		11 Aug 1847	Lindorf	Krch.	Apr 1861	N.-Amer	835946
Lutz, Jacob		30 Jul 1856	Gebersheim	Leon.	Jul 1873	N.-Amer	837953
Lutz, Johann			Weil der Stadt	Leon.	Mar 1858	N.-Amer	837966
Lutz, Johann Balthas		2 Aug 1842	Oberjesingen	Herr.	May 1868	N.-Amer	834630
Lutz, Johann Georg			Heimsheim	Leon.	bef 1870	N.-Amer	837955
Lutz, Johann Georg		20 Jan 1826	Ueberberg	Nag.	1843	N.-Amer	838488
Lutz, Johann Jacob			Ueberberg	Nag.	1838	N.-Amer	838488
Lutz, Johannes		11 Dec 1863	Oberjesingen	Herr.	May 1868	N.-Amer	834630
Lutz, Johannes		7 Sep 1849	Gaertringen	Herr.	Jun 1867	N.-Amer	834630
Lutz, Johannes		21 Nov 1852	Lindorf	Krch.	May 1867	N.-Amer	835946
Lutz, Kunigunda		22 Apr 1828	Ueberberg	Nag.	1843	N.-Amer	838488
Lutz, Maria Catharina		24 Dec 1865	Oberjesingen	Herr.	May 1868	N.-Amer	834630
Lutz, Philipp		10 Sep 1842	Lindorf	Krch.	Aug 1857	N.-Amer	835946
Luz, Anna Maria		22 yrs.	Ditzingen	Leon.	May 1817	Russia	835788
Luz, Johann Gottlieb		18 Feb 1849	Gomaringen	Rtl.	Aug 1867	N.-Amer	841055
Luz, Johannes & F			Ditzingen	Leon.	Feb 1827	N.-Amer	835788
Luz, Joseph			Gomaringen	Rtl.	Feb 1867	N.-Amer	841055
Luz, Katharina		29 yrs.	Gomaringen	Rtl.	May 1832	N.-Amer	841051
Luz, Konrad		3 Jan 1852	Gomaringen	Rtl.	May 1869	N.-Amer	841055
Mack, Maria Katharina		20 Mar 1820	Bissingen	Krch.	bef 1884	N.-Amer	835943
Mader, Adolf		7 Nov 1849	Kirchheim	Krch.	Jul 1865	N.-Amer	835941

Mader, Caroline Luise	5 Sep 1843	Pfullingen	Rtl.	Dec 1862	N.-Amer	841055
Mader, Jacob Friedrich		Pfullingen	Rtl.	Jul 1836	N.-Amer	841051
Mader, Johann Georg	9 Dec 1839	Pfullingen	Rtl.	Dec 1862	N.-Amer	841055
Mader, Johann Georg & F	3 Mar 1810	Pfullingen	Rtl.	Dec 1862	N.-Amer	841055
Mader, Katharina Barbara	27 Apr 1835	Pfullingen	Rtl.	Dec 1862	N.-Amer	841055
Mader, Louise Friderike	6 Dec 1832	Kirchheim	Krch.	Jan 1870	N.-Amer	835941
Mader, Maria Barbara (wife)	27 Nov 1814	Goenningen	Rtl.	Dec 1862	N.-Amer	841055
Mader, Maria Mathilde	11 Jan 1834	Pfullingen	Rtl.	Dec 1862	N.-Amer	841055
Maeckle, Johannes	24 yrs.	Geislingen	Gsl.	May 1852	N.-Amer	572041
Maeckle, Stephan		Geislingen	Gsl.	Sep 1852	N.-Amer	572041
Maenner, Johann Michael	18 Dec 1832	Bissingen	Krch.	Feb 1855	N.-Amer	835943
Maentele, Ludwig	29 Aug 1847	Aichhalden	Obd.	May 1865	N.-Amer	838629
Maerdter, Anna	28 Apr 1836	Grosssuessen	Gsl.	Sep 1854	N.-Amer	572042
Maerz, Johannes	23 Nov 1834	Neidlingen	Krch.	Feb 1860	N.-Amer	835946
Maestling, Regina	4 Nov 1847	Bondorf	Herr.	Feb 1869	Hesse	834630
Maeugele, Christian Wilhelm		Leonberg	Leon.	Feb 1817	N.-Amer	835785
Maeule, Carl Gottlob	6 Aug 1858	Weil im Dorf	Loen.	Sep 1874	N.-Amer	837967
Maeule, Johann Christian	27 Sep 1826	Weil im Dorf	Loen.	Nov 1871	N.-Amer	837967
Maeule, Joseph	25 Jul 1835	Weil im Dorf	Loen.	Jan 1854	N.-Amer	837967
Maeulen, Adolph	1 Apr 1849	Heimerdingen	Leon.	May 1867	N.-Amer	837954
Maeulen, Albert Friedrich	30 Jun 1851	Heimerdingen	Leon.	Nov 1872	N.-Amer	837954
Maeulen, Paul Heinrich	28 Oct 1855	Heimerdingen	Leon.	Feb 1871	N.-Amer	837954
Mahle, Christian August	12 Nov 1866	Kirchheim	Krch.	Oct 1882	N.-Amer	548403
Mahler, Johannes	24 yrs.	Boehmenkirch	Gsl.	Aug 1854	N.-Amer	572042
Mahler, Joseph	25 Jan 1827	Boehmenkirch	Gsl.	Feb 1854	N.-Amer	572042
Maibauer, Christian Ernst	30 Apr 1864	Oetlingen	Krch.	Mar 1881	N.-Amer	548403
Maibauer, Hermann Immanuel	9 Apr 1862	Oetlingen	Krch.	Aug 1878	N.-Amer	835948
Maibauer, Imanuel	9 Apr 1862	Oetlingen	Krch.	Aug 1878	N.-Amer	548403
Maibauer, Robert David	12 Oct 1865	Oetlingen	Krch.	Mar 1882	N.-Amer	548403
Maienknecht, Michael & F	46 yrs.	Moensheim	Leon.	Apr 1818	Hungary	837960
Maier, Albert Christian Wilh.	16 Oct 1867	Kirchheim	Krch.	Apr 1884	N.-Amer	835942
Maier, Andreas	23 Jun 1832	Moensheim	Leon.	Oct 1852	N.-Amer	837960
Maier, Andreas	27 Nov 1873	Oberlenningen	Krch.	1881	N.-Amer	548403
Maier, Andreas	27 Nov 1871	Oberlenningen	Krch.	1881	N.-Amer	835947
Maier, Andreas & F	15 Feb 1842	Oberlenningen	Krch.	1881	N.-Amer	835947
Maier, Anna Maria (wife)	3 Jun 1841	Willmandingen	Rtl.	Oct 1865	N.-Amer	841055
Maier, Anna Maria Katharina	9 Feb 1869	Oberlenningen	Krch.	1881	N.-Amer	548403
Maier, August	15 yrs.	Reutlingen	Rtl.	Apr 1834	N.-Amer	841051
Maier, August Friedrich	16 Aug 1867	Kirchheim	Krch.	Aug 1884	N.-Amer	548403
Maier, Barbara		Merklingen	Leon.	1859	N.-Amer	837959
Maier, Carl	27 Aug 1847	Kirchheim	Krch.	1865	N.-Amer	835941
Maier, Carl	20 Jun 1854	Kirchheim	Krch.	May 1882	N.-Amer	548403
Maier, Carl Albert	18 Feb 1841	Leonberg	Leon	Mar 1860	N.-Amer	835786
Maier, Caroline	11 May 1846	Owen	Krch.	Feb 1869	N.-Amer	835948
Maier, Catharina	15 Mar 1852	Bissingen	Krch.	Oct 1865	N.-Amer	835943
Maier, Catharina Barbara	4 Jun 1860	Gueltstein	Herr.	Sep 1867	N.-Amer	834631
Maier, Christian	17 Nov 1848	Kirchheim	Krch.	Jul 1866	N.-Amer	835941
Maier, Christian	18 Mar 1870	Oberlenningen	Krch.	1881	N.-Amer	548403
Maier, Christian Adolf	16 May 1836	Kirchheim	Krch.	Sep 1870	N.-Amer	835941
Maier, Christian Friedrich	15 Apr 1822	Kirchheim	Krch.	Aug 1860	N.-Amer	835940

Name		Birth		Emigration			Film
Last	First	Date	Place	O'amt	Appl. Date	Dest.	Number
Maier, Christian Gottlieb		30 Dec 1862	Kirchheim	Krch.	Feb 1882	N.-Amer	548403
Maier, Christian Heinrich		9 Jul 1852	Kirchheim	Krch.	bef 1880	Switz.	835942
Maier, Christian Jacob		7 Apr 1867	Zell	Krch.	1884	N.-Amer	548403
Maier, Christiana		9 Oct 1850	Owen	Krch.	Feb 1869	N.-Amer	835948
Maier, Christina			Merklingen	Leon.	1856	N.-Amer	837959
Maier, Christine (wife)			Moessingen	Rtl.	Jul 1869	N.-Amer	841055
Maier, Christoph Conrad		30 May 1873	Oberlenningen	Krch.	1881	N.-Amer	835947
Maier, Christoph Friedrich		10 May 1815	Kirchheim	Krch.	bef 1865	A-dam	835941
Maier, Conrad & F			Dusslingen	Rtl.	Jul 1869	N.-Amer	841055
Maier, Elisabeth Cathar. (wife)		28 Nov 1832	Oberlenningen	Krch.	Mar 1858	N.-Amer	835947
Maier, Emilie Heinrike		12 May 1884	Zell	Krch.	Apr 1886	N.-Amer	548403
Maier, Ernst Gottlieb		4 Jan 1859	Muenklingen	Leon.	Jun 1881	N.-Amer	837962
Maier, Friedrich		13 yrs.	Reutlingen	Rtl.	Apr 1834	N.-Amer	841051
Maier, Friedrich		13 Nov 1850	Notzingen	Krch.	Nov 1870	N.-Amer	835947
Maier, Georg Michael			Malmsheim	Leon.	bef 1826	N.-Amer	837958
Maier, Gottfried Heinrich		27 May 1829	Dettingen	Krch.	bef 1867	N.-Amer	835940
Maier, Gottlieb		30 yrs.	Flacht	Leon.	May 1854	N.-Amer	835790
Maier, Gottlieb		9 yrs.	Reutlingen	Rtl.	Apr 1834	N.-Amer	841051
Maier, Gottlob		2 Apr 1846	Malmsheim	Leon.	May 1852	N.-Amer	837958
Maier, Gottlob		23 Jan 1844	Reutlingen	Rtl.	Mar 1863	N.-Amer	841055
Maier, Gottlob Conrad & W		17 Jan 1829	Oberlenningen	Krch.	Mar 1858	N.-Amer	835947
Maier, Gottlob Friedrich			Merklingen	Leon.	Aug 1871	N.-Amer	837959
Maier, Gustav Friedrich		13 Feb 1878	Zell	Krch.	Apr 1886	N.-Amer	548403
Maier, Jacob & F		3 Aug 1826	Zell	Krch.	Apr 1886	N.-Amer	548403
Maier, Jacob Friedrich		4 Jul 1843	Malmsheim	Leon.	May 1852	N.-Amer	837958
Maier, Jakob Friedrich		5 Apr 1806	Herrenberg	Herr.	Sep 1862	N.-Amer	834629
Maier, Jakob Friedrich			Merklingen	Leon.	Apr 1853	N.-Amer	837959
Maier, Jakob Friedrich		13 Jan 1853	Kirchheim	Krch.	1871	N.-Amer	835942
Maier, Johann Andreas		24 Feb 1846	Kirchheim	Krch.	Mar 1862	N.-Amer	835941
Maier, Johann Christoph		4 Aug 1839	Malmsheim	Leon.	May 1852	N.-Amer	837958
Maier, Johann Daniel		3 Oct 1845	Bissingen	Krch.	Oct 1867	N.-Amer	835943
Maier, Johann David		10 Dec 1842	Owen	Krch.	Feb 1869	N.-Amer	835948
Maier, Johann Friedrich		29 Jan 1873	Brucken	Krch.	Sep 1887	N.-Amer	835944
Maier, Johann Friedrich & W		4 Jul 1831	Bissingen	Krch.	Mar 1866	N.-Amer	835943
Maier, Johann Georg		27 Oct 1847	Merklingen	Leon.	Mar 1862	N.-Amer	837959
Maier, Johann Georg		24 yrs.	Geislingen	Gsl.	Jul 1850	N.-Amer	577788
Maier, Johann Georg		22 yrs.	Deggingen	Gsl.	Feb 1855	N.-Amer	572043
Maier, Johann Georg		30 Apr 1851	Aufhausen	Gsl.	Feb 1870	N.-Amer	572047
Maier, Johann Georg		24 Oct 1864	Moessingen	Rtl.	Jul 1869	N.-Amer	841055
Maier, Johann Georg		1 Feb 1886	Zell	Krch.	Apr 1886	N.-Amer	548403
Maier, Johann Georg		22 Sep 1818	Brucken	Krch.	Jun 1866	N.-Amer	835944
Maier, Johann Georg		22 Jul 1844	Owen	Krch.	Sep 1863	N.-Amer	835948
Maier, Johann Georg & F			Malmsheim	Leon.	Mar 1817	N.-Amer	837958
Maier, Johann Georg & F			Reutlingen	Rtl.	Apr 1834	N.-Amer	841051
Maier, Johann Gottfried		19 Nov 1827	Dettingen	Krch.	bef 1867	N.-Amer	835940
Maier, Johann Gottlob		12 Jan 1871	Zell	Krch.	Apr 1886	N.-Amer	548403
Maier, Johann Jacob		23 Feb 1856	Gueltstein	Herr.	Sep 1867	N.-Amer	834631
Maier, Johann Jacob		11 Dec 1839	Malmsheim	Leon.	Aug 1869	N.-Amer	837958
Maier, Johann Michael			Ohmenhausen	Rtl.	May 1832	N.-Amer	841051
Maier, Johanna		2 Apr 1872	Zell	Krch.	Apr 1886	N.-Amer	548403

Name	Date	Place	Region	Date2	Destination	Number
Maier, Johanna (wife)	5 Aug 1840	Oberlenningen	Krch.	1881	N.-Amer	835947
Maier, Johanne Christ. (wife)	2 Jan 1843	Zell	Krch.	Apr 1886	N.-Amer	548403
Maier, Johannes	14 Feb 1851	Bach-Altenberg	Obd.	Feb 1868	N.-Amer	838631
Maier, Johannes	2 Oct 1854	Gueltstein	Herr.	Sep 1867	N.-Amer	834631
Maier, Johannes		Hemmingen	Leon.	Jun 1854	N.-Amer	837956
Maier, Johannes	14 Sep 1848	Malmsheim	Leon.	May 1852	N.-Amer	837958
Maier, Johannes	19 Oct 1849	Eningen	Rtl.	Jun 1865	N.-Amer	841055
Maier, Johannes	12 Oct 1840	Kirchheim	Krch.	Jul 1871	N.-Amer	835942
Maier, Johannes	5 Aug 1845	Oetlingen	Krch.	jun 1864	N.-Amer	835948
Maier, Johannes	17 Aug 1830	Bissingen	Krch.	bef 1863	N.-Amer	835943
Maier, Johannes & F	20 Jan 1822	Moenchberg	Herr.	Sep 1867	N.-Amer	834631
Maier, Johannes (wid.) & F	10 Nov 1788	Bissingen	Krch.	Oct 1865	N.-Amer	835943
Maier, Joseph	17 Jan 1821	Muenklingen	Leon.	Feb 1883	N.-Amer	837962
Maier, Joseph	13 Apr 1857	Muenklingen	Leon.	Oct 1880	N.-Amer	837962
Maier, Joseph		Reichenbach	Gsl.	Nov 1867	N.-Amer	572046
Maier, Julius	29 Jun 1837	Kirchheim	Krch.	Aug 1856	N.-Amer	835940
Maier, Justine	13 Feb 1859	Gueltstein	Herr.	Sep 1867	N.-Amer	834631
Maier, Karl	6 Apr 1860	Bitz/Bal.	Krch.	bef 1889	N.-Amer	835942
Maier, Karl August	3 Aug 1848	Kirchheim	Krch.	Sep 1867	N.-Amer	835941
Maier, Karl Friedrich	21 Feb 1867	Muenklingen	Leon.	Mar 1882	N.-Amer	837962
Maier, Katharina	30 Aug 1841	Malmsheim	Leon.	May 1852	N.-Amer	837958
Maier, Katharina (wife)	17 Jan 1812	Malmsheim	Leon.	May 1852	N.-Amer	837958
Maier, Luise Pauline	30 Apr 1880	Oberlenningen	Krch.	1881	N.-Amer	835947
Maier, Magdalena	19 Feb 1821	Ueberkingen	Gsl.	Feb 1855	N.-Amer	572043
Maier, Magdalena (wife)	22 Apr 1832	Bissingen	Krch.	Mar 1866	N.-Amer	835943
Maier, Margaretha	27 May 1832	Deggingen	Gsl.	Feb 1857	N.-Amer	572043
Maier, Maria	8 Jan 1829	Altenstadt-Gsl.	Gsl.	Mar 1854	N.-Amer	572042
Maier, Maria	28 Oct 1830	Oetlingen	Krch.	bef 1864	N.-Amer	835948
Maier, Maria & C	25 Oct 1844	Merklingen	Leon.	Jun 1868	N.-Amer	837959
Maier, Maria Agnes (wife)	14 Apr 1823	Gueltstein	Herr.	Sep 1867	N.-Amer	834631
Maier, Maria Dorothea		Dettingen	Krch.	bef 1867	N.-Amer	835940
Maier, Maria Regina	11 Aug 1867	Merklingen	Leon.	1869	N.-Amer	837959
Maier, Maria Sofia Barbara	18 Apr 1868	Gingen	Gsl.	Oct 1873	N.-Amer	572047
Maier, Mariana		Donzdorf	Gsl.	Mar 1852	N.-Amer	572041
Maier, Mathaeus & F	20 Jul 1810	Malmsheim	Leon.	May 1852	N.-Amer	837958
Maier, Matthaeus	30 Jun 1850	Merklingen	Leon.	Jun 1868	N.-Amer	837959
Maier, Michael	12 Jul 1835	Grosssuessen	Gsl.	Mar 1854	N.-Amer	572042
Maier, Michael & F		Lauterbach	Obd.	Apr 1817	N.-Amer	838634
Maier, Otto	3 Nov 1865	Boettingen/Muens.	Krch.	Oct 1880	N.-Amer	548403
Maier, Otto	3 Nov 1865	Kirchheim	Krch.	Oct 1880	N.-Amer	835942
Maier, Otto Eugen	27 Jan 1883	Zell	Krch.	Apr 1886	N.-Amer	548403
Maier, Otto Karl August	11 Feb 1839	Kirchheim	Krch.	Nov 1859	N.-Amer	835940
Maier, Paul	21 Feb 1847	Reutlingen	Rtl.	Jul 1867	N.-Amer	841055
Maier, Regina	8 Jun 1836	Bissingen	Krch.	bef 1863	N.-Amer	835943
Maier, Rosine	23 Feb 1827	Kirchheim	Krch.	Aug 1857	N.-Amer	835940
Maier, Rosine Katharine	26 Jul 1837	Moensheim	Leon.	Oct 1852	N.-Amer	837960
Maier, Simon	21 Aug 1862	Gingen	Gsl.	Oct 1873	N.-Amer	572047
Maier, Sophia	10 Jan 1834	Altenstadt-Gsl.	Gsl.	Sep 1854	N.-Amer	572042
Maier, Stanislaus		Seedorf	Obd.	May 1862	France	838637
Maier, Theresia	15 Nov 1842	Wiesensteig	Gsl.	Nov 1867	N.-Amer	572046

Name		Birth		Emigration			Film
Last	First	Date	Place	O'amt	Appl. Date	Dest.	Number
Maier, Wilhelm		14 Apr 1872	Merklingen	Leon.	Dec 1888	N.-Amer	837959
Maier, Wilhelm		20 Sep 1864	Muenklingen	Leon.	Mar 1882	N.-Amer	837962
Maier, Wilhelm		6 yrs.	Reutlingen	Rtl.	Apr 1834	N.-Amer	841051
Maier, Wilhelm		26 May 1866	Kirchheim	Krch.	May 1882	N.-Amer	548403
Maier, Wilhelm		23 Dec 1871	Oetlingen	Krch.	Oct 1884	N.-Amer	835948
Maier, Wilhelm Gottlob		18 Apr 1855	Kirchheim	Krch.	1871	N.-Amer	835942
Maisch, Anna Barbara		18 yrs.	Hausen a.d. Wurm	Leon.	Feb 1817	Russia	837954
Maisch, Anna Elisabethe		9 Oct 1878	Renningen	Leon.	May 1880	N.-Amer	837963
Maisch, Anna Regina (wid.) & F		63 yrs.	Gerlingen	Leon.	May 1873	Hamburg	837953
Maisch, Barbara (wife)		46 yrs.	Hausen a.d. Wurm	Leon.	Feb 1817	Russia	837954
Maisch, Christian Gottlob		22 Oct 1841	Renningen	Leon.	Sep 1860	N.-Amer	837963
Maisch, Christina Katharina		20 Dec 1847	Renningen	Leon.	May 1880	N.-Amer	837963
Maisch, Christof		61 yrs.	Ditzingen	Leon.	Aug 1853	N.-Amer	835788
Maisch, Christoph			Gerlingen	Leon.	1804	Russia	837953
Maisch, Elisabeth			Gerlingen	Leon.	Mar 1847	Austria	837953
Maisch, Georg Gottlob		28 Feb 1846	Gerlingen	Leon.	May 1873	Hamburg	837953
Maisch, Georg Jacob		19 Apr 1871	Renningen	Leon.	May 1880	N.-Amer	837963
Maisch, Jakob Friedrich & F		10 Jul 1844	Renningen	Leon.	May 1880	N.-Amer	837963
Maisch, Johann Georg		15 yrs.	Hausen a.d. Wurm	Leon.	Feb 1817	Russia	837954
Maisch, Johann Georg			Gerlingen	Leon.	Apr 1831	N.-Amer	837953
Maisch, Johann Georg		17 yrs.	Gerlingen	Leon.	1827	Hungary	837953
Maisch, Johann Georg & F		51 yrs.	Hausen a.d. Wurm	Leon.	Feb 1817	Russia	837954
Maisch, Johannes		3 yrs.	Gerlingen	Leon.	Apr 1857	N.-Amer	837953
Maisch, Karl August		18 Jan 1876	Renningen	Leon.	May 1880	N.-Amer	837963
Maisch, Marie Luisa		3 Nov 1849	Gerlingen	Leon.	May 1873	Hamburg	837953
Maisch, Rosina Barbara		6 Jun 1838	Renningen	Leon.	Aug 1857	N.-Amer	837963
Maisch, Rosina Dorothea		20 Jan 1826	Renningen	Leon.	Jul 1854	N.-Amer	837963
Maizmann. Barbara		6 Dec 1815	Grosssuessen	Gsl.	Feb 1854	N.-Amer	572042
Mall, Christoph		15 May 1845	Gutenberg	Krch.	May 1865	N.-Amer	835945
Mammel, Hermann		21 Aug 1829	Malmsheim	Leon.	Jul 1849	N.-Amer	837958
Mammele, August Friedrich		8 Nov 1819	Kirchheim	Krch.	Aug 1859	N.-Amer	835940
Mammele, Catharina Frid. (wife)		19 Sep 1821	Kirchheim	Krch.	bef 1869	N.-Amer	835941
Mammele, Jacob & W		19 Nov 1820	Kirchheim	Krch.	Dec 1869	N.-Amer	835941
Mammele, Rosine Louise			Kirchheim	Krch.	bef 1869	N.-Amer	835941
Mandel, Christine Catharine		2 Apr 1839	Reutlingen	Rtl.	Nov 1864	Saxony	841055
Mandel, Gottlieb		7 Nov 1845	Eltingen	Leon.	Sep 1865	N.-Amer	835789
Mangold, Katharina & C		28 yrs.	Hepsisau	Krch.	Jun 1853	N.-Amer	835945
Mann, Andreas		20 yrs.	Hirschlanden	Leon.	Apr 1851	N.-Amer	837956
Mann, Andreas & F			Schoeckingen	Leon.	Mar 1833	Rus-Pol	837964
Mann, Anna		16 Jun 1823	Muenchingen	Leon.	May 1855	N.-Amer	837961
Mann, Anna Margaretha		28 yrs.	Hirschlanden	Leon.	Jun 1853	N.-Amer	837956
Mann, Anna Margaretha		5 yrs.	Hirschlanden	Leon.	May 1834	Rus-Pol	837956
Mann, Anna Maria		31 May 1839	Muenchingen	Leon.	1857	N.-Amer	837961
Mann, Anna Maria			Hirschlanden	Leon.	Jul 1853	N.-Amer	837956
Mann, Anna Maria		24 yrs.	Hirschlanden	Leon.	Jun 1853	N.-Amer	837956
Mann, Anna Maria (wid.) & F		49 yrs.	Hirschlanden	Leon.	Jul 1853	N.-Amer	837956
Mann, Anna Maria (wife)			Hirschlanden	Leon.	Jun 1853	N.-Amer	837956
Mann, Christian		16 yrs.	Flacht	Leon.	Mar 1830	N.-Amer	835790
Mann, Christian		11 Dec 1831	Hirschlanden	Leon.	Mar 1852	N.-Amer	837956
Mann, Christine Marg. (wife)			Schoeckingen	Leon.	Mar 1833	Rus-Pol	837964

Mann, Christoph Ada	18 yrs.	Flacht	Leon.	Jan 1854	N.-Amer	835790
Mann, Friedrich	3 Mar 1850	Muenchingen	Leon.	May 1855	N.-Amer	837961
Mann, Friedrich	2 Oct 1838	Hirschlanden	Leon.	Apr 1855	N.-Amer	837956
Mann, Gottliebin	13 yrs.	Hirschlanden	Leon.	Jun 1853	N.-Amer	837956
Mann, Jakob Friedrich	23 yrs.	Flacht	Leon.	Jan 1854	N.-Amer	835790
Mann, Jakob Friedrich		Flacht	Leon.	bef 1857	N.-Amer	835790
Mann, Johann	17 Apr 1803	Weilheim	Krch.	1843	N.-Amer	835950
Mann, Johann Georg	15 May 1835	Muenchingen	Leon.	May 1855	N.-Amer	837961
Mann, Johann Georg	2 yrs.	Hirschlanden	Leon.	May 1834	Rus-Pol	837956
Mann, Johann Georg & F	40 yrs.	Hirschlanden	Leon.	May 1834	Rus-Pol	837956
Mann, Johann Jakob	16 Jun 1837	Muenchingen	Leon.	May 1855	N.-Amer	837961
Mann, Johann Jakob		Ditzingen	Leon.	bef 1859	N.-Amer	835788
Mann, Johann Jakob		Hirschlanden	Leon.	Jul 1853	N.-Amer	837956
Mann, Johann Jakob & W		Flacht	Leon.	Mar 1830	N.-Amer	835790
Mann, Johann Konrad		Schoeckingen	Leon.	Mar 1833	Rus-Pol	837964
Mann, Johann Konrad	14 yrs.	Hirschlanden	Leon.	Jun 1853	N.-Amer	837956
Mann, Johann Konrad	14 yrs.	Hirschlanden	Leon.	May 1834	Rus-Pol	837956
Mann, Johann Michael	19 Jun 1831	Muenchingen	Leon.	May 1855	N.-Amer	837961
Mann, Johannes	11 Jun 1880	Zell	Krch.	bef 1898	N.-Amer	835774
Mann, Johannes	29 yrs.	Hirschlanden	Leon.	Jun 1853	N.-Amer	837956
Mann, Johannes	19 yrs.	Hirschlanden	Leon.	Mar 1853	N.-Amer	837956
Mann, Johannes & F		Hirschlanden	Leon.	Jun 1853	N.-Amer	837956
Mann, Katharine	17 yrs.	Hirschlanden	Leon.	Jun 1853	N.-Amer	837956
Mann, Konrad	36 yrs.	Hirschlanden	Leon.	Jan 1852	N.-Amer	837956
Mann, Kristina	6 yrs.	Hirschlanden	Leon.	May 1834	Rus-Pol	837956
Mann, Magdalena & C	8 Jan 1819	Muenchingen	Leon.	May 1855	N.-Amer	837961
Mann, Margaretha Catharina	10 yrs.	Hirschlanden	Leon.	May 1834	Rus-Pol	837956
Mann, Maria Barbara	16 yrs.	Hirschlanden	Leon.	Jun 1853	N.-Amer	837956
Mann, Maria Barbara (wife)		Flacht	Leon.	Mar 1830	N.-Amer	835790
Mann, Maria Magdalena	11 yrs.	Hirschlanden	Leon.	May 1834	Rus-Pol	837956
Mann, Maria Magdalena (wife)	35 yrs.	Hirschlanden	Leon.	May 1834	Rus-Pol	837956
Mann, Philipp Friedrich	36 yrs.	Flacht	Leon.	Sep 1820	France	835790
Mann, Regina Katharina	15 yrs.	Hirschlanden	Leon.	May 1834	Rus-Pol	837956
Mann, Regine	19 yrs.	Hirschlanden	Leon.	Jun 1853	N.-Amer	837956
Mann, Ulrich	51 yrs.	Muehlhausen	Gsl.	May 1852	N.-Amer	572041
Mannal, Barbara	13 yrs.	Hemmingen	Leon.	Apr 1833	Rus-Pol	837956
Mannal, Christina Margretha	10 yrs.	Hemmingen	Leon.	Apr 1833	Rus-Pol	837956
Mannal, Dorothea (wife)		Hemmingen	Leon.	Apr 1833	Rus-Pol	837956
Mannal, Johann Georg	14 yrs.	Hemmingen	Leon.	Apr 1833	Rus-Pol	837956
Mannal, Wilhelm	7 yrs.	Hemmingen	Leon.	Apr 1833	Rus-Pol	837956
Mannal, johann Georg & F	42 yrs.	Hemmingen	Leon.	Apr 1833	Rus-Pol	837956
Mantel, Ferdinand	32 yrs.	Schramberg	Obd.	Jun 1852	Switz.	838637
Mantel, Johann Baptist		Schramberg	Obd.	Jan 1854	Austria	838636
Mantel, Monika		Schramberg	Obd.	May 1817	A.-Amer	838637
Mantel, Severin		Schramberg	Obd.	Jun 1852	Switz.	838637
Manz, Andreas		Fluorn	Obd.	bef 1843	Austria	838632
Manz, Barbara	23 Oct 1842	Fluorn	Obd.	Sep 1868	France	838632
Marci, Magdalena	18 Aug 1834	Grosssuessen	Gsl.	Feb 1854	N.-Amer	572042
Marey, Georg	12 Apr 1834	Steinenkirch	Gsl.	Mar 1854	N.-Amer	572042
Marschall, Johannes	19 yrs.	Weil im Dorf	Loen.	Apr 1847	N.-Amer	837967

| Name | | Birth | | Emigration | | | Film |
Last	First	Date	Place	O'amt	Appl. Date	Dest.	Number
Marte, Augusta			Aichhalden	Obd.	Sep 1850	N.-Amer	838629
Marte, Paul		23 yrs.	Aichhalden	Obd.	Jun 1860	N.-Amer	838629
Martenitz, Christian		2 Mar 1850	Oberhausen	Rtl.	Jun 1866	N.-Amer	841055
Martin, Christian			Reichenbach	Gsl.	Feb 1853	N.-Amer	572041
Martin, Fanny		7 Jan 1827	Korntal	Leon.	Apr 1854	Hesse	837957
Marx, Johann Georg		21 Apr 1841	Bissingen	Krch.	Jun 1860	N.-Amer	835943
Marx, Maria Barbara		14 Dec 1864	Bissingen	Krch.	Apr 1881	N.-Amer	835943
Marzel, Johannes		3 Jan 1850	Weiler	Krch.	Feb 1866	N.-Amer	835949
Maser, Christine		13 Aug 1824	Alpirsbach	Obd.	Jun 1852	Switz.	838630
Maser, Jacob Heinrich		18 Aug 1826	Alpirsbach	Obd.	Jul 1853	N.-Amer	838630
Maser, Maria Catharina			Alpirsbach	Obd.	bef 1851	France	838630
Maser, Matthias		8 Feb 1846	Seedorf	Obd.	Sep 1866	N.-Amer	838637
Mast, Barbara & C			Enztal	Nag.	Dec 1850	N.-Amer	838488
Mast, Johann Georg		23 Apr 1828	Gaertringen	Herr.	1850	N.-Amer	834630
Mast, Johann Martin		9 Aug 1847	Bondorf	Herr.	Apr 1867	N.-Amer	834630
Matsch, Bernhard		24 Feb 1851	Boehmenkirch	Gsl.	Jun 1854	N.-Amer	572042
Matsch, Bernhard & F		20 Apr 1826	Boehmenkirch	Gsl.	Sep 1853	N.-Amer	572041
Matsch, Creszentia		2 Jun 1844	Boehmenkirch	Gsl.	Jun 1854	N.-Amer	572042
Matsch, Genovefa (wife)			Boehmenkirch	Gsl.	Sep 1853	N.-Amer	572041
Matsch, Gertraud		28 Apr 1852	Boehmenkirch	Gsl.	Sep 1853	N.-Amer	572041
Matsch, Josef		18 Apr 1848	Boehmenkirch	Gsl.	Sep 1853	N.-Amer	572041
Matsch, Joseph		3 Jun 1848	Boehmenkirch	Gsl.	Jun 1854	N.-Amer	572042
Matsch, Karl		26 Jul 1815	Boehmenkirch	Gsl.	Jun 1854	N.-Amer	572042
Matsch, Katharina		15 Sep 1834	Boehmenkirch	Gsl.	Sep 1853	N.-Amer	572041
Matsch, Marianna		14 Mar 1843	Boehmenkirch	Gsl.	Jun 1854	N.-Amer	572042
Matsch, Walburga		13 Feb 1812	Boehmenkirch	Gsl.	Jun 1854	N.-Amer	572042
Mattheis, Johann Georg		5 Aug 1834	Altenstadt-Gsl.	Gsl.	May 1854	N.-Amer	572042
Mattheiss, Johann Georg		18 Mar 1851	Unterlenningen	Krch.	May 1867	N.-Amer	835949
Mattich, Barbara & C		2 May 1836	Jesingen	Krch.	Aug 1866	N.-Amer	835946
Mattich, Jacob Friedrich		3 Feb 1845	Jesingen	Krch.	Nov 1872	N.-Amer	835946
Mattich, Johannes		14 Jul 1862	Jesingen	Krch.	Aug 1866	N.-Amer	835946
Mattich, Johannes		14 Apr 1826	Jesingen	Krch.	Apr 1865	Russia	835946
Mattich, Maria Margaretha		22 Jan 1843	Jesingen	Krch.	bef 1866	N.-Amer	835946
Mau, Michael		15 Sep 1840	Krebsstein	Krch.	Jul 1857	N.-Amer	835945
Mauch, Anna Maria		24 Dec 1846	Renningen	Leon.	Apr 1867	N.-Amer	837963
Mauch, August		2 Jul 1826	Muenchingen	Leon.	1854	N.-Amer	837961
Mauch, Barbara (wife)			Muenchingen	Leon.	Jan 1854	N.-Amer	837961
Mauch, Carl Anton		6 Oct 1834	Weil der Stadt	Leon.	Feb 1854	N.-Amer	837966
Mauch, Caroline Catharine		6 May 1839	Renningen	Leon.	Jun 1870	Austria	837963
Mauch, Franz Heinrich		11 May 1838	Kirchheim	Krch.	Aug 1857	N.-Amer	835940
Mauch, Franz Xaver		28 Jul 1829	Schramberg	Obd.	bef 1863	N.-Amer	838636
Mauch, Jakob		19 Mar 1836	Hirschlanden	Leon.	Dec 1862	France	837956
Mauch, Jakob Friedrich		11 Nov 1856	Renningen	Leon.	bef 1888	N.-Amer	837963
Mauch, Johann Conrad			Malmsheim	Leon.	bef 1850	N.-Amer	837958
Mauch, Johann Georg		31 May 1833	Muenchingen	Leon.	Feb 1853	N.-Amer	837961
Mauch, Johann Georg & W		5 Jun 1825	Muenchingen	Leon.	Jan 1854	N.-Amer	837961
Mauch, Johannes		27 Jul 1850	Seedorf	Obd.	Sep 1867	N.-Amer	838637
Mauch, Karl August		4 Oct 1848	Renningen	Leon.	Jul 1867	N.-Amer	837963
Mauch, Leonhard		3 Jan 1833	Muenchingen	Leon.	Feb 1853	N.-Amer	837961
Mauch, Maria Barbara		19 Apr 1849	Renningen	Leon.	Apr 1868	Prussia	837963

Mauch, Michael	23 Feb 1814	Weil im Dorf	Loen.	Feb 1854	N.-Amer	837967
Mauch, Regina (wid.)	12 Jun 1806	Muenchingen	Leon.	Jul 1864	N.-Amer	837961
Mauer, Mathias		Hardt	Obd.	May 1855	N.-Amer	838633
Mauerhahn, Gottlob	22 Mar 1845	Reutlingen	Rtl.	Aug 1864	N.-Amer	841055
Mauerhahn, Karl		Reutlingen	Rtl.	Aug 1864	N.-Amer	841055
Mauerhahn, Robert	15 Apr 1839	Reutlingen	Rtl.	Feb 1862	France	841055
Maug, Johann Michael		Malmsheim	Leon.	Jun 1854	N.-Amer	837958
Maurer, Anna	15 May 1802	Muenchingen	Leon.	Mar 1848	N.-Amer	837961
Maurer, Anna (wife)		Alt Oberndorf	Obd.	Sep 1851	N.-Amer	838631
Maurer, Carl	6 May 1853	Schramberg	Obd.	Dec 1870	N.-Amer	838636
Maurer, Friedrich	3 Jun 1879	Herrenberg	Herr.	May 1896	N.-Amer	834629
Maurer, Georg Friedrich & F		Gebersheim	Leon.	Jun 1852	N.-Amer	837953
Maurer, Jacob		Reutlingen	Rtl.	Apr 1834	N.-Amer	841051
Maurer, Jakob		Stoetten	Gsl.	Mar 1852	N.-Amer	572041
Maurer, Johann & W		Alt Oberndorf	Obd.	Sep 1851	N.-Amer	838631
Maurer, Johann Jakob		Malmsheim	Leon.	Apr 1854	N.-Amer	837958
Maurer, Joseph	47 yrs.	Aichhalden	Obd.	Feb 1857	N.-Amer	838629
Maurer, Leonhardt	48 yrs.	Stoetten	Gsl.	Jan 1852	N.-Amer	572041
Maurer, Maria	3 Jan 1845	Reutlingen	Rtl.	Jul 1865	N.-Amer	841055
Maurer, Paul Julius	19 Jul 1859	Herrenberg	Herr.	1886	N.-Amer	834629
Mauser, Adam Friedrich & F		Erpfingen	Rtl.	Dec 1862	N.-Amer	841055
Mauser, Gottlieb	14 yrs.	Erpfingen	Rtl.	Dec 1862	N.-Amer	841055
Mauser, Johann Martin	6 yrs.	Erpfingen	Rtl.	Dec 1862	N.-Amer	841055
Mauser, Johann Wendel	8 yrs.	Erpfingen	Rtl.	Dec 1862	N.-Amer	841055
Mauser, Katharina (wife)		Erpfingen	Rtl.	Dec 1862	N.-Amer	841055
Mayer, Agnes	19 yrs.	Tuerkheim	Gsl.	Jan 1853	N.-Amer	572041
Mayer, Andreas	21 May 1833	Betzweiler	Obd.	May 1847	N.-Amer	838631
Mayer, Anna	4 Feb 1830	Betzweiler	Obd.	May 1847	N.-Amer	838631
Mayer, Anna		Brucken	Krch.	bef 1868	N.-Amer	835940
Mayer, Anna (wife)	22 Sep 1801	Unterbraendi	Obd.	May 1847	N.-Amer	838631
Mayer, Anna Catharina	2 yrs.	Tuerkheim	Gsl.	Jan 1853	N.-Amer	572041
Mayer, Anna Margaretha (wife)	8 Jan 1805	Zell	Krch.	Feb 1857	N.-Amer	835774
Mayer, Anna Maria	18 Jul 1836	Bondorf	Herr.	bef 1865	N.-Amer	834630
Mayer, Anna Maria (wife)	34 yrs.	Malmsheim	Leon.	Sep 1852	N.-Amer	837958
Mayer, Barbara	16 yrs.	Tuerkheim	Gsl.	Jan 1853	N.-Amer	572041
Mayer, Carolina		Heimerdingen	Leon.	Apr 1833	N.-Amer	837954
Mayer, Catharina Dorothea	7 yrs.	Malmsheim	Leon.	Sep 1852	N.-Amer	837958
Mayer, Christian & F		Leonberg	Leon.	Apr 1833	Poland	835786
Mayer, Christian Gottlob	7 Nov 1837	Kirchheim	Krch.	Oct 1856	N.-Amer	835940
Mayer, Christoph Heinrich	24 Jan 1801	Kirchheim	Krch.	Jul 1855	N.-Amer	835940
Mayer, Cordula	25 May 1838	Betzweiler	Obd.	May 1847	N.-Amer	838631
Mayer, Daniel (wid.) & F		Tuerkheim	Gsl.	Jan 1853	N.-Amer	572041
Mayer, Eduard		Oetlingen	Krch.	bef 1866	N.-Amer	835948
Mayer, Elisabeth	18 Sep 1825	Betzweiler	Obd.	May 1847	N.-Amer	838631
Mayer, Elisabeth (wife)		Deggingen	Gsl.	Sep 1851	Hesse	577788
Mayer, Ernst Wilhelm Heinrich	27 Sep 1839	Kirchheim	Krch.	Oct 1857	Brasil	835940
Mayer, Franz Xaver	32 yrs.	Oberndorf	Obd.	Jul 1857	N.-Amer	838635
Mayer, Friedrich	4 Apr 1835	Betzweiler	Obd.	May 1847	N.-Amer	838631
Mayer, Friedrich & F	8 Aug 1800	Betzweiler	Obd.	May 1847	N.-Amer	838631
Mayer, Friedrich Christian	8 Jul 1833	Bondorf	Herr.	1858	N.-Amer	834630

| Name | | Birth | | Emigration | | | Film |
Last	First	Date	Place	O'amt	Appl. Date	Dest.	Number
Mayer, Gabriel		2 yrs.	Malmsheim	Leon.	Sep 1852	N.-Amer	837958
Mayer, Georg		11 Oct 1831	Zell	Krch.	Nov 1860	N.-Amer	835774
Mayer, Georg			Merklingen	Leon.	bef 1816	Poland	837959
Mayer, Georg & F			Deggingen	Gsl.	Sep 1851	Hesse	577788
Mayer, Gottlieb		21 Sep 1825	Heimerdingen	Leon.	Apr 1833	N.-Amer	837954
Mayer, Gottlieb Christian		22 Nov 1848	Rutesheim	Leon.	Oct 1866	N.-Amer	837964
Mayer, Gottlieb Friedrich		4 Aug 1835	Heimerdingen	Leon.	Mar 1854	N.-Amer	837954
Mayer, Gustav Albert		25 Mar 1867	Lindorf	Krch.	Feb 1884	N.-Amer	548403
Mayer, Jacob Martin		6 Jun 1815	Heimerdingen	Leon.	Apr 1833	N.-Amer	837954
Mayer, Jacob Martin & F		18 Nov 1791	Heimerdingen	Leon.	Apr 1833	N.-Amer	837954
Mayer, Jakob		11 Jan 1827	Neidlingen	Krch.	Aug 1859	N.-Amer	835946
Mayer, Johann			Hemmingen	Leon.	Mar 1832	N.-Amer	837956
Mayer, Johann & W			Deggingen	Gsl.	Apr 1851	N.-Amer	577788
Mayer, Johann Conrad		16 Jul 1822	Heimerdingen	Leon.	Apr 1833	N.-Amer	837954
Mayer, Johann Georg		3 May 1866	Schlattstall	Krch.	Jun 1883	N.-Amer	835949
Mayer, Johann Georg & W		15 Feb 1809	Zell	Krch.	Feb 1857	N.-Amer	835774
Mayer, Johann Jakob		4 yrs.	Malmsheim	Leon.	Sep 1852	N.-Amer	837958
Mayer, Johann Jakob & F			Malmsheim	Leon.	Sep 1852	N.-Amer	837958
Mayer, Johann Michael		1 Oct 1828	Eckwaelden	Krch.	bef 1860	N.-Amer	835774
Mayer, Johann Michael		24 Sep 1837	Bondorf	Herr.	1858	N.-Amer	834630
Mayer, Johann Michael		29 Jun 1857	Aichelberg	Krch.	Apr 1883	N.-Amer	548403
Mayer, Johannes		25 Jan 1841	Betzweiler	Obd.	May 1847	N.-Amer	838631
Mayer, Johannes		14 yrs.	Tuerkheim	Gsl.	Jan 1853	N.-Amer	572041
Mayer, Johannes		27 yrs.	Geislingen	Gsl.	Oct 1851	N.-Amer	577788
Mayer, Johannes		5 Nov 1836	Hohenstadt	Gsl.	Feb 1854	N.-Amer	573622
Mayer, Joseph		16 yrs.	Deggingen	Gsl.	Sep 1851	Hesse	577788
Mayer, Joseph		11 Jun 1817	Donzdorf	Gsl.	May 1861	N.-Amer	572044
Mayer, Josepha		24 yrs.	Wiesensteig	Gsl.	Mar 1853	N.-Amer	572041
Mayer, Josepha (wife)			Deggingen	Gsl.	Apr 1851	N.-Amer	577788
Mayer, Margaretha		11 yrs.	Tuerkheim	Gsl.	Jan 1853	N.-Amer	572041
Mayer, Maria		22 yrs.	Wiesensteig	Gsl.	Mar 1853	N.-Amer	572041
Mayer, Maria Elisabeth		14 yrs.	Deggingen	Gsl.	Sep 1851	Hesse	577788
Mayer, Maria Margaretha (wife)		15 Jul 1787	Heimerdingen	Leon.	Apr 1833	N.-Amer	837954
Mayer, Michael		19 Nov 1825	Brucken	Krch.	bef 1868	N.-Amer	835940
Mayer, Michael & F			Eltingen	Leon.	May 1830	N.-Amer	835789
Mayer, Regina		26 Jul 1826	Moensheim	Leon.	Oct 1852	N.-Amer	837960
Mayer, Sabina		23 May 1836	Deggingen	Gsl.	Feb 1856	N.-Amer	572043
Mayer, Sophia Christina		12 Jul 1831	Neidlingen	Krch.	bef 1857	N.-Amer	835946
Mayer, Thomas		25 Jan 1820	Heimerdingen	Leon.	Apr 1833	N.-Amer	837954
Mayer, Thomas		37 yrs.	Heimerdingen	Leon.	May 1831	N.-Amer	837954
Mayer, Thomas (wid.)		20 Feb 1770	Heimerdingen	Leon.	May 1843	N.-Amer	837954
Mayer, Ursula		5 yrs.	Tuerkheim	Gsl.	Jan 1853	N.-Amer	572041
Mayer, Wilhelm		23 Dec 1871	Oetlingen	Krch.	Oct 1884	N.-Amer	548403
Mayer, Wilhelmine Barbara		8 Jun 1832	Oetlingen	Krch.	Nov 1866	N.-Amer	835948
Mazenhan, Bartolomaeus		14 Aug 1848	Winzeln	Obd.	Dec 1867	N.-Amer	841016
Mazenhan, Paulina			Winzeln	Obd.	Nov 1860	N.-Amer	841016
Mehrer, Catharina		44 yrs.	Hoefingen	Leon.	Jan 1854	N.-Amer	837957
Mehrer, Friedrich			Hoefingen	Leon.	bef 1825	Austria	837957
Mehrer, Johann Konrad			Leonberg	Leon.	May 1850	N.-Amer	835786
Mehrer, Johann Michael			Hoefingen	Leon.	Nov 1851	Switz.	837957

Meier, Anton		Winzeln	Obd.	Apr 1866	N.-Amer 841016
Meier, Barbara	13 Mar 1841	Rosswaelden	Krch.	May 1855	N.-Amer 835949
Meier, Johanna	19 Sep 1836	Moensheim	Leon.	Jul 1854	N.-Amer 837960
Meier, Louise Magdalena	30 May 1830	Heimerdingen	Leon.	Aug 1853	N.-Amer 837954
Meier, Marie Louise	20 Mar 1831	Kirchheim	Krch.	Jul 1857	N.-Amer 835940
Meier, Protasius		Reichenbach	Gsl.	Aug 1866	N.-Amer 572045
Meier, Wilhelm August	28 Jun 1835	Heimerdingen	Leon.	Aug 1853	N.-Amer 837954
Meirer, Johannes & F		Ohmenhausen	Rtl.	May 1831	N.-Amer 841051
Meis, Christoph Friedrich		Pfullingen	Rtl.	Apr 1864	N.-Amer 841051
Meissnest, Anna Maria	2 Oct 1863	Weiler	Krch.	Apr 1864	N.-Amer 835949
Meissnest, Barbara (wife)	31 Aug 1824	Weiler	Krch.	Apr 1864	N.-Amer 835949
Meissnest, Johann Georg & F	16 Mar 1802	Weiler	Krch.	Apr 1864	N.-Amer 835949
Melber, Balbina	29 Mar 1814	Winzeln	Obd.	Oct 1847	N.-Amer 841016
Melber, Johannes		Winzeln	Obd.	Nov 1860	N.-Amer 841016
Melber, Samuel	27 Aug 1831	Winzeln	Obd.	Sep 1851	N.-Amer 841016
Melber, Thomas		Winzeln	Obd.	Nov 1860	N.-Amer 841016
Meng, Andreas	25 Sep 1842	Roetenbach	Obd.	Jan 1859	N.-Amer 838636
Meng, Barbara		Roetenbach	Obd.	Jan 1860	N.-Amer 838636
Meng, Christian		Roetenbach	Obd.	Jan 1860	N.-Amer 838636
Meng, David	1 Feb 1836	Hildrizhausen	Herr.	bef 1864	N.-Amer 834631
Meng, Dorothea	5 Mar 1845	Roetenbach	Obd.	Jan 1859	N.-Amer 838636
Meng, Dorothea (wife)		Roetenbach	Obd.	Jan 1860	N.-Amer 838636
Meng, Jakob		Roetenbach	Obd.	Jan 1860	N.-Amer 838636
Meng, Johann Christian & F		Roetenbach	Obd.	Jan 1860	N.-Amer 838636
Meng, Johann Georg & F		Roetenbach	Obd.	Jan 1860	N.-Amer 838636
Meng, Johannes	1 Jun 1827	Hildrizhausen	Herr.	bef 1864	N.-Amer 834631
Mentele, Konrad	15 yrs.	Aichhalden	Obd.	Dec 1854	N.-Amer 838629
Menz, Johannes	28 yrs,	Peterzell	Obd.	Nov 1846	N.-Amer 838635
Merk, Eva Barbara (wife)	20 Apr 1817	Heimerdingen	Leon.	May 1854	N.-Amer 837954
Merk, Louise Friederike	17 Nov 1848	Heimerdingen	Leon.	May 1854	N.-Amer 837954
Merk, Mathaeus & F	25 Jul 1820	Heimerdingen	Leon.	May 1854	N.-Amer 837954
Merk, Wilhelm Friedrich	30 Jan 1853	Heimerdingen	Leon.	May 1854	N.-Amer 837954
Merkh, Gottfried	9 Feb 1823	Reutlingen	Rtl.	bef 1864	N.-Amer 841055
Merkle, Amalie Sophie (wid.) & F	15 Jul 1835	Aichelberg	Krch.	Jul 1888	N.-Amer 835943
Merkle, Anna Maria & C	28 Oct 1823	Bissingen	Krch.	May 1865	N.-Amer 835943
Merkle, Barbara	13 Nov 1868	Aichelberg	Krch.	Jul 1888	N.-Amer 835943
Merkle, Christian	12 Jun 1866	Aichelberg	Krch.	Nov 1882	N.-Amer 548403
Merkle, Johannes	3 Dec 1832	Bissingen	Krch.	Mar 1860	N.-Amer 835943
Merkle, Maria Elisabeth	8 Mar 1852	Bissingen	Krch.	May 1865	N.-Amer 835943
Merklin, Luise		Schramberg	Obd.	Oct 1812	Switz. 838637
Merkt, Anna Maria	5 Oct 1809	Fluorn	Obd.	Aug 1817	N.-Amer 838629
Merkt, Barbara	8 Jun 1815	Fluorn	Obd.	Aug 1817	N.-Amer 838629
Merkt, Caroline	20 Sep 1855	Wannweil	Rtl.	Apr 1866	N.-Amer 841055
Merkt, Christina	5 Nov 1807	Fluorn	Obd.	Aug 1817	N.-Amer 838629
Merkt, Christina Friederike	19 Sep 1846	Wannweil	Rtl.	Apr 1866	N.-Amer 841055
Merkt, Gottfried	10 Nov 1865	Wannweil	Rtl.	Apr 1866	N.-Amer 841055
Merkt, Gottlieb	3 Feb 1850	Wannweil	Rtl.	Apr 1866	N.-Amer 841055
Merkt, Johannes	29 Aug 1858	Wannweil	Rtl.	Apr 1866	N.-Amer 841055
Merkt, Juditha (wife)	19 Jan 1824	Wannweil	Rtl.	Apr 1866	N.-Amer 841055
Merkt, Lucia	2 Nov 1812	Fluorn	Obd.	Aug 1817	N.-Amer 838629

Name		Birth		Emigration			Film
Last	First	Date	Place	O'amt	Appl. Date	Dest.	Number
Merkt, Margaretha (wife)		16 Feb 1786	Fluorn	Obd.	Aug 1817	N.-Amer	838629
Merkt, Michael		10 May 1868	Hemmingen	Leon.	Jan 1884	N.-Amer	837956
Merkt, Nikolaus & F		6 Dec 1776	Fluorn	Obd.	Aug 1817	N.-Amer	838629
Merkt, Wenzelaus & F		30 Jun 1813	Isenburg/Horb	Rtl.	Apr 1866	N.-Amer	841055
Merkt, Wilhelm		18 Nov 1848	Wannweil	Rtl.	Apr 1866	N.-Amer	841055
Merz, Adele		11 yrs.	Alpirsbach	Obd.	Jan 1858	France	838630
Merz, Albertina		27 Nov 1845	Seedorf	Obd.	Feb 1854	N.-Amer	838637
Merz, Augustina (wife)		18 Oct 1821	Seedorf	Obd.	Feb 1854	N.-Amer	838637
Merz, Bonaventura		14 Jul 1847	Seedorf	Obd.	Feb 1854	N.-Amer	838637
Merz, Catharina Margaretha		12 Jan 1839	Renningen	Leon.	Apr 1852	N.-Amer	837963
Merz, Christoph Ludwig		27 Feb 1816	Alpirsbach	Obd.	May 1855	Frankf.	838630
Merz, Elisabetha Rosina & C			Alpirsbach	Obd.	Jan 1858	France	838630
Merz, Genovefa & C		27 Feb 1811	Epfendorf	Obd.	May 1847	N.-Amer	838632
Merz, Jacob Friedrich		26 Aug 1796	Pfullingen	Rtl.	Sep 1865	N.-Amer	841055
Merz, Johann Evangelist		1 Aug 1821	Epfendorf	Obd.	May 1854	N.-Amer	838632
Merz, Johann Georg			Hozelfingen	Rtl.	Nov 1827	N.-Amer	841051
Merz, Johann Jacob & F			Notzingen	Krch.	Mar 1784	Pr.-Pol	550804
Merz, Johann Jacob & F			Oetlingen	Krch.	Mar 1784	Pr.-Pol	550804
Merz, Johannes		32 yrs.	Epfendorf	Obd.	May 1854	N.-Amer	838632
Merz, Karl Friedrich		5 May 1865	Herrenberg	Herr.	Apr 1883	N.-Amer	834629
Merz, Konrad			Epfendorf	Obd.	bef 1852	Austria	838632
Merz, Maria		27 Mar 1843	Bach-Altenberg	Obd.	Jan 1866	N.-Amer	838631
Merz, Maria		23 Mar 1827	Epfendorf	Obd.	May 1847	N.-Amer	838632
Merz, Maria		24 Mar 1849	Seedorf	Obd.	Feb 1854	N.-Amer	838637
Merz, Mathaeus		18 Sep 1793	Epfendorf	Obd.	May 1847	N.-Amer	838632
Merz, Matthias		8 Jan 1839	Renningen	Leon.	bef 1869	Bavaria	837963
Merz, Pauline		30 Aug 1832	Epfendorf	Obd.	Oct 1861	N.-Amer	838632
Merz, Rupert		26 Mar 1840	Epfendorf	Obd.	May 1847	N.-Amer	838632
Merz, Sebastian & F		26 May 1812	Seedorf	Obd.	Feb 1854	N.-Amer	838637
Merz, Theresia		28 Sep 1851	Seedorf	Obd.	Feb 1854	N.-Amer	838637
Merz, Walburga		23 Feb 1845	Epfendorf	Obd.	May 1847	N.-Amer	838632
Merz, Wendelin		18 Sep 1834	Seedorf	Obd.	Feb 1854	N.-Amer	838637
Messerschmid, Adolph		4 yrs.	Wiesensteig	Gsl.	Dec 1852	N.-Amer	572041
Messerschmid, Anna Maria (wife)			Wiesensteig	Gsl.	Dec 1852	N.-Amer	572041
Messerschmid, Balthas & F			Wiesensteig	Gsl.	Dec 1852	N.-Amer	572041
Messmer, Kristian		15 Dec 1839	Epfendorf	Obd.	Jun 1869	N.-Amer	838632
Metteler, August Friedrich		28 yrs.	Pfullingen	Rtl.	Apr 1880	N.-Amer	841051
Metzger, Alexander Friedrich		13 Feb 1854	Kirchheim	Krch.	Jul 1870	N.-Amer	835941
Metzger, Carl Heinrich		7 Jan 1849	Ludwigsburg	Herr.	bef 1880	Prussia	834629
Metzger, Carl Heinrich		20 Jun 1826	Herrenberg	Herr.	bef 1862	N.-Amer	834629
Metzger, Christine		4 Aug 1847	Kirchheim	Krch.	Jul 1870	N.-Amer	835941
Metzger, Friederike		5 Oct 1858	Kirchheim	Krch.	Mar 1873	N.-Amer	835942
Metzger, Gottlieb		27 Dec 1840	Kirchheim	Krch.	Feb 1860	N.-Amer	835940
Metzger, Johann Georg		20 Oct 1844	Pfullingen	Rtl.	Nov 1865	N.-Amer	841055
Metzger, Johannes		6 Nov 1852	Dettingen	Krch.	Feb 1869	N.-Amer	835944
Metzger, Maria Margaretha		29 Aug 1818	Herrenberg	Herr.	1863	Austral	834629
Metzger, Otto		24 Mar 1851	Kirchheim	Krch.	Apr 1869	N.-Amer	835941
Metzger, Pauline		11 Feb 1852	Kirchheim	Krch.	Jul 1870	N.-Amer	835941
Metzger, Robert		18 Jan 1849	Kirchheim	Krch.	Apr 1866	N.-Amer	835941
Meyer, David		28 May 1845	Kuchen	Gsl.	Jul 1865	N.-Amer	572045

Meyer, Johann Georg	23 yrs.	Heimerdingen	Leon.	bef 1818	N.-Amer	837954
Meyer, Johann Jakob Friedrich	21 yrs.	Oberhausen	Rtl.	May 1880	N.-Amer	841051
Meyer, Johannes	5 Nov 1836	Hohenstadt	Gsl.	Feb 1854	N.-Amer	572042
Meyer, Josef		Oberndorf	Obd.	Mar 1849	N.-Amer	838635
Meyer, Louise	23 yrs.	Wiesensteig	Gsl.	Mar 1854	N.-Amer	572042
Meyer, Maria Anna	1 Sep 1830	Deggingen	Gsl.	Feb 1855	N.-Amer	572043
Meyer, Theresia	26 Jul 1830	Schramberg	Obd.	Aug 1865	N.-Amer	838636
Mezger, Friederike		Herrenberg	Herr.	bef 1867	N.-Amer	834629
Mezger, Gustav Adolph	5 Oct 1847	Herrenberg	Herr.	Dec 1867	N.-Amer	834629
Mezger, Johann Gottlieb	30 Oct 1855	Dettingen	Krch.	Mar 1872	N.-Amer	835944
Mezger, Michael		Oberhausen	Rtl.	Jan 1836	N.-Amer	841051
Mezger, Wilhelm Friedrich	9 Nov 1843	Leonberg	Leon.	Mar 1860	N.-Amer	835786
Michler, Johann Gottlob	29 Sep 1867	Altenstadt-Gsl.	Gsl.	Jun 1884	N.-Amer	572049
Mick, Anna Maria	3 yrs.	Willmandingen	Rtl.	Jan 1880	N.-Amer	841051
Mick, Beata Margaretha Barb.	1 yrs.	Willmandingen	Rtl.	Jan 1880	N.-Amer	841051
Mick, Gottlieb	21 yrs.	Willmandingen	Rtl.	Jan 1880	N.-Amer	841051
Mick, Johann Georg Friedrich	5 yrs.	Willmandingen	Rtl.	Jan 1880	N.-Amer	841051
Mick, Magdalene Christine	22 Dec 1825	Alpirsbach	Obd.	Sep 1858	France	838630
Mick, Mathess & F	35 yrs.	Willmandingen	Rtl.	Jan 1880	N.-Amer	841051
Mick, Wilhelmine (wife)	31 yrs.	Willmandingen	Rtl.	Jan 1880	N.-Amer	841051
Micol, Jacob Friedrich	27 Oct 1857	Serres	Leon.	Aug 1881	N.-Amer	837959
Miehle, Simon		Epfendorf	Obd.	Mar 1817	France	838632
Mik, Johannes	18 yrs.	Willmandingen	Rtl.	Jun 1880	N.-Amer	841051
Miller, Franz	15 Oct 1850	Hochmoessingen	Obd.	Aug 1869	N.-Amer	838633
Miller, Johannes	13 May 1835	Waldmoessingen	Obd.	Mar 1853	N.-Amer	841015
Mink, Joseph	25 yrs.	Beffendorf	Obd.	Sep 1854	N.-Amer	838631
Mitschele, Anna Maria	13 yrs.	Malmsheim	Leon.	Mar 1830	N.-Amer	837958
Mitschele, Anna Maria & C	8 Nov 1796	Malmsheim	Leon.	Apr 1843	N.-Amer	837958
Mitschele, Catharina	22 May 1822	Malmsheim	Leon.	Apr 1843	N.-Amer	837958
Mitschele, Catharina Barbara		Malmsheim	Leon.	1830	N.-Amer	837958
Mitschele, Catharina Barbara	11 yrs.	Malmsheim	Leon.	Mar 1830	N.-Amer	837958
Mitschele, Christina C. (wife)	36 yrs.	Malmsheim	Leon.	Apr 1818	N.-Amer	837958
Mitschele, Christina Margar.	7 yrs.	Malmsheim	Leon.	Mar 1830	N.-Amer	837958
Mitschele, Friederika		Malmsheim	Leon.	May 1853	N.-Amer	837958
Mitschele, Georg Michael	4 yrs.	Malmsheim	Leon.	Mar 1830	N.-Amer	837958
Mitschele, Gottlieb		Leonberg	Leon.	Apr 1849	N.-Amer	835786
Mitschele, Jakob	7 yrs.	Malmsheim	Leon.	Apr 1818	N.-Amer	837958
Mitschele, Johann Jak. (wid.) & F		Malmsheim	Leon.	Mar 1830	N.-Amer	837958
Mitschele, Johann Jakob	9 yrs.	Malmsheim	Leon.	Mar 1830	N.-Amer	837958
Mitschele, Johann Konrad	3 yrs.	Malmsheim	Leon.	Apr 1818	N.-Amer	837958
Mitschele, Johann Salomon		Malmsheim	Leon.	bef 1843	N.-Amer	837958
Mitschele, Johannes	19 yrs.	Malmsheim	Leon.	Mar 1830	N.-Amer	837958
Mitschele, Johannes	11 yrs.	Malmsheim	Leon.	Apr 1818	N.-Amer	837958
Mitschele, Johannes & F	37 yrs.	Malmsheim	Leon.	Apr 1818	N.-Amer	837958
Mitschele, Luise	22 yrs.	Leonberg	Leon.	Jul 1841	N.-Amer	835786
Mitschele, Magdalena	13 yrs.	Malmsheim	Leon.	Apr 1818	N.-Amer	837958
Mitschele, Maria Catharina	9 May 1832	Malmsheim	Leon.	Apr 1843	N.-Amer	837958
Mittnacht, Elisabetha Sophie		Flacht	Leon.	May 1853	N.-Amer	835790
Mittnacht, Gottlieb	11 Jul 1831	Flacht	Leon.	Mar 1850	N.-Amer	835790
Mittnacht, Jakob	29 Aug 1823	Flacht	Leon.	Mar 1850	N.-Amer	835790

Name		Birth		Emigration			Film
Last	First	Date	Place	O'amt	Appl. Date	Dest.	Number
Mittnacht, Magdalena			Wimsheim	Loen.	Apr 1854	N.-Amer	837967
Mittnacht, – (wid.)			Flacht	Leon.	Mar 1854	N.-Amer	835790
Mochel, Carl		9 Aug 1849	Leonberg	Leon.	Nov 1862	N.-Amer	835787
Mochel, Christiane Frieder.			Leonberg	Leon.	Dec 1863	N.-Amer	835787
Mochel, Heinrich		22 Dec 1846	Leonberg	Leon.	Nov 1862	N.-Amer	835787
Moeck, Margaretha		19 Jul 1819	Willmandingen	Rtl.	bef 1863	N.-Amer	841058
Moegle, Michael			Muenchingen	Leon.	Dec 1853	N.-Amer	837961
Moehrle, Jakob			Unterschwandorf	Nag.	Jul 1852	N.-Amer	838488
Moek, Andreas		27 Oct 1841	Willmandingen	Rtl.	Apr 1860	N.-Amer	841055
Moek, Anna Maria (wife)		7 Mar 1817	Thalheim	Rtl.	Aug 1864	N.-Amer	841055
Moek, Gottlieb & W		4 Sep 1833	Willmandingen	Rtl.	Oct 1865	N.-Amer	841055
Moek, Johann Bernhard		1 Oct 1827	Willmandinger	Rtl.	Apr 1867	N.-Amer	841055
Moek, Johann Georg		28 Oct 1832	Willmandingen	Rtl.	Aug 1864	N.-Amer	841055
Moek, Johann Georg		19 Sep 1842	Willmandingen	Rtl.	Feb 1862	N.-Amer	841055
Moek, Johann Georg		29 Nov 1850	Willmandingen	Rtl.	Apr 1860	N.-Amer	841055
Moek, Johann Wilhelm		15 Sep 1839	Willmandingen	Rtl.	1857	N.-Amer	841055
Moek, Johannes		27 Feb 1831	Willmandingen	Rtl.	Aug 1864	N.-Amer	841055
Moek, Johannes		2 May 1841	Willmandingen	Rtl.	Apr 1860	N.-Amer	841055
Moek, Johannes		26 Aug 1841	Willmandingen	Rtl.	Apr 1860	N.-Amer	841055
Moek, Johannes		4 Oct 1846	Willmandingen	Rtl.	Apr 1860	N.-Amer	841055
Moek, Johannes & F		17 Jan 1799	Willmandingen	Rtl.	Aug 1864	N.-Amer	841055
Moek, Johannes & F		16 Aug 1817	Willmandingen	Rtl.	Apr 1860	N.-Amer	841055
Moek, Margaretha		17 Jun 1846	Willmandingen	Rtl.	Aug 1864	N.-Amer	841055
Moek, Michael		21 Aug 1848	Willmandingen	Rtl.	Apr 1860	N.-Amer	841055
Moek, Regina		12 Aug 1841	Willmandingen	Rtl.	1857	N.-Amer	841055
Moek, Regina (wid.)		15 Jan 1805	Willmandingen	Rtl.	Aug 1864	N.-Amer	841055
Moek, Rosine (wife)		8 Nov 1818	Willmandingen	Rtl.	Apr 1860	N.-Amer	841055
Moeller, Lukas		19 yrs.	Bochingen	Obd.	Oct 1856	N.-Amer	838632
Moench, Christoph Ludwig		43 yrs.	Owen	Krch.	Mar 1860	N.-Amer	835948
Moench, Karl August		1 Nov 1864	Owen	Krch.	Jul 1880	N.-Amer	548403
Moench, Louis Wilhelm		18 Apr 1865	Eltingen	Leon.	Sep 1889	N.-Amer	835789
Moench, Ludwig Friedrich		15 May 1875	Owen	Krch.	Dec 1889	N.-Amer	835948
Moench, Wilhelm Nicolaus		9 Oct 1846	Owen	Krch.	Sep 1865	N.-Amer	835948
Moerk, Anna Friederike & F			Gebersheim	Leon.	Jan 1852	N.-Amer	837953
Moerk, Christiane		10 Jan 1844	Gebersheim	Leon.	Jun 1852	N.-Amer	837953
Moerk, Ernst Friedrich			Eltingen	Leon.	bef 1859	N.-Amer	835789
Moerk, Ernst Gottlob		4 May 1835	Renningen	Leon.	bef 1855	N.-Amer	837963
Moerk, Friederika & F			Gebersheim	Leon.	Jun 1852	N.-Amer	837963
Moerk, Friederike		21 Jan 1848	Gebersheim	Leon.	Jun 1852	N.-Amer	837953
Moerk, Johann Georg & W			Renningen	Leon.	Jan 1853	N.-Amer	837963
Moerk, Johannes			Gebersheim	Leon.	bef 1852	N.-Amer	837953
Moerk, Maria Louisa (wife)			Renningen	Leon.	Jan 1853	N.-Amer	837963
Moerk, Traugott Christian		3 Mar 1833	Renningen	Leon.	Feb 1851	N.-Amer	837963
Moess, Johannes			Willmandingen	Rtl.	Jun 1834	N.-Amer	841051
Moessner, Carl August		8 Feb 1850	Kirchheim	Krch.	Feb 1870	N.-Amer	835941
Moessner, Johann Martin		13 Jan 1823	Affstaett	Herr.	bef 1862	N.-Amer	834630
Moessner, Johanna Elisabeth		27 Nov 1804	Altenstadt-Gsl.	Gsl.	Aug 1853	N.-Amer	572041
Mogger, Matthaeus		28 Apr 1828	Waldmoessingen	Obd.	Jun 1861	N.-Amer	841015
Mohr, Anna Maria (wife)		53 yrs.	Malmsheim	Leon.	Apr 1818	N.-Amer	837958
Mohr, Catharina Magdalena		18 yrs.	Malmsheim	Leon.	Apr 1818	N.-Amer	837958

Mohr, Georg Friedrich & F	28 yrs.	Malmsheim	Leon.	Mar 1820	N.-Amer	837958
Mohr, Johann Georg	16 yrs.	Malmsheim	Leon.	Apr 1818	N.-Amer	837958
Mohr, Johann Georg & F		Heimsheim	Leon.	Apr 1818	N.-Amer	837955
Mohr, Johann Konrad	19 yrs.	Malmsheim	Leon.	Apr 1818	N.-Amer	837958
Mohr, Konrad & F	53 yrs.	Malmsheim	Leon.	Apr 1818	N.-Amer	837958
Mohr, Margaretha	22 yrs.	Heimsheim	Leon.	Apr 1818	N.-Amer	837955
Mohr, Maria Catharina (wife)	26 yrs.	Malmsheim	Leon.	Mar 1820	N.-Amer	837958
Mohring, Conrad & F	27 Jul 1829	Weilheim	Krch.	Feb 1870	N.-Amer	835950
Mohring, Johannes	22 Aug 1866	Weilheim	Krch.	Feb 1870	N.-Amer	835950
Mohring, Maria Dorothea (wife)	27 Aug 1825	Weilheim	Krch.	Feb 1870	N.-Amer	835950
Moll, Barbara	13 Aug 1830	Aichelberg	Krch.	May 1873	N.-Amer	548403
Moll, Georg Jacob	25 Oct 1841	Weilheim	Krch.	Apr 1859	England	835949
Moll, Johann	10 Nov 1844	Weilheim	Krch.	Apr 1871	England	835774
Moll, Johann Christoph	9 May 1848	Weilheim	Krch.	Aug 1866	N.-Amer	835950
Moll, Johann Georg	21 Apr 1875	Weilheim	Krch.	Jun 1882	N.-Amer	548403
Moll, Johann Michael	13 Jun 1826	Zell	Krch.	Apr 1855	N.-Amer	835774
Moll, Johann Michael	25 Nov 1846	Weilheim	Krch.	Aug 1866	N.-Amer	835950
Moll, Johann Wilhelm	14 Apr 1830	Kirchheim	Krch.	Jan 1856	N.-Amer	835940
Moll, Maria Magdalena	14 May 1877	Weilheim	Krch.	Jun 1882	N.-Amer	548403
Mollenkopf, Albert	2 Oct 1847	Tuebingen	Rtl.	Mar 1867	N.-Amer	841055
Mollenkopf, Anna Barbara		Pfullingen	Rtl.	Apr 1830	N.-Amer	841051
Mollenkopf, Elisabeth (wife)		Pfullingen	Rtl.	bef 1864	N.-Amer	841055
Mollenkopf, Ferdinand	4 Feb 1850	Pfullingen	Rtl.	Mar 1869	N.-Amer	841055
Mollenkopf, Heinrich	8 Jul 1845	Tuebingen	Rtl.	Mar 1867	N.-Amer	841055
Mollenkopf, Johann Georg		Pfullingen	Rtl.	Aug 1835	N.-Amer	841051
Mollenkopf, Johann Jacob		Pfullingen	Rtl.	Aug 1834	N.-Amer	841051
Mollenkopf, Johann Jacob	27 Aug 1845	Pfullingen	Rtl.	Sep 1865	N.-Amer	841055
Mollenkopf, Johannes	14 May 1847	Pfullingen	Rtl.	Sep 1866	N.-Amer	841055
Mollenkopf, Matthaeus & W		Pfullingen	Rtl.	bef 1864	N.-Amer	841055
Moosmann, Anton	11 May 1833	Aichhalden	Obd.	Aug 1853	N.-Amer	838629
Moosmann, Carl Heinrich	13 Jul 1847	Schramberg	Obd.	Feb 1867	N.-Amer	838636
Moosmann, Caroline		Schramberg	Obd.	Apr 1851	France	838637
Moosmann, Casimir	20 yrs.	Fluorn	Obd.	Mar 1857	N.-Amer	838632
Moosmann, Felix	6 Jan 1842	Aichhalden	Obd.	Aug 1858	N.-Amer	838629
Moosmann, Franziska		Schramberg	Obd.	Aug 1857	N.-Amer	838636
Moosmann, Franziska	23 yrs.	Schramberg	Obd.	Aug 1853	N.-Amer	838636
Moosmann, Franziska		Schramberg	Obd.	Feb 1851	France	838637
Moosmann, Johannes	13 Sep 1844	Lauterbach	Obd.	Jun 1864	N.-Amer	838634
Moosmann, Josepha		Schramberg	Obd.	Aug 1815	Prag	838637
Moosmann, Philipp		Schramberg	Obd.	bef 1860	N.-Amer	838636
Moosmann, Philipp	24 yrs.	Schramberg	Obd.	Apr 1854	N.-Amer	838636
Moosmann, Valentin	18 yrs.	Aichhalden	Obd.	Feb 1853	N.-Amer	838629
Moosmann, Wendelin		Aichhalden	Obd.	Feb 1859	Africa	838629
Moosmann, Wendelin	5 Jul 1839	Aichhalden	Obd.	Mar 1856	N.-Amer	838629
Morlock, Friedrich	17 Sep 1880	Herrenberg	Herr.	Jan 1896	N.-Amer	834629
Mornhinweg, Jakob	4 yrs.	Malmsheim	Leon.	Jul 1857	N.-Amer	837958
Mornhinweg, Johanna Barb. (wife)	33 yrs.	Malmsheim	Leon.	Jul 1857	N.-Amer	837958
Mornhinweg, Johannes	9 yrs.	Malmsheim	Leon.	Jul 1857	N.-Amer	837958
Mornhinweg, Johannes & F		Malmsheim	Leon.	Jul 1857	N.-Amer	837958
Mornhinweg, Joseph	28 Jul 1856	Gaertringen	Herr.	Feb 1880	N.-Amer	834630

Name		Birth		Emigration			Film
Last	First	Date	Place	O'amt	Appl. Date	Dest.	Number
Mornhinweg, Karl		18 Apr 1859	Gaertringen	Herr.	Feb 1880	N.-Amer	834630
Mornhinweg, Wilhelm		6 yrs.	Malmsheim	Leon.	Jul 1857	N.-Amer	837958
Morof, Jakob Friedrich			Flacht	Leon.	Nov 1866	N.-Amer	835790
Morof, Johann Jakob			Flacht	Leon.	bef 1858	N.-Amer	835790
Mosbacher, Franz Sales		17 yrs.	Epfendorf	Obd.	Sep 1853	N.-Amer	838632
Mosbacher, Werner		16 Apr 1838	Epfendorf	Obd.	Mar 1853	N.-Amer	838632
Moser, Anna Maria		1 Jan 1835	Roemlinsdorf	Obd.	Aug 1869	France	838635
Moser, Bernhard Michael & F			Fuenfbronn	Nag.	Jul 1852	N.-Amer	838488
Moser, Christian		19 Nov 1845	Schramberg	Obd.	Sep 1863	N.-Amer	838636
Moser, Christian		5 Apr 1862	Hochdorf	Krch.	Aug 1868	N.-Amer	835945
Moser, Georg Friedrich		20 Nov 1815	Alpirsbach	Obd.	Dec 1844	Paris	838630
Moser, Jacob			Hochdorf	Krch.	1867	N.-Amer	835945
Moser, Jacob Heinrich & F			Alpirsbach	Obd.	Apr 1817	N.-Amer	838631
Moser, Jakob		9 Jun 1821	Hochdorf	Krch.	Jun 1867	N.-Amer	835945
Moser, Jakob		24 Jun 1852	Hochdorf	Krch.	Jun 1867	N.-Amer	835945
Moser, Johann Georg		16 Sep 1847	Fluorn	Obd.	Nov 1867	N.-Amer	838632
Moser, Johann Georg		31 Jan 1856	Hochdorf	Krch.	Aug 1868	N.-Amer	835945
Moser, Johann Gottfried		11 Mar 1860	Hochdorf	Krch.	Aug 1868	N.-Amer	835945
Moser, Magdalena		8 Jan 1839	Roemlinsdorf	Obd.	Feb 1870	France	838635
Moser, Rosine		2 Nov 1835	Hochdorf	Krch.	Aug 1868	N.-Amer	835945
Moser, Wilhelm		24 Dec 1866	Hochdorf	Krch.	Aug 1868	N.-Amer	835945
Mosner, Friedrich Wilhelm		1 Oct 1843	Kirchheim	Krch.	Jan 1858	N.-Amer	835940
Mosser, Matthias		5 Jul 1849	Peterzell	Obd.	Jan 1869	N.-Amer	838635
Mouris, Jaguas & F			Perouse	Leon.	Mar 1830	N.-Amer	837962
Mozer, Friedrich		9 Mar 1851	Gomaringen	Rtl.	Jul 1865	N.-Amer	841055
Mozer, Jacob		17 Jul 1848	Gomaringen	Rtl.	Apr 1867	N.-Amer	841055
Mozer, Johannes		22 Feb 1849	Gomaringen	Rtl.	Sep 1859	N.-Amer	841055
Mozer, Katharina Dorothea		22 yrs.	Flacht	Leon.	Mar 1828	N.-Amer	835790
Muckenfuss, Maria Agnes		13 May 1828	Gutenberg	Krch.	May 1857	N.-Amer	835945
Mueck, Christian Friedrich		24 Jan 1845	Rutesheim	Leon.	Apr 1862	N.-Amer	837964
Mueck, Johann Georg		28 yrs.	Rutesheim	Leon.	Feb 1854	N.-Amer	837964
Muehleis, Adelheid		30 May 1830	Wiesensteig	Gsl.	May 1865	Austria	572045
Muehleisen, Andreas		4 May 1839	Eningen	Rtl.	Dec 1860	N.-Amer	841055
Muehleisen, Elisabetha & C		11 Sep 1845	Eningen	Rtl.	Jun 1866	N.-Amer	841055
Muehlhaeuser, August Wilhelm		30 Oct 1852	Notzingen	Krch.	Mar 1867	N.-Amer	835947
Muehlhaeuser, Bartholomaeus		16 Aug 1835	Altenstadt-Gsl.	Gsl.	Jul 1854	N.-Amer	572042
Muehlhaeuser, Johannes Gottl.		20 Sep 1865	Notzingen	Krch.	May 1882	N.-Amer	548403
Muehlhauser, Adolf		19 Sep 1841	Notzingen	Krch.	Jul 1857	N.-Amer	835940
Muehlich, Arthur		17 Mar 1862	Grosssuessen	Gsl.	Dec 1866	Prussia	572045
Muehlich, Friederika		21 Sep 1836	Kuchen	Gsl.	Jan 1854	N.-Amer	572042
Muehlich, Ida Louise Eugenie		31 Dec 1864	Grosssuessen	Gsl.	Dec 1866	Prussia	572045
Muehlich, Johannes		11 Jul 1835	Steinenkirch	Gsl.	Jun 1854	N.-Amer	572042
Muehlich, Leonhardt		9 Mar 1827	Steinenkirch	Gsl.	Feb 1854	N.-Amer	572042
Muehlich, Louise (wife)		5 Apr 1838	Grosssuessen	Gsl.	Dec 1866	Prussia	572045
Muehlich, Matthaeus		26 May 1832	Kuchen	Gsl.	May 1854	N.-Amer	572042
Muehlich, Michael & F		8 Dec 1838	Grosssuessen	Gsl.	Dec 1866	Prussia	572045
Muehlich, Timotheus Wilhelm			Gingen	Gsl.	Aug 1853	N.-Amer	572041
Mueller, Andreas		21 Sep 1835	Moensheim	Leon.	Jan 1847	N.-Amer	837960
Mueller, Andreas		12 Sep 1835	Moensheim	Leon.	Feb 1846	Austria	837960
Mueller, Andreas		13 Dec 1827	Moensheim	Leon.	Mar 1830	N.-Amer	837960

Mueller, Andreas		Wimsheim	Loen.	Oct 1858	N.-Amer	837967
Mueller, Andreas & F	42 yrs.	Moensheim	Leon.	Feb 1846	Austria	837960
Mueller, Anna Katharina (wife)	32 yrs.	Moensheim	Leon.	Mar 1830	N.-Amer	837960
Mueller, Anton & F		Epfendorf	Obd.	May 1817	N.-Amer	838632
Mueller, Anton & F		Sulgen	Obd.	Apr 1817	N.-Amer	838638
Mueller, Barbara	24 Mar 1833	Moensheim	Leon.	Feb 1846	Austria	837960
Mueller, Barbara & C	24 yrs.	Wimsheim	Loen.	Nov 1853	N.-Amer	837967
Mueller, Bartholomaeus	24 Aug 1809	Epfendorf	Obd.	Aug 1817	N.-Amer	838629
Mueller, Carl	66 yrs.	Oberndorf	Obd.	May 1852	N.-Amer	838635
Mueller, Carl Gotthilf	15 Jun 1815	Eltingen	Leon.	Mar 1842	N.-Amer	835789
Mueller, Catharina Friederike	10 Dec 1848	Unterlenningen	Krch.	Feb 1869	N.-Amer	835949
Mueller, Christian	31 Dec 1834	Seedorf	Obd.	Sep 1853	N.-Amer	838637
Mueller, Christian Friedrich	39 yrs.	Nabern	Krch.	Dec 1864	N.-Amer	835946
Mueller, Christian Heinrich	21 Apr 1814	Renningen	Leon.	Dec 1842	Berlin	837963
Mueller, Christian Sigmund & F	43 yrs.	Heimsheim	Leon.	Aug 1819	N.-Amer	837955
Mueller, Christian Wilhelm		Heimsheim	Leon.	Jun 1819	France	837955
Mueller, Christina	8 Nov 1825	Moensheim	Leon.	Mar 1830	N.-Amer	837960
Mueller, Christine Barb. (wife)	10 Jun 1811	Muenchingen	Leon.	Mar 1837	N.-Amer	837961
Mueller, Christine Doro. (wife)	42 yrs.	Heimsheim	Leon.	Aug 1819	N.-Amer	837955
Mueller, Christine Regine	5 yrs.	Heimsheim	Leon.	Aug 1819	N.-Amer	837955
Mueller, Conrad & F		Muenchingen	Leon.	Mar 1852	N.-Amer	837961
Mueller, Cyprian		Epfendorf	Obd.	Apr 1866	N.-Amer	838632
Mueller, Dorothea & C	21 Nov 1843	Donzdorf	Gsl.	Jul 1871	N.-Amer	572047
Mueller, Eduard		Donzdorf	Gsl.	Jan 1865	N.-Amer	572045
Mueller, Ehrenreich & F	25 Jul 1840	Weiler	Krch.	Apr 1884	N.-Amer	835949
Mueller, Emma	21 yrs.	Schramberg	Obd.	Sep 1854	N.-Amer	838636
Mueller, Emmerich	20 yrs.	Schramberg	Obd.	Sep 1854	N.-Amer	838636
Mueller, Ernst Gottlieb	18 Oct 1847	Gueltstein	Herr.	Apr 1869	N.-Amer	834631
Mueller, Ferdinand Robert		Geislingen	Gsl.	Apr 1866	England	572045
Mueller, Francisca	24 May 1816	Epfendorf	Obd.	Aug 1817	N.-Amer	838629
Mueller, Franz Hugo	8 May 1858	Nabern	Krch.	Jun 1874	England	835946
Mueller, Friederika	9 yrs.	Moensheim	Leon.	Aug 1851	N.-Amer	837960
Mueller, Friedrich	26 Apr 1838	Muenchingen	Leon.	Nov 1861	N.-Amer	837961
Mueller, Friedrich	17 Apr 1830	Muenchingen	Leon.	1854	N.-Amer	837961
Mueller, Friedrich	21 Dec 1866	Gutenberg	Krch.	Aug 1883	N.-Amer	548403
Mueller, Georg Friedrich	2 yrs.	Heimsheim	Leon.	Aug 1819	N.-Amer	837955
Mueller, Gottfried & F	35 yrs.	Moensheim	Leon.	Jan 1847	N.-Amer	837960
Mueller, Gottlieb	5 May 1808	Muenchingen	Leon.	Mar 1837	N.-Amer	837961
Mueller, Gottlob	4 Feb 1850	Muenchingen	Leon.	Mar 1852	N.-Amer	837961
Mueller, Hieronymus	3 Dec 1865	Donzdorf	Gsl.	Jul 1871	N.-Amer	572047
Mueller, Jacob		Muenchingen	Leon.	1853	N.-Amer	837961
Mueller, Jacob		Malmsheim	Leon.	May 1847	N.-Amer	837958
Mueller, Jacob	36 yrs.	Reutlingen	Rtl.	May 1880	N.-Amer	841051
Mueller, Jacob Friedrich	1785	Alpirsbach	Obd.	Nov 1824	France	838631
Mueller, Jacob Friedrich	10 Oct 1838	Hoefingen	Leon.	Feb 1857	N.-Amer	837957
Mueller, Jakob	15 Feb 1834	Alpirsbach	Obd.	Dec 1867	France	838630
Mueller, Jakob	2 May 1819	Moensheim	Leon.	Mar 1830	N.-Amer	837960
Mueller, Johann	17 Jun 1834	Moensheim	Leon.	Jan 1847	N.-Amer	837960
Mueller, Johann	1 yrs.	Westerheim	Gsl.	May 1853	N.-Amer	572041
Mueller, Johann Andreas	8 Mar 1839	Heimerdingen	Leon.	bef 1867	N.-Amer	837954

Name		Birth		Emigration			Film
Last	First	Date	Place	O'amt	Appl. Date	Dest.	Number
Mueller, Johann Christoph		15 yrs.	Heimsheim	Leon.	Aug 1819	N.-Amer	837955
Mueller, Johann Eberhard		24 Feb 1841	Owen	Krch.	bef 1871	N.-Amer	835948
Mueller, Johann Georg		23 Oct 1839	Moensheim	Leon.	Sep 1856	N.-Amer	837960
Mueller, Johann Georg		18 Sep 1830	Moensheim	Leon.	Feb 1846	Austria	837960
Mueller, Johann Georg		11 yrs.	Heimsheim	Leon.	Aug 1819	N.-Amer	837955
Mueller, Johann Georg		11 Apr 1819	Hochdorf	Krch.	May 1861	N.-Amer	835945
Mueller, Johann Georg & F			Moensheim	Leon.	Aug 1851	N.-Amer	837960
Mueller, Johann Georg & F		33 yrs.	Moensheim	Leon.	Mar 1830	N.-Amer	837960
Mueller, Johann Gottfried		19 Dec 1837	Moensheim	Leon.	Jan 1847	N.-Amer	837960
Mueller, Johann Jakob		10 Mar 1835	Muenchingen	Leon.	Mar 1837	N.-Amer	837961
Mueller, Johann Jakob		28 Oct 1812	Renningen	Leon.	bef 1841	Berlin	837963
Mueller, Johann Kristian			Leonberg	Leon.	Jan 1817	Russia	835785
Mueller, Johann Mathaeus		8 yrs.	Heimsheim	Leon.	Aug 1819	N.-Amer	837955
Mueller, Johanna		10 Mar 1835	Moensheim	Leon.	Sep 1856	N.-Amer	837960
Mueller, Johanna		27 Mar 1843	Moensheim	Leon.	Feb 1846	Austria	837960
Mueller, Johanna (wife)			Muenchingen	Leon.	Mar 1852	N.-Amer	837961
Mueller, Johanna Dorothea		9 Dec 1826	Moensheim	Leon.	Mar 1830	N.-Amer	837960
Mueller, Johanna Katharina		3 Jun 1844	Moensheim	Leon.	Jan 1847	N.-Amer	837960
Mueller, Johanna Maria		23 Oct 1838	Kirchheim	Krch.	Apr 1864	Austria	835941
Mueller, Johanne Catrine		6 yrs.	Heimsheim	Leon.	Aug 1819	N.-Amer	837955
Mueller, Johannes		19 Aug 1804	Epfendorf	Obd.	Aug 1817	N.-Amer	838629
Mueller, Johannes		27 Jun 1840	Moensheim	Leon.	Feb 1846	Austria	837960
Mueller, Johannes		27 Jun 1881	Eckwaelden	Krch.	Mar 1898	N.-Amer	835774
Mueller, Johannes		21 Sep 1835	Kuchen	Gsl.	Feb 1854	N.-Amer	572042
Mueller, Johannes		4 Aug 1840	Weissenstein	Gsl.	Feb 1857	N.-Amer	572043
Mueller, Johannes		7 Feb 1811	Hemmingen	Leon.	bef 1840	Holland	837956
Mueller, Johannes		30 Sep 1849	Donzdorf	Gsl.	Jul 1869	N.-Amer	572047
Mueller, Johannes		10 Jul 1848	Owen	Krch.	Oct 1866	N.-Amer	835948
Mueller, Joseph		16 yrs.	Lauterbach	Obd.	Oct 1852	N.-Amer	838634
Mueller, Joseph		17 Jul 1867	Donzdorf	Gsl.	Jul 1871	N.-Amer	572047
Mueller, Julius		17 Oct 1832	Geislingen	Gsl.	bef 1861	Hesse	572044
Mueller, Julius		16 yrs.	Kirchheim	Krch.	Aug 1872	N.-Amer	548403
Mueller, Julius		24 Feb 1856	Kirchheim	Krch.	Jul 1872	N.-Amer	835942
Mueller, Karolina		6 Jul 1822	Hemmingen	Leon.	Apr 1841	Bavaria	837956
Mueller, Katharina (wife)		2 Nov 1842	Wellingen	Krch.	Apr 1884	N.-Amer	835949
Mueller, Katharina Dorothea		– Sep 1828	Moensheim	Leon.	Feb 1846	Austria	837960
Mueller, Katharina Dorothea		14 Nov 1823	Moensheim	Leon.	Mar 1830	N.-Amer	837960
Mueller, Katharina Dorothea		16 May 1847	Heimsheim	Leon.	Mar 1869	N.-Amer	837955
Mueller, Konrad		18 Nov 1840	Lauterbach	Obd.	Apr 1864	Prussia	838634
Mueller, Konrad			Hirschlanden	Leon.	May 1849	N.-Amer	837956
Mueller, Leonhard Friedrich		28 yrs.	Leonberg	Leon.	Nov 1850	N.-Amer	835786
Mueller, Leonhardt		14 Nov 1842	Moensheim	Leon.	Jan 1847	N.-Amer	837960
Mueller, Leonhardt		24 Nov 1829	Moensheim	Leon.	Mar 1830	N.-Amer	837960
Mueller, Louise (wife)			Moensheim	Leon.	Aug 1851	N.-Amer	837960
Mueller, Ludwig		28 Oct 1847	Holzelfingen	Rtl.	Apr 1864	N.-Amer	841055
Mueller, Margaretha		21 May 1808	Kuchen	Gsl.	Mar 1852	N.-Amer	572041
Mueller, Margaretha		9 Mar 1870	Bissingen	Krch.	Apr 1884	N.-Amer	835949
Mueller, Margaretha Barb. (wife)		36 yrs.	Moensheim	Leon.	Feb 1846	Austria	837960
Mueller, Maria		1 Aug 1834	Weiler	Krch.	Jul 1857	N.-Amer	835949
Mueller, Maria Agnes & C		22 Mar 1844	Weiler	Krch.	Apr 1866	N.-Amer	835949

Mueller, Marie Margarethe	9 Mar 1870	Weiler	Krch.	Apr 1884	N.-Amer	548403
Mueller, Mathaeus	9 Apr 1836	Donzdorf	Gsl.	bef 1865	France	572045
Mueller, Matthias	2 Apr 1844	Fluorn	Obd.	Feb 1867	N.-Amer	838632
Mueller, Michael	7 Aug 1840	Moensheim	Leon.	Jan 1847	N.-Amer	837960
Mueller, Michael	13 Mar 1816	Moensheim	Leon.	Mar 1830	N.-Amer	837960
Mueller, Michael & F	37 yrs.	Moensheim	Leon.	Mar 1830	N.-Amer	837960
Mueller, Pauline		Muenchingen	Leon.	bef 1855	N.-Amer	837961
Mueller, Philipp	26 Sep 1839	Bondorf	Herr.	Jan 1865	N.-Amer	834630
Mueller, Rosina	10 yrs.	Moensheim	Leon.	Aug 1851	N.-Amer	837960
Mueller, Rosina Barbara (wife)		Moensheim	Leon.	Jan 1847	N.-Amer	837960
Mueller, Rosina Catharina	16 Apr 1829	Moensheim	Leon.	Mar 1830	N.-Amer	837960
Mueller, Rosina Dorothea	20 Dec 1846	Moensheim	Leon.	Jan 1847	N.-Amer	837960
Mueller, Rosine Barbara		Renningen	Leon.	May 1854	N.-Amer	837963
Mueller, Theresa (wife)		Epfendorf	Obd.	Aug 1817	N.-Amer	838629
Mueller, Walpurga & F	36 yrs.	Oberndorf	Obd.	May 1852	N.-Amer	838635
Mueller, Wendelin	20 Oct 1853	Seedorf	Obd.	Aug 1868	N.-Amer	838637
Mueller, Wilhelm Christian	20 Mar 1877	Eckwaelden	Krch.	Nar 1893	N.-Amer	835774
Mueller, Wilhelm Friedrich	20 Jul 1840	Kirchheim	Krch.	Feb 1855	N.-Amer	835940
Muellerschoen, Wilhelm	24 Dec 1868	Kirchheim	Krch.	Sep 1884	England	835942
Muenchinger, August	16 Aug 1871	Hoefingen	Leon.	Feb 1887	N.-Amer	837957
Muenchinger, Johannes	11 Feb 1857	Pliensbach	Krch.	Dec 1872	N.-Amer	835774
Muendler, Johannes		Altenstadt-Gsl.	Gsl.	bef 1868	N.-Amer	572046
Muensinger, Wilhelm Julius	29 Apr 1876	Aichelberg	Krch.	Apr 1892	N.-Amer	835943
Mukenfuss, Eberhard	18 Mar 1845	Pfullingen	Rtl.	Apr 1864	N.-Amer	841055
Mukenfuss, Eberhard Ludwig	24 Mar 1850	Pfullingen	Rtl.	Apr 1868	N.-Amer	841055
Mundinger, Anna Maria	6 May 1830	Warmbronn	Leon.	Jul 1854	N.-Amer	837965
Mundinger, Catharina	17 yrs.	Warmbronn	Leon.	Mar 1849	N.-Amer	837965
Mundinger, Friederike	3 yrs.	Eltingen	Leon.	Dec 1851	N.-Amer	835789
Mundinger, Johanna	7 yrs.	Eltingen	Leon.	Dec 1851	N.-Amer	835789
Mundinger, Johannes	18 Mar 1833	Leonberg	Leon.	May 1859	Switz.	835786
Mundinger, Johannes	8 yrs.	Eltingen	Leon.	Dec 1851	N.-Amer	835789
Mundinger, Johannes & F		Eltingen	Leon.	Dec 1851	N.-Amer	835789
Mundinger, Leonhardt Gotthilf	4 Dec 1854	Warmbronn	Leon.	May 1871	N.-Amer	837965
Mundinger, Luise Katharina	13 Jul 1839	Warmbronn	Leon.	1879	Switz.	837965
Mundinger, Magdalena (wife)		Eltingen	Leon.	Dec 1851	N.-Amer	835789
Munk, Barbara	10 Sep 1831	Owen	Krch.	bef 1873	N.-Amer	835948
Munk, Caspar	18 Oct 1804	Unterlenningen	Krch.	Jun 1857	N.-Amer	835949
Munk, Christina (wife)	10 Feb 1840	Oberlenningen	Krch.	Apr 1881	N.-Amer	548403
Munk, Friederike	2 Mar 1863	Oberlenningen	Krch.	Apr 1881	N.-Amer	548403
Munk, Gottlieb	2 Aug 1864	Oberlenningen	Krch.	Apr 1881	N.-Amer	835947
Munk, Gottlob Friedrich	26 Mar 1871	Oberlenningen	Krch.	Apr 1881	N.-Amer	548403
Munk, Johann Bernhard	14 Jul 1866	Oberlenningen	Krch.	Apr 1881	N.-Amer	548403
Munk, Johann Bernhard & F	16 Mar 1838	Oberlenningen	Krch.	Apr 1881	N.-Amer	548403
Munk, Johann Konrad	21 Mar 1830	Owen	Krch.	bef 1873	N.-Amer	835948
Munk, Johannes	18 May 1868	Oberlenningen	Krch.	Apr 1881	N.-Amer	835947
Munz, Adolph	25 Aug 1840	Schramberg	Obd.	bef 1867	N.-Amer	838636
Munz, Amalie	3 Aug 1845	Schramberg	Obd.	bef 1869	N.-Amer	838636
Munz, Angelika	17 May 1830	Geislingen	Gsl.	Sep 1854	N.-Amer	572042
Munz, Carl	6 Oct 1843	Weilheim	Krch.	Feb 1867	N.-Amer	835950
Munz, David	10 May 1839	Oetlingen	Krch.	bef 1869	N.-Amer	835948

| Name | | Birth | | Emigration | | | Film |
Last	First	Date	Place	O'amt	Appl. Date	Dest.	Number
Munz,	Ernestine Rosine	15 Aug 1873	Oetlingen	Krch.	Apr 1883	N.-Amer	835948
Munz,	Johannes		Winzeln	Obd.	Sep 1851	N.-Amer	841016
Munz,	Karl & F	14 May 1843	Oetlingen	Krch.	Apr 1883	N.-Amer	835948
Munz,	Karl Hermann	19 Jun 1870	Oetlingen	Krch.	Apr 1883	N.-Amer	835948
Munz,	Karl Wilhelm	1 Nov 1868	Oetlingen	Krch.	Apr 1883	N.-Amer	835948
Munz,	Luise Mathilde	13 Jun 1880	Oetlingen	Krch.	Apr 1883	N.-Amer	835948
Munz,	Luise Mathilde (wife)	21 Aug 1842	Cannstadt	Krch.	Apr 1883	N.-Amer	835948
Munz,	Marie Luise	18 Feb 1876	Oetlingen	Krch.	Apr 1883	N.-Amer	835948
Munz,	Matthaeus	18 Sep 1834	Winzeln	Obd.	Nov 1853	N.-Amer	841016
Munz,	Nikolaus	4 Dec 1837	Winzeln	Obd.	Sep 1857	N.-Amer	841016
Munz,	Rosine Luise	9 Jan 1878	Oetlingen	Krch.	Apr 1883	N.-Amer	835948
Muscheller,	Anna Katharina	30 Jan 1837	Tuerkheim	Gsl.	Aug 1869	Paris	572047
Muth,	Lorenz	9 Oct 1838	Weilheim	Krch.	bef 1867	N.-Amer	835950
Mutschelknauss,	Gottlieb	26 yrs.	Flacht	Leon.	Sep 1853	N.-Amer	835790
Mutschler,	Andreas	18 Sep 1836	Betzweiler	Obd.	May 1847	N.-Amer	838631
Mutschler,	Andreas & F		Boll	Obd.	May 1847	N.-Amer	838631
Mutschler,	Anna Maria	2 Mar 1844	Betzweiler	Obd.	May 1847	N.-Amer	838631
Mutschler,	Catharina	11 Aug 1846	Betzweiler	Obd.	May 1847	N.-Amer	838631
Mutschler,	Christian	8 Feb 1834	Betzweiler	Obd.	Apr 1854	N.-Amer	838631
Mutschler,	Christine	15 Sep 1837	Betzweiler	Obd.	May 1847	N.-Amer	838631
Mutschler,	Ernest	26 Jul 1849	Kirchheim	Krch.	Jul 1869	N.-Amer	835941
Mutschler,	Georg	29 Apr 1839	Peterzell	Obd.	Aug 1854	N.-Amer	838635
Mutschler,	Georg & F		Effringen	Nag.	Jul 1852	N.-Amer	838488
Mutschler,	Johann	14 Nov 1851	Betzweiler	Obd.	Oct 1868	N.-Amer	838631
Mutschler,	Johann Mich. Gott.	26 Sep 1846	Hochdorf	Krch.	Mar 1876	N.-Amer	835945
Mutschler,	Johannes	26 Dec 1838	Betzweiler	Obd.	May 1847	N.-Amer	838631
Mutschler,	Johannes	4 Mar 1846	Undingen	Rtl.	Oct 1866	N.-Amer	841055
Mutschler,	Margaretha (wife)	23 May 1812	Betzweiler	Obd.	May 1847	N.-Amer	838631
Mutschler,	Matthias	10 Dec 1839	Betzweiler	Obd.	May 1847	N.-Amer	838631
Mutschler,	Wilhelm Friedrich	19 Jul 1826	Unterlenningen	Krch.	1845	N.-Amer	835949
Muttschler,	Johann Michael G.	26 Sep 1846	Hochdorf	Krch.	Apr 1876	N.-Amer	548403
Nachbauer,	Johs & F		Weil der Stadt	Leon.	May 1853	N.-Amer	837966
Nachbauer,	Theresia	10 Jul 1837	Weil der Stadt	Leon.	Oct 1859	Prussia	837966
Naegele,	Anton & F		Weissenstein	Gsl.	Dec 1852	N.-Amer	573622
Naegele,	Augustin	1 Oct 1822	Weissenstein	Gsl.	Aug 1848	Wien	577788
Naegele,	Carl Friedr. Conrad	26 Apr 1846	Jesingen	Krch.	Oct 1865	N.-Amer	835946
Naegele,	Christian Gottlieb	7 Jan 1855	Dettingen	Krch.	Feb 1868	N.-Amer	835944
Naegele,	Christiana	26 Dec 1848	Jesingen	Krch.	bef 1886	N.-Amer	835946
Naegele,	Elisabetha (wife)	17 May 1812	Ulm	Gsl.	Mar 1853	N.-Amer	572041
Naegele,	Franz	1 Dec 1847	Treffelhausen	Gsl.	Oct 1866	N.-Amer	572045
Naegele,	Jakob	3 Mar 1836	Donzdorf	Gsl.	Jun 1854	N.-Amer	572042
Naegele,	Johann	8 Mar 1843	Lindorf	Krch.	Jun 1867	N.-Amer	835946
Naegele,	Johann Bap. Joa. & F	20 Mar 1813	Eybach	Gsl.	Mar 1853	N.-Amer	572041
Naegele,	Johann Georg & F	1 Mar 1821	Dettingen	Krch.	Feb 1868	N.-Amer	835944
Naegele,	Johann Wilhelm	3 Apr 1863	Dettingen	Krch.	Mar 1880	N.-Amer	835944
Naegele,	Johannes	30 Mar 1844	Ulm	Gsl.	Mar 1853	N.-Amer	572041
Naegele,	Johannes	29 Jul 1856	Bissingen	Krch.	Feb 1879	N.-Amer	548403
Naegele,	Johannes	29 Jul 1856	Bissingen	Krch.	Feb 1879	N.-Amer	835943
Naegele,	Joseph Anton		Eybach	Gsl.	Mar 1852	N.-Amer	572041
Naegele,	Ludwig	17 Aug 1832	Weissenstein	Gsl.	Jul 1851	N.-Amer	577788

Naegele, Marie Louise	23 Apr 1850	Ulm	Gsl.	Mar 1853	N.-Amer	572041
Naegele, Michael	4 May 1835	Jesingen	Krch.	May 1877	N.-Amer	548403
Naegele, Wunibald	14 Jun 1832	Weissenstein	Gsl.	Jan 1854	N.-Amer	572042
Naeher, Friedrich	25 Jan 1833	Geislingen	Gsl.	bef 1863	N.-Amer	572044
Naeher, Jakob	9 APr 1813	Grosssuessen	Gsl.	Feb 1854	N.-Amer	572042
Naeher, Simon	26 Oct 1830	Geislingen	Gsl.	bef 1863	N.-Amer	572044
Nagel, Alois	1822	Schramberg	Obd.	Mar 1848	N.-Amer	838637
Nagel, Andreas	30 Nov 1836	Donzdorf	Gsl.	Jun 1854	N.-Amer	572042
Nagel, Anna Katharina		Ueberkingen	Gsl.	Dec 1853	N.-Amer	572041
Nagel, Bernhard	18 yrs.	Donzdorf	Gsl.	Mar 1852	N.-Amer	572041
Nagel, Bernhard & F	11 Oct 1794	Donzdorf	Gsl.	Aug 1854	N.-Amer	572042
Nagel, Crescenz	1 Mar 1845	Donzdorf	Gsl.	Aug 1854	N.-Amer	572042
Nagel, Elisabetha	29 Jul 1830	Donzdorf	Gsl.	Feb 1853	N.-Amer	572041
Nagel, Franziska & C		Schnittlingen	Gsl.	Mar 1860	Hungary	572044
Nagel, Friederich	4 Jan 1846	Gaertringen	Herr.	Nov 1866	N.-Amer	834630
Nagel, Friedrich		Schramberg	Obd.	Jun 1862	Poland	838636
Nagel, Jacob & F		Schramberg	Obd.	Oct 1852	N.-Amer	838637
Nagel, Johann Peter	7 Nov 1852	Gaertringen	Herr.	Jun 1873	N.-Amer	834630
Nagel, Johannes	18 Mar 1839	Sulgen	Obd.	Oct 1868	Bavaria	838638
Nagel, Johannes	26 yrs.	Treffelhausen	Gsl.	May 1852	N.-Amer	572041
Nagel, Johannes		Donzdorf	Gsl.	bef 1865	N.-Amer	572045
Nagel, Joseph	27 yrs.	Donzdorf	Gsl.	Mar 1852	N.-Amer	572041
Nagel, Joseph	26 May 1834	Donzdorf	Gsl.	Feb 1853	N.-Amer	572041
Nagel, Josepha	3 Dec 1816	Sulgen	Obd.	Jun 1867	Bavaria	838638
Nagel, Josepha	11 Aug 1804	Donzdorf	Gsl.	Aug 1854	N.-Amer	572042
Nagel, Josepha	12 May 1854	Donzdorf	Gsl.	Aug 1854	N.-Amer	572042
Nagel, Josephine		Schramberg	Obd.	Sep 1862	France	838636
Nagel, Katharina	19 Sep 1838	Donzdorf	Gsl.	Aug 1854	N.-Amer	572042
Nagel, Katharina	17 Jan 1849	Donzdorf	Gsl.	Jul 1871	N.-Amer	572047
Nagel, Leonhard	3 Dec 1847	Schnittlingen	Gsl.	Oct 1869	N.-Amer	572047
Nagel, Lorenz	21 Mar 1866	Treffelhausen	Gsl.	Feb 1883	N.-Amer	572049
Nagel, Maria Anna	11 Oct 1829	Donzdorf	Gsl.	Aug 1854	N.-Amer	572042
Nagel, Maria Barbara		Ueberkingen	Gsl.	Dec 1853	N.-Amer	572041
Nagel, Marianna		Donzdorf	Gsl.	bef 1864	N.-Amer	572045
Nagel, Mathias	3 Sep 1836	Donzdorf	Gsl.	Feb 1853	N.-Amer	572041
Nagel, Matthias	18 Feb 1865	Treffelhausen	Gsl.	Feb 1883	N.-Amer	572049
Nagel, Xaver	20 Nov 1837	Donzdorf	Gsl.	Jun 1854	N.-Amer	572042
Nagels, Sabina		Boehmenkirch	Gsl.	Oct 1852	N.-Amer	572041
Naspel, Wilhelm	28 yrs.	Reutlingen	Rtl.	Dec 1880	N.-Amer	841051
Nass, Johann Jakob	9 Feb 1835	Renningen	Leon.	Jul 1854	N.-Amer	837963
Nast, Albert	21 Feb 1850	Leonberg	Leon.	Apr 1853	N.-Amer	835786
Nast, Albert David	28 Oct 1838	Leonberg	Leon.	Sep 1853	N.-Amer	835786
Nast, Bertha Augusta	3 Jan 1836	Leonberg	Leon.	Aug 1865	Hesse	835787
Nast, Carl Friedrich	5 yrs.	Geislingen	Gsl.	Aug 1853	N.-Amer	572041
Nast, Caroline		Leonberg	Leon.	May 1829	Saxony	835786
Nast, Christian August	28 Jul 1816	Leonberg	Leon.	Mar 1867	Hesse	835787
Nast, Gottlob & F		Leonberg	Leon.	Apr 1853	N.-Amer	835786
Nast, Karl Heinrich	29 Jun 1830	Leonberg	Leon.	Aug 1852	N.-Amer	835786
Nast, Louise	30 May 1852	Leonberg	Leon.	Apr 1853	N.-Amer	835786
Nast, Pauline (wife)		Leonberg	Leon.	Apr 1853	N.-Amer	835786

Name		Birth		Emigration			Film
Last	First	Date	Place	O'amt	Appl. Date	Dest.	Number
Nast, Rudolf		20 Aug 1842	Leonberg	Leon.	Jan 1861	N.-Amer	835787
Natter, Johann Nepomuk		27 May 1868	Muehlhausen	Gsl.	Feb 1883	N.-Amer	572049
Natter. Franz Anton		30 yrs.	Drackenstein	Gsl.	Sep 1862	Hungary	572044
Naumer, Mathilde Jakobine		18 Oct 1839	Malmsheim	Leon.	Aug 1856	N.-Amer	837958
Nedele, Jakob		11 Feb 1848	Betzingen	Rtl.	Apr 1867	N.-Amer	841055
Nedele, Johannes		10 May 1848	Betzingen	Rtl.	Jun 1866	N.-Amer	841055
Neeb, Barbara		19 Dec 1842	Alpirsbach	Obd.	Jan.1869	France	838630
Neef, Anton		7 Jan 1837	Schramberg	Obd.	Feb 1856	N.-Amer	838636
Neef, Theresia			Schramberg	Obd.	Aug 1861	Austria	838636
Neff, Balthasar			Schramberg	Obd.	Mar 1817	A.-Amer	838637
Neff, Moriz			Winzeln	Obd.	Aug 1860	N.-Amer	841016
Neidhardt, Carl Gottlieb		24 Oct 1860	Kirchheim	Krch.	May 1878	N.-Amer	835942
Neidhardt, Johann Friedrich		25 Aug 1836	Kirchheim	Krch.	Feb 1866	N.-Amer	835941
Neidhardt, Sophie Friederike		3 Apr 1846	Kirchheim	Krch.	May 1868	N.-Amer	835941
Neser, Carl			Schramberg	Obd.	Dec 1837	Switz.	838637
Nestel, Catharina (wife)		27 Apr 1799	Epfendorf	Obd.	Aug 1817	N.-Amer	838629
Nestel, Christian		17 Feb 1808	Epfendorf	Obd.	Aug 1817	N.-Amer	838629
Nestel, Crescenzia		21 Nov 1813	Epfendorf	Obd.	Aug 1817	N.-Amer	838629
Nestel, Johannes		27 Nov 1816	Epfendorf	Obd.	Aug 1817	N.-Amer	838629
Nestel, Maria (wife)			Epfendorf	Obd.	Aug 1817	N.-Amer	838629
Nestel, Maria Anna		22 Apr 1801	Epfendorf	Obd.	Aug 1817	N.-Amer	838629
Nestel, Martin		13 May 1841	Betzingen	Rtl.	Apr 1862	N.-Amer	841055
Nestel, Sebastian & F			Epfendorf	Obd.	Aug 1817	N.-Amer	838629
Nestle, Carl Friedrich		1 yr.	Oberndorf	Obd.	Mar 1865	N.-Amer	838635
Nestle, Catharina (wid.) & F			Altenstaig	Nag.	Jul 1852	N.-Amer	838488
Nestle, Emilie		4 yrs.	Oberndorf	Obd.	Mar 1865	N.-Amer	838635
Nestle, Friedrich & F			Oberndorf	Obd.	Mar 1865	N.-Amer	838635
Nestle, Josepha (wife)			Oberndorf	Obd.	Mar 1865	N.-Amer	838635
Nestle, Pauline		3 yrs.	Oberndorf	Obd.	Mar 1865	N.-Amer	838635
Nestler, August		9 Jun 1839	Weil der Stadt	Leon.	Jul 1850	N.-Amer	837966
Nestler, Boneventur & F			Weil der Stadt	Leon.	May 1847	N.-Amer	837965
Nestler, Caroline		3 Jan 1847	Weil der Stadt	Leon.	May 1847	N.-Amer	837965
Nestler, Hermann		21 Jan 1835	Weil der Stadt	Leon.	May 1847	N.-Amer	837965
Nestler, Johannes Nicolaus		22 Jan 1840	Weil der Stadt	Leon.	bef 1860	N.-Amer	837966
Nestler, Joseph			Weil der Stadt	Leon.	Jan 1854	N.-Amer	837966
Nestler, Joseph			Weil der Stadt	Leon.	1848	N.-Amer	837966
Nestler, Joseph		22 Nov 1824	Weil der Stadt	Leon.	May 1847	N.-Amer	837965
Nestler, Joseph Anton		21 Mar 1836	Weil der Stadt	Leon.	Jul 1850	N.-Amer	837966
Nestler, Marianne		10 Apr 1829	Weil der Stadt	Leon.	Jul 1850	N.-Amer	837966
Nestler, Sophie & F			Weil der Stadt	Leon.	Jul 1850	N.-Amer	837966
Nestler, Therese		18 Feb 1839	Weil der Stadt	Leon.	May 1847	N.-Amer	837965
Nettlinger, Martin			Geislingen	Gsl.	bef 1854	N.-Amer	572042
Nettlinger, Ursula (wife)		34 yrs.	Geislingen	Gsl.	Sep 1854	N.-Amer	572042
Neubrander, Jakob		26 Feb 1841	Unterhausen	Rtl.	May 1866	N.-Amer	841055
Neubrander, Johann Martin & F		3 May 1816	Unterhausen	Rtl.	Nov 1867	N.-Amer	841055
Neubrander, Johann Stephan		3 Jun 1845	Unterhausen	Rtl.	Apr 1864	N.-Amer	841055
Neubrander, Margaretha		22 Jul 1845	Unterhausen	Rtl.	1865	N.-Amer	841055
Neubrander, Maria Barb. (wife)		21 Dec 1822	Undingen	Rtl.	Nov 1867	N.-Amer	841055
Neubrander, Maria Barbara		21 Mar 1848	Unterhausen	Rtl.	Nov 1867	N.-Amer	841055
Neubrander, Maria Elisab. & C		21 Jul 1842	Unterhausen	Rtl.	Nov 1867	N.-Amer	841055

Neubrander, Martin	21 Nov 1843	Unterhausen	Rtl.	bef 1867	N.-Amer	841055
Neuffer, Carl Gottl. Fruecht.	12 Jan 1848	Unterlenningen	Krch.	Nov 1866	N.-Amer	835949
Neuffer, Johannes	15 Jul 1831	Grosssuessen	Gsl.	1854	N.-Amer	572043
Neuffer, Paul Wilhelm	5 Nov 1855	Unterlenningen	Krch.	Aug 1871	N.-Amer	835949
Neuffer, Wilhelm Eduard	2 Mar 1851	Unterlenningen	Krch.	Mar 1867	N.-Amer	835949
Neuhaeuser, Johannes Christ.	14 Apr 1867	Bissingen	Krch.	Apr 1883	N.-Amer	548403
Neuhauser, Christian Ludwig	2 Sep 1866	Dettingen	Krch.	Mar 1883	N.-Amer	835944
Neuschwanger, Bartholomaeus	19 yrs.	Harthausen	Obd.	Sep 1853	N.-Amer	838633
Neuschwanger, Magdalena	17 yrs.	Harthausen	Obd.	Sep 1853	N.-Amer	838633
Nibel, Robert	1 Jun 1850	Winzeln	Obd.	Sep 1867	N.-Amer	841016
Nick, Andreas	25 Oct 1798	Schoeckingen	Leon.	bef 1859	Wien	837964
Nick, Anna Maria		Hoefingen	Leon.	1822	Russia	837957
Nick, Carl Ernst Rudolf	16 Apr 1838	Leonberg	Leon.	Sep 1852	N.-Amer	835786
Nick, Carl Heinrich	15 Dec 1844	Leonberg	Leon.	Nov 1866	N.-Amer	835787
Nick, Christian & F		Hoefingen	Leon.	1822	Russia	837957
Nick, Christine Barbara & C		Hoefingen	Leon.	Feb 1854	N.-Amer	837957
Nick, Georg Heinrich	4 Jul 1829	Leonberg	Leon.	Feb 1861	Algier	835787
Nick, Gottlieb	20 yrs.	Hoefingen	Leon.	Sep 1853	N.-Amer	837957
Nick, Gottlieb & W	28 Apr 1838	Peterzell	Obd.	Apr 1865	N.-Amer	838635
Nick, Jacob	12 Aug 1849	Schoeckingen	Leon.	Mat 1868	N.-Amer	837964
Nick, Johann Georg	32 yrs.	Hoefingen	Leon.	May 1854	N.-Amer	837957
Nick, Katharina (wife)	16 Jul 1835	Reutin	Obd.	Apr 1865	N.-Amer	838635
Nick, Leonarda		Leonberg	Leon.	Oct 1853	Switz.	835786
Nick, Margaretha (wife)		Hoefingen	Leon.	1822	Russia	837957
Nick, Margreta		Hoefingen	Leon.	1822	Russia	837957
Nick, Maria Caroline	18 Jun 1835	Leonberg	Leon.	bef 1855	N.-Amer	835786
Nick, Michael		Hoefingen	Leon.	Jun 1829	Holland	837957
Nick, Philipp Arnold	10 May 1833	Leonberg	Leon.	Feb 1861	Algier	835787
Nick, Sophie	8 yrs.	Hoefingen	Leon.	Feb 1854	N.-Amer	837957
Nick, Theodor Wilhelm	22 Dec 1829	Heimsheim	Leon.	Apr 1849	N.-Amer	837955
Nickel, Gottlieb	4 Aug 1838	Hoefingen	Leon.	Mar 1853	N.-Amer	837957
Niebel, Anna Maria		Roetenbach	Obd.	bef 1863	N.-Amer	838636
Niebel, Christian		Alpirsbach	Obd.	Aug 1849	N.-Amer	838630
Niebel, Christian	8 May 1846	Waldmoessingen	Obd.	Apr 1866	N.-Amer	841015
Niebel, Christian Friedrich	5 Mar 1809	Alpirsbach	Obd.	Aug 1854	N.-Amer	838630
Niebel, Christiane & C	18 Dec 1816	Alpirsbach	Obd.	Apr 1856	N.-Amer	838630
Niebel, Christina		Roetenbach	Obd.	Jun 1857	N.-Amer	838636
Niebel, Jacob Friedrich	8 Dec 1821	Alpirsbach	Obd.	Sep 1848	N.-Amer	838630
Niebel, Wilhelm	6 yrs.	Alpirsbach	Obd.	Apr 1856	N.-Amer	838630
Niefer, Anna Katharina	28 Dec 1843	Notzingen	Krch.	Mar 1869	N.-Amer	835947
Niefer, Carola	25 Oct 1832	Notzingen	Krch.	bef 1861	Austria	835947
Niefer, Johann	6 Feb 1840	Notzingen	Krch.	May 1867	N.-Amer	835947
Niefer, Johann Carl	11 Oct 1835	Notzingen	Krch.	bef 1861	Austria	835947
Niefer, Johann Georg	18 Nov 1825	Notzingen	Krch.	May 1855	N.-Amer	835947
Niefer, Josepha	27 Nov 1839	Notzingen	Krch.	bef 1861	Austria	835947
Niefer, Wilhelm	1 Nov 1850	Notzingen	Krch.	Sep 1869	N.-Amer	835947
Nieffer, Georg Heinrich	6 Oct 1869	Cannstatt/Stutt.	Krch.	Apr 1884	N.-Amer	548403
Niess, Euphrosine	23 yrs.	Geislingen	Gsl.	Aug 1853	N.-Amer	572041
Niethammer, Wilhelm Friedr.	10 Feb 1845	Herrenberg	Herr.	Aug 1872	N.-Amer	834629
Nik, Christian & F		Hoefingen	Leon.	May 1832	Poland	837957

Name		Birth		Emigration			Film
Last	First	Date	Place	O'amt	Appl. Date	Dest.	Number
Nill, – (wife)		27 yrs.	Reutlingen	Rtl.	Apr 1880	N.-Amer	841051
Nill, Henrich & F		30 yrs.	Reutlingen	Rtl.	Apr 1880	N.-Amer	841051
Nill, Johann Eugen		2 yrs.	Reutlingen	Rtl.	Apr 1880	N.-Amer	841051
Nill, Johann Reinhold		infant	Reutlingen	Rtl.	Apr 1880	N.-Amer	841051
Nilli, Johannes		2 Aug 1837	Kirchheim	Krch.	Mar 1857	N.-Amer	835940
Nilli, Wilhelm Friedrich		15 Mar 1854	Kirchheim	Krch.	1875	N.-Amer	835942
Nilli, Xaver		15 Mar 1838	Wiesensteig	Gsl.	Apr 1855	N.-Amer	573622
Nissle, Carl		15 May 1838	Leonberg	Leon.	Jul 1854	N.-Amer	835786
Noelsch, Johann David		25 Sep 1840	Oetlingen	Krch.	Jun 1866	N.-Amer	835948
Noll, Albin & F		27 Feb 1830	Alt Oberndorf	Obd.	Sep 1868	N.-Amer	838631
Noll, Magdalena			Alt Oberndorf	Obd.	Sep 1868	N.-Amer	838631
Noll, Mathilde (wife)			Alt Oberndorf	Obd.	Sep 1868	N.-Amer	838631
Nonnenmacher, Jakob			Hausen a.d. Wurm	Leon.	Apr 1831	N.-Amer	837954
Nonnenmann, Caroline Chr. Lo.		3 Apr 1838	Brucken	Krch.	Feb 1854	N.-Amer	835944
Nonnenmann, Joh. Christoph Ad.		16 May 1841	Brucken	Krch.	Jul 1863	N.-Amer	835944
Notheis, Johannes		28 Apr 1837	Seedorf	Obd.	Sep 1862	France	838637
Notheis, Leander		17 Nov 1834	Waldmoessingen	Obd.	Mar 1853	N.-Amer	841015
Nothenius, Caroline Dorothea		12 May 1848	Warmbronn	Leon.	bef 1869	N.-Amer	837965
Nothenius, Johann Jacob		27 Aug 1841	Warmbronn	Leon.	Mar 1867	N.-Amer	837965
Nothenius, Johannes		5 Apr 1851	Warmbronn	Leon.	Mar 1867	N.-Amer	837965
Noz, Karl Gotthilf		28 Jan 1859	Esslingen	Krch.	bef 1883	Belgien	835942
Nuding, Anton			Weissenstein	Gsl.	Aug 1864	N.-Amer	572045
Nuding, Christina		23 Apr 1843	Geislingen	Gsl.	Sep 1867	Austria	572046
Nuding, Christoph Friedrich			Heimsheim	Leon.	bef 1818	Poland	837955
Nuebel, Adelheid		5 yrs.	Fluorn	Obd.	Nov 1846	N.-Amer	838632
Nuebel, Anna		infant	Fluorn	Obd.	Nov 1846	N.-Amer	838632
Nuebel, Anna		17 yrs.	Fluorn	Obd.	Nov 1846	N.-Amer	838632
Nuebel, Anna Maria		19 yrs.	Fluorn	Obd.	Nov 1846	N.-Amer	838632
Nuebel, Anna Maria		15 yrs.	Fluorn	Obd.	Nov 1846	N.-Amer	838632
Nuebel, Anna Maria		3 Jun 1861	Dornhan	Obd.	Mar 1869	N.-Amer	838638
Nuebel, Anna Maria (wife)		41 yrs.	Fluorn	Obd.	Nov 1846	N.-Amer	838632
Nuebel, Barbara		4 yrs.	Fluorn	Obd.	Nov 1846	N.-Amer	838632
Nuebel, Christine		13 yrs.	Fluorn	Obd.	Nov 1846	N.-Amer	838632
Nuebel, Christine		14 yrs.	Fluorn	Obd.	Nov 1846	N.-Amer	838632
Nuebel, Dorothea		7 yrs.	Fluorn	Obd.	Nov 1846	N.-Amer	838632
Nuebel, Dorothea (wife)		31 May 1825	Dornhan	Obd.	Mar 1869	N.-Amer	838638
Nuebel, Jakob		2 yrs.	Fluorn	Obd.	Nov 1846	N.-Amer	838632
Nuebel, Johann Georg		2 Jul 1859	Dornhan	Obd.	Mar 1869	N.-Amer	838638
Nuebel, Johann Georg & F			Fluorn	Obd.	Nov 1846	N.-Amer	838632
Nuebel, Johann Jakob & F			Fluorn	Obd.	Apr 1845	N.-Amer	838632
Nuebel, Johann Martin & F		3 Feb 1817	Dornhan	Obd.	Mar 1869	N.-Amer	838638
Nuebel, Johanna (wife)		27 yrs.	Fluorn	Obd.	Nov 1846	N.-Amer	838632
Nuebel, Johannes		9 yrs.	Fluorn	Obd.	Nov 1846	N.-Amer	838632
Nuebel, Johannes & F			Fluorn	Obd.	Nov 1846	N.-Amer	838632
Nuebel, Justine		11 yrs.	Fluorn	Obd.	Nov 1846	N.-Amer	838632
Nuebel, Katharina		16 yrs.	Fluorn	Obd.	Nov 1846	N.-Amer	838632
Nuebel, Magdalena Barbara		12 yrs.	Fluorn	Obd.	Nov 1846	N.-Amer	838632
Nuebel, Mathias		25 Nov 1845	Fluorn	Obd.	Oct 1869	N.-Amer	838632
Nuebel, Rosine		9 yrs.	Fluorn	Obd.	Nov 1846	N.-Amer	838632
Nueding, Kristine Heinrike			Heimsheim	Leon.	Apr 1831	N.-Amer	837955

Nuffer, Christian Peter	14 Jan 1825	Renningen	Leon.	Feb 1852	N.-Amer	837963
Oberle, Josef	13 yrs.	Winzeln	Obd.	Sep 1852	N.-Amer	841016
Oberle, Maria (wid.) & F		Winzeln	Obd.	Sep 1852	N.-Amer	841016
Oberle, Susanna	13 Aug 1837	Winzeln	Obd.	Mar 1852	N.-Amer	841016
Ochsenwadel, Andreas	5 Dec 1834	Aufhausen	Gsl.	Apr 1856	N.-Amer	572043
Ochsenwadel, Anna Kathar. & F	13 Mar 1801	Aufhausen	Gsl.	Apr 1856	N.-Amer	572043
Ochsenwadel, Helene Magdalene	8 Jun 1843	Aufhausen	Gsl.	Apr 1856	N.-Amer	572043
Ochsenwadel, Johann Georg	29 Apr 1828	Eckwaelden	Krch.	Jun 1866	N.-Amer	835774
Ochsenwadel, Johann Michael	9 Jul 1823	Zell	Krch.	Apr 1859	N.-Amer	835774
Ochsenwadel, Johannes	22 May 1838	Aufhausen	Gsl.	Apr 1856	N.-Amer	572043
Ochsenwadel, Matthaeus	3 Mar 1836	Aufhausen	Gsl.	Apr 1856	N.-Amer	572043
Ocker, August	1827	Treffelhausen	Gsl.	Apr 1852	N.-Amer	572041
Ocker, Valentin		Treffelhausen	Gsl.	Apr 1852	N.-Amer	572041
Oechsle, Anna Maria		Geislingen	Gsl.	Feb 1853	N.-Amer	572041
Oechsle, Anna Maria - twin	20 May 1826	Kuchen	Gsl.	Feb 1854	N.-Amer	572042
Oechsle, Konrad	28 Oct 1838	Kuchen	Gsl.	Feb 1854	N.-Amer	572042
Oechsle, Margaretha - twin	20 May 1826	Kuchen	Gsl.	Feb 1854	N.-Amer	572042
Oechsle, Michael	21 Jun 1853	Kuchen	Gsl.	Aug 1879	N.-Amer	572048
Oeffinger, Johann & F		Sulgen	Obd.	May 1817	N.-Amer	838638
Oehler, Anton	21 Mar 1849	Weil der Stadt	Leon.	Aug 1868	N.-Amer	837966
Oehler, Barnabas	9 Jun 1833	Lauterbach	Obd.	Dec 1853	N.-Amer	838634
Oehler, Bernhard	7 Aug 1837	Lauterbach	Obd.	Dec 1865	Prussia	838634
Oehler, Carl Emmerich	10 Jul 1845	Sulgen	Obd.	Oct 1865	N.-Amer	838638
Oehler, David	21 Mar 1844	Weil der Stadt	Leon.	Mar 1847	N.-Amer	837965
Oehler, David & F		Weil der Stadt	Leon.	Mar 1847	N.-Amer	837965
Oehler, Elias		Lauterbach	Obd.	Sep 1854	Prussia	838634
Oehler, Elisabetha	10 Jan 1846	Schramberg	Obd.	Nov 1857	N.-Amer	838636
Oehler, Engelbert	6 Sep 1838	Schramberg	Obd.	Nov 1857	N.-Amer	838636
Oehler, Franz Joseph	9 Dec 1839	Weil der Stadt	Leon.	Mar 1847	N.-Amer	837965
Oehler, Herrmann	12 Jan 1841	Weil der Stadt	Leon.	Mar 1847	N.-Amer	837965
Oehler, Johannes	24 Jun 1840	Lauterbach	Obd.	Oct 1867	Prussia	838634
Oehler, Mathias		Lauterbach	Obd.	Apr 1859	N.-Amer	838634
Oehler, Nikolaus	28 Nov 1814	Schramberg	Obd.	Oct 1852	Austria	838637
Oehler, Robert	5 Jun 1844	Schramberg	Obd.	Mar 1861	N.-Amer	838636
Oehler, Victoria (wife)		Weil der Stadt	Leon.	Mar 1847	N.-Amer	837965
Oehrlich, Catharina Wilhelm.	7 Mar 1862	Bondorf	Herr.	1852	N.-Amer	834630
Oehrlich, Jacobine (wife)	26 Aug 1837	Bondorf	Herr.	1852	N. Amer	834630
Oehrlich, Johann Michael & F	8 May 1835	Bondorf	Herr.	1852	N.-Amer	834630
Oesterlin, Marx	16 Mar 1835	Tuerkheim	Gsl.	Mar 1853	N.-Amer	572041
Off, Johann Friedrich	25 Jul 1864	Gebersheim	Leon.	Apr 1880	N.-Amer	837953
Ohnmacht, Christina	34 yrs.	Epfendorf	Obd.	Mar 1858	N.-Amer	838632
Ohnmacht, Maria	2 yrs.	Epfendorf	Obd.	Mar 1858	N.-Amer	838632
Olpp, Christina		Merklingen	Leon.	May 1853	N.-Amer	837959
Olpp, Johannes		Merklingen	Leon.	Oct 1853	N.-Amer	837959
Olpp, Karl Wilhelm	19 yrs.	Merklingen	Leon.	Feb 1854	N.-Amer	837959
Ortlieb, Rosa	1 Aug 1813	Oberndorf	Obd.	Jan 1859	Bavaria	838635
Osiander, Ernst Heinrich	2 Jan 1835	Alpirsbach	Obd.	Mar 1854	N.-Amer	838630
Osiander, Henriette Ernestine		Alpirsbach	Obd.	bef 1851	France	838630
Osiander, Otto Gustav	30 Nov 1823	Kirchheim	Krch.	bef 1860	N.-Amer	835940
Osiander, Robert	14 Apr 1839	Kirchheim	Krch.	1857	N.-Amer	835940

| Name | | Birth | | Emigration | | | Film |
Last	First	Date	Place	O'amt	Appl. Date	Dest.	Number
Osswald, Christian			Leonberg	Leon.	Jul 1853	N.-Amer	835786
Osswald, Christian & F			Leonberg	Leon.	Apr 1833	Poland	835786
Osswald, Conrad Heinrich & W			Leonberg	Leon.	Apr 1831	N.-Amer	835786
Osswald, Johann Adam Friedr.		1 Jan 1843	Kirchheim	Krch.	Aug 1862	N.-Amer	835941
Osswald, Johann Christian			Leonberg	Leon.	1853	N.-Amer	835786
Osswald, Johanna Maria		10 Nov 1857	Kirchheim	Krch.	Apr 1874	N.-Amer	835942
Osswald, Louise Marie		25 Jan 1831	Leonberg	Leon.	Apr 1860	Mainz	835786
Osswald, Ludwig Friedrich		2 Mar 1846	Owen	Krch.	Aug 1867	N.-Amer	835948
Osswald, Wilhelmine		20 Aug 1826	Leonberg	Leon.	Sep 1852	N.-Amer	835786
Ost, Bertha		16 Feb 1842	Geislingen	Gsl.	Mar 1863	Hesse	572046
Ostermaier, Christian			Unterboehringen	Gsl.	Nov 1863	Austral	572044
Oswald, Christian		1 Feb 1812	Schoeckingen	Leon.	bef 1839	France	837964
Oswald, Christoph			Schoeckingen	Leon.	bef 1838	France	837964
Ott, Agnes Margaretha		29 Nov 1834	Dettingen	Krch.	bef 1868	N.-Amer	835944
Ott, Albertine		20 Apr 1850	Winzeln	Obd.	May 1866	N.-Amer	841016
Ott, Anna Maria		12 Mar 1852	Hochdorf	Krch.	Jul 1878	N.-Amer	835945
Ott, Christine Magdalena		12 Jan 1820	Weilheim	Krch.	bef 1863	N.-Amer	835950
Ott, Dorothea (wid.)		11 Nov 1798	Hochdorf	Krch.	Mar 1866	N.-Amer	835945
Ott, Elisabetha		19 Nov 1832	Winzeln	Obd.	Sep 1854	N.-Amer	841016
Ott, Elisabetha Margaretha		4 Jun 1829	Weilheim	Krch.	bef 1863	N.-Amer	835950
Ott, Engelbert			Winzeln	Obd.	Sep 1863	N.-Amer	841016
Ott, Georg & F		14 Dec 1841	Hochdorf	Krch.	Mar 1866	N.-Amer	835945
Ott, Johann Georg		7 Oct 1831	Notzingen	Krch.	Jul 1863	Austral	835947
Ott, Karl Friedrich		3 Nov 1870	Dettingen	Krch.	May 1887	N.-Amer	835944
Ott, Magdalena			Bronnen	Rtl.	Nov 1835	N.-Amer	841051
Ott, Maria Barbara		17 Sep 1833	Dettingen	Krch.	bef 1868	N.-Amer	835944
Ott, Maria Catharina		15 Apr 1865	Hochdorf	Krch.	Mar 1866	N.-Amer	835945
Ott, Wilhelmine (wife)		21 May 1843	Hochdorf	Krch.	Mar 1866	N.-Amer	835945
Ott, Xaver		2 Jul 1835	Winzeln	Obd.	Nov 1855	N.-Amer	841016
Otto, Christian Heinrich		23 Sep 1830	Heimsheim	Leon.	Jun 1850	Prussia	837955
Otto, Magdalena		26 Dec 1828	Kuchen	Gsl.	Feb 1854	N.-Amer	572042
Palmer, Friederike		24 Oct 1837	Leonberg	Leon.	May 1864	N.-Amer	835787
Palmer, Jacob Heinrich		26 Dec 1874	Weilheim	Krch.	Feb 1890	N.-Amer	835774
Pandtle, Karl Friedrich		2 Nov 1833	Heimsheim	Leon.	bef 1870	Austria	837955
Pankenhorn, Johann Georg			Pfullingen	Rtl.	Jan 1832	England	841051
Paulus, Christoph		16 Feb 1842	Leonberg	Leon.	Jun 1866	Switz.	835787
Pfaeffle, Anna Maria		9 Oct 1822	Muenklingen	Leon.	May 1853	N.-Amer	837962
Pfaeffle, Anna Maria (wife)			Merklingen	Leon.	May 1827	N.-Amer	837959
Pfaeffle, Jakob Friedrich		13 Jun 1830	Muenklingen	Leon.	Feb 1852	N.-Amer	837962
Pfaeffle, Johannes & F			Merklingen	Leon.	May 1827	N.-Amer	837958
Pfaeffle, Johannes & W			Merklingen	Leon.	May 1827	N.-Amer	837959
Pfaefflin, Elisabetha		26 May 1827	Friolzheim	Leon.	Mar 1854	N.-Amer	835791
Pfaender, Johann Michael		11 Dec 1825	Kirchheim	Krch.	May 1857	N.-Amer	835940
Pfannenschmid, Friedrich		6 Mar 1858	Hemmingen	Leon.	Jul 1882	N.-Amer	837956
Pfannenschmid, Johannes			Hemmingen	Leon.	bef 1840	N.-Amer	837956
Pfau, Adam & F		28 Feb 1839	Schopfloch	Krch.	bef 1872	N.-Amer	835943
Pfau, Andreas		11 Dec 1838	Roemlinsdorf	Obd.	Nov 1866	N.-Amer	838635
Pfau, Anna Barbara		1 Apr 1814	Roemlinsdorf	Obd.	Sep 1847	N.-Amer	838635
Pfau, Anna Maria			Roemlinsdorf	Obd.	Jun 1857	N.-Amer	838635
Pfau, Barbara			Roemlinsdorf	Obd.	Mar 1852	N.-Amer	838635

Pfau, Christian	15 yrs.	Peterzell	Obd.	Aug 1850	N.-Amer	838635
Pfau, Christina	1 yr.	Fluorn	Obd.	Aug 1867	N.-Amer	838632
Pfau, Dorothea	13 Oct 1825	Roemlinsdorf	Obd.	Apr 1849	N.-Amer	838635
Pfau, Eva	17 yrs.	Betzweiler	Obd.	Jun 1854	N.-Amer	838631
Pfau, Jakob	16 yrs.	Roetenbach	Obd.	Sep 1857	N.-Amer	838636
Pfau, Johann Adam	28 Dec 1839	Schopfloch	Krch.	Feb 1858	N.-Amer	835949
Pfau, Johann Georg	18 Aug 1839	Roetenbach	Obd.	Jul 1854	N.-Amer	838636
Pfau, Johann Martin	4 Apr 1845	Gutenberg	Krch.	Jun 1864	N.-Amer	835945
Pfau, Johanne (wife)	5 Jul 1845	Bissingen	Krch.	bef 1872	N.-Amer	835943
Pfau, Johannes	18 yrs.	Roemlinsdorf	Obd.	Apr 1852	N.-Amer	838635
Pfau, Margaretha	7 Feb 1847	Gutenberg	Krch.	Aug 1867	N.-Amer	835945
Pfau, Maria Barbara	28 Oct 1865	Bissingen	Krch.	bef 1872	N.-Amer	835943
Pfau, Salome & C	16 Feb 1845	Fluorn	Obd.	Aug 1867	N.-Amer	838632
Pfeffer, Christian	14 Jan 1844	Dettingen	Krch.	Aug 1866	N.-Amer	835944
Pfeffer, Maria	19 Apr 1846	Epfendorf	Obd.	bef 1870	N.-Amer	838632
Pfeifer, Anna Magdalena	10 yrs.	Gingen	Gsl.	Aug 1853	N.-Amer	572041
Pfeifer, Barbara	15 yrs.	Gingen	Gsl.	Aug 1853	N.-Amer	572041
Pfeifer, Barbara & F		Gingen	Gsl.	Aug 1853	N.-Amer	572041
Pfeifer, Christoph Heinr. & F		Gomaringen	Rtl.	May 1832	N.-Amer	841051
Pfeifer, Jakob		Gingen	Gsl.	bef 1853	N.-Amer	572041
Pfeifer, Jakob	17 yrs.	Gingen	Gsl.	Feb 1853	N.-Amer	572041
Pfeifer, Johann Georg	11 Nov 1825	Oetlingen	Krch.	Dec 1855	N.-Amer	835948
Pfeifer, Johann Peter	19 yrs.	Gingen	Gsl.	Aug 1853	N.-Amer	572041
Pfeiffer, Christoph Friedrich	14 Nov 1840	Kirchheim	Krch.	Apr 1858	N.-Amer	835940
Pfeiffer, Emmanuel Ehrenreich	17 Nov 1846	Kirchheim	Krch.	Jul 1860	N.-Amer	835940
Pfeiffer, Eugen	29 May 1849	Muenchingen	Leon.	Apr 1866	N.-Amer	837961
Pfeiffer, Johann David Fried.	1 Nov 1846	Gomaringen	Rtl.	Dec 1866	N.-Amer	841055
Pfeiffer, Johann Georg	24 Sep 1830	Eybach	Gsl.	Jun 1854	N.-Amer	572042
Pfeiffer, Johann Jacob	29 Sep 1853	Gomaringen	Rtl.	Sep 1869	N.-Amer	841055
Pfeiffer, Katharina	28 Oct 1825	Gomaringen	Rtl.	1854	N.-Amer	841055
Pfeifle, Johannes	20 Feb 1834	Betzweiler	Obd.	Dec 1854	N.-Amer	838631
Pfennig, Johannes		Betzweiler	Obd.	Apr 1817	France	838631
Pfister, Johannes	15 Jul 1816	Weil der Stadt	Leon.	Jun 1852	N.-Amer	837966
Pfister, Susanna Margar. & F	4 Apr 1809	Dettingen	Krch.	Mar 1856	N.-Amer	835948
Pfisterer, Christine Cathar.	- 1840	Oetlingen	Krch.	Mar 1856	N.-Amer	835948
Pfisterer, David		Oetlingen	Krch.	1854	N.-Amer	835948
Pfisterer, Eva Rosina	- 1845	Oetlingen	Krch.	Mar 1856	N.-Amer	835948
Pfisterer, Johann David	- 1843	Oetlingen	Krch.	Mar 1856	N.-Amer	835948
Pfisterer, Johann Georg	30 Aug 1832	Oetlingen	Krch.	Mar 1856	N.-Amer	835948
Pfisterer, Johannes	12 Jul 1849	Oetlingen	Krch.	Jul 1867	N.-Amer	835948
Pfizenmaier, Caroline		Heimerdingen	Leon.	bef 1855	N.-Amer	837954
Pfizenmaier, Gottfried	10 Jan 1863	Eltingen	Leon.	Sep 1880	N.-Amer	835789
Pfizenmeier, Louis	8 Jan 1833	Heimerdingen	Leon.	May 1852	N.-Amer	837954
Pfizer, Amalia	15 yrs.	Reutlingen	Rtl.	May 1880	N.-Amer	841051
Pflinger, Karl	7 Feb 1851	Warmbronn	Leon.	Apr 1867	N.-Amer	837965
Pflueger, Adam & F	11 Oct 1814	Warmbronn	Leon.	May 1867	N.-Amer	837965
Pflueger, Christian	30 Oct 1843	Warmbronn	Leon.	May 1867	N.-Amer	837965
Pflueger, Christian & F	25 Dec 1822	Neidlingen	Krch.	Oct 1860	N.-Amer	835946
Pflueger, Christian Jakob	23 Oct 1850	Neidlingen	Krch.	Oct 1860	N.-Amer	835946
Pflueger, Dorothea (wife)	18 Jan 1817	Stuttgart	Leon.	May 1867	N.-Amer	837965

| Name | | Birth | | Emigration | | | Film |
Last	First	Date	Place	O'amt	Appl. Date	Dest.	Number
Pflueger, Friedrich		3 Nov 1843	Flacht	Leon.	Apr 1865	N.-Amer	835790
Pflueger, Georg Michael		30 Mar 1784	Renningen	Leon.	bef 1828	France	837963
Pflueger, Gottliebin		16 Jan 1832	Eltingen	Leon.	Feb 1852	N.-Amer	835789
Pflueger, Johann Friedrich		12 Oct 1829	Eltingen	Leon.	Mar 1853	N.-Amer	835789
Pflueger, Johannes & F		21 Mar 1844	Oberlenningen	Krch.	Apr 1883	N.-Amer	835946
Pflueger, Josef		11 Jan 1839	Eltingen	Leon.	Mar 1853	N.-Amer	835789
Pflueger, Maria Rosina		25 May 1853	Neidlingen	Krch.	Oct 1860	N.-Amer	835946
Pflueger, Marie Lou. (wid.) & F			Eltingen	Leon.	1852	N.-Amer	835789
Pflueger, Philipp Friedrich			Rutesheim	Leon.	bef 1869	N.-Amer	837964
Pflueger, Sophia Marg. (wife)		14 Jun 1824	Neidlingen	Krch.	Oct 1860	N.-Amer	835946
Pflueger, Sophie Dorothea		6 Jul 1834	Eltingen	Leon.	Mar 1853	N.-Amer	835789
Pflueger, Sophie Rosine		29 Dec 1878	Neidlingen	Krch.	Apr 1883	N.-Amer	548403
Pflueger, Sophie Rosine		29 Dec 1878	Oberlenningen	Krch.	Apr 1883	N.-Amer	835946
Pflueger, Sophie Rosine (wife)		27 Nov 1844	Oberlenningen	Krch.	Apr 1883	N.-Amer	835946
Pflueger, Wilhelm Heinrich		18 Mar 1881	Oberlenningen	Krch.	Apr 1883	N.-Amer	835946
Pflug, Michael		20 Mar 1834	Geislingen	Gsl.	Jan 1853	N.-Amer	572041
Pflugfelder, Johann Friedrich		23 Feb 1867	Hirschlanden	Leon.	May 1883	N.-Amer	837956
Pflumm, Jakob		12 Mar 1827	Ohmden	Krch.	bef 1866	N.-Amer	835948
Pflumm, Jakob Friedrich		5 Feb 1833	Heimsheim	Leon.	Apr 1853	N.-Amer	837955
Pflumm, Johann Ludwig		6 Oct 1823	Ohmden	Krch.	Oct 1866	N.-Amer	835948
Pflumm, Johann Michael		5 Apr 1847	Gomaringen	Rtl.	Dec 1863	N.-Amer	841055
Pflumm, Johann Michael		18 Sep 1824	Ohmden	Krch.	bef 1866	N.-Amer	835948
Pflumm, Johannes		17 Mar 1822	Ohmden	Krch.	bef 1866	N.-Amer	835948
Pfundstein, Jacobine		13 May 1835	Lauterbach	Obd.	Aug 1864	N.-Amer	838634
Pfundstein, Lorenz & F			Schramberg	Obd.	May 1817	A.-Amer	838637
Pfundstein, Teresia		10 Jan 1833	Lauterbach	Obd.	Oct 1853	N.-Amer	838634
Plankenhorn, Anna Barb. (wife)		15 Nov 1820	Pfullingen	Rtl.	Sep 1865	N.-Amer	841055
Plankenhorn, Anna Marg. (wid.)		10 Apr 1811	Pfullingen	Rtl.	Sep 1867	N.-Amer	841054
Plankenhorn, Anna Maria (wife)		26 Jun 1833	Pfullingen	Rtl.	Jan 1866	N.-Amer	841055
Plankenhorn, Christof Fr. & F		17 May 1792	Pfullingen	Rtl.	Jan 1866	N.-Amer	841055
Plankenhorn, Friederike Magda.		7 Dec 1820	Pfullingen	Rtl.	Jan 1866	N.-Amer	841055
Plankenhorn, Georg Friedrich			Pfullingen	Rtl.	Apr 1867	N.-Amer	841055
Plankenhorn, Imanuel Benedikt		30 Jul 1844	Pfullingen	Rtl.	May 1864	N.-Amer	841055
Plankenhorn, Johann Friedrich		20 Nov 1858	Pfullingen	Rtl.	Sep 1865	N.-Amer	841055
Plankenhorn, Johann Georg		1 Jun 1852	Pfullingen	Rtl.	Sep 1865	N.-Amer	841055
Plankenhorn, Johann Georg		21 Feb 1860	Lindorf	Krch.	Feb 1868	N.-Amer	835946
Plankenhorn, Johannes		18 Mar 1857	Pfullingen	Rtl.	Sep 1865	N.-Amer	841055
Plankenhorn, Johannes & W		18 Mar 1828	Pfullingen	Rtl.	Jan 1866	N.-Amer	841055
Plankenhorn, Maria Barbara		11 Mar 1855	Pfullingen	Rtl.	Sep 1865	N.-Amer	841055
Plankenhorn, Matthaeus		14 Jun 1850	Pfullingen	Rtl.	Sep 1865	N.-Amer	841055
Plankenhorn, Matthaeus & F		14 Aug 1820	Pfullingen	Rtl.	Sep 1865	N.-Amer	841055
Plankenhorn, Matthias		28 Feb 1831	Pfullingen	Rtl.	Jan 1866	N.-Amer	841055
Pleikocher, Johannes			Pfullingen	Rtl.	Apr 1830	N.-Amer	841051
Plessing, Elisabeth			Weilheim	Krch.	May 1753	N.-Amer	550804
Plessing, Johannes		5 Sep 1857	Weilheim	Krch.	May 1873	N.-Amer	548403
Plessing, Mathaeus			Notzingen	Krch.	Mar 1784	Pr.-Pol	550804
Pletschinger, Joseph		9 Aug 1849	Degginger	Gsl.	Apr 1877	Austria	572048
Poepple, Anna Barbara		5 Jun 1844	Eybach	Gsl.	May 1867	N.-Amer	572046
Pollius, Johann Friedrich			Gomaringen	Rtl.	Mar 1834	N.-Amer	841051
Potteler, Magdalena		25 yrs.	Reutlingen	Rtl.	Apr 1880	N.-Amer	841051

Pouet, Catharina	14 Dec 1822	Perouse	Leon.	Feb 1855	N.-Amer	837962
Precher, Moritz	21 Nov 1840	Weil im Dorf	Loen.	Jan 1864	N.-Amer	837967
Press-Albrecht, Johannes	10 Jan 1853	Kuchen	Gsl.	Feb 1854	N.-Amer	572042
Pressmar, Johann	9 Mar 1842	Geislingen	Gsl.	Jun 1867	France	572046
Pressner, Apolonia & C		Altenstadt-Gsl.	Gsl.	May 1872	N.-Amer	572047
Prinzinger, Bernhard	25 Sep 1824	Boehmenkirch	Gsl.	Apr 1853	N.-Amer	572041
Prinzinger, Elisabetha & F	24 yrs.	Boehmenkirch	Gsl.	Sep 1854	N.-Amer	572042
Prinzinger, Genovefa	1 yrs.	Boehmenkirch	Gsl.	Sep 1854	N.-Amer	572042
Prinzinger, Marianna	2 yrs.	Boehmenkirch	Gsl.	Sep 1854	N.-Amer	572042
Probst, Anna Maria	18 Nov 1805	Gaertringen	Herr.	Jul 1869	N.-Amer	834630
Probst, Karl Adolf	30 May 1853	Gmuend	Krch.	Jun 1882	Austral	548403
Prophet, Georg Friedrich		Merklingen	Leon.	bef 1816	Poland	837959
Pulvermueller, Adolf	18 yrs.	Esslingen	Gsl.	Oct 1867	S.-Amer	572046
Pulvermueller, Dominik		Reichenbach	Gsl.	Mar 1853	N.-Amer	572041
Pulvermueller, Ludwig	18 yrs.	Reichenbach	Gsl.	Aug 1851	N.-Amer	577788
Queck, Georg Jacob & F	40 yrs.	Gerlingen	Leon.	Apr 1833	Poland	837953
Queck, Johann Georg		Gerlingen	Leon.	bef 1860	N.-Amer	837953
Raach, Gottlob	55 yrs.	Reutlingen	Rtl.	Jul 1880	N.-Amer	841051
Raach, Johann Klarus		Grossengstingen	Rtl.	May 1832	N.-Amer	841051
Rabel, Christian	7 Jun 1851	Brucken	Krch.	Mar 1870	N.-Amer	835944
Rabel, Christine Barb. (wife)	13 Aug 1838	Dettingen	Krch.	May 1868	N.-Amer	835944
Rabel, Eduard	1 Sep 1841	Owen	Krch.	Oct 1870	Prussia	835948
Rabel, Johann Jakob	26 Apr 1864	Dettingen	Krch.	May 1868	N.-Amer	835944
Rabel, Johann Jakob & F	10 May 1835	Dettingen	Krch.	May 1868	N.-Amer	835944
Rabel, Johann Michael	26 Dec 1861	Dettingen	Krch.	May 1868	N.-Amer	835944
Rabel, Johann Wilhelm	14 Jun 1867	Dettingen	Krch.	May 1868	N.-Amer	835944
Radel, Johann Georg	31 Jan 1827	Notzingen	Krch.	Sep 1856	N.-Amer	835947
Raezle, Johannes	14 Dec 1823	Merklingen	Leon.	1853	N.-Amer	837959
Raff, Dorothea Louise	12 Aug 1848	Reutlingen	Rtl.	Nov 1868	Bohemia	841056
Raff, Johann Ludwig	29 Apr 1850	Weilheim	Krch.	Nov 1870	N.-Amer	835774
Raff, Theodor	19 yrs.	Bochingen	Obd.	Mar 1856	N.-Amer	838632
Raible, Caecelie (wife)		Oberndorf	Obd.	Oct 1852	N.-Amer	838635
Raible, Kaspar & F		Oberndorf	Obd.	Oct 1852	N.-Amer	838635
Raichle, Christian Friedrich	2 Apr 1841	Owen	Krch.	Apr 1857	N.-Amer	835948
Raichle, Christian Gottl.	6 Nov 1840	Dettingen	Krch.	Mar 1869	N.-Amer	835944
Raichle, Christina Friederika	10 yrs.	Goeppingen	Krch.	Jun 1804	Russia	550804
Raichle, Eva Catharina & C	27 Apr 1830	Owen	Krch.	Mar 1860	N.-Amer	835948
Raichle, Gottlieb Hermann	11 Aug 1842	Owen	Krch.	Jul 1860	N.-Amer	835948
Raichle, Gustav Wilhelm	14 Jan 1868	Owen	Krch.	Jun 1882	N.-Amer	835948
Raichle, Jakob Friedrich	15 Jun 1848	Dettingen	Krch.	Jul 1868	N.-Amer	835944
Raichle, Johann Georg	6 Feb 1854	Owen	Krch.	Mar 1860	N.-Amer	835948
Raichle, Johannes	11 Apr 1864	Owen	Krch.	Mar 1881	N.-Amer	835948
Raichle, Johannes	24 May 1850	Owen	Krch.	Feb 1867	N.-Amer	835948
Raichle, Maximillian	6 Jan 1845	Owen	Krch.	Jun 1864	N.-Amer	835948
Raichle, Nikolaus Friedrich	18 yrs.	Goeppingen	Krch.	Jun 1804	Russia	550804
Raidt, Johannes	16 May 1850	Hochmoessingen	Obd.	Jan 1869	N.-Amer	838633
Raisch, Catharina	12 yrs.	Eltingen	Leon.	Sep 1852	N.-Amer	835789
Raisch, Christiane		Eltingen	Leon.	Mar 1852	N.-Amer	835789
Raisch, Dorothea (wife)		Eltingen	Leon.	Sep 1852	N.-Amer	835789
Raisch, Johannes & F		Eltingen	Leon.	Sep 1852	N.-Amer	835789

Name		Birth		Emigration			Film
Last	First	Date	Place	O'amt	Appl. Date	Dest.	Number
Raisch, Maria		10 yrs.	Eltingen	Leon.	Sep 1852	N.-Amer	835789
Raisch, Rosina		5 yrs.	Eltingen	Leon.	Sep 1852	N.-Amer	835789
Raisch, Susanna			Eltingen	Leon.	Apr 1830	N.-Amer	835789
Raiser, Barbara		38 yrs.	Hemmingen	Leon.	Nov 1860	N.-Amer	837956
Raiser, Georg			Pfullingen	Rtl.	Oct 1831	Hannov.	841051
Raiser, Matthias		1 Jan 1825	Pfullingen	Rtl.	Feb 1863	London	841056
Raiser, Rosine & C		23 Feb 1832	Kirchheim	Krch.	Mar 1868	N.-Amer	835941
Raiser, Wilhelm		20 Jan 1857	Kirchheim	Krch.	Mar 1868	N.-Amer	835941
Raiser, Wilhelm Friedrich		18 Aug 1842	Pfullingen	Rtl.	Dec 1866	N.-Amer	841056
Raiser, Wilhelm Friedrich		25 Jul 1845	Pfullingen	Rtl.	Dec 1865	N.-Amer	841056
Raitbauer, Xaver		24 Oct 1848	Grossengstingen	Rtl.	Apr 1868	N.-Amer	841056
Raith, Caroline			Weil im Dorf	Loen.	Mar 1853	N.-Amer	837967
Raith, Catharina			Hoefingen	Leon.	bef 1870	N.-Amer	837957
Raith, Eberhard & F			Weil im Dorf	Loen.	Mar 1853	N.-Amer	837967
Raith, Friedrich		19 Jul 1842	Hoefingen	Leon.	Mar 1862	N.-Amer	837957
Raith, Georg Friedrich		2 Mar 1847	Weil im Dorf	Loen.	Mar 1853	N.-Amer	837967
Raith, Johann Georg		31 Mar 1851	Weil im Dorf	Loen.	Mar 1853	N.-Amer	837967
Raith, Johann Jakob		4 Nov 1855	Weil im Dorf	Loen.	Feb 1881	N.-Amer	837967
Raith, Margaretha		28 yrs.	Hoefingen	Leon.	Aug 1854	N.-Amer	837957
Rall, David		25 May 1833	Eningen	Rtl.	Sep 1865	N.-Amer	841056
Rall, David Gotthilf Kaspar		22 yrs.	Eningen	Rtl.	Jul 1863	N.-Amer	841056
Rall, David Martin		23 Jan 1843	Eningen	Rtl.	Jul 1863	N.-Amer	841056
Rall, Eduard		27 Oct 1851	Waldmoessingen	Obd.	Mar 1865	N.-Amer	841015
Rall, Elisabeth			Seedorf	Obd.	bef 1855	N.-Amer	838637
Rall, Emma		22 Dec 1848	Eningen	Rtl.	May 1866	N.-Amer	841056
Rall, Gottlob		12 Nov 1845	Eningen	Rtl.	Jun 1864	N.-Amer	841056
Rall, Heinrich		13 Apr 1848	Reutlingen	Rtl.	1867	N.-Amer	841056
Rall, Hektor Julius		27 Sep 1851	Eningen	Rtl.	Jul 1869	N.-Amer	841056
Rall, Hugo Otto		14 Nov 1843	Eningen	Rtl.	1863	N.-Amer	841056
Rall, Jakob Friedrich		18 Oct 1832	Eningen	Rtl.	bef 1859	N.-Amer	841056
Rall, Johanne Friederike		30 Nov 1831	Eningen	Rtl.	bef 1864	N.-Amer	841056
Rall, Johannes		14 Apr 1846	Dettingen	Krch.	Feb 1861	N.-Amer	835944
Rall, Katharina			Reutlingen	Leon.	bef 1862	N.-Amer	841057
Rall, Kraft Gustav Eberhart		31 Aug 1849	Eningen	Rtl.	Jun 1867	N.-Amer	841056
Rall, Maria Agnes		14 Sep 1832	Eningen	Rtl.	bef 1862	Bavaria	841056
Rall, Maria Magdalena		11 Mar 1840	Eningen	Rtl.	May 1869	N.-Amer	841056
Rall, Maria Margaretha		25 Dec 1847	Eningen	Rtl.	May 1869	N.-Amer	841056
Rall, Melchior		21 Oct 1831	Eningen	Rtl.	Nov 1861	France	841056
Rall, Reinhard		1 Apr 1837	Waldmoessingen	Obd.	Sep 1856	N.-Amer	841015
Rall/Kraft, Heinrich		28 Mar 1847	Heimsheim	Leon.	Jul 1860	N.-Amer	837955
Rammenstein, Christian Gottfr.			Eltingen	Leon.	Feb 1843	N.-Amer	835789
Rammenstein, Friedrich		30 Jul 1854	Eltingen	Leon.	May 1869	N.-Amer	835789
Rammenstein, Maria		21 Feb 1839	Eltingen	Leon.	Feb 1864	Berlin	835789
Ramminger, Anna Maria		11 mon.	Wiesensteig	Gsl.	Mar 1853	N.-Amer	572041
Ramminger, Ignaz & F			Wiesensteig	Gsl.	Mar 1853	N.-Amer	572041
Ramminger, Josef		5 Dec 1826	Reichenbach	Gsl.	Nov 1862	Prussia	572044
Ramminger, Josef		10 Feb 1859	Hohenstadt	Gsl.	Nov 1866	N.-Amer	572045
Ramminger, Josef & F		4 Jul 1828	Hohenstadt	Gsl.	Nov 1866	N.-Amer	572045
Ramminger, Josepha (wife)			Wiesensteig	Gsl.	Mar 1853	N.-Amer	572041
Ramminger, Lorenz		12 Aug 1833	Westerheim	Gsl.	Apr 1854	N.-Amer	572042

Ramminger, Margaretha (wife)	21 Jul 1827	Hohenstadt	Gsl.	Nov 1866	N.-Amer	572045
Ramminger, Marianna	16 May 1857	Hohenstadt	Gsl.	Nov 1866	N.-Amer	572045
Ramminger, Theresia	20 Dec 1831	Westerheim	Gsl.	Apr 1854	N.-Amer	572042
Rampf, Josepha	30 Jan 1846	Donzdorf	Gsl.	Aug 1867	N.-Amer	572046
Ramsauer, Ernst Gottlob	29 Jul 1862	Warmbronn	Leon.	Jan 1888	N.-Amer	837965
Ramsayer, Nikolaus		Muenchingen	Leon.	bef 1856	France	837961
Ramweiler, Bernhard	17 May 1823	Boehmenkirch	Gsl.	May 1850	N.-Amer	577788
Ramweiler, Kreszenzia	18 yrs.	Boehmenkirch	Gsl.	Mar 1852	N.-Amer	572041
Ramweiler, Michael	29 Sep 1817	Boehmenkirch	Gsl.	May 1850	N.-Amer	577788
Ranalder, Eva Rosina	9 Dec 1830	Dettingen	Krch.	Apr 1868	N.-Amer	835944
Rapp, Adam	8 Jul 1851	Gomaringen	Rtl.	Jun 1869	N.-Amer	841056
Rapp, Anastasia	10 Apr 1848	Seedorf	Obd.	Sep 1866	N.-Amer	838637
Rapp, Anna Barbara		Eybach	Gsl.	Jun 1867	N.-Amer	572046
Rapp, Anna Maria	14 Sep 1837	Eybach	Gsl.	Dec 1867	Bavaria	572046
Rapp, Antonius & F		Beffendorf	Obd.	Apr 1817	N.-Amer	838631
Rapp, Barbara	13 yrs.	Hemmingen	Leon.	Feb 1834	Rus-Pol	837956
Rapp, Caroline	8 Apr 1842	Schramberg	Obd.	Mar 1864	N.-Amer	838636
Rapp, Christian	29 Apr 1841	Ueberkingen	Gsl.	Mar 1869	N.-Amer	572047
Rapp, Christina	24 yrs.	Hemmingen	Leon.	Feb 1834	Rus-Pol	837956
Rapp, Christina (wife)	47 yrs.	Hemmingen	Leon.	Feb 1834	Rus-Pol	837956
Rapp, Conrad		Hemmingen	Leon.	bef 1858	N.-Amer	837956
Rapp, Conrad & F		Hemmingen	Leon.	Mar 1852	N.-Amer	837956
Rapp, Dorothea	16 yrs.	Hemmingen	Leon.	Feb 1834	Rus-Pol	837956
Rapp, Franz Joseph	17 Oct 1830	Mariazell	Obd.	Oct 1856	Hungary	838634
Rapp, Friederika	4 yrs.	Hemmingen	Leon.	Feb 1834	Rus-Pol	837956
Rapp, Friedrich		Hemmingen	Leon.	Jul 1853	N.-Amer	837956
Rapp, Gottlieb	9 Jan 1814	Hemmingen	Leon.	Mar 1846	Prussia	837956
Rapp, Jakob Friedrich		Neidlingen	Krch.	bef 1860	N.-Amer	835946
Rapp, Johann	2 Nov 1862	Oberndorf	Obd.	Oct 1864	Austria	838635
Rapp, Johann & F	28 yrs.	Oberndorf	Obd.	Oct 1864	Austria	838635
Rapp, Johann Christoph		Hemmingen	Leon.	Mar 1857	N.-Amer	837956
Rapp, Johann Georg	21 yrs.	Hemmingen	Leon.	Feb 1834	Rus-Pol	837956
Rapp, Johann Georg & F	58 yrs.	Hemmingen	Leon.	Feb 1834	Rus-Pol	837956
Rapp, Johann Georg & W	10 Aug 1827	Gomaringen	Rtl.	1865	Frankf.	841056
Rapp, Johanna	8 yrs.	Hemmingen	Leon.	Feb 1834	Rus-Pol	837956
Rapp, Johanna Dorothea (wife)	27 Jan 1820	Winnenden	Rtl.	1865	Frankf.	841056
Rapp, Johannes		Waldmoessingen	Obd.	1854	N.-Amer	841015
Rapp, Johannes	18 yrs.	Hemmingen	Leon.	Feb 1834	Rus-Pol	837956
Rapp, Joseph	8 Jan 1845	Schramberg	Obd.	May 1864	N.-Amer	838636
Rapp, Joseph	24 yrs.	Schramberg	Obd.	Oct 1854	N.-Amer	838636
Rapp, Joseph & F		Mariazell	Obd.	May 1817	N.-Amer	838634
Rapp, Josepha		Schramberg	Obd.	Feb 1860	N.-Amer	838636
Rapp, Josephine (wife) & F		Waldmoessingen	Obd.	1855	N.-Amer	841015
Rapp, Katharina		Mariazell	Obd.	Jan 1859	Prussia	838634
Rapp, Klemens & F		Mariazell	Obd.	May 1817	N.-Amer	838634
Rapp, Konrad		Schramberg	Obd.	Nov 1811	France	838637
Rapp, Ludwig	18 Oct 1850	Unterhausen	Rtl.	Nov 1867	N.-Amer	841056
Rapp, Maria	8 Dec 1843	Bach-Altenberg	Obd.	Mar 1868	France	838631
Rapp, Maria Magdalena	18 mon.	Waldmoessingen	Obd.	1855	N.-Amer	841015
Rapp, Marianna		Mariazell	Obd.	Jul 1860	France	838634

Name		Birth		Emigration			Film
Last	First	Date	Place	O'amt	Appl. Date	Dest.	Number
Rapp, Michael		20 Jan 1838	Nabern	Krch.	Feb 1857	N.-Amer	835946
Rapp, Pauline (wife)			Oberndorf	Obd.	Oct 1864	Austria	838635
Rapp, Sebastian & F			Mariazell	Obd.	May 1817	N.-Amer	838634
Rapp, Wilhelm Friedrich		29 Jun 1853	Gomaringen	Rtl.	Sep 1869	N.-Amer	841056
Rasser, Charlotte (wife)		33 yrs.	Gutenberg	Krch.	May 1804	Pr.-Pol	550804
Rasser, Christina Rosina		4 yrs.	Gutenberg	Krch.	May 1804	Pr.-Pol	550804
Rasser, Eberhard & F		35 yrs.	Gutenberg	Krch.	May 1804	Pr.-Pol	550804
Rasser, Friederike Auguste		8 yrs.	Gutenberg	Krch.	May 1804	Pr.-Pol	550804
Rattenmann, Nepomuk			Weil der Stadt	Leon.	Apr 1841	Prussia	837965
Rau, Christian		27 Jul 1849	Rosswaelden	Krch.	Mar 1867	N.-Amer	835949
Rau, Friedrich Ferdinand		16 Aug 1868	Kirchheim	Krch.	Feb 1885	N.-Amer	835942
Rau, Friedrich Wilhelm		26 Nov 1822	Oberlenningen	Krch.	bef 1860	N.-Amer	835947
Rau, Josef		12 Mar 1868	Zimmern	Rtw.	Mar 1885	N.-Amer	841117
Rau, Karl Albert		31 Aug 1875	Weiler	Krch.	Apr 1889	N.-Amer	548323
Rau, Karl Albert		31 Aug 1875	Weiler	Krch.	May 1889	N.-Amer	835949
Rau, Louise			Rotfelden	Nag.	Sep 1851	N.-Amer	838488
Rau, Magdalena		11 Sep 1823	Sulpach	Krch.	bef 1860	N.-Amer	835949
Rauch , Johann & F			Mariazell	Obd.	May 1817	N.-Amer	838634
Rauer, Gottlieb		24 Sep 1856	Oberlenningen	Krch.	Aug 1879	N.-Amer	835940
Rausch, Christiana		23 Jun 1857	Jesingen	Krch.	Jun 1859	N.-Amer	835946
Rausch, Maria Barbara & C			Jesingen	Krch.	Jun 1859	N.-Amer	835946
Rauschenberger, Maria (wid.) & F			Aichhalden	Obd.	Nov 1855	N.-Amer	838629
Rauschenberger, Michael Friedr		19 Mar 1839	Aichhalden	Obd.	Nov 1855	N.-Amer	838629
Rauschenberger, Wilhelmine		23 Oct 1833	Aichhalden	Obd.	Nov 1855	N.-Amer	838629
Rauscher, Gottlob		3 Feb 1844	Gutenberg	Krch.	May 1862	N.-Amer	835945
Rauscher, Johann Georg		20 Dec 1835	Gutenberg	Krch.	Nov 1862	N.-Amer	835945
Rauscher, Rosine			Reutlingen	Rtl.	bef 1862	N.-Amer	841056
Rauschmaier, Philipp Jacob		30 Apr 1835	Westerheim	Gsl.	1852	N.-Amer	572043
Rauschmayer, Andreas		19 yrs.	Westerheim	Gsl.	bef 1856	N.-Amer	572043
Rauschmayer, Elias		20 Jul 1848	Westerheim	Gsl.	Feb 1856	N.-Amer	572043
Rauschmayer, Joseph & F		10 May 1804	Westerheim	Gsl.	Feb 1856	N.-Amer	572043
Rauschmayer, Justina		17 Jun 1832	Westerheim	Gsl.	Feb 1856	N.-Amer	572043
Rauschmayer, Katharina (wife)		7 Nov 1804	Westerheim	Gsl.	Feb 1856	N.-Amer	572043
Rauschmayer, Maria		13 Sep 1840	Westerheim	Gsl.	Feb 1856	N.-Amer	572043
Rauschmayer, Theresia		2 Jun 1842	Westerheim	Gsl.	Feb 1856	N.-Amer	572043
Rauschmayer, Xaverus		17 May 1839	Westerheim	Gsl.	Feb 1856	N.-Amer	572043
Rauschmeier, Andreas		11 Jul 1836	Westerheim	Gsl.	Mar 1854	N.-Amer	572042
Rauschmeier, Balthasar		6 Jan 1836	Westerheim	Gsl.	Mar 1854	N.-Amer	572042
Rauschmeyer, Christina			Westerheim	Gsl.	Sep 1851	N.-Amer	577788
Rauser, Katharina		19 Dec 1848	Pfullingen	Rtl.	Sep 1868	Switz.	841056
Rauss, Christine			Hoefingen	Leon.	bef 1857	N.-Amer	837957
Rauss, Margaretha & C		28 yrs.	Hoefingen	Leon.	Sep 1853	N.-Amer	837957
Rautter, Johann Michael		12 Nov 1871	Bissingen	Krch.	Mar 1888	N.-Amer	548323
Rayher, Gottlieb Friedr. & F			Kirchheim	Krch.	bef 1860	Russia	835940
Rayher, Rosine		23 Feb 1832	Kirchheim	Krch.	Jul 1859	N.-Amer	835940
Rebstock, Johannes & W		14 Oct 1814	Gueltstein	Herr.	Apr 1866	N.-Amer	834631
Rebstock, Maria Magdal. (wife)		9 Apr 1818	Gueltstein	Herr.	Apr 1866	N.-Amer	834631
Recker, Johann Georg		24 Jul 1827	Oberlenningen	Krch.	Oct 1866	N.-Amer	835947
Redwitz, Carl			Malmsheim	Leon.	Aug 1854	N.-Amer	837958
Redwitz, Philipp Heinr. (wid.)			Malmsheim	Leon.	Mar 1818	N.-Amer	837958

Reebenz, Carl	24 yrs.	Reutlingen	Rtl.	Sep 1879	N.-Amer	841051
Regel, Elisabetha		Kirchheim	Krch.	1859	N.-Amer	835940
Regel, Johanna Margaretha		Kirchheim	Krch.	1859	N.-Amer	835940
Rehkugel, Friederike Dorothea	12 Jun 1822	Owen	Krch.	Dec 1862	N.-Amer	835948
Rehm, Christian Friedrich	25 Oct 1835	Pfullingen	Rtl.	Mar 1869	N.-Amer	841056
Rehm, Christoph Friedrich	22 Aug 1820	Pfullingen	Rtl.	bef 1865	Austria	841056
Rehm, Georg Friedrich	11 Dec 1847	Pfullingen	Rtl.	Feb 1865	N.-Amer	841056
Rehm, Johann Georg	26 Apr 1849	Pfullingen	Rtl.	Apr 1866	N.-Amer	841056
Rehm, Johann Georg		Reutlingen	Rtl.	Jun 1829	France	841051
Rehm, Johannes		Pfullingen	Rtl.	Apr 1830	N.-Amer	841051
Reich, Andreas	24 May 1827	Dornhan	Obd.	Jan 1866	N.-Amer	838638
Reich, Anna Catharina	11 Jul 1830	Renningen	Leon.	Apr 1852	N.-Amer	837963
Reich, Catharina	17 yrs.	Heimsheim	Loen.	May 1853	N.-Amer	837967
Reich, Georg Jakob	19 Jul 1850	Heimsheim	Leon.	Apr 1869	N.-Amer	837955
Reich, Jacob	27 yrs.	Betzweiler	Obd.	Apr 1851	N.-Amer	838631
Reich, Johann Georg	12 Dec 1828	Betzweiler	Obd.	Apr 1851	N.-Amer	838631
Reich, Margaretha		Oetlingen	Krch.	1855	N.-Amer	835940
Reichardt, Johann Georg	12 Jul 1828	Hildrizhausen	Herr.	1852	N.-Amer	834631
Reichele, Johann Christoph	6 Dec 1854	Oberlenningen	Krch.	Jan 1870	N.-Amer	835947
Reichert, Andreas		Alpirsbach	Obd.	Sep 1848	N.-Amer	838630
Reichert, Andreas	18 yrs.	Flacht	Leon.	Oct 1866	N.-Amer	835790
Reichert, Christian	11 Apr 1796	Friolzheim	Leon.	bef 1818	N.-Amer	835791
Reichert, Christian Friedrich	9 Nov 1857	Flacht	Leon.	Mar 1881	N.-Amer	835790
Reichert, Christian Gottlob	21 yrs.	Friolzheim	Leon.	Aug 1865	N.-Amer	835791
Reichert, Friederike	20 yrs.	Friolzheim	Leon.	Apr 1852	N.-Amer	835791
Reichert, Gottlieb	45 yrs.	Hoefingen	Leon.	May 1867	N.-Amer	837957
Reichert, Heinrich	20 Jul 1846	Warmbronn	Leon.	Nov 1866	N.-Amer	837965
Reichert, Heinrich Albert	13 Mar 1852	Hildrizhausen	Herr.	May 1876	N.-Amer	834631
Reichert, Johann Georg		Reutlingen	Rtl.	May 1835	N.-Amer	841051
Reichert, Johann Gottlieb	14 Apr 1825	Alpirsbach	Obd.	Apr 1854	N.-Amer	838630
Reichert, Johann Michael	12 Feb 1826	Friolzheim	Leon.	1852	N.-Amer	835791
Reichert, Johannes	17 Jul 1832	Grosssuessen	Gsl.	Jan 1854	N.-Amer	572042
Reichert, Johannes	28 Jan 1818	Bissingen	Krch.	bef 1866	N.-Amer	835940
Reichert, Katharina	11 Jun 1845	Grosssuessen	Gsl.	Jun 1865	N.-Amer	572045
Reichert, Margaretha	28 yrs.	Friolzheim	Leon.	Aug 1851	N.-Amer	835791
Reichert, Michael		Hoefingen	Leon.	bef 1809	Poland	837957
Reichert, Rahel	7 Sep 1820	Friolzheim	Leon.	1852	N.-Amer	835791
Reicherter, August	1 Aug 1848	Reutlingen	Rtl.	bef 1867	London	841056
Reicherter, Johann Ludwig	24 Jul 1850	Reutlingen	Rtl.	Jun 1869	N.-Amer	841056
Reicherter, Johann Ulrich		Reutlingen	Rtl.	Jan 1829	Switz.	841051
Reicherter, Johannes	12 Mar 1848	Reutlingen	Rtl.	Oct 1867	N.-Amer	841056
Reicherter, Mathilde	11 Dec 1838	Tailfingen	Rtl.	Mar 1860	Switz.	841056
Reichle, Anna Maria (wife)	5 May 1839	Unterlenningen	Krch.	Mar 1867	N.-Amer	835949
Reichle, Carl Gottlob	20 Apr 1864	Oberlenningen	Krch.	Apr 1872	N.-Amer	835947
Reichle, Christian	1 Feb 1867	Oberlenningen	Krch.	Apr 1872	N.-Amer	835947
Reichle, Christian		Oberlenningen	Krch.	bef 1865	Prussia	835947
Reichle, Christiane Catharine	24 Jul 1857	Oberlenningen	Krch.	Apr 1872	N.-Amer	835947
Reichle, Christiane Sophie	20 Jan 1860	Oberlenningen	Krch.	Apr 1872	N.-Amer	835947
Reichle, Christoph	22 Oct 1865	Unterlenningen	Krch.	Mar 1867	N.-Amer	835949
Reichle, Christoph & F	12 Sep 1841	Unterlenningen	Krch.	Mar 1867	N.-Amer	835949

Name		Birth		Emigration			Film
Last	First	Date	Place	O'amt	Appl. Date	Dest.	Number
Reichle, Euphrosine Carloline		24 Jul 1871	Oberlenningen	Krch.	Apr 1872	N.-Amer	835947
Reichle, Euphrosine Pauline		20 Oct 1862	Oberlenningen	Krch.	Apr 1872	N.-Amer	835947
Reichle, Friederike Louise		29 Nov 1869	Oberlenningen	Krch.	Apr 1872	N.-Amer	835947
Reichle, Gottlob		12 Oct 1864	Gutenberg	Krch.	Dec 1880	N.-Amer	835945
Reichle, Jakob		16 Mar 1820	Bissingen	Krch.	bef 1858	N.-Amer	835943
Reichle, Johann Gottlieb		19 Apr 1856	Oberlenningen	Krch.	Apr 1872	N.-Amer	835947
Reichle, Johann Jakob		23 Aug 1858	Oberlenningen	Krch.	Apr 1872	N.-Amer	835947
Reichle, Johann Jakob & F			Oberlenningen	Krch.	Apr 1872	N.-Amer	835947
Reichle, Johann Ludwig		2 Oct 1837	Payern/Switz.	Krch.	Dec 1857	N.-Amer	835940
Reichle, Johannes		11 Apr 1864	Owen	Krch.	Mar 1881	N.-Amer	548403
Reichle, Johannes		22 Oct 1863	Unterlenningen	Krch.	Mar 1867	N.-Amer	835949
Reichle, Sophie (wife)			Oberlenningen	Krch.	Apr 1872	N.-Amer	835947
Reichstadt, Isidor		30 yrs.	Aichhalden	Obd.	Sep 1853	France	838629
Reichstadt, Joseph		8 Jan 1829	Winzeln	Obd.	Sep 1854	N.-Amer	841016
Reiff, Andreas		15 Jul 1849	Oberhausen	Rtl.	Jun 1866	N.-Amer	841056
Reiff, Baltas		21 Aug 1839	Unterhausen	Rtl.	Mar 1860	N.-Amer	841056
Reiff, Elisabetha (wid.) & F		17 Jan 1832	Honau	Rtl.	Apr 1867	N.-Amer	841056
Reiff, Jakob		14 Mar 1859	Willmandingen	Rtl.	Jul 1879	N.-Amer	841051
Reiff, Johann Christian		19 yrs.	Oberhausen	Rtl.	Feb 1880	N.-Amer	841051
Reiff, Johann Georg			Unterhausen	Rtl.	May 1835	N.-Amer	841051
Reiff, Johannes		4 May 1815	Oberhausen	Rtl.	1857	N.-Amer	841056
Reiff, Julie		16 Oct 1859	Honau	Rtl.	Apr 1867	N.-Amer	841056
Reiff, Katharina		26 Nov 1832	Holzelfingen	Rtl.	Apr 1865	N.-Amer	841056
Reiff, Margaretha Barbara & F		6 May 1826	Oberhausen	Rtl.	1860	N.-Amer	841056
Reiff, Maria Agnes		6 Feb 1847	Unterhausen	Rtl.	Sep 1866	N.-Amer	841056
Reiff, Mathilda		29 Apr 1841	Unterhausen	Rtl.	Sep 1861	Switz.	841056
Reiff, Michael		3 Jul 1846	Oberhausen	Rtl.	1860	N.-Amer	841056
Reiff, Rosine Louise		15 Feb 1857	Honau	Rtl.	Apr 1867	N.-Amer	841056
Reiff, Wilhelm Gottfried		17 Nov 1828	Unterhausen	Rtl.	bef 1862	N.-Amer	841056
Reiff, Wilhelmine Johanna		11 May 1854	Oberhausen	Rtl.	1860	N.-Amer	841056
Reifsteck, Johann & F			Lauterbach	Obd.	Feb 1817	N.-Amer	838634
Reik, Johannes		18 Feb 1848	Neidlingen	Krch.	Apr 1866	N.-Amer	835946
Reik, Wilhelm Friedrich		10 Nov 1851	Notzingen	Krch.	Feb 1872	N.-Amer	835947
Rein, Anna Barbara		7 Mar 1827	Willmandingen	Rtl.	bef 1861	N.-Amer	841056
Rein, Christiane			Jesingen	Krch.	bef 1856	N.-Amer	835946
Rein, Friederike Rosine		10 Feb 1848	Lindorf	Krch.	Feb 1868	N.-Amer	835946
Rein, Friedrich Wilhelm		21 Jan 1848	Jesingen	Krch.	Jul 1867	N.-Amer	835946
Rein, Jacob		25 May 1845	Willmandingen	Rtl.	May 1864	N.-Amer	841056
Rein, Johann Martin		16 Oct 1790	Jesingen	Krch.	Aug 1860	N.-Amer	835946
Rein, Johannes		31 Jan 1840	Willmandingen	Rtl.	1860	N.-Amer	841056
Rein, Karl Ludwig		18 Sep 1843	Undingen	Rtl.	Oct 1866	N.-Amer	841056
Rein, Maria Barbara		21 Jul 1839	Undingen	Rtl.	Jun 1865	N.-Amer	841056
Rein, Rosina		9 Jun 1836	Willmandingen	Rtl.	bef 1861	N.-Amer	841056
Reinauer, Anton		22 Mar 1850	Hochmoessingen	Obd.	Mar 1867	N.-Amer	838633
Reinert, Christian			Altenstadt-Gsl.	Gsl.	Feb 1853	N.-Amer	572041
Reinert, Daniel		19 Jun 1825	Moensheim	Leon.	bef 1856	N.-Amer	837960
Reinert, Johann Friedrich		8 Nov 1833	Moensheim	Leon.	Nov 1853	N.-Amer	837960
Reinert, Johanna		3 Apr 1843	Ditzingen	Leon.	Aug 1866	N.-Amer	835788
Reinert, Johannes		14 Mar 1824	Ditzingen	Leon.	bef 1854	N.-Amer	835788
Reinhardt, Anna		16 Dec 1848	Gomaringen	Rtl.	May 1869	N.-Amer	841056

Reinhardt, Anna Barbara (wife)	23 Feb 1820	Gomaringen	Rtl.	May 1869	N.-Amer	841056
Reinhardt, Catharina	14 Nov 1851	Gomaringen	Rtl.	May 1869	N.-Amer	841056
Reinhardt, Conrad & F	30 Dec 1821	Gomaringen	Rtl.	May 1869	N.-Amer	841056
Reinhardt, Friederika	4 Aug 1859	Gomaringen	Rtl.	May 1869	N.-Amer	841056
Reinhardt, Johann Georg	15 Jul 1855	Gomaringen	Rtl.	May 1869	N.-Amer	841056
Reinhardt, Johanna Barbara	4 Mar 1851	Malmsheim	Leon.	Jun 1869	N.-Amer	837958
Reinhardt, Johannes	6 Mar 1839	Gomaringen	Rtl.	Jul 1859	N.-Amer	841056
Reinhardt, Karl Jakob	8 May 1869	Malmsheim	Leon.	Nov 1889	N.-Amer	837958
Reinhardt, Magdalena Dorothea	22 May 1830	Dettingen	Krch.	Apr 1869	N.-Amer	835944
Reinhardt, Rosine	8 May 1833	Moensheim	Leon.	Sep 1856	N. Amer	837960
Reinhardt, Rosine	1 Oct 1826	Malmsheim	Leon.	May 1851	N.-Amer	837958
Reinhardt, Samuel	12 Mar 1862	Gomaringen	Rtl.	May 1869	N.-Amer	841056
Reinhardt, Wilhelm Friedrich		Leonberg	Leon.	bef 1820	N.-Amer	835787
Reinhardt, Wilhelm Friedrich	31 Oct 1847	Pfullingen	Rtl.	Oct 1866	N.-Amer	841056
Reininger, Johann Georg	19 Oct 1829	Ditzingen	Leon.	1854	N.-Amer	835788
Reinoehl, Carl Wilhelm		Kirchheim	Krch.	bef 1858	N.-Amer	835940
Reinoehl, Christian		Kirchheim	Krch.	bef 1858	N.-Amer	835940
Reinoehl, Christian	19 Jan 1846	Kirchheim	Krch.	May 1866	N.-Amer	835941
Reinoehl, Maria Louise	22 Oct 1825	Kirchheim	Krch.	Dec 1857	N.-Amer	835940
Reinoehl, Rosine		Kirchheim	Krch.	bef 1858	N. Amer	835940
Reinoel, Wilhelm Georg	30 Jun 1847	Burrach/Rav.	Krch.	Feb 1867	N.-Amer	835943
Reis, Johannes & F		Merklingen	Leon.	Mar 1817	Russia	837959
Reis, Michael		Merklingen	Leon.	Mar 1817	Russia	837959
Reiser, Georg	27 Feb 1837	Ueberkingen	Gsl.	Dec 1863	N.-Amer	572044
Reiser, Paul Christian	31 Aug 1820	Leonberg	Leon.	Jul 1845	N.-Amer	835786
Reiss, Angelika		Altensteig	Gsl.	Mar 1867	N.-Amer	572046
Reisser, Christoph	11 Nov 1847	Ueberkingen	Gsl.	Mar 1866	N.-Amer	572045
Reiter, Anton	14 Aug 1861	Boehmenkirch	Gsl.	Aug 1867	N.-Amer	572046
Reiter, Gertrude	6 Nov 1859	Boehmenkirch	Gsl.	Aug 1867	N.-Amer	572046
Reiter, Johann Baptist	3 Sep 1864	Boehmenkirch	Gsl.	Aug 1867	N.-Amer	572046
Reiter, Johann Georg & F		Boehmenkirch	Gsl.	Aug 1867	N.-Amer	572046
Reiter, Josef	13 Jul 1867	Boehmenkirch	Gsl.	Aug 1867	N.-Amer	572046
Reiter, Poteriz	16 May 1863	Boehmenkirch	Gsl.	Aug 1867	N.-Amer	572046
Reiter, Theresia (wife)		Boehmenkirch	Gsl.	Aug 1867	N.-Amer	572046
Reitter, Albert Eb. Aug.	30 Oct 1856	Muenchingen	Leon.	bef 1862	Russia	837961
Reitter, August Karl Adolph	19 Apr 1858	Muenchingen	Leon.	bef 1862	Russia	837961
Reitter, Karl	3 Nov 1845	Reutlingen	Rtl.	Jun 1865	N.-Amer	841056
Rekenberger, Friedrich Ludwig		Gerlingen	Leon.	May 1831	N.-Amer	837953
Remminger, August		Reichenbach	Gsl.	Aug 1868	Prussia	572046
Remminger, Theresia & C		Hohenstadt	Gsl.	bef 1868	W.-Prs.	572046
Remp, Anna Friederika	20 Feb 1828	Moensheim	Leon.	Jul 1854	N.-Amer	837960
Remp, Heinrich		Moensheim	Leon.	bef 1865	N.-Amer	837960
Remp, Israel	16 yrs.	Moensheim	Leon.	Apr 1852	N.-Amer	837960
Remp, Israel & F		Moensheim	Leon.	Apr 1852	N.-Amer	837960
Remp, Justina		Moensheim	Leon.	bef 1865	N.-Amer	837960
Remp, Justina Magdalena	15 yrs.	Moensheim	Leon.	Apr 1852	N.-Amer	837960
Rempfer, Anna	11 Jul 1877	Herrenberg	Herr.	Jun 1896	N.-Amer	834629
Rempp, Caroline	18 Apr 1851	Heimerdingen	Leon.	Mar 1852	N.-Amer	837954
Rempp, Christian	3 Jul 1847	Heimerdingen	Leon.	Mar 1852	N.-Amer	837954
Rempp, Christina		Peterzell	Obd.	Sep 1860	N.-Amer	838635

Name		Birth		Emigration			Film
Last	First	Date	Place	O'amt	Appl. Date	Dest.	Number
Rempp, Conrad		8 Jan 1845	Heimerdingen	Leon.	Mar 1852	N.-Amer	837954
Rempp, Friederich		12 Jan 1849	Heimerdingen	Leon.	Mar 1852	N.-Amer	837954
Rempp, Friederike		5 yrs.	Leonberg	Leon.	Jan 1852	N.-Amer	835786
Rempp, Friederike (wife)			Leonberg	Leon.	Jan 1852	N.-Amer	835786
Rempp, Gottlieb		3 yrs.	Leonberg	Leon.	Jan 1852	N.-Amer	835786
Rempp, Jakob & F			Leonberg	Leon.	Jan 1852	N.-Amer	835786
Rempp, Johann Friedrich		8 Jul 1838	Heimerdingen	Leon.	bef 1862	N.-Amer	837954
Rempp, Johann Ulrich & F		14 Sep 1815	Heimerdingen	Leon.	Mar 1852	N.-Amer	837954
Rempp, Margaretha (wife)		23 Jan 1819	Heimerdingen	Leon.	Mar 1852	N.-Amer	837954
Rempp, Maria		infant	Leonberg	Leon.	Jan 1852	N.-Amer	835786
Rempp, Wilhelm		23 yrs.	Fluorn	Obd.	Mar 1861	N.-Amer	838632
Rempp, Wilhelm		2 Jul 1843	Heimerdingen	Leon.	Mar 1852	N.-Amer	837954
Renfle, Katharina		17 yrs.	Geislingen	Gsl.	Jun 1852	Switz.	572044
Renftle, Johann Georg		4 May 1847	Gingen	Gsl.	Jul 1866	N.-Amer	572045
Renftle, Lukas		20 Feb 1849	Gingen	Gsl.	Jul 1868	N.-Amer	572046
Renkenberger, – (wife)		50 yrs.	Schoeckingen	Leon.	Mar 1818	N.-Amer	837964
Renkenberger, Barbara		4 yrs.	Schoeckingen	Leon.	Mar 1818	N.-Amer	837964
Renkenberger, Catharina		20 yrs.	Schoeckingen	Leon.	Mar 1818	N.-Amer	837964
Renkenberger, Christina		13 yrs.	Schoeckingen	Leon.	Mar 1818	N.-Amer	837964
Renkenberger, Christoph		16 yrs.	Schoeckingen	Leon.	Mar 1818	N.-Amer	837964
Renkenberger, Friederika		2 yrs.	Schoeckingen	Leon.	Mar 1818	N.-Amer	837964
Renkenberger, Jakob			Gerlingen	Leon.	Jan 1830	N.-Amer	837953
Renkenberger, Johann Georg		11 yrs.	Schoeckingen	Leon.	Mar 1818	N.-Amer	837964
Renkenberger, Johann Georg & F		52 yrs.	Schoeckingen	Leon.	Mar 1818	N.-Amer	837964
Renkenberger, Johannes		17 yrs.	Schoeckingen	Leon.	Mar 1818	N.-Amer	837964
Renner, Christian Ludwig		10 Jan 1829	Renningen	Leon.	Jan 1852	N.-Amer	837963
Renner, Dorothea		5 Nov 1845	Moensheim	Leon.	Jun 1847	Austria	837960
Renner, Johann Daniel & F		34 yrs.	Moensheim	Leon.	Jun 1847	Austria	837960
Renner, Johann Friedrich		23 Sep 1839	Moensheim	Leon.	Jun 1847	Austria	837960
Renner, Johann Wilhelm		18 Dec 1851	Willmandingen	Rtl.	Apr 1867	N.-Amer	841056
Renner, Johanna Catharina			Moensheim	Leon.	Jun 1847	Austria	837960
Renner, Louise		17 Feb 1858	Willmandingen	Rtl.	Apr 1861	N.-Amer	841056
Renner, Maria Magdalena		10 May 1846	Moensheim	Leon.	Jun 1847	Austria	837960
Renner, Michael		28 Jan 1838	Moensheim	Leon.	Jun 1847	Austria	837960
Renner, Regina Catharina		16 Jul 1855	Willmandingen	Rtl.	Apr 1861	N.-Amer	841056
Renner, Regina Catharina & C		21 Aug 1827	Willmandingen	Rtl.	Apr 1861	N.-Amer	841056
Renschler, Anna Maria		11 yrs.	Rutesheim	Leon.	Feb 1852	N.-Amer	837964
Renschler, Catharina		10 yrs.	Rutesheim	Leon.	Feb 1852	N.-Amer	837964
Renschler, Johann Martin		15 yrs.	Rutesheim	Leon.	Feb 1852	N.-Amer	837964
Renschler, Johannes		16 yrs.	Rutesheim	Leon.	Feb 1852	N.-Amer	837964
Renschler, Johannes & F			Rutesheim	Leon.	Feb 1852	N.-Amer	837964
Renschler, Magdalena		6 yrs.	Rutesheim	Leon.	Feb 1852	N.-Amer	837964
Rentz, Johann Jakob & F			Perouse	Leon.	Nov 1853	N.-Amer	837962
Renz, Amand		9 yrs.	Gomaringen	Rtl.	Sep 1859	N.-Amer	841056
Renz, Anna Maria		7 yrs.	Gomaringen	Rtl.	Sep 1859	N.-Amer	841056
Renz, Anna Maria (wife)		46 yrs.	Gomaringen	Rtl.	Sep 1859	N.-Amer	841056
Renz, Barbara		18 Nov 1838	Gomaringen	Rtl.	1854	N.-Amer	841056
Renz, Barbara		18 yrs.	Gomaringen	Rtl.	Sep 1859	N.-Amer	841056
Renz, Carl Friedrich		26 Aug 1864	Unterlenningen	Krch.	May 1881	N.-Amer	548403
Renz, Catharina		14 Jun 1837	Gomaringen	Rtl.	1854	N.-Amer	841056

Renz, Christian	12 Nov 1886	Unterlenningen	Krch.	Apr 1884	N.-Amer	548403
Renz, Christian	12 Nov 1868	Unterlenningen	Krch.	Mar 1884	N.-Amer	835949
Renz, Christian	21 Dec 1865	Unterlenningen	Krch.	Jan 1882	N.-Amer	835949
Renz, Conrad	20 Aug 1835	Gomaringen	Rtl.	bef 1864	Holland	841056
Renz, Dieterich	8 Oct 1846	Unterlenningen	Krch.	Apr 1856	N.-Amer	835949
Renz, Elisabetha	17 yrs.	Gomaringen	Rtl.	Sep 1859	N.-Amer	841056
Renz, Elise Paulina	18 May 1859	Pfullingen	Rtl.	Sep 1865	N.-Amer	841056
Renz, Eva Rosine (wife)	5 Sep 1823	Unterlenningen	Krch.	Apr 1856	N.-Amer	835949
Renz, Friderika Paulina	11 Jan 1863	Pfullingen	Rtl.	Sep 1865	N.-Amer	841056
Renz, Jeremias	30 Jan 1862	Unterlenningen	Krch.	Feb 1881	N.-Amer	835949
Renz, Johann Adam	20 Apr 1853	Unterlenningen	Krch.	Sep 1871	Palest.	835949
Renz, Johann Caspar	21 May 1848	Unterlenningen	Krch.	Oct 1865	N.-Amer	835949
Renz, Johann Caspar & F	28 Feb 1819	Unterlenningen	Krch.	Apr 1856	N.-Amer	835949
Renz, Johann Friedrich	11 Aug 1865	Pfullingen	Rtl.	Sep 1865	N.-Amer	841056
Renz, Johann Georg	2 Sep 1847	Zell	Krch.	Aug 1867	N.-Amer	835774
Renz, Johann Georg	8 Feb 1848	Pfullingen	Rtl.	May 1865	N.-Amer	841056
Renz, Johann Georg	1 Nov 1837	Gomaringen	Rtl.	Sep 1859	N.-Amer	841056
Renz, Johann Jacob	28 Apr 1870	Unterlenningen	Krch.	Mar 1884	N.-Amer	548403
Renz, Johannes	12 Mar 1849	Pfullingen	Rtl.	Apr 1867	N.-Amer	841056
Renz, Johannes	20 Jan 1821	Pfullingen	Rtl.	Dec 1862	N.-Amer	841056
Renz, Johannes	13 Nov 1845	Unterlenningen	Krch.	Apr 1856	N.-Amer	835949
Renz, Johannes	4 Jul 1867	Unterlenningen	Krch.	Mar 1884	N.-Amer	835949
Renz, Johannes	19 Aug 1857	Unterlenningen	Krch.	Aug 1872	N.-Amer	835949
Renz, Johannes	12 Apr 1855	Unterlenningen	Krch.	Sep 1869	N.-Amer	835949
Renz, Karl Friedrich	2 Aug 1864	Unterlenningen	Krch.	Apr 1881	N.-Amer	835949
Renz, Karoline	11 Feb 1867	Herrenberg	Herr.	Dec 1894	N.-Amer	834629
Renz, Ludwig Friedrich & F	16 Mar 1833	Pfullingen	Rtl.	Sep 1865	N.-Amer	841056
Renz, Luisa Barbara (wife)		Pfullingen	Rtl.	Sep 1865	N.-Amer	841056
Renz, Magdalena	8 yrs.	Gomaringen	Rtl.	Sep 1859	N.-Amer	841056
Renz, Michael & F	43 yrs.	Gomaringen	Rtl.	Sep 1859	N.-Amer	841056
Renz, Regine Wilhelmine	14 Aug 1855	Unterlenningen	Krch.	Apr 1856	N.-Amer	835949
Renz, Sebastian		Bronnweiler	Rtl.	May 1832	N.-Amer	841051
Renz, Wilhelm	25 Dec 1851	Zell	Krch.	Jul 1868	N.-Amer	835774
Renz, Wilhelm	30 Mar 1857	Unterlenningen	Krch.	Feb 1871	N.-Amer	835949
Renz, Wilhelmine	23 Sep 1854	Unterlenningen	Krch.	May 1870	N.-Amer	835949
Retter, Carl	17 Aug 1841	Oetlingen	Krch.	Jun 1868	N.-Amer	835948
Retter, Gottlib Friedrich	2 May 1867	Flacht	Leon.	Sep 1883	N.-Amer	835790
Retter, Johann Wilhelm	13 Oct 1824	Oetlingen	Krch.	May 1865	N.-Amer	835948
Retter, Regina		Flacht	Leon.	May 1854	N.-Amer	835790
Rettich, Johanna Margaretha	- 1832	Kirchheim	Krch.	Nov 1859	N.-Amer	835940
Reuelspacher, Johann Georg	12 Mar 1853	Zell	Krch.	Oct 1879	N.-Amer	835940
Reule, Jacob Friedrich		Berneck	Nag.	Sep 1851	N.-Amer	838488
Reule, Johann Jacob		Berneck	Nag.	Aug 1852	N.-Amer	838488
Reuter, Gottliebin & F		Groembach/Freudenst.	Obd.	Apr 1848	N.-Amer	838632
Reuter, Jakob		Groembach/Freudenst.	Obd.	Apr 1848	N.-Amer	838632
Reuter, Johannes	3 Jun 1850	Aichhalden	Obd.	Nov 1866	N.-Amer	838629
Reuter, Josephine (wife)		Schramberg	Obd.	Aug 1855	N.-Amer	838636
Reuter, Maria		Aichhalden	Obd.	Aug 1863	France	838629
Reuter, Severin & W		Schramberg	Obd.	Aug 1855	N.-Amer	838636
Reutter, Johannes	2 Nov 1850	Schramberg	Obd.	Dec 1870	N.-Amer	838636

Name		Birth		Emigration			Film
Last	First	Date	Place	O'amt	Appl. Date	Dest.	Number
Rexer, Anna Maria (wid.) & F			Malmsheim	Leon.	Jun 1869	N.-Amer	837958
Rexer, Christian Friedrich		23 yrs.	Malmsheim	Leon.	Feb 1854	N.-Amer	837958
Rexer, Christiana		24 yrs.	Warmbronn	Leon.	Jan 1867	Prussia	837965
Rexer, Gottlob			Malmsheim	Leon.	Feb 1854	N.-Amer	837958
Rexer, Jakob Friedrich & W			Malmsheim	Leon.	Sep 1867	N.-Amer	837958
Rexer, Johann Friedrich			Malmsheim	Leon.	Feb 1854	N.-Amer	837958
Rexer, Katharina (wife)			Malmsheim	Leon.	Sep 1867	N.-Amer	837958
Rexer, Ludwig			Ruetesheim	Leon.	1869	N.-Amer	837956
Rexer, Ludwig		17 Sep 1844	Malmsheim	Leon.	Jun 1869	N.-Amer	837958
Rexer, Magdalena Friederike		24 May 1821	Malmsheim	Leon.	Jun 1848	N.-Amer	837958
Rexer, Maria Catharina		20 yrs.	Malmsheim	Leon.	Jun 1869	N.-Amer	837958
Rexer, Rosine			Warmbronn	Leon.	Apr 1853	N.-Amer	837965
Reyle, Christian & W		18 Jul 1785	Perouse	Leon.	Jan 1852	N.-Amer	837962
Reyle, Christine Agnes		27 Feb 1844	Perouse	Leon.	Jan 1852	N.-Amer	837962
Reyle, Elisabetha (wife)		1 Feb 1812	Perouse	Leon.	Jan 1852	N.-Amer	837962
Reyle, Eva Margaretha		19 yrs.	Wimsheim	Loen.	Feb 1851	N.-Amer	837967
Reyle, Friederike		30 Mar 1845	Perouse	Leon.	Jan 1852	N.-Amer	837962
Reyle, Jakob		22 Feb 1849	Perouse	Leon.	Jan 1852	N.-Amer	837962
Reyle, Jakob Friedrich			Malmsheim	Leon.	bef 1841	N.-Amer	837958
Reyle, Johann Georg		17 yrs.	Wimsheim	Loen.	Feb 1851	N.-Amer	837967
Reyle, Johannes & F		6 Dec 1811	Perouse	Leon.	Jan 1852	N.-Amer	837962
Reyle, Margaretha (wife)			Wimsheim	Loen.	Feb 1851	N.-Amer	837967
Reyle, Marie Agnes (wife)		8 Nov 1785	Perouse	Leon.	Jan 1852	N.-Amer	837962
Reyle, Mathias & F			Wimsheim	Loen.	Feb 1851	N.-Amer	837967
Reyle, Michael			Wimsheim	Loen.	Apr 1834	Rus-Pol	837967
Rhenz, Jakob Friedrich		22 yrs.	Merklingen	Leon.	Apr 1852	N.-Amer	837959
Richt, Andreas		18 yrs.	Moensheim	Leon.	Mar 1852	N.-Amer	837960
Richt, Anna Maria		16 yrs.	Moensheim	Leon.	Mar 1852	N.-Amer	837960
Richt, Anna Maria (wife)			Moensheim	Leon.	Mar 1852	N.-Amer	837960
Richt, Christina		25 Jun 1851	Moensheim	Leon.	Apr 1866	N.-Amer	837960
Richt, Christine		14 yrs.	Moensheim	Leon.	Mar 1852	N.-Amer	837960
Richt, Friedrich		31 Oct 1848	Moensheim	Leon.	Apr 1866	N.-Amer	837960
Richt, Helene		12 yrs.	Moensheim	Leon.	Mar 1852	N.-Amer	837960
Richt, Jonathan		24 yrs.	Moensheim	Leon.	Mar 1852	N.-Amer	837960
Richt, Leonhardt & F			Moensheim	Leon.	Mar 1852	N.-Amer	837960
Richt, Michael		28 Aug 1844	Moensheim	Leon.	Jul 1864	N.-Amer	837960
Richt, Rosine Katharine		9 yrs.	Moensheim	Leon.	Mar 1852	N.-Amer	837960
Riedaisch, Georg			Owen	Krch.	bef 1872	N.-Amer	835948
Riedaisch, Johann Jacob		24 Nov 1849	Owen	Krch.	Jul 1872	N.-Amer	835948
Riedaisch, Johannes		19 Oct 1816	Owen	Krch.	bef 1872	N.-Amer	835948
Riedaisch, Jokob Friedrich		5 Dec 1855	Owen	Krch.	Jun 1872	N.-Amer	835948
Riedaisch, Wilhelm		1 Jun 1866	Hepsisau	Krch.	May 1883	N.-Amer	835948
Riedel, Thomas			Hirschlanden	Leon.	bef 1828	Hungary	837956
Riefler, Johann Georg		19 Sep 1846	Gomaringen	Rtl.	Nov 1866	N.-Amer	841056
Riefler, Johann Georg		9 Jun 1835	Gomaringen	Rtl.	May 1869	N.-Amer	841056
Riefler, Kaspar & F			Gomaringen	Rtl.	May 1832	N.-Amer	841051
Rieger, Anna			Donzdorf	Gsl.	Jul 1865	N.-Amer	572045
Rieger, Carl August		29 Oct 1840	Alpirsbach	Obd.	Jul 1853	N.-Amer	838630
Rieger, Franz Johann		30 Oct 1839	Alpirsbach	Obd.	Jul 1853	N.-Amer	838630
Rieger, Johann & F			Fluorn	Obd.	Apr 1817	N.-Amer	838631

Name	Date	Place	Region	Date	Destination	Film
Rieger, Johann Georg	12 Feb 1831	Moensheim	Leon.	Feb 1857	Austral	837960
Rieger, Johannes		Fluorn	Obd.	bef 1865	N.-Amer	838632
Rieger, Josef Emil	25 Apr 1854	Bach-Altenberg	Obd.	Feb 1869	N.-Amer	838631
Rieger, Sebastian	21 Jan 1845	Donzdorf	Gsl.	Sep 1866	N.-Amer	572045
Riegert, Augustin	19 Nov 1867	Schnittlingen	Gsl.	May 1884	N.-Amer	572049
Riegert, Jacob	3 Nov 1865	Schnittlingen	Gsl.	Sep 1883	N.-Amer	572049
Riegert, Joseph		Gingen	Gsl.	Mar 1853	N.-Amer	572041
Riegert, Maria Anna		Boehmenkirch	Gsl.	Mar 1852	N.-Amer	572041
Riegle, Christian		Muenchingen	Leon.	bef 1830	Switz.	837961
Riek, Pius	11 Jul 1836	Gosbach	Gsl.	Feb 1853	N.-Amer	572041
Rieker, Peter	9 Jan 1828	Neidlingen	Krch.	Apr 1857	N.-Amer	835946
Rielneker, Dorotea (wife)	42 yrs.	Burcken	Krch.	Mar 1804	Rus-Pol	550804
Rielneker, Jacob & F	42 yrs.	Burcken	Krch.	Mar 1804	Rus-Pol	550804
Rielneker, Johann Adam	5 yrs.	Burcken	Krch.	Mar 1804	Rus-Pol	550804
Riepert, Carl	19 yrs.	Reutlingen	Rtl.	Jun 1880	N.-Amer	841051
Riepert, Jakob	14 Feb 1842	Reutlingen	Rtl.	Jan 1862	N.-Amer	841056
Riepert, Justus	21 Sep 1844	Reutlingen	Rtl.	Jun 1864	N.-Amer	841056
Ries, Johann Jacob & F		Hausen a.d. Wurm	Leon.	Sep 1853	N.-Amer	837954
Ries, Johann Jakob	28 Mar 1849	Unterhausen	Rtl.	Sep 1866	N.-Amer	841056
Riesch, Barbara (wife)	4 Aug 1817	Heimerdingen	Leon.	Feb 1852	N.-Amer	837954
Riesch, Carolina	13 Feb 1849	Heimerdingen	Leon.	Feb 1852	N.-Amer	837954
Riesch, Christian Friedrich	15 Aug 1843	Heimerdingen	Leon.	Feb 1852	N.-Amer	837954
Riesch, Christiane	30 Jan 1849	Heimerdingen	Leon.	May 1853	N.-Amer	837954
Riesch, Gottfried	4 Apr 1851	Heimerdingen	Leon.	May 1853	N.-Amer	837954
Riesch, Gottfried & F	22 Sep 1810	Heimerdingen	Leon.	May 1853	N.-Amer	837954
Riesch, Gottlieb	24 Jan 1835	Heimerdingen	Leon.	Aug 1853	N.-Amer	837954
Riesch, Johanna Friederike	4 Jul 1846	Heimerdingen	Leon.	May 1853	N.-Amer	837954
Riesch, Margaretha (wife)	28 Jun 1819	Heimerdingen	Leon.	May 1853	N.-Amer	837954
Riesch, Maria Catharina	20 Oct 1844	Heimerdingen	Leon.	Feb 1852	N.-Amer	837954
Riesch, Thomas & F	4 Dec 1817	Heimerdingen	Leon.	Feb 1852	N.-Amer	837954
Rietheimer, Friederike	11 Feb 1832	Oetlingen	Krch.	bef 1864	N.-Amer	835948
Rietheimer, Georg Robert	12 Jul 1866	Oetlingen	Krch.	Apr 1883	N.-Amer	548403
Rietheimer, Georg Wilhelm	24 Oct 1851	Oetlingen	Krch.	bef 1864	N.-Amer	835948
Rietheimer, Johannes		Oetlingen	Krch.	bef 1860	N.-Amer	835940
Rietheimer, Wilhelm Gottlob	3 Nov 1871	Oetlingen	Krch.	Nov 1886	N.-Amer	835948
Riethmueller, Caroline		Eltingen	Leon.	Dec 1850	N.-Amer	835789
Riethmueller, Caroline Fried.	21 Sep 1817	Eltingen	Leon.	Jun 1846	N.-Amer	835789
Riethmueller, Friederike	33 yrs.	Eltingen	Leon.	Dec 1850	N.-Amer	835789
Riethmueller, Hermann	22 Oct 1834	Kirchheim	Krch.	bef 1861	Hungary	835940
Riethmueller, Johann Jakob	8 Nov 1839	Gueltstein	Herr.	Aug 1867	N.-Amer	834631
Riethmueller, Marie Frieder.	4 Apr 1842	Kirchheim	Krch.	Jan 1866	N.-Amer	835941
Riethmueller, Xristiana Kath.	21 Aug 1838	Gueltstein	Herr.	Aug 1867	N.-Amer	834631
Riexinger, Andreas	9 mon.	Merklingen	Leon.	Apr 1852	N.-Amer	837959
Riexinger, Anna Maria	7 yrs.	Merklingen	Leon.	May 1854	N.-Amer	837959
Riexinger, Anna Maria (wife)		Merklingen	Leon.	Apr 1852	N.-Amer	837959
Riexinger, Friederika	4 yrs.	Merklingen	Leon.	Apr 1852	N.-Amer	837959
Riexinger, Friederika (wife)		Merklingen	Leon.	Apr 1852	N.-Amer	837959
Riexinger, Friederike & C		Merklingen	Leon.	May 1851	N.-Amer	837959
Riexinger, Friedrich	3 yrs.	Merklingen	Leon.	Apr 1852	N.-Amer	837959
Riexinger, Friedrich	2 yrs.	Merklingen	Leon.	Apr 1852	N.-Amer	837959

Name		Birth		Emigration			Film
Last	First	Date	Place	O'amt	Appl. Date	Dest.	Number
Riexinger, Georg Friedrich & F			Merklingen	Leon.	Apr 1852	N.-Amer	837959
Riexinger, Jakob		3 Jan 1835	Merklingen	Leon.	bef 1863	France	837959
Riexinger, Jakob		10 Dec 1825	Merklingen	Leon.	Sep 1859	N.-Amer	837959
Riexinger, Johann Michael			Merklingen	Leon.	Apr 1852	N.-Amer	837959
Riexinger, Joseph		9 yrs.	Merklingen	Leon.	Apr 1852	N.-Amer	837959
Riexinger, Joseph & F			Merklingen	Leon.	Apr 1852	N.-Amer	837959
Riexinger, Lorenz		8 yrs.	Merklingen	Leon.	Apr 1852	N.-Amer	837959
Riexinger, Margaretha		8 yrs.	Merklingen	Leon.	Apr 1852	N.-Amer	837959
Riexinger, Maria Catharina		12 yrs.	Merklingen	Leon.	Apr 1852	N.-Amer	837959
Riexinger, Michael		6 yrs.	Merklingen	Leon.	Apr 1852	N.-Amer	837959
Riexinger, Regina Dorothea		11 yrs.	Merklingen	Leon.	Apr 1852	N.-Amer	837959
Rilling, Christian		27 Apr 1848	Gomaringen	Rtl.	Aug 1867	N.-Amer	841056
Rilling, David Gottlob		20 Nov 1850	Gomaringen	Rtl.	Aug 1865	N.-Amer	841056
Rilling, Elisabetha		12 Jan 1829	Gomaringen	Rtl.	Mar 1866	N.-Amer	841056
Rilling, Jakob		28 May 1845	Gomaringen	Rtl.	Oct 1859	N.-Amer	841056
Rilling, Johann Georg		9 Sep 1827	Gomaringen	Rtl.	Nov 1859	France	841056
Rilling, Johann Martin		5 Sep 1835	Gomaringen	Rtl.	Sep 1859	N.-Amer	841056
Rilling, Johann Michael		14 Jun 1839	Gomaringen	Rtl.	Nov 1859	N.-Amer	841056
Rilling, Karl Friedrich		21 Mar 1846	Pfullingen	Rtl.	Aug 1866	N.-Amer	841056
Rilling, Maria Elisabetha		24 Apr 1847	Gomaringen	Rtl.	Aug 1865	N.-Amer	841056
Rimpis, Johann Georg		7 Jun 1846	Notzingen	Krch.	Dec 1863	N.-Amer	835947
Rinck, Christian		18 May 1853	Alpirsbach	Obd.	Feb 1870	N.-Amer	838630
Rinck, Eduard		10 Aug 1853	Alpirsbach	Obd.	May 1870	N.-Amer	838630
Rinck, Karoline Wilhelmine			Alpirsbach	Obd.	Oct 1860	France	838630
Rinck, Wilhelm		4 Sep 1851	Alpirsbach	Obd.	May 1868	N.-Amer	838630
Rinck, Wilhelm Christian		31 Jul 1830	Roetenbach	Obd.	Mar 1866	France	838636
Ringle, Joseph Anton			Weil der Stadt	Leon.	Jun 1852	N.-Amer	837966
Rink, Adolf		3 Jun 1846	Donzdorf	Gsl.	May 1867	N.-Amer	572046
Rink, Christiane		6 May 1819	Alpirsbach	Obd.	Aug 1852	France	838630
Rink, Friedrich Wilhelm		18 Oct 1835	Alpirsbach	Obd.	Feb 1854	N.-Amer	838630
Rink, Johann Baptist		8 Jun 1849	Gosbach	Gsl.	Apr 1866	N.-Amer	572045
Ritter, Adolf Michael		28 May 1853	Geislingen	Gsl.	Oct 1880	N.-Amer	572048
Ritter, Justina			Geislingen	Gsl.	Mar 1851	N.-Amer	577788
Ritz, Alois		17 Jan 1854	Boehmenkirch	Gsl.	Apr 1870	N.-Amer	572047
Ritz, Bernhard		22 Mar 1846	Boehmenkirch	Gsl.	Apr 1867	N.-Amer	572046
Ritz, Josef		2 Jan 1850	Boehmenkirch	Gsl.	May 1869	N.-Amer	572047
Ritz, Marianna		12 Dec 1851	Boehmenkirch	Gsl.	Apr 1870	N.-Amer	572047
Ritz, Nikolaus		3 Jul 1832	Boehmenkirch	Gsl.	Sep 1853	N.-Amer	572041
Ritz, Theresia		17 Oct 1848	Treffelhausen	Gsl.	May 1868	Austria	572046
Rockenbauch, Dorothea		8 yrs.	Schoeckingen	Leon.	Mar 1852	N.-Amer	837964
Rockenbauch, Friedrich			Hoefingen	Leon.	1822	Austria	837957
Rockenbauch, Georg Michael		6 Dec 1825	Ditzingen	Leon.	1853	N.-Amer	835788
Rockenbauch, Jakob & F		40 yrs.	Schoeckingen	Leon.	Mar 1852	N.-Amer	837964
Rockenbauch, Magdaline Catha.		1 yrs.	Schoeckingen	Leon.	Mar 1852	N.-Amer	837964
Rockenbauch, Margaretha		25 yrs.	Hoefingen	Leon.	Aug 1854	N.-Amer	837957
Rockenbauch, Marie Kath. (wife)			Schoeckingen	Leon.	Mar 1852	N.-Amer	837964
Rodociusky, Adolf Karl		1 Oct 1872	Gingen	Gsl.	Oct 1873	N.-Amer	572047
Rodociusky, Christina (wife)		9 May 1835	Gingen	Gsl.	Oct 1873	N.-Amer	572047
Rodociusky, Gustav Ad.Wil. & F		11 Feb 1833	Gingen	Gsl.	Oct 1873	N.-Amer	572047
Rodociusky, Sophia Maria		12 May 1871	Gingen	Gsl.	Oct 1873	N.-Amer	572047

Roebele, Thimothaeus Wilhelm	9 Jun 1829	Gingen	Gsl.	Jul 1874	Austria	572048
Roebelen, Carl Heinrich	18 Apr 1840	Altenstadt-Gsl.	Gsl.	May 1853	N.-Amer	572041
Roebelen, Euphrosine (wife)	8 Apr 1809	Altenstadt-Gsl.	Gsl.	May 1853	N.-Amer	572041
Roebelen, Ferdinand Gottlieb	28 Dec 1848	Altenstadt-Gsl.	Gsl.	May 1853	N.-Amer	572041
Roebelen, Georg Friedrich	1 Aug 1838	Altenstadt-Gsl.	Gsl.	May 1853	N.-Amer	572041
Roebelen, Imanuel Gottfried	12 Feb 1843	Altenstadt-Gsl.	Gsl.	May 1853	N.-Amer	572041
Roebelen, Karoline Barbara	11 Dec 1844	Altenstadt-Gsl.	Gsl.	May 1853	N.-Amer	572041
Roebelen, Maria	6 Oct 1830	Altenstadt-Gsl.	Gsl.	May 1853	N.-Amer	572041
Roebelen, Theodor August	11 Mar 1832	Altenstadt-Gsl.	Gsl.	May 1853	N.-Amer	572041
Roebelen, Theodor August	26 May 1801	Altenstadt-Gsl.	Gsl.	bef 1853	N.-Amer	572041
Roecker, Friedrich Albert	9 Nov 1840	Leonberg	Leon.	Jul 1859	N.-Amer	835786
Roecker, Jakob Friedrich & F		Flacht	Leon.	Sep 1850	N.-Amer	835790
Roeckle, Anna Maria	10 May 1826	Eltingen	Leon.	bef 1861	N.-Amer	835789
Roeckle, Johannes	36 yrs.	Eltingen	Leon.	May 1860	N.-Amer	835789
Roeckle, Katharina	8 Apr 1820	Eltingen	Leon.	May 1867	N.-Amer	835789
Roeckle, Katharina	5 Jun 1854	Eltingen	Leon.	May 1867	N.-Amer	835789
Roeckle, Katharina (wid.) & F		Eltingen	Leon.	May 1867	N.-Amer	835789
Roeckle, Maria Barbara (wife)		Eltingen	Leon.	May 1867	N.-Amer	835789
Roeckle, Philipp & W		Eltingen	Leon.	May 1867	N.-Amer	835789
Roeder, Andreas	32 yrs.	Steinenkirch	Gsl.	Apr 1866	N.-Amer	572045
Roeder, Dorothea	3 Nov 1842	Steinenkirch	Gsl.	Apr 1870	N.-Amer	572047
Roeder, Georg	31 Mar 1842	Steinenkirch	Gsl.	Jul 1869	N.-Amer	572047
Roeder, Philipp	21 Jan 1849	Steinenkirch	Gsl.	Aug 1871	N.-Amer	572047
Roehm, Anna Margaretha	18 Jul 1838	Reutlingen	Rtl.	Dec 1869	Prussia	841056
Roehm, Carl Wilhelm	15 Jul 1841	Wiesensteig	Gsl.	Aug 1860	N.-Amer	572044
Roehm, Christiane		Reutlingen	Rtl.	Mar 1866	France	841056
Roehm, Johannes	27 Jan 1848	Wiesensteig	Gsl.	Oct 1866	N.-Amer	572045
Roehm, Johannes	27 yrs.	Reutlingen	Rtl.	Jun 1880	N.-Amer	841051
Roehm, Wilhelm	1841	Hoefingen	Leon.	Jun 1869	Palest.	837957
Roehner, Jakob Friedrich Wilh.	30 Nov 1844	Oetlingen	Krch.	Jun 1862	N.-Amer	835948
Roehner, Johann Friedrich	12 Sep 1849	Weilheim	Krch.	Apr 1867	N.-Amer	835950
Roehr, August	16 yrs.	Ditzenbach	Gsl.	Feb 1853	N.-Amer	573622
Roehr, Conrad	21 yrs.	Ditzenbach	Gsl.	Feb 1853	N.-Amer	573622
Roehr, Conrad & F	50 yrs.	Ditzenbach	Gsl.	Feb 1853	N.-Amer	573622
Roehr, Magdalena (wife)	51 yrs.	Ditzenbach	Gsl.	Feb 1853	N.-Amer	573622
Roehr, Marianna	15 yrs.	Ditzenbach	Gsl.	Feb 1853	N.-Amer	573622
Roehr, Martina	23 yrs.	Ditzenbach	Gsl.	Feb 1853	N.-Amer	573622
Roehr, Paulina	10 yrs.	Ditzenbach	Gsl.	Feb 1853	N.-Amer	573622
Roehr, Wilhelm	13 yrs.	Ditzenbach	Gsl.	Feb 1853	N.-Amer	573622
Roeker, Jakob Friedrich		Flacht	Leon.	bef 1855	N.-Amer	835790
Roekle, Adam Jakob	25 Jul 1854	Eltingen	Leon.	May 1880	N.-Amer	835789
Roekle, Anna Maria		Warmbronn	Leon.	May 1857	N.-Amer	837965
Roekle, Anna Maria & C	25 yrs.	Eltingen	Leon.	Apr 1852	N.-Amer	835789
Roekle, Catharina		Eltingen	Leon.	Aug 1854	N.-Amer	835789
Roekle, Catharina Barb. (wife)		Eltingen	Leon.	Oct 1854	N.-Amer	835789
Roekle, Christian Abraham		Eltingen	Leon.	bef 1853	N.-Amer	835789
Roekle, Conradt & F		Eltingen	Leon.	Apr 1830	N.-Amer	835789
Roekle, Eberhard		Eltingen	Leon.	bef 1832	N.-Amer	835789
Roekle, Georg Wilhelm	infant	Eltingen	Leon.	Apr 1852	N.-Amer	835789
Roekle, Jacob	8 yrs.	Eltingen	Leon.	Oct 1854	N.-Amer	835789

Name		Birth		Emigration			Film
Last	First	Date	Place	O'amt	Appl. Date	Dest.	Number
Roekle, Jacob & F			Eltingen	Leon.	Oct 1854	N.-Amer	835789
Roekle, Johann Christian		11 Oct 1832	Eltingen	Leon.	Oct 1869	Bavaria	835789
Roekle, Margaretha			Eltingen	Leon.	Aug 1854	N.-Amer	835789
Roekle, Margaretha (wife)			Eltingen	Leon.	Aug 1854	N.-Amer	835789
Roekle, Maria Magdalena			Eltingen	Leon.	1850	N.-Amer	835789
Roekle, Philipp			Eltingen	Leon.	Aug 1854	N.-Amer	835789
Roekle, Philipp			Eltingen	Leon.	Apr 1830	N.-Amer	835789
Roekle, Philipp & F			Eltingen	Leon.	Aug 1854	N.-Amer	835789
Roekle, Samuel		10 Aug 1833	Eltingen	Leon.	Oct 1853	N.-Amer	835789
Roekle, Sebastian & F			Eltingen	Leon.	Apr 1830	N.-Amer	835789
Roemer, Elise		18 Oct 1824	Leonberg	Leon.	Apr 1856	Bavaria	835786
Roemer, Emma		7 Nov 1822	Leonberg	Leon.	Jan 1846	Switz.	835786
Roemer, Maria Auguste			Leonberg	Leon.	May 1858	Switz.	835787
Roesch, Christoph Fr. Gotth.		25 Nov 1862	Oetlingen	Krch.	Feb 1881	N.-Amer	548403
Roesch, Georg Friedrich		4 Dec 1846	Reutlingen	Rtl.	Aug 1865	N.-Amer	841056
Roesch, Gottlob		17 Dec 1842	Reutlingen	Rtl.	Apr 1864	N.-Amer	841056
Roesch, Johann Jacob			Neidlingen	Krch.	1853	N.-Amer	835940
Roesch, Johannes		20 Sep 1840	Gomaringen	Rtl.	Apr 1867	N.-Amer	841056
Roeser, Johannes		31 Oct 1853	Gomaringen	Rtl.	May 1869	N.-Amer	841056
Roesle, Friedrich			Geislingen	Gsl.	bef 1859	N.-Amer	573622
Roessler, Rosine		11 Sep 1836	Oetlingen	Krch.	Dec 1861	N.-Amer	835948
Roetter, Johannes		27 Nov 1844	Weissenstein	Gsl.	Jan 1862	N.-Amer	572044
Roetter, Kreszenzia		7 Feb 1831	Weissenstein	Gsl.	Feb 1850	Wien	577788
Roetter, Lukas			Steinenkirch	Gsl.	Feb 1867	N.-Amer	572046
Roetter, Michael		3 Sep 1834	Weissenstein	Gsl.	Apr 1854	N.-Amer	572042
Roggenbauch, Theodor			Malmsheim	Leon.	Apr 1854	N.-Amer	837958
Rohr, Andreas			Hochmoessingen	Obd.	1857	N.-Amer	838633
Rohr, Michael			Oberndorf	Obd.	Jul 1849	N.-Amer	838635
Rohr, Pauline		30 yrs.	Oberndorf	Obd.	Feb 1862	Switz.	838635
Rohrer, Andreas		1 Jan 1840	Peterzell	Obd.	Nov 1853	N.-Amer	838635
Rohrer, Barbara & F			Peterzell	Obd.	Apr 1855	N.-Amer	838635
Rohrer, Christina			Peterzell	Obd.	Apr 1855	N.-Amer	838635
Rohrer, Franz Xaver		30 Nov 1847	Bochingen	Obd.	Dec 1867	N.-Amer	838632
Rohrer, Johann Georg			Peterzell	Obd.	Apr 1855	N.-Amer	838635
Rohrer, Johannes		9 Jan 1837	Peterzell	Obd.	Nov 1853	N.-Amer	838635
Rohrer, Johannes		- Dec 1819	Kirchheim	Krch.	bef 1867	N.-Amer	835940
Rokenbauch, Johann Bernhard		4 Feb 1828	Ditzingen	Leon.	Feb 1854	N.-Amer	835788
Rokenbauch, Rosina Dorothea		23 Jul 1815	Ditzingen	Leon.	Aug 1853	N.-Amer	835788
Roll, Johann Michael		24 Jan 1875	Bondorf	Herr.	Feb 1881	N.-Amer	834630
Roll, Johann Michael & F		12 Jul 1830	Bondorf	Herr.	Feb 1881	N.-Amer	834630
Roll, Karl Heinrich		3 Apr 1842	Bondorf	Herr.	Mar 1873	N.-Amer	834630
Roll, Katharina		19 Jun 1872	Bondorf	Herr.	Feb 1881	N.-Amer	834630
Roll, Maria Magdalena		9 Feb 1880	Bondorf	Herr.	Feb 1881	N.-Amer	834630
Roll, Maria Magdalena (wife)			Bondorf	Herr.	Feb 1881	N.-Amer	834630
Roller, Emilie		4 Apr 1834	Rosswaelden	Krch.	Jun 1859	Italy	835949
Roller, Gustav		25 Dec 1847	Herrenberg	Herr.	Jan 1877	Holland	834629
Rometsch, Barbara		12 yrs.	Gerlingen	Leon.	Mar 1855	Austral	837953
Rometsch, Christian		11 yrs.	Gerlingen	Leon.	Mar 1855	Austral	837953
Rometsch, Christian & F			Gerlingen	Leon.	Mar 1855	Austral	837953
Rometsch, Christoph		4 Jul 1823	Alpirsbach	Obd.	May 1870	N.-Amer	838630

Rometsch, Georg Gottlieb	11 yrs.	Gerlingen	Leon.	Mar 1855	Austral	837953
Rometsch, Gottlieb	9 Feb 1873	Gerlingen	Leon.	Jan 1889	N.-Amer	837953
Rometsch, Gottlieb	15 Jan 1847	Gerlingen	Leon.	Mar 1882	N.-Amer	837953
Rometsch, Gottlieb	2 yrs.	Gerlingen	Leon.	Mar 1855	Austral	837953
Rometsch, Jacob Friedrich	11 Feb 1835	Alpirsbach	Obd.	Feb 1855	N.-Amer	838630
Rometsch, Jakob Friedrich	3 Aug 1834	Gerlingen	Leon.	Apr 1854	N.-Amer	837953
Rometsch, Johann Georg		Gerlingen	Leon.	Mar 1855	Austral	837953
Rometsch, Johannes	17 yrs.	Gerlingen	Leon.	Mar 1855	Austral	837953
Rometsch, Johannes & F		Gerlingen	Leon.	Mar 1855	Austral	837953
Rometsch, Katharina (wife)		Gerlingen	Leon.	Mar 1855	Austral	837953
Rometsch, Magdalena (wife)		Gerlingen	Leon.	Mar 1855	Austral	837953
Rometsch, Rosina	4 Jun 1841	Alpirsbach	Obd.	Mar 1864	France	838630
Romig, Michael		Sulgen	Obd.	Oct 1816	France	838638
Romig, Reinhold		Perouse	Leon.	bef 1861	Koeln	837962
Roming, Wendelin	4 Jul 1837	Hochmoessingen	Obd.	Jul 1870	Poland	838634
Rommel, Franz Karl Eduard	31 Jan 1866	Weissenstein	Gsl.	Feb 1881	N.-Amer	572048
Rommel, Friedrich	19 yrs.	Hemmingen	Leon.	Jul 1859	N.-Amer	837956
Rommelsbacher, Thomas	4 May 1834	Hirschlanden	Leon.	1857	N.-Amer	837956
Roos, Caroline & C	5 Apr 1832	Sulpach	Krch.	Feb 1857	N.-Amer	835949
Roos, Friederike	20 Aug 1804	Alpirsbach	Obd.	Jun 1858	France	838630
Roos, Johann	11 Mar 1854	Sulpach	Krch.	Feb 1857	N.-Amer	835949
Roos, Johann Georg	27 Jul 1829	Sulpach	Krch.	Feb 1857	N.-Amer	835949
Roos, Magdalena	23 Feb 1821	Sulpach	Krch.	Feb 1857	N.-Amer	835949
Roos, Maria Magdalena	30 Mar 1856	Sulpach	Krch.	Feb 1857	N.-Amer	835949
Roth, Adam & F	7 Mar 1809	Plattenhard	Leon.	Feb 1853	N.-Amer	837954
Roth, Albert	26 Sep 1831	Seedorf	Obd.	Feb 1869	Prussia	838637
Roth, Andreas	29 Nov 1811	Seedorf	Obd.	Apr 1847	N.-Amer	838637
Roth, Anna Catharina	17 yrs.	Heimerdingen	Leon.	Sep 1851	N.-Amer	837954
Roth, Anna Maria (wife)	11 Nov 1807	Plattenhard	Leon.	Feb 1853	N.-Amer	837954
Roth, August		Flacht	Leon.	Jul 1811	Austria	835790
Roth, Balthasar		Seedorf	Obd.	bef 1863	N.-Amer	838637
Roth, Carolina	4 Sep 1837	Plattenhard	Leon.	Feb 1853	N.-Amer	837954
Roth, Christian	16 Sep 1816	Kirchheim	Krch.	Dec 1862	N.-Amer	835941
Roth, Conrad	3 May 1844	Plattenhard	Leon.	Feb 1853	N.-Amer	837954
Roth, Elisabetha Margaretha	11 Jan 1835	Weilheim	Krch.	Mar 1856	N.-Amer	835949
Roth, Euphrosine	14 Sep 1843	Seedorf	Obd.	Apr 1847	N.-Amer	838637
Roth, Franziska (wife)	2 Feb 1821	Seedorf	Obd.	Apr 1847	N.-Amer	838637
Roth, Fridolin	1 Mar 1847	Lauterbach	Obd.	May 1859	N.-Amer	838634
Roth, Fridolin	5 Mar 1849	Waldmoessingen	Obd.	May 1869	N.-Amer	841015
Roth, Johann Georg		Gerlingen	Leon.	May 1847	Hesse	837953
Roth, Johann Georg & F		Betzweiler	Obd.	Jun 1817	Hungary	838631
Roth, Johann Georg & W	25 yrs.	Gerlingen	Leon.	Sep 1853	N.-Amer	837953
Roth, Johann Jacob	17 Jul 1837	Alpirsbach	Obd.	Jun 1866	N.-Amer	838630
Roth, Johann Jacob		Gerlingen	Leon.	Jul 1836	N.-Amer	837953
Roth, Johann Michael & F	29 Apr 1798	Weilheim	Krch.	Mar 1856	N.-Amer	835949
Roth, Johanna (wife)	24 yrs.	Gerlingen	Leon.	Sep 1853	N.-Amer	837953
Roth, Johanne Rosine (wife)	6 May 1795	Weilheim	Krch.	Mar 1856	N.-Amer	835949
Roth, Johannes	4 Jul 1840	Plattenhard	Leon.	Feb 1853	N.-Amer	837954
Roth, Johannes & F		Merklingen	Leon.	Sep 1853	N.-Amer	837959
Roth, Joseph	19 Mar 1850	Alt Oberndorf	Obd.	Jun 1869	N.-Amer	838631

Name		Birth		Emigration			Film
Last	First	Date	Place	O'amt	Appl. Date	Dest.	Number
Roth, Joseph		18 Feb 1844	Lauterbach	Obd.	May 1859	N.-Amer	838634
Roth, Joseph		29 Jan 1836	Seedorf	Obd.	Feb 1854	N.-Amer	838637
Roth, Josepha			Fluorn	Obd.	Apr 1817	N.-Amer	838631
Roth, Peter Paul		5 Jun 1850	Bach-Altenberg	Obd.	Jun 1867	N.-Amer	838631
Roth, Silvester & F		19 May 1815	Seedorf	Obd.	Apr 1847	N.-Amer	838637
Roth, Valentin			Beffendorf	Obd.	1835	Austria	838631
Roth, Waldburga		26 yrs.	Aichhalden	Obd.	Apr 1857	N.-Amer	838629
Roth, Wendelin			Seedorf	Obd.	bef 1863	N.-Amer	838637
Roth, Wilhelm		13 Jan 1850	Plattenhard	Leon.	Feb 1853	N.-Amer	837954
Rothoehler, David			Seedorf	Obd.	bef 1846	Hamburg	838637
Rothoehler, Katharina		22 Apr 1847	Seedorf	Obd.	Oct 1867	N.-Amer	838637
Rottler, Karoline Luise		28 Feb 1846	Seedorf	Obd.	Jul 1867	Austria	838637
Roux, Johann Peter		2 Mar 1834	Perouse	Leon.	1853	N.-Amer	837962
Ruedt, Andreas Heinrich		30 Nov 1807	Heimsheim	Leon.	bef 1842	Saxony	837955
Ruef, Catharina		4 yrs.	Beffendorf	Obd.	Jul 1853	N.-Amer	838631
Ruef, Franz Xaver & F			Beffendorf	Obd.	Jul 1853	N.-Amer	838631
Ruef, Joseph		12 yrs.	Beffendorf	Obd.	Jul 1853	N.-Amer	838631
Ruef, Juliana		10 yrs.	Beffendorf	Obd.	Jul 1853	N.-Amer	838631
Ruef, Konstantin		7 yrs.	Beffendorf	Obd.	Jul 1853	N.-Amer	838631
Rueffer, Anna Barbara (wife)		3 Jul 1829	Bissingen	Krch.	1855	N.-Amer-	835943
Ruehle, Eberhard Martin		28 Apr 1828	Pfullingen	Rtl.	Sep 1865	N.-Amer	841056
Ruehle, Georg Bernhard			Heimsheim	Leon.	Aug 1867	Holland	837955
Ruehle, Georg Bernhardt			Merklingen	Leon.	1843	France	837959
Ruehle, Gottfried			Boehmenkirch	Gsl.	Jul 1853	N.-Amer	572041
Ruehle, Gottlob Jakob Fried.		1 Nov 1864	Stuttgart	Leon.	Sep 1881	England	837959
Ruehle, Johann Georg & F		36 yrs.	Merklingen	Leon.	May 1852	France	837959
Ruehle, Johannes			Merklingen	Leon.	bef 1854	France	837959
Ruehle, Johannes		18 mon.	Merklingen	Leon.	Apr 1852	S.-Amer	837959
Ruehle, Katharina			Boehmenkirch	Gsl.	May 1852	N.-Amer	572041
Ruehle, Maria		6 mon.	Merklingen	Leon.	Apr 1852	S.-Amer	837959
Ruehle, Regina (wife)			Merklingen	Leon.	Apr 1852	S.-Amer	837959
Ruehle, Wilhelm & F			Merklingen	Leon.	Apr 1852	S.-Amer	837959
Ruehlwein, Johannes		3 Jul 1847	Geislingen	Gsl.	Jul 1867	N.-Amer	572046
Ruess, Georg		11 Mar 1828	Oetlingen	Krch.	Mar 1865	N.-Amer	835948
Ruess, Jakob		29 Jan 1829	Oetlingen	Krch.	bef 1861	N.-Amer	835948
Ruess, Johann		20 Oct 1831	Oetlingen	Krch.	bef 1861	N.-Amer	835948
Ruess, Johann David		3 Jun 1826	Oetlingen	Krch.	Mar 1865	N.-Amer	835948
Ruettger, Anna - (wid.) & F			Bochingen	Obd.	Apr 1860	N.-Amer	838632
Ruettger, August		9 yrs.	Bochingen	Obd.	Apr 1860	N.-Amer	838632
Ruettger, Juliana		7 yrs.	Bochingen	Obd.	Apr 1860	N.-Amer	838632
Ruf, Agnes			Winzeln	Obd.	Sep 1863	N.-Amer	841016
Ruf, Anna Maria		15 Nov 1832	Muenchingen	Leon.	Aug 1863	N.-Amer	837961
Ruf, Caroline		3 yrs.	Winzeln	Obd.	Feb 1850	N.-Amer	841016
Ruf, Ernst		19 yrs.	Oberndorf	Obd.	Mar 1856	N.-Amer	838635
Ruf, Hedwig			Winzeln	Obd.	Feb 1850	N.-Amer	841016
Ruf, Ignaz & F			Winzeln	Obd.	Feb 1850	N.-Amer	841016
Ruf, Jakob			Winzeln	Obd.	Jul 1862	Switz.	841016
Ruf, Johann Jakob		20 Nov 1829	Muenchingen	Leon.	Aug 1863	N.-Amer	837961
Ruf, Johanna (wife)			Hemmingen	Leon.	Apr 1833	N.-Amer	837956
Ruf, Johannes		2 Mar 1850	Winzeln	Obd.	Sep 1869	N.-Amer	841016

Ruf, Johannes & F		Hemmingen	Leon.	Apr 1833	N.-Amer 837956
Ruf, Katharina	30 Nov 1836	Winzeln	Obd.	1870	France 841016
Ruf, Kilian & F		Winzeln	Obd.	Mar 1860	N.-Amer 841016
Ruf, Maria	21 Aug 1842	Epfendorf	Obd.	Feb 1870	N.-Amer 838632
Ruf, Maria	24 Nov 1842	Winzeln	Obd.	Mar 1858	N.-Amer 841016
Ruf, Maria	4 mon.	Winzeln	Obd.	Apr 1857	N.-Amer 841016
Ruf, Maria	2 yrs.	Winzeln	Obd.	Feb 1850	N.-Amer 841016
Ruf, Pauline & C	26 Nov 1837	Winzeln	Obd.	Apr 1857	N.-Amer 841016
Ruf, Pius	18 yrs.	Oberndorf	Obd.	Mar 1856	N.-Amer 838635
Ruf, Roman	1 Mar 1836	Epfendorf	Obd.	Feb 1870	N.-Amer 838632
Ruf, Sabina		Winzeln	Obd.	Jun 1866	France 841016
Ruff, Bernhard	25 Dec 1835	Deggingen	Gsl.	Jun 1854	N.-Amer 572042
Ruff, Blandina	8 Nov 1839	Deggingen	Gsl.	Jun 1854	N.-Amer 572042
Ruff, Lukas	13 Oct 1831	Winzeln	Obd.	Sep 1854	N.-Amer 841016
Ruff, Otto Mathias	23 Feb 1844	Deggingen	Gsl.	Sep 1866	N.-Amer 572045
Ruh, Johann Peter		Perouse	Leon.	1853	N.-Amer 837962
Ruisch, Magdalena	14 Jul 1846	Eltingen	Leon.	Sep 1870	N.-Amer 835789
Ruisinger, Johann Jakob	31 Aug 1833	Eybach	Gsl.	Aug 1860	Austria 572044
Ruisinger, Konrad		Eybach	Gsl.	Jul 1867	N.-Amer 572046
Rukenbrod, Georg Friedrich		Malmsheim	Leon.	Mar 1818	N.-Amer 837958
Rummel, Carl Gottlob Johannes	31 Dec 1851	Weissenstein	Gsl.	Jul 1869	N.-Amer 572047
Rummel, Engelbert	6 Nov 1846	Wiesensteig	Gsl.	Oct 1866	N.-Amer 572045
Rund, Franz Anton & F	10 Feb 1816	Weil der Stadt	Leon.	Apr 1848	N.-Amer 837965
Rund, Franz Ferdinand	23 Sep 1844	Weil der Stadt	Leon.	Apr 1848	N.-Amer 837965
Rund, Johann Anton	18 Oct 1847	Weil der Stadt	Leon.	Apr 1848	N.-Amer 837965
Rund, Maria Antonia	16 Jul 1846	Weil der Stadt	Leon.	Apr 1848	N.-Amer 837965
Rund, Theresia (wife)	27 Apr 1818	Weil der Stadt	Leon.	Apr 1848	N.-Amer 837965
Ruof, Jakob	40 yrs.	Alt Oberndorf	Obd.	Feb 1863	N.-Amer 838631
Ruof, Johannes	16 yrs.	Hochmoessingen	Obd.	Sep 1854	N.-Amer 838633
Ruof, Johannes	18 yrs.	Hochmoessingen	Obd.	Apr 1853	N.-Amer 838633
Ruof, Johannes & F		Winzeln	Obd.	May 1817	N.-Amer 841016
Ruof, Joseph & F		Bochingen	Obd.	Mar 1839	N.-Amer 838632
Ruof, Nikolaus & F		Winzeln	Obd.	May 1817	N.-Amer 841016
Ruof, Severin	22 yrs.	Alt Oberndorf	Obd.	Jan 1853	N.-Amer 838631
Ruof, Simon	28 Oct 1807	Hochmoessingen	Obd.	Aug 1853	Austria 838633
Ruof, Stephan & F		Alt Oberndorf	Obd.	Jan 1853	N.-Amer 838631
Ruoff, Christian Friedrich	14 Feb 1868	Kirchheim	Krch.	Sep 1883	N.-Amer 548403
Ruoff, Christian Jacob		Undingen	Rtl.	May 1835	N.-Amer 841051
Ruoff, Gottlob	16 Oct 1844	Reutlingen	Rtl.	Jul 1864	N.-Amer 841056
Ruoff, Matthias	31 Jan 1852	Fluorn	Obd.	Jun 1870	N.-Amer 838632
Ruos, Catharina (wife)	17 Dec 1784	Fluorn	Obd.	Aug 1817	Russia 838629
Ruos, Jakob Balthas	26 Apr 1812	Fluorn	Obd.	Aug 1817	Russia 838629
Ruos, Johann Peter & F	29 Jun 1779	Fluorn	Obd.	Aug 1817	Russia 838629
Ruoss, Benony	14 Feb 1835	Eybach	Gsl.	May 1852	N.-Amer 572041
Ruoss, Johann Peter & F		Fluorn	Obd.	Apr 1817	N.-Amer 838631
Ruoss, Leonhard	11 Aug 1830	Eybach	Gsl.	May 1852	N.-Amer 572041
Ruoss, Margaretha	20 Jan 1826	Eybach	Gsl.	bef 1852	N.-Amer 572041
Ruoss, Matheus	30 Aug 1832	Eybach	Gsl.	May 1852	N.-Amer 572041
Rupp, Andreas	9 yrs.	Wimsheim	Loen.	Jul 1851	N.-Amer 837967
Rupp, Dorothea & C		Wimsheim	Loen.	Jul 1851	N.-Amer 837967

Name		Birth		Emigration			Film
Last	First	Date	Place	O'amt	Appl. Date	Dest.	Number
Rupp, Friedrich Wilhelm		15 May 1852	Reutlingen	Rtl.	Aug 1869	N.-Amer	841056
Rupp, Louise (wife)		39 yrs.	Kirchheim	Krch.	Feb 1860	N.-Amer	835940
Rupp, Ludwig & W		43 yrs.	Kirchheim	Krch.	Feb 1860	N.-Amer	835940
Ruschmaier, Andreas & F			Hohenstadt	Gsl.	Jan 1853	N.-Amer	572041
Russ, Christoph		7 Dec 1866	Oberlenningen	Krch.	Aug 1883	N.-Amer	548403
Russ, Gottlieb Heinrich		29 Nov 1840	Oberlenningen	Krch.	Jun 1866	N.-Amer	835947
Russ, Jacob		26 Jan 1824	Oberlenningen	Krch.	Jan 1865	N.-Amer	835947
Russ, Jakob		1 sep 1849	Gingen	Gsl.	Jul 1869	N.-Amer	572047
Russ, Ludwig David		29 Aug 1844	Oberlenningen	Krch.	Oct 1866	N.-Amer	835947
Ruthardt, Catharina Margar.			Renningen	Leon.	Jul 1854	N.-Amer	837963
Ruthardt, Christiane Frieder.		19 May 1835	Renningen	Leon.	Jul 1854	N.-Amer	837963
Ruthardt, Christiane Kathar.		16 Apr 1835	Renningen	Leon.	Jul 1854	N.-Amer	837963
Ruthardt, Christoph Friedr.& F			Renningen	Leon.	Jul 1854	N.-Amer	837963
Ruthardt, Johann Jakob		22 Aug 1830	Renningen	Leon.	Feb 1849	N.-Amer	837963
Ruthfelder, Gottlieb		3 Nov 1829	Rutesheim	Leon.	1853	N.-Amer	837964
Ruthfelder, Gottlieb Friedr.		22 yrs.	Rutesheim	Leon.	Feb 1852	N.-Amer	837964
Saal, Anna Maria		30 Sep 1783	Friolzheim	Leon.	Mar 1831	N.-Amer	835791
Saal, Christina Dorothea & C			Friolzheim	Leon.	Mar 1830	N.-Amer	835791
Saal, Friederike		18 yrs.	Friolzheim	Leon.	Mar 1830	N.-Amer	835791
Saeckinger, Andreas			Peterzell	Obd.	bef 1855	N.-Amer	838635
Saeckinger, Johannes		21 yrs.	Peterzell	Obd.	Aug 1854	N.-Amer	838635
Saender, Gottlob		20 Jul 1869	Flacht	Leon.	Aug 1884	N.-Amer	835790
Saessle, Friederika			Oberlenningen	Krch.	1853	N.-Amer	835947
Saessle, Gottlieb			Oberlenningen	Krch.	1853	N.-Amer	835947
Saessle, Johann Gottlieb		13 Feb 1832	Oberlenningen	Krch.	1852	N.-Amer	835947
Saib, Johannes		23 May 1864	Owen	Krch.	Mar 1881	N.-Amer	548403
Saile, Magda		12 Jul 1851	Harthausen	Obd.	Aug 1869	N.-Amer	838633
Sailer, Johann Georg & F		13 Sep 1809	Darkenstein	Gsl.	Apr 1853	N.-Amer	572041
Sailer, Joseph		15 May 1820	Westerheim	Gsl.	Feb 1854	N.-Amer	572042
Sailer, Marianna		21 Apr 1845	Darkenstein	Gsl.	Apr 1853	N.-Amer	572041
Sailer, Zezilia (wife)		24 Jun 1807	Darkenstein	Gsl.	Apr 1853	N.-Amer	572041
Salber, Anton			Boehmenkirch	Gsl.	Oct 1866	N.-Amer	572045
Salzer, Johann Georg		25 Feb 1813	Bissingen	Krch.	bef 1864	N.-Amer	835943
Salzmann, Anna		28 May 1814	Unterboehringen	Gsl.	May 1854	N.-Amer	572042
Sanzi, Gustav Adolph		25 Jan 1869	Pfaeffingen	Herr.	Mar 1887	N.-Amer	834630
Sapper, Christian Friedrich			Merklingen	Leon.	bef 1854	N.-Amer	837959
Sattler, Carl Friedrich		22 Jan 1849	Holzmaden	Krch.	Apr 1867	N.-Amer	835945
Sattler, Johann Friedrich		13 Apr 1815	Kirchheim	Krch.	Feb 1855	N.-Amer	835940
Sattler, Johann Friedrich		27 Oct 1843	Dettingen	Krch.	Jun 1862	N.-Amer	835944
Sauer, Andreas		21 Nov 1791	Fluorn	Obd.	Aug 1817	N.-Amer	838629
Sauer, Andreas		4 yrs.	Fluorn	Obd.	Nov 1846	N.-Amer	838632
Sauer, Andreas		22 Oct 1842	Roemlinsdorf	Obd.	May 1846	N.-Amer	838635
Sauer, Anna Barbara		1 Aug 1814	Fluorn	Obd.	Aug 1817	N.-Amer	838629
Sauer, Anna Maria		12 Feb 1812	Fluorn	Obd.	Aug 1817	N.-Amer	838629
Sauer, Anna Maria		9 yrs.	Fluorn	Obd.	Nov 1846	N.-Amer	838632
Sauer, Anna Maria (wife)		36 yrs.	Fluorn	Obd.	Nov 1846	N.-Amer	838632
Sauer, Barbara		21 yrs.	Pfullingen	Rtl.	Apr 1880	N.-Amer	841051
Sauer, Barbara (wife)			Roemlinsdorf	Obd.	May 1846	N.-Amer	838635
Sauer, Barbara (wife)		15 Sep 1778	Fluorn	Obd.	Aug 1817	N.-Amer	838629
Sauer, Christian		29 May 1810	Fluorn	Obd.	Aug 1817	N.-Amer	838629

Sauer, Christian	6 yrs.	Fluorn	Obd.	Nov 1846	N.-Amer	838632
Sauer, Christian & F		Fluorn	Obd.	Nov 1846	N.-Amer	838632
Sauer, Christina	2 Sep 1813	Fluorn	Obd.	Aug 1817	N.-Amer	838629
Sauer, Christine	28 Sep 1785	Fluorn	Obd.	Aug 1817	N.-Amer	838629
Sauer, Christine	21 Feb 1845	Roemlinsdorf	Obd.	May 1846	N.-Amer	838635
Sauer, Friedrich	2 yrs.	Fluorn	Obd.	Nov 1846	N.-Amer	838632
Sauer, Johann Georg	19 Feb 1760	Fluorn	Obd.	Aug 1817	N.-Amer	838629
Sauer, Johann Georg	3 Feb 1809	Fluorn	Obd.	Aug 1817	N.-Amer	838629
Sauer, Johann Ludwig	11 Mar 1832	Honau	Rtl.	Aug 1869	N.-Amer	841057
Sauer, Johannes	11 yrs.	Fluorn	Obd.	Nov 1846	N.-Amer	838632
Sauer, Johannes	6 Jun 1846	Betzingen	Rtl.	Oct 1866	N.-Amer	841057
Sauer, Martin		Betzingen	Rtl.	May 1835	N.-Amer	841051
Sauer, Martin	21 Mar 1844	Betzingen	Rtl.	Jul 1864	N.-Amer	841057
Sauer, Matthias & F	24 Jul 1812	Roemlinsdorf	Obd.	May 1846	N.-Amer	838635
Saur, Gustav	28 May 1862	Kleinengstingen	Rtl.	Apr 1880	N.-Amer	841051
Sauter, Albert	14 Jan 1857	Gaertringen	Herr.	Jul 1872	N.-Amer	834630
Sauter, Blasius & F		Aichhalden	Obd.	Oct 1854	N.-Amer	838629
Sauter, Carl Konrad Alfred	4 Aug 1867	Ditzingen	Leon.	bef 1886	N.-Amer	835788
Sauter, Jacob Friedrich	19 Aug 1821	Rutesheim	Leon.	Feb 1852	N.-Amer	837964
Sauter, Johanna (wife)		Aichhalden	Obd.	Oct 1854	N.-Amer	838629
Sauter, Karoline	15 yrs.	Rutesheim	Leon.	Apr 1857	N.-Amer	837964
Sauter, Katharina Pauline	18 yrs.	Rutesheim	Leon.	May 1866	N.-Amer	837964
Sauter, Maria Luisa		Aichhalden	Obd.	Oct 1854	N.-Amer	838629
Sautter, Amalie	22 Aug 1831	Ditzingen	Leon.	Apr 1851	N.-Amer	835788
Sautter, Anna Maria	26 Jan 1829	Ditzingen	Leon.	Apr 1854	N.-Amer	835788
Sautter, Christof Friedrich	1 Feb 1797	Schoeckingen	Leon.	bef 1839	France	837964
Sautter, Edelbert Aug. Otto	13 Nov 1841	Eningen	Rtl.	bef 1862	N.-Amer	841057
Sautter, Gottlob	18 Aug 1848	Malmsheim	Leon.	Jun 1870	N.-Amer	837958
Sautter, Jakob Friedrich		Ditzingen	Leon.	Dec 1819	Austria	835788
Sautter, Johann Georg	8 Aug 1843	Haslach	Herr.	Mar 1869	N.-Amer	834631
Sautter, Johannes	8 Jan 1876	Herrenberg	Herr.	Jun 1896	N.-Amer	834629
Sautter, Maria	15 Aug 1843	Kirchheim	Krch.	Oct 1868	N.-Amer	835941
Sautter, Wilhelm	2 Apr 1845	Malmsheim	Leon.	Jun 1870	N.-Amer	837958
ScHwarz, Sophie Friederike	1 May 1834	Wimsheim	Loen.	Mar 1856	N.-Amer	837967
Schaaf, Christian	11 Aug 1832	Muehlhausen	Gsl.	Apr 1864	Saxony	572045
Schaaf, Louise	9 yrs.	Leonberg	Leon.	Apr 1851	N.-Amer	835786
Schaaf, Pauline	8 yrs.	Leonberg	Leon.	Apr 1851	N.-Amer	835786
Schaal, Gottlieb	2 Apr 1848	Reutlingen	Rtl.	Apr 1867	N.-Amer	841057
Schabel, Ignaz		Donzdorf	Gsl.	bef 1851	N.-Amer	577788
Schaber, Johann Georg		Heimerdingen	Leon.	May 1834	Russia	837954
Schaber, Johanne Chr. Fried.	11 Jun 1827	Renningen	Leon.	Mar 1852	N.-Amer	837963
Schaber, Rosine Katharine	11 Oct 1867	Renningen	Leon.	Sep 1888	N.-Amer	837963
Schach, Barbara & F		Leonberg	Leon.	Sep 1856	N.-Amer	835786
Schach, Friedrich		Leonberg	Leon.	bef 1856	N.-Amer	835786
Schach, Gottlieb Friedrich	11 Mar 1836	Leonberg	Leon.	May 1856	N.-Amer	835786
Schach, Gottlieb Heinrich	6 Jun 1844	Leonberg	Leon.	Sep 1856	N.-Amer	835786
Schach, Jakob Heinrich	7 Nov 1846	Leonberg	Leon.	Sep 1856	N.-Amer	835786
Schach, Sophie Friederike	8 May 1850	Leonberg	Leon.	Sep 1856	N.-Amer	835786
Schaedel, Jacob	25 Nov 1841	Zell	Krch.	Oct 1858	N.-Amer	835774
Schaedel, Maria Barbara	14 Nov 1839	Zell	Krch.	Jul 1856	N.-Amer	835774

Name		Birth		Emigration			Film
Last	First	Date	Place	O'amt	Appl. Date	Dest.	Number
Schaedler, Pauline			Unterlenningen	Krch.	bef 1861	N.-Amer	835949
Schaedler, Regine		1 Nov 1820	Unterlenningen	Krch.	bef 1862	N.-Amer	835949
Schaedler, Wilhelm		8 Dec 1855	Unterlenningen	Krch.	Sep 1871	N.-Amer	835949
Schaedler, Wilhelmine		18 Oct 1824	Unterlenningen	Krch.	bef 1864	N.-Amer	835940
Schaefer, Adolf		24 yrs.	Reutlingen	Rtl.	Jun 1880	N.-Amer	841051
Schaefer, Agnes Cathar. (wife)			Weil i. Schoenbuch	Leon.	bef 1859	N.-Amer	837953
Schaefer, Barbara		23 Aug 1847	Lindorf	Krch.	Aug 1868	N.-Amer	835946
Schaefer, Caroline Friederike		22 Jan 1832	Hoefingen	Leon.	Mar 1860	N.-Amer	837957
Schaefer, Catharina Barbara		5 Oct 1839	Nabern	Krch.	1867	N.-Amer	835946
Schaefer, Charlotte (wife)		29 yrs.	Schoeckingen	Leon.	Nov 1852	N.-Amer	837964
Schaefer, Christian		18 yrs.	Betzweiler	Obd.	Apr 1861	N.-Amer	838631
Schaefer, Christian & F			Renningen	Leon.	Apr 1852	N.-Amer	837963
Schaefer, Christian Immanuel		28 Jul 1843	Renningen	Leon.	Apr 1852	N.-Amer	837963
Schaefer, Christiane Carolie		18 Jul 1851	Schoeckingen	Leon.	Apr 1853	N.-Amer	837964
Schaefer, Christiane Luise			Schoeckingen	Leon.	Jul 1852	N.-Amer	837964
Schaefer, Christiane (wid.) & F			Hoefingen	Leon.	Mar 1860	N.-Amer	837957
Schaefer, Christina Gottlieb.		26 Oct 1849	Renningen	Leon.	Apr 1852	N.-Amer	837963
Schaefer, Christof Heinrich			Schoeckingen	Leon.	bef 1849	N.-Amer	837964
Schaefer, Conrad		12 Apr 1848	Nabern	Krch.	dec 1871	N.-Amer	835946
Schaefer, David		11 Nov 1818	Lindorf	Krch.	1855	N.-Amer	835946
Schaefer, Emilie		28 Feb 1845	Schoeckingen	Leon.	Apr 1853	N.-Amer	837964
Schaefer, Ernst Gottlieb		26 Feb 1849	Dettingen	Krch.	Sep 1866	N.-Amer	835944
Schaefer, Friederike		15 yrs.	Schoeckingen	Leon.	Mar 1852	N.-Amer	837964
Schaefer, Friederike		28 yrs.	Hemmingen	Leon.	Feb 1852	N.-Amer	837956
Schaefer, Friedrich & F			Gebersheim	Leon.	May 1805	Russia	837953
Schaefer, Friedrich & F			Reutlingen	Rtl.	Apr 1831	N.-Amer	841051
Schaefer, Georg Michael		29 May 1841	Gaertringen	Herr.	Jul 1866	N.-Amer	834630
Schaefer, Gottlieb			Gebersheim	Leon.	Nov 1854	N.-Amer	837953
Schaefer, Gottlieb			Eltingen	Leon.	Mar 1821	N.-Amer	835789
Schaefer, Gottlieb Friedrich		15 May 1847	Hoefingen	Leon.	Mar 1860	N.-Amer	837957
Schaefer, Gottliebin (wife)			Renningen	Leon.	Apr 1852	N.-Amer	837963
Schaefer, Gustav		21 yrs.	Reutlingen	Rtl.	1879	N.-Amer	841051
Schaefer, Jacob			Eltingen	Leon.	Feb 1858	N.-Amer	835789
Schaefer, Jacob			Ohmenhausen	Rtl.	Apr 1831	France	841051
Schaefer, Jakob Friedrich & F		38 yrs.	Schoeckingen	Leon.	Nov 1852	N.-Amer	837964
Schaefer, Johann Andreas		9 Dec 1846	Renningen	Leon.	Apr 1852	N.-Amer	837963
Schaefer, Johann Georg		Sep 1834	Alpirsbach	Obd.	Dec 1854	N.-Amer	838630
Schaefer, Johann Georg			Hoefingen	Leon.	May 1843	N.-Amer	837957
Schaefer, Johann Georg & F			Hoefingen	Leon.	May 1843	N.-Amer	837957
Schaefer, Johann Georg & W			Gebersheim	Leon.	bef 1859	N.-Amer	837953
Schaefer, Johann Gottl.			Jesingen	Krch.	Oct 1861	France	835946
Schaefer, Johann Gottlob		27 Nov 1837	Schoeckingen	Leon.	bef 1864	Austria	837964
Schaefer, Johann Jakob		1 yrs.	Schoeckingen	Leon.	Mar 1852	N.-Amer	837964
Schaefer, Johannes'		11 May 1840	Schoeckingen	Leon.	Mar 1864	N.-Amer	837964
Schaefer, Libor & F		-	Weil der Stadt	Leon.	Feb 1854	N.-Amer	837966
Schaefer, Lorenz			Ohmenhausen	Rtl.	Jun 1865	France	841057
Schaefer, Margaretha		26 yrs.	Hoefingen	Leon.	Jul 1853	N.-Amer	837957
Schaefer, Maria Catharina		26 Aug 1848	Gaertringen	Herr.	Feb 1870	N.-Amer	834630
Schaefer, Marie Sophie		23 Jun 1843	Schoeckingen	Leon.	Apr 1853	N.-Amer	837964
Schaefer, Marie Sophie (wife)		21 Sep 1816	Schoeckingen	Leon.	Apr 1853	N.-Amer	837964

Schaefer, Valentin	14 Feb 1867	Boehmenkirch	Gsl.	Feb 1884	N.-Amer	572049
Schaefer, Wilhelm & F	29 Apr 1809	Schoeckingen	Leon.	Apr 1853	N.-Amer	837964
Schaefer, Wilhelmine Margar.		Hoefingen	Leon.	May 1843	N.-Amer	837957
Schaeff, Johann Jakob	5 Jan 1847	Hausen a.d. Fils	Gsl.	Feb 1870	Prussia	572047
Schaeffer, Bartholomaeus	16 May 1825	Bondorf	Herr.	bef 1871	N.-Amer	834630
Schaeffer, Christiane Wilhelm.	18 Feb 1830	Alpirsbach	Obd.	Aug 1854	N.-Amer	838630
Schaeffer, Johannes & F		Eltingen	Leon.	Apr 1830	N.-Amer	835789
Schaeffer, Lorentz & F		Eltingen	Leon.	Apr 1830	N.-Amer	835789
Schaenzlin, Wilhelm Friedr.	8 Nov 1849	Pfullingen	Rtl.	Aug 1869	N.-Amer	841057
Schaepperle, Albert	1 Dec 1845	Hochdorf	Krch.	May 1864	N.-Amer	835945
Schaerer, Johann Georg & F		Hoefingen	Leon.	bef 1831	Russia	837957
Schaerer, Marie Josephine	23 Aug 1825	Schoeckingen	Leon.	bef 1852	Prag	837964
Schaettle, Albertine	18 yrs.	Oberndorf	Obd.	Sep 1850	N.-Amer	838635
Schaettle, Albertine (wife)		Oberndorf	Obd.	May 1849	N.-Amer	838635
Schaettle, Blandine	23 yrs.	Oberndorf	Obd.	Oct 1862	Prussia	838635
Schaettle, Franz	3 Oct 1843	Oberndorf	Obd.	May 1849	N.-Amer	838635
Schaettle, Franziska	9 Mar 1841	Oberndorf	Obd.	May 1849	N.-Amer	838635
Schaettle, Friedrich Paul	19 yrs.	Oberndorf	Obd.	Apr 1852	N.-Amer	838635
Schaettle, Gertrud & F		Oberndorf	Obd.	May 1849	N.-Amer	838635
Schaettle, Johann & F		Oberndorf	Obd.	May 1849	N.-Amer	838635
Schaettle, Julius	9 Feb 1834	Oberndorf	Obd.	Dec 1860	Austria	838635
Schaettle, Maximillian	23 Nov 1839	Oberndorf	Obd.	May 1849	N.-Amer	838635
Schaettle, Otto	19 yrs.	Oberndorf	Obd.	May 1854	N.-Amer	838635
Schaettle, Paul	9 yrs.	Oberndorf	Obd.	Jul 1860	N.-Amer	838635
Schaettle, Pauline	21 yrs.	Oberndorf	Obd.	Sep 1850	N.-Amer	838635
Schaettle, Simon & F		Oberndorf	Obd.	Sep 1850	N.-Amer	838635
Schaettle, Theresia	May 1825	Oberndorf	Obd.	Apr 1863	Prussia	838635
Schaettle, Vincentia & F		Oberndorf	Obd.	Jul 1860	N.-Amer	838635
Schaeuble, Johann Gottlieb	14 Aug 1844	Reutlingen	Rtl.	Jun 1864	N.-Amer	841057
Schaeufele, Carl August	4 yrs.	Hirschlanden	Leon.	Jan 1852	N.-Amer	837956
Schaeufele, Carl August	13 Aug 1860	Dettingen	Krch.	Apr 1871	N.-Amer	835944
Schaeufele, Christina Cathar.	25 Dec 1867	Dettingen	Krch.	Apr 1871	N.-Amer	835944
Schaeufele, David	20 Nov 1860	Nabern	Krch.	Jul 1876	N.-Amer	835946
Schaeufele, Friedrich	49 yrs.	Hoefingen	Leon.	Jun 1852	N.-Amer	837957
Schaeufele, Friedrich	26 Mar 1834	Hirschlanden	Leon.	1853	N.-Amer	837956
Schaeufele, Friedrich	17 yrs.	Hirschlanden	Leon.	Jan 1852	N.-Amer	837956
Schaeufele, Gottfried	10 Jul 1861	Dettingen	Krch.	Apr 1871	N.-Amer	835944
Schaeufele, Gottlob	20 Feb 1867	Hoefingen	Leon.	Mar 1888	N.-Amer	837957
Schaeufele, Johanna (wife)	41 yrs.	Hirschlanden	Leon.	Jan 1852	N.-Amer	837956
Schaeufele, Johanna Luise	16 Sep 1837	Ohmden	Krch.	May 1856	N.-Amer	835948
Schaeufele, Johannes & F		Gebersheim	Leon.	Aug 1822	Russia	837953
Schaeufele, Karl Gustav	18 Aug 1877	Zell	Krch.	Jun 1894	N.-Amer	835774
Schaeufele, Mathaeus		Hirschlanden	Leon.	Apr 1828	Hungary	837956
Schaeufele, Mathaeus & F	47 yrs.	Hirschlanden	Leon.	Jan 1852	N.-Amer	837956
Schaeufele, Matthaeus	4 Oct 1843	Ochsenwang	Krch.	Mar 1864	N.-Amer	835947
Schaeufele, Regina Margaretha	8 Dec 1870	Dettingen	Krch.	Apr 1871	N.-Amer	835944
Schaeufele, Thomas	13 yrs.	Hirschlanden	Leon.	Jan 1852	N.-Amer	837956
Schaeuffele, Wilhelm Gottlieb	4 Dec 1849	Gebersheim	Leon.	Oct 1869	N.-Amer	837953
Schaible, Anna	14 Sep 1800	Fluorn	Obd.	Aug 1817	N.-Amer	838629
Schaible, Anna Maria (wife)	24 Aug 1774	Fluorn	Obd.	Aug 1817	N.-Amer	838629

Name		Birth		Emigration			Film
Last	First	Date	Place	O'amt	Appl. Date	Dest.	Number
Schaible, August Adolf		13 Mar 1858	Gerlingen	Leon.	Oct 1881	N.-Amer	837953
Schaible, Barbaras		25 Nov 1804	Fluorn	Obd.	Aug 1817	N.-Amer	838629
Schaible, Conrad & F		7 Feb 1801	Weilheim	Krch.	Apr 1867	N.-Amer	835950
Schaible, Dorothea		20 Nov 1802	Fluorn	Obd.	Aug 1817	N.-Amer	838629
Schaible, Friedrich		10 Sep 1838	Gerlingen	Leon.	May 1873	N.-Amer	837953
Schaible, Gottfried		27 Apr 1851	Gerlingen	Leon.	Nov 1865	N.-Amer	837953
Schaible, Gottlieb		27 Apr 1849	Gerlingen	Leon.	Jun 1882	N.-Amer	837953
Schaible, Heinrike Regine		31 Aug 1842	Weilheim	Krch.	Apr 1867	N.-Amer	835950
Schaible, Johann Georg		25 Oct 1845	Gerlingen	Leon.	Nov 1865	N.-Amer	837953
Schaible, Johann Michael		18 Jan 1845	Weilheim	Krch.	Jan 1860	N.-Amer	835949
Schaible, Johannes		13 Nov 1809	Fluorn	Obd.	Aug 1817	N.-Amer	838629
Schaible, Johannes & F		24 Jun 1772	Fluorn	Obd.	Aug 1817	N.-Amer	838629
Schaible, Joseph		infant	Gerlingen	Leon.	Apr 1860	N.-Amer	837953
Schaible, Katharine & C		27 yrs.	Gerlingen	Leon.	Apr 1860	N.-Amer	837953
Schaible, Lukas		16 yrs.	Geislingen	Gsl.	Apr 1866	N.-Amer	572045
Schaible, Maria		5 yrs.	Gerlingen	Leon.	Apr 1860	N.-Amer	837953
Schaible, Rosina		13 Oct 1797	Fluorn	Obd.	Aug 1817	N.-Amer	838629
Schaible, Ursula Cathar. (wife)		1 Dec 1800	Weilheim	Krch.	Apr 1867	N.-Amer	835950
Schaible, Wilhelm		18 yrs.	Geislingen	Gsl.	Apr 1866	N.-Amer	572045
Schaich, Carl Lorenz		18 Jan 1847	Weilheim	Krch.	Mar 1862	N.-Amer	835950
Schaich, Elisabetha Maria		2 Sep 1852	Weilheim	Krch.	Mar 1862	N.-Amer	835950
Schaich, Heinrich Hugo		16 Jan 1850	Weilheim	Krch.	Mar 1862	N.-Amer	835950
Schaich, Lorenz & F		24 Jan 1823	Weilheim	Krch.	Mar 1862	N.-Amer	835950
Schaich, Regine Rosine Cath.		8 Nov 1848	Weilheim	Krch.	Mar 1862	N.-Amer	835950
Schaich, Rosine Cathar. (wife)		6 Oct 1824	Weilheim	Krch.	Mar 1862	N.-Amer	835950
Schall, Caroline Wilhelmine		23 Mar 1864	Zell	Krch.	Oct 1865	N.-Amer	835774
Schall, Christiana & C		9 Jun 1840	Zell	Krch.	Oct 1865	N.-Amer	835774
Schall, Jacob		2 Jan 1838	Tuerkheim	Gsl.	bef 1863	N.-Amer	572044
Schall, Jakob		15 Feb 1848	Altenstadt-Gsl.	Gsl.	Jun 1866	N.-Amer	572045
Schaller, Johann Baptist			Aichhalden	Obd.	bef 1852	Austria	838629
Schaller, Susanna			Schramberg	Obd.	Mar 1848	N.-Amer	838637
Schanz, Joseph Adam		12 Jul 1861	Gaertringen	Herr.	Aug 1863	N.-Amer	834630
Schanz, Margaretha Magdal. & C		6 Nov 1827	Gaertringen	Herr.	Aug 1863	N.-Amer	834630
Schanz, Marx Gottlob		19 Oct 1845	Gomaringen	Rtl.	Aug 1865	N.-Amer	841057
Scharpf, Anna Maria		14 Mar 1839	Rosswaelden	Krch.	Apr 1862	N.-Amer	835949
Scharpf, Euphrosine		28 Feb 1835	Rosswaelden	Krch.	Apr 1862	N.-Amer	835949
Scharpf, Johannes		15 Sep 1825	Rosswaelden	Krch.	Mar 1864	N.-Amer	835949
Scharpf, Ludwig		15 Oct 1823	Rosswaelden	Krch.	May 1855	N.-Amer	835949
Scharpf, Margaretha		5 Sep 1843	Rosswaelden	Krch.	Apr 1862	N.-Amer	835949
Schattle, Wilhelm		26 Jul 1829	Oberndorf	Obd.	Dec 1860	Austria	838635
Schatz, Barbara		12 Jan 1841	Betzweiler	Obd.	Apr 1856	N.-Amer	838631
Schatz, Christina		26 Sep 1829	Betzweiler	Obd.	Sep 1855	N.-Amer	838631
Schatz, Johann Georg		6 Jul 1833	Betzweiler	Obd.	Apr 1856	N.-Amer	838631
Schatz, Matthias			Betzweiler	Obd.	Aug 1854	N.-Amer	838631
Schau, Georg		19 yrs.	Tuerkheim	Gsl.	bef 1862	N.-Amer	572044
Schau, Hermann		22 Jun 1835	Tuerkheim	Gsl.	bef 1862	N.-Amer	572044
Schauecker, Friedrich		2 Dec 1827	Ditzingen	Leon.	May 1847	N.-Amer	835788
Schaufler, Anna Maria & C		22 May 1823	Hepsisau	Krch.	May 1857	N.-Amer	835945
Schaufler, Barbara		8 May 1830	Hepsisau	Krch.	bef 1868	N.-Amer	835940
Schaufler, Barbara		18 Feb 1848	Hepsisau	Krch.	May 1857	N.-Amer	835945

Schaufler, Caspar		Hepsisau	Krch.	Dec 1829	N.-Amer	835945
Schaufler, Christiana	18 Jan 1823	Hepsisau	Krch.	bef 1868	N.-Amer	835940
Schaufler, Conrad		Lindorf	Krch.	bef 1868	N.-Amer	835940
Schaufler, Elisabetha	5 Dec 1844	Hepsisau	Krch.	May 1857	N.-Amer	835945
Schaufler, Georg	6 May 1828	Hepsisau	Krch.	bef 1868	N.-Amer	835940
Schaufler, Jac.Theo.Bernh.Con.	31 May 1849	Hepsisau	Krch.	Dec 1867	N.-Amer	835945
Schaufler, Johann Michael	19 Feb 1957	Hepsisau	Krch.	May 1857	N.-Amer	835945
Schaufler, Johannes	11 Nov 1831	Hepsisau	Krch.	bef 1868	N.-Amer	835940
Schaufler, Johannes	14 Apr 1826	Bissingen	Krch.	bef 1866	N.-Amer	835943
Schaufler, Karl Theodor	2 Apr 1854	Hepsisau	Krch.	Jan 1871	N.-Amer	835945
Schaufler, Maria	22 May 1824	Hepsisau	Krch.	bef 1868	N.-Amer	835940
Schaufler, Wilhelm	25 Aug 1871	Weilheim	Krch.	Mar 1888	N.-Amer	835774
Schaum, Wilhelm	27 Sep 1849	Notzingen	Krch.	May 1867	N.-Amer	835947
Schaupp, Adam	18 yrs.	Reutlingen	Rtl.	Jul 1879	N.-Amer	841051
Schaupp, Gottlob	12 Sep 1849	Reutlingen	Rtl.	Jun 1868	N.-Amer	841057
Schauwecker, Carl Christian	12 Dec 1848	Reutlingen	Rtl.	Nov 1867	N.-Amer	841057
Schauwecker, Christoph Pet.& F	57 yrs.	Reutlingen	Rtl.	Apr 1879	N.-Amer	841051
Schauwecker, Ernst, Friedrich	9 yrs.	Reutlingen	Rtl.	Apr 1879	N.-Amer	841051
Schauwecker, Gottlieb	28 Jan 1819	Reutlingen	Rtl.	bef 1863	N.-Amer	841057
Schauwecker, Johann Jakob		Reutlingen	Rtl.	bef 1866	N.-Amer	841057
Schauwecker, Johannes	18 Oct 1845	Reutlingen	Rtl.	Nov 1865	N.-Amer	841057
Schauwecker, Karl Friedrich	5 Mat 1840	Reutlingen	Rtl.	Oct 1860	N.-Amer	841057
Schauwecker, Michael		Reutlingen	Rtl.	bef 1866	N.-Amer	841057
Schauwecker, Robert August	12 Aug 1850	Reutlingen	Rtl.	Sep 1869	N.-Amer	841057
Schauweker, Christina	24 Feb 1850	Deggingen	Gsl.	Oct 1852	N.-Amer	572041
Schauweker, Gottlob		Deggingen	Gsl.	Oct 1852	N.-Amer	572041
Schauweker, Johann Jakob Fr.	14 Jul 1841	Deggingen	Gsl.	Oct 1852	N.-Amer	572041
Schauweker, Johannes	1 Feb 1845	Deggingen	Gsl.	Oct 1852	N.-Amer	572041
Schauweker, Johannes		Reutlingen	Rtl.	Apr 1828	N.-Amer	841051
Schauweker, Margaretha		Deggingen	Gsl.	Oct 1852	N.-Amer	572041
Schauweker, Rosina	6 Apr 1843	Deggingen	Gsl.	Oct 1852	N.-Amer	572041
Schaz, Christia & F		Eltingen	Leon.	Mar 1831	N.-Amer	835789
Schazmann, Anton	1834	Schramberg	Obd.	Jan 1854	N.-Amer	838636
Scheck, Anna Maria (wife)	7 Jun 1839	Rutesheim	Leon.	Jun 1882	N.-Amer	837964
Scheck, Catharina Paulina	3 yrs.	Rutesheim	Leon.	Feb 1852	N.-Amer	837964
Scheck, Christian Friedrich	11 yrs.	Rutesheim	Leon.	Feb 1852	N.-Amer	837964
Scheck, Friedrich & F		Wimsheim	Loen.	Jul 1851	N.-Amer	837967
Scheck, Gottlieb & W	25 Aug 1838	Rutesheim	Leon.	Jun 1882	N.-Amer	837964
Scheck, Gottlob	21 May 1851	Ditzingen	Leon.	Jan 1881	N.-Amer	835788
Scheck, Johann Gottlieb	2 yrs.	Rutesheim	Leon.	Feb 1852	N.-Amer	837964
Scheck, Johann Jacob	3 yrs.	Rutesheim	Leon.	Feb 1852	N.-Amer	837964
Scheck, Johann Jacob	12 yrs.	Rutesheim	Leon.	Feb 1852	N.-Amer	837964
Scheck, Johann Jacob & F	33 yrs.	Rutesheim	Leon.	Feb 1852	N.-Amer	837964
Scheck, Maria Barbara	17 yrs.	Rutesheim	Leon.	Feb 1852	N.-Amer	837964
Scheck, Maria Cathar. (wife)	40 yrs.	Rutesheim	Leon.	Feb 1852	N.-Amer	837964
Scheck, Paul & F		Rutesheim	Leon.	Feb 1852	N.-Amer	837964
Scheck, Regina	13 yrs.	Rutesheim	Leon.	Feb 1852	N.-Amer	837964
Scheck, Rosina Barbara	27 Apr 1821	Eltingen	Leon.	Jan 1854	N.-Amer	835789
Schedel, Karl	22 Jan 1846	Oetlingen	Krch.	Nov 1866	N.-Amer	835948
Scheel, Johann		Gingen	Gsl.	Mar 1853	N.-Amer	572041

Name		Birth		Emigration			Film
Last	First	Date	Place	O'amt	Appl. Date	Dest.	Number
Scheerer, Barbara & C		1 Dec 1823	Seedorf	Obd.	Apr 1847	N.-Amer	838637
Scheerer, Desiderius		10 Feb 1844	Seedorf	Obd.	Apr 1847	N.-Amer	838637
Scheerer, Maria			Seedorf	Obd.	Apr 1847	N.-Amer	838637
Scheerer, Martin		27 Jan 1846	Betzingen	Rtl.	Mar 1864	N.-Amer	841057
Schefer, Georg Michael			Pfullingen	Rtl.	Apr 1830	N.-Amer	841051
Scheffel, Marie Christine		27 Jan 1838	Leonberg	Leon.	Nov 1871	Austria	835787
Scheible, Georg			Gebersheim	Leon.	Sep 1851	N.-Amer	837953
Scheifele, Georg		16 yrs.	Gingen	Gsl.	Jan 1853	N.-Amer	572041
Scheifele, Jakob			Gingen	Gsl.	1849	N.-Amer	572043
Scheifele, Johannes			Gingen	Gsl.	Mar 1853	N.-Amer	572041
Scheifele, Mathaeus		3 May 1842	Ueberkingen	Gsl.	bef 1877	Switz.	572048
Scheifele, Stephan		19 Feb 1836	Ueberkingen	Gsl.	Feb 1853	N.-Amer	572041
Scheifle, Lukas		6 Jul 1838	Gingen	Gsl.	Sep 1853	N.-Amer	572041
Schek, Anna Maria		16 Oct 1847	Rutesheim	Leon.	Mar 1851	N.-Amer	837964
Schek, Catharina		15 yrs.	Eltingen	Leon.	May 1818	Russia	835789
Schek, Christian		26 Aug 1844	Rutesheim	Leon.	Mar 1851	N.-Amer	837964
Schek, Friederich			Eltingen	Leon.	Feb 1856	N.-Amer	835789
Schek, Friedrich		21 Aug 1838	Rutesheim	Leon.	Mar 1851	N.-Amer	837964
Schek, Georg & F			Rutesheim	Leon.	Mar 1851	N.-Amer	837964
Schek, Heinrike		13 Oct 1840	Rutesheim	Leon.	Mar 1851	N.-Amer	837964
Schek, Jakob		5 Nov 1842	Rutesheim	Leon.	Mar 1851	N.-Amer	837964
Schek, Johann Georg		18 yrs.	Eltingen	Leon.	May 1818	Russia	835789
Schek, Johann Jacob		14 Jul 1837	Eltingen	Leon.	Jun 1853	N.-Amer	835789
Schek, Johannes		6 yrs.	Eltingen	Leon.	May 1818	Russia	835789
Schek, Johannes & F		55 yrs.	Eltingen	Leon.	May 1818	Russia	835789
Schek, Magdalena (wife)		15 Oct 1813	Rutesheim	Leon.	Mar 1851	N.-Amer	837964
Schek, Maria Barbara (wife)		50 yrs.	Eltingen	Leon.	May 1818	Russia	835789
Schek, Martin		28 yrs.	Rutesheim	Leon.	Aug 1857	N.-Amer	837964
Schele, Jakob			Pfullingen	Rtl.	Dec 1831	N.-Amer	841051
Scheller, Gertrude (wife)		25 Jun 1805	Moensheim	Leon.	Feb 1844	N.-Amer	837960
Scheller, Wilhelm & F			Moensheim	Leon.	Feb 1844	N.-Amer	837960
Schellhammer, Bonifazius		6 Jun 1844	Beffendorf	Obd.	Nov 1861	N.-Amer	838631
Schelling, Elisabeth			Oberndorf	Obd.	May 1849	N.-Amer	838635
Schelling, Johann & F			Oberndorf	Obd.	May 1849	N.-Amer	838635
Schelling, Juliane (wife)			Oberndorf	Obd.	May 1849	N.-Amer	838635
Schelling, Marianne			Oberndorf	Obd.	May 1849	N.-Amer	838635
Schelling, Mathilde			Oberndorf	Obd.	May 1849	N.-Amer	838635
Schelling, Paulina Maria		16 May 1857	Kirchheim	Krch.	Aug 1875	N.-Amer	835942
Schempp, Carl Ludwig		24 Mar 1851	Kirchheim	Krch.	Apr 1867	N.-Amer	835941
Schempp, Catharina & F			Weilheim	Krch.	1850	N.-Amer	835949
Schempp, Christian		30 Mar 1845	Willmandingen	Rtl.	Feb 1860	N.-Amer	841057
Schempp, Christopf		25 Jun 1829	Ohmden	Krch.	bef 1865	N.-Amer	835948
Schempp, Cunrad			Bissingen	Krch.	Apr 1858	N.-Amer	835943
Schempp, Cyriakus (wid.) & F		20 Oct 1799	Bissingen	Krch.	Apr 1858	N.-Amer	835943
Schempp, Fanny		20 Apr 1848	Weilheim	Krch.	1850	N.-Amer	835949
Schempp, Johann Cunrad		17 Sep 1836	Bissingen	Krch.	Dec 1856	N.-Amer	835943
Schempp, Johann Georg		29 Aug 1841	Willmandingen	Rtl.	May 1860	N.-Amer	841057
Schempp, Johanna Friederika			Bissingen	Krch.	Apr 1858	N.-Amer	835943
Schempp, Johannes		2 Apr 1871	Bissingen	Krch.	Mar 1888	N.-Amer	835943
Schempp, Michael		22 mar 1835	Holzmaden	Krch.	Mar 1870	N.-Amer	835945

Schempp, Wilhelm Friedrich	7 Aug 1848	Willmandingen	Rtl.	Feb 1867	N.-Amer	841057
Schenk, Adolph	13 yrs.	Winzeln	Obd.	Dec 1852	N.-Amer	841016
Schenk, Agathe & F		Winzeln	Obd.	Mar 1852	N.-Amer	841016
Schenk, Apolonia		Winzeln	Obd.	Dec 1852	N.-Amer	841016
Schenk, Christiane		Perouse	Leon.	bef 1847	France	837962
Schenk, Franziska	9 yrs.	Winzeln	Obd.	Dec 1852	N.-Amer	841016
Schenk, Georg	5 Oct 1852	Kirchheim	Krch.	Jul 1870	N.-Amer	835941
Schenk, Johann David	1 Sep 1854	Perouse	Leon.	bef 1879	N.-Amer	837962
Schenk, Maria & C	20 Mar 1817	Winzeln	Obd.	Sep 1865	N.-Amer	841016
Schenk, Mathaeus & F		Winzeln	Obd.	Dec 1852	N.-Amer	841016
Schenk, Wilhelm	9 May 1860	Kleinengstingen	Rtl.	Jul 1879	N.-Amer	841051
Schenkel, Andreas & W		Moensheim	Leon.	Apr 1854	N.-Amer	837960
Schenkel, Georg Friedrich	1830	Friolzheim	Leon.	Dec 1850	N.-Amer	835791
Schenkel, Jakob	5 Nov 1814	Moensheim	Leon.	bef 1844	France	837960
Schenkel, Johann Joseph	27 Oct 1849	Friolzheim	Leon.	Jul 1874	N.-Amer	835791
Schenkel, Marie Salome	4 Oct 1837	Moensheim	Leon.	Dec 1853	N.-Amer	837960
Schenkel, Rosine Catharine	8 Aug 1835	Moensheim	Leon.	Dec 1853	N.-Amer	837960
Scherer, Andreas	26 Oct 1840	Alpiersbach	Obd.	Sep 1858	N.-Amer	838638
Scherer, Caroline Louise	25 May 1876	Rutesheim	Leon.	Apr 1879	N.-Amer	837964
Scherer, Christian	21 yrs.	Dornhan	Obd.	Aug 1854	N.-Amer	838638
Scherer, Edeltrud		Winzeln	Obd.	bef 1863	N.-Amer	841016
Scherer, Egidius	22 Jan 1830	Seedorf	Obd.	Apr 1847	N.-Amer	838637
Scherer, Georg		Winzeln	Obd.	May 1861	N.-Amer	841016
Scherer, Isidor	31 Mar 1812	Seedorf	Obd.	Apr 1847	N.-Amer	838637
Scherer, Jacob	30 Apr 1819	Seedorf	Obd.	Apr 1847	N.-Amer	838637
Scherer, Jakob Friedrich & F	15 Jun 1853	Rutesheim	Leon.	Apr 1879	N.-Amer	837964
Scherer, Ludwig	22 May 1828	Betzingen	Rtl.	Apr 1861	N.-Amer	841057
Scherer, Margaretha Lou. (wife)	20 Jan 1850	Heimsheim	Leon.	Apr 1879	N.-Amer	837964
Scherer, Martin		Betzingen	Rtl.	bef 1858	N.-Amer	841057
Scherer, Pauline Rosine	11 Jul 1877	Rutesheim	Leon.	Apr 1879	N.-Amer	837964
Scherer, Sebald		Winzeln	Obd.	Nov 1860	N.-Amer	841016
Scherraus, Martin	6 Sep 1829	Stubersheim	Gsl.	Aug 1874	N.-Amer	572048
Scherrbacher, Johann	6 Apr 1824	Deggingen	Gsl.	Sep 1857	N.-Amer	572043
Schettle, Johannes		Oberndorf	Obd.	bef 1860	N.-Amer	838635
Scheu, Christian	15 Mar 1839	Owen	Krch.	1867	N.-Amer	835948
Scheu, Johann Andreas		Owen	Krch.	bef 1865	N.-Amer	835940
Scheu, Maria Rosina & F		Owen	Krch.	bef 1865	N.-Amer	835940
Scheuerl, Joseph	25 Jul 1833	Weissenstein	Gsl.	Apr 1866	N.-Amer	572045
Scheufele, Angelika (wid.)	18 Aug 1838	Eltingen	Leon.	Feb 1870	Bavaria	835789
Scheufele, Carl Friedrich	15 Jun 1867	Weilheim	Krch.	Jun 1883	N.-Amer	548403
Scheufele, Christoph	10 Jan 1823	Weilheim	Krch.	Aug 1859	N.-Amer	835949
Scheufele, Heinrich	16 Sep 1826	Weilheim	Krch.	Dec 1869	N.-Amer	835950
Scheufele, Jacob Heinrich	1 May 1846	Weilheim	Krch.	Apr 1866	N.-Amer	835950
Scheufele, Johann Caspar	6 Dec 1827	Weilheim	Krch.	bef 1863	N.-Amer	835950
Scheufele, Johann Friedrich	29 Jul 1857	Weilheim	Krch.	Mar 1873	N.-Amer	835774
Scheufele, Johann Friedrich	14 Sep 1863	Weilheim	Krch.	Sep 1868	N.-Amer	835950
Scheufele, Johann Gottlieb	17 Feb 1856	Weilheim	Krch.	May 1870	N.-Amer	835950
Scheufele, Johannes	7 Oct 1847	Weilheim	Krch.	May 1867	N.-Amer	835950
Scheufele, Matheus	4 Oct 1843	Weilheim	Krch.	bef 1867	N.-Amer	835940
Scheurer, Gottlob	24 Sep 1882	Bondorf	Herr.	Apr 1899	N.-Amer	834630

Name		Birth		Emigration			Film
Last	First	Date	Place	O'amt	Appl. Date	Dest.	Number
Scheurer, Johann Georg (wid.)		28 Jun 1798	Bondorf	Herr.	1868	N.-Amer	834630
Scheuring, Christian		1 Dec 1867	Holzmaden	Krch.	Apr 1883	N.-Amer	548403
Scheutle, Friedrich & W		29 Sep 1798	Ohmden	Krch.	Apr 1857	N.-Amer	835948
Scheutle, Johann Georg		20 Oct 1839	Ohmden	Krch.	Feb 1865	N.-Amer	835948
Scheutle, Margaretha (wife)			Ohmden	Krch.	Apr 1857	N.-Amer	835948
Scheville, Friedrich		50 yrs.	Reutlingen	Rtl.	Apr 1880	N.-Amer	841051
Schick, Andreas Gottfried		4 Jan 1849	Ditzingen	Leon.	Jun 1867	N.-Amer	835788
Schick, Sophia		14 Jan 1857	Kirchheim	Krch.	May 1877	N.-Amer	835942
Schickler, Adam			Notzingen	Krch.	bef 1864	N.-Amer	835940
Schickler, Adam		22 Mar 1827	Notzingen	Krch.	bef 1856	N.-Amer	835947
Schieber, Nikolaus		34 yrs.	Wiesensteig	Gsl.	Sep 1870	N.-Amer	572047
Schiefer, Christian Friedrich		28 Jan 1843	Dettingen	Krch.	Dec 1862	N.-Amer	835944
Schiefer, Christina (wid.)		65 yrs.	Dettingen	Krch.	Apr 1868	N.-Amer	835944
Schiefer, Hermann		16 Mar 1871	Dettingen	Krch.	Feb 1888	N.-Amer	835944
Schiefer, Louise & C		26 Dec 1836	Owen	Krch.	Aug 1864	N.-Amer	835948
Schiek, Anna Maria		2 Jun 1836	Gosbach	Gsl.	Oct 1859	N.-Amer	572043
Schiek, Barbara		30 May 1833	Gosbach	Gsl.	Feb 1853	N.-Amer	572041
Schiek, Franz Anton		19 yrs.	Gosbach	Gsl.	Feb 1851	N.-Amer	577788
Schiek, Joseph (wid.) & F		58 yrs.	Gosbach	Gsl.	Feb 1853	N.-Amer	572041
Schiek, Magdalena		22 Jul 1829	Hohenstadt	Gsl.	Mar 1854	N.-Amer	572042
Schiek, Michael		15 Dec 1833	Gosbach	Gsl.	bef 1853	N.-Amer	572041
Schiek, Simon		30 Oct 1840	Gosbach	Gsl.	Feb 1853	N.-Amer	572041
Schiek, Theresia			Hohenstadt	Gsl.	Apr 1853	N.-Amer	572041
Schiek, Theresia		10 Aug 1845	Gosbach	Gsl.	Oct 1859	N.-Amer	572043
Schiek, Wendelin		8 Jul 1843	Gosbach	Gsl.	Oct 1859	N.-Amer	572043
Schielein, Albert		3 Aug 1850	Weissenstein	Gsl.	Apr 1869	N.-Amer	572047
Schifer, Johann Samuel		7 May 1849	Owen	Krch.	Mar 1866	N.-Amer	835948
Schill, Robert		13 Mar 1850	Reutlingen	Rtl.	Mar 1867	N.-Amer	841057
Schilling, Carl Albert		12 Jun 1867	Kirchheim	Krch.	Aug 1870	Austria	835941
Schilling, Elisabetha			Schramberg	Obd.	Mar 1854	N.-Amer	838636
Schilling, Ferdinand		13 Aug 1847	Schramberg	Obd.	Jul 1866	N.-Amer	838636
Schilling, Friederike & C		14 Feb 1845	Kirchheim	Krch.	Aug 1870	Austria	835941
Schilling, Gottlieb		5 Jun 1841	Neidlingen	Krch.	May 1856	N.-Amer	835946
Schilling, Heinrich (wid.)		12 Jul 1809	Neidlingen	Krch.	Feb 1859	N.-Amer	835946
Schilling, Isedor		1 Jan 1835	Schramberg	Obd.	Mar 1854	N.-Amer	838636
Schilling, Johann & F			Alpirsbach	Obd.	May 1817	N.-Amer	838631
Schilling, Joseph & W			Schramberg	Obd.	Mar 1854	N.-Amer	838636
Schilling, Pauline		22 Feb 1870	Kirchheim	Krch.	Aug 1870	Austria	835941
Schilling, Rosalie (wife)			Schramberg	Obd.	Mar 1854	N.-Amer	838636
Schillinger, Michael Wilhelm		25 yrs.	Hoenweiler	Obd.	Nov 1840	Austria	838635
Schimming, Johanne Friederike			Kirchheim	Krch.	bef 1866	N.-Amer	835940
Schimpf, Catharina Barb. (wife)			Muenklingen	Leon.	Feb 1847	Austria	837962
Schimpf, Johannes & F			Muenklingen	Leon.	Feb 1847	Austria	837962
Schimpf, Magdalena & C		35 yrs.	Eltingen	Leon.	Mar 1851	N.-Amer	835789
Schirm, Christine Katharine		30 Apr 1846	Reutlingen	Rtl.	Oct 1865	N.-Amer	841057
Schirm, Friedrich		10 May 1847	Betzingen	Rtl.	Apr 1866	N.-Amer	841057
Schirm, Jacob			Betzingen	Rtl.	Mar 1833	N.-Amer	841051
Schirm, Johann Georg		26 Nov 1851	Betzingen	Rtl.	Jan 1869	N.-Amer	841057
Schirm, Johann Georg		20 Feb 1840	Betzingen	Rtl.	Jun 1860	N.-Amer	841057
Schirm, Johannes		8 Apr 1845	Betzingen	Rtl.	Mar 1864	N.-Amer	841057

Schirm, Martin	20 Dec 1830	Betzingen	Rtl.	1853	N.-Amer	841057
Schirodt, Julius	12 Apr 1867	Weil der Stadt	Leon.	Mar 1884	N.-Amer	837966
Schirott, Andreas		Weil der Stadt	Leon.	Aug 1853	N.-Amer	837966
Schirott, Philipp Jacob		Weil der Stadt	Leon.	Oct 1853	N.-Amer	837966
Schittenhelm, Anna Barbara		Malmsheim	Leon.	Jan 1854	N.-Amer	837958
Schittenhelm, Georg		Malmsheim	Leon.	Jan 1854	N.-Amer	837958
Schittenhelm, Gottlob		Malmsheim	Leon.	Jan 1854	N.-Amer	837958
Schittenhelm, Johann Jakob		Malmsheim	Leon.	Apr 1854	N.-Amer	837958
Schittenhelm, Johann Peter & F		Malmsheim	Leon.	Jan 1854	N.-Amer	837958
Schittenhelm, Juliana (wife)		Malmsheim	Leon.	Jan 1854	N.-Amer	837958
Schittenhelm, Peter		Malmsheim	Leon.	Jan 1854	N.-Amer	837958
Schlaich, Elisabetha Friedrika	24 Dec 1814	Alpirsbach	Obd.	Feb 1848	Switz.	838630
Schlatter, Anna Maria	25 May 1830	Gutenberg	Krch.	Dec 1860	N.-Amer	835945
Schlatter, Christian	28 Nov 1826	Krebsstein	Krch.	Jun 1855	N.-Amer	835945
Schlatter, Dorothea	10 May 1830	Kuchen	Gsl.	Feb 1854	N.-Amer	572042
Schlatter, Michael	9 Aug 1849	Gutenberg	Krch.	Feb 1869	N.-Amer	835945
Schlatterer, Johann Conrad	18 Feb 1835	Muenchingen	Leon.	Nov 1863	N.-Amer	837961
Schlayer, Auguste & C	13 Jul 1836	Weilheim	Krch.	Sep 1868	N.-Amer	835950
Schlegel, August Ulrich	30 May 1846	Honau	Rtl.	Oct 1866	N.-Amer	841057
Schlegel, Christof Friedrich	4 Feb 1873	Beuren/Nuert.	Krch.	Oct 1889	N.-Amer	835942
Schlegel, Friedrich	4 Feb 1873	Kirchheim	Krch.	Oct 1889	N.-Amer	548323
Schlegel, Georg Friedrich	15 Jan 1848	Pfullingen	Rtl.	Apr 1866	N.-Amer	841057
Schlegel, Johann Georg	16 Jul 1850	Eningen	Rtl.	Jun 1867	N.-Amer	841057
Schlegel, Karl	23 Jan 1849	Honau	Rtl.	Oct 1866	N.-Amer	841057
Schleicher, Johann Sebastian	22 Jun 1821	Schnittlingen	Gsl.	Sep 1867	Hannov.	572046
Schleicher, Johannes	28 Oct 1861	Schalkstetten	Gsl.	May 1873	N.-Amer	572047
Schleicher, Johannes & W		Treffelhausen	Gsl.	Mar 1852	N.-Amer	572041
Schleicher, Katharina		Treffelhausen	Gsl.	Mar 1852	N.-Amer	572041
Schleicher, Marianna		Treffelhausen	Gsl.	1853	N.-Amer	572041
Schlempp, Julius	23 Jul 1855	Kirchheim	Krch.	Apr 1869	N.-Amer	835941
Schlenk, Georg	25 Jun 1847	Brucken	Krch.	Apr 1867	N.-Amer	835944
Schlenker, Gottlob Eug.Im.	3 Mar 1856	Kirchheim	Krch.	Feb 1873	N.-Amer	835942
Schlenker, Samuel	18 Sep 1853	Kirchheim	Krch.	Oct 1870	N.-Amer	835941
Schlientz, Johann	14 May 1822	Kirchheim	Krch.	Jul 1859	N.-Amer	835940
Schlienz, Carl Friedrich		Friolzheim	Leon.	Apr 1831	N.-Amer	835791
Schlipf, Wilhelm	4 Jul 1850	Kirchheim	Krch.	Jul 1867	N.-Amer	835941
Schloth, Gotthilf Wilhelm	14 yrs.	Reutlingen	Rtl.	May 1880	N.-Amer	841051
Schlotterbek, Martin	29 Jun 1842	Betzingen	Rtl.	May 1862	N.-Amer	841057
Schmalzried, Agnes (wife)	42 yrs.	Hemmingen	Leon.	Mar 1827	N.-Amer	837956
Schmalzried, Anna Catarina	11 yrs.	Hemmingen	Leon.	Mar 1827	N.-Amer	837956
Schmalzried, Jakob	2 yrs.	Hemmingen	Leon.	Mar 1827	N.-Amer	837956
Schmalzried, Jakob Friedr. (wid.)	20 Mar 1798	Muenchingen	Leon.	Apr 1837	N.-Amer	837961
Schmalzried, Johanna & C	27 Dec 1829	Muenchingen	Leon.	Jun 1852	N.-Amer	837961
Schmalzried, Johannes	11 Jan 1852	Muenchingen	Leon.	Jun 1852	N.-Amer	837961
Schmalzried, Konrad	4 yrs.	Hemmingen	Leon.	Mar 1827	N.-Amer	837956
Schmalzried, Konrad & F	42 yrs.	Hemmingen	Leon.	Mar 1827	N.-Amer	837956
Schmalzried, Sibyla	15 yrs.	Hemmingen	Leon.	Mar 1827	N.-Amer	837956
Schmalzriedt, Johannes	3 Feb 1842	Muenchingen	Leon.	bef 1867	N.-Amer	837961
Schmalzriedt, Pauline	30 Jan 1843	Muenchingen	Leon.	bef 1865	N.-Amer	837961
Schmalzrieth, Jakob Friedrich	20 Jun 1843	Muenchingen	Leon.	Jul 1869	N.-Amer	837961

Name		Birth		Emigration			Film
Last	First	Date	Place	O'amt	Appl. Date	Dest.	Number
Schmauder, Georg Philipp & W			Leonberg	Leon.	Apr 1834	N.-Amer	835786
Schmauder, Gottfried Friedr.			Leonberg	Leon.	Mar 1824	Prussia	835786
Schmauder, Jakob Gottlieb		26 Aug 1840	Leonberg	Leon.	Nov 1862	N.-Amer	835787
Schmauder, Katharine Chr. (wife)			Leonberg	Leon.	Apr 1834	N.-Amer	835786
Schmauder, Marie Louise		26 Oct 1831	Leonberg	Leon.	Feb 1852	N.-Amer	835786
Schmetterer, Wilhelm			Miltenberg/Bavaria	Gsl.	Aug 1851	N.-Amer	577788
Schmid, Agnes		18 Jan 1841	Winzeln	Obd.	Mar 1865	N.-Amer	841016
Schmid, Albert		20 Apr 1846	Winzeln	Obd.	Sep 1864	N.-Amer	841016
Schmid, Albertine			Waldmoessingen	Obd.	bef 1862	N.-Amer	841015
Schmid, Ambrosius		6 Dec 1852	Winzeln	Obd.	Jul 1869	N.-Amer	841016
Schmid, Andreas		14 Jan 1874	Weilheim	Krch.	Jul 1890	N.-Amer	835774
Schmid, Angelika		29 May 1832	Kuchen	Gsl.	Apr 1852	N.-Amer	572041
Schmid, Anna		28 Jul 1839	Winzeln	Obd.	Mar 1846	N.-Amer	841016
Schmid, Anna			Tuerkheim	Gsl.	1854	N.-Amer	572047
Schmid, Anna Maria			Oberndorf	Obd.	Jan 1857	N.-Amer	838635
Schmid, Anna Maria		18 Sep 1829	Bissingen	Krch.	bef 1862	N.-Amer	835943
Schmid, Anna Maria (wife)		40 yrs.	Hausen a.d. Wurm	Leon.	Feb 1817	Russia	837954
Schmid, Anton		13 Jun 1864	Winzeln	Obd.	Oct 1865	N.-Amer	841016
Schmid, Anton		17 Apr 1845	Donzdorf	Gsl.	Apr 1867	N.-Amer	572046
Schmid, Anton & W			Boehmenkirch	Gsl.	May 1850	N.-Amer	577788
Schmid, Apolonia (wife)			Winzeln	Obd.	Mar 1846	N.-Amer	841016
Schmid, August		18 Apr 1823	Schoeckingen	Leon.	Jul 1848	N.-Amer	837964
Schmid, Barbara		5 Dec 1849	Winzeln	Obd.	Sep 1868	N.-Amer	841016
Schmid, Bernhard		12 Jul 1832	Schramberg	Obd.	Sep 1867	Prussia	838636
Schmid, Carl		10 Jan 1839	Winzeln	Obd.	Dec 1869	N.-Amer	841016
Schmid, Caroline		6 Dec 1827	Schoeckingen	Leon.	bef 1849	Bavaria	837964
Schmid, Caroline		22 yrs.	Leonberg	Leon.	Apr 1852	N.-Amer	835786
Schmid, Catharina Dorothea		25 Mar 1841	Kirchheim	Krch.	Feb 1856	N.-Amer	835940
Schmid, Catharine		17 Sep 1820	Schoeckingen	Leon.	Aug 1849	N.-Amer	837964
Schmid, Catharine Elisabeth		8 Apr 1830	Leonberg	Leon.	May 1861	N.-Amer	835787
Schmid, Christian		23 Dec 1851	Winzeln	Obd.	Feb 1868	N.-Amer	841016
Schmid, Christian & F		1 May 1798	Winzeln	Obd.	Oct 1865	N.-Amer	841016
Schmid, Christian Jacob		31 May 1825	Herrenberg	Herr.	1849	N.-Amer	834629
Schmid, Christiane Friederike		- Jun 1830	Eltingen	Leon.	Apr 1854	N.-Amer	835789
Schmid, Christina		33 yrs.	Hemmingen	Leon.	Apr 1853	N.-Amer	837956
Schmid, Christina Dorothea		21 Aug 1843	Brucken	Krch.	Mar 1860	N.-Amer	835944
Schmid, Christine (wife)		28 Sep 1827	Grosssuessen	Gsl.	Jun 1854	N.-Amer	572042
Schmid, Christof Adam		18 Dec 1821	Kirchheim	Krch.	bef 1860	N.-Amer	835940
Schmid, Christoph			Schoeckingen	Leon.	bef 1849	N.-Amer	837964
Schmid, Christoph (wid.) & F		25 Dec 1795	Schoeckingen	Leon.	Aug 1849	N.-Amer	837964
Schmid, Christoph Adam		18 Dec 1827	Kirchheim	Krch.	Mar 1862	N.-Amer	835941
Schmid, Conrad		17 Feb 1860	Winzeln	Obd.	Oct 1865	N.-Amer	841016
Schmid, Cunrad		17 Sep 1832	Bissingen	Krch.	bef 1860	N.-Amer	835943
Schmid, Eduard		21 Apr 1842	Winzeln	Obd.	Mar 1846	N.-Amer	841016
Schmid, Elias		18 yrs.	Winzeln	Obd.	Apr 1851	N.-Amer	841016
Schmid, Elisabeth & C		18 Nov 1837	Winzeln	Obd.	Oct 1865	N.-Amer	841016
Schmid, Elisabetha		16 Mar 1845	Winzeln	Obd.	Mar 1865	N.-Amer	841016
Schmid, Emma (wife)			Kirchheim	Krch.	Jul 1866	N.-Amer	835941
Schmid, Engelbert		14 Nov 1848	Winzeln	Obd.	Oct 1866	N.-Amer	841016
Schmid, Erhard			Winzeln	Obd.	Aug 1861	N.-Amer	841016

Schmid, Ernst August	7 Mar 1846	Oberndorf	Obd.	Aug 1862	N.-Amer	838635
Schmid, Ernst Hermann	2 Dec 1871	Kirchheim	Krch.	Nov 1888	N.-Amer	835942
Schmid, Felix	10 Jan 1840	Winzeln	Obd.	Sep 1859	N.-Amer	841016
Schmid, Ferdinand & F	51 yrs.	Hausen a.d. Wurm	Leon.	Feb 1817	Russia	837954
Schmid, Friederika	11 yrs.	Hausen a.d. Wurm	Leon.	Feb 1817	Russia	837954
Schmid, Friederike	7 Dec 1828	Leonberg	Leon.	bef 1855	N.-Amer	835786
Schmid, Friederike		Leonberg	Leon.	bef 1871	N.-Amer	835787
Schmid, Friedrich & F		Reutlingen	Rtl.	May 1832	N.-Amer	841051
Schmid, Georg	8 Oct 1823	Kuchen	Gsl.	Apr 1852	N.-Amer	572041
Schmid, Georg Adam	26 Jun 1849	Notzingen	Krch.	Apr 1867	N.-Amer	835947
Schmid, Georg Friedrich	16 Aug 1833	Notzingen	Krch.	1866	N.-Amer	835947
Schmid, Gottlieb Friedrich	16 Dec 1846	Owen	Krch.	Mar 1866	N.-Amer	835948
Schmid, Gottliebin Rosine	14 Apr 1836	Eltingen	Leon.	Jul 1860	N.-Amer	835789
Schmid, Gustav Friedrich	27 Nov 1837	Heimsheim	Leon.	Sep 1854	N.-Amer	837955
Schmid, Hermann	6 Apr 1825	Schopfloch	Krch.	1848	N.-Amer	835949
Schmid, Hermann Friedrich A.	27 Aug 1833	Geislingen	Gsl.	Aug 1853	N.-Amer	572041
Schmid, Hilarius	9 Jan 1809	Hochmoessingen	Obd.	May 1867	N.-Amer	838633
Schmid, Ignaz	27 Jul 1840	Oberndorf	Obd.	Jan 1857	N.-Amer	838635
Schmid, Isedor & F		Winzeln	Obd.	Mar 1846	N.-Amer	841016
Schmid, Jacob	4 Aug 1832	Eltingen	Leon.	Nov 1851	N.-Amer	835789
Schmid, Jakob	2 Feb 1866	Schopfloch	Krch.	May 1882	N.-Amer	548403
Schmid, Jakob Friedrich	14 Oct 1819	Muenchingen	Leon.	bef 1848	N.-Amer	837961
Schmid, Jakob Ulrich	14 yrs.	Hausen a.d. Wurm	Leon.	Feb 1817	Russia	837954
Schmid, Johann	24 Jun 1818	Tuerkheim	Gsl.	Apr 1852	N.-Amer	572041
Schmid, Johann Christian	8 Oct 1850	Kirchheim	Krch.	Dec 1870	N.-Amer	835941
Schmid, Johann Friedrich	15 Jun 1801	Herrenberg	Herr.	1831	N.-Amer	834629
Schmid, Johann Friedrich	26 Mar 1844	Leonberg	Leon.	Sep 1856	N.-Amer	835786
Schmid, Johann Georg	29 Nov 1830	Gueltstein	Herr.	bef 1862	N.-Amer	834631
Schmid, Johann Georg	15 Apr 1832	Wiesensteig	Gsl.	Dec 1852	N.-Amer	572041
Schmid, Johann Georg	21 Nov 1829	Grosssuessen	Gsl.	Mar 1852	N.-Amer	572041
Schmid, Johann Georg		Donzdorf	Gsl.	Mar 1850	N.-Amer	577788
Schmid, Johann Georg		Heimerdingen	Leon.	1828	N.-Amer	837954
Schmid, Johann Georg	1 Jul 1820	Nabern	Krch.	1846	N.-Amer	835946
Schmid, Johann Georg	13 Oct 1840	Owen	Krch.	Apr 1857	N.-Amer	835948
Schmid, Johann Jacob	7 Feb 1838	Unterlenningen	Krch.	Feb 1867	N.-Amer	835949
Schmid, Johann Jakob	3 Dec 1835	Kuchen	Gsl.	May 1854	N.-Amer	572042
Schmid, Johann Martin	18 yrs.	Hausen a.d. Wurm	Leon.	Feb 1817	Russia	837954
Schmid, Johann Michael	3 Jul 1829	Owen	Krch.	Mar 1855	N.-Amer	835948
Schmid, Johanna	23 May 1857	Winzeln	Obd.	Oct 1865	N.-Amer	841016
Schmid, Johanna	14 Nov 1828	Schoeckingen	Leon.	Jul 1848	N.-Amer	837964
Schmid, Johanna	31 yrs.	Hemmingen	Leon.	Apr 1859	Switz.	837956
Schmid, Johanna (wid.)		Gerlingen	Leon.	1817	Russia	837953
Schmid, Johannes	22 Dec 1849	Grosssuessen	Gsl.	Jun 1854	N.-Amer	572042
Schmid, Johannes	6 Mar 1830	Schoeckingen	Leon.	Jul 1848	N.-Amer	837964
Schmid, Johannes	13 yrs.	Hausen a.d. Wurm	Leon.	Feb 1817	Russia	837954
Schmid, Johannes	22 Dec 1844	Boehmenkirch	Gsl.	Mar 1868	N.-Amer	572046
Schmid, Johannes	18 Aug 1818	Hochdorf	Krch.	Apr 1864	N.-Amer	835945
Schmid, Johannes	9 Oct 1827	Hochdorf	Krch.	May 1854	N.-Amer	835945
Schmid, Johannes	11 Mar 1842	Owen	Krch.	May 1858	N.-Amer	835948
Schmid, Josef		Lauterbach	Obd.	1850	England	838634

Name		Birth		Emigration			Film
Last	First	Date	Place	O'amt	Appl. Date	Dest.	Number
Schmid, Josef		10 Mar 1853	Winzeln	Obd.	Sep 1868	N.-Amer	841016
Schmid, Josef		3 Mar 1832	Winzeln	Obd.	Sep 1852	N.-Amer	841016
Schmid, Josefa & C		14 Mar 1825	Winzeln	Obd.	Oct 1865	N.-Amer	841016
Schmid, Joseph			Beffendorf	Obd.	Feb 1861	N.-Amer	838631
Schmid, Joseph		11 Mar 1847	Oberndorf	Obd.	Aug 1867	N.-Amer	838635
Schmid, Joseph		infant	Hausen a.d. Wurm	Leon.	Feb 1817	Russia	837954
Schmid, Joseph Bernt		9 Dec 1859	Donzdorf	Gsl.	Feb 1866	N.-Amer	572045
Schmid, Josepha		20 Dec 1824	Donzdorf	Gsl.	Apr 1854	N.-Amer	572042
Schmid, Josepha & C		18 Mar 1833	Donzdorf	Gsl.	Feb 1866	N.-Amer	572045
Schmid, Josepha (wid.) & F			Aichhalden	Obd.	Jun 1853	N.-Amer	838629
Schmid, Juliana		2 Jan 1846	Donzdorf	Gsl.	Dec 1868	N.-Amer	572046
Schmid, Karl		5 Jan 1854	Winzeln	Obd.	Feb 1869	N.-Amer	841016
Schmid, Karl August		19 Jun 1852	Wiesensteig	Gsl.	Mar 1869	N.-Amer	572047
Schmid, Karl Constantin		6 Feb 1845	Stuttgart	Rtl.	Mar 1864	N.-Amer	841057
Schmid, Konrad		22 Nov 1844	Weissenstein	Gsl.	May 1872	N.-Amer	572047
Schmid, Landidus		30 Sep 1849	Winzeln	Obd.	Jul 1869	N.-Amer	841016
Schmid, Leonhard		27 Jul 1851	Grosssuessen	Gsl.	Jun 1854	N.-Amer	572042
Schmid, Lorenz		7 Aug 1847	Winzeln	Obd.	Apr 1867	N.-Amer	841016
Schmid, Louise (wife)			Donzdorf	Gsl.	Mar 1850	N.-Amer	577788
Schmid, Magdalena		4 Jan 1834	Bissingen	Krch.	bef 1862	N.-Amer	835943
Schmid, Maria		1 Aug 1859	Winzeln	Obd.	Feb 1868	N.-Amer	841016
Schmid, Maria		7 Sep 1847	Grosssuessen	Gsl.	Jun 1854	N.-Amer	572042
Schmid, Maria		25 Mar 1849	Weissenstein	Gsl.	Aug 1869	N.-Amer	572047
Schmid, Maria Rosina		30 Dec 1798	Renningen	Leon.	Apr 1818	N.-Amer	837963
Schmid, Mariana (wife)			Boehmenkirch	Gsl.	May 1850	N.-Amer	577788
Schmid, Marie		9 Oct 1834	Kirchheim	Krch.	Aug 1869	Saxony	835941
Schmid, Mathias & W			Aichhalden	Obd.	May 1817	N.-Amer	838629
Schmid, Matthias & F			Winzeln	Obd.	Feb 1850	N.-Amer	841016
Schmid, Maximilian Emil		6 Nov 1828	Wiesensteig	Gsl.	Mar 1858	Prussia	572043
Schmid, Nikodemus		3 Jun 1853	Winzeln	Obd.	Oct 1868	N.-Amer	841016
Schmid, Otto		16 yrs.	Reutlingen	Rtl.	Apr 1880	N.-Amer	841051
Schmid, Paul		7 Nov 1834	Geislingen	Gsl.	Jul 1863	Sweden	572044
Schmid, Peter & F		3 Apr 1820	Grosssuessen	Gsl.	Jun 1854	N.-Amer	572042
Schmid, Philipp			Oberndorf	Obd.	Jan 1857	N.-Amer	838635
Schmid, Rahel		12 Mar 1835	Schoeckingen	Leon.	Aug 1849	N.-Amer	837964
Schmid, Regina			Winzeln	Obd.	Aug 1859	N.-Amer	841016
Schmid, Rosalia			Winzeln	Obd.	Mar 1866	N.-Amer	841016
Schmid, Rosina		23 yrs.	Geislingen	Gsl.	Dec 1851	N.-Amer	577788
Schmid, Salome		25 Dec 1844	Schoeckingen	Leon.	bef 1866	N.-Amer	837964
Schmid, Sebastian & F			Sulgen	Obd.	Apr 1817	N.-Amer	838638
Schmid, Sophia Barbara		10 Apr 1863	Bissingen	Krch.	Apr 1869	N.-Amer	835943
Schmid, Susanna		17 Feb 1838	Winzeln	Obd.	Mar 1846	N.-Amer	841016
Schmid, Theresia		21 yrs.	Aichhalden	Obd.	Sep 1854	N.-Amer	838629
Schmid, Ursula		20 Oct 1848	Winzeln	Obd.	Feb 1869	N.-Amer	841016
Schmid, Vincenz		16 yrs.	Aichhalden	Obd.	Jun 1853	N.-Amer	838629
Schmid, Wilhelm		3 May 1850	Leonberg	Leon.	Feb 1867	N.-Amer	835787
Schmid, Wilhelm		21 yrs.	Willmandingen	Rtl.	Jan 1880	N.-Amer	841051
Schmid, Wilhelm & W		30 May 1829	Kirchheim	Krch.	Jul 1866	N.-Amer	835941
Schmid, Wilhelm Friedrich		18 yrs.	Heimerdingen	Leon.	May 1831	N.-Amer	837954
Schmidt, Catharina		44 yrs.	Hoefingen	Leon.	Aug 1853	N.-Amer	837957

Schmidt, Christiane	30 Nov 1852	Hoefingen	Leon.	Nov 1855	Hungary	837957
Schmidt, Christina Maria	12 yrs.	Malmsheim	Leon.	Mar 1830	N.-Amer	837958
Schmidt, Christoph Friedrich	1 yrs.	Hemmingen	Leon.	May 1821	N.-Amer	837956
Schmidt, Conrad		Hoefingen	Leon.	Jan 1852	N.-Amer	837957
Schmidt, Dorothea (wife)	30 yrs.	Hemmingen	Leon.	May 1821	N.-Amer	837956
Schmidt, Dorothea (wife)	25 yrs.	Hemmingen	Leon.	Feb 1818	N.-Amer	837956
Schmidt, Friedrich & F	31 yrs.	Hemmingen	Leon.	May 1821	N.-Amer	837956
Schmidt, Friedrich & W	29 yrs.	Hemmingen	Leon.	Feb 1818	N.-Amer	837956
Schmidt, Gottlob	5 Dec 1848	Hoefingen	Leon.	Nov 1855	Hungary	837957
Schmidt, Jakob	13 Mar 1839	Muenchingen	Leon.	Jul 1860	N.-Amer	837961
Schmidt, Johann Albrecht	14 Apr 1819	Renningen	Leon.	bef 1852	Prussia	837963
Schmidt, Johann Christian	10 Oct 1843	Hoefingen	Leon.	Nov 1855	Hungary	837957
Schmidt, Johann Georg	24 Oct 1845	Hoefingen	Leon.	Nov 1855	Hungary	837957
Schmidt, Johannes	13 Jul 1817	Renningen	Leon.	Feb 1848	Prussia	837963
Schmidt, Johannes	Jul 1816	Renningen	Leon.	bef 1848	Prussia	837963
Schmidt, Johannes	8 Dec 1840	Hoefingen	Leon.	Nov 1855	Hungary	837957
Schmidt, Johannes & F		Hoefingen	Leon.	bef 1855	Hungary	837957
Schmidt, Johannes Gotthilf	2 May 1863	Renningen	Leon.	Apr 1880	N.-Amer	837963
Schmidt, Karoline	12 Mar 1850	Hoefingen	Leon.	Nov 1855	Hungary	837957
Schmidt, Katharina (wife)		Hoefingen	Leon.	Nov 1855	Hungary	837957
Schmidt, Katharina Wilhelmine	16 Apr 1842	Hoefingen	Leon.	Nov 1855	Hungary	837957
Schmidt, Maria Agnes (wid.) & F		Malmsheim	Leon.	Mar 1830	N.-Amer	837958
Schmidt, Philippina Magdalena	18 yrs.	Malmsheim	Leon.	Mar 1830	N.-Amer	837958
Schmidt, Sibbila	2 yrs.	Hemmingen	Leon.	May 1821	N.-Amer	837956
Schmied, Andreas	29 Aug 1832	Muenchingen	Leon.	bef 1852	N.-Amer	837961
Schmied, Johann Georg	1 Apr 1852	Muenchingen	Leon.	1852	N.-Amer	837961
Schmiedt, Jakob Friedrich	14 Jun 1823	Muenchingen	Leon.	1853	N.-Amer	837961
Schmiedt, Michael	22 Oct 1823	Muenchingen	Leon.	1853	N.-Amer	837961
Schmoker, Josef	27 Dec 1826	Mariazell	Obd.	Mar 1867	Munich	838634
Schmueckle, Friedrich	- 1839	Kirchheim	Krch.	Apr 1859	N.-Amer	835940
Schnabel, Ignaz		Donzdorf	Gsl.	bef 1869	N.-Amer	572047
Schnarrenberger, Anna Maria	1 Jul 1840	Gingen	Gsl.	Aug 1851	N.-Amer	577788
Schnarrenberger, Johannes & F	15 Jan 1799	Gingen	Gsl.	Aug 1851	N.-Amer	577788
Schnarrenberger, Lukas	30 Oct 1846	Gingen	Gsl.	Aug 1851	N.-Amer	577788
Schnarrenberger, Margar. (wife)	7 Dec 1805	Gingen	Gsl.	Aug 1851	N.-Amer	577788
Schnaufer, Anna Barbara	7 yrs.	Malmsheim	Leon.	May 1853	N.-Amer	837958
Schnaufer, Anna Barbara	infant	Malmsheim	Leon.	Mar 1830	N.-Amer	837958
Schnaufer, Anna Maria	12 yrs.	Malmsheim	Leon.	Mar 1830	N.-Amer	837958
Schnaufer, Anna Maria (wife)	43 yrs.	Malmsheim	Leon.	May 1853	N.-Amer	837958
Schnaufer, Anna Maria (wife)		Malmsheim	Leon.	Mar 1830	N.-Amer	837958
Schnaufer, Carl Heinrich	4 Jul 1823	Heimsheim	Leon.	Aug 1848	N.-Amer	837955
Schnaufer, Catharina	5 yrs.	Malmsheim	Leon.	Mar 1830	N.-Amer	837958
Schnaufer, Catharina Barbara	18 yrs.	Malmsheim	Leon.	May 1853	N.-Amer	837958
Schnaufer, Christiana Johanna	19 yrs.	Malmsheim	Leon.	Mar 1830	N.-Amer	837958
Schnaufer, Christina Bar. (wife)		Malmsheim	Leon.	Mar 1830	N.-Amer	837958
Schnaufer, Christina Maria	5 yrs.	Malmsheim	Leon.	Mar 1830	N.-Amer	837958
Schnaufer, Dorothea	11 yrs.	Malmsheim	Leon.	May 1853	N.-Amer	837958
Schnaufer, Elisabetha Barb.	19 yrs.	Malmsheim	Leon.	Mar 1830	N.-Amer	837958
Schnaufer, Friedrich	11 yrs.	Malmsheim	Leon.	Mar 1830	N.-Amer	837958
Schnaufer, Georg Friedrich	28 yrs.	Malmsheim	Leon.	May 1829	N.-Amer	837958

Name		Birth		Emigration			Film
Last	First	Date	Place	O'amt	Appl. Date	Dest.	Number
Schnaufer, Gottlob Friedrich			Malmsheim	Leon.	1839	N.-Amer	837958
Schnaufer, Jakob Friedrich		17 Jan 1847	Malmsheim	Leon.	Aug 1867	N.-Amer	837958
Schnaufer, Johann Friedr. & F			Malmsheim	Leon.	Mar 1830	N.-Amer	837958
Schnaufer, Johann Georg		23 yrs.	Malmsheim	Leon.	Mar 1830	N.-Amer	837958
Schnaufer, Johann Heinrich		14 yrs.	Malmsheim	Leon.	May 1853	N.-Amer	837958
Schnaufer, Johann Marx. & F			Malmsheim	Leon.	Mar 1830	N.-Amer	837958
Schnaufer, Johann Michael & F			Malmsheim	Leon.	May 1853	N.-Amer	837958
Schnaufer, Johanna Friederika		6 yrs.	Malmsheim	Leon.	Mar 1830	N.-Amer	837958
Schnaufer, Johannes		9 yrs.	Malmsheim	Leon.	May 1853	N.-Amer	837958
Schnaufer, Johannes		9 yrs.	Malmsheim	Leon.	Mar 1830	N.-Amer	837958
Schnaufer, Johannes & F			Malmsheim	Leon.	Mar 1830	N.-Amer	837958
Schnaufer, Jonathan		14 yrs.	Malmsheim	Leon.	Mar 1830	N.-Amer	837958
Schnaufer, Luise		2 yrs.	Malmsheim	Leon.	Mar 1830	N.-Amer	837958
Schnaufer, Regina Catharina		3 yrs.	Malmsheim	Leon.	Mar 1830	N.-Amer	837958
Schnauffer, Ernst Ludwig		10 Sep 1836	Stuttgart	Leon.	Feb 1864	Bavaria	837963
Schnauffer, Johanna Louisa W.		20 Jul 1845	Stuttgart	Leon.	Jan 1864	Bavaria	837963
Schnauffer, Maria Rosina		22 Sep 1806	Renningen	Leon.	May 1854	N.-Amer	837963
Schnauffer, Wilhelm Friedrich		20 Jul 1835	Heimsheim	Leon.	Feb 1854	N.-Amer	837955
Schnee, Catharina		15 Mar 1828	Muenchingen	Leon.	May 1855	N.-Amer	837961
Schneeweiss, Anna Maria		11 Jun 1825	Weilheim	Krch.	Nov 1859	N.-Amer	835949
Schneeweiss, Eva Maria		27 Sep 1827	Weilheim	Krch.	bef 1856	N.-Amer	835949
Schneider, Adelbert		13 Sep 1847	Waldmoessingen	Obd.	Apr 1867	N.-Amer	841015
Schneider, Alois		16 Jun 1818	Lauterbach	Obd.	Apr 1840	N.-Amer	838634
Schneider, Aloys		29 Apr 1848	Waldmoessingen	Obd.	Aug 1865	N.-Amer	841015
Schneider, Andreas			Roetenbach	Obd.	Feb 1860	N.-Amer	838636
Schneider, Andreas		26 yrs.	Moensheim	Leon.	Mar 1831	N.-Amer	837960
Schneider, Anna		7 yrs.	Geislingen	Gsl.	Jan 1853	N.-Amer	572041
Schneider, Anna Magdalena		7 yrs.	Eltingen	Leon.	Jul 1820	N.-Amer	835789
Schneider, Anna Maria (wife)			Malmsheim	Leon.	Mar 1821	N.-Amer	837958
Schneider, Anton			Waldmoessingen	Obd.	Apr 1862	N.-Amer	841015
Schneider, Barbara (wife)			Eltingen	Leon.	Jul 1820	N.-Amer	835789
Schneider, Bernhardt & F			Malmsheim	Leon.	Mar 1821	N.-Amer	837958
Schneider, Carl Friedrich		18 Jul 1832	Gomaringen	Rtl.	bef 1866	France	841057
Schneider, Catharina		12 Nov 1846	Seedorf	Obd.	Apr 1847	N.-Amer	838637
Schneider, Catharina Barbara		22 Jun 1817	Malmsheim	Leon.	Jul 1831	N.-Amer	837958
Schneider, Catharina Walpurga		6 yrs.	Geislingen	Gsl.	Jan 1853	N.-Amer	572041
Schneider, Christiane & C			Enztal	Nag.	Jul 1852	N.-Amer	838488
Schneider, Christina Bar. (wife)			Malmsheim	Leon.	Mar 1821	N.-Amer	837958
Schneider, Constantin			Sulgen	Obd.	bef 1861	France	838638
Schneider, Eduard		19 yrs.	Alt Oberndorf	Obd.	Oct 1860	N.-Amer	838631
Schneider, Eusebius		14 Aug 1837	Winzeln	Obd.	Sep 1853	N.-Amer	841016
Schneider, Fridolin			Waldmoessingen	Obd.	Apr 1860	N.-Amer	841015
Schneider, Friederika		5 yrs.	Malmsheim	Leon.	Mar 1821	N.-Amer	837958
Schneider, Friederike		16 yrs.	Eltingen	Leon.	Jul 1820	N.-Amer	835789
Schneider, Friedrich		31 yrs.	Alt Oberndorf	Obd.	Apr 1860	N.-Amer	838631
Schneider, Friedrich			Renningen	Leon.	Apr 1817	N.-Amer	837963
Schneider, Georg			Seedorf	Obd.	Mar 1841	Austria	838637
Schneider, Gottfried		11 Jun 1835	Eltingen	Leon.	Sep 1854	N.-Amer	835789
Schneider, Isidor		31 Mar 1812	Seedorf	Obd.	Apr 1847	N.-Amer	838637
Schneider, Jakob		30 Apr 1819	Seedorf	Obd.	Apr 1847	N.-Amer	838637

Schneider, Jakob & F		Malmsheim	Leon.	Mar 1821	N.-Amer	837958
Schneider, Jakob Benjamin	15 Apr 1832	Eningen	Rtl.	bef 1860	France	841057
Schneider, Jakob Friedrich	15 Sep 1831	Eltingen	Leon.	1852	N.-Amer	835789
Schneider, Joachim & F		Winzeln	Obd.	Mar 1866	N.-Amer	841016
Schneider, Johann	4 yrs.	Geislingen	Gsl.	Jan 1853	N.-Amer	572041
Schneider, Johann Conrad	20 Aug 1818	Malmsheim	Leon.	Jul 1831	N.-Amer	837958
Schneider, Johann Georg	34 yrs.	Malmsheim	Leon.	Sep 1851	N.-Amer	837958
Schneider, Johann Georg & F		Eltingen	Leon.	Aug 1851	N.-Amer	835789
Schneider, Johann Jakob	8 Mar 1813	Malmsheim	Leon.	Jul 1831	N.-Amer	837958
Schneider, Johann Jakob	1 yrs.	Malmsheim	Leon.	Mar 1821	N.-Amer	837958
Schneider, Johann Jakob	3 yrs.	Malmsheim	Leon.	Mar 1821	N.-Amer	837958
Schneider, Johannes	5 May 1847	Winzeln	Obd.	Nov 1867	N.-Amer	841016
Schneider, Johannes		Winzeln	Obd.	Sep 1852	N.-Amer	841016
Schneider, Johannes	23 Aug 1830	Eltingen	Leon.	1851	N.-Amer	835789
Schneider, Johannes & F		Geislingen	Gsl.	Jan 1853	N.-Amer	572041
Schneider, Josef	12 Nov 1848	Mariazell	Obd.	Aug 1868	N.-Amer	838634
Schneider, Joseph	21 Feb 1847	Hochmoessingen	Obd.	Apr 1867	N.-Amer	838633
Schneider, Joseph	5 May 1825	Seedorf	Obd.	bef 1866	N.-Amer	838637
Schneider, Karl	2 Mar 1850	Mariazell	Obd.	Aug 1868	N.-Amer	838634
Schneider, Lorenz & F		Eltingen	Leon.	Jul 1830	N.-Amer	835789
Schneider, Lorenz & F		Eltingen	Leon.	Jul 1820	N.-Amer	835789
Schneider, Lukas	18 Oct 1836	Harthausen	Obd.	Dec 1866	Bavaria	838633
Schneider, Margaretha		Eltingen	Leon.	Apr 1854	N.-Amer	835789
Schneider, Maria	2 yrs.	Geislingen	Gsl.	Jan 1853	N.-Amer	572041
Schneider, Maria (wife)		Winzeln	Obd.	Mar 1866	N.-Amer	841016
Schneider, Maria Anna		Winzeln	Obd.	Mar 1866	N.-Amer	841016
Schneider, Maria Barbara & F		Malmsheim	Leon.	Jul 1831	N.-Amer	837958
Schneider, Maria Magdalena	30 Nov 1846	Eltingen	Leon.	1867	N.-Amer	835789
Schneider, Marianne	16 Jul 1816	Lauterbach	Obd.	Apr 1840	N.-Amer	838634
Schneider, Martin		Alt Oberndorf	Obd.	Aug 1841	Austria	838631
Schneider, Martin	57 yrs.	Waldmoessingen	Obd.	Apr 1852	N.-Amer	841015
Schneider, Mathaeus		Bochingen	Obd.	bef 1845	Austria	838632
Schneider, Matthaeus	5 Sep 1835	Seedorf	Obd.	Mar 1853	N.-Amer	838637
Schneider, Matthaeus	19 yrs.	Winzeln	Obd.	Apr 1851	N.-Amer	841016
Schneider, Michael & W		Aichhalden	Obd.	May 1817	N.-Amer	838629
Schneider, Paul	26 May 1820	Seedorf	Obd.	Jul 1858	N.-Amer	838637
Schneider, Raimund	21 Jan 1836	Aichhalden	Obd.	Aug 1853	N.-Amer	838629
Schneider, Rosa	24 Aug 1845	Seedorf	Obd.	Apr 1847	N.-Amer	838637
Schneider, Salomon	33 yrs.	Eltingen	Leon.	Jul 1820	N.-Amer	835789
Schneider, Severin	26 Oct 1836	Seedorf	Obd.	Feb 1854	N.-Amer	838637
Schneider, Stanislaus & F		Mariazell	Obd.	May 1817	N.-Amer	838634
Schneider, Wendelin		Alt Oberndorf	Obd.	Jan 1854	N.-Amer	838631
Schneider, Wilhelmine Joseph.	27 yrs.	Alt Oberndorf	Obd.	Sep 1854	N.-Amer	838631
Schnell, Gregor	35 yrs.	Alt Oberndorf	Obd.	Feb 1857	N.-Amer	838631
Schnell, Johann Nepomuk	8 May 1803	Epfendorf	Obd.	May 1847	N.-Amer	838632
Schnell, Johann Nepomuk	9 May 1832	Seedorf	Obd.	Sep 1866	France	838637
Schnell, Valentin	11 Feb 1825	Hochmoessingen	Obd.	Jan 1853	N.-Amer	838633
Schnell, Valentin	1 Feb 1825	Seedorf	Obd.	1852	N.-Amer	838637
Schnell, Xaver		Seedorf	Obd.	Sep 1863	N.-Amer	838637
Schneller, Christian-	20 May 1845	Heimerdingen	Leon.	May 1849	N.-Amer	837954

Name		Birth		Emigration			Film
Last	First	Date	Place	O'amt	Appl. Date	Dest.	Number
Schneller, Christoph Friedr.		7 Jul 1841	Heimerdingen	Leon.	May 1849	N.-Amer	837954
Schneller, Wilhelmine		14 Feb 1848	Heimerdingen	Leon.	May 1849	N.-Amer	837954
Schneller, Wilhelmine & F		8 Jan 1815	Heimerdingen	Leon.	May 1849	N.-Amer	837954
Schnizler, Jakob Baltas		26 Apr 1823	Gomaringen	Rtl.	Jul 1862	N.-Amer	841057
Schober, Barbara Marg. (wife)		5 Jun 1831	Malmsheim	Leon.	Sep 1871	N.-Amer	837958
Schober, Catharina Dorothea		1 Jul 1852	Malmsheim	Leon.	Sep 1871	N.-Amer	837958
Schober, Christiane Louise		25 Dec 1862	Malmsheim	Leon.	Sep 1871	N.-Amer	837958
Schober, Gottfried & F		31 Dec 1828	Malmsheim	Leon.	Sep 1871	N.-Amer	837958
Schober, Ludwig		19 Nov 1855	Malmsheim	Leon.	Sep 1871	N.-Amer	837958
Schock, Friedrich Christian		18 Jul 1885	Zell	Krch.	May 1899	N.-Amer	835774
Schoeck, Katharina Barbara		9 Jan 1831	Renningen	Leon.	bef 1856	Switz.	837963
Schoeffel, Gotttlob Wilhelm		18 Sep 1866	Hirschlanden	Leon.	Jul 1882	N.-Amer	837956
Schoeffel, Karl Gottfried		16 Mar 1846	Malmsheim	Leon.	Jun 1870	N.-Amer	837958
Schoeffel, Karl Jacob		10 Jul 1865	Hirschlanden	Leon.	Jul 1880	N.-Amer	837956
Schoeffel, Konrad Friedrich		10 Aug 1867	Hirschlanden	Leon.	Feb 1883	N.-Amer	837956
Schoek, Anna Magdalena		1 Oct 1828	Renningen	Leon.	Apr 1852	N.-Amer	837963
Schoek, Catharina Margaretha		31 Oct 1833	Renningen	Leon.	Apr 1852	N.-Amer	837963
Schoek, Christina Friederika		22 Jul 1838	Renningen	Leon.	Apr 1852	N.-Amer	837963
Schoek, Johann Christ.Friedr.		11 Dec 1841	Renningen	Leon.	Apr 1852	N.-Amer	837963
Schoek, Johann Karl Friedrich		1 Apr 1831	Renningen	Leon.	Apr 1852	N.-Amer	837963
Schoek, Louise Dorothea		30 Jan 1845	Renningen	Leon.	Apr 1852	N.-Amer	837963
Schoek, Louise Friederike		8 Jul 1848	Renningen	Leon.	Apr 1852	N.-Amer	837963
Schoek, Margaretha (wife)		14 Aug 1806	Renningen	Leon.	Apr 1852	N.-Amer	837963
Schoek, Michael & F			Renningen	Leon.	Apr 1852	N.-Amer	837963
Schoelkopf, Caroline Louise		7 Apr 1821	Leonberg	Leon.	Sep 1853	N.-Amer	835786
Schoelkopf, Friedrich			Leonberg	Leon.	Oct 1852	N.-Amer	835786
Schoelkopf, Karolina Wilhelm.		6 Oct 1841	Leonberg	Leon.	Nov 1864	Switz.	835787
Schoellkopf, Anna Maria		23 Sep 1871	Rosswaelden	Krch.	Feb 1881	N.-Amer	835949
Schoellkopf, Barbara (wife)		18 Jun 1842	Oberurbach	Krch.	Feb 1881	N.-Amer	835949
Schoellkopf, Barbara Lou. (wife)		18 Jun 1842	Rosswaelden	Krch.	Feb 1881	N.-Amer	548403
Schoellkopf, Charlotte Gottl.			Herrenberg	Herr.	1845	N.-Amer	834629
Schoellkopf, Christian L.		28 Jan 1823	Herrenberg	Herr.	1853	N.-Amer	834629
Schoellkopf, David & F			Bronnweiler	Rtl.	Sep 1847	N.-Amer	841057
Schoellkopf, Gottlieb Heinr.		- Sep 1849	Kirchheim	Krch.	Jul 1866	N.-Amer	835941
Schoellkopf, Gottlob Friedr.		23 yrs.	Leonberg	Leon.	Apr 1825	Austria	835786
Schoellkopf, Jacob Friedrich		15 Nov 1819	Kirchheim	Krch.	Feb 1861	N.-Amer	835940
Schoellkopf, Johann Georg		27 Jan 1870	Rosswaelden	Krch.	Feb 1881	N.-Amer	548403
Schoellkopf, Johann Georg		27 Jan 1870	Rosswaelden	Krch.	Feb 1881	N.-Amer	835949
Schoellkopf, Johann Georg & F		17 Feb 1843	Rosswaelden	Krch.	Feb 1881	N.-Amer	548403
Schoellkopf, Johann Georg & F		17 Feb 1843	Rosswaelden	Krch.	Feb 1881	N.-Amer	835949
Schoellkopf, Johann Martin & F		6 Feb 1825	Geislingen	Gsl.	Jan 1854	N.-Amer	572042
Schoellkopf, Johann Michael		7 Nov 1839	Oberlenningen	Krch.	Aug 1859	N.-Amer	835947
Schoellkopf, Louise Sophie		16 Jul 1868	Rosswaelden	Krch.	Feb 1881	N.-Amer	548403
Schoellkopf, Margaretha		7 Feb 1829	Kuchen	Gsl.	Feb 1854	N.-Amer	572042
Schoellkopf, Maria (wife)		18 Jul 1823	Kuchen	Gsl.	Jan 1854	N.-Amer	572042
Schoellkopf, Marie Caroline		26 Mar 1825	Herrenberg	Herr.	bef 1864	N.-Amer	834629
Schoellkopf, Martin		17 Feb 1851	Geislingen	Gsl.	Jan 1854	N.-Amer	572042
Schoelple, Conrad Heinrich		20 Sep 1832	Weilheim	Krch.	Oct 1865	N.-Amer	835950
Schoelpple, Johann		17 Nov 1847	Weilheim	Krch.	Dec 1866	N.-Amer	835950
Schoelpple, Johann Georg		16 Oct 1874	Weilheim	Krch.	Jul 1890	England	835774

Name	Date	Place	Region	Emig. Date	Destination	No.
Schoelpple, Mathaeus	7 Jul 1829	Weilheim	Krch.	Nov 1865	N.-Amer	835950
Schoemperle, Barbara Marg. & C	36 yrs.	Hoefingen	Leon.	Apr 1853	N.-Amer	837957
Schoempperle, Johann Christoph		Hoefingen	Leon.	bef 1842	Hamburg	837957
Schoenfeld, Maria Pauline	3 Apr 1866	Eningen	Rtl.	Jun 1866	N.-Amer	841055
Schoeninger, Adolf		Weil der Stadt	Leon.	Dec 1853	N.-Amer	837966
Schoeninger, August		Weil der Stadt	Leon.	Jun 1854	N.-Amer	837966
Schoeninger, Conrad		Weil der Stadt	Leon.	Jan 1854	N.-Amer	837966
Schoeninger, Joseph Anton	1 Apr 1839	Weil der Stadt	Leon.	bef 1859	N.-Amer	837966
Schoeninger, Leo	21 Jan 1811	Weil der Stadt	Leon.	bef 1840	Bavaria	837966
Schoenleber, Jakob Friedr. Ph.	8 Feb 1863	Hoefingen	Leon.	Feb 1880	N.-Amer	837957
Schoenleber, Karl Eberh. Chr.	28 Apr 1870	Kirchheim	Krch.	Sep 1887	N.-Amer	835942
Schoenleber, Louise Kath. & F	21 Mar 1837	Kirchheim	Krch.	Sep 1887	N.-Amer	835942
Schoenleber, Maria Karolina	10 May 1877	Kirchheim	Krch.	Sep 1887	N.-Amer	835942
Schoenleber, Wilhelm Friedr.	30 Jul 1866	Kirchheim	Krch.	Mar 1881	N.-Amer	548403
Schoenwalter, Johann Christ.		Weil im Dorf	Loen.	1865	N.-Amer	837967
Schoepf, Alexander	8 Apr 1841	Renningen	Leon.	Feb 1854	N.-Amer	837963
Schoepf, Andreas	30 Apr 1869	Gutenberg	Krch.	Oct 1885	N.-Amer	548403
Schoepf, Anna Catharina		Renningen	Leon.	Apr 1852	N.-Amer	837963
Schoepf, Anna Maria (wife)	14 Jul 1815	Renningen	Leon.	Jul 1854	N.-Amer	837963
Schoepf, Anna Maria Philipp.	29 Jan 1873	Gutenberg	Krch.	Apr 1882	N.-Amer	835945
Schoepf, Christina		Renningen	Leon.	Apr 1852	N.-Amer	837963
Schoepf, Daniel		Renningen	Leon.	Feb 1854	N.-Amer	837963
Schoepf, David	25 Feb 1871	Gutenberg	Krch.	Oct 1887	N.-Amer	835945
Schoepf, Friedrich	13 Jan 1878	Gutenberg	Krch.	Apr 1882	N.-Amer	548403
Schoepf, Johann Adam	29 Oct 1880	Gutenberg	Krch.	Apr 1882	N.-Amer	548403
Schoepf, Johann Adam	29 Oct 1880	Gutenberg	Krch.	Apr 1882	N.-Amer	835945
Schoepf, Johann Adam & F	3 Apr 1847	Gutenberg	Krch.	Apr 1882	N.-Amer	835945
Schoepf, Johann Daniel & W	11 Feb 1810	Renningen	Leon.	Jul 1854	N.-Amer	837963
Schoepf, Johann Karl	22 Mar 1838	Renningen	Leon.	Apr 1852	N.-Amer	837963
Schoepf, Sophia	1 Mar 1882	Gutenberg	Krch.	Apr 1882	N.-Amer	835945
Schoepf, Sophie	1 Mar 1882	Gutenberg	Krch.	Apr 1882	N.-Amer	548403
Schoepf, Sophie (wife)	2 Feb 1849	Gutenberg	Krch.	Apr 1882	N.-Amer	548403
Schoepfer, Friederike	24 Jan 1839	Owen	Krch.	Jul 1857	N.-Amer	835948
Schoerle, Christian Friedrich	6 Apr 1827	Heimsheim	Leon.	bef 1861	N.-Amer	837955
Schoettle, Auguste	16 yrs.	Oberndorf	Obd.	Apr 1847	N.-Amer	838635
Schoettle, Bertha	12 yrs.	Oberndorf	Obd.	Apr 1847	N.-Amer	838635
Schoettle, Carl	20 yrs.	Oberndorf	Obd.	Apr 1847	N.-Amer	838635
Schoettle, Eleonore	26 yrs.	Oberndorf	Obd.	Apr 1847	N.-Amer	838635
Schoettle, Ferdinand Eberhard	16 Mar 1839	Weilheim	Krch.	Jun 1859	N.-Amer	835949
Schoettle, Franziska	15 yrs.	Oberndorf	Obd.	Apr 1847	N.-Amer	838635
Schoettle, Joseph & F		Oberndorf	Obd.	Apr 1847	N.-Amer	838635
Schoettle, Louise (wife)	25 yrs.	Oberndorf	Obd.	Apr 1847	N.-Amer	838635
Schoettle, Wilhelm	27 Sep 1849	Oberndorf	Obd.	Nov 1868	N.-Amer	838635
Schoettle, Wilhelm Gottlieb	1 Dec 1846	Merklingen	Leon.	Jul 1866	N.-Amer	837959
Schoffer, Heinrich	21 Aug 1847	Kirchheim	Krch.	Jul 1856	N.-Amer	835940
Scholder, Christian Gottlieb	19 Jan 1838	Alpirsbach	Obd.	Dec 1852	N.-Amer	838630
Scholder, Emma	28 Jun 1836	Alpirsbach	Obd.	Jul 1863	Hesse	838630
Scholder, Friedrich	7 May 1833	Alpirsbach	Obd.	Jul 1853	N.-Amer	838630
Scholder, Wilhelm	27 Mar 1836	Alpirsbach	Obd.	Feb 1854	N.-Amer	838630
Scholl, Jakob	14 Jan 1839	Muenchingen	Leon.	bef 1867	N.-Amer	837961

| Name | | Birth | | Emigration | | | Film |
Last	First	Date	Place	O'amt	Appl. Date	Dest.	Number
Scholl, Johann Georg		26 Sep 1819	Muenchingen	Leon.	bef 1855	N.-Amer	837961
Scholl, Maria Catharina		15 Dec 1804	Ditzingen	Leon.	Jan 1827	N.-Amer	835788
Scholtz, Leonhard		12 Sep 1849	Sulpach	Krch.	Sep 1869	N.-Amer	835949
Scholz, Friedrich Wilhelm		6 Jun 1870	Oetlingen	Krch.	Aug 1884	N.-Amer	548403
Scholz, Johann		16 Oct 1831	Reutlingen	Rtl.	Jan 1870	N.-Amer	841057
Schopf, Anna Maria Philipp.		29 Jan 1873	Gutenberg	Krch.	Apr 1882	N.-Amer	548403
Schopf, Caroline		2 Jul 1835	Heimerdingen	Leon.	May 1854	N.-Amer	837954
Schopf, Gottlieb Friedrich		24 Jan 1845	Heimerdingen	Leon.	Apr 1864	N.-Amer	837954
Schopf, Jakob			Muenchingen	Leon.	Feb 1852	N.-Amer	837961
Schopf, Jakob Friedrich		26 Feb 1871	Ditzingen	Leon.	Jun 1886	Africa	835788
Schopf, Jakob Friedrich		29 Apr 1837	Heimerdingen	Leon.	Jul 1855	N.-Amer	837954
Schopf, Johannes		12 Jan 1815	Muenchingen	Leon.	Nov 1851	N.-Amer	837961
Schopf, Katharina Margar. & C		6 Mar 1807	Schoeckingen	Leon.	Apr 1833	Rus-Pol	837964
Schopf, Maria Catharina		4 Mar 1841	Muenchingen	Leon.	Dec 1870	Switz.	837961
Schopf, Maria Katharina		31 Mar 1851	Gerlingen	Leon.	Mar 1873	N.-Amer	837953
Schorpf, Anna (wife)			Altenstadt-Gsl.	Gsl.	Aug 1853	N.-Amer	572041
Schorpf, Carl Friedrich			Altenstadt-Gsl.	Gsl.	Aug 1853	N.-Amer	572041
Schorpf, Samuel & F			Altenstadt-Gsl.	Gsl.	Aug 1853	N.-Amer	572041
Schott, Barbara		27 Jul 1849	Bissingen	Krch.	Apr 1870	N.-Amer	835943
Schott, Carl Franz		25 Nov 1837	Kirchheim	Krch.	Feb 1857	N.-Amer	835940
Schott, Carolina Friederike		13 Oct 1856	Leonberg	Leon.	Mar 1874	N.-Amer	835787
Schott, Catharina (wife)		23 Nov 1812	Hochdorf	Krch.	Jan 1854	N.-Amer	835945
Schott, Christian Friedrich			Hemmingen	Leon.	bef 1849	N.-Amer	837956
Schott, Christiane		26 Mar 1854	Oberlenningen	Krch.	Aug 1869	N.-Amer	835947
Schott, Christoph (wid.) & F		14 Mar 1819	Oberlenningen	Krch.	Aug 1869	N.-Amer	835947
Schott, Ernst Gottlieb		6 Feb 1847	Kirchheim	Krch.	May 1867	N.-Amer	835941
Schott, Johannes		1 Nov 1840	Hochdorf	Krch.	Jan 1854	N.-Amer	835945
Schott, Johannes		22 Sep 1849	Feldstetten/Muen.	Krch.	Sep 1869	N.-Amer	835943
Schott, Wilhelm & F		29 Jun 1811	Hochdorf	Krch.	Jan 1854	N.-Amer	835945
Schott, Wilhelm Gottfried		2 Feb 1838	Hochdorf	Krch.	Mar 1856	N.-Amer	835945
Schott, Wilhelmine Catharine		20 Jun 1851	Hochdorf	Krch.	Jan 1854	N.-Amer	835945
Schraag, Christian			Schoeckingen	Leon.	bef 1837	N.-Amer	837964
Schraag, Georg Wilhelm		18 Dec 1816	Schoeckingen	Leon.	bef 1844	N.-Amer	837964
Schrade, Adolf		10 Aug 1866	Oetlingen	Krch.	Sep 1881	N.-Amer	548403
Schrade, Anna Maria		14 Aug 1857	Willmandingen	Rtl.	Mar 1860	N.-Amer	841057
Schrade, Anna Maria (wife)		30 Mar 1834	Willmandingen	Rtl.	Mar 1860	N.-Amer	841057
Schrade, Catharina		13 Jul 1850	Willmandingen	Rtl.	Mar 1860	N.-Amer	841057
Schrade, Elisabetha Margar.		10 Apr 1848	Thalheim	Rtl.	Aug 1864	N.-Amer	841055
Schrade, Gottfried		6 Feb 1865	Oetlingen	Krch.	Mar 1881	N.-Amer	548403
Schrade, Johannes & F		23 Jan 1823	Willmandingen	Rtl.	Mar 1860	N.-Amer	841057
Schrade, Karl Wilhelm		7 Sep 1854	Oetlingen	Krch.	May 1878	Holland	835948
Schrade, Katharina		10 Jun 1852	Thalheim	Rtl.	Aug 1864	N.-Amer	841055
Schrade, Rosina Magdalena		24 Sep 1835	Willmandingen	Rtl.	Feb 1861	Switz.	841057
Schradin, Carl Julius		22 Oct 1841	Reutlingen	Rtl.	Feb 1861	N.-Amer	841057
Schradin, Johannes		24 Jun 1847	Reutlingen	Rtl.	Jul 1867	N.-Amer	841057
Schraft, Karl Wilhelm		1 Aug 1869	Garrweiler/Nag.	Krch.	May 1886	N.-Amer	548403
Schraft, Karl Wilhelm		1 Aug 1869	Dettingen	Krch.	Apr 1886	N.-Amer	835944
Schrag, Georg		28 May 1834	Hofstett-Emerbuch	Gsl.	Apr 1854	N.-Amer	572042
Schrag, Theodorus		1 Oct 1835	Hofstett-Emerbuch	Gsl.	Apr 1854	N.-Amer	572042
Schramm, Amalie Sophie		15 Jul 1835	Aichelberg	Krch.	Jul 1888	N.-Amer	835943

Schray, Wilhelmine	9 Jul 1881	Alpirsbach	Obd.	Nov 1859	Switz.	838630
Schrayshuen, Chr. Friedrich	7 Nov 1833	Moensheim	Leon.	Nov 1853	N.-Amer	837960
Schreiner, Felix & F		Aichhalden	Obd.	May 1817	N.-Amer	838629
Schrenk, Carl	19 Apr 1850	Hoefingen	Leon.	Oct 1861	Hesse	837957
Schrenk, Frisderike Louise	16 Apr 1852	Hoefingen	Leon.	Oct 1861	Hesse	837957
Schrenk, Gottfried	14 Sep 1823	Hoefingen	Leon.	Aug 1862	N.-Amer	837957
Schrenk, Jacob & F		Hoefingen	Leon.	Oct 1861	Hesse	837957
Schrenk, Jacob Friedrich & W		Hoefingen	Leon.	Feb 1851	N.-Amer	837957
Schrenk, Johann David	29 Oct 1857	Hoefingen	Leon.	Mar 1882	N.-Amer	837957
Schrenk, Maria Barbar (wife)		Hoefingen	Leon.	Oct 1861	Hesse	837957
Schrenk, Sophie	1 Mar 1832	Hoefingen	Leon.	bef 1861	Switz.	837957
Schrenk, Sophie Auguste (wife)		Hoefingen	Leon.	Feb 1851	N.-Amer	837957
Schrenk. Martin Friedrich	2 Aug 1833	Hoefingen	Leon.	Oct 1861	Russia	837957
Schuber, Catharina (wife)		Malmsheim	Leon.	Jan 1852	N.-Amer	837958
Schuber, Georg Michael & F		Malmsheim	Leon.	Jan 1852	N.-Amer	837958
Schuber, Johannes		Malmsheim	Leon.	Jan 1852	N.-Amer	837958
Schuele, Catharina		Merklingen	Leon.	Mar 1868	N.-Amer	837959
Schuele, Johannes		Merklingen	Leon.	bef 1833	Switz.	837959
Schuele, Karl	22 yrs.	Geislingen	Gsl.	Aug 1853	N.-Amer	572041
Schuele, Karl Wilhelm		Merklingen	Leon.	Aug 1871	N.-Amer	837959
Schuele, Maria Christine		Merklingen	Leon.	Sep 1868	Bavaria	837959
Schuessler, Wilhelm	25 May 1849	Wannweil	Rtl.	May 1867	N.-Amer	841057
Schuetz, David	24 Aug 1842	Weil der Stadt	Leon.	Oct 1859	N.-Amer	837966
Schuez, Carl Friedrich Chr.	7 Oct 1861	Herrenberg	Herr.	Feb 1886	N.-Amer	834629
Schuez, Johann Georg	21 Aug 1845	Hildrizhausen	Herr.	Jul 1865	N.-Amer	834631
Schule, Adolf	31 Oct 1832	Kirchheim	Krch.	1853	N.-Amer	835940
Schuler, Andreas	30 Aug 1827	Roetenbach	Obd.	Nov 1853	N.-Amer	838636
Schuler, Friedrich	12 Jan 1847	Moensheim	Leon.	bef 1867	N.-Amer	837960
Schuler, Gotthilf Eduard	18 May 1846	Reutlingen	Rtl.	Nov 1866	N.-Amer	841057
Schuler, Gottlieb Friedrich	2 Mar 1801	Heimsheim	Leon.	bef 1826	Holland	837955
Schuler, Heinrika	3 Mar 1821	Moensheim	Leon.	Mar 1831	N.-Amer	837960
Schuler, Heinrika (wife)	48 yrs.	Moensheim	Leon.	Mar 1831	N.-Amer	837960
Schuler, Johann Conrad	20 Mar 1834	Muenchingen	Leon.	Apr 1853	N.-Amer	837961
Schuler, Leonhardt & F	41 yrs.	Moensheim	Leon.	Mar 1831	N.-Amer	837960
Schuler, Michael		Schoenbronn	Obd.	Feb 1859	Austria	838637
Schuler, Regina Ernestina	13 Oct 1815	Moensheim	Leon.	Mar 1831	N.-Amer	837960
Schulerm, Johannes	2 Jun 1848	Geislingen	Gsl.	Apr 1866	N.-Amer	572045
Schult, Johannes	10 May 1822	Schopfloch	Krch.	bef 1859	N.-Amer	835949
Schultes, Jakob		Wannweil	Rtl.	May 1832	N.-Amer	841051
Schulz, Isedor	30 Dec 1853	Westerheim	Gsl.	Feb 1872	N.-Amer	572047
Schulz, Matthaeus	21 Sep 1837	Westerheim	Gsl.	Jul 1857	N.-Amer	572043
Schulz, Stephan	22 May 1826	Westerheim	Gsl.	Feb 1854	N.-Amer	572042
Schulz, Thimotheus	20 Jan 1850	Westerheim	Gsl.	Mar 1867	N.-Amer	572046
Schumacher, Andreas	27 Nov 1840	Epfendorf	Obd.	Oct 1847	N.-Amer	838632
Schumacher, Apolonia	30 Jan 1810	Epfendorf	Obd.	Aug 1817	N.-Amer	838629
Schumacher, Christian	15 Nov 1807	Epfendorf	Obd.	Aug 1817	N.-Amer	838629
Schumacher, Christian	15 Dec 1836	Epfendorf	Obd.	Oct 1847	N.-Amer	838632
Schumacher, Eva	24 Dec 1842	Epfendorf	Obd.	Oct 1847	N.-Amer	838632
Schumacher, Fidelis & F		Epfendorf	Obd.	Aug 1817	N.-Amer	838629
Schumacher, Georg	12 Feb 1835	Weilheim	Krch.	1852	N.-Amer	548403

Name		Birth		Emigration			Film
Last	First	Date	Place	O'amt	Appl. Date	Dest.	Number
Schumacher, Heinrich Conrad		28 Feb 1825	Weilheim	Krch.	May 1867	N.-Amer	835950
Schumacher, Johann		12 Feb 1835	Weilheim	Krch.	bef 1880	N.-Amer	835774
Schumacher, Johann Georg			Weilheim	Krch.	1854	N.-Amer	835949
Schumacher, Johann Jakob		9 Jul 1932	Dettingen	Krch.	1852	N.-Amer	835944
Schumacher, Johannes		30 Nov 1830	Weilheim	Krch.	Mar 1857	N.-Amer	835949
Schumacher, Joseph		7 Feb 1814	Epfendorf	Obd.	Aug 1817	N.-Amer	838629
Schumacher, Kristian & F		15 Nov 1807	Epfendorf	Obd.	Oct 1847	N.-Amer	838632
Schumacher, Maria		8 Sep 1816	Epfendorf	Obd.	Aug 1817	N.-Amer	838629
Schumacher, Maria Anna (wife)			Epfendorf	Obd.	Oct 1847	N.-Amer	838632
Schumacher, Michael		24 Sep 1811	Epfendorf	Obd.	Aug 1817	N.-Amer	838629
Schumacher, Puis		10 Jul 1835	Epfendorf	Obd.	Oct 1847	N.-Amer	838632
Schumacher, Rupertus		20 Mar 1846	Epfendorf	Obd.	Oct 1847	N.-Amer	838632
Schumacher, Therese (wife)			Epfendorf	Obd.	Aug 1817	N.-Amer	838629
Schumann, Georg		17 Jan 1821	Hepsisau	Krch.	May 1846	N.-Amer	835945
Schumann, Johann Carl		2 Jan 1848	Hepsisau	Krch.	Apr 1867	N.-Amer	835945
Schumann, Johannes		23 Aug 1865	Hepsisau	Krch.	Jun 1882	N.-Amer	548403
Schumann, Johannes		23 Aug 1868	Hepsisau	Krch.	Jun 1882	N.-Amer	835945
Schumann, Johannes		19 yrs.	Hepsisau	Krch.	May 1863	N.-Amer	835945
Schumann, Magdalena		5 Dec 1832	Hepsisau	Krch.	1852	N.-Amer	835945
Schumann, Wilhelm		29 Aug 1867	Hepsisau	Krch.	Apr 1884	N.-Amer	835945
Schunter, Willibald			Donzdorf	Gsl.	bef 1851	N.-Amer	577788
Schurr, Agnes		12 Sep 1851	Gingen	Gsl.	Jul 1854	N.-Amer	572042
Schurr, Andreas & F			Geislingen	Gsl.	Jul 1851	N.-Amer	577788
Schurr, Barbara			Sulpach	Krch.	1851	N.-Amer	835949
Schurr, Carl August & F		17 Oct 1857	Notzingen	Krch.	Jan 1884	N.-Amer	835947
Schurr, Caroline Friederike			Geislingen	Gsl.	Jul 1851	N.-Amer	577788
Schurr, Caroline Friederike		5 Jul 1859	Notzingen	Krch.	Jan 1884	N.-Amer	835947
Schurr, Catharina			Geislingen	Gsl.	Jul 1851	N.-Amer	577788
Schurr, Catharina			Rosswaelden	Krch.	bef 1867	N.-Amer	835940
Schurr, Christian		28 May 1849	Sulpach	Krch.	May 1869	N.-Amer	835949
Schurr, Christina			Geislingen	Gsl.	Jul 1851	N.-Amer	577788
Schurr, Clara Frida		9 Mar 1881	Basel/Switz.	Krch.	Jan 1884	N.-Amer	835947
Schurr, Clara Frieda		9 Mar 1881	Notzingen	Krch.	Jan 1884	N.-Amer	548403
Schurr, Emilie Caroline		13 Feb 1882	Notzingen	Krch.	Jan 1884	N.-Amer	835947
Schurr, Johann Georg		15 Sep 1861	Sulpach	Krch.	Feb 1876	N.-Amer	835949
Schurr, Julius		25 yrs.	Reutlingen	Rtl.	Sep 1879	N.-Amer	841051
Schurr, Karl August & F		17 Oct 1857	Notzingen	Krch.	Jan 1884	N.-Amer	548403
Schurr, Karoline Fried. (wife)		5 Jul 1859	Notzingen	Krch.	Jan 1884	N.-Amer	548403
Schurr, Leonhard		26 Nov 1816	Gingen	Gsl.	bef 1854	N.-Amer	572042
Schurr, Leonhardt		27 Feb 1848	Gingen	Gsl.	Jul 1854	N.-Amer	572042
Schurr, Ludwig		17 Dec 1841	Sulpach	Krch.	Jan 1864	N.-Amer	835949
Schurr, Lukas		6 Nov 1841	Gingen	Gsl.	Mar 1867	N.-Amer	572046
Schurr, Margaretha		27 Sep 1849	Gingen	Gsl.	Jul 1854	N.-Amer	572042
Schurr, Margaretha & F		20 Dec 1811	Gingen	Gsl.	Jul 1854	N.-Amer	572042
Schurr, Maria (wife)			Geislingen	Gsl.	Jul 1851	N.-Amer	577788
Schurr, Maria Magdalena			Geislingen	Gsl.	Jul 1851	N.-Amer	577788
Schurr, Martin		9 Mar 1846	Gingen	Gsl.	Jul 1854	N.-Amer	572042
Schurtenburger, Carl		19 Nov 1842	Schramberg	Obd.	Dec 1860	N.-Amer	838636
Schuster, Andreas & W		28 yrs.	Moensheim	Leon.	Apr 1831	Russia	837960
Schuster, Christina Dor. (wife)		46 yrs.	Moensheim	Leon.	Apr 1831	Russia	837960

Schuster, Eva Barbara	28 Oct 1812	Merklingen	Leon.	1851	N.-Amer	837959
Schuster, Israel & W	39 yrs.	Moensheim	Leon.	Mar 1830	N.-Amer	837960
Schuster, Johann Michael	27 Mar 1827	Merklingen	Leon.	Sep 1868	N.-Amer	837959
Schuster, Johanna (wife)	30 yrs.	Moensheim	Leon.	Mar 1830	N.-Amer	837960
Schuster, Johanna Frieder. & C	33 yrs.	Merklingen	Leon.	Sep 1846	N.-Amer	837959
Schuster, Johanna Friederike	7 yrs.	Merklingen	Leon.	Sep 1846	N.-Amer	837959
Schuster, Karl Ludw. Gottfr.	8 Aug 1866	Leonberg	Leon.	Mar 1882	N.-Amer	835787
Schuster, Louise	3 yrs.	Merklingen	Leon.	Sep 1846	N.-Amer	837959
Schuwerk, Katharina	10 Feb 1834	Alt Oberndorf	Obd.	May 1869	Switz.	838631
Schwab, Andreas	3 Jul 1819	Alpirsbach	Obd.	Sep 1851	Prussia	838630
Schwab, Andreas	27 yrs.	Bach-Altenberg	Obd.	1854	N.-Amer	838631
Schwab, Anna Maria	13 yrs.	Betzweiler	Obd.	Sep 1856	N.-Amer	838631
Schwab, Barbara	12 Sep 1833	Betzweiler	Obd.	Oct 1854	N.-Amer	838631
Schwab, Christina	18 Oct 1831	Betzweiler	Obd.	Oct 1854	N.-Amer	838631
Schwab, Jakob	18 Sep 1849	Fluorn	Obd.	Dec 1869	N.-Amer	838632
Schwab, Johann Georg	27 May 1834	Bochingen	Obd.	Aug 1853	N.-Amer	838632
Schwab, Johanna	14 May 1833	Leonberg	Leon.	Mar 1854	N.-Amer	835786
Schwab, Julius Albert	18 Mar 1856	Leonberg	Leon.	Sep 1872	N.-Amer	835787
Schwab, Marie Wilhelmine & C	25 Oct 1825	Leonberg	Leon.	Mar 1854	N.-Amer	835786
Schwaegler, Johannes	6 Dec 1831	Bondorf	Herr.	1869	Switz.	834630
Schwaemle, Christiane		Fuenfbronn	Nag.	Jul 1852	N.-Amer	838488
Schwahr, Maria	27 Feb 1844	Grosssuessen	Gsl.	May 1869	N.-Amer	572047
Schwank, Barbara	13 Jul 1848	Dettingen	Krch.	May 1867	N.-Amer	835944
Schwank, Johann Georg	26 Apr 1850	Dettingen	Krch.	May 1869	N.-Amer	835944
Schwanz, Sibilla	26 Mar 1839	Peterzell	Obd.	Apr 1862	N.-Amer	838635
Schwartz, Christine Margar.		Hirschlanden	Leon.	bef 1856	N.-Amer	837956
Schwarz, Agnes	2 Dec 1806	Heimerdingen	Leon.	Apr 1831	N.-Amer	837954
Schwarz, Andreas		Peterzell	Obd.	Aug 1854	N.-Amer	838635
Schwarz, Andreas	24 Oct 1840	Heimerdingen	Leon.	May 1854	N.-Amer	837954
Schwarz, Anna Katharina	9 Apr 1822	Schoeckingen	Leon.	Apr 1833	Rus-Pol	837964
Schwarz, Anna Maria (wife)	6 May 1777	Heimerdingen	Leon.	Apr 1831	N.-Amer	837954
Schwarz, Barbara	24 Aug 1829	Weissenstein	Gsl.	Mar 1854	N.-Amer	572042
Schwarz, Barbara (wife)		Muenchingen	Leon.	Aug 1853	N.-Amer	837961
Schwarz, Carl Adolf Gottf. & F	11 Jun 1831	Grosssuessen	Gsl.	Apr 1880	N.-Amer	572048
Schwarz, Carl Albert		Augsburg/Bav.	Gsl.	Apr 1880	N.-Amer	572048
Schwarz, Carl Ernst	6 Mar 1845	Oberlenningen	Krch.	Sep 1865	N.-Amer	835947
Schwarz, Carl Friedrich	22 Mar 1851	Muenchingen	Leon.	Aug 1853	N.-Amer	837961
Schwarz, Carl Friedrich	10 Mar 1838	Kornwestheim	Leon.	Apr 1839	Russia	837954
Schwarz, Carl Joseph & F		Muenchingen	Leon.	Aug 1853	N.-Amer	837961
Schwarz, Carolina	25 Apr 1805	Heimerdingen	Leon.	Apr 1831	N.-Amer	837954
Schwarz, Caroline	16 Feb 1853	Muenchingen	Leon.	Oct 1853	N.-Amer	837961
Schwarz, Caroline	26 Jan 1826	Schoeckingen	Leon.	Apr 1833	Rus-Pol	837964
Schwarz, Caroline	4 Apr 1843	Heimerdingen	Leon.	May 1854	N.-Amer	837954
Schwarz, Caspar	17 Dec 1838	Winzeln	Obd.	Nov 1853	N.-Amer	841016
Schwarz, Catharina	9 Oct 1845	Heimerdingen	Leon.	May 1854	N.-Amer	837954
Schwarz, Catharina & C	13 Apr 1798	Rutesheim	Leon.	Apr 1830	N.-Amer	837964
Schwarz, Catharina Margaretha	20 Mar 1831	Kornwestheim	Leon.	Apr 1839	Russia	837954
Schwarz, Catharine (wife)		Muenchingen	Leon.	Oct 1853	N.-Amer	837961
Schwarz, Christian	12 Sep 1831	Schoeckingen	Leon.	Apr 1833	Rus-Pol	837964
Schwarz, Christian & F		Muenchingen	Leon.	Oct 1853	N.-Amer	837961

Name		Birth		Emigration			Film
Last	First	Date	Place	O'amt	Appl. Date	Dest.	Number
Schwarz, Christian Franz		29 Jan 1867	Weilheim	Krch.	Feb 1881	N.-Amer	548403
Schwarz, Christian Friedrich		5 Feb 1830	Wimsheim	Loen.	Mar 1869	N.-Amer	837967
Schwarz, Christian Friedrich		5 Aug 1839	Heimerdingen	Leon.	May 1854	N.-Amer	837954
Schwarz, Christiana		25 Dec 1821	Heimerdingen	Leon.	Apr 1831	N.-Amer	837954
Schwarz, Christiane		4 Feb 1849	Muenchingen	Leon.	Aug 1853	N.-Amer	837961
Schwarz, Christiane			Weilheim	Krch.	bef 1864	N.-Amer	835940
Schwarz, Christiane Jacobine		22 Nov 1825	Kornwestheim	Leon.	Apr 1839	Russia	837954
Schwarz, Christina		25 Dec 1851	Weilheim	Krch.	Apr 1865	N.-Amer	835950
Schwarz, Christina Barba. (wife)			Kornwestheim	Leon.	Apr 1839	Russia	837954
Schwarz, Christina Margaretha		24 Dec 1797	Heimerdingen	Leon.	bef 1818	N.-Amer	837954
Schwarz, Christine		28 Aug 1834	Muenchingen	Leon.	Apr 1863	Prussia	837961
Schwarz, Christine Barbara		15 Dec 1847	Muenchingen	Leon.	Aug 1853	N.-Amer	837961
Schwarz, Christoph		24 Jun 1855	Oberlenningen	Krch.	Apr 1872	N.-Amer	835947
Schwarz, Eduard Wilhelm		4 Jul 1843	Pfullingen	Rtl.	Nov 1863	London	841057
Schwarz, Emil Jacob			Augsburg/Bav.	Gsl.	Apr 1880	N.-Amer	572048
Schwarz, Franziskus			Winzeln	Obd.	Jun 1860	N.-Amer	841016
Schwarz, Friederike		7 Dec 1828	Schoeckingen	Leon.	Apr 1833	Rus-Pol	837964
Schwarz, Friedrich			Wimsheim	Loen.	Jun 1851	N.-Amer	837967
Schwarz, Georg		21 Apr 1825	Heimerdingen	Leon.	bef 1854	Switz.	837954
Schwarz, Gottlieb & F			Schoeckingen	Leon.	Apr 1833	Rus-Pol	837964
Schwarz, Gottlieb Friederich		19 Nov 1824	Schoeckingen	Leon.	Apr 1833	Rus-Pol	837964
Schwarz, Gottlob		19 Mar 1862	Oberlenningen	Krch.	Jan 1879	N.-Amer	835947
Schwarz, Gustav Friedrich		18 Jul 1822	Grosssuessen	Gsl.	Sep 1854	Bavaria	572042
Schwarz, Jacobina		15 Nov 1811	Heimerdingen	Leon.	Apr 1831	N.-Amer	837954
Schwarz, Jakob Friedrich		3 Aug 1827	Schoeckingen	Leon.	Apr 1833	Rus-Pol	837964
Schwarz, Jakob Friedrich		31 Mar 1824	Kornwestheim	Leon.	Apr 1839	Russia	837954
Schwarz, Johann			Aichhalden	Obd.	bef 1860	N.-Amer	838629
Schwarz, Johann Friedrich		28 Jun 1842	Eltingen	Leon.	Mar 1851	N.-Amer	835789
Schwarz, Johann Georg		18 yrs.	Fluorn	Obd.	Feb 1861	N.-Amer	838632
Schwarz, Johann Georg		23 Feb 1846	Gaertringen	Herr.	Jul 1866	N.-Amer	834630
Schwarz, Johann Georg		23 yrs.	Muenchingen	Leon.	Jan 1855	N.-Amer	837961
Schwarz, Johann Georg			Muenchingen	Leon.	Jan 1854	N.-Amer	837961
Schwarz, Johann Georg		2 Dec 1815	Heimerdingen	Leon.	Apr 1831	N.-Amer	837954
Schwarz, Johann Georg			Pfullingen	Rtl.	May 1828	N.-Amer	841051
Schwarz, Johann Georg		26 Aug 1850	Weilheim	Krch.	Dec 1866	N.-Amer	835950
Schwarz, Johann Hermann		24 Jun 1848	Muenchingen	Leon.	Aug 1867	N.-Amer	837961
Schwarz, Johann Jakob		12 Oct 1852	Muenchingen	Leon.	Aug 1853	N.-Amer	837961
Schwarz, Johann Ludwig		23 Dec 1863	Weiheim	Krch.	Apr 1882	N.-Amer	548403
Schwarz, Johann Martin		24 Aug 1848	Pfullingen	Rtl.	Aug 1865	N.-Amer	841057
Schwarz, Johann Ulrich		17 Sep 1836	Kornwestheim	Leon.	Apr 1839	Russia	837954
Schwarz, Johannes			Weilheim	Krch.	May 1753	N.-Amer	550804
Schwarz, Johannes		24 Apr 1830	Oberlenningen	Krch.	Dec 1868	N.-Amer	835940
Schwarz, Johannes & F		7 Sep 1777	Heimerdingen	Leon.	Apr 1831	N.-Amer	837954
Schwarz, Katharina			Rutesheim	Leon.	Jul 1866	Switz.	837964
Schwarz, Kunigunde & F			Aichhalden	Obd.	Dec 1860	N.-Amer	838629
Schwarz, Magdalena		4 Aug 1827	Rutesheim	Leon.	Apr 1830	N.-Amer	837964
Schwarz, Maria Agnes		7 Sep 1755	Heimerdingen	Leon.	Apr 1831	N.-Amer	837954
Schwarz, Maria Christine		10 Sep 1823	Schoeckingen	Leon.	Apr 1833	Rus-Pol	837964
Schwarz, Mathaeus		21 Sep 1822	Heimerdingen	Leon.	Jun 1853	N.-Amer	837954
Schwarz, Mathaeus		33 yrs.	Heimerdingen	Leon.	May 1851	N.-Amer	837954

Schwarz, Michael	6 Jun 1822	Muenchingen	Leon.	1853	N.-Amer	837961
Schwarz, Sibyla	18 Jun 1808	Heimerdingen	Leon.	Apr 1831	N.-Amer	837954
Schwarz, Sophie Barbara	27 Jan 1833	Kornwestheim	Leon.	Apr 1839	Russia	837954
Schwarz, Tobias		Rutesheim	Leon.	1847	Switz.	837964
Schwarz, Ulrich & F		Heimerdingen	Leon.	Apr 1839	Russia	837954
Schwarz, Valentin	12 Feb 1833	Winzeln	Obd.	Nov 1853	N.-Amer	841016
Schwarz, Wilhelm	3 May 1876	Weilheim	Krch.	Apr 1890	N.-Amer	835774
Schwarz, Wilhelm Gustav	16 May 1847	Heimerdingen	Leon.	Mar 1867	N.-Amer	837954
Schwarz, Wilhelmine	17 Apr 1848	Oberlenningen	Krch.	Sep 1865	N.-Amer	835947
Schwarzenberger, Ludwig		Hemmingen	Leon.	Apr 1825	N.-Amer	837956
Schwarzkopf, Barbara		Nenningen	Gsl.	Dec 1852	N.-Amer	572041
Schwarzkopf, Bernhardt & F		Nenningen	Gsl.	Dec 1852	N.-Amer	572041
Schwarzkopf, Bernhart		Nenningen	Gsl.	Dec 1852	N.-Amer	572041
Schwarzkopf, Johann Ludwig	24 Mar 1835	Weissenstein	Gsl.	Jun 1854	N.-Amer	572042
Schwarzkopf, Maria		Nenningen	Gsl.	Dec 1852	N.-Amer	572041
Schwarzkopf, Maria & C		Nenningen	Gsl.	Dec 1852	N.-Amer	572041
Schwarzkopf, Marianna		Nenningen	Gsl.	Dec 1852	N.-Amer	572041
Schwarzkopf, Paulus		Nenningen	Gsl.	Dec 1852	N.-Amer	572041
Schwarzkopf, Petrus		Nenningen	Gsl.	Dec 1852	N.-Amer	572041
Schwarzkopf, Rosina		Nenningen	Gsl.	Dec 1852	N.-Amer	572041
Schwarzkopf, Wilhelm		Nenningen	Gsl.	Dec 1852	N.-Amer	572041
Schwarzmaier, Barbara (wife)		Friolzheim	Leon.	Oct 1865	N.-Amer	835791
Schwarzmaier, Carl Michael		Affstaett	Herr.	May 1862	N.-Amer	834630
Schwarzmaier, Friedrich	6 yrs.	Friolzheim	Leon.	Oct 1865	N.-Amer	835791
Schwarzmaier, Georg & F		Friolzheim	Leon.	Oct 1865	N.-Amer	835791
Schwarzmaier, Gottlieb	infant	Friolzheim	Leon.	Oct 1865	N.-Amer	835791
Schwarzmaier, Heinrike	3 yrs.	Friolzheim	Leon.	Oct 1865	N.-Amer	835791
Schwarzmaier, Johannes	9 yrs.	Friolzheim	Leon.	Oct 1865	N.-Amer	835791
Schwarzmann, Christiana	18 Jan 1830	Neidlingen	Krch.	Jun 1862	N.-Amer	835946
Schwarzmann, Johann Adam	28 Dec 1840	Ochsenwang	Krch.	Mar 1864	N.-Amer	835947
Schwegler, Elias	1 Jan 1862	Schalkstetten	Gsl.	Jun 1880	N.-Amer	572048
Schwegler, Friedrich	20 May 1805	Heimerdingen	Leon.	Feb 1854	N.-Amer	837954
Schwegler, Friedrich	30 Mar 1805	Heimerdingen	Leon.	Feb 1853	N.-Amer	837954
Schweiger, – (wid.) & F		Westerheim	Gsl.	Mar 1852	N.-Amer	572041
Schweiger, August	17 yrs.	Westerheim	Gsl.	Mar 1852	N.-Amer	572041
Schweiger, Stefan	10 yrs.	Westerheim	Gsl.	Mar 1852	N.-Amer	572041
Schweiger, Theresia	15 yrs.	Westerheim	Gsl.	Mar 1852	N.-Amer	572041
Schweigert, Euphrosine		Unterboehringen	Gsl.	Aug 1853	N.-Amer	572041
Schweikert, Albert	31 Dec 1836	Winzeln	Obd.	Mar 1846	N.-Amer	841016
Schweikert, Andreas & F		Winzeln	Obd.	May 1817	N.-Amer	841016
Schweikert, Carl	19 Feb 1835	Winzeln	Obd.	Mar 1846	N.-Amer	841016
Schweikert, Caspar	11 Jan 1826	Winzeln	Obd.	bef 1855	N.-Amer	841016
Schweikert, Emilia	2 Oct 1842	Winzeln	Obd.	Mar 1846	N.-Amer	841016
Schweikert, Engelbert	9 Oct 1845	Winzeln	Obd.	Mar 1846	N.-Amer	841016
Schweikert, Eva	24 Dec 1842	Winzeln	Obd.	Mar 1865	France	841016
Schweikert, Gebhard	23 Aug 1845	Winzeln	Obd.	Oct 1865	N.-Amer	841016
Schweikert, Georg	9 Apr 1832	Winzeln	Obd.	Apr 1851	N.-Amer	841016
Schweikert, Jacob Friedr. & F		Oetlingen	Krch.	Mar 1804	Russia	550804
Schweikert, Johannes & F	1 Feb 1805	Winzeln	Obd.	Mar 1846	N.-Amer	841016
Schweikert, Josef		Winzeln	Obd.	Mar 1866	N.-Amer	841016

Name		Birth		Emigration			Film
Last	First	Date	Place	O'amt	Appl. Date	Dest.	Number
Schweikert, Justina (wife)			Winzeln	Obd.	Mar 1846	N.-Amer	841016
Schweikert, Konstantin		6 Feb 1849	Winzeln	Obd.	Aug 1868	N.-Amer	841016
Schweikert, Krescenz		5 Mar 1833	Winzeln	Obd.	Mar 1846	N.-Amer	841016
Schweikert, Liberata		22 Aug 1833	Winzeln	Obd.	Mar 1852	N.-Amer	841016
Schweikert, Magdalena			Winzeln	Obd.	Mar 1866	N.-Amer	841016
Schweikert, Maria		30 Jan 1846	Winzeln	Obd.	Nov 1865	N.-Amer	841016
Schweikert, Maria		1 Nov 1829	Winzeln	Obd.	Mar 1846	N.-Amer	841016
Schweikert, Martina		11 Jun 1829	Winzeln	Obd.	1852	N.-Amer	841016
Schweikert, Martina		22 Feb 1840	Winzeln	Obd.	Mar 1846	N.-Amer	841016
Schweikert, Mathias & F			Winzeln	Obd.	May 1817	N.-Amer	841016
Schweikert, Nothburga & F			Winzeln	Obd.	Oct 1847	N.-Amer	841016
Schweikert, Peter		28 Dec 1823	Winzeln	Obd.	1851	N.-Amer	841016
Schweikert, Reinhold		24 Dec 1849	Winzeln	Obd.	May 1868	N.-Amer	841016
Schweikert, Reinhold		12 Jan 1848	Winzeln	Obd.	Mar 1867	N.-Amer	841016
Schweikert, Sigmund		15 Jan 1842	Beffendorf	Obd.	Oct 1847	N.-Amer	841016
Schweikert, Simon		3 Feb 1841	Winzeln	Obd.	Sep 1859	N.-Amer	841016
Schweikert, Thomas		20 Dec 1831	Winzeln	Obd.	1853	N.-Amer	841016
Schweitzer, Anna Maria		6 yrs.	Muehlhausen	Gsl.	Oct 1853	N.-Amer	572041
Schweitzer, Anna Maria & F		42 yrs.	Muehlhausen	Gsl.	Oct 1853	N.-Amer	572041
Schweitzer, Carl		2 yrs.	Muehlhausen	Gsl.	Oct 1853	N.-Amer	572041
Schweitzer, Georg		13 yrs.	Muehlhausen	Gsl.	Oct 1853	N.-Amer	572041
Schweitzer, Johann Michael		28 Mar 1807	Muenchingen	Leon.	bef 1841	Russia	837961
Schweitzer, Joseph		3 Oct 1831	Deggingen	Gsl.	Jul 1859	N.-Amer	572043
Schweitzer, Maria Anna		31 Dec 1824	Deggingen	Gsl.	Sep 1855	N.-Amer	572043
Schweitzer, Melchior			Muehlhausen	Gsl.	bef 1853	N.-Amer	572041
Schweizer, Anton		2 Sep 1862	Deggingen	Gsl.	Nov 1874	N.-Amer	572048
Schweizer, Barbara		28 yrs.	Geislingen	Gsl.	Feb 1857	N.-Amer	572043
Schweizer, Caspar		22 Sep 1849	Weilheim	Krch.	Apr 1869	N.-Amer	835950
Schweizer, Christian & F			Gerlingen	Leon.	Sep 1854	N.-Amer	837953
Schweizer, Christian Jacob		15 yrs.	Gerlingen	Leon.	Sep 1854	N.-Amer	837953
Schweizer, Christoph			Gerlingen	Leon.	Mar 1855	Austral	837953
Schweizer, Elisabetha		14 Jul 1814	Geislingen	Gsl.	Jun 1854	N.-Amer	572042
Schweizer, Friederike		21 Jul 1830	Leonberg	Leon.	Feb 1850	N.-Amer	835786
Schweizer, Friederike		12 Jan 1852	Heimerdingen	Leon.	Mar 1872	N.-Amer	837954
Schweizer, Friedrich		15 Mar 1837	Geislingen	Gsl.	May 1854	N.-Amer	572042
Schweizer, Friedrich		1811	Leonberg	Leon.	Sep 1857	Austria	835786
Schweizer, Georg Friedrich		4 Jul 1847	Weilheim	Krch.	May 1867	N.-Amer	835950
Schweizer, Gotthilf Friedrich			Eltingen	Leon.	Nov 1866	N.-Amer	835789
Schweizer, Gustav Adolph		2 Jul 1846	Gerlingen	Leon.	Feb 1864	N.-Amer	837953
Schweizer, Helena			Boehmenkirch	Gsl.	Mar 1852	N.-Amer	572041
Schweizer, Jakob			Rutesheim	Leon.	bef 1855	N.-Amer	837964
Schweizer, Johann Georg		19 Jul 1835	Deggingen	Gsl.	Sep 1852	N.-Amer	572042
Schweizer, Johann Georg		11 yrs.	Gerlingen	Leon.	Jun 1818	Hungary	837953
Schweizer, Johann Georg			Berneck	Nag.	Sep 1851	N.-Amer	838488
Schweizer, Johann Heinrich		28 Jan 1833	Eltingen	Leon.	Oct 1866	N.-Amer	835789
Schweizer, Johannes			Hausen a. d. Fils	Gsl.	Mar 1853	N.-Amer	572041
Schweizer, Julie (wife)			Gerlingen	Leon.	Sep 1854	N.-Amer	837953
Schweizer, Karl August		26 Jan 1849	Geislingen	Gsl.	Mar 1854	N.-Amer	572042
Schweizer, Karl Friedrich		26 Jun 1855	Heimerdingen	Leon.	Jan 1872	N.-Amer	837954
Schweizer, Karl Theodor		12 Dec 1859	Wiesensteig	Gsl.	Mar 1880	N.-Amer	572048

Schweizer, Katharina	25 Sep 1835	Geislingen	Gsl.	Jul 1854	N.-Amer	572042
Schweizer, Margaretha	67 yrs.	Geislingen	Gsl.	Sep 1864	N.-Amer	572045
Schweizer, Maria Anna	31 Mar 1845	Boehmenkirch	Gsl.	Jan 1867	N.-Amer	572046
Schweizer, Maximilian	10 Oct 1848	Degginger	Gsl.	Apr 1866	N.-Amer	572045
Schweizer, Otto	23 Dec 1846	Degginger	Gsl.	Apr 1866	N.-Amer	572045
Schweizer, Pauline		Kirchheim	Krch.	bef 1864	N.-Amer	835940
Schweizer, Regina Katharina	25 yrs.	Gerlingen	Leon.	Apr 1863	Prussia	837953
Schweizer, Regine		Kirchheim	Krch.	1868	N.-Amer	835940
Schweizer, Rudolph	14 Apr 1850	Schramberg	Obd.	Jun 1869	N.-Amer	838636
Schweizer, Sophie Pauline	1 yrs.	Gerlingen	Leon.	Sep 1854	N.-Amer	837953
Schweizer, Therese	3 Mar 1826	Leonberg	Leon.	bef 1869	N.-Amer	835787
Schweizer, Thomas		Geislingen	Gsl.	Jan 1854	N.-Amer	572042
Schweizer, Ulrich	24 May 1835	Kuchen	Gsl.	May 1853	N.-Amer	572041
Schwenk, Andreas	8 May 1837	Dornhan	Obd.	Feb 1854	N.-Amer	838638
Schwenk, Barbara (wid.) & F	6 Jan 1801	Bollerberg	Obd.	Feb 1854	N.-Amer	838638
Schwenk, Christian Daniel	11 May 1871	Bissingen	Krch.	Mar 1887	N.-Amer	835943
Schwenk, Christina	3 Jun 1842	Dornhan	Obd.	Feb 1854	N.-Amer	838638
Schwenk, Dorothea	9 Feb 1836	Dornhan	Obd.	Feb 1854	N.-Amer	838638
Schwenk, Georg	26 Jun 1833	Dornhan	Obd.	Sep 1853	N.-Amer	838638
Schwenk, Johannes	9 May 1832	Dornhan	Obd.	Sep 1852	N.-Amer	838638
Schwenk, Matthias	4 Aug 1829	Dornhan	Obd.	Feb 1854	N.-Amer	838638
Schwenk, Michael	10 Feb 1846	Dornhan	Obd.	Feb 1854	N.-Amer	838638
Schwerer, Elisabetha		Harthausen	Obd.	Jun 1870	N.-Amer	838633
Schwerer, Maria		Harthausen	Obd.	Jun 1870	N.-Amer	838633
Schwerer, Maria (wife)		Harthausen	Obd.	Jun 1870	N.-Amer	838633
Schwerer, Mathias & F	26 Feb 1828	Harthausen	Obd.	Jun 1870	N.-Amer	838633
Schwerer, Waldburga		Harthausen	Obd.	Jun 1870	N.-Amer	838633
Schwille, Johann Georg	24 Oct 1846	Pfullingen	Rtl.	Aug 1865	N.-Amer	841057
Schwille, Johannes	22 Nov 1851	Pfullingen	Rtl.	Jan 1869	N.-Amer	841057
Schwille, Karl	9 Dec 1841	Pfullingen	Rtl.	Nov 1860	N.-Amer	841057
Schwindel, Jacob	24 Jun 1850	Hemmingen	Leon.	Jan 1870	N.-Amer	837956
Schwrz, Sebastian Ulrich	30 Dec 1846	Pfullingen	Rtl.	Nov 1866	N.-Amer	841057
Schzeufele, Barbara (wid.) & F		Dettingen	Krch.	Apr 1871	N.-Amer	835944
Seeger, Anna Maria	20 yrs.	Bach-Altenberg	Obd.	Feb 1854	N.-Amer	838631
Seeger, Christian Friedrich	26 Nov 1843	Renningen	Leon.	May 1854	N.-Amer	837963
Seeger, Christiane Katharina	21 Dec 1841	Renningen	Leon.	May 1854	N.-Amer	837963
Seeger, Ernst Gottlob	24 Jun 1840	Renningen	Leon.	May 1854	N.-Amer	837963
Seeger, Johann Friedrich		Renningen	Leon.	bef 1854	N.-Amer	837963
Seeger, Katharina Marg. (wid.) & F		Renningen	Leon.	May 1854	N.-Amer	837963
Seeger, Rosina		Betzweiler	Obd.	Dec 1852	France	838631
Seehofer, Johannes	9 Feb 1851	Donzdorf	Gsl.	May 1875	N.-Amer	572048
Seehofer, Michael	19 yrs.	Donzdorf	Gsl.	Mar 1852	N.-Amer	572041
Seemann, Christian David	31 Mar 1856	Ditzingen	Leon.	Oct 1886	N.-Amer	835788
Seibel, Friedrich Robert	23 Sep 1867	Kirchheim	Krch.	Sep 1882	N.-Amer	548403
Seibold, Johannes	6 yrs.	Grosssuessen	Gsl.	May 1851	N.-Amer	577788
Seibold, Johannes & F	30 yrs.	Grosssuessen	Gsl.	May 1851	N.-Amer	577788
Seibold, Katharina (wife)		Grosssuessen	Gsl.	May 1851	N.-Amer	577788
Seibold, Konrad	2 mon.	Grosssuessen	Gsl.	May 1851	N.-Amer	577788
Seibold, Ludwig & F	14 Sep 1821	Ditzingen	Leon.	1853	N.-Amer	835788
Seidel, Margaretha	8 Nov 1843	Owen	Krch.	bef 1873	N.-Amer	835948

Name		Birth		Emigration			Film
Last	First	Date	Place	O'amt	Appl. Date	Dest.	Number
Seidenspinner, Anna Maria		17 Jun 1850	Korntal	Leon.	Oct 1871	N.-Amer	837957
Seidenspinner, Gottlob Isaak		12 Feb 1853	Korntal	Leon.	Oct 1871	N.-Amer	837957
Seiter, Christoph Gottlob			Wimsheim	Locn.	bef 1854	N.-Amer	837967
Seiter, Rosina Sophie		12 Sep 1838	Leonberg	Leon.	Jul 1861	Switz.	835787
Seitter, Johann Georg			Flacht	Leon.	bef 1865	N.-Amer	835790
Seitter, Johannes		18 Jul 1803	Flacht	Leon.	Apr 1830	N.-Amer	835790
Seitter, Marie Louise			Leonberg	Leon.	Nov 1857	Switz.	835786
Seitz, Adolph		6 Apr 1849	Herrenberg	Herr.	Apr 1866	N.-Amer	834629
Seitz, Albert		14 yrs.	Rutesheim	Leon.	Jun 1853	N.-Amer	837964
Seitz, Crezenz		29 Jul 1850	Boehmenkirch	Gsl.	Sep 1853	N.-Amer	572041
Seitz, Friederike Wilhelmine		29 Dec 1846	Herrenberg	Herr.	bef 1867	N.-Amer	834629
Seitz, Johann			Boehmenkirch	Gsl.	bef 1853	N.-Amer	572041
Seitz, Johannes		11 Jan 1843	Boehmenkirch	Gsl.	Sep 1853	N.-Amer	572041
Seitz, Joseph		24 Oct 1841	Boehmenkirch	Gsl.	Sep 1853	N.-Amer	572041
Seitz, Katharina (wife) & F			Boehmenkirch	Gsl.	Sep 1853	N.-Amer	572041
Seitz, Theresia		24 Apr 1845	Boehmenkirch	Gsl.	Sep 1853	N.-Amer	572041
Seiz, Anna		20 Mar 1848	Leonberg	Leon.	Apr 1869	N.-Amer	835787
Seiz, Friederike		10 Feb 1853	Leonberg	Leon.	Apr 1869	N.-Amer	835787
Seiz, Friederike (wid.) & F			Leonberg	Leon.	Apr 1869	N.-Amer	835787
Seiz, Georg Christoph & F			Pfullingen	Rtl.	Jun 1830	N.-Amer	841051
Seiz, Gottlob		11 Apr 1859	Leonberg	Leon.	Apr 1869	N.-Amer	835787
Seizinger, Christian		19 Mar 1830	Steinenkirch	Gsl.	Apr 1879	Switz.	572048
Sekinger, Elisabetha & C			Winzeln	Obd.	Aug 1859	Switz.	841016
Sekinger, Genovefa			Winzeln	Obd.	Nov 1862	Switz.	841016
Sekinger, Helena (wid.)		6 May 1808	Winzeln	Obd.	Nov 1866	N.-Amer	841016
Sekinger, Johannes		17 yrs.	Aichhalden	Obd.	Dec 1854	N.-Amer	838629
Sekinger, Johannes		21 Dec 1835	Sulgen	Obd.	Sep 1853	N.-Amer	838638
Sekinger, Karl			Winzeln	Obd.	Aug 1859	N.-Amer	841016
Sekinger, Magdalena			Aichhalden	Obd.	Sep 1860	France	838629
Sekinger, Magdalena			Winzeln	Obd.	Aug 1859	N.-Amer	841016
Sekinger, Simon		7 Oct 1842	Winzeln	Obd.	Oct 1865	N.-Amer	841016
Sekler, Johann Klaus & F			Weissenstein	Gsl.	Jan 1854	N.-Amer	573622
Sellner, Albert Christian		20 Mar 1840	Weil im Dorf	Loen.	Apr 1859	N.-Amer	837967
Sellner, Karl		25 Oct 1825	Weil im Dorf	Loen.	Apr 1849	N.-Amer	837967
Sellner, Pauline		17 Jan 1833	Weil im Dorf	Loen.	Oct 1853	N.-Amer	837967
Sellner, Wilhelm Friedrich		1 Mar 1838	Weil im Dorf	Loen.	Sep 1858	N.-Amer	837967
Semmendinger, Christiana & C			Kleinengstingen	Rtl.	Apr 1860	N.-Amer	841057
Semmendinger, Paulina			Kleinengstingen	Rtl.	Apr 1860	N.-Amer	841057
Seng, Johannes			Winzeln	Obd.	Aug 1862	Austria	841016
Seng, Karolina		31 Oct 1843	Winzeln	Obd.	Sep 1865	N.-Amer	841016
Seng, Leopold			Winzeln	Obd.	Feb 1861	N.-Amer	841016
Senner, Jakob Friedrich		28 Jan 1846	Pfullingen	Rtl.	Apr 1864	N.-Amer	841057
Senner, Johannes		12 Feb 1846	Pfullingen	Rtl.	Oct 1866	London	841057
Senner, Louise Heinrike		18 Sep 1848	Pfullingen	Rtl.	Jul 1868	N.-Amer	841057
Sepper, Anna Maria (wife)			Muenchingen	Leon.	Feb 1851	N.-Amer	837961
Sepper, Johann Georg & F			Muenchingen	Leon.	Feb 1851	N.-Amer	837961
Sesso, Heinrich		16 Nov 1842	Reutlingen	Rtl.	bef 1862	N.-Amer	841057
Seubert, Christian Gottlieb		15 Dec 1850	Kirchheim	Krch.	Aug 1868	N.-Amer	835941
Seufer, Anna Regina		14 Mar 1837	Gingen	Gsl.	Jul 1854	N.-Amer	572042
Seybold, Johann Adolf		8 Dec 1843	Hofstett	Gsl.	1857	N.-Amer	572044

Seyfang, Barbara	8 Mar 1827	Aichelberg	Krch.	bef 1857	N.-Amer	835774
Seyfang, Christian Gottlieb		Dettingen	Krch.	Sep 1857	N.-Amer	835944
Seyfang, Christiane	8 Mar 1866	Aichelberg	Krch.	Mar 1886	N.-Amer	548403
Seyfang, Heinrike (wife)	5 Feb 1837	Albershausen	Krch.	Mar 1886	N.-Amer	835943
Seyfang, Johann Georg & F	10 Oct 1837	Aichelberg	Krch.	Mar 1886	N.-Amer	835943
Seyfang, Johannes	24 Jan 1837	Altenstadt-Gsl.	Gsl.	bef 1873	Switz.	572048
Seyfang, Johannes	21 May 1868	Aichelberg	Krch.	Mar 1886	N.-Amer	548403
Seyfang, Stephan	21 Dec 1836	Aichelberg	Krch.	Aug 1855	N.-Amer	835774
Sichler, Johann Evangelist	19 Dec 1837	Rottweil	Rtw.	bef 1870	Switz.	841117
Sichler, Karl Viktor	19 Jan 1843	Rottweil	Rtw.	bef 1870	Switz.	841117
Sickinger, Christian Konrad	6 Dec 1865	Gerlingen	Leon.	Aug 1887	N.-Amer	837953
Sickinger, Jakob		Gerlingen	Leon.	bef 1850	N.-Amer	837953
Sickinger, Karl Friedrich	18 Jan 1871	Heimerdingen	Leon.	Mar 1887	N.-Amer	837954
Siebenhaar, Adam	3 Mar 1822	Reutlingen	Rtl.	Mar 1864	N.-Amer	841057
Siebenhaar, Arduin		Reutlingen	Rtl.	1858	N.-Amer	841057
Sieber, Anna	22 yrs.	Fluorn	Obd.	Apr 1856	N.-Amer	838632
Sieber, Anton & F	37 yrs.	Alt Oberndorf	Obd.	Jun 1852	N.-Amer	838631
Sieber, Johann Georg	15 Apr 1841	Fluorn	Obd.	Jul 1865	N.-Amer	838632
Sieber, Mathias	5 Feb 1849	Fluorn	Obd.	Oct 1869	N.-Amer	838632
Sieber, Waldburga (wife)		Alt Oberndorf	Obd.	Jun 1852	N.-Amer	838631
Sieffermann, Carolina Magdal.		Eltingen	Leon.	Jun 1826	N.-Amer	835789
Sieffermann, Elisabeth Sabina	16 yrs.	Eltingen	Leon.	Jun 1826	N.-Amer	835789
Sieffermann, Friedrich (wid.) & F		Eltingen	Leon.	Jun 1826	N.-Amer	835789
Sieffermann, Johanna Cathar.	19 yrs.	Eltingen	Leon.	Jun 1826	N.-Amer	835789
Sieffermann, Rosina Carolina	17 yrs.	Eltingen	Leon.	Jun 1826	N.-Amer	835789
Siegel, Christian Gottlieb		Hoefingen	Leon.	Nov 1869	N.-Amer	837957
Siegel, Conrad & F		Ditzingen	Leon.	Feb 1829	N.-Amer	835788
Siegel, Franz Gustav	25 Nov 1837	Oberlenningen	Krch.	Dec 1858	N.-Amer	835947
Siegle, Andreas	17 yrs.	Weil der Stadt	Leon.	Sep 1851	N.-Amer	837966
Siegle, Anna Margaretha		Pfullingen	Rtl.	Feb 1832	France	841051
Siegle, Carl	21 yrs.	Ditzingen	Leon.	Jun 1875	N.-Amer	835788
Siegle, Caroline	20 yrs.	Weil der Stadt	Leon.	Sep 1851	N.-Amer	837966
Siegle, Conrad	14 Apr 1837	Ditzingen	Leon.	Jul 1862	N.-Amer	835788
Siegle, Daniel	7 Aug 1842	Ditzingen	Leon.	Jul 1869	N.-Amer	835788
Siegle, Elisabetha	28 yrs.	Weil der Stadt	Leon.	Sep 1851	N.-Amer	837966
Siegle, Ezechiel Ludwig	1 Sep 1832	Ditzingen	Leon.	1851	S.-Amer	835788
Siegle, Friederike	6 yrs.	Ditzingen	Leon.	Mar 1852	N.-Amer	835788
Siegle, Gottfried	infant	Ditzingen	Leon.	Mar 1852	N.-Amer	835788
Siegle, Gottlieb	3 Apr 1823	Ditzingen	Leon.	May 1851	N.-Amer	835788
Siegle, Jakob & F		Ditzingen	Leon.	May 1851	N.-Amer	835788
Siegle, Jakob Friedrich		Ditzingen	Leon.	Oct 1853	N.-Amer	835788
Siegle, Johann Georg	2 Jul 1849	Ditzingen	Leon.	May 1851	N.-Amer	835788
Siegle, Johann Georg & F		Ditzingen	Leon.	Mar 1852	N.-Amer	835788
Siegle, Johann Jakob	7 Jan 1845	Ditzingen	Leon.	May 1851	N.-Amer	835788
Siegle, Johann Michael		Altensteig	Nag.	Jul 1852	N.-Amer	838488
Siegle, Johanna Karoline	3 May 1847	Ditzingen	Leon.	May 1851	N.-Amer	835788
Siegle, Katharina	12 yrs.	Ditzingen	Leon.	Mar 1852	N.-Amer	835788
Siegle, Katharina		Ditzingen	Leon.	bef 1842	Austria	835788
Siegle, Rosina	14 yrs.	Ditzingen	Leon.	Mar 1852	N.-Amer	835788
Siegle, Rosina Dorothea		Ditzingen	Leon.	bef 1868	Austria	835788

Name		Birth		Emigration			Film
Last	First	Date	Place	O'amt	Appl. Date	Dest.	Number
Siegle, Wilhelmine Fried. (wife)		1 Feb 1813	Ditzingen	Leon.	May 1851	N.-Amer	835788
Siegler, Catharina & C		2 Sep 1830	Kirchheim	Krch.	Aug 1868	N.-Amer	835941
Siegler, Christina Sophie		4 Jan 1856	Kirchheim	Krch.	Aug 1868	N.-Amer	835941
Siegmeyer, Carl Friedrich		27 Sep 1828	Gosbach	Gsl.	Sep 1851	N.-Amer	577788
Siehler, Mathaeus			Unterboehringen	Gsl.	Oct 1865	N.-Amer	572045
Sigel, Alexander		7 Feb 1858	Kirchheim	Krch.	Sep 1874	N.-Amer	835942
Sigel, Amalie Bertha		23 Jan 1856	Kirchheim	Krch.	Sep 1874	N.-Amer	835942
Sigel, Anna Margaetha		18 Aug 1831	Weilheim	Krch.	bef 1857	N.-Amer	835949
Sigel, Anna Maria (wife)		21 Mar 1815	Weilheim	Krch.	Jan 1861	N.-Amer	835949
Sigel, Carl Christian		12 Nov 1848	Kirchheim	Krch.	Apr 1867	N.-Amer	835941
Sigel, Carl Heinrich		29 Mar 1844	Weilheim	Krch.	Aug 1866	N.-Amer	835950
Sigel, Christoph Heinrich & W		22 Feb 1846	Weilheim	Krch.	Feb 1872	N.-Amer	835774
Sigel, Dorothea (wife)		1 Jul 1840	Weilheim	Krch.	Feb 1872	N.-Amer	835774
Sigel, Eva Maria		5 Sep 1833	Weilheim	Krch.	bef 1857	N.-Amer	835949
Sigel, Friederike		3 Aug 1847	Weilheim	Krch.	Jan 1861	N.-Amer	835949
Sigel, Georg Adam		1 Aug 1829	Weilheim	Krch.	bef 1853	N.-Amer	835949
Sigel, Georg Friedrich		8 Jul 1828	Weilheim	Krch.	Feb 1862	N.-Amer	835950
Sigel, Gottfried		25 Jun 1854	Weilheim	Krch.	Jan 1861	N.-Amer	835949
Sigel, Johann Georg		24 Mar 1814	Weilheim	Krch.	bef 1860	N.-Amer	835940
Sigel, Johann Georg		23 Oct 1836	Weilheim	Krch.	Mar 1856	N.-Amer	835949
Sigel, Johann Heinrich		17 Dec 1850	Kirchheim	Krch.	Jan 1870	N.-Amer	835941
Sigel, Johann Michael		22 Mar 1847	Weilheim	Krch.	Dec 1866	N.-Amer	835950
Sigel, Johannes		26 Jun 1863	Zell	Krch.	Apr 1880	England	835940
Sigel, Johannes		1 Dec 1827	Weilheim	Krch.	Mar 1862	N.-Amer	835950
Sigel, Johannes & F		27 Jan 1814	Weilheim	Krch.	Jan 1861	N.-Amer	835949
Sigel, Josephine Stephanie		6 Jun 1845	Weilheim	Krch.	Jan 1861	N.-Amer	835949
Sigel, Karl Friedrich		11 Apr 1872	Kirchheim	Krch.	Jan 1889	N.-Amer	835942
Sigel, Marie Elise		18 Dec 1851	Weilheim	Krch.	Jan 1861	N.-Amer	835949
Sigel, Robert Theodor		20 Dec 1849	Kirchheim	Krch.	Jul 1868	N.-Amer	835941
Sigel, Wilhelm		21 Sep 1830	Kirchheim	Krch.	1852	N.-Amer	835940
Siger, Maria Magdalena		31 yrs.	Heimerdingen	Leon.	Apr 1818	N.-Amer	837954
Sigle, Catharina (wife)			Muenchingen	Leon.	Feb 1850	N.-Amer	837961
Sigle, Christian		14 Apr 1844	Muenchingen	Leon.	Feb 1851	N.-Amer	837961
Sigle, Georg		2 Mar 1827	Muenchingen	Leon.	Feb 1850	N.-Amer	837961
Sigle, Gottlieb		5 Mar 1820	Muenchingen	Leon.	Feb 1850	N.-Amer	837961
Sigle, Gottlieb & F			Muenchingen	Leon.	Feb 1850	N.-Amer	837961
Sigle, Margaretha & C		36 yrs.	Muenchingen	Leon.	Feb 1851	N.-Amer	837961
Sigle, Maria		9 May 1825	Muenchingen	Leon.	Feb 1850	N.-Amer	837961
Sigle, Philipp Jakob		9 Sep 1829	Muenchingen	Leon.	Feb 1850	N.-Amer	837961
Sikeler, Albert		28 Mar 1845	Beffendorf	Obd.	Sep 1865	N.-Amer	838631
Sikeler, Johannes		25 Jan 1826	Beffendorf	Obd.	Mar 1864	N.-Amer	838631
Sikeler, Karl Robert		28 Mar 1850	Bach-Altenberg	Obd.	Feb 1869	N.-Amer	838631
Sikeler, Sebastian		31 Jan 1827	Beffendorf	Obd.	Oct 1853	N.-Amer	838631
Sikinger, Caroline			Heimerdingen	Leon.	1849	N.-Amer	837954
Sikinger, Christiana		16 Jan 1825	Heimerdingen	Leon.	Feb 1854	N.-Amer	837954
Sikinger, Eva Maria			Heimerdingen	Leon.	1831	N.-Amer	837954
Sikinger, Gottlieb		12 May 1820	Heimerdingen	Leon.	1849	N.-Amer	837954
Simmendinger, Johannes		12 Feb 1842	Maegerkingen	Rtl.	Sep 1867	France	841057
Simondet, Anna Maria (wife)			Malmsheim	Leon.	Jul 1857	N.-Amer	837958
Simondet, Anna Wilhelmine		20 Aug 1874	Friolzheim	Leon.	Feb 1881	N.-Amer	835791

Simondet, Catharina Louise	19 Feb 1846	Malmsheim	Leon.	Jul 1857	N.-Amer	837958
Simondet, Catharine Judith	2 Mar 1849	Malmsheim	Leon.	Jul 1857	N.-Amer	837958
Simondet, Emma Bertha	7 Nov 1876	Friolzheim	Leon.	Feb 1881	N.-Amer	835791
Simondet, Friederike Dorothea	4 Jan 1873	Friolzheim	Leon.	Feb 1881	N.-Amer	835791
Simondet, Gottlob Friedrich	24 Nov 1869	Friolzheim	Leon.	Feb 1881	N.-Amer	835791
Simondet, Jacob & F	10 Jul 1832	Friolzheim	Leon.	Feb 1881	N.-Amer	835791
Simondet, Jakob Friedrich	1 Apr 1871	Friolzheim	Leon.	Feb 1881	N.-Amer	835791
Simondet, Jakob Heinrich	2 Mar 1854	Malmsheim	Leon.	Jul 1857	N.-Amer	837958
Simondet, Karl Anton & F		Malmsheim	Leon.	Jul 1857	N.-Amer	837958
Simondet, Karoline Dorothea	24 Sep 1866	Friolzheim	Leon.	Feb 1881	N.-Amer	835791
Simondet, Louise Karoline	10 Jan 1864	Friolzheim	Leon.	Feb 1881	N.-Amer	835791
Simondet, Maria Karoline	17 Dec 1847	Malmsheim	Leon.	Jul 1857	N.-Amer	837958
Simondet, Marie Friederike	14 Feb 1865	Friolzheim	Leon.	Feb 1881	N.-Amer	835791
Simondet, Marie Magdalena (wife)	31 May 1842	Friolzheim	Leon.	Feb 1881	N.-Amer	835791
Simondet, Pauline Wilhelmine	22 Sep 1875	Friolzheim	Leon.	Feb 1881	N.-Amer	835791
Simondet, Rosine Magdalena	8 Jan 1863	Friolzheim	Leon.	Feb 1881	N.-Amer	835791
Sindlinger, Elisabetha Marg.	16 Jul 1839	Weilheim	Krch.	Feb 1870	Weimar	835950
Sindlinger, Johann Gottfried	2 Nov 1849	Weilheim	Krch.	1866	N.-Amer	835950
Sindlinger, Johann Michael	9 Jan 1843	Weilheim	Krch.	Jan 1860	N.-Amer	835949
Sindlinger, Johanna Dorothea	28 Feb 1837	Weilheim	Krch.	1862	N.-Amer	835940
Sindlinger, Johannes	5 Mar 1832	Weilheim	Krch.	Jul 1867	N.-Amer	835950
Sindlinger, Katharine Rosine	8 Jun 1880	Weilheim	Krch.	Jun 1882	N.-Amer	548403
Sindlinger, Matthaeus & F	18 May 1850	Weilheim	Krch.	Jun 1882	N.-Amer	548403
Sindlinger, Michael		Weilheim	Krch.	1853	N.-Amer	835940
Sindlinger, Michael	25 Aug 1818	Weilheim	Krch.	Mar 1856	N.-Amer	835949
Sindlinger, Sophie Magd. (wife)	1 Oct 1850	Weilheim	Krch.	Jun 1882	N.-Amer	548403
Sindlinger, Wilhelm Heinrich	2 Nov 1855	Weilheim	Krch.	Mar 1872	N.-Amer	835774
Singer, Barbara	22 yrs.	Deggingen	Gsl.	Mar 1854	N.-Amer	572042
Siokovich, Charlotte Karoline	1 Jul 1840	Eybach	Gsl.	May 1869	Austria	572047
Sohmer, Anna (wife)	38 yrs.	Sulgen	Obd.	Apr 1868	N.-Amer	838638
Sohmer, Blandina	3 Nov 1843	Winzeln	Obd.	Feb 1868	N.-Amer	841016
Sohmer, Carl August	20 Jan 1849	Schramberg	Obd.	bef 1870	N.-Amer	838636
Sohmer, Fidel & F		Sulgen	Obd.	May 1815	N.-Amer	838638
Sohmer, Fridolin & F	25 Sep 1835	Sulgen	Obd.	Apr 1868	N.-Amer	838638
Sohmer, Gebhard	11 May 1867	Sulgen	Obd.	Apr 1868	N.-Amer	838638
Sohmer, Johann Georg	9 Mar 1835	Sulgen	Obd.	Jan 1852	N.-Amer	838638
Sohmer, Johannes		Hochmoessingen	Obd.	bef 1848	N.-Amer	838633
Sohmer, Joseph	26 Jan 1845	Sulgen	Obd.	Aug 1865	N.-Amer	838638
Sohmer, Konrad	25 Nov 1845	Hardt	Obd.	Apr 1865	N.-Amer	838633
Sohmer, Ursula	16 Jul 1864	Sulgen	Obd.	Apr 1868	N.-Amer	838638
Sohmer, Valentin	13 Feb 1850	Winzeln	Obd.	Oct 1868	N.-Amer	841016
Soller, Caroline	20 yrs.	Leonberg	Leon.	Jul 1855	N.-Amer	835786
Soller, Christian	29 Oct 1835	Leonberg	Leon.	Jul 1852	N.-Amer	835786
Soller, Friederike (wife)		Leonberg	Leon.	Jul 1855	N.-Amer	835786
Soller, Joseph & F		Leonberg	Leon.	Jul 1855	N.-Amer	835786
Sommer, Andreas		Oberndorf	Obd.	May 1849	N.-Amer	838635
Sommer, Friedrich Wilhelm	23 Feb 1834	Reutlingen	Rtl.	bef 1861	Saxony	841057
Sommer, Johann Jakob	17 Nov 1850	Pfullingen	Rtl.	Aug 1868	N.-Amer	841057
Sommer, Maria Catharina	17 Jun 1833	Heimerdingen	Leon.	Oct 1854	N.-Amer	837954
Sommer, Mathias & F		Mariazell	Obd.	Jan 1817	N.-Amer	838634

Name		Birth		Emigration			Film
Last	First	Date	Place	O'amt	Appl. Date	Dest.	Number
Sonntag, Jakob Philipp		4 Oct 1856	Sternenfels/Maulb.	Rtl.	Jan 1860	N.-Amer	841057
Sonntag, Katharina		14 Apr 1853	Leonbronn/Maulb.	Rtl.	Jan 1860	N.-Amer	841057
Sonntag, Katharina & C			Eningen	Rtl.	Jan 1860	N.-Amer	841057
Sonntag, Maria		24 Jan 1850	Sternenfels/Maulb.	Rtl.	Jan 1860	N.-Amer	841057
Sonntag, Sophie		9 mon.	Eningen	Rtl.	Jan 1860	N.-Amer	841057
Spadi, Christian Albert		25 Apr 1843	Muenchingen	Leon.	Apr 1866	N.-Amer	837961
Spadi, Conrad		28 Aug 1836	Muenchingen	Leon.	Feb 1853	N.-Amer	837961
Spaeht, Carl Wolf		26 Dec 1840	Kirchheim	Krch.	Sep 1869	Hannov.	835941
Spaeht, Gottlob		8 Dec 1826	Reutlingen	Rtl.	bef 1864	Berlin	841057
Spaeth, Anton		23 Jan 1828	Treffelhausen	Gsl.	Mar 1866	N.-Amer	572045
Spaeth, Christina Lou. (wife)		1 Apr 1841	Friolzheim	Leon.	Jul 1881	N.-Amer	835791
Spaeth, Ernst Julius		6 Aug 1879	Friolzheim	Leon.	Jul 1881	N.-Amer	835791
Spaeth, Friederich			Ditzenbach	Gsl.	Oct 1854	N.-Amer	572042
Spaeth, Friederike			Leonberg	Leon.	Jul 1854	N.-Amer	835786
Spaeth, Gottlob Friedrich		3 Jun 1863	Friolzheim	Leon.	Jul 1881	N.-Amer	835791
Spaeth, Jacob Friedrich		30 Sep 1833	Friolzheim	Leon.	Jul 1881	N.-Amer	835791
Spaeth, Jakob Wilhelm		11 Jan 1873	Friolzheim	Leon.	Jul 1881	N.-Amer	835791
Spaeth, Johannes Friedrich		23 Mar 1868	Friolzheim	Leon.	Jul 1881	N.-Amer	835791
Spaeth, Joseph		30 Sep 1829	Leonberg	Leon.	Jul 1854	N.-Amer	835786
Spaeth, Karl August		7 Feb 1870	Friolzheim	Leon.	Jul 1881	N.-Amer	835791
Spaeth, Karl Gustav		5 Aug 1874	Friolzheim	Leon.	Jul 1881	N.-Amer	835791
Spaeth, Katharina Wilhelmine		24 Oct 1865	Friolzheim	Leon.	Jul 1881	N.-Amer	835791
Spaeth, Leonhardt		13 Feb 1844	Kuchen	Gsl.	Sep 1866	N.-Amer	572045
Spaeth, Louise		1 Aug 1849	Leonberg	Leon.	Jul 1854	N.-Amer	835786
Spaeth, Wilhelm		18 Apr 1846	Kuchen	Gsl.	Apr 1865	N.-Amer	572045
Spaeth, Wilhelmine & C		27 yrs.	Leonberg	Leon.	Jul 1854	N.-Amer	835786
Spannagel, Jakob		12 Jul 1846	Reutlingen	Rtl.	Feb 1862	N.-Amer	841057
Spanninger, Joseph		11 Feb 1846	Schramberg	Obd.	Oct 1866	N.-Amer	838636
Speckhardt, Catharina		7 yrs.	Gerlingen	Leon.	Sep 1854	N.-Amer	837953
Speidel, Christian Wilhelm		14 May 1840	Bondorf	Herr.	Oct 1864	Paris	834630
Speidel, Judith			Pfullingen	Rtl.	bef 1861	Wien	841057
Speilmann, Anna Maria		12 Jun 1813	Malmsheim	Leon.	Jul 1831	N.-Amer	837958
Speilmann, Anna Maria (wife)			Malmsheim	Leon.	Jul 1831	N.-Amer	837958
Speilmann, Christina		27 Nov 1825	Malmsheim	Leon.	Jul 1831	N.-Amer	837958
Speilmann, Christina Judith		11 Nov 1814	Malmsheim	Leon.	Jul 1831	N.-Amer	837958
Speilmann, Johann Georg		28 Mar 1812	Malmsheim	Leon.	Jul 1831	N.-Amer	837958
Speilmann, Johann Georg & F			Malmsheim	Leon.	Jul 1831	N.-Amer	837958
Speilmann, Johann Heinrich		15 Jul 1820	Malmsheim	Leon.	Jul 1831	N.-Amer	837958
Speilmann, Margaretha		7 Nov 1818	Malmsheim	Leon.	Jul 1831	N.-Amer	837958
Speilmann, Maria Agnes		21 Dec 1816	Malmsheim	Leon.	Jul 1831	N.-Amer	837958
Speiser, Heinrich David		20 May 1850	Jesingen	Krch.	Jul 1869	N.-Amer	835946
Speisser, David		9 Jul 1822	Hochdorf	Krch.	1852	N.-Amer	835940
Spengler, Johann Michael		6 Jan 1831	Neidlingen	Krch.	Jul 1867	N.-Amer	835946
Spiegelhalter, Josef		19 yrs.	Oberndorf	Obd.	Apr 1854	N.-Amer	838635
Spielmann, Johannes		26 Sep 1813	Hochdorf	Krch.	bef 1865	N.-Amer	835945
Spielmann, Josef		10 Nov 1865	Hochdorf	Krch.	May 1882	N.-Amer	835945
Spiess, Georg Friedrich		28 Jan 1828	Hoefingen	Leon.	bef 1867	N.-Amer	837957
Spiess, Johann Georg & F			Hoefingen	Leon.	bef 1867	N.-Amer	837957
Spiess, Johannes		21 Oct 1850	Weil im Dorf	Loen.	Apr 1869	N.-Amer	837967
Spiess, Maria Magdalena			Weil im Dorf	Loen.	1855	N.-Amer	837967

Name	Date/Age	Place	Dist.	Emig.	Dest.	Film
Spiess, Martin	1 Feb 1858	Hoefingen	Leon.	Jun 1876	N.-Amer	837957
Spindler, Friedrich	5 Mar 1848	Kirchheim	Krch.	Aug 1866	N.-Amer	835941
Spindler, Johann Adam	10 Nov 1865	Neidlingen	Krch.	May 1882	N.-Amer	548403
Spittel, Andreas	6 yrs.	Leonberg	Leon.	Feb 1853	N.-Amer	835786
Spittel, Andreas & W		Leonberg	Leon.	Apr 1853	N.-Amer	835786
Spittel, Heinrich		Leonberg	Leon.	Feb 1853	N.-Amer	835786
Spittel, Heinrich & F		Leonberg	Leon.	Feb 1853	N.-Amer	835786
Spittel, Katharina		Leonberg	Leon.	Oct 1853	N.-Amer	835786
Spittel, Magdalena Ros. (wife)		Leonberg	Leon.	Apr 1853	N.-Amer	835786
Spittel, Wilhelm Friedrich	3 yrs.	Leonberg	Leon.	Feb 1853	N.-Amer	835786
Spittel, Wilhelmine Louise	4 yrs.	Leonberg	Leon.	Feb 1853	N.-Amer	835786
Spitz, Wilhelm	5 Dec 1828	Kirchheim	Krch.	Jul 1856	N.-Amer	835940
Spitzemberg von , Gustav Adol.	10 Apr 1839	Zell	Krch.	Jun 1859	Austria	835774
Spizig, Angelika (wife)	23 Sep 1805	Altenstadt-Gsl.	Gsl.	Mar 1857	N.-Amer	572043
Spizig, Johannes	18 Jun 1834	Altenstadt-Gsl.	Gsl.	Jan 1854	N.-Amer	572042
Spizig, Johannes & F	20 Aug 1806	Altenstadt-Gsl.	Gsl.	Mar 1857	N.-Amer	572043
Spizig, Rosina	24 Sep 1840	Altenstadt-Gsl.	Gsl.	Mar 1857	N.-Amer	572043
Spohr, Georg & W		Altenstadt-Gsl.	Gsl.	Feb 1854	N.-Amer	572042
Spohr, Susanna (wife)		Altenstadt-Gsl.	Gsl.	Feb 1854	N.-Amer	572042
Sprandel, Anna Maria (wife)	10 Mar 1824	Pfullingen	Rtl.	Aug 1868	N.-Amer	841057
Sprandel, Elisabetha Margar.	20 Jan 1864	Pfullingen	Rtl.	Aug 1868	N.-Amer	841057
Sprandel, Jakob Friedrich	23 Nov 1850	Pfullingen	Rtl.	Aug 1868	N.-Amer	841057
Sprandel, Jakob Friedrich & F	16 Jan 1824	Pfullingen	Rtl.	Aug 1868	N.-Amer	841057
Sprandel, Karl Friedrich	9 Aug 1859	Pfullingen	Rtl.	Aug 1868	N.-Amer	841057
Sprandel, Maria	21 Nov 1855	Pfullingen	Rtl.	Aug 1868	N.-Amer	841057
Sprandel, Wilhelm	20 Sep 1861	Pfullingen	Rtl.	Aug 1868	N.-Amer	841057
Sprengler, Gottlieb		Neidlingen	Krch.	bef 1867	N.-Amer	835940
Sprengler, Michael		Neidlingen	Krch.	bef 1867	N.-Amer	835940
Springer, Ottmer	11 Nov 1832	Herrenberg	Herr.	1858	N.-Amer	834629
Springmann, Johannes		Betzweiler	Obd.	Apr 1861	N.-Amer	838631
Springmann, Xaver	24 yrs.	Lauterbach	Obd.	Apr 1857	France	838634
Staeb, Franziska		Deggingen	Gsl.	Dec 1867	N.-Amer	572046
Staeb, Ida & C	1 Oct 1841	Deggingen	Gsl.	Aug 1865	N.-Amer	572045
Staeb, Otto	26 May 1863	Deggingen	Gsl.	Aug 1865	N.-Amer	572045
Staeb, Viktoria	3 Feb 1839	Deggingen	Gsl.	Jun 1862	N.-Amer	572044
Staebler, Maria Catharina	18 Nov 1829	Gerlingen	Leon.	Apr 1855	N.-Amer	837953
Staegle, Carl	11 May 1840	Alpirsbach	Obd.	Aug 1854	N.-Amer	838630
Staehle, Catharine		Kirchheim	Krch.	bef 1864	N.-Amer	835940
Staehle, Christian Gottlieb	7 Jan 1844	Renningen	Leon.	Apr 1852	N.-Amer	837963
Staehle, Christina Barba. (wife)		Renningen	Leon.	Aug 1844	N.-Amer	837963
Staehle, Christina Katharina	27 Jun 1839	Renningen	Leon.	Apr 1852	N.-Amer	837963
Staehle, Christina Magdalena	29 Aug 1836	Renningen	Leon.	Apr 1852	N.-Amer	837963
Staehle, Elias Wilhelm		Geislingen	Gsl.	Sep 1851	N.-Amer	577788
Staehle, Georg Michael	17 Apr 1834	Renningen	Leon.	Apr 1852	N.-Amer	837963
Staehle, Johann Christian	11 Oct 1838	Alpirsbach	Obd.	Dec 1858	N.-Amer	838630
Staehle, Johann Christoph	51 yrs.	Renningen	Leon.	Apr 1852	N.-Amer	837963
Staehle, Johannes & F		Renningen	Leon.	Apr 1852	N.-Amer	837963
Staehle, Johannes & F		Renningen	Leon.	Aug 1844	N.-Amer	837963
Staehle, Katharina (wife)		Renningen	Leon.	Apr 1852	N.-Amer	837963
Staehle, Louise Friederika	25 Feb 1842	Renningen	Leon.	Apr 1852	N.-Amer	837963

| Name | | Birth | | Emigration | | | Film |
Last	First	Date	Place	O'amt	Appl. Date	Dest.	Number
Staehle, Louise Friederike		31 Jul 1843	Renningen	Leon.	Aug 1844	N.-Amer	837963
Staehle, Ludwig		9 Jun 1815	Heimsheim	Leon.	Jun 1851	N.-Amer	837955
Staehle, Marie Catharina		2 Feb 1842	Renningen	Leon.	Aug 1844	N.-Amer	837963
Staehle, Wilhelm Friedrich		21 Apr 1846	Alpirsbach	Obd.	Sep 1866	N.-Amer	838630
Staehle, Wilhelm Gottlob		29 Mar 1849	Renningen	Leon.	Apr 1852	N.-Amer	837963
Staehlin, Anna Maria			Alpirsbach	Obd.	Oct 1845	France	838630
Staehlin, Catharina & C		17 Jun 1826	Alpirsbach	Obd.	bef 1846	Switz.	838630
Staehlin, Rosina		29 yrs.	Alpirsbach	Obd.	Oct 1844	Hz.-Pr.	838630
Stahl, Barbara (wife)		44 yrs.	Hemmingen	Leon.	Feb 1818	N.-Amer	837956
Stahl, Catarina		16 yrs.	Hemmingen	Leon.	Feb 1818	N.-Amer	837956
Stahl, Dorothea (wife)		3 Jan 1842	Geislingen	Gsl.	Mar 1867	N.-Amer	572046
Stahl, Georg & W		16 Sep 1836	Geislingen	Gsl.	Mar 1867	N.-Amer	572046
Stahl, Jacob			Gomaringen	Rtl.	Jul 1829	Switz.	841051
Stahl, Jakob & F			Rutesheim	Leon.	Oct 1853	N.-Amer	837964
Stahl, Jakob & F			Ditzingen	Leon.	Mar 1830	N.-Amer	835788
Stahl, Johann Georg & F			Hemmingen	Leon.	Feb 1853	N.-Amer	837956
Stahl, Johann Martin		23 yrs.	Rutesheim	Leon.	Feb 1852	N.-Amer	837964
Stahl, Johannes		1 May 1800	Hemmingen	Leon.	Feb 1818	N.-Amer	837956
Stahl, Johannes & F		45 yrs.	Hemmingen	Leon.	Feb 1818	N.-Amer	837956
Stahl, Michael			Rutesheim	Leon.	May 1856	N.-Amer	837964
Stahl, Pauline		7 May 1840	Stuttgart	Herr.	bef 1868	Wien	834630
Stahl, Sebastian		9 Sep 1812	Wiesensteig	Gsl.	bef 1862	N.-Amer	572044
Stahle, Johann Martin		8 Sep 1842	Bondorf	Herr.	May 1869	N.-Amer	834630
Stahlecker, Anna Barbara & F			Honau	Rtl.	May 1859	N.-Amer	841057
Stahlecker, Carl			Dettingen	Krch.	bef 1868	N.-Amer	835940
Stahlecker, Carl		17 Nov 1828	Kirchheim	Krch.	Nov 1868	N.-Amer	835941
Stahlecker, Daniel			Honau	Rtl.	bef 1859	N.-Amer	841057
Stahlecker, Jakob Heinrich		8 Oct 1837	Honau	Rtl.	Oct 1866	N.-Amer	841057
Stahlecker, Johannes		19 Mar 1866	Honau	Rtl.	Oct 1866	N.-Amer	841057
Stahlecker, Katharina (wife)		29 May 1844	Ochsenwang	Rtl.	Oct 1866	N.-Amer	841057
Stahlecker, Philipp Gottfried		6 Apr 1816	Oberhausen	Rtl.	1853	N.-Amer	841057
Staib, Anna		3 Oct 1835	Bissingen	Krch.	bef 1855	N.-Amer	835943
Staib, Anna Catharina		6 Sep 1838	Bissingen	Krch.	1854	N.-Amer	835943
Staib, Anna Maria		6 Apr 1851	Bissingen	Krch.	Feb 1855	N.-Amer	835943
Staib, Anna Maria (wife)		15 Oct 1810	Owen	Krch.	Feb 1855	N.-Amer	835943
Staib, Catharina		8 Mar 1846	Bissingen	Krch.	May 1867	N.-Amer	835943
Staib, Catharina (wife)			Bissingen	Krch.	Mar 1874	N.-Amer	835943
Staib, Christoph		11 Apr 1854	Bissingen	Krch.	Jun 1865	N.-Amer	835943
Staib, Christoph & F		33 yrs.	Bissingen	Krch.	Mar 1874	N.-Amer	548403
Staib, Christoph & F		9 Nov 1841	Bissingen	Krch.	Mar 1874	N.-Amer	835943
Staib, Conrad			Bissingen	Krch.	Mar 1864	N.-Amer	835943
Staib, Cyriakus		14 Aug 1844	Bissingen	Krch.	Jun 1865	N.-Amer	835943
Staib, Daniel		18 Dec 1847	Bissingen	Krch.	Jun 1865	N.-Amer	835943
Staib, Georg		12 Aug 1850	Bissingen	Krch.	Jun 1865	N.-Amer	835943
Staib, Johann Conrad		17 Jul 1846	Bissingen	Krch.	Oct 1866	N.-Amer	835943
Staib, Johann Conrad		30 Mar 1844	Bissingen	Krch.	Mar 1864	N.-Amer	835943
Staib, Johann Conrad		23 Sep 1829	Bissingen	Krch.	bef 1862	N.-Amer	835943
Staib, Johann Conrad		31 Dec 1836	Bissingen	Krch.	bef 1855	N.-Amer	835943
Staib, Johann Gottlieb		15 Feb 1850	Bissingen	Krch.	Feb 1855	N.-Amer	835943
Staib, Johann Jakob		2 Dec 1852	Dettingen	Krch.	May 1866	N.-Amer	835944

Staib, Johann Jakob	11 Oct 1845	Bissingen	Krch.	Feb 1855	N.-Amer	835943
Staib, Johann Jakob	10 Sep 1812	Bissingen	Krch.	bef 1855	N.-Amer	835943
Staib, Johann Michael	23 Apr 1819	Bissingen	Krch.	bef 1868	N.-Amer	835940
Staib, Johannes	23 May 1864	Owen	Krch.	Mar 1881	N.-Amer	835948
Staib, Johannes	23 Sep 1816	Bissingen	Krch.	1837	N.-Amer	835943
Staib, Karl Friedrich	12 Sep 1873	Kirchheim	Krch.	Jul 1890	N.-Amer	835942
Staib, Kathrina (wife)	8 Mar 1846	Bissingen	Krch.	Mar 1874	N.-Amer	548403
Staib, Margaretha	2 yrs.	Bissingen	Krch.	Mar 1874	N.-Amer	548403
Staib, Margaretha	17 Feb 1872	Bissingen	Krch.	Mar 1874	N.-Amer	835943
Staib, Margaretha	12 Dec 1842	Bissingen	Krch.	May 1867	N.-Amer	835943
Staib, Margaretha	11 Nov 1841	Bissingen	Krch.	Jun 1865	N.-Amer	835943
Staib, Margaretha	11 Nov 1841	Bissingen	Krch.	Feb 1861	N.-Amer	835943
Staib, Maria Barbara	18 Jun 1843	Bissingen	Krch.	1854	N.-Amer	835943
Staib, Paulina	30 Mar 1873	Bissingen	Krch.	Mar 1874	N.-Amer	835943
Staib, Pauline	1 yrs.	Bissingen	Krch.	Mar 1874	N.-Amer	548403
Staib, Ursula (wid.) & F	2 Apr 1814	Bissingen	Krch.	Jun 1865	N.-Amer	835943
Staib, Wilhelm	4 yrs.	Bissingen	Krch.	Mar 1874	N.-Amer	548403
Staib, Wilhelm	5 Mar 1870	Bissingen	Krch.	Mar 1874	N.-Amer	835943
Staiber, Bernhardine	42 yrs.	Donzdorf	Gsl.	Jul 1854	N.-Amer	572042
Staiger, Albert Wilhelm	17 Feb 1862	Leonberg	Leon.	Oct 1879	France	835787
Staiger, Anna Maria	14 Dec 1844	Schlattstall	Krch.	Jul 1865	N.-Amer	835949
Staiger, Balthasar	8 Feb 1841	Fluorn	Obd.	May 1858	N.-Amer	838632
Staiger, Catharina	Feb 1844	Fluorn	Obd.	Feb 1864	N.-Amer	838632
Staiger, Christian	29 Jan 1848	Weil im Dorf	Loen.	Apr 1858	N.-Amer	837967
Staiger, Christian	25 Dec 1825	Weil im Dorf	Loen.	Jan 1854	N.-Amer	837967
Staiger, Eduard Gottlob	15 Jan 1822	Reutlingen	Leon.	bef 1862	Hamburg	837964
Staiger, Friedrich	23 Mar 1849	Fluorn	Obd.	Feb 1864	N.-Amer	838632
Staiger, Friedrich	20 May 1842	Weil im Dorf	Loen.	Aug 1852	N.-Amer	837967
Staiger, Friedrich	44 yrs.	Weil im Dorf	Loen.	Nov 1851	N.-Amer	837967
Staiger, Georg & F	49 yrs.	Weil im Dorf	Loen.	Apr 1858	N.-Amer	837967
Staiger, Hermann	28 Jul 1840	Schramberg	Obd.	Aug 1865	Bavaria	838636
Staiger, Johann Friedrich	15 Jun 1850	Gerlingen	Leon.	Mar 1885	N.-Amer	837953
Staiger, Johann Georg	29 Dec 1845	Weil im Dorf	Loen.	Apr 1858	N.-Amer	837967
Staiger, Johann Georg		Hoefingen	Leon.	Sep 1871	N.-Amer	837957
Staiger, Johann Jakob	23 Jun 1846	Fluorn	Obd.	Feb 1864	N.-Amer	838632
Staiger, Johannes	7 Mar 1839	Fluorn	Obd.	Feb 1864	N.-Amer	838632
Staiger, Johannes	8 Apr 1837	Fluorn	Obd.	Feb 1861	N.-Amer	838632
Staiger, Johannes	7 Apr 1816	Leonberg	Leon.	Apr 1862	Holst.	835787
Staiger, Maria Katharina (wid.)	27 Feb 1806	Fluorn	Obd.	Feb 1864	N.-Amer	838632
Staiger, Marie Sophie	26 Apr 1844	Weil im Dorf	Loen.	Apr 1858	N.-Amer	837967
Staiger, Wilhelm Carl		Weil im Dorf	Loen.	bef 1860	France	837967
Stanger, Georg Friedrich	19 Oct 1825	Muenklingen	Leon.	Feb 1847	Hungary	837962
Stanger, Gottlieb	32 yrs.	Friolzheim	Leon.	1852	N.-Amer	835791
Stanger, Jakob	12 Apr 1833	Muenklingen	Leon.	Feb 1847	Hungary	837962
Stanger, Johann Georg	17 Jun 1827	Muenklingen	Leon.	Feb 1847	Hungary	837962
Stanger, Johann Georg & F		Muenklingen	Leon.	Feb 1847	Hungary	837962
Stanger, Johannes		Korntal	Leon.	Apr 1853	Austral	837957
Stanger, Margaretha Barb. (wife)		Muenklingen	Leon.	Feb 1847	Hungary	837962
Stark, August Heinrich	9 May 1874	Holzmaden	Krch.	Dec 1889	N.-Amer	835945
Stark, Barbara	30 yrs.	Notzingen	Krch.	Apr 1864	Hesse	835947

Name		Birth		Emigration			Film
Last	First	Date	Place	O'amt	Appl. Date	Dest.	Number
Stark, Catharina		30 Dec 1830	Jesingen	Krch.	Jun 1867	N.-Amer	835946
Stark, Christian Heinrich & F			Heimsheim	Leon.	Apr 1853	N.-Amer	837955
Stark, Christiane Friederike			Heimsheim	Leon.	Apr 1853	N.-Amer	837955
Stark, Gottlob		26 Nov 1875	Holzmaden	Krch.	Jul 1889	N.-Amer	835945
Stark, Jakob		9 Jun 1834	Grosssuessen	Gsl.	Feb 1854	N.-Amer	572042
Stark, Johann Georg			Jesingen	Krch.	bef 1860	N.-Amer	835940
Stark, Johann Georg & F		9 Aug 1811	Notzingen	Krch.	Apr 1866	N.-Amer	835947
Stark, Johanne Sophia		17 yrs.	Heimsheim	Leon.	Apr 1853	N.-Amer	837955
Stark, Johannes			Jesingen	Krch.	bef 1860	N.-Amer	835940
Stark, Johannes		14 Feb 1850	Holzmaden	Krch.	May 1867	N.-Amer	835945
Stark, Magdalena			Holzmaden	Krch.	May 1753	N.-Amer	550804
Stark, Martin			Jesingen	Krch.	bef 1860	N.-Amer	835940
Stark, Michael			Holzmaden	Krch.	bef 1889	N.-Amer	835945
Stark, Paul Heinrich		11 yrs.	Heimsheim	Leon.	Apr 1853	N.-Amer	837955
Staub, Elisabetha			Schramberg	Obd.	Mar 1854	N.-Amer	838636
Staub, Pauline			Ueberkingen	Gsl.	Dec 1863	Switz.	572044
Stauch, Gottlieb		20 Apr 1857	Muenklingen	Leon.	Oct 1880	N.-Amer	837962
Stauch, Maria Magdalena		15 Sep 1844	Tuebingen	Rtl.	Mar 1861	N.-Amer	841055
Staudemann, Johann Michael			Treffelhausen	Gsl.	Apr 1852	N.-Amer	572041
Staudenmaier, Aloys		29 Mar 1869	Boehmenkirch	Gsl.	Sep 1883	N.-Amer	572049
Staudenmaier, Franz		5 Jul 1822	Donzdorf	Gsl.	bef 1856	N.-Amer	572043
Staudenmaier, Johannes		18 yrs.	Donzdorf	Gsl.	Mar 1852	N.-Amer	572041
Staudenmaier, Johannes		17 Jun 1842	Boehmenkirch	Gsl.	Apr 1867	N.-Amer	572046
Staudenmaier, Joseph		14 Feb 1856	Boehmenkirch	Gsl.	Jul 1872	N.-Amer	572047
Staudenmaier, Konrad		20 Sep 1849	Nenningen	Gsl.	Feb 1869	N.-Amer	572047
Staudenmaier, Maria Josepha		4 Jun 1843	Weissenstein	Gsl.	Sep 1869	N.-Amer	572047
Staudenmaier, Michael		11 Sep 1867	Boehmenkirch	Gsl.	Aug 1883	N.-Amer	572049
Staudenmaier, Carl		27 Feb 1849	Donzdorf	Gsl.	Mar 1873	N.-Amer	572047
Staudenmayer, Georg		27 yrs.	Treffelhausen	Gsl.	Mar 1852	N.-Amer	572041
Staudenmayer, Joseph		24 Jun 1842	Schnittlinger	Gsl.	Mar 1869	N.-Amer	572047
Staudenmayer, Maria (wife)			Treffelhausen	Gsl.	Feb 1852	N.-Amer	572041
Staudenmayer, Sebastian & F			Treffelhausen	Gsl.	Feb 1852	N.-Amer	572041
Staudenmeier, Bernhard		21 yrs.	Boehmenkirch	Gsl.	Mar 1852	N.-Amer	572041
Staudenmeier, Coezilia		22 May 1829	Boehmenkirch	Gsl.	Feb 1854	N.-Amer	572042
Staudenmeier, Josepha		23 yrs.	Boehmenkirch	Gsl.	Mar 1852	N.-Amer	572041
Staudenmeier, Kreszenz			Boehmenkirch	Gsl.	Feb 1853	N.-Amer	572041
Stecher, Anton & F			Westerheim	Gsl.	Mar 1852	N.-Amer	572041
Stecher, Maria Theresia		13 yrs.	Westerheim	Gsl.	Mar 1852	N.-Amer	572041
Steck, Christina		3 Nov 1821	Tuerkheim	Gsl.	Sep 1854	N.-Amer	572042
Steffan, Gottfried Hermann		16 Nov 1865	Kirchheim	Krch.	Aug 1882	N.-Amer	548403
Steffan, Heinrich		2 Sep 1864	Kirchheim	Krch.	Mar 1881	N.-Amer	835942
Stegmaier, Christian		11 May 1846	Buenzwangen	Krch.	May 1881	N.-Amer	548403
Stegmaier, Johann Georg		9 Feb 1828	Kuchen	Gsl.	Mar 1857	N.-Amer	572043
Stegmueller, Gottlieb		9 Mar 1872	Stuttgart	Leon.	Nov 1886	N.-Amer	835789
Stehle, Caroline		15 Sep 1835	Bissingen	Krch.	bef 1868	Austria	835943
Stehle, Daniel		11 Feb 1822	Hepsisau	Krch.	Jun 1852	N.-Amer	835945
Stehle, Franz Xaver		30 Nov 1849	Oberndorf	Obd.	Aug 1867	N.-Amer	838635
Stehle, Franz Xaver		24 May 1838	Gosbach	Gsl.	Feb 1854	N.-Amer	572042
Stehle, Friedrich		2 Mar 1846	Oberndorf	Obd.	Sep 1866	N.-Amer	838635
Stehle, Georg			Wiesensteig	Gsl.	Apr 1852	N.-Amer	572041

Stehle, Maria Theresia	1 Apr 1840	Bissingen	Krch.	Jul 1880	N.-Amer	548403
Steib, Eberhard	3 Mar 1822	Gingen	Gsl.	Mar 1852	N.-Amer	572041
Steiblin, Barbara	28 yrs.	Gebersheim	Leon.	Mar 1853	N.-Amer	837953
Steidinger, Anna Maria	2 Feb 1833	Betzweiler	Obd.	Apr 1856	N.-Amer	838631
Steidinger, Christian		Betzweiler	Obd.	Apr 1816	-	838631
Steidinger, Christina	25 Jul 1837	Betzweiler	Obd.	Apr 1856	N.-Amer	838631
Steidinger, Dorothea	24 Oct 1834	Betzweiler	Obd.	Apr 1856	N.-Amer	838631
Steidinger, Eva	28 Jan 1842	Betzweiler	Obd.	Apr 1856	N.-Amer	838631
Steiflinger, Andreas	19 yrs.	Gosbach	Gsl.	1851	N.-Amer	577788
Steiger, Christine Regine		Pfullingen	Rtl.	Jun 1832	N.-Amer	841051
Steiger, Hildebert	17 May 1839	Schramberg	Obd.	bef 1869	N.-Amer	838636
Steiger, Johannes		Pfullingen	Rtl.	Aug 1835	N.-Amer	841051
Steiger, Wilhelm	20 Aug 1851	Schramberg	Obd.	Apr 1869	N.-Amer	838636
Stein von, Leopoldina		Harthausen	Obd.	Oct 1835	Prussia	838633
Stein, Johannes	30 Jun 1847	Owen	Krch.	Nov 1865	N.-Amer	835948
Steinbrueck, Otto	7 Oct 1859	Gutenberg	Krch.	Jun 1876	N.-Amer	548403
Steinbrueck, Otto	7 Oct 1859	Esslingen	Krch.	Jun 1876	N.-Amer	835945
Steiner, Florian & F		Weil der Stadt	Leon.	Jul 1854	N.-Amer	837966
Steinhardt, Johann Gottlob	10 Mar 1840	Reutlingen	Rtl.	Jun 1859	N.-Amer	841057
Steinhuber, Theodor	14 Jan 1860	Kirchheim	Krch.	Sep 1878	N.-Amer	835942
Steinmann, Anne Cathar. (wife)		Muenchingen	Leon.	Mar 1848	N.-Amer	837961
Steinmann, Jacob Friedrich & F		Muenchingen	Leon.	Mar 1848	N.-Amer	837961
Steinmann, Jakob	3 Oct 1844	Muenchingen	Leon.	Mar 1848	N.-Amer	837961
Steinmann, Jakob & F		Muenchingen	Leon.	Mar 1848	N.-Amer	837961
Steinmann, Johann Georg	4 Jul 1830	Muenchingen	Leon.	Mar 1848	N.-Amer	837961
Steinmann, Johann Michael	5 Mar 1820	Muenchingen	Leon.	Mar 1848	N.-Amer	837961
Steinmann, Johanna	23 Jul 1833	Muenchingen	Leon.	Mar 1848	N.-Amer	837961
Steinmann, Katharina Barbara	12 Mar 1827	Muenchingen	Leon.	Mar 1848	N.-Amer	837961
Steinmann, Margaretha	29 Jan 1835	Muenchingen	Leon.	Mar 1848	N.-Amer	837961
Steinmann, Wilhelm	20 Dec 1846	Muenchingen	Leon.	Mar 1848	N.-Amer	837961
Steinmayer, Michael Robert	15 Oct 1840	Eningen	Rtl.	Sep 1860	N.-Amer	841057
Steinwandel, Nikodemus	1 Apr 1842	Seedorf	Obd.	Mar 1861	N.-Amer	838637
Steisslinger, Andreas		Gosbach	Gsl.	bef 1853	N.-Amer	572041
Stelzer, Magdalena	24 Sep 1842	Kirchheim	Krch.	Mar 1868	N.-Amer	835941
Stempfle, Ludwig	7 Mar 1832	Ueberkingen	Gsl.	Dec 1853	N.-Amer	572041
Sterr, Christian	6 Jan 1855	Holzmaden	Krch.	Apr 1871	N.-Amer	835945
Sterr, Georg Friedrich	6 Jul 1864	Holzmaden	Krch.	Mar 1881	N.-Amer	835945
Sterr, Michael	16 Jul 1857	Holzmaden	Krch.	Mar 1874	N.-Amer	835945
Steudele, Johann David Martin	11 Dec 1820	Gutenberg	Krch.	Apr 1874	N.-Amer	835945
Steudle, Johann Georg	1 Nov 1848	Brucken	Krch.	Jul 1864	N.-Amer	835944
Steudle, Johann Georg	10 Oct 1843	Schlattstall	Krch.	1869	N.-Amer	835949
Steudle, Johann Jakob	11 Aug 1839	Brucken	Krch.	Mar 1859	N.-Amer	835944
Steudle, Johann Michael	17 Jul 1845	Brucken	Krch.	Mar 1860	N.-Amer	835944
Steudle, Karl Friedrich	8 Feb 1839	Schlattstall	Krch.	1868	N.-Amer	835949
Steudle, Luise	24 Mar 1849	Gutenberg	Krch.	Sep 1867	N.-Amer	835945
Stief, Karl Gottfried	30 yrs.	Warmbronn	Leon.	Mar 1854	N.-Amer	837965
Stiefbold, Georg David		Gerlingen	Leon.	Nov 1846	Hesse	837953
Stiefbold, Georg Martin		Gerlingen	Leon.	Aug 1837	Hesse	837953
Stiefbold, Johann Conrad		Hoefingen	Leon.	May 1832	France	837957
Stiefbold, Johann Jacob		Gerlingen	Leon.	Jun 1843	France	837953

Name		Birth		Emigration			Film
Last	First	Date	Place	O'amt	Appl. Date	Dest.	Number
Stiefbold, Johann Jacob		18 Aug 1814	Gebersheim	Leon.	Dec 1832	France	837953
Stiefelmaier, Melchior		25 Apr 1841	Gingen	Gsl.	Oct 1857	N.-Amer	572043
Stiefelmayer, Christina Wilh.		19 Sep 1846	Gingen	Gsl.	Mar 1867	N.-Amer	572046
Stimmler, Andreas (wid.) & F			Oberndorf	Obd.	Mar 1863	Austria	838635
Stimmler, Barbara		5 yrs.	Oberndorf	Obd.	Mar 1863	Austria	838635
Stirmlinger, Johannes		5 Aug 1831	Ditzenbach	Gsl.	Mar 1852	N.-Amer	572041
Stockburger, Andreas		18 Oct 1833	Bach-Altenberg	Obd.	Oct 1855	N.-Amer	838631
Stockburger, Johann Georg		17 Aug 1828	Roemlinsdorf	Obd.	Sep 1864	N.-Amer	838635
Stockemer, Johannes & W		30 Dec 1826	Gomaringen	Rtl.	Jun 1865	N.-Amer	841057
Stockemer, Maria Barbara (wife)		12 Dec 1833	Gomaringen	Rtl.	Jun 1865	N.-Amer	841057
Stocker, Albert		2 May 1851	Pfullingen	Rtl.	Sep 1869	N.-Amer	841057
Stocker, Karl Gustav			Leonberg	Leon.	Apr 1866	Austria	835787
Stockinger, Georg Wilhelm			Altenstaig	Nag.	Jul 1852	N.-Amer	838488
Stockinger, Johann Michael			Altenstaig	Nag.	Jul 1852	N.-Amer	838488
Stoeckinger, Andreas			Betzweiler	Obd.	Jun 1848	N.-Amer	838631
Stoeckinger, Christina		21 Jun 1826	Betzweiler	Obd.	Jun 1848	N.-Amer	838631
Stoeckle, Johann Jacob		11 Dec 1826	Leonberg	Leon.	Apr 1857	France	835786
Stoeffer, Maria Friederike		23 May 1845	Oberndorf	Obd.	Apr 1872	Hesse	838635
Stoeffler, Wilhelm Heinrich		24 Jul 1837	Oberndorf	Obd.	1852	N.-Amer	838635
Stoehrer, Andreas		1 May 1823	Moensheim	Leon.	Apr 1829	N.-Amer	837960
Stoehrer, Dorothea Margaretha		16 Jul 1809	Moensheim	Leon.	Apr 1829	N.-Amer	837960
Stoehrer, Friederika Christina		13 Sep 1811	Moensheim	Leon.	Apr 1829	N.-Amer	837960
Stoehrer, Jacob Martin		1 Dec 1820	Moensheim	Leon.	Apr 1829	N.-Amer	837960
Stoehrer, Jacob Martin & F		53 yrs.	Moensheim	Leon.	Apr 1829	N.-Amer	837960
Stoehrer, Johanna Rosina		17 Jul 1818	Moensheim	Leon.	Apr 1829	N.-Amer	837960
Stoehrer, Justina		8 Jun 1814	Moensheim	Leon.	Apr 1829	N.-Amer	837960
Stoehrer, Justina (wife)		44 yrs.	Moensheim	Leon.	Apr 1829	N.-Amer	837960
Stoehrer, Regina		25 Jul 1826	Moensheim	Leon.	Apr 1829	N.-Amer	837960
Stoekle, Caroline Louise		26yrs.	Leonberg	Leon.	Sep 1853	N.-Amer	835786
Stoekle, Friedrich		1 Feb 1834	Leonberg	Leon.	Jul 1852	N.-Amer	835786
Stoekle, Gottlieb Friedrich		5 Dec 1835	Leonberg	Leon.	May 1853	N.-Amer	835786
Stoeriz, Johann Georg		9 Aug 1826	Dettingen	Krch.	Sep 1069	N.-Amer	835944
Stoeriz, Regina Margaretha			Dettingen	Krch.	bef 1860	N.-Amer	835944
Stoerker, Karl Gustav		11 Aug 1845	Leonberg	Leon.	Nov 1865	N.-Amer	835787
Stoetter, Anna Barbara		28 Jul 1836	Steinenkirch	Gsl.	Aug 1854	N.-Amer	572042
Stoetter, Ernst Karl		1 Mar 1854	Steinenkirch	Gsl.	Aug 1854	N.-Amer	572042
Stoetter, Maria & C		13 Aug 1823	Steinenkirch	Gsl.	Aug 1854	N.-Amer	572042
Stoetter, Marianna		7 Feb 1851	Steinenkirch	Gsl.	Aug 1854	N.-Amer	572042
Stohleker, Anna Barbara			Honau	Rtl.	May 1833	N.-Amer	841051
Stohleker, Gottfried			Honau	Rtl.	May 1833	N.-Amer	841051
Stokburger, Friedrich			Bach-Altenberg	Obd.	Nov 1854	N.-Amer	838631
Stokburger, Jakob		30 Jul 1848	Peterzell	Obd.	Dec 1868	N.-Amer	838635
Stokburger, Johann Georg		3 Oct 1836	Bach-Altenberg	Obd.	Aug 1856	N.-Amer	838631
Stokemer, Bartholomaeus & F			Gomaringen	Rtl.	May 1832	N.-Amer	841051
Stoll, Johann Martin		8 May 1847	Pfullingen	Rtl.	Sep 1867	N.-Amer	841057
Stoll, Johannes		12 yrs.	Schaafhausen	Leon.	Apr 1833	Rus-Pol	837956
Stoll, Maria Katharina & C		15 Feb 1841	Pfullingen	Rtl.	Jul 1867	N.-Amer	841057
Stoll, Martin		7 Jan 1867	Pfullingen	Rtl.	Jul 1867	N.-Amer	841057
Stolz, Klemenz		2 Feb 1853	Kleinengstingen	Rtl.	Jun 1880	N.-Amer	841051
Stooss, Clemens		18 Nov 1839	Holzelfingen	Rtl.	Mar 1864	N.-Amer	841057

Stooss, Wilhelm	13 Mar 1847	Kleinengstingen	Rtl.	Feb 1866	N.-Amer	841057
Storker, Jacob	13 Jul 1821	Friolzheim	Leon.	bef 1850	N.-Amer	835791
Storr, Albert	22 Apr 1838	Wiesensteig	Gsl.	Mar 1853	N.-Amer	572041
Storz, Amalia	13 yrs.	Aichhalden	Obd.	Sep 1854	N.-Amer	838629
Storz, Anastasia	2 yrs.	Sulgau	Obd.	Sep 1852	N.-Amer	838637
Storz, Anastasia (wife)		Sulgau	Obd.	Sep 1852	N.-Amer	838637
Storz, Andreas	17 Jan 1849	Fluorn	Obd.	Oct 1866	N.-Amer	838632
Storz, Anna		Betzweiler	Obd.	Jul 1816	France	838631
Storz, Anna	10 Jun 1851	Fluorn	Obd.	May 1866	N.-Amer	838632
Storz, Barbara	7 Aug 1845	Fluorn	Obd.	Feb 1867	N.-Amer	838632
Storz, Christoph	4 Apr 1841	Alpirsbach	Obd.	Sep 1856	N.-Amer	838630
Storz, Emmerich	18 Sep 1838	Schramberg	Obd.	Aug 1868	Hungary	838636
Storz, Eva	22 Mar 1860	Fluorn	Obd.	May 1860	Saxony	838632
Storz, Ferdinand		Aichhalden	Obd.	bef 1861	N.-Amer	838629
Storz, Ferdinand	17 yrs.	Schramberg	Obd.	Sep 1854	N.-Amer	838636
Storz, Friedrich	28 Jul 1843	Peterzell	Obd.	Dec 1869	N.-Amer	838635
Storz, Jacob		Beffendorf	Obd.	bef 1858	N.-Amer	838631
Storz, Jakob & F		Sulgau	Obd.	Sep 1852	N.-Amer	838637
Storz, Johannes	17 Aug 1841	Hoenweiler	Obd.	Apr 1869	N.-Amer	838635
Storz, Magda - (wid.) & F		Aichhalden	Obd.	Sep 1854	N.-Amer	838629
Storz, Martin		Fluorn	Obd.	Jan 1861	N.-Amer	838632
Storz, Mathias		Beffendorf	Obd.	bef 1858	N.-Amer	838631
Storz, Richard		Lauterbach	Obd.	Jun 1860	N.-Amer	838634
Storz, Simon		Aichhalden	Obd.	Nov 1851	N.-Amer	838629
Stradinger, Bernhardine	10 May 1838	Seedorf	Obd.	Apr 1847	N.-Amer	838637
Stradinger, Carolina	2 Mar 1832	Seedorf	Obd.	Apr 1847	N.-Amer	838637
Stradinger, Catharina (wife)	25 Nov 1809	Seedorf	Obd.	Apr 1847	N.-Amer	838637
Stradinger, Constantin	20 May 1834	Seedorf	Obd.	Apr 1847	N.-Amer	838637
Stradinger, Crescentia	4 Jun 1841	Seedorf	Obd.	Apr 1847	N.-Amer	838637
Stradinger, Johann Baptist	20 Jun 1839	Seedorf	Obd.	Apr 1847	N.-Amer	838637
Stradinger, Philipp & F	4 May 1808	Seedorf	Obd.	Apr 1847	N.-Amer	838637
Stradinger, Pia	10 Jul 1834	Seedorf	Obd.	Apr 1847	N.-Amer	838637
Stradinger, Xaver	3 Aug 1845	Seedorf	Obd.	Apr 1847	N.-Amer	838637
Straehle, Anna	29 Jun 1879	Dettingen	Krch.	May 1882	N.-Amer	835944
Straehle, Anna Maria	8 Sep 1867	Dettingen	Krch.	May 1882	N.-Amer	835944
Straehle, Anna Maria (wife)	16 Mar 1843	Dettingen	Krch.	May 1882	N.-Amer	835944
Straehle, Christian	11 Jan 1878	Dettingen	Krch.	May 1882	N.-Amer	835944
Straehle, Christian Gottlieb	1 Feb 1869	Dettingen	Krch.	May 1882	N.-Amer	835944
Straehle, Christian Gottlieb	21 Jul 1831	Dettingen	Krch.	bef 1863	N.-Amer	835944
Straehle, Christiane	11 Jan 1878	Dettingen	Krch.	May 1882	N.-Amer	548403
Straehle, Christina Katharina	24 Jun 1872	Dettingen	Krch.	May 1882	N.-Amer	548403
Straehle, Georg Friedrich & F	18 Apr 1836	Dettingen	Krch.	May 1882	N.-Amer	835944
Straehle, Jacob Friedrich	15 Sep 1873	Dettingen	Krch.	May 1890	N.-Amer	835944
Straehle, Jakob Friedrich	16 Oct 1842	Kirchheim	Krch.	Feb 1862	N.-Amer	835941
Straehle, Johann Wilhelm	19 Nov 1817	Dettingen	Krch.	bef 1864	N.-Amer	835940
Straehle, Johann Wilhelm	2 Jun 1876	Dettingen	Krch.	May 1882	N.-Amer	548403
Straehle, Johann Wilhelm	29 Apr 1843	Dettingen	Krch.	Feb 1876	N.-Amer	548403
Straehle, Johannes	9 Feb 1846	Altenstadt-Gsl.	Gsl.	Oct 1866	N.-Amer	572045
Straehle, Michael		Kuchen	Gsl.	Aug 1866	Austral	572045
Straehle, Rosina	29 Oct 1870	Dettingen	Krch.	May 1882	N.-Amer	548403

Name		Birth		Emigration			Film
Last	First	Date	Place	O'amt	Appl. Date	Dest.	Number
Straehle, Wilhelm		19 Nov 1817	Dettingen	Krch.	Jan 1867	N.-Amer	835944
Straehle, Wilhelm Friedrich		13 Nov 1869	Dettingen	Krch.	Mar 1886	Austria	548403
Straub, Albrecht		5 May 1835	Oberndorf	Obd.	Apr 1847	N.-Amer	838635
Straub, Dorothea		34 yrs.	Amstetten	Gsl.	May 1857	N.-Amer	572043
Straub, Franziska		27 Feb 1830	Deggingen	Gsl.	Feb 1854	N.-Amer	572042
Straub, Friedrich & F		37 yrs.	Oberndorf	Obd.	Apr 1847	N.-Amer	838635
Straub, Johann Georg		24 May 1881	Zell	Krch.	Feb 1893	N.-Amer	835774
Straub, Johannes		31 Mar 1868	Zell	Krch.	Feb 1885	N.-Amer	548403
Straub, Maria Kreszensia		17 Sep 1845	Westerheim	Gsl.	May 1868	N.-Amer	572046
Straub, Philippina (wife)		30 yrs.	Oberndorf	Obd.	Apr 1847	N.-Amer	838635
Straub, Theodor		9 Nov 1841	Westerheim	Gsl.	Aug 1859	N.-Amer	572043
Straubmueller, Alfons		29 Oct 1865	Donzdorf	Gsl.	Aug 1882	N.-Amer	572048
Straum, Franz Anton		21 Jan 1821	Wiesensteig	Gsl.	Oct 1851	N.-Amer	577788
Strauss, Christina		9 mon.	Geislingen	Gsl.	Apr 1853	N.-Amer	572041
Strauss, Christina		24 yrs.	Geislingen	Gsl.	Apr 1853	N.-Amer	572041
Strauss, Friederike & C		26 yrs.	Geislingen	Gsl.	Apr 1853	N.-Amer	572041
Strauss, Gottlieb Friedrich			Heimsheim	Leon.	Mar 1826	Austria	837955
Strehler, Johannes			Berneck	Nag.	Aug 1852	N.-Amer	838488
Stroehle, Anna (wife)		28 May 1814	Aufhausen	Gsl.	May 1854	N.-Amer	572042
Stroehle, Anna Maria		6 Dec 1848	Kuchen	Gsl.	Feb 1853	N.-Amer	572041
Stroehle, Barbara		21 Dec 1838	Aufhausen	Gsl.	May 1854	N.-Amer	572042
Stroehle, Jakob		30 Jan 1832	Geislingen	Gsl.	Aug 1852	N.-Amer	572041
Stroehle, Johann Michael		8 May 1842	Aufhausen	Gsl.	May 1854	N.-Amer	572042
Stroehle, Johannes			Ueberkingen	Gsl.	Dec 1853	N.-Amer	572041
Stroehle, Johannes		20 May 1824	Geislingen	Gsl.	Mar 1853	Bavaria	572041
Stroehle, Johannes & F		18 Jan 1809	Aufhausen	Gsl.	May 1854	N.-Amer	572042
Stroehle, Kaspar		5 Nov 1841	Steinenkirch	Gsl.	Apr 1869	N.-Amer	572047
Stroehle, Katharina		14 Jul 1846	Kuchen	Gsl.	Feb 1853	N.-Amer	572041
Stroehle, Maria		5 Jun 1837	Aufhausen	Gsl.	May 1854	N.-Amer	572042
Stroehle, Marie		21 Mar 1821	Unterboehringen	Gsl.	Feb 1854	N.-Amer	572042
Stroehle, Regina (wid.) & F			Kuchen	Gsl.	Feb 1853	N.-Amer	572041
Stroehle, Sabina		23 Jul 1826	Ueberkingen	Gsl.	Jul 1856	N.-Amer	572043
Stroehle, Ursula		25 Oct 1840	Aufhausen	Gsl.	May 1854	N.-Amer	572042
Stroehles, Johannes		30 Jul 1819	Ueberkingen	Gsl.	Jul 1856	N.-Amer	572043
Stroele, Gottlob Hermann		11 Oct 1872	Oberlenningen	Krch.	Apr 1883	N.-Amer	835946
Stroele, Paulina		26 Nov 1862	Oberlenningen	Krch.	May 1880	N.-Amer	835940
Stroezer, Johann Martin			Pfullingen	Rtl.	Mar 1860	N.-Amer	841057
Strohecker, Andreas			Wimsheim	Loen.	bef 1854	N.-Amer	837967
Strohecker, Anna Maria		17 yrs.	Wimsheim	Loen.	Jul 1855	N.-Amer	837967
Strohecker, Johann Michael		16 yrs.	Wimsheim	Loen.	Jul 1855	N.-Amer	837967
Strohecker, Michael			Wimsheim	Loen.	Oct 1854	N.-Amer	837967
Strohecker, Sara (wife) & F			Wimsheim	Loen.	Oct 1854	N.-Amer	837967
Strohhecker, Elisabetha (wife)			Wimsheim	Loen.	Jun 1838	N.-Amer	837967
Strohhecker, Eva		24 yrs.	Wimsheim	Loen.	Feb 1861	N.-Amer	837967
Strohhecker, Matthias & W			Wimsheim	Loen.	Jun 1838	N.-Amer	837967
Strohm, Andreas		21 Jul 1829	Moensheim	Leon.	Apr 1854	N.-Amer	837960
Strohm, Christiane Regina		18 Mar 1841	Moensheim	Leon.	Mar 1854	N.-Amer	837960
Strohm, Christine Dorothea		3 Jan 1845	Moensheim	Leon.	Mar 1854	N.-Amer	837960
Strohm, Dorothea Carolina		7 Sep 1853	Moensheim	Leon.	Mar 1854	N.-Amer	837960
Strohm, Georg Jakob		23 Feb 1837	Moensheim	Leon.	Sep 1853	N.-Amer	837960

Strohm, Johann Georg	21 Jan 1839	Moensheim	Leon.	Sep 1853	N.-Amer	837960
Strohm, Katharina	7 Mar 1851	Moensheim	Leon.	Mar 1854	N.-Amer	837960
Strohm, Simon	21 Nov 1842	Moensheim	Leon.	Mar 1854	N.-Amer	837960
Strohm, Simon & F		Moensheim	Leon.	Mar 1854	N.-Amer	837960
Strohm, Wilhelm	20 Nov 1854	Perouse	Leon.	bef 1880	N.-Amer	837962
Strohmayer, Katharina		Neidlingen	Krch.	bef 1865	N.-Amer	835940
Strohmeier, Adam	11 Jan 1851	Gomaringen	Rtl.	Jun 1869	N.-Amer	841057
Strohmeier, Jakob & F		Gomaringen	Rtl.	1853	N.-Amer	841057
Strohmeier, Johann		Gomaringen	Rtl.	1853	N.-Amer	841057
Strohmeier, Julius	22 Jun 1851	Gomaringen	Rtl.	Jun 1869	N.-Amer	841057
Strohmeier, Margaretha		Gomaringen	Rtl.	1853	N.-Amer	841057
Strohmeier, Maria (wife)		Gomaringen	Rtl.	1853	N.-Amer	841057
Strohmer, Jacob		Jesingen	Krch.	Jul 1787	Hungary	550804
Stuber, Dorothea & C	31 yrs.	Wimsheim	Loen.	Jul 1850	N.-Amer	837967
Stuber, Michael	7 yrs.	Wimsheim	Loen.	Jul 1850	N.-Amer	837967
Stucke, Christian Friedrich	16 Oct 1849	Herrenberg	Herr.	Sep 1868	N.-Amer	834629
Stueckel, Gottfried		Ditzingen	Leon.	Apr 1858	N.-Amer	835788
Stueckle, Anna Maria	5 Aug 1834	Michelbach	Herr.	Jan 1864	France	834629
Stuempfle, Johann Jakob	29 Jul 1839	Brucken	Krch.	Jul 1863	Austria	835944
Stuempfle, Johann Michael	29 Aug 1837	Brucken	Krch.	Oct 1866	N.-Amer	835944
Stuempfle, Johann Michael	11 Jan 1844	Brucken	Krch.	Mar 1859	N.-Amer	835944
Stuetz, Bernhard		Boehmenkirch	Gsl.	Sep 1853	N.-Amer	572041
Stuetz, Johannes	31 Jul 1836	Boehmenkirch	Gsl.	Dec 1856	N.-Amer	572043
Stuetz, Josefa	2 yrs.	Boehmenkirch	Gsl.	Sep 1853	N.-Amer	572041
Stuetz, Joseph	6 yrs.	Boehmenkirch	Gsl.	Sep 1853	N.-Amer	572041
Stuetz, Kaspar & F		Boehmenkirch	Gsl.	Sep 1853	N.-Amer	572041
Stuetz, Marianna (wife)		Boehmenkirch	Gsl.	Sep 1853	N.-Amer	572041
Stuetz, Michael	4 yrs.	Boehmenkirch	Gsl.	Sep 1853	N.-Amer	572041
Stuible, Andreas	20 Feb 1844	Moensheim	Leon.	Jul 1853	N.-Amer	837960
Stuible, Andreas	17 Jul 1837	Moensheim	Leon.	Feb 1847	N.-Amer	837960
Stuible, Andreas & F		Moensheim	Leon.	Jul 1853	N.-Amer	837960
Stuible, Anna Maria	21 Jul 1852	Moensheim	Leon.	Jul 1853	N.-Amer	837960
Stuible, Anna Maria	3 Mar 1845	Moensheim	Leon.	Feb 1847	N.-Amer	837960
Stuible, Anna Maria (wife)		Moensheim	Leon.	Jul 1853	N.-Amer	837960
Stuible, Anna Maria (wife)		Moensheim	Leon.	Feb 1847	N.-Amer	837960
Stuible, Augustin & F	39 yrs.	Moensheim	Leon.	Feb 1847	N.-Amer	837960
Stuible, Christine Margaretha	13 Jun 1840	Moensheim	Leon.	Feb 1847	N.-Amer	837960
Stuible, Johann Mathaeus	4 Jan 1850	Moensheim	Leon.	Jul 1853	N.-Amer	837960
Stuible, Johanna Catharina	19 Jul 1834	Moensheim	Leon.	Feb 1847	N.-Amer	837960
Stuible, Johanna Magdalena	14 Nov 1822	Moensheim	Leon.	Apr 1854	N.-Amer	837960
Stuible, Johanna Margaretha	12 Jan 1842	Moensheim	Leon.	Jul 1853	N.-Amer	837960
Stuible, Rosina Catharina	9 Nov 1839	Moensheim	Leon.	Jul 1853	N.-Amer	837960
Stuible, Samuel Friedrich	16 Apr 1842	Moensheim	Leon.	Feb 1847	N.-Amer	837960
Stumpp, Carl August	24 Oct 1865	Holzmaden	Krch.	Aug 1880	N.-Amer	835945
Stumpp, Karl	21 Nov 1841	Bronnen	Rtl.	Sep 1869	Prussia	841057
Stutzmann, Johannes	3 Dec 1833	Friolzheim	Leon.	May 1880	N.-Amer	835791
Suelzle, Johann Georg		Moensheim	Leon.	1873	N.-Amer	837960
Suess, Alfred	31 Mar 1850	Oetlingen	Krch.	Dec 1867	N.-Amer	835948
Suess, Christian August	29 Apr 1846	Oetlingen	Krch.	Jul 1866	N.-Amer	835948
Sulger, Friedrich	9 May 1850	Gomaringen	Rtl.	Dec 1866	N.-Amer	841057

Name		Birth		Emigration			Film
Last	First	Date	Place	O'amt	Appl. Date	Dest.	Number
Sulzmann, Johann Christian			Leonberg	Leon.	bef 1860	N.-Amer	835787
Summ, Andreas		28 Jun 1850	Betzweiler	Obd.	Dec 1870	N.-Amer	838631
Summ, Andreas		17 Dec 1859	Peterzell	Obd.	Apr 1862	N.-Amer	838635
Summ, Anna Maria		13 Nov 1839	Peterzell	Obd.	Apr 1862	N.-Amer	838635
Summ, Georg		18 yrs.	Peterzell	Obd.	Mar 1854	N.-Amer	838635
Summ, Johannes		3 Mar 1843	Peterzell	Obd.	Feb 1861	N.-Amer	838635
Supper, Anna Barbara		19 Aug 1800	Muenchingen	Leon.	Apr 1848	N.-Amer	837961
Supper, Georg Friedrich		29 Nov 1838	Heimerdingen	Leon.	bef 1869	N.-Amer	837954
Supper, Johannes			Heimerdingen	Leon.	bef 1872	N.-Amer	837954
Supper, Wilhelm Friedrich		29 Oct 1857	Heimerdingen	Leon.	Dec 1880	N.-Amer	837954
Tafel, Ida Johanna Maria		16 Dec 1841	Flacht	Leon.	Jan 1864	Prussia	835790
Tafelmayer, Hans Jerg			Oberlenningen	Krch.	May 1771	Hungary	550804
Taigel, Georg Friedrich		7 Jul 1835	Pfullingen	Rtl.	Nov 1855	London	841057
Teck, Martina			Winzeln	Obd.	Apr 1866	N.-Amer	841016
Teufel, Agathe			Bronnen	Rtl.	Oct 1828	N.-Amer	841051
Teufel, Barbara (wife)		50 yrs.	Hochmoessingen	Obd.	Nov 1846	N.-Amer	838633
Teufel, Elisabetha		1 Apr 1839	Hochmoessingen	Obd.	Nov 1846	N.-Amer	838633
Teufel, Jakob		16 Jul 1835	Hochmoessingen	Obd.	Nov 1846	N.-Amer	838633
Teufel, Johann Georg		31 Mar 1847	Bondorf	Herr.	Dec 1866	N.-Amer	834630
Teufel, Johannes		13 Feb 1820	Hochmoessingen	Obd.	Nov 1846	N.-Amer	838633
Teufel, Joseph		25 Jul 1821	Hochmoessingen	Obd.	Nov 1846	N.-Amer	838633
Teufel, Karoline		20 Dec 1831	Hochmoessingen	Obd.	Nov 1846	N.-Amer	838633
Teufel, Katharina		11 Dec 1824	Hochmoessingen	Obd.	Nov 1846	N.-Amer	838633
Teufel, Matheus & F		1 Nov 1799	Hochmoessingen	Obd.	Nov 1846	N.-Amer	838633
Thalmann, Ernst Robert		28 Feb 1868	Kirchheim	Krch.	Apr 1884	N.-Amer	548403
Thalmann, Karl Heinrich		10 Oct 1870	Kirchheim	Krch.	Sep 1887	N.-Amer	548323
Theilfahrt, Georg			Ditzingen	Leon.	Mar 1852	N.-Amer	835788
Theurer, Barbara			Alpirsbach	Obd.	Apr 1859	France	838630
Theurer, Christiane			Alpirsbach	Obd.	Jun 1862	France	838630
Theurer, Friederike Rosine			Alpirsbach	Obd.	Mar 1859	France	838630
Theurer, Georg Jacob		3 Sep 1817	Alpirsbach	Obd.	Aug 1844	France	838630
Theurer, Lorenz Heinrich		22 Mar 1819	Leonberg	Leon.	1852	N.-Amer	835787
Thierer, Bernhard		22 Apr 1845	Boehmenkirch	Gsl.	Jan 1867	N.-Amer	572046
Thierer, Franz		6 Dec 1817	Treffelhausen	Gsl.	Jun 1851	N.-Amer	577788
Thierer, Joseph		27 Feb 1849	Treffelhausen	Gsl.	Mar 1869	N.-Amer	572047
Thoni, Charlotte Caroline		8 yrs.	Muenchingen	Leon.	Feb 1854	N.-Amer	837961
Thoni, Christine			Muenchingen	Leon.	Feb 1854	N.-Amer	837961
Thoni, Johann Georg & F			Muenchingen	Leon.	Feb 1854	N.-Amer	837961
Thudium, Barbara		9 Nov 1831	Aichelberg	Krch.	bef 1866	N.-Amer	835940
Tochtermann, Albert		6 Dec 1848	Reutlingen	Rtl.	bef 1868	N.-Amer	841057
Tochtermann, Bertha		29 Jun 1841	Reutlingen	Rtl.	bef 1868	Switz.	841057
Tochtermann, Caroline		19 Apr 1846	Reutlingen	Rtl.	Jul 1865	N.-Amer	841057
Tochtermann, Gottlob August		3 Aug 1847	Reutlingen	Rtl.	Apr 1866	N.-Amer	841057
Tochtermann, Johannes		16 May 1849	Reutlingen	Rtl.	Jul 1865	N.-Amer	841057
Tochtermann, Julie Marie		3 Apr 1842	Reutlingen	Rtl.	May 1866	N.-Amer	841057
Tompert, Johann Ernst Christ.		1 Apr 1824	Renningen	Leon.	Jun 1854	N.-Amer	837963
Tondel, Johannes		17 yrs.	Oberhausen	Rtl.	Feb 1880	N.-Amer	841051
Tondel, Matheus		46 yrs.	Oberhausen	Rtl.	Jun 1880	N.-Amer	841051
Traub, Christof Friedrich & F		11 Apr 1859	Oberlenningen	Krch.	Apr 1888	N.-Amer	835947
Traub, Friederike Karoline		23 Mar 1885	Oberlenningen	Krch.	Apr 1888	N.-Amer	835947

Traub, Gustav	25 Jun 1856	Kirchheim	Krch.	Jun 1873	N.-Amer	548403
Traub, Jacob		Wellingen	Krch.	bef 1771	N.-Amer	550804
Traub, Johann Stephan	5 Jun 1849	Unterhausen	Rtl.	Apr 1864	N.-Amer	841057
Traub, Johannes	3 Mar 1847	Oberlenningen	Krch.	Nov 1866	N.-Amer	835947
Traub, Juliana	1 Oct 1810	Pfullingen	Rtl.	bef 1866	N.-Amer	841057
Traub, Karoline Frieder. (wife)	18 Nov 1859	Oberlenningen	Krch.	Apr 1888	N.-Amer	835947
Traub, Katharina Karolina	17 Mar 1887	Oberlenningen	Krch.	Apr 1888	N.-Amer	835947
Traub, Wilhelmine	7 Mar 1886	Oberlenningen	Krch.	Apr 1888	N.-Amer	835947
Trautman, Katharina	11 Jun 1843	Willmandingen	Rtl.	bef 1866	N.-Amer	841057
Trautmann, Albert	5 mon.	Reutlingen	Rtl.	Mar 1860	N.-Amer	841057
Trautmann, Anna Katharina	21 Aug 1836	Willmandingen	Rtl.	bef 1860	Switz.	841057
Trautmann, Anna Maria	38 yrs.	Alpirsbach	Obd.	Nov 1849	France	838630
Trautmann, Friedrich	2 yrs.	Reutlingen	Rtl.	Mar 1860	N.-Amer	841057
Trautmann, Friedrich & F		Reutlingen	Rtl.	Mar 1860	N.-Amer	841057
Trautmann, Johannes	3 Feb 1830	Willmandingen	Rtl.	1851	N.-Amer	841057
Trautmann, Maria Barbara	17 Sep 1837	Willmandingen	Rtl.	Feb 1860	N.-Amer	841057
Trautmann, Marie (wife)		Reutlingen	Rtl.	Mar 1860	N.-Amer	841057
Trautwein, Friedrich		Alpirsbach	Obd.	Nov 1861	N.-Amer	838630
Trautwein, Jacob Friedrich	29 Mar 1818	Alpirsbach	Obd.	Jun 1847	France	838630
Trefz, Gustav Adolf	5 Jan 1871	Ditzingen	Loen.	Oct 1887	N.-Amer	837967
Tressel, Christian	14 Dec 1828	Bochingen	Obd.	Oct 1863	Austria	838632
Trick, Andreas Wilhelm	27 May 1835	Alpirsbach	Obd.	Mar 1854	N.-Amer	838630
Trick, Anna Maria	4 Sep 1828	Alpirsbach	Obd.	Jun 1856	France	838630
Trick, Christiane	19 Feb 1821	Alpirsbach	Obd.	Oct 1855	Switz.	838630
Trick, Christoph Friedrich		Alpirsbach	Obd.	Jun 1821	France	838631
Trick, Friederike		Alpirsbach	Obd.	May 1862	France	838630
Trick, Jacob Franz	2 May 1837	Alpirsbach	Obd.	Aug 1856	N.-Amer	838630
Trick, Rosina	14 Aug 1833	Alpirsbach	Obd.	Jun 1858	Switz.	838630
Trick, Wilhelm	14 Sep 1856	Hoenweiler	Obd.	May 1867	N.-Amer	838635
Trik, Josef	19 yrs.	Aichhalden	Obd.	Mar 1855	N.-Amer	838629
Trissler, Eberhard Friedr. & W		Reutlingen	Rtl.	Dec 1859	N.-Amer	841057
Trissler, Gustav Theodor	28 Oct 1840	Reutlingen	Rtl.	Sep 1867	Prussia	841057
Trissler, Heinrich	6 Mar 1848	Reutlingen	Rtl.	Nov 1867	N.-Amer	841057
Trissler, Hermann	10 Jan 1848	Reutlingen	Rtl.	Aug 1864	N.-Amer	841057
Trissler, Katharina (wife)		Reutlingen	Rtl.	Dec 1859	N.-Amer	841057
Tritschler, Johann Carl	27 Dec 1826	Kirchheim	Krch.	Feb 1856	Prussia	835940
Tritschler, Johannes	11 Jun 1848	Schramberg	Obd.	May 1864	N.-Amer	838636
Tritschler, Leo	22 yrs.	Lauterbach	Obd.	Oct 1852	N.-Amer	838634
Troester, Agnes Barbara	2 Jan 1848	Reutlingen	Rtl.	Oct 1865	N.-Amer	841057
Troester, Johann Friedrich	31 Oct 1830	Pfullingen	Rtl.	Jul 1868	N.-Amer	841057
Troester, Johann Jakob	26 Oct 1852	Pfullingen	Rtl.	Oct 1868	N.-Amer	841057
Troester, Johann Jakob	6 Feb 1837	Pfullingen	Rtl.	bef 1868	France	841057
Trommeter, Franz Anton & F		Westerheim	Gsl.	Apr 1853	N.-Amer	572041
Trommeter, Georg	2 yrs.	Westerheim	Gsl.	Apr 1853	N.-Amer	572041
Trommeter, Maria Anna	1 yrs.	Westerheim	Gsl.	Apr 1853	N.-Amer	572041
Trost, Karl Adolf	30 May 1853	Oetlingen	Krch.	Jun 1883	Austral	835948
Trotter, Caroline	36 yrs.	Oberndorf	Obd.	Mar 1856	France	838635
Trotter, Cuno	9 Aug 1841	Oberndorf	Obd.	Sep 1854	N.-Amer	838635
Trotter, Johann Baptist	15 May 1847	Oberndorf	Obd.	Jul 1867	N.-Amer	838635
Trotter, Josefa	13 Apr 1826	Oberndorf	Obd.	Jun 1847	Austria	838635

Name		Birth		Emigration			Film
Last	First	Date	Place	O'amt	Appl. Date	Dest.	Number
Trotter, Max			Oberndorf	Obd.	Dec 1850	N.-Amer	838635
Truchsess, Carl Christian		11 Sep 1847	Kirchheim	Krch.	Apr 1866	N.-Amer	835941
Truchsess, Ernst		7 Aug 1842	Kirchheim	Krch.	1852	N.-Amer	835941
Trucksaess, Johann Georg		30 Sep 1807	Schoeckingen	Leon.	bef 1828	N.-Amer	837964
Trudel, Jacob		30 Jan 1835	Oberhausen	Rtl.	1858	N.-Amer	841057
Truek, Magda			Aichhalden	Obd.	Mar 1863	France	838629
Truek, Maria		29 yrs.	Aichhalden	Obd.	Sep 1862	N.-Amer	838629
Truksaess, Jacob & F			Hemmingen	Leon.	Feb 1853	N.-Amer	837956
Uhl, Anna Maria			Geislingen	Gsl.	Jan 1854	N.-Amer	572042
Uhl, Anna Maria & C			Renningen	Leon.	Apr 1852	N.-Amer	837963
Uhl, Christina Barbara		31 Mar 1833	Renningen	Leon.	Apr 1852	N.-Amer	837963
Uhl, Johann Georg			Renningen	Leon.	Apr 1852	N.-Amer	837963
Uhl, Johannes		6 mon.	Geislingen	Gsl.	Jan 1854	N.-Amer	572042
Uhl, Johannes & F			Geislingen	Gsl.	Jan 1854	N.-Amer	572042
Uhl, Margaretha		18 mon.	Geislingen	Gsl.	Jan 1854	N.-Amer	572042
Uhl, Mathias & F			Sulgen	Obd.	Apr 1817	N.-Amer	838631
Uhle, Adam & F			Heimsheim	Leon.	Feb 1853	N.-Amer	837955
Uhlmann, Georg Gottlieb & W			Gerlingen	Leon.	Dec 1842	Austria	837953
Ulmer, Carl		2 Oct 1850	Kirchheim	Krch.	Jul 1870	N.-Amer	835941
Ulmer, Eva		15 Aug 1825	Willmandingen	Rtl.	bef 1863	N.-Amer	841057
Ulmer, Friedrich Wilhelm		26 Feb 1843	Pfullingen	Rtl.	Nov 1860	England	841057
Ulmer, Georg Friedrich		25 Apr 1843	Willmandingen	Rtl.	Feb 1860	N.-Amer	841057
Ulmer, Gottlieb		15 Sep 1848	Willmandingen	Rtl.	Apr 1867	N.-Amer	841057
Ulmer, Heinrich		18 Mar 1848	Willmandingen	Rtl.	Feb 1861	N.-Amer	841057
Ulmer, Heinrich Sr. & F		16 Oct 1806	Willmandingen	Rtl.	Feb 1861	N.-Amer	841057
Ulmer, Immanuel & W		24 Sep 1837	Pfullingen	Rtl.	Aug 1865	Saxony	841057
Ulmer, Jacob		11 Mar 1830	Willmandingen	Rtl.	bef 1863	N.-Amer	841057
Ulmer, Jakob		22 Aug 1840	Gomaringen	Rtl.	Sep 1859	N.-Amer	841057
Ulmer, Johann Georg		18 Oct 1874	Weilheim	Krch.	Apr 1890	N.-Amer	835774
Ulmer, Johann Jacob		19 Jul 1840	Stockach	Rtl.	Nov 1869	Bremen	841057
Ulmer, Johannes		30 Jan 1846	Willmandingen	Rtl.	Apr 1866	N.-Amer	841057
Ulmer, Johannes		29 Jan 1814	Pfullingen	Rtl.	Nov 1860	Austral	841057
Ulmer, Johannes		20 Apr 1844	Willmandingen	Rtl.	Feb 1860	N.-Amer	841057
Ulmer, Johannes		11 Oct 1838	Weilheim	Krch.	Mar 1856	N.-Amer	835949
Ulmer, Ludwig		22 yrs.	Willmandingen	Rtl.	Apr 1880	N.-Amer	841051
Ulmer, Maria Magdalena		9 Dec 1836	Pfullingen	Rtl.	Aug 1865	Saxony	841057
Ulmer, Matthaeus		14 Nov 1789	Willmandingen	Rtl.	Mar 1860	N.-Amer	841057
Ulmer, Michael		24 Jan 1843	Kuchen	Gsl.	Jul 1865	N.-Amer	572045
Ulmer, Ursula		6 Feb 1832	Kuchen	Gsl.	Sep 1860	Switz.	572044
Ulmer, Ursula Cathar. (wife)		14 Sep 1811	Willmandingen	Rtl.	Feb 1861	N.-Amer	841057
Ulmer, Ursula Catharina		4 Jul 1850	Willmandingen	Rtl.	Feb 1861	N.-Amer	841057
Ulmer, Wilhelm Friedrich		1 Apr 1871	Kirchheim	Krch.	Dec 1887	N.-Amer	835942
Ulmschneider, Theresia			Sulgen	Obd.	Jun 1859	N.-Amer	838638
Ulrich, Anna Catharina		12 May 1829	Muenchingen	Leon.	Mar 1848	N.-Amer	837961
Ulrich, Anna Maria			Moensheim	Leon.	Feb 1854	N.-Amer	837960
Ulrich, Catharina		27 May 1829	Muenchingen	Leon.	1849	N.-Amer	837961
Ulrich, Christiane		8 Aug 1830	Muenchingen	Leon.	1849	N.-Amer	837961
Ulrich, Christine Johanne		21 May 1836	Muenchingen	Leon.	Mar 1848	N.-Amer	837961
Ulrich, Johann Georg		21 Dec 1844	Muenchingen	Leon.	Mar 1848	N.-Amer	837961
Ulrich, Johanne		19 May 1838	Muenchingen	Leon.	Mar 1848	N.-Amer	837961

Name	Date	Place	Dist.	Emigr.	Dest.	Film
Ulrich, Johannes & F		Muenchingen	Leon.	Mar 1848	N.-Amer	837961
Ulrich, Maria Barbara	17 Mar 1827	Muenchingen	Leon.	Mar 1848	N.-Amer	837961
Ulrich, Maria Barbara (wife)		Muenchingen	Leon.	Mar 1848	N.-Amer	837961
Unckle, Christian Eduard	2 Aug 1849	Herrenberg	Herr.	Apr 1866	N.-Amer	834629
Unger, Anna Maria	25 Jul 1831	Hochdorf	Krch.	Apr 1854	N.-Amer	835945
Unger, Barbara Wilhel. (wife)	26 Mar 1834	Hochdorf	Krch.	Jul 1876	N.-Amer	835945
Unger, Christiane Kunigunde	25 Jan 1853	Hochdorf	Krch.	bef 1861	N.-Amer	835945
Unger, Elisabetha Dorothea	1 Nov 1836	Hochdorf	Krch.	bef 1861	N.-Amer	835945
Unger, Friedrich & F		Hochdorf	Krch.	bef 1861	N.-Amer	835945
Unger, Gottlieb	27 Oct 1847	Holzmaden	Krch.	Feb 1866	N.-Amer	835945
Unger, Johann Christian	23 Dec 1841	Hochdorf	Krch.	bef 1861	N.-Amer	835945
Unger, Johann Georg	23 Jan 1841	Holzmaden	Krch.	Feb 1866	N.-Amer	835945
Unger, Johanna Katharina	13 Jan 1864	Hochdorf	Krch.	Jul 1876	N.-Amer	548403
Unger, Josef Friedrich	11 May 1840	Hochdorf	Krch.	Apr 1854	N.-Amer	835945
Unger, Ludwig & F	24 Mar 1838	Hochdorf	Krch.	Jul 1876	N.-Amer	835945
Unger, Salome Wilhelmine	26 Mar 1839	Hochdorf	Krch.	Jul 1876	N.-Amer	548403
Unger, Wilhelm	26 Aug 1847	Hochdorf	Krch.	bef 1861	N.-Amer	835945
Unger, Wilhelm Friedrich	26 Mar 1870	Hochdorf	Krch.	Jul 1876	N.-Amer	835945
Unger, Wilhelmine Barbara	1 Jan 1868	Hochdorf	Krch.	Jul 1876	N.-Amer	548403
Urban, Martin	25 yrs.	Oppingen	Gsl.	bef 1852	N.-Amer	572041
Valet, Wilhelm	14 Feb 1859	Friedrichshafen/Tett	Krch.	bef 1883	N.-Amer	835942
Varnbueler, Pauline		Hemmingen	Leon.	Apr 1841	Bavaria	837956
Vatter, Johann Matthaeus	20 Sep 1865	Owen	Krch.	Jul 1882	N.-Amer	548403
Veil, Michael & F		Gutenberg	Krch.	Apr 1804	Pr.-Pol	550804
Veit, Ehrenreich		Leonberg	Leon.	Jan 1814	Poland	835786
Veit, Jacob	25 May 1835	Boehmenkirch	Gsl.	Mar 1861	N.-Amer	572044
Velm, Christiane Cathar. & F		Schoeckingen	Leon.	Mar 1851	N.-Amer	837964
Velm, Heinrich Wilhelm	1 yrs.	Schoeckingen	Leon.	Mar 1851	N.-Amer	837964
Velm, Johann Gottlieb	3 yrs.	Schoeckingen	Leon.	Mar 1851	N.-Amer	837964
Velte, Anna & C	13 Aug 1824	Muenchingen	Leon.	Apr 1849	N.-Amer	837961
Velte, Catharina	1 Apr 1830	Muenchingen	Leon.	Mar 1852	N.-Amer	837961
Velte, Jakob	22 Sep 1849	Muenchingen	Leon.	Mar 1852	N.-Amer	837961
Velte, Jakob Friedrich	16 Jan 1836	Muenchingen	Leon.	Mar 1852	N.-Amer	837961
Velte, Jakob Friedrich & F		Muenchingen	Leon.	Mar 1852	N.-Amer	837961
Velte, Johann (wife)		Muenchingen	Leon.	Mar 1852	N.-Amer	837961
Velte, Johann Georg	25 Mar 1845	Muenchingen	Leon.	Mar 1852	N.-Amer	837961
Velte, Johann Georg & F		Muenchingen	Leon.	Mar 1852	N.-Amer	837961
Velte, Johanna Maria (wife)		Muenchingen	Leon.	Mar 1852	N.-Amer	837961
Velte, Johannes	15 Dec 1850	Muenchingen	Leon.	Mar 1852	N.-Amer	837961
Velte, Karl Ernst	10 Feb 1849	Muenchingen	Leon.	Apr 1849	N.-Amer	837961
Velte, Maria	23 Aug 1846	Muenchingen	Leon.	Mar 1852	N.-Amer	837961
Velte, Wilhelm	20 Mar 1846	Muenchingen	Leon.	Apr 1849	N.-Amer	837961
Veltin, Johanna	19 Apr 1845	Muenchingen	Leon.	Jan 1854	N.-Amer	837961
Vesenmaier, Johann Georg		Donzdorf	Gsl.	Sep 1852	N.-Amer	572041
Vetter, Agatha	22 Aug 1849	Kuchen	Gsl.	May 1854	N.-Amer	572042
Vetter, Andreas	20 Oct 1841	Ueberkingen	Gsl.	Dec 1881	Switz.	572048
Vetter, Andreas	8 Jul 1851	Boehmenkirch	Gsl.	Mar 1868	N.-Amer	572046
Vetter, Apollonia	10 Sep 1825	Kuchen	Gsl.	Apr 1854	N.-Amer	572042
Vetter, Barbara		Kuchen	Gsl.	Feb 1853	N.-Amer	572041
Vetter, Elisabetha & C	21 Apr 1824	Kuchen	Gsl.	May 1854	N.-Amer	572042

Name		Birth		Emigration			Film
Last	First	Date	Place	O'amt	Appl. Date	Dest.	Number
Vetter, Georg			Ueberkingen	Gsl.	Apr 1853	N.-Amer	572041
Vetter, Georg			Altenstadt-Gsl.	Gsl.	Feb 1853	N.-Amer	572041
Vetter, Georg			Grosssuessen	Gsl.	May 1851	N.-Amer	577788
Vetter, Gertrude (wife)		36 yrs.	Boehmenkirch	Gsl.	Sep 1854	N.-Amer	572042
Vetter, Jacob & F		41 yrs.	Boehmenkirch	Gsl.	Sep 1854	N.-Amer	572042
Vetter, Johannes			Kuchen	Gsl.	Feb 1853	N.-Amer	572041
Vetter, Johannes		4 yrs.	Boehmenkirch	Gsl.	Sep 1854	N.-Amer	572042
Vetter, Johannes		11 Nov 1804	Unterboehringen	Gsl.	Mar 1854	N.-Amer	572042
Vetter, Joseph		7 mon.	Boehmenkirch	Gsl.	Sep 1854	N.-Amer	572042
Vetter, Karl		19 Sep 1835	Unterboehringen	Gsl.	Jul 1854	N.-Amer	572042
Vetter, Karl		22 Jan 1863	Renningen	Leon.	Apr 1880	N.-Amer	837963
Vetter, Kaspar		9 Nov 1834	Kuchen	Gsl.	Sep 1853	N.-Amer	572041
Vetter, Leonhard		2 yrs.	Boehmenkirch	Gsl.	Sep 1854	N.-Amer	572042
Vetter, Lukas			Kuchen	Gsl.	Jul 1851	N.-Amer	577788
Vetter, Magdalena			Kuchen	Gsl.	Feb 1853	N.-Amer	572041
Vetter, Mathias		24 May 1848	Kuchen	Gsl.	Oct 1865	N.-Amer	572045
Vetter, Nikolaus		18 Jun 1830	Kuchen	Gsl.	Feb 1853	N.-Amer	572041
Vetter, Regina		20 Mar 1849	Kuchen	Gsl.	Aug 1866	N.-Amer	572045
Vetter, Simon			Kuchen	Gsl.	1849	N.-Amer	572044
Vialkowitsch, Engelbert		18 Sep 1849	Winzeln	Obd.	Jul 1867	N.-Amer	841016
Vialkowitsch, Louise		8 Sep 1846	Winzeln	Obd.	Jul 1867	N.-Amer	841016
Vialkowitsch, Michael & F			Winzeln	Obd.	May 1817	N.-Amer	841016
Vielkawitsch, Jakobina		27 Jun 1838	Winzeln	Obd.	Sep 1854	N.-Amer	841016
Vielkovitsch, Andreas		7 Nov 1817	Winzeln	Obd.	bef 1858	N.-Amer	841016
Vielkovitsch, Caspar		1 Jun 1843	Winzeln	Obd.	Mar 1858	N.-Amer	841016
Vielkovitsch, Johannes		17 Jun 1844	Winzeln	Obd.	Mar 1858	N.-Amer	841016
Vielkovitsch, Karolina		29 Apr 1848	Winzeln	Obd.	Mar 1858	N.-Amer	841016
Vielkovitsch, Matthias		25 Feb 1852	Winzeln	Obd.	Mar 1858	N.-Amer	841016
Vielkovitsch, Paulina		28 May 1850	Winzeln	Obd.	Mar 1858	N.-Amer	841016
Vielkovitsch, Rosa		19 Aug 1846	Winzeln	Obd.	Mar 1858	N.-Amer	841016
Vielkovitsch, Rosa & F		6 Aug 182-	Winzeln	Obd.	Mar 1858	N.-Amer	841016
Vielkowitsch, Nothburga		2 Oct 1811	Winzeln	Obd.	Oct 1847	N.-Amer	841016
Villforth, Anna Maria		14 Dec 1777	Unterboehringen	Gsl.	Feb 1854	N.-Amer	572042
Voegele, Georg Jakob			Renningen	Leon.	1852	N.-Amer	837963
Voegele, Johann Michael		27 yrs.	Renningen	Leon.	1856	Hesse	837963
Voehringer, Anna Barbara		9 Aug 1845	Bissingen	Krch.	Mar 1864	N.-Amer	835943
Voehringer, Barbara		18 May 1841	Bronnweiler	Rtl.	Apr 1863	N.-Amer	841057
Voehringer, Friedrich		27 Feb 1849	Bronnweiler	Rtl.	Apr 1863	N.-Amer	841057
Voehringer, Jakob		2 Dec 1845	Bronnweiler	Rtl.	Apr 1863	N.-Amer	841057
Voehringer, Johannes & F		12 Oct 1838	Wittlingen	Leon.	Sep 1884	N.-Amer	837964
Voehringer, Karl August		9 Aug 1870	Rutesheim	Leon.	Sep 1884	N.-Amer	837964
Voehringer, Maria Agnes		23 Apr 1837	Unterhausen	Rtl.	Jan 1859	N.-Amer	841057
Voehringer, Rosina		1 Dec 1843	Bronnweiler	Rtl.	Apr 1863	N.-Amer	841057
Voelker, Christine Caroline		29 Jun 1839	Leonberg	Leon.	Oct 1856	N.-Amer	835786
Voelker, Gotthilf Heinrich		30 Oct 1840	Leonberg	Leon.	Sep 1865	N.-Amer	835787
Voelker, Gottlob		21 Jul 1837	Leonberg	Leon.	Sep 1854	N.-Amer	835786
Voelker, Johannes		19 Oct 1845	Leonberg	Leon.	Oct 1865	N.-Amer	835787
Voelker, Karoline		29 Jun 1839	Leonberg	Leon.	Feb 1863	N.-Amer	835787
Voell, Christian		4 Mar 1860	Gomaringen	Rtl.	May 1880	N.-Amer	841051
Voell, Katharina		10 Dec 1862	Gomaringen	Rtl.	May 1880	N.-Amer	841051

Name	Date	Place	Dist.	Emig.	Dest.	Film
Voell, Margaretha		Gomaringen	Rtl.	May 1880	N.-Amer	841051
Voeller, Anna Maria	9 Nov 1828	Hildrizhausen	Herr.	bef 1862	N.-Amer	834631
Voeller, Johanna Dorothea	15 Oct 1826	Hildrizhausen	Herr.	bef 1862	N.-Amer	834631
Voellm, Caroline	23 Apr 1820	Leonberg	Leon.	May 1859	N.-Amer	835786
Voelm, Christiane Cathar. & C	26 Dec 1817	Leonberg	Leon.	Jul 1847	Prussia	835786
Voelm, Heinrich	5 yrs.	Leonberg	Leon.	Jul 1847	Prussia	835786
Voelm, Johann Gottlieb	17 Jan 1824	Leonberg	Leon.	Feb 1852	N.-Amer	835786
Voetterle, Anna Maria		Gueltstein	Herr.	1863	Leipzig	834631
Voetterlin, Margaretha	23 Aug 1817	Herrenberg	Herr.	Apr 1865	N.-Amer	834629
Voettiner, Johannes & F	12 Apr 1828	Bissingen	Krch.	Oct 1865	N.-Amer	835943
Voettiner, Regina (wife)		Bissingen	Krch.	Oct 1865	N.-Amer	835943
Voettiner, Viktor	7 Feb 1830	Bissingen	Krch.	Apr 1857	N.-Amer	835943
Vogel, Christine & C	16 Oct 1840	Lindorf	Krch.	Feb 1869	France	835946
Vogel, David Martin	24 Jun 1822	Oetlingen	Krch.	Dec 1855	N.-Amer	835948
Vogel, Friedrich	2 Nov 1821	Rutesheim	Leon.	Dec 1862	N.-Amer	837964
Vogel, Gustav Albert	25 Mar 1867	Lindorf	Krch.	Feb 1869	France	835946
Vogel, Jacobine	12 Oct 1803	Weilheim	Krch.	bef 1870	N.-Amer	835950
Vogel, Johann Ferdinand	4 Oct 1835	Kirchheim	Krch.	Oct 1855	N.-Amer	835940
Vogel, Maria Catharina	13 Oct 1824	Weilheim	Krch.	bef 1868	N.-Amer	835950
Vogelweid, Wilhelm	15 Nov 1840	Reutlingen	Rtl..	Jan 1859	N.-Amer	841057
Vogenberger, Catharina	25 yrs.	Eltingen	Leon.	Feb 1854	N.-Amer	835789
Vogenberger, Catharina (wife)	39 yrs.	Eltingen	Leon.	Dec 1816	Russia	835789
Vogenberger, Christian		Eltingen	Leon.	bef 1861	N.-Amer	837955
Vogenberger, Christian	5 Jul 1826	Eltingen	Leon.	Nov 1861	N.-Amer	835789
Vogenberger, Gottlieb	10 yrs.	Eltingen	Leon.	Dec 1816	Russia	835789
Vogenberger, Helene	2 yrs.	Eltingen	Leon.	Dec 1816	Russia	835789
Vogenberger, Jacob		Eltingen	Leon.	Mar 1817	Russia	835789
Vogenberger, Jacob & F	42 yrs.	Eltingen	Leon.	Dec 1816	Russia	835789
Vogenberger, Johann Eberhard	27 yrs.	Eltingen	Leon.	Feb 1854	N.-Amer	835789
Vogenberger, Johann Georg	18 yrs.	Eltingen	Leon.	Dec 1816	Russia	835789
Vogenberger, Johann Ulrich		Eltingen	Leon.	bef 1823	Hungary	835789
Vogt, Daniel	3 Mar 1822	Rosswaelden	Krch.	bef 1879	France	548403
Vogt, Dorothea		Malmsheim	Leon.	May 1853	N.-Amer	837958
Vogt, Emma	7 Oct 1854	Anwihl/Switz.	Krch.	May 1858	Africa	835949
Vogt, Ferdinand	3 Feb 1847	Anwihl/Switz.	Krch.	May 1858	Africa	835949
Vogt, Ferdinand & F	6 Oct 1814	Weiler	Krch.	May 1858	Africa	835949
Vogt, Gustav Adolph	13 Jan 1850	Anwihl/Switz.	Krch.	May 1858	Africa	835949
Vogt, Johann	16 Sep 1848	Anwihl/Switz.	Krch.	May 1858	Africa	835949
Vogt, Johannes		Geislingen	Gsl.	Apr 1853	N.-Amer	572041
Vogt, Margaretha (wife)	29 May 1814	Anwihl/Switz.	Krch.	May 1858	Africa	835949
Vogt, Wilhelm	6 Oct 1852	Anwihl/Switz.	Krch.	May 1858	Africa	835949
Vohrer, Anna Maria	8 Mar 1865	Pfullingen	Rtl.	Oct 1865	N.-Amer	841057
Vohrer, Johann Heinr. Conrad		Reutlingen	Rtl.	bef 1866	N.-Amer	841057
Vohrer, Johann Jacob & F	6 Oct 1836	Pfullingen	Rtl.	Oct 1865	N.-Amer	841057
Vohrer, Maria Ursula (wife)	26 Sep 1834	Pfullingen	Rtl.	Oct 1865	N.-Amer	841057
Vohrer, Philippina Heinrike	22 Nov 1842	Reutlingen	Rtl.	Aug 1865	Prussia	841057
Volk, Christian Friedrich	19 Jun 1838	Leonberg	Leon.	Apr 1854	N.-Amer	835786
Volk, Filicitas	4 Jul 1837	Schramberg	Obd.	bef 1858	N.-Amer	838636
Volk, Theresia	31 Jul 1831	Schramberg	Obd.	bef 1858	N.-Amer	838636
Vollmer, Amalie Mathilde	19 Jul 1841	Unterhausen	Rtl.	Sep 1863	Switz.	841057

Name		Birth		Emigration			Film
Last	First	Date	Place	O'amt	Appl. Date	Dest.	Number
Vollmer, Andreas		3 May 1859	Owen	Krch.	Jan 1874	N.-Amer	835948
Vollmer, Anna Barbara		21 Jan 1829	Unterhausen	Rtl.	1868	Switz.	841057
Vollmer, Anna Christina		29 May 1879	Weiler	Krch.	Apr 1882	N.-Amer	548403
Vollmer, Anna Christine		29 May 1879	Goeppingen	Krch.	Apr 1882	N.-Amer	835949
Vollmer, Anna Maria		13 Jun 1831	Owen	Krch.	Jul 1856	Hamburg	835948
Vollmer, Carl		30 Jul 1849	Oberhausen	Rtl.	Apr 1866	N.-Amer	841057
Vollmer, Carl Wilhelm		22 Sep 1862	Reutlingen	Rtl.	May 1880	N.-Amer	841051
Vollmer, Christof Friedrich			Unterhausen	Rtl.	Jul 1830	Switz.	841057
Vollmer, Christoph & F		20 Jan 1842	Weiler	Krch.	Sep 1871	N.-Amer	835949
Vollmer, Christoph Carl			Reutlingen	Rtl.	Apr 1827	N.-Amer	841051
Vollmer, Friederike (wid.)		2 Feb 1829	Gerlingen	Leon.	Feb 1872	N.-Amer	837953
Vollmer, Friedrich		20 Apr 1864	Owen	Krch.	Dec 1880	N.-Amer	835948
Vollmer, Gottlob Eugen		22 Jan 1881	Goeppingen	Krch.	Apr 1882	N.-Amer	835949
Vollmer, Joh. Jacob Friedr.		21 Jul 1846	Honau	Rtl.	Sep 1868	N.-Amer	841057
Vollmer, Johann		3 Jul 1870	Weiler	Krch.	Sep 1871	N.-Amer	835949
Vollmer, Johann Jakob & F		16 Oct 1853	Weiler	Krch.	Apr 1882	N.-Amer	548403
Vollmer, Johann Michael		7 Nov 1830	Brucken	Krch.	Feb 1854	N.-Amer	835944
Vollmer, Johanna		18 Jun 1836	Unterhausen	Rtl..	Feb 1859	N.-Amer	841057
Vollmer, Johannes		11 Oct 1855	Owen	Krch.	May 1871	N.-Amer	835948
Vollmer, Katharina			Rottenburg	Rtl.	bef 1862	N.-Amer	841057
Vollmer, Katharina (wife)		27 Sep 1859	Weiler	Krch.	Apr 1882	N.-Amer	548403
Vollmer, Katharina (wife)		27 Nov 1859	Uhingen	Krch.	Apr 1882	N.-Amer	835949
Vollmer, Ludwig		10 May 1831	Unterhausen	Rtl.	bef 1865	N.-Amer	841057
Vollmer, Ludwig Carl		10 May 1880	Goeppingen	Krch.	Apr 1882	N.-Amer	835949
Vollmer, Maria (wid.)			Brucken	Krch.	Sep 1866	N.-Amer	835944
Vollmer, Maria Cathar. (wife)		15 Nov 1841	Weiler	Krch.	Sep 1871	N.-Amer	835949
Vollmer, Philipp Friedrich		14 Jan 1846	Owen	Krch.	Jun 1865	N.-Amer	835948
Vollmer, Rosina Barbara			Weiler	Krch.	bef 1857	N.-Amer	835949
Vollmer, Rosine Barbara			Weiler	Krch.	bef 1862	N.-Amer	835949
Vollmer, Stephan		18 yrs.	Oberhausen	Rtl.	Feb 1880	N.-Amer	841051
Volz, Christian Albrecht		16 Apr 1851	Renningen	Leon.	Apr 1852	N.-Amer	837963
Volz, Christian Albrecht & F			Renningen	Leon.	Apr 1852	N.-Amer	837963
Volz, Christian Moritz		26 Feb 1840	Renningen	Leon.	Apr 1852	N.-Amer	837963
Volz, Egidius & F			Enztal	Nag.	Apr 1851	N.-Amer	838488
Volz, Gottlieb Friedrich		17 Jan 1850	Renningen	Leon.	Apr 1852	N.-Amer	837963
Volz, Johann Jakob		10 Dec 1846	Renningen	Leon.	Apr 1852	N.-Amer	837963
Volz, Johann Jakob		21 Jul 1808	Renningen	Leon.	bef 1840	Bavaria	837963
Volz, Julie		31 Jul 1843	Reutlingen	Leon.	May 1863	N.-Amer	841057
Volz, Maria (wife)			Renningen	Leon.	Apr 1852	N.-Amer	837963
Volz, Maria Catharina		28 Nov 1845	Renningen	Leon.	Apr 1852	N.-Amer	837963
Volz, Maria Catharina		12 Aug 1844	Renningen	Leon.	Apr 1852	N.-Amer	837963
Volz, Maria Christina		18 Nov 1849	Renningen	Leon.	Apr 1852	N.-Amer	837963
Volz, Maria Rosina		2 Apr 1833	Renningen	Leon.	Jul 1851	N.-Amer	837963
Volz, Philipp Jakob		16 Jul 1843	Renningen	Leon.	Apr 1852	N.-Amer	837963
Volz, Philipp Jakob & F			Renningen	Leon.	Apr 1852	N.-Amer	837963
Volz, Rosina (wife)			Renningen	Leon.	Apr 1852	N.-Amer	837963
Volz, Siegfried Moritz		22 Jun 1843	Renningen	Leon.	Apr 1852	N.-Amer	837963
Votteler, Gustav		12 Jun 1844	Reutlingen	Rtl.	Dec 1868	Prussia	841057
Votteler, Karl Wilhelm		7 Mar 1849	Reutlingen	Rtl.	Nov 1866	N.-Amer	841057
Votteler, Ulrich		8 Jan 1849	Pfullingen	Rtl.	Apr 1868	N.-Amer	841057

Waag, Eberhardine		Malmsheim	Leon.	Sep 1852	N.-Amer	837958
Waag, Johann Jacob	1 May 1809	Malmsheim	Leon.	Apr 1831	N.-Amer	837958
Waag, Karl August	9 Feb 1867	Malmsheim	Leon.	Apr 1882	N.-Amer	837958
Waag, Michael	20 yrs.	Malmsheim	Leon.	Nov 1865	N.-Amer	837958
Wachele, Catharina	9 yrs.	Hoefingen	Leon.	1821	Russia	837957
Wachele, Conrad	16 yrs.	Hoefingen	Leon.	1821	Russia	837957
Wachele, Georg	20 yrs.	Hoefingen	Leon.	1821	Russia	837957
Wachele, Gottlieb	1 Aug 1847	Hoefingen	Leon.	Oct 1867	N.-Amer	837957
Wachele, Gottlieb		Hoefingen	Leon.	Jan 1854	N.-Amer	837957
Wachele, Gottlieb	12 yrs.	Hoefingen	Leon.	1821	Russia	837957
Wachele, Hans Jerg & F	44 yrs.	Hoefingen	Leon.	1821	Russia	837957
Wachele, Jacob	14 yrs.	Hoefingen	Leon.	1821	Russia	837957
Wachele, Johann Georg & F		Hoefingen	Leon.	Oct 1853	N.-Amer	837957
Wachele, Johanna (wife)	44 yrs.	Hoefingen	Leon.	1821	Russia	837957
Wachele, Ludwig	19 yrs.	Hoefingen	Leon.	Jan 1854	N.-Amer	837957
Wachele, Ludwig	18 yrs.	Hoefingen	Leon.	1821	Russia	837957
Wachele, Maria Catharina		Hoefingen	Leon.	Dec 1853	N.-Amer	837957
Wachendorfer, Barbara (wife)	9 Dec 1810	Weil der Stadt	Leon.	Mar 1848	N.-Amer	837965
Wachendorfer, Johann Bapt. & F	15 Nov 1813	Weil der Stadt	Leon.	Mar 1848	N.-Amer	837965
Wachter, Anna Elisabetha		Geislingen	Gsl.	Feb 1853	N.-Amer	572041
Wachter, Anna Elisabetha (wife)		Schalkstetten	Gsl.	Apr 1852	N.-Amer	572041
Wachter, Christian		Geislingen	Gsl.	bef 1853	N.-Amer	572041
Wachter, Christian & W		Schalkstetten	Gsl.	Apr 1852	N.-Amer	572041
Wachter, Christoph	27 Nov 1850	Stubersheim	Gsl.	Jul 1869	N.-Amer	572047
Wachter, Johann Caspar		Stubersheim	Gsl.	Jun 1853	N.-Amer	572041
Wachter, Leonhard	2 Oct 1836	Holzheim/Goeppingen	Gsl.	May 1854	N.-Amer	572042
Wacker, Albert Theodor	20 Oct 1841	Reutlingen	Rtl.	Oct 1866	Prussia	841058
Waechter, Carl Ferdinand	7 Aug 1859	Owen	Krch.	bef 1886	N.-Amer	835948
Waegenbauer, Christine (wife)	29 Nov 1812	Dettingen	Krch.	Jun 1863	France	835944
Waegenbauer, Christine Margar.	9 Dec 1932	Dettingen	Krch.	Jun 1863	France	835944
Waegenbauer, Gottlieb Friedr.	28 Dec 1829	Dettingen	Krch.	Jun 1863	France	835944
Waegenbauer, Johannes & F	24 Apr 1798	Dettingen	Krch.	Jun 1863	France	835944
Wagenbauer, Andreas		Dettingen u. T.	Krch.	bef 1809	France	550804
Wagenbauer, Andreas	21 Dec 1825	Dettingen	Krch.	bef 1872	N.-Amer	835944
Wagenbauer, Johann Georg	11 Oct 1855	Dettingen	Krch.	Mar 1870	N.-Amer	835944
Wagner, Adelheid	27 May 1837	Geislingen	Gsl.	Aug 1859	Switz.	572043
Wagner, Adolph	13 yrs.	Geislingen	Gsl.	Mar 1851	N.-Amer	577788
Wagner, Anna Maria		Westerheim	Gsl.	May 1853	N.-Amer	572041
Wagner, Anna Maria	8 May 1837	Kuchen	Gsl.	Feb 1857	N.-Amer	572043
Wagner, Anna Maria	30 Dec 1840	Heimerdingen	Leon.	Nov 1862	N.-Amer	837954
Wagner, Anna Maria & C	28 yrs.	Hoefingen	Leon.	Jul 1868	N.-Amer	837957
Wagner, Carl	6 Dec 1844	Kuchen	Gsl.	Feb 1857	N.-Amer	572043
Wagner, Carl	27 Dec 1843	Leonberg	Leon.	Jun 1868	Berlin	835787
Wagner, Carl Gottlieb	2 yrs.	Hoefingen	Leon.	Feb 1854	N.-Amer	837957
Wagner, Catharina (wid.) & F		Geislingen	Gsl.	Mar 1851	N.-Amer	577788
Wagner, Christian	6 May 1858	Gaertringen	Herr.	bef 1884	Switz.	834630
Wagner, Christian	18 Aug 1849	Willmandingen	Rtl.	Jun 1868	N.-Amer	841058
Wagner, Christiane		Gerlingen	Leon.	Mar 1852	N.-Amer	837953
Wagner, Christoph	2 yrs.	Gerlingen	Leon.	Apr 1857	N.-Amer	837953
Wagner, Christoph Friedrich		Gerlingen	Leon.	Mar 1852	N.-Amer	837953

Name		Birth		Emigration			Film
Last	First	Date	Place	O'amt	Appl. Date	Dest.	Number
Wagner, Conrad & F			Gerlingen	Leon.	Mar 1852	N.-Amer	837953
Wagner, Elisabetha			Westerheim	Gsl.	May 1853	N.-Amer	572041
Wagner, Franz		1 Oct 1837	Westerheim	Gsl.	Mar 1854	N.-Amer	572042
Wagner, Franz Xaver		8 Dec 1835	Deggingen	Gsl.	Sep 1854	N.-Amer	572042
Wagner, Friederike		23 Apr 1839	Heimerdingen	Leon.	Jun 1856	N.-Amer	837954
Wagner, Friederike Barbara			Gerlingen	Leon.	Mar 1852	N.-Amer	837953
Wagner, Friedrich		8 Oct 1836	Ruteslieim	Leon.	Mar 1862	N.-Amer	837964
Wagner, Friedrich		21 Feb 1830	Hoefingen	Leon.	1851	N.-Amer	837957
Wagner, Friedrich Adolph		28 Feb 1828	Ditzingen	Leon.	Apr 1851	N.-Amer	835788
Wagner, Georg			Heimerdingen	Leon.	bef 1862	N.-Amer	837954
Wagner, Georg Michael & F			Willmandingen	Rtl.	Apr 1831	N.-Amer	841051
Wagner, Gottlieb		17 Nov 1835	Heimerdingen	Leon.	Jul 1852	N.-Amer	837954
Wagner, Gottlieb		7 Mar 1848	Gerlingen	Leon.	Feb 1866	N.-Amer	837953
Wagner, Gottlieb			Gerlingen	Leon.	Mar 1852	N.-Amer	837953
Wagner, Gottlob			Gerlingen	Leon.	Mar 1852	N.-Amer	837953
Wagner, Heinrich & W			Leonberg	Leon.	Mar 1870	N.-Amer	835787
Wagner, Heinrike		28 yrs.	Hoefingen	Leon.	Apr 1852	N.-Amer	837957
Wagner, Heinrike Wilhelmine		23 Dec 1837	Reutlingen	Rtl.	Dec 1861	Switz.	841058
Wagner, Hermann		17 Aug 1834	Geislingen	Gsl.	Jul 1864	Switz.	572045
Wagner, Hermann			Reutlingen	Rtl.	bef 1866	N.-Amer	841058
Wagner, Jacob & F			Eltingen	Leon.	Apr 1830	N.-Amer	835789
Wagner, Jacob Friedrich			Gerlingen	Leon.	Mar 1852	N.-Amer	837953
Wagner, Jacobine			Gerlingen	Leon.	Mar 1852	N.-Amer	837953
Wagner, Jakob		6 yrs.	Gerlingen	Leon.	Apr 1857	N.-Amer	837953
Wagner, Jakob Gottlob		10 Oct 1855	Heimerdingen	Leon.	Jul 1872	N.-Amer	837954
Wagner, Jerg (wid.)		50 yrs.	Hoefingen	Leon.	Jan 1819	N.-Amer	837957
Wagner, Johann Conrad		infant	Hoefingen	Leon.	Feb 1854	N.-Amer	837957
Wagner, Johann David			Gerlingen	Leon.	bef 1858	N.-Amer	837953
Wagner, Johann Friedrich		28 Jan 1849	Weilheim	Krch.	Oct 1863	N.-Amer	835950
Wagner, Johann Georg		8 Aug 1871	Zell	Krch.	bef 1894	Berlin	835774
Wagner, Johann Georg			Heimerdingen	Leon.	bef 1864	N.-Amer	837954
Wagner, Johann Georg		3 Jun 1834	Heimerdingen	Leon.	Jul 1852	N.-Amer	837954
Wagner, Johann Georg			Heimerdingen	Leon.	Jun 1851	N.-Amer	837954
Wagner, Johann Georg		7 Jul 1840	Hoefingen	Leon.	Feb 1860	N.-Amer	837957
Wagner, Johann Georg			Hoefingen	Leon.	Apr 1816	France	837957
Wagner, Johann Jacob		11 Apr 1846	Weilheim	Krch.	Oct 1865	N.-Amer	835950
Wagner, Johann Michael		13 Nov 1851	Weilheim	Krch.	Dec 1870	N.-Amer	835950
Wagner, Johann Michael		2 Feb 1839	Weilheim	Krch.	Oct 1863	N.-Amer	835950
Wagner, Johanna Friederike		9 Dec 1849	Schoeckingen	Leon.	Nov 1872	N.-Amer	837964
Wagner, Johannes		10 Jun 1838	Westerheim	Gsl.	Mar 1854	N.-Amer	572042
Wagner, Johannes			Warmbronn	Leon.	bef 1859	Saxony	837965
Wagner, Johannes		18 Jun 1812	Hemmingen	Leon.	Nov 1840	N.-Amer	837956
Wagner, Johannes		31 yrs.	Willmandingen	Rtl.	Jan 1880	N.-Amer	841051
Wagner, Johannes & F			Gerlingen	Leon.	Apr 1857	N.-Amer	837953
Wagner, Joseph Willibald			Ditzenbach	Gsl.	Aug 1851	N.-Amer	577788
Wagner, Julius			Ditzenbach	Gsl.	Feb 1853	N.-Amer	572041
Wagner, Karl Eberhardt & F			Kuchen	Gsl.	Feb 1857	N.-Amer	572043
Wagner, Karl Gottieb		4 Feb 1850	Hoefingen	Leon.	Sep 1869	N.-Amer	837957
Wagner, Karoline Magdalena			Gerlingen	Leon.	Mar 1852	N.-Amer	837953
Wagner, Katharina Regina			Gerlingen	Leon.	Mar 1852	N.-Amer	837953

Wagner, Konrad	28 May 1834	Kuchen	Gsl.	Feb 1854	N.-Amer	572042
Wagner, Louise	16 yrs.	Geislingen	Gsl.	Mar 1851	N.-Amer	577788
Wagner, Louise (wife)		Leonberg	Leon.	Mar 1870	N.-Amer	835787
Wagner, Margaretha & C	21 yrs.	Hoefingen	Leon.	Feb 1854	N.-Amer	837957
Wagner, Maria Catharina	23 Jul 1837	Heimerdingen	Leon.	Aug 1853	N.-Amer	837954
Wagner, Maria Catharina	7 Feb 1812	Weilheim	Krch.	Apr 1862	N.-Amer	835950
Wagner, Maria Katharina		Gerlingen	Leon.	Mar 1852	N.-Amer	837953
Wagner, Marie	7 yrs.	Gerlingen	Leon.	Apr 1857	N.-Amer	837953
Wagner, Max Joseph	28 Apr 1850	Deggingen	Gsl.	Dec 1868	N.-Amer	572046
Wagner, Maximilian	12 Oct 1839	Deggingen	Gsl.	Sep 1855	N.-Amer	572043
Wagner, Sara	27 yrs.	Geislingen	Gsl.	Mar 1854	N.-Amer	572042
Wagner, Sebastian		Reichenbach	Gsl.	Mar 1852	N.-Amer	572041
Wagner, Thomas	6 Sep 1847	Schoeckingen	Leon.	Nov 1872	N.-Amer	837964
Wagner, Ursula Maria Cathar.	7 Aug 1837	Weilheim	Krch.	Mar 1860	N.-Amer	835949
Wagner, Wilhelm	2 Mar 1841	Deggingen	Gsl.	Feb 1857	N.-Amer	572043
Wagner, Wilhelm Christian		Heimerdingen	Leon.	Apr 1864	N.-Amer	837954
Wagner, Wilhelm Michael & W	27 yrs.	Geislingen	Gsl.	Mar 1854	N.-Amer	572042
Wagner, Xaver	26 Oct 1850	Westerheim	Gsl.	May 1868	N.-Amer	572046
Wahl, Anna Margaretha (wid.)		Hausen a.d.Lauchert	Rtl.	Oct 1828	N.-Amer	841051
Wahl, Catharina	22 Sep 1822	Leonberg	Leon.	Mar 1846	N.-Amer	835786
Wahl, Christine	1 Mar 1828	Schoeckingen	Leon.	Jan 1852	N.-Amer	837964
Wahl, Elisabetha		Weissenstein	Gsl.	bef 1850	Wien	577788
Wahl, Friederike	1 Dec 1829	Schoeckingen	Leon.	Jan 1852	N.-Amer	837964
Wahl, Friedrich	1 Jan 1829	Leonberg	Leon.	Aug 1854	N.-Amer	835786
Wahl, Gottlieb	6 Jul 1825	Weil im Dorf	Loen.	Jan 1854	N.-Amer	837967
Wahl, Gottlieb	17 Mar 1835	Schoeckingen	Leon.	Apr 1855	N.-Amer	837964
Wahl, Heinrich	23 Oct 1824	Schoeckingen	Leon.	Apr 1855	N.-Amer	837964
Wahl, Johanna Christina	25 Mar 1849	Leonberg	Leon.	Jul 1870	Bavaria	835787
Wahl, Josef	6 Apr 1805	Weissenstein	Gsl.	bef 1863	Austria	572044
Wahl, Luise Caroline	21 Mar 1838	Leonberg	Leon.	Feb 1864	Prussia	835787
Wahl, Maria		Leonberg	Leon.	Dec 1859	Hesse	835786
Wahlheim, Alois		Beffendorf	Obd.	Apr 1844	France	838631
Wahlheim, Brigitta	1 Feb 1837	Bochingen	Obd.	Sep 1866	N.-Amer	838632
Wahlheim, Maria & C	15 Dec 1835	Bach-Altenberg	Obd.	May 1870	Prussia	838631
Wahlheim, Valentin	9 Feb 1857	Bach-Altenberg	Obd.	May 1870	Prussia	838631
Waibel, Alois		Weissenstein	Gsl.	Apr 1867	N.-Amer	572046
Waidele, Maria Anna	9 Apr 1829	Hochmoessingen	Obd.	Jul 1870	France	838634
Waidele, Maria Eva		Lauterbach	Obd.	Oct 1859	France	838634
Waidmann, Carl Friedrich Eug.	28 Feb 1851	Rutesheim	Leon.	Apr 1851	N.-Amer	837964
Waidmann, Catharina (wife)	25 Mar 1833	Rutesheim	Leon.	Apr 1851	N.-Amer	837964
Waidmann, Johann Peter & F	13 Oct 1818	Rutesheim	Leon.	Apr 1851	N.-Amer	837964
Waik, Wilhelm Heinrich	7 Feb 1835	Herrenberg	Herr.	Dec 1868	N.-Amer	834629
Waldemaier, Johann Michael	10 Dec 1817	Eltingen	Leon.	Apr 1846	N.-Amer	835789
Waldner, Gottlieb Wilhelm	5 Jan 1840	Kirchheim	Krch.	May 1857	N.-Amer	835940
Waldner, Wilhelm	12 Sep 1823	Kirchheim	Krch.	Jan 1861	N.-Amer	835940
Waldvogel, Agnes		Mariazell	Obd.	Apr 1866	Hesse	838634
Walheim, Agatha (wid.) & F		Bochingen	Obd.	Jun 1860	N.-Amer	838632
Walheim, Joseph	14 Mar 1849	Bochingen	Obd.	Jun 1860	N.-Amer	838632
Walheim, Katharina	6 Apr 1849	Bochingen	Obd.	Jun 1860	N.-Amer	838632
Walheim, Walburga (wid.) & F		Bochingen	Obd.	Jun 1860	N.-Amer	838632

Name		Birth		Emigration			Film
Last	First	Date	Place	O'amt	Appl. Date	Dest.	Number
Walheim, Wilhelm		26 Oct 1844	Bochingen	Obd.	Jun 1860	N.-Amer	838632
Walker, Christian Friedrich		13 Mar 1829	Kirchheim	Krch.	Feb 1870	N.-Amer	835941
Walker, Johann Albert		16 May 1861	Immenhausen	Krch.	Jan 1870	N.-Amer	835940
Walker, Johann Georg & F			Immenhausen	Krch.	Jan 1870	N.-Amer	835940
Walker, Maria		8 May 1832	Gomaringen	Rtl.	Dec 1864	N.-Amer	841058
Walker, Marie		6 Jan 1865	Immenhausen	Krch.	Jan 1870	N.-Amer	835940
Wall, Anna Christine		29 Dec 1835	Owen	Krch.	Aug 1856	N.-Amer	835948
Wall, Anna Maria & C		24 Jan 1833	Owen	Krch.	Jun 1864	N.-Amer	835948
Wall, Barbara (wid.)		2 May 1804	Owen	Krch.	Jun 1862	N.-Amer	835948
Wall, Christian Friedrich		12 Apr 1867	Owen	Krch.	Jul 1889	N.-Amer	835948
Wall, Christine Friederike		19 Jan 1828	Owen	Krch.	Jun 1862	N.-Amer	835948
Wall, Johann Andreas		9 Nov 1839	Owen	Krch.	Apr 1858	N.-Amer	835948
Wall, Johann Georg		3 Feb 1845	Owen	Krch.	Aug 1865	N.-Amer	835948
Wall, Johann Jacob		19 Oct 1842	Owen	Krch.	Aug 1872	N.-Amer	835948
Wall, Johann Jacob		27 Jun 1843	Owen	Krch.	Apr 1859	N.-Amer	835948
Wall, Wilhelm		16 Dec 1842	Owen	Krch.	Feb 1862	N.-Amer	835948
Waller, Hermann		15 Jun 1850	Schramberg	Obd.	Mar 1870	N.-Amer	838636
Waller, Leopoldine		8 Feb 1839	Lauterbach	Obd.	Sep 1860	Austria	838634
Waller, Ludwig August		8 Aug 1847	Sulgen	Obd.	Nov 1867	Romania	838638
Waller, Sebastian		18 Jan 1835	Hochmoessingen	Obd.	Jul 1870	Berlin	838634
Waller, Theodor		1 Oct 1852	Schramberg	Obd.	Sep 1867	N.-Amer	838636
Walliser, Johann Baptiste			Oberndorf	Obd.	Jun 1852	N.-Amer	838635
Wallum, Johannes			Hochmoessingen	Obd.	Mar 1864	N.-Amer	838633
Walter, Andreas		8 Dec 1838	Betzweiler	Obd.	1852	N.-Amer	838631
Walter, Barbara (wife)		6 May 1815	Betzweiler	Obd.	May 1847	N.-Amer	838631
Walter, Catharina		30 Jun 1842	Betzweiler	Obd.	May 1847	N.-Amer	838631
Walter, Catharine Christine		26 yrs.	Alpirsbach	Obd.	Apr 1855	N.-Amer	838630
Walter, Christian		27 yrs.	Roemlinsdorf	Obd.	bef 1858	N.-Amer	838635
Walter, Friederike			Alpirsbach	Obd.	bef 1847	Switz.	838630
Walter, Georg Friedrich			Alpirsbach	Obd.	Jun 1861	Prussia	838630
Walter, Georg Friedrich		14 yrs.	Alpirsbach	Obd.	Apr 1855	N.-Amer	838630
Walter, Jacob		25 Aug 1832	Dornhan	Obd.	Oct 1852	N.-Amer	838638
Walter, Johann Georg		16 Jun 1845	Betzweiler	Obd.	May 1847	N.-Amer	838631
Walter, Johann Georg & F		30 Aug 1811	Betzweiler	Obd.	May 1847	N.-Amer	838631
Walter, Johann Jacob & F			Reutlingen	Rtl.	May 1832	N.-Amer	841051
Walter, Johannes		11 Sep 1839	Betzweiler	Obd.	May 1847	N.-Amer	838631
Walter, Johannes			Dornhan	Obd.	Apr 1866	England	838638
Walter, Martin		28 Jul 1845	Willmandingen	Rtl.	Apr 1860	N.-Amer	841058
Walter, Matthias		18 yrs.	Dornhan	Obd.	Dec 1852	N.-Amer	838638
Walter, Otto		13 Oct 1848	Kirchheim	Krch.	bef 1868	N.-Amer	835941
Walz, Anna		28 Jun 1835	Ohmenhausen	Rtl.	bef 1861	Basel	841058
Walz, Anna Catharina		12 Jan 1860	Ohmenhausen	Rtl.	Dec 1860	Switz.	841058
Walz, Anna Maria		3 Jun 1849	Ohmenhausen	Rtl.	Feb 1867	N.-Amer	841058
Walz, Carl Friedrich		19 Aug 1830	Eltingen	Leon.	Dec 1850	N.-Amer	835789
Walz, Carolina (wife)			Friolzheim	Leon.	Sep 1868	N.-Amer	835791
Walz, Christian			Eltingen	Leon.	Feb 1870	N.-Amer	835789
Walz, Christian Gottlob		36 yrs.	Reutlingen	Rtl.	1879	N.-Amer	841051
Walz, Christina Magdalena & C		4 Feb 1827	Ohmenhausen	Rtl.	Dec 1860	Switz.	841058
Walz, Friederike		12 Jan 1837	Wannweil	Rtl.	Apr 1864	N.-Amer	841058
Walz, Friederike Sara (wife)		18 Feb 1853	Friolzheim	Leon.	Jan 1880	N.-Amer	835791

Walz, Friedrich	16 Apr 1833	Renningen	Leon.	Sep 1853	N.-Amer	837963
Walz, Friedrich & F		Friolzheim	Leon.	Sep 1868	N.-Amer	835791
Walz, Friedrich (wid.)	66 yrs.	Leonberg	Leon.	Dec 1816	Russia	835789
Walz, Georg Gottlob & F	24 Jul 1854	Friolzheim	Leon.	Jan 1880	N.-Amer	835791
Walz, Gottlieb	26 yrs.	Eltingen	Leon.	Mar 1868	Prussia	835789
Walz, Gottlieb	10 yrs.	Eltingen	Leon.	Oct 1853	N.-Amer	835789
Walz, Gottlob Friedrich	18 Jun 1877	Friolzheim	Leon.	Jan 1880	N.-Amer	835791
Walz, Jakob	27 Nov 1859	Reutlingen	Rtl.	Jan 1861	N.-Amer	841058
Walz, Johann Christoph	24 yrs.	Friolzheim	Leon.	Feb 1864	N.-Amer	835791
Walz, Johann Friedrich	infant	Friolzheim	Leon.	Sep 1868	N.-Amer	835791
Walz, Johann Georg		Eltingen	Leon.	Mar 1851	N.-Amer	835789
Walz, Johann Georg		Eltingen	Leon.	Apr 1830	N.-Amer	835789
Walz, Johann Georg	25 May 1844	Wannweil	Rtl.	Apr 1861	N.-Amer	841058
Walz, Johann Georg	22 Feb 1839	Bissingen	Krch.	Mar 1856	N.-Amer	835943
Walz, Johann Gottlob	24 Feb 1873	Bissingen	Krch.	Mar 1889	N.-Amer	835943
Walz, Johann Martin	3 Aug 1852	Ohmenhausen	Rtl.	Sep 1866	N.-Amer	841058
Walz, Johann Martin & F		Ohmenhausen	Rtl.	May 1831	N.-Amer	841051
Walz, Johann Michael	7 May 1856	Bissingen	Krch.	Sep 1881	N.-Amer	835943
Walz, Johannes		Eltingen	Leon.	Apr 1830	N.-Amer	835789
Walz, Johannes	17 May 1851	Ohmenhausen	Rtl.	Apr 1880	N.-Amer	841051
Walz, Johannes & F		Hemmingen	Leon.	Apr 1833	N.-Amer	837956
Walz, Karl Johannes	11 Apr 1879	Friolzheim	Leon.	Jan 1880	N.-Amer	835791
Walz, Louise & C		Eltingen	Leon.	Oct 1853	N.-Amer	835789
Walz, Margaretha		Eltingen	Leon.	Apr 1830	N.-Amer	835789
Walz, Margaretha & C	8 Jul 1834	Reutlingen	Rtl.	Jan 1861	N.-Amer	841058
Walz, Maria		Eltingen	Leon.	May 1853	N.-Amer	835789
Walz, Maria	20 Feb 1853	Bissingen	Krch.	Aug 1869	N.-Amer	835943
Walz, Marie Louise	15 yrs.	Eltingen	Leon.	Oct 1853	N.-Amer	835789
Walz, Martin	25 Sep 1855	Ohmenhausen	Rtl.	Apr 1880	N.-Amer	841051
Walz, Michael	25 Apr 1846	Eltingen	Leon.	Apr 1866	N.-Amer	835789
Walz, Philippine	18 Mar 1859	Kleinengstingen	Rtl.	Jan 1880	N.-Amer	841051
Walz, Robert	21 Nov 1860	Reutlingen	Rtl.	Jan 1861	N.-Amer	841058
Walz, Sibyla (wife)		Hemmingen	Leon.	Apr 1833	N.-Amer	837956
Walz, Wilhelm	8 Feb 1874	Gaertringen	Herr.	bef 1897	Switz.	834630
Wandel, Carl	20 Feb 1815	Kirchheim	Krch.	Jan 1857	N.-Amer	835940
Wankmueller, Gottlieb	9 Feb 1817	Eltingen	Leon.	Aug 1842	France	835789
Wankmueller, Jakob Friedrich	26 Apr 1815	Eltingen	Leon.	Aug 1842	France	835789
Wankmueller, Karl Friedrich	19 Aug 1829	Eltingen	Leon.	Jun 1865	N.-Amer	835789
Wanner, Johann Georg	16 Jun 1836	Moensheim	Leon.	Oct 1854	N.-Amer	837960
Wanner, Johannes	10 Mar 1834	Moensheim	Leon.	Oct 1854	N.-Amer	837960
Wanner, Johannes	31 yrs.	Moensheim	Leon.	Mar 1831	N.-Amer	837960
Wanner, Johannes & F		Moensheim	Leon.	Oct 1854	N.-Amer	837960
Wanner, Rosina Barbara (wife)		Moensheim	Leon.	Oct 1854	N.-Amer	837960
Wanner, Wilhelmine		Gerlingen	Leon.	Nov 1842	Saxony	837953
Weber, Albert	24 Mar 1841	Winzeln	Obd.	Sep 1847	N.-Amer	841016
Weber, Anna Maria & C	29 Jun 1827	Bissingen	Krch.	Feb 1866	N.-Amer	835943
Weber, Anna Maria Catharina	16 Oct 1842	Bissingen	Krch.	Jan 1868	France	835943
Weber, Anton	10 yrs.	Donzdorf	Gsl.	Sep 1854	N.-Amer	572042
Weber, Blandina	3 Nov 1846	Winzeln	Obd.	Sep 1847	N.-Amer	841016
Weber, Carl	18 Jan 1852	Neidlingen	Krch.	bef 1866	N.-Amer	835940

Name		Birth		Emigration			Film
Last	First	Date	Place	O'amt	Appl. Date	Dest.	Number
Weber, Catharina - twin		4 Jan 1853	Neidlingen	Krch.	bef 1866	N.-Amer	835940
Weber, Christian & F			Neidlingen	Krch.	bef 1866	N.-Amer	835940
Weber, Christian Albrecht			Kuchen	Gsl.	bef 1862	N.-Amer	572044
Weber, Christoph		20 Sep 1836	Owen	Krch.	Dec 1856	N.-Amer	835948
Weber, Franz			Hochmoessingen	Obd.	Apr 1847	N.-Amer	838633
Weber, Franziska & F			Donzdorf	Gsl.	Sep 1854	N.-Amer	572042
Weber, Franziska (wife) & F			Donzdorf	Gsl.	Mar 1852	N.-Amer	572041
Weber, Gotthardt			Waldmoessingen	Obd.	Mar 1865	N.-Amer	841015
Weber, Gottlieb Friedrich		12 Sep 1813	Gutenberg	Krch.	bef 1859	N.-Amer	835945
Weber, Hermann		14 Mar 1828	Gutenberg	Krch.	bef 1859	N.-Amer	835945
Weber, Jakob		12 Aug 1842	Hochdorf	Krch.	Jun 1867	N.-Amer	835945
Weber, Johann		6 Jul 1847	Schramberg	Obd.	Sep 1867	N.-Amer	838636
Weber, Johann - twin		4 Jan 1853	Neidlingen	Krch.	bef 1866	N.-Amer	835940
Weber, Johann Baptist		13 Nov 1826	Boehmenkirch	Gsl.	Feb 1854	N.-Amer	572042
Weber, Johann Friedrich		28 Feb 1857	Ohmden	Krch.	Jun 1873	N.-Amer	548403
Weber, Johann Georg		30 Jun 1862	Ohmden	Krch.	Apr 1879	N.-Amer	548403
Weber, Johann Georg		8 Mar 1846	Bissingen	Krch.	Jul 1865	N.-Amer	835943
Weber, Johann Venziez		17 Jan 1847	Donzdorf	Gsl.	Mar 1852	N.-Amer	572041
Weber, Johannes		1 Jun 1833	Haslach	Herr.	Sep 1867	N.-Amer	834631
Weber, Johannes			Drachenstein	Gsl.	Sep 1851	N.-Amer	577788
Weber, Johannes		28 Aug 1843	Unterlenningen	Krch.	Jul 1864	N.-Amer	835949
Weber, Josef		5 yrs.	Donzdorf	Gsl.	Sep 1854	N.-Amer	572042
Weber, Joseph		23 Sep 1832	Hochmoessingen	Obd.	May 1851	N.-Amer	838633
Weber, Karl Moritz			Waldmoessingen	Obd.	Apr 1862	N.-Amer	841015
Weber, Katharina (wife)		25 Apr 1809	Winzeln	Obd.	Sep 1847	N.-Amer	841016
Weber, Lorenz		6 yrs.	Donzdorf	Gsl.	Sep 1854	N.-Amer	572042
Weber, Margaretha		19 Jul 1819	Willmandingen	Rtl.	bef 1863	N.-Amer	841058
Weber, Margaretha		5 Oct 1846	Weilheim	Krch.	Mar 1866	N.-Amer	835950
Weber, Marianne			Donzdorf	Gsl.	bef 1863	N.-Amer	572044
Weber, Michael			Aichhalden	Obd.	May 1817	N.-Amer	838629
Weber, Michael			Donzdorf	Gsl.	bef 1852	N.-Amer	572041
Weber, Michael		23 yrs.	Donzdorf	Gsl.	Dec 1851	N.-Amer	572041
Weber, Michael			Donzdorf	Gsl.	1851	N.-Amer	572042
Weber, Nikomend & F		15 Sep 1813	Winzeln	Obd.	bef 1847	N.-Amer	841016
Weber, Paul		28 Jan 1844	Donzdorf	Gsl.	Sep 1865	N.-Amer	572045
Weber, Pauline		5 Jan 1828	Geislingen	Gsl.	Oct 1854	N.-Amer	572042
Weber, Peter		24 yrs.	Gerlingen	Leon.	Apr 1856	N.-Amer	837953
Weber, Philipp		10 Nov 1820	Bissingen	Krch.	bef 1856	Austria	835943
Weber, Regina		16 Nov 1848	Bissingen	Krch.	Feb 1866	N.-Amer	835943
Weber, Wilhelm			Waldmoessingen	Obd.	Apr 1862	N.-Amer	841015
Weber, Wilhelm		9 Mar 1845	Oetlingen	Krch.	Jun 1865	N.-Amer	835948
Weber, family - 3 s.& 1 d.			Aichhalden	Obd.	May 1817	N.-Amer	838629
Weckerlin, Euphrosine		3 May 1830	Geislingen	Gsl.	Mar 1854	N.-Amer	572042
Weckerlin, Katharina		2 Jan 1816	Geislingen	Gsl.	Mar 1854	N.-Amer	572042
Weckherlin, Regina		29 yrs.	Geislingen	Gsl.	Mar 1857	N.-Amer	572043
Weegmann, Carl Gottlieb		19 Jun 1858	Kirchheim	Krch.	Apr 1875	N.-Amer	548403
Weeh, Johann Michael		1 Jan 1832	Gebersheim	Leon.	Oct 1864	N.-Amer	837953
Weger, Barbara			Bissingen	Krch.	bef 1861	N.-Amer	835943
Weger, Gustav		18 Sep 1849	Bissingen	Krch.	Jun 1861	N.-Amer	835943
Wegner, Wilhelm		3 Dec 1849	Reichenbach	Gsl.	Sep 1874	N.-Amer	572048

Weh, Friedrich	74 yrs.	Rutesheim	Leon.	May 1866	N.-Amer	837964
Weh, Johann Georg	22 Apr 1821	Rutesheim	Leon.	Mar 1848	N.-Amer	837964
Wehle, Benedikt	26 Feb 1845	Beffendorf	Obd.	Dec 1865	N.-Amer	838631
Wehle, Eduard	20 yrs.	Beffendorf	Obd.	Jun 1854	N.-Amer	838631
Wehr, Christina		Reichenbach	Leon.	1854	N.-Amer	837959
Weidle, Andreas	26 Nov 1858	Gerlingen	Leon.	Jun 1882	N.-Amer	837953
Weidle, Andreas		Gerlingen	Leon.	bef 1847	N.-Amer	837953
Weidle, Johann Gottlob	19 Sep 1858	Gerlingen	Leon.	Jun 1882	N.-Amer	837953
Weigele, Anna Maria	5 May 1832	Ohmenhausen	Rtl.	Apr 1868	N.-Amer	841058
Weigele, Christian	13 Jun 1875	Aichelberg	Krch.	Jan 1890	N.-Amer	835943
Weigele, Heinrich	18 Oct 1876	Aichelberg	Krch.	May 1893	N.-Amer	835943
Weigele, Johannes	22 Jul 1867	Aichelberg	Krch.	Feb 1884	N.-Amer	835943
Weigold, Johann Georg	1 Feb 1849	Dornhan	Obd.	Mar 1867	N.-Amer	838638
Weihrich, Magdalena		Geislingen	Gsl.	Sep 1852	N.-Amer	572041
Weik, Andreas	40 yrs.	Merklingen	Leon.	Sep 1871	N.-Amer	837959
Weik, Paulus		Merklingen	Leon.	1815	France	837959
Weil, Anna Christina	7 Feb 1850	Muenchingen	Leon.	Oct 1851	N.-Amer	837961
Weil, Anna Maria	18 Jan 1836	Muenchingen	Leon.	Oct 1851	N.-Amer	837961
Weil, Anna Maria	27 Sep 1833	Unterlenningen	Krch.	Sep 1861	N.-Amer	835949
Weil, Christina	3 Feb 1839	Muenchingen	Leon.	Oct 1851	N.-Amer	837961
Weil, Christina (wife)		Muenchingen	Leon.	Oct 1851	N.-Amer	837961
Weil, Friedrich	13 Jan 1843	Muenchingen	Leon.	Oct 1851	N.-Amer	837961
Weil, Heinrich	6 Feb 1845	Ochsenwang	Krch.	May 1861	N.-Amer	835947
Weil, Jakob	4 Apr 1837	Muenchingen	Leon.	Oct 1851	N.-Amer	837961
Weil, Jakob & F		Muenchingen	Leon.	Oct 1851	N.-Amer	837961
Weil, Johann Georg	4 Nov 1845	Muenchingen	Leon.	Oct 1851	N.-Amer	837961
Weil, Johann Georg	26 Dec 1827	Oetlingen	Krch.	bef 1859	N.-Amer	835948
Weil, Johann Jacob	4 Apr 1867	Owen	Krch.	Jan 1884	N.-Amer	548403
Weil, Johann Jacob	10 Jul 1823	Oetlingen	Krch.	bef 1859	N.-Amer	835948
Weil, Johann Jacob	4 Apr 1867	Owen	Krch.	Dec 1883	N.-Amer	835948
Weil, Johannes	24 Jul 1841	Muenchingen	Leon.	Oct 1851	N.-Amer	837961
Weil, Johannes	28 Nov 1842	Ochsenwang	Krch.	Apr 1861	N.-Amer	835947
Weil, Konrad	28 Sep 1843	Ochsenwang	Krch.	May 1861	N.-Amer	835947
Weiland, Jacob & F		Leonberg	Leon.	Apr 1831	N.-Amer	835786
Weiler, Hermann	6 Apr 1871	Heiningen/Back.	Krch.	Jun 1887	N.-Amer	835949
Weimann, Jakob Friedrich		Malmsheim	Leon.	Jan 1817	N.-Amer	837958
Weimer, Barbara	1 Feb 1835	Geislingen	Gsl.	May 1859	Switz.	572043
Weimer, Catharina	12 Oct 1822	Eltingen	Leon.	Apr 1854	N.-Amer	835789
Weimer, Christian	31 Dec 1824	Eltingen	Leon.	Apr 1854	N.-Amer	835789
Weimer, Christian Adam	12 May 1842	Eltingen	Leon.	Jul 1865	N.-Amer	835789
Weimer, Johann Christian	25 Jan 1843	Bissingen	Krch.	Feb 1869	N.-Amer	835943
Weimer, Johann Gottlieb	5 Jun 1845	Eltingen	Leon.	Sep 1865	N.-Amer	835789
Weimer, Johann Jacob	11 Sep 1820	Oeschelbronn	Leon.	Dec 1862	Bavaria	834624
Weimer, Johann Jakob	16 Nov 1845	Bondorf	Herr.	Aug 1869	N.-Amer	834630
Weimer, Johann Jakob	23 Mar 1837	Bondorf	Herr.	May 1867	France	834630
Weimer, Johann Martin	14 Mar 1827	Bondorf	Herr.	1846	N.-Amer	834630
Weimer, Johannes	17 Jan 1833	Eltingen	Leon.	May 1851	N.-Amer	835789
Weimer, Leonhardt & F		Geislingen	Gsl.	Oct 1866	N.-Amer	572045
Weimer, Louise	infant	Geislingen	Gsl.	Oct 1866	N.-Amer	572045
Weimer, Maria Magdalena	4 Jun 1848	Bissingen	Krch.	Oct 1866	N.-Amer	835943

Name		Birth		Emigration			Film
Last	First	Date	Place	O'amt	Appl. Date	Dest.	Number
Weimer, Mathilde (wife)		25 yrs.	Geislingen	Gsl.	Oct 1866	N.-Amer	572045
Weinberg, Albert		11 Feb 1853	Roetenbach	Obd.	Jan 1864	N.-Amer	838636
Weinberg, Eduard		22 Aug 1855	Roetenbach	Obd.	Jan 1864	N.-Amer	838636
Weinberg, Eduard & F			Roetenbach	Obd.	Jan 1864	N.-Amer	838636
Weinberg, Max		9 Oct 1851	Roetenbach	Obd.	Jan 1864	N.-Amer	838636
Weinhardt, Conrad Gottlieb		13 Oct 1840	Kirchheim	Krch.	Jul 1859	N.-Amer	835940
Weinmann, Gottlob		7 Mar 1849	Reutlingen	Rtl.	Apr 1867	N.-Amer	841058
Weinmann, Johann Martin		10 Nov 1851	Reutlingen	Rtl.	Apr 1867	N.-Amer	841058
Weirich, Melchior		12 Apr 1819	Altenstadt-Gsl.	Gsl.	Feb 1863	N.-Amer	572044
Weishardt, Johann Martin			Pfullingen	Rtl.	Jul 1836	N.-Amer	841051
Weismann, Tobias Friedrich			Alpirsbach	Obd.	Nov 1821	Frankf.	838631
Weiss, Andreas Michael Fried.		22 yrs.	Rutesheim	Leon.	Feb 1852	N.-Amer	837964
Weiss, Anna		12 Jul 1877	Rosswaelden	Krch.	Feb 1881	N.-Amer	835949
Weiss, Anna Maria		3 Jan 1837	Rosswaelden	Krch.	Jun 1857	N.-Amer	835949
Weiss, Carolina Catharina		17 Jun 1873	Rosswaelden	Krch.	Mar 1881	N.-Amer	548403
Weiss, Catharina		29 Jul 1880	Rosswaelden	Krch.	Mar 1881	N.-Amer	548403
Weiss, Catharina (wife)		17 May 1824	Rosswaelden	Krch.	Aug 1858	Africa	835949
Weiss, Christian		1 May 1876	Rosswaelden	Krch.	Mar 1881	N.-Amer	548403
Weiss, Christiana		8 Apr 1875	Rosswaelden	Krch.	Feb 1881	N.-Amer	835949
Weiss, Christine		7 Oct 1850	Rosswaelden	Krch.	Aug 1858	Africa	835949
Weiss, Elisabetha		24 Dec 1842	Rosswaelden	Krch.	Sep 1858	N.-Amer	835949
Weiss, Elisabetha & C		7 Feb 1828	Gaertringen	Herr.	Nov 1865	France	834630
Weiss, Eva Rosina			Unterboehringen	Gsl.	Jul 1856	N.-Amer	572043
Weiss, Friederike Carol. (wife)		28 Oct 1846	Rosswaelden	Krch.	Mar 1881	N.-Amer	548403
Weiss, Friedrich			Rutesheim	Leon.	Feb 1852	N.-Amer	837964
Weiss, Georg Michael		31 Aug 1849	Reutlingen	Rtl.	Aug 1869	N.-Amer	841058
Weiss, Jakob			Moensheim	Leon.	Feb 1854	N.-Amer	837960
Weiss, Jakob Friedrich		19 yrs.	Rutesheim	Leon.	Feb 1852	N.-Amer	837964
Weiss, Johann		2 Jul 1848	Rosswaelden	Krch.	Aug 1858	Africa	835949
Weiss, Johann & F		15 Feb 1813	Rosswaelden	Krch.	Aug 1858	Africa	835949
Weiss, Johann Friedrich		36 yrs.	Rutesheim	Leon.	Apr 1839	N.-Amer	837964
Weiss, Johann Georg		17 yrs.	Rutesheim	Leon.	Feb 1852	N.-Amer	837964
Weiss, Johann Gottlieb		13 yrs.	Rutesheim	Leon.	Feb 1852	N.-Amer	837964
Weiss, Johann Jacob		9 mon.	Rutesheim	Leon.	Feb 1852	N.-Amer	837964
Weiss, Johann Jakob		6 Nov 1848	Pfullingen	Rtl.	Feb 1868	N.-Amer	841058
Weiss, Johann Michael		27 Jan 1815	Rosswaelden	Krch.	May 1863	N.-Amer	835949
Weiss, Johannes		12 Apr 1845	Pfullingen	Rtl.	Feb 1865	N.-Amer	841058
Weiss, Johannes			Wenden	Nag.	Apr 1853	N.-Amer	838488
Weiss, Joseph Richard		16 Jan 1868	Oetlingen	Krch.	Apr 1883	N.-Amer	548403
Weiss, Karoline Catharine		17 Jun 1873	Kirchheim	Krch.	Feb 1881	N.-Amer	835949
Weiss, Katharina		29 Jul 1880	Rosswaelden	Krch.	Feb 1881	N.-Amer	835949
Weiss, Katharina Jacobine		31 Oct 1851	Rosswaelden	Krch.	Aug 1858	Africa	835949
Weiss, Konrad Friedrich		27 Jul 1849	Eltingen	Leon.	Sep 1869	N.-Amer	835789
Weiss, Maria Agnes		24 yrs.	Rutesheim	Leon.	Feb 1852	N.-Amer	837964
Weiss, Maria Agnes (wife)		55 yrs.	Rutesheim	Leon.	Feb 1852	N.-Amer	837964
Weiss, Maria Magdalena		26 yrs.	Rutesheim	Leon.	Feb 1852	N.-Amer	837964
Weiss, Matthaeus		25 Dec 1834	Rosswaelden	Krch.	Feb 1863	N.-Amer	835949
Weiss, Michael		9 Sep 1849	Rosswaelden	Krch.	Aug 1858	Africa	835949
Weiss, Michael & F		8 Mar 1850	Rosswaelden	Krch.	Mar 1881	N.-Amer	548403
Weiss, Robert		26 Jul 1878	Rosswaelden	Krch.	Mar 1881	N.-Amer	548403

Weiss, Theodor Christian	23 Aug 1860	Herrenberg	Herr.	Dec 1881	N.-Amer	834629
Weiss, Thomas & F	55 yrs.	Rutesheim	Leon.	Feb 1852	N.-Amer	837964
Weisser, Amandus	10 yrs.	Aichhalden	Obd.	Feb 1853	N.-Amer	838629
Weisser, Anna	28 May 1843	Betzweiler	Obd.	May 1847	N.-Amer	838631
Weisser, Anna Maria	29 Jun 1846	Betzweiler	Obd.	May 1847	N.-Amer	838631
Weisser, Christian Emanuel A.	11 Oct 1838	Heimsheim	Leon.	Jul 1863	N.-Amer	837955
Weisser, Christiane		Alpirsbach	Obd.	Mar 1820	Frankf.	838631
Weisser, Christina	11 Jan 1845	Betzweiler	Obd.	May 1847	N.-Amer	838631
Weisser, Jakob		Aichhalden	Obd.	Aug 1857	N.-Amer	838629
Weisser, Johann & F		Aichhalden	Obd.	May 1817	N.-Amer	838629
Weisser, Johann Christoph		Alpirsbach	Obd.	Oct 1821	Frankf.	838631
Weisser, Konstantin	3 Feb 1851	Aichhalden	Obd.	Jul 1869	N.-Amer	838629
Weisser, Konstantin		Aichhalden	Obd.	Oct 1854	N.-Amer	838629
Weisser, Louisa	17 yrs.	Aichhalden	Obd.	Aug 1857	N.-Amer	838629
Weisser, Ludwig Friedrich	13 Jul 1802	Heimsheim	Leon.	bef 1864	Switz.	837955
Weisser, Margaretha & C	15 Apr 1820	Kappel/Baden	Obd.	May 1847	N.-Amer	838631
Weisser, Rosina		Ueberberg	Nag.	1847	N.-Amer	838488
Weisser, Wendelin	15 Oct 1847	Aichhalden	Obd.	May 1865	N.-Amer	838629
Weisser, Wilhelm	27 Jul 1846	Aichhalden	Obd.	May 1865	N.-Amer	838629
Weissinger, Heinrich Wilhelm	7 Nov 1872	Weilheim	Krch.	Mar 1889	N.-Amer	835774
Weissinger, Johann Adam	11 Aug 1874	Weilheim	Krch.	Jul 1890	N.-Amer	835774
Weissinger, Johann Adam	18 Mar 1843	Weilheim	Krch.	Dec 1863	N.-Amer	835950
Weissinger, Johann Georg	16 May 1844	Weilheim	Krch.	Aug 1866	N.-Amer	835940
Weissinger, Johann Georg	24 Oct 1841	Weilheim	Krch.	Jan 1857	N.-Amer	835949
Weissinger, Johann Michael	15 Jun 1839	Weilheim	Krch.	Jun 1855	N.-Amer	835949
Welcker, August	22 Jun 1834	Balmannsweiler	Leon.	1859	Oldenb.	837954
Welsch, Gustav Adolph	5 Dec 1846	Leonberg	Leon.	Aug 1866	N.-Amer	835787
Wencher, Johannes	19 Feb 1874	Gaertringen	Herr.	Aug 1891	N.-Amer	834631
Wendel, David Johannes	31 Aug 1865	Eltingen	Leon.	Nov 1882	N.-Amer	835789
Wendel, Friederich & F		Leonberg	Leon.	Apr 1851	N.-Amer	835786
Wendel, Friederike (wife)		Leonberg	Leon.	Apr 1851	N.-Amer	835786
Wendel, Friederike Sabine		Leonberg	Leon.	Feb 1837	Hesse	835786
Wendel, Friedrich	24 yrs.	Leonberg	Leon.	Apr 1852	N.-Amer	835786
Wendel, Friedrich & F		Leonberg	Leon.	Apr 1833	Poland	835786
Wendel, Friedrich & W		Leonberg	Leon.	Apr 1843	N.-Amer	835786
Wendel, Gottlieb Friedrich	2 yrs.	Leonberg	Leon.	Apr 1851	N.-Amer	835786
Wendel, Jacob	19 yrs.	Eltingen	Leon.	May 1851	N.-Amer	835789
Wendel, Johann Conrad		Leonberg	Leon.	Aug 1833	Hesse	835786
Wendel, Karl Gottlieb	17 Jan 1842	Leonberg	Leon.	Jun 1864	N.-Amer	835787
Wendel, Margaretha (wife)		Leonberg	Leon.	Apr 1843	N.-Amer	835786
Wendel, Maria Catharina	24 Feb 1839	Leonberg	Leon.	Jun 1859	N.-Amer	835786
Wendel, Michael & F		Eltingen	Leon.	Apr 1830	N.-Amer	835789
Wendel, Rosine	16 Jul 1832	Leonberg	Leon.	Apr 1852	N.-Amer	835786
Wendler, Christian	7 Sep 1827	Reutlingen	Rtl.	Mar 1867	N.-Amer	841058
Wendler, Franz Jakob		Eningen	Rtl.	Feb 1866	Switz.	841058
Wendler, Gottliebin Louise	18 Jun 1844	Weil	Rtl.	May 1867	N.-Amer	841058
Wendler, Johann Georg	27 Apr 1803	Reutlingen	Rtl.	Sep 1864	N.-Amer	841058
Wendler, Johann Georg		Reutlingen	Rtl.	Apr 1831	N.-Amer	841051
Wendler, Maria	24 Jul 1845	Reutlingen	Rtl.	May 1865	N.-Amer	841058
Wendler, Regina		Reutlingen	Rtl.	Jun 1860	N.-Amer	841058

Name		Birth		Emigration			Film
Last	First	Date	Place	O'amt	Appl. Date	Dest.	Number
Wendler, Rosine		2 Sep 1825	Pfullingen	Rtl.	May 1867	N.-Amer	841058
Wendnagel, Paul		15 Feb 1861	Kirchheim	Krch.	May 1878	N.-Amer	835942
Wenk, Anna Maria		17 yrs.	Fluorn	Obd.	Feb 1861	N.-Amer	838632
W'enrad, Crescentia		3 Jul 1823	Donzdorf	Gsl.	1854	N.-Amer	572043
Wenz, Johann Georg		25 Dec 1857	Undingen	Rtl.	Jun 1879	N.-Amer	841051
Wenz, Johann Martin		21 Aug 1859	Undingen	Rtl.	Jan 1880	N.-Amer	841051
Weoppert, Elisabetha Cathar.		21 Mar 1805	Weilheim	Krch.	bef 1866	N.-Amer	835950
Wepfer, Friedrich		17 May 1832	Kirchheim	Krch.	Apr 1858	France	835940
Werner, Anna Maria (wife)		2 Aug 1840	Bondorf	Herr.	Apr 1872	N.-Amer	834630
Werner, Anna Rosine (wife)		10 Nov 1853	Dusslingen	Herr.	1881	N.-Amer	834630
Werner, Barbara		20 Apr 1867	Bondorf	Herr.	Apr 1872	N.-Amer	834630
Werner, Carl Friedrich		1 Mar 1842	Bondorf	Herr.	Oct 1866	N.-Amer	834630
Werner, Christian		1 Feb 1848	Bondorf	Herr.	bef 1868	N.-Amer	834630
Werner, Christiane		21 Jul 1864	Bondorf	Herr.	Apr 1872	N.-Amer	834630
Werner, David		32 yrs.	Lindorf	Krch.	1857	N.-Amer	835946
Werner, Jacob		3 Mar 1839	Genkingen	Rtl.	Jun 1880	N.-Amer	841051
Werner, Jakob		22 Jul 1879	Bondorf	Herr.	1881	N.-Amer	834630
Werner, Jakob		13 Apr 1842	Betzingen	Rtl.	May 1862	N.-Amer	841058
Werner, Johann Christian		9 Dec 1832	Bondorf	Herr.	1852	N.-Amer	834630
Werner, Johann Georg		24 Aug 1840	Bondorf	Herr.	Dec 1864	N.-Amer	834630
Werner, Johann Jakob & F		12 Sep 1854	Bondorf	Herr.	1881	N.-Amer	834630
Werner, Johann Martin		24 Sep 1849	Bondorf	Herr.	Oct 1866	N.-Amer	834630
Werner, Johannes		17 Aug 1849	Bondorf	Herr.	bef 1877	Switz.	834630
Werner, Johannes		27 Jan 1845	Unterhausen	Rtl.	Aug 1865	N.-Amer	841058
Werner, Johannes		22 Aug 1841	Unterhausen	Rtl.	Apr 1864	N.-Amer	841058
Werner, Johannes & F		2 Oct 1841	Bondorf	Herr.	Apr 1872	N.-Amer	834630
Werner, Johannes & F		2 May 1838	Honau	Rtl.	Oct 1866	N.-Amer	841058
Werner, Luise (wife)		8 Mar 1836	Honau	Rtl.	Oct 1866	N.-Amer	841058
Werner, Sophie			Waldmoessingen	Obd.	bef 1864	N.-Amer	841015
Werner, Wilhelm Jacob		24 Aug 1865	Honau	Rtl.	Oct 1866	N.-Amer	841058
Wernle, Carl		17 Nov 1840	Kirchheim	Krch.	Oct 1866	S.-Amer	835941
Wernle, Johanna Magdalena		24 May 1824	Kirchheim	Krch.	May 1868	France	835941
Wernz, Alois			Aichhalden	Obd.	Sep 1861	N.-Amer	838629
Wernz, Marzell		19 yrs.	Aichhalden	Obd.	Jun 1869	N.-Amer	838629
Werz, Adam		11 Oct 1847	Kleinengstingen	Rtl.	Feb 1866	N.-Amer	841058
Werz, Christian		16 Oct 1846	Kleinengstingen	Rtl.	Feb 1869	N.-Amer	841058
Werz, Johann Martin		4 Jul 1847	Ohmenhausen	Rtl.	Apr 1867	N.-Amer	841058
Westenberger, Josephine Soph.		27 yrs.	Honau	Rtl.	Mar 1862	N.-Amer	841058
Wetzel, Karoline		2 Nov 1842	Oberndorf	Obd.	Apr 1861	N.-Amer	838635
Wetzel, Philipp Friedrich & F			Enztal	Nag.	Apr 1851	N.-Amer	838488
Weyhl, Heinrich		15 Aug 1849	Kirchheim	Krch.	Jul 1869	N.-Amer	835941
Weyhrich, Christine		28 Sep 1827	Gammelshausen	Gsl.	Jun 1854	N.-Amer	572042
Weysing, Elisabetha		18 Oct 1808	Gomaringen	Rtl.	Apr 1867	N.-Amer	841058
Weysing, Johann Daniel		1 Jan 1849	Gomaringen	Rtl.	Jun 1865	N.-Amer	841058
Weysing, Simon & W		3 Sep 1812	Gomaringen	Rtl.	Apr 1867	N.-Amer	841058
Wezel, Caecilie			Oberndorf	Obd.	Mar 1849	N.-Amer	838635
Wezel, Josefa			Oberndorf	Obd.	Mar 1849	N.-Amer	838635
Wezel, Marianne & C			Oberndorf	Obd.	Mar 1849	N.-Amer	838635
Wichtermann, Johann Michael		20 Mar 1847	Hildrizhausen	Herr.	bef 1874	N.-Amer	834631
Wick, David Gottlob		18 Sep 1844	Eningen	Rtl.	May 1863	N.-Amer	841058

Widmaier, – (wife)	17 Nov 1825	Eltingen	Leon.	Mar 1851	N.-Amer	835789
Widmaier, Abraham	19 Dec 1814	Eltingen	Leon.	Aug 1851	N.-Amer	835789
Widmaier, Alexander & F		Renningen	Leon.	Apr 1852	N.-Amer	837963
Widmaier, Anna Barbara (wife)		Renningen	Leon.	Apr 1852	N.-Amer	837963
Widmaier, Catharina	10 yrs.	Heimsheim	Leon.	Sep 1852	N.-Amer	837955
Widmaier, Christian	12 Apr 1838	Renningen	Leon.	Jul 1854	N.-Amer	837963
Widmaier, Christian	13 May 1828	Eltingen	Leon.	Jan 1852	N.-Amer	835789
Widmaier, Christiana (wife)		Eltingen	Leon.	Sep 1852	N.-Amer	835789
Widmaier, Christof Friedrich	20 Nov 1848	Eltingen	Leon.	Mar 1851	N.-Amer	835789
Widmaier, Christoph	2 yrs.	Heimsheim	Leon.	Sep 1852	N.-Amer	837955
Widmaier, Eva Catharina	22 Jan 1832	Renningen	Leon.	Apr 1852	N.-Amer	837963
Widmaier, Friedrich	5 yrs.	Heimsheim	Leon.	Sep 1852	N.-Amer	837955
Widmaier, Georg Adam & F		Heimsheim	Leon.	May 1851	N.-Amer	837955
Widmaier, Georg Heinrich	13 Dec 1835	Heimsheim	Leon.	May 1851	N.-Amer	837955
Widmaier, Gottfried	18 Apr 1854	Eltingen	Leon.	Aug 1880	N.-Amer	835789
Widmaier, Gottfried	1 yrs.	Eltingen	Leon.	Sep 1852	N.-Amer	835789
Widmaier, Gottlieb	3 yrs.	Eltingen	Leon.	Sep 1852	N.-Amer	835789
Widmaier, Gottlieb	22 yrs.	Eltingen	Leon.	Mar 1851	N.-Amer	835789
Widmaier, Gottlieb	20 May 1846	Eltingen	Leon.	Mar 1851	N.-Amer	835789
Widmaier, Gottliebin		Eltingen	Leon.	Jul 1855	N.-Amer	835789
Widmaier, Gottlob & F	25 Mar 1818	Eltingen	Leon.	Mar 1851	N.-Amer	835789
Widmaier, Gottlob Friedrich	17 yrs.	Malmsheim	Leon.	Apr 1854	N.-Amer	837958
Widmaier, Helene	21 yrs.	Eltingen	Leon.	Mar 1851	N.-Amer	835789
Widmaier, Jacob	16 Nov 1836	Heimsheim	Leon.	Oct 1854	N.-Amer	837955
Widmaier, Jacob	15 yrs.	Heimsheim	Leon.	Sep 1852	N.-Amer	837955
Widmaier, Jacob & F		Eltingen	Leon.	Sep 1852	N.-Amer	835789
Widmaier, Johann Jacob	13 Feb 1849	Eltingen	Leon.	Sep 1869	N.-Amer	835789
Widmaier, Johann Jakob	6 Dec 1826	Renningen	Leon.	Apr 1852	N.-Amer	837963
Widmaier, Johanne Margaretha	13 yrs.	Heimsheim	Leon.	Sep 1852	N.-Amer	837955
Widmaier, Johannes		Eltingen	Leon.	Oct 1854	N.-Amer	835789
Widmaier, Johannes	1 May 1808	Eltingen	Leon.	Aug 1851	N.-Amer	835789
Widmaier, Leonhard	17 Aug 1828	Eltingen	Leon.	Nov 1864	N.-Amer	835789
Widmaier, Louise	5 yrs.	Eltingen	Leon.	Sep 1852	N.-Amer	835789
Widmaier, Maria		Eltingen	Leon.	Jul 1855	N.-Amer	835789
Widmaier, Michael	8 yrs.	Heimsheim	Leon.	Sep 1852	N.-Amer	837955
Widmaier, Michael & F		Heimsheim	Leon.	Sep 1852	N.-Amer	837955
Widmaier, Pauline Friederike	28 Aug 1838	Renningen	Leon.	Apr 1852	N.-Amer	837963
Widmaier, Rosina Margaretha	1 Jan 1829	Renningen	Leon.	Apr 1852	N.-Amer	837963
Widmaier, Sara (wife)		Heimsheim	Leon.	Sep 1852	N.-Amer	837955
Widmaier, Sebastian	18 Mar 1859	Eltingen	Leon.	Aug 1889	N.-Amer	835789
Widman, Conrad & F		Moensheim	Leon.	Aug 1851	N.-Amer	837960
Widman, Josef	17 Jan 1832	Boehmenkirch	Gsl.	1854	N.-Amer	573622
Widman, Marianna & C		Wiesensteig	Gsl.	Dec 1852	N.-Amer	572041
Widman, Sophia (wife)		Moensheim	Leon.	Aug 1851	N.-Amer	837960
Widmann, – & W	25 yrs.	Oberhausen	Rtl.	Jun 1879	N.-Amer	841051
Widmann, Albert		Weissenstein	Gsl.	Apr 1853	N.-Amer	572041
Widmann, Alexander & W		Moensheim	Leon.	Jul 1819	Russia	837960
Widmann, Andreas	9 Jun 1843	Moensheim	Leon.	Mar 1854	N.-Amer	837960
Widmann, Anna	12 yrs.	Westerheim	Gsl.	Mar 1852	N.-Amer	572041
Widmann, Anna Maria	24 Apr 1853	Moensheim	Leon.	Mar 1854	N.-Amer	837960

Name		Birth		Emigration			Film
Last	First	Date	Place	O'amt	Appl. Date	Dest.	Number
Widmann, Anton		21 yrs.	Deggingen	Gsl.	May 1851	N.-Amer	577788
Widmann, Anton		19 May 1842	Boehmenkirch	Gsl.	Mar 1861	N.-Amer	572044
Widmann, Carolina			Weissenstein	Gsl.	Apr 1853	N.-Amer	572041
Widmann, Christian		23 Oct 1818	Alpirsbach	Obd.	bef 1851	Paris	838630
Widmann, Christian & F		6 Oct 1815	Moensheim	Leon.	Mar 1854	N.-Amer	837960
Widmann, Christina		16 yrs.	Westerheim	Gsl.	Mar 1852	N.-Amer	572041
Widmann, Conrad		1 yrs.	Moensheim	Leon.	Aug 1851	N.-Amer	837960
Widmann, Elias		3 yrs.	Westerheim	Gsl.	Mar 1852	N.-Amer	572041
Widmann, Elisabetha (wife)			Westerheim	Gsl.	Mar 1852	N.-Amer	572041
Widmann, Franziska		7 yrs.	Westerheim	Gsl.	Mar 1852	N.-Amer	572041
Widmann, Franziska			Boehmenkirch	Gsl.	Feb 1852	N.-Amer	572044
Widmann, Friedrich		14 Dec 1865	Hochdorf	Krch.	May 1882	N.-Amer	548403
Widmann, Gottfried		17 Jul 1835	Rosswaelden	Krch.	Mar 1867	N.-Amer	835949
Widmann, Gottlieb		1 mon.	Moensheim	Leon.	Aug 1851	N.-Amer	837960
Widmann, Jakob		2 Jun 1832	Moensheim	Leon.	Aug 1851	N.-Amer	837960
Widmann, Jakob Wilhelm		11 Jun 1875	Oetlingen	Krch.	Jul 1877	N.-Amer	548403
Widmann, Johann Robert		2 Jun 1874	Oetlingen	Krch.	Jul 1877	N.-Amer	835948
Widmann, Johanna (wife)		19 yrs.	Oberhausen	Rtl.	Jun 1879	N.-Amer	841051
Widmann, Johanna Catharina		1 Nov 1845	Moensheim	Leon.	Mar 1854	N.-Amer	837960
Widmann, Johannes			Weissenstein	Gsl.	Apr 1853	N.-Amer	572041
Widmann, Johannes & F		20 Aug 1850	Beuren	Krch.	Jul 1877	N.-Amer	835948
Widmann, Joseph			Weissenstein	Gsl.	Apr 1853	N.-Amer	572041
Widmann, Joseph & F			Westerheim	Gsl.	Mar 1852	N.-Amer	572041
Widmann, Joseph Anton & F		1 Nov 1804	Weissenstein	Gsl.	Apr 1853	N.-Amer	572041
Widmann, Karl Hermann		14 Jan 1860	Gaertringen	Herr.	1882	N.-Amer	834630
Widmann, Katharina		9 yrs.	Westerheim	Gsl.	Mar 1852	N.-Amer	572041
Widmann, Kreszenz		26 Feb 1847	Boehmenkirch	Gsl.	Jan 1867	N.-Amer	572046
Widmann, Ludwig Jacob Friedr.			Hemmingen	Leon.	Nov 1833	France	837956
Widmann, Ludwik		13 yrs.	Westerheim	Gsl.	Mar 1852	N.-Amer	572041
Widmann, Margaretha (wife)			Weissenstein	Gsl.	Apr 1853	N.-Amer	572041
Widmann, Maria Josepha			Weissenstein	Gsl.	Apr 1853	N.-Amer	572041
Widmann, Michael		31 yrs.	Unterboehringen	Gsl.	Apr 1852	N.-Amer	572041
Widmann, Philipp			Moensheim	Leon.	Dec 1851	N.-Amer	837960
Widmann, Philipp			Weissenstein	Gsl.	Apr 1853	N.-Amer	572041
Widmann, Rosina (wife)		19 May 1849	Oetlingen	Krch.	Jul 1877	N.-Amer	548403
Widmann, Sara Friederike & C		11 Jun 1819	Heimsheim	Leon.	Jun 1851	N.-Amer	837955
Widmann, Sophia Margaretha		17 Dec 1850	Moensheim	Leon.	Mar 1854	N.-Amer	837960
Widmayer, Anna Maria (wife)			Renningen	Leon	Mar 1830	N.-Amer	837963
Widmayer, Gottlob & F			Eltingen	Leon.	Mar 1831	N.-Amer	835789
Widmayer, Jakob Friedrich & W			Renningen	Leon.	Mar 1830	N.-Amer	837963
Widmayer, Johannes			Heimsheim	Leon.	bef 1827	Hamburg	837963
Widmayer, Lorenz & F			Eltingen	Leon.	Mar 1831	N.-Amer	835789
Widmayer, Wilhelm Gottl.		24 Apr 1845	Renningen	Leon.	Jun 1865	N.-Amer	837963
Widmer, Andreas Adolph		3 Nov 1864	Alpirsbach	Obd.	Dec 1865	Prussia	838630
Widmer, Anna Margaretha & C			Alpirsbach	Obd.	Dec 1865	Prussia	838630
Widmer, Christiane & C		7 Apr 1828	Alpirsbach	Obd.	Apr 1864	Switz.	838630
Widmer, Elise		20 Aug 1861	Alpirsbach	Obd.	Apr 1864	Switz.	838630
Widmer, Friederike		26 Apr 1834	Alpirsbach	Obd.	Dec 1858	Switz.	838630
Widmer, Jacob			Alpirsbach	Obd.	Apr 1863	America	838630
Widmer, Johann Georg		25 Oct 1847	Alpirsbach	Obd.	Apr 1863	America	838630

Widmer, Karl Christoph	2 Aug 1849	Alpirsbach	Obd.	Jul 1867	N.-Amer	838630
Widmer, Wilhelm	24 Mar 1851	Alpirsbach	Obd.	Feb 1867	N.-Amer	838630
Wied, Albert	24 Apr 1865	Ueberkingen	Gsl.	Mar 1882	N.-Amer	572048
Wiedemann, Michael	18 Sep 1834	Grosssuessen	Gsl.	Feb 1854	N.-Amer	572042
Wiedenhoefer, Friederike	25 Sep 1844	Kirchheim	Krch.	Jan 1860	N.-Amer	835940
Wiedenhoefer, Gottlieb		Kirchheim	Krch.	Jan 1860	N.-Amer	835940
Wiedenhoefer, Gustav Adolph	14 Jul 1844	Kirchheim	Krch.	Aug 1864	N.-Amer	835941
Wiedenhoefer, Johann Wilhelm	13 Jul 1831	Kirchheim	Krch.	May 1857	N.-Amer	835940
Wiedmaier, Friedrich	25 Jun 1838	Leonberg	Leon.	Apr 1855	N.-Amer	835786
Wiedmaier, Georg Adam	22 Jan 1832	Heimsheim	Leon.	Jan 1864	N.-Amer	837955
Wiedmaier, Marianna	4 May 1838	Donzdorf	Gsl.	Jan 1865	Switz.	572045
Wiedmaier, Wilhelm	26 Nov 1834	Leonberg	Leon.	Mar 1853	N.-Amer	835786
Wiedmann, Friedrich Carl	16 yrs.	Reutlingen	Rtl.	Jun 1880	N.-Amer	841051
Wiedmann, Georg & F		Weilheim	Krch.	1784	Hungary	550804
Wiedmann, Johannes		Weilheim	Krch.	May 1753	N.-Amer	550804
Wiedmann, Maria Doro. (wife)		Weilheim	Krch.	1784	Hungary	550804
Wiedmann, Michael	18 Sep 1834	Grosssuessen	Gsl.	1854	N.-Amer	572044
Wieland, Anna Magdalena	11 yrs.	Eltingen	Leon.	May 1818	Russia	835789
Wieland, Anna Maria	16 yrs.	Eltingen	Leon.	May 1818	Russia	835789
Wieland, Catharina	2 Nov 1848	Dettingen	Krch.	Nov 1871	N.-Amer	835944
Wieland, Christian	5 Aug 1842	Dettingen	Krch.	Dec 1868	N.-Amer	835944
Wieland, Christian (wid.) & F	10 Dec 1804	Dettingen	Krch.	Nov 1871	N.-Amer	835944
Wieland, Christian Friedrich	6 Dec 1822	Ditzingen	Leon.	Mar 1853	N.-Amer	835788
Wieland, Dorothea	31 Mar 1853	Dettingen	Krch.	Nov 1871	N.-Amer	835944
Wieland, Elise Frieder. Soph.	19 Feb 1845	Leonberg	Leon.	Oct 1870	Switz.	835787
Wieland, Friedericke Magdal.	11 Jul 1843	Schlattstall	Krch.	Jul 1883	N.-Amer	835949
Wieland, Gustav Theodor	10 Sep 1835	Hochdorf	Krch.	Mar 1857	N.-Amer	835945
Wieland, Johann Georg	25 yrs.	Eltingen	Leon.	May 1818	Russia	835789
Wieland, Katharina	17 May 1845	Schlattstall	Krch.	Jul 1865	N.-Amer	835949
Wieland, Leonhardt & F	52 yrs.	Eltingen	Leon.	May 1818	Russia	835789
Wieland, Louise	10 Apr 1848	Leonberg	Leon.	Jan 1872	Switz.	835787
Wieland, Regine (wife)	54 yrs.	Eltingen	Leon.	May 1818	Russia	835789
Wieland, Rosine Barbara	16 Aug 1839	Dettingen	Krch.	Nov 1871	N.-Amer	835944
Wieland, Sara (divorced) & F		Malmsheim	Leon.	Apr 1854	N.-Amer	837958
Wielandt, Carl Aug. Dav. Fr.	31 Aug 1836	Kirchheim	Krch.	bef 1867	N.-Amer	835941
Wild, Agatha	1 Sep 1826	Elchingen	Gsl.	Jul 1853	N.-Amer	572041
Wild, Christine Barbara	10 Mar 1822	Alpirsbach	Obd.	Nov 1849	France	838630
Wild, Johann	26 yrs.	Perouse	Leon.	Sep 1853	N.-Amer	837962
Wild, Johannes	19 Apr 1829	Aufhausen	Gsl.	Jan 1854	N.-Amer	572042
Wild, Johannes	24 Dec 1822	Wellingen	Krch.	May 1862	N.-Amer	835947
Wildbrett, Bertha	31 Dec 1844	Leonberg	Leon.	Aug 1868	Austria	835787
Wilhelm, Agatha	5 Mar 1845	Harthausen	Obd.	Aug 1866	N.-Amer	838633
Wilhelm, Agnes & C	13 Jan 1821	Harthausen	Obd.	Sep 1869	N.-Amer	838633
Wilhelm, Christian	28 yrs.	Hochmoessingen	Obd.	bef 1843	Austria	838633
Wilhelm, Elisabeth	24 yrs.	Hochmoessingen	Obd.	Dec 1845	Austria	838633
Wilhelm, Franz	1 Dec 1836	Harthausen	Obd.	May 1864	N.-Amer	838633
Wilhelm, Franziska	9 Mar 1838	Harthausen	Obd.	May 1863	N.-Amer	838633
Wilhelm, Johanna	23 May 1855	Harthausen	Obd.	Sep 1869	N.-Amer	838633
Wilhelm, Joseph	22 Jan 1811	Hochmoessingen	Obd.	Aug 1842	Austria	838633
Wille, Joseph Robert	16 Nov 1848	Pfullingen	Rtl.	Aug 1867	N.-Amer	841058

Name		Birth		Emigration			Film
Last	First	Date	Place	O'amt	Appl. Date	Dest.	Number
Wille, Karl Adolph		22 Sep 1860	Pfullingen	Rtl.	Jul 1867	N.-Amer	841058
Willot, Friederike Katharine		26 Apr 1850	Pfullingen	Rtl.	Nov 1860	N.-Amer	841058
Winkler, Friederika		10 Oct 1875	Moensheim	Leon.	Apr 1885	N.-Amer	837960
Winkler, Georg Friedrich & F		21 Jul 1838	Moensheim	Leon.	Apr 1885	N.-Amer	837960
Winkler, Katharina (wife)		28 May 1855	Moensheim	Leon.	Apr 1885	N.-Amer	837960
Winkler, Ludwig		3 Mar 1831	Moensheim	Leon.	Feb 1844	N.-Amer	837960
Winkler, Marie Wilhelmine		25 Feb 1873	Moensheim	Leon.	Apr 1885	N.-Amer	837960
Winkler, Wilhelmine		10 Sep 1874	Moensheim	Leon.	Apr 1885	N.-Amer	837960
Winter, Christian Carl		15 Aug 1846	Flacht	Leon.	Jan 1861	N.-Amer	835790
Winter, Christian Helmuth		28 Jun 1844	Flacht	Leon.	Jan 1861	N.-Amer	835790
Winter, Friedrich Ludwig & F			Flacht	Leon.	Jan 1861	N.-Amer	835790
Winter, Johann Friedrich		18 Oct 1838	Flacht	Leon.	Jan 1861	N.-Amer	835790
Winter, Johann Gottlob		13 Apr 1840	Flacht	Leon.	Jan 1861	N.-Amer	835790
Winter, Maria Catharina		13 Sep 1834	Weilheim	Krch.	Apr 1859	N.-Amer	835949
Winter, Mathilde		29 Sep 1842	Pfullingen	Rtl.	Feb 1863	Prussia	841058
Wirth, Gottfried		9 yrs.	Heimsheim	Leon.	Aug 1853	N.-Amer	837955
Wirth, Jakob Friedrich		8 yrs.	Heimsheim	Leon.	Aug 1853	N.-Amer	837955
Wissmann, Christian Andreas		14 Feb 1827	Renningen	Leon.	Jul 1865	N.-Amer	837963
Wittel, Christian			Stockach	Rtl.	bef 1859	N.-Amer	841058
Wittel, Elisabetha		9 Jul 1809	Betzingen	Rtl.	Sep 1859	N.-Amer	841058
Wittel, Heinrich		10 Apr 1840	Stockach	Rtl.	Jul 1859	N.-Amer	841058
Wittel, Jakob			Stockach	Rtl.	Apr 1859	N.-Amer	841058
Wittel, Maria			Stockach	Rtl.	Mar 1859	N.-Amer	841058
Wittel, Rosina			Stockach	Rtl.	Apr 1859	N.-Amer	841058
Wittlinger, Johann Georg			Unterboehringen	Gsl.	May 1854	N.-Amer	572042
Wittlinger, Johannes		18 Feb 1864	Geislingen	Gsl.	Jan 1881	N.-Amer	572048
Wittlinger, Leonhard		2 Mar 1843	Eybach	Gsl.	May 1873	N.-Amer	572047
Wittlinger, Max		9 Jan 1863	Geislingen	Gsl.	Dec 1879	N.-Amer	572048
Witz, Lorenz		23 yrs.	Seedorf	Obd.	Apr 1857	N.-Amer	838637
Wizemann, Gustav		11 Nov 1849	Kirchheim	Krch.	May 1869	France	835941
Wochele, Jakob & F			Heimsheim	Leon.	Sep 1853	N.-Amer	837955
Wochele, Johann Georg & F			Hoefingen	Leon.	Mar 1831	N.-Amer	837957
Wochele, Johann Jakob			Merklingen	Leon.	bef 1853	Switz.	837959
Wochele, Julius		19 Feb 1847	Rosenfeld	Leon.	Aug 1865	N.-Amer	837959
Wochele, Margaretha (wife)			Heimsheim	Leon.	Sep 1853	N.-Amer	837955
Woehr, Adam			Eltingen	Leon.	Nov 1866	N.-Amer	835787
Woehr, Adam		11 Oct 1846	Eltingen	Leon.	Aug 1866	N.-Amer	835789
Woehr, Barbara (wife)		62 yrs.	Eltingen	Leon.	Mar 1817	Russia	835789
Woehr, Carola Wilhelmine (wife)			Leonberg	Leon.	Mar 1847	Austria	835786
Woehr, Caroline Rosine		21 Sep 1846	Leonberg	Leon.	Mar 1847	Austria	835786
Woehr, Catharina			Leonberg	Leon.	Mar 1861	N.-Amer	835787
Woehr, Catharina		7 yrs.	Leonberg	Leon.	Dec 1816	Russia	835789
Woehr, Elisabeth Catharina		24 yrs.	Eltingen	Leon.	Mar 1817	Russia	835789
Woehr, Friederich Georg		20 Jun 1841	Leonberg	Leon.	Mar 1847	Austria	835786
Woehr, Friederike (wife)		45 yrs.	Leonberg	Leon.	Dec 1816	Russia	835789
Woehr, Friedrich		7 Aug 1822	Leonberg	Leon.	May 1856	N.-Amer	835786
Woehr, Friedrich		22 yrs.	Eltingen	Leon.	Mar 1817	Russia	835789
Woehr, Georg Christian		28 May 1840	Leonberg	Leon.	Mar 1847	Austria	835786
Woehr, Georg Christian & F			Leonberg	Leon.	Mar 1847	Austria	835786
Woehr, Gottlieb		18 yrs.	Eltingen	Leon.	Mar 1817	Russia	835789

Woehr, Jacob & F	38 yrs.	Eltingen	Leon.	Mar 1817	Russia	835789
Woehr, Johann Jacob	1 yrs.	Eltingen	Leon.	Mar 1817	Russia	835789
Woehr, Johanna & C	19 yrs.	Eltingen	Leon.	Mar 1817	N.-Amer	835789
Woehr, Louise Catharine	7 Aug 1844	Leonberg	Leon.	Mar 1847	Austria	835786
Woehr, Louise Wilhelmine	11 Feb 1843	Leonberg	Leon.	Mar 1847	Austria	835786
Woehr, Magdalena	infant	Leonberg	Leon.	Dec 1816	Russia	835789
Woehr, Margaretha	11 yrs.	Eltingen	Leon.	Mar 1817	Russia	835789
Woehr, Margaretha (wife)	29 yrs.	Eltingen	Leon.	Mar 1817	Russia	835789
Woehr, Margaretha Barbara	3 yrs.	Eltingen	Leon.	Mar 1817	Russia	835789
Woehr, Margaretha Barbara & C	26 yrs.	Eltingen	Leon.	Mar 1817	Russia	835789
Woehr, Michael	28 yrs.	Eltingen	Leon.	Mar 1817	Russia	835789
Woehr, Philipp & F	33 yrs.	Leonberg	Leon.	Dec 1816	Russia	835789
Woehr, Ulrich & F	64 yrs.	Eltingen	Leon.	Mar 1817	Russia	835789
Woehrle, Agatha	27 Jun 1847	Weil der Stadt	Leon.	Jul 1847	N.-Amer	837965
Woehrle, Anna Maria		Reichenbaechle	Obd.	Aug 1856	N.-Amer	838636
Woehrle, Anton Johann		Weil der Stadt	Leon.	Jul 1847	N.-Amer	837965
Woehrle, Barbara	18 Mar 1788	Weil der Stadt	Leon.	Jul 1847	N.-Amer	837965
Woehrle, Christine Friedrich	1 Jan 1830	Notzingen	Krch.	bef 1855	N.-Amer	835943
Woehrle, Franz Felix		Weil der Stadt	Leon.	Jul 1847	N.-Amer	837965
Woehrle, Jacob	12 Nov 1831	Roetenbach	Obd.	Mar 1854	N.-Amer	838636
Woehrle, Johann Anton	14 Nov 1845	Weil der Stadt	Leon.	Jul 1847	N.-Amer	837965
Woehrle, Johann Baptist & F		Weil der Stadt	Leon.	Jul 1847	N.-Amer	837965
Woehrle, Johann Georg Adam		Weil der Stadt	Leon.	Jul 1847	N.-Amer	837965
Woehrle, Joseph Anton & F		Weil der Stadt	Leon.	Jul 1847	N.-Amer	837965
Woehrle, Julie (wife)		Weil der Stadt	Leon.	Jul 1847	N.-Amer	837965
Woehrle, Maria Anna Agnes		Weil der Stadt	Leon.	Jul 1847	N.-Amer	837965
Woehrle, Maria Eva & F		Weil der Stadt	Leon.	Jul 1847	N.-Amer	837965
Woehrle, Maria Rosa		Weil der Stadt	Leon.	Jul 1847	N.-Amer	837965
Woehrle, Maria Rosa	1 Jun 1846	Weil der Stadt	Leon.	Jul 1847	N.-Amer	837965
Woehrle, Sophia		Weil der Stadt	Leon.	Jul 1847	N.-Amer	837965
Woehrlen, Maria	18 yrs.	Kirchheim	Krch.	Sep 1869	N.-Amer	835941
Woerner, Anna Maria (wife)	24 Dec 1844	Hildrizhausen	Herr.	Feb 1870	N.-Amer	834631
Woerner, Carl	14 Nov 1850	Alpirsbach	Obd.	Jul 1853	N.-Amer	838630
Woerner, Carl August	13 Jul 1843	Herrenberg	Herr.	Dec 1868	N.-Amer	834629
Woerner, Catarina	11 yrs.	Hemmingen	Leon.	Mar 1827	N.-Amer	837956
Woerner, Catarina Margar. (wife)	47 yrs.	Hemmingen	Leon.	Mar 1827	N.-Amer	837956
Woerner, Dorothea	8 Jan 1843	Dornhan	Obd.	Sep 1868	France	838638
Woerner, Friedrich	14 yrs.	Hemmingen	Leon.	Mar 1827	N.-Amer	837956
Woerner, Georg	34 yrs.	Hemmingen	Leon.	Oct 1864	Austral	837956
Woerner, Jakob	7 yrs.	Hemmingen	Leon.	Mar 1827	N.-Amer	837956
Woerner, Jakob & F		Hausen a.d. Wurm	Leon.	Sep 1853	N.-Amer	837954
Woerner, Johann August	3 May 1866	Hildrizhausen	Herr.	Feb 1870	N.-Amer	834631
Woerner, Johann Christian	14 Apr 1845	Roetenbach	Obd.	Aug 1865	N.-Amer	838636
Woerner, Johann Georg		Hemmingen	Leon.	Nov 1827	N.-Amer	837956
Woerner, Johann Georg & F	26 Dec 1842	Hildrizhausen	Herr.	Feb 1870	N.-Amer	834631
Woerner, Johann Jacob Friedr.	27 Apr 1827	Nufringen	Herr.	bef 1869	N.-Amer	834629
Woerner, Johannes	19 Sep 1806	Fluorn	Obd.	Nov 1847	Austria	838632
Woerner, Johannes	19 yrs.	Hemmingen	Leon.	Mar 1827	N.-Amer	837956
Woerner, Johannes & F	22 Aug 1826	Alpirsbach	Obd.	Jul 1853	N.-Amer	838630
Woerner, Johannes & F	48 yrs.	Hemmingen	Leon.	Mar 1827	N.-Amer	837956

Name		Birth		Emigration			Film
Last	First	Date	Place	O'amt	Appl. Date	Dest.	Number
Woerner, Lisette (wife)		22 Dec 1826	Alpirsbach	Obd.	Jul 1853	N.-Amer	838630
Woerner, Louise		22 Sep 1852	Alpirsbach	Obd.	Jul 1853	N.-Amer	838630
Woerner, Michael		1 Jun 1850	Roetenbach	Obd.	Apr 1868	N.-Amer	838636
Woerner, Wilhelmine		16 Mar 1846	Dornhan	Obd.	Sep 1868	France	838638
Woertz, Matthaeus		16 Jul 1829	Ueberkingen	Gsl.	Mar 1854	N.-Amer	572042
Woerz, Johann Georg		9 Mar 1827	Ueberkingen	Gsl.	Nov 1854	N.-Amer	572042
Woessner, Andreas		7 yrs.	Fluorn	Obd.	Nov 1846	N.-Amer	838632
Woessner, Andreas		23 yrs.	Peterzell	Obd.	bef 1857	N.-Amer	838635
Woessner, Andreas & F		25 yrs.	Fluorn	Obd.	Mar 1847	N.-Amer	838632
Woessner, Andreas & F			Fluorn	Obd.	Nov 1846	N.-Amer	838632
Woessner, Anna		18 months	Fluorn	Obd.	Mar 1847	N.-Amer	838632
Woessner, Anna Barbara		5 Jun 1837	Alpirsbach	Obd.	Jan 1866	Berlin	838630
Woessner, Anna Maria			Aichhalden	Obd.	May 1817	N.-Amer	838629
Woessner, Anna Maria		12 yrs.	Fluorn	Obd.	Nov 1846	N.-Amer	838632
Woessner, Anna Maria			Peterzell	Obd.	May 1862	N.-Amer	838635
Woessner, Anna Maria & C			Roetenbach	Obd.	Aug 1854	N.-Amer	838636
Woessner, Anna Maria (wife)		41 yrs.	Fluorn	Obd.	Nov 1846	N.-Amer	838632
Woessner, Barbara		9 yrs.	Fluorn	Obd.	Nov 1846	N.-Amer	838632
Woessner, Barbara			Peterzell	Obd.	May 1862	N.-Amer	838635
Woessner, Barbara		21 Mar 1850	Roemlinsdorf	Obd.	May 1868	N.-Amer	838635
Woessner, Barbara		28 Mar 1842	Roetenbach	Obd.	Sep 1866	N.-Amer	838636
Woessner, Carl		29 Sep 1848	Schramberg	Obd.	May 1864	N.-Amer	838636
Woessner, Christian		21 Feb 1852	Peterzell	Obd.	May 1868	N.-Amer	838635
Woessner, Christian			Peterzell	Obd.	May 1862	N.-Amer	838635
Woessner, Christian		11 Apr 1840	Reichenbaechle	Obd.	Sep 1855	N.-Amer	838636
Woessner, Christian			Roetenbach	Obd.	bef 1854	N.-Amer	838636
Woessner, Christina		25 Apr 1848	Roemlinsdorf	Obd.	Jun 1865	N.-Amer	838635
Woessner, Christina & C			Betzweiler	Obd.	Jul 1863	Hesse	838631
Woessner, Christine			Alpirsbach	Obd.	bef 1848	France	838630
Woessner, Christine		6 yrs.	Fluorn	Obd.	Nov 1846	N.-Amer	838632
Woessner, Christine (wife)			Fluorn	Obd.	Mar 1847	N.-Amer	838632
Woessner, Friedrich		infant	Fluorn	Obd.	Mar 1847	N.-Amer	838632
Woessner, Friedrich		26 Feb 1845	Roemlinsdorf	Obd.	Jun 1865	N.-Amer	838635
Woessner, Georg		18 Aug 1832	Alpirsbach	Obd.	Nov 1858	Austria	838630
Woessner, Jacob			Peterzell	Obd.	bef 1868	N.-Amer	838635
Woessner, Jacob & F		4 Feb 1840	Bach-Altenberg	Obd.	Sep 1869	N.-Amer	838631
Woessner, Jakob Friedrich		4 Apr 1867	Bach-Altenberg	Obd.	Sep 1869	N.-Amer	838631
Woessner, Johann Georg			Peterzell	Obd.	May 1862	N.-Amer	838635
Woessner, Johann Georg		24 Aug 1837	Roetenbach	Obd.	Sep 1855	N.-Amer	838636
Woessner, Johann Georg & F			Peterzell	Obd.	May 1862	N.-Amer	838635
Woessner, Johannes		16 Aug 1848	Peterzell	Obd.	Apr 1865	N.-Amer	838635
Woessner, Johannes		14 Mar 1849	Roetenbach	Obd.	Sep 1866	N.-Amer	838636
Woessner, Johannes		7 Dec 1850	Seedorf	Obd.	Mar 1868	N.-Amer	838637
Woessner, Joseph			Fluorn	Obd.	Dec 1853	N.-Amer	838632
Woessner, Karoline			Peterzell	Obd.	May 1862	N.-Amer	838635
Woessner, Lucia (wife)			Peterzell	Obd.	May 1862	N.-Amer	838635
Woessner, Mathaeus		9 Dec 1834	Fluorn	Obd.	Sep 1853	N.-Amer	838632
Woessner, Matthias		25 Jul 1840	Fluorn	Obd.	Jul 1866	France	838632
Woessner, Matthias		28 Dec 1850	Roetenbach	Obd.	Apr 1869	N.-Amer	838636
Woessner, Matthias		26 Sep 1842	Roetenbach	Obd.	Aug 1854	N.-Amer	838636

Woessner, Matthias & F		Roetenberg	Obd.	Apr 1817	N.-Amer	838636
Woessner, Pauline Wilhelmine	5 Mar 1866	Bach-Altenberg	Obd.	Sep 1869	N.-Amer	838631
Woessner, Sophie	1 yr.	Fluorn	Obd.	Nov 1846	N.-Amer	838632
Woessner, Wilhelm	9 Apr 1817	Alpirsbach	Obd.	Dec 1858	France	838630
Woessner, Wilhelm Friedrich	9 Apr 1817	Alpirsbach	Obd.	Sep 1858	France	838630
Woessner, Wilhelmine (wife)	29 Sep 1844	Bach-Altenberg	Obd.	Sep 1869	N.-Amer	838631
Wohlbold, Dorothea	4 Oct 1834	Gaertringen	Herr.	Dec 1866	N.-Amer	834630
Wohlboldt, Maria Katharina	29 Sep 1841	Renningen	Leon.	Apr 1857	N.-Amer	837963
Wohlfahrt, Andreas	30 Nov 1837	Hohenstadt	Gsl.	Mar 1854	N.-Amer	572042
Wohlfahrt, Barbara	24 May 1824	Hohenstadt	Gsl.	Mar 1854	N.-Amer	572042
Wohlfahrt, Clemens	12 Jun 1842	Hohenstadt	Gsl.	Mar 1854	N.-Amer	572042
Wohlfahrt, Georg	17 Oct 1839	Hohenstadt	Gsl.	Mar 1854	N.-Amer	572042
Wohlfahrt, Joseph	25 Oct 1836	Hohenstadt	Gsl.	Mar 1854	N.-Amer	572042
Wohlfahrt, Karoline	20 Jan 1844	Hohenstadt	Gsl.	Mar 1854	N.-Amer	572042
Wohlfahrt, Marcharius (wid.) & F	2 Jan 1810	Hohenstadt	Gsl.	Mar 1854	N.-Amer	572042
Wohlfahrt, Wilhelmine	21 Mar 1851	Hohenstadt	Gsl.	Mar 1854	N.-Amer	572042
Wohlleber, Dorothea	18 yrs.	Merklingen	Leon.	Apr 1852	N.-Amer	837959
Wohlleber, Friedrich		Merklingen	Leon.	Apr 1852	N.-Amer	837959
Wohnus, Juliana (wid.)	1 Oct 1810	Pfullingen	Rtl.	Jan 1866	N.-Amer	841057
Wohnuss, Catharina		Pfullingen	Rtl.	Apr 1829	Switz.	841051
Wolber, Anastasia (wife)		Oberndorf	Obd.	bef 1842	Austria	838635
Wolber, Carl	29 Nov 1851	Schramberg	Obd.	Dec 1870	N.-Amer	838636
Wolber, Christiane Margarethe	26 Jun 1863	Alpirsbach	Obd.	Jan 1866	Prussia	838630
Wolber, Christine	31 May 1823	Alpirsbach	Obd.	Apr 1858	Switz.	838630
Wolber, Heinrich	17 yrs.	Sulgen	Obd.	Oct 1854	N.-Amer	838638
Wolber, Jacob		Oberndorf	Obd.	bef 1842	Austria	838635
Wolber, Johann		Oberndorf	Obd.	bef 1842	Austria	838635
Wolber, Johann Baptist & F		Oberndorf	Obd.	bef 1842	Austria	838635
Wolber, Karolina	17 Apr 1838	Sulgen	Obd.	Oct 1854	N.-Amer	838638
Wolber, Katharine Friederike	27 Jun 1839	Alpirsbach	Obd.	Jan.1869	France	838630
Wolber, Nikolaus	18 Nov 1813	Schramberg	Obd.	Nov 1857	France	838636
Wolber, Rosa	26 Aug 1835	Sulgen	Obd.	Oct 1854	N.-Amer	838638
Wolber, Wilhelm	30 May 1835	Hemmingen	Leon.	Aug 1858	S.-Amer	837956
Wolf, Andreas		Weil der Stadt	Leon.	Aug 1853	N.-Amer	837966
Wolf, Anton	20 yrs.	Weil der Stadt	Leon.	Oct 1853	N.-Amer	837966
Wolf, Carl		Hochdorf	Krch.	bef 1854	N.-Amer	835945
Wolf, Catharina Margaretha	17 yrs.	Eltingen	Leon.	bef 1817	Russia	835789
Wolf, David & W		Weil der Stadt	Leon.	Mar 1851	N.-Amer	837966
Wolf, Ernst	1 Apr 1864	Weil der Stadt	Leon.	Dec 1881	N.-Amer	837966
Wolf, Jakob Friedrich	1 Dec 1867	Friolzheim	Leon.	Apr 1884	N.-Amer	835791
Wolf, Joseph		Weil der Stadt	Leon.	Aug 1852	N.-Amer	837966
Wolf, Louis		Alpirsbach	Obd.	bef 1854	N.-Amer	838630
Wolf, Louise	36 yrs.	Alpirsbach	Obd.	bef 1852	N.-Amer	838630
Wolf, Lukas		Weil der Stadt	Leon.	bef 1867	N.-Amer	837966
Wolf, Walburga (wife)		Weil der Stadt	Leon.	Mar 1851	N.-Amer	837966
Wolf, Wilhelmine	16 May 1827	Hochdorf	Krch.	bef 1854	N.-Amer	835945
Wolfangel Johann Conrad	9 Aug 1824	Weil im Dorf	Loen.	bef 1857	Switz.	837967
Wolfangel, – (wife)	51 yrs.	Eltingen	Leon.	Jun 1853	N.-Amer	835789
Wolfangel, Barbara	14 Mar 1835	Eltingen	Leon.	Jun 1853	N.-Amer	835789
Wolfangel, Barbara (wife)	5 Jun 1828	Eltingen	Leon.	1866	N.-Amer	835789

Name		Birth		Emigration			Film
Last	First	Date	Place	O'amt	Appl. Date	Dest.	Number
Wolfangel, Catharina		2 Jul 1838	Eltingen	Leon.	Jun 1853	N.-Amer	835789
Wolfangel, Catharina (wife)			Eltingen	Leon.	May 1853	N.-Amer	835789
Wolfangel, Catharina Frieder.		60 yrs.	Heimerdingen	Leon.	Jan 1852	N.-Amer	837954
Wolfangel, Christian & F			Eltingen	Leon.	Apr 1830	N.-Amer	835789
Wolfangel, Christian Friedrich		19 Oct 1852	Eltingen	Leon.	1866	N.-Amer	835789
Wolfangel, Christina Barbara		2 Mar 1850	Muenchingen	Leon.	May 1852	N.-Amer	837961
Wolfangel, Elisabeth Barbara		17 yrs.	Heimerdingen	Leon.	bef 1818	N.-Amer	837954
Wolfangel, Friederike			Eltingen	Leon.	bef 1861	N.-Amer	837955
Wolfangel, Friederike		29 Jul 1831	Eltingen	Leon.	Nov 1861	N.-Amer	835789
Wolfangel, Friedrich		10 Dec 1840	Muenchingen	Leon.	May 1852	N.-Amer	837961
Wolfangel, Friedrich		1 yrs.	Eltingen	Leon.	Jun 1853	N.-Amer	835789
Wolfangel, Friedrich & F			Muenchingen	Leon.	May 1852	N.-Amer	837961
Wolfangel, Georg		24 Sep 1855	Eltingen	Leon.	1866	N.-Amer	835789
Wolfangel, Georg Jakob & F			Malmsheim	Leon.	Jan 1817	N.-Amer	837958
Wolfangel, Gottlieb		19 yrs.	Weil im Dorf	Loen.	Feb 1854	N.-Amer	837967
Wolfangel, Gottlieb		8 Aug 1849	Eltingen	Leon.	1866	N.-Amer	835789
Wolfangel, Gottlieb & F		7 Jul 1827	Eltingen	Leon.	1866	N.-Amer	835789
Wolfangel, Gottliebin		18 Nov 1832	Eltingen	Leon.	Jun 1853	N.-Amer	835789
Wolfangel, Jakob		6 Dec 1858	Eltingen	Leon.	1866	N.-Amer	835789
Wolfangel, Johann Andreas		17 Mar 1871	Nussdorf	Loen.	Jul 1887	N.-Amer	837967
Wolfangel, Johann Georg		21 Jan 1835	Weil im Dorf	Loen.	Aug 1853	N.-Amer	837967
Wolfangel, Johann Georg		14 Jul 1841	Eltingen	Leon.	Jun 1853	N.-Amer	835789
Wolfangel, Johann Georg & F		48 yrs.	Eltingen	Leon.	Jun 1853	N.-Amer	835789
Wolfangel, Johann Jacob		2 Sep 1831	Eltingen	Leon.	Jun 1853	N.-Amer	835789
Wolfangel, Johann Michael		23 Jan 1834	Malmsheim	Leon.	May 1852	N.-Amer	837958
Wolfangel, Johanna (wife)			Muenchingen	Leon.	May 1852	N.-Amer	837961
Wolfangel, Johannes			Muenchingen	Leon.	May 1853	N.-Amer	837961
Wolfangel, Johannes		12 Nov 1850	Eltingen	Leon.	1866	N.-Amer	835789
Wolfangel, Johannes & F			Eltingen	Leon.	May 1853	N.-Amer	835789
Wolfangel, Kardina Katharina		20 Mar 1862	Eltingen	Leon.	1866	N.-Amer	835789
Wolfangel, Karl		34 yrs.	Eltingen	Leon.	May 1853	N.-Amer	835789
Wolfangel, Margaretha & C		9 May 1826	Eltingen	Leon.	Jun 1853	N.-Amer	835789
Wolfangel, Maria Catharina		31 Jul 1803	Weil im Dorf	Loen.	bef 1869	Wien	837967
Wolfangel, Michael			Heimerdingen	Leon.	bef 1818	N.-Amer	837954
Wolfangel, Michael			Eltingen	Leon.	Oct 1854	N.-Amer	835789
Wolfnagel, Catharina Barbara			Muenchingen	Leon.	1855	N.-Amer	837961
Wolfnagel, Margaretha			Muenchingen	Leon.	1857	N.-Amer	837961
Wollpert, Jakob		30 Sep 1846	Wannweil	Rtl.	Nov 1866	N.-Amer	841058
Wollpert, Martin		7 Jan 1842	Wannweil	Rtl.	Jun 1862	N.-Amer	841058
Wolpert, August		17 Feb 1845	Alpirsbach	Obd.	Nov 1868	Prussia	838630
Wolpert, Johann Georg			Wannweil	Rtl.	Apr 1833	N.-Amer	841051
Wolpert, Martin		29 Sep 1853	Wannweil	Rtl.	Mar 1869	N.-Amer	841058
Wolpp, Jakob			Brucken	Krch.	bef 1868	N.-Amer	835940
Wossner, Elisabetha		5 Jan 1837	Alpirsbach	Obd.	Aug 1867	France	838630
Wuercker, Christian		5 Mar 1829	Alpirsbach	Obd.	bef 1853	N.-Amer	838630
Wuertele, Heinrich		29 Jul 1870	Schoeckingen	Leon.	Apr 1881	N.-Amer	837964
Wuertele, Heinrich & F		6 Jan 1849	Schoeckingen	Leon.	Apr 1881	N.-Amer	837964
Wuertele, Pauline		23 May 1872	Schoeckingen	Leon.	Apr 1881	N.-Amer	837964
Wuertele, Wilhelmine C. (wife)		21 Aug 1842	Schoeckingen	Leon.	Apr 1881	N.-Amer	837964
Wuest, Johann Georg		22 Jun 1834	Ditzingen	Leon.	Aug 1854	N.-Amer	835788

Wuest, Johann Gottlieb	7 May 1842	Jesingen	Krch.	May 1857	N.-Amer	835946
Wuest, Johannes	18 May 1844	Kirchheim	Krch.	Dec 1864	N.-Amer	835941
Wuest, Maria Luise Pauline	3 Jun 1842	Jesingen	Krch.	Jun 1865	Russia	835946
Wulle, Max Gustav	7 Feb 1875	Kirchheim	Krch.	May 1891	N.-Amer	548323
Wunderlich, Friederike	13 May 1843	Alpirsbach	Obd.	Nov 1866	France	838630
Wurst, Gottlob Heinrich	14 Aug 1838	Heimsheim	Leon.	Jan 1852	N.-Amer	837955
Wurst, Jakob	2 yrs.	Heimsheim	Leon.	Aug 1853	N.-Amer	837955
Wurst, Johann Georg	23 Feb 1841	Betzingen	Rtl.	Jun 1860	N.-Amer	841058
Wurst, Karl Christoph	21 Jan 1829	Heimsheim	Leon.	Jan 1852	N.-Amer	837955
Wurst, Regine Sophie & C	30 yrs.	Heimsheim	Leon.	Aug 1853	N.-Amer	837955
Wurst, Wilhelm	24 Oct 1864	Unterhausen	Rtl.	Nov 1867	N.-Amer	841055
Wurst, Wilhelmina Margaretha	19 Feb 1822	Heimsheim	Leon.	Jan 1852	N.-Amer	837955
Wurster, C. F.		Berneck	Nag.	Aug 1852	N.-Amer	838488
Wurster, Carl		Wenden	Nag.	Apr 1853	N.-Amer	838488
Zahn, Ehrhardt	7 Jan 1864	Wiesensteig	Gsl.	Jan 1881	N.-Amer	572048
Zahn, Erhard	7 Jan 1864	Wiesensteig	Gsl.	Jun 1881	N.-Amer	572048
Zahn, Franz Josef	13 Mar 1854	Wiesensteig	Gsl.	Jan 1881	N.-Amer	572048
Zaininger, Christiana	2 May 1840	Gutenberg	Krch.	Feb 1868	N.-Amer	835945
Zaininger, Johann Georg	11 Jan 1866	Gutenberg	Krch.	Apr 1882	N.-Amer	835945
Zaininger, Jophann Georg	11 Jan 1866	Gutenberg	Krch.	Apr 1882	N.-Amer	548403
Zanger, Johann Martin	4 Feb 1821	Unterhausen	Rtl.	Sep 1867	N.-Amer	841058
Zanger, Josef	17 Mar 1851	Aichhalden	Obd.	Apr 1865	N.-Amer	838629
Zanger, Maria	18 yrs.	Schramberg	Obd.	Mar 1848	N.-Amer	838637
Zanger, Matthaeus	15 Mar 1824	Unterhausen	Rtl.	Sep 1865	N.-Amer	841058
Zanger, Wendelin	30 Oct 1847	Aichhalden	Obd.	Apr 1865	N.-Amer	838629
Zanker, Gottlob	11 Jul 1838	Weilheim	Krch.	Sep 1857	N.-Amer	835949
Zanker, Katharina	8 Mar 1838	Zell	Krch.	Jun 1864	N.-Amer	835774
Zebele, Anastasia	24 Dec 1821	Epfendorf	Obd.	May 1847	N.-Amer	838632
Zebele, Anselm	16 Apr 1819	Epfendorf	Obd.	May 1847	N.-Amer	838632
Zebele, Eduard & F	13 Oct 1778	Epfendorf	Obd.	May 1847	N.-Amer	838632
Zebele, Kolumbus	14 Nov 1809	Epfendorf	Obd.	May 1847	N.-Amer	838632
Zebele, Priska (wife)	29 Jan 1784	Epfendorf	Obd.	May 1847	N.-Amer	838632
Zeeb, Albert	26 Jun 1860	Wannweil	Rtl.	Apr 1861	N.-Amer	841058
Zeeb, Anna Maria (wife)	22 Mar 1841	Gomaringen	Rtl.	Dec 1866	N.-Amer	841058
Zeeb, Barbara	7 Apr 1848	Wannweil	Rtl.	Apr 1861	N.-Amer	841058
Zeeb, Catharina	8 Feb 1866	Gomaringen	Rtl.	Dec 1866	N.-Amer	841058
Zeeb, Christina	16 May 1852	Wannweil	Rtl.	Apr 1861	N.-Amer	841058
Zeeb, Elisabetha (wife)	24 Apr 1815	Wannweil	Rtl.	Apr 1861	N.-Amer	841058
Zeeb, Gottlieb Friedrich	22 Dec 1855	Wannweil	Rtl.	Apr 1861	N.-Amer	841058
Zeeb, Jacob	33 yrs.	Hirschlanden	Leon.	Feb 1853	Austria	837956
Zeeb, Jakob	29 Aug 1846	Wannweil	Rtl.	Apr 1861	N.-Amer	841058
Zeeb, Johann Georg	16 Oct 1835	Wannweil	Rtl.	bef 1861	N.-Amer	841058
Zeeb, Johann Martin & F	9 May 1838	Gomaringen	Rtl.	Dec 1866	N.-Amer	841058
Zeeb, Maria	8 Jun 1854	Wannweil	Rtl.	Apr 1861	N.-Amer	841058
Zeeb, Michael & F		Gomaringen	Rtl.	May 1832	N.-Amer	841051
Zeeb, Paul Wilhelm	2 Apr 1875	Ladenburg	Herr.	Sep 1891	N.-Amer	834629
Zeeb, Veit	5 Aug 1844	Wannweil	Rtl.	Apr 1861	N.-Amer	841058
Zeeb, Veit & F	4 Apr 1808	Wannweil	Rtl.	Apr 1861	N.-Amer	841058
Zeeb, Wilhelm	8 Jan 1837	Wannweil	Rtl.	bef 1861	N.-Amer	841058
Zeh, Carl Wilhelm	29 Mar 1837	Kirchheim	Krch.	Jul 1857	N.-Amer	835940

Name		Birth		Emigration			Film
Last	First	Date	Place	O'amt	Appl. Date	Dest.	Number
Zehender, Daniel		16 Jun 1823	Schramberg	Obd.	Dec 1845	Bavaria	837637
Zehnder, Anna Margar. (wife)		22 Dec 1846	Bissingen	Krch.	Apr 1881	N.-Amer	548403
Zehnder, Jacob		19 Sep 1867	Weilheim	Krch.	Apr 1881	N.-Amer	548403
Zehnder, Josef		28 Feb 1846	Aichhalden	Obd.	Apr 1869	N.-Amer	838629
Zehnder, Kaspar		5 Jan 1839	Mariazell	Obd.	Mar 1859	France	838634
Zehnder, Michael & F		16 Aug 1839	Weilheim	Krch.	Apr 1881	N.-Amer	548403
Zeile, Adolph Robert		17 Oct 1840	Weil der Stadt	Leon.	Sep 1858	N.-Amer	837966
Zeile, Carl			Weil der Stadt	Leon.	Jul 1854	N.-Amer	837966
Zeile, Georg David		11 Nov 1829	Reutlingen	Rtl.	Mar 1860	N.-Amer	841058
Zeile, Lorenz Friedrich		17 Sep 1833	Reutlingen	Rtl.	bef 1861	N.-Amer	841058
Zeitler, Karl		10 May 1863	Geislingen	Gsl.	Apr 1880	N.-Amer	572048
Zeller, Anna		7 yrs.	Bach-Altenberg	Obd.	Oct 1855	N.-Amer	838631
Zeller, Bernhard		10 Dec 1841	Weissenstein	Gsl.	Mar 1873	Austria	572047
Zeller, Christian		8 yrs.	Bach-Altenberg	Obd.	Oct 1855	N.-Amer	838631
Zeller, Christine & F		35 yrs.	Bach-Altenberg	Obd.	Oct 1855	N.-Amer	838631
Zeller, Franz Xaver			Weissenstein	Gsl.	bef 1867	Austria	572046
Zeller, Johann Georg			Bach-Altenberg	Obd.	1852	N.-Amer	838631
Zeller, Johannes		19 Jun 1846	Betzweiler	Obd.	Mar 1864	N.-Amer	838631
Zeller, Johannes		46 yrs.	Fluorn	Obd.	1864	N.-Amer	838632
Zeller, Johannes		11 May 1844	Weissenstein	Gsl.	Aug 1872	Austria	572047
Zeller, Maria Theresia		28 yrs.	Wiesensteig	Gsl.	Jul 1866	Switz.	572045
Zeller, Marianna		28 Nov 1832	Boehmenkirchen	Gsl.	May 1856	N.-Amer	572043
Zeller, Mathias		9 yrs.	Bach-Altenberg	Obd.	Oct 1855	N.-Amer	838631
Zenneck, Adolf Christian		5 Jun 1849	Reutlingen	Rtl.	Jul 1869	N.-Amer	841058
Zepf, Marie Frieder. Therese		14 Dec 1840	Reutlingen	Rtl.	Nov 1852	Switz.	841058
Zerrweik, Karl Friedrich		25 Jun 1871	Esslingen	Krch.	Mar 1888	N.-Amer	835942
Zerweck, Christ. David Carl		26 Jul 1848	Herrenberg	Herr.	Nov 1868	N.-Amer	834629
Ziedel, Christiane Regine			Reutlingen	Rtl.	Sep 1835	N.-Amer	841051
Ziegler, Aloisia & F			Oberndorf	Obd.	Sep 1854	N.-Amer	838635
Ziegler, Anna Emilie		18 Oct 1879	Dettingen	Krch.	Jul 1882	N.-Amer	835944
Ziegler, Barbara		4 Mar 1849	Kuchen	Gsl.	Feb 1854	N.-Amer	572042
Ziegler, Carl		5 Feb 1835	Kuchen	Gsl.	Feb 1854	N.-Amer	572042
Ziegler, Caroline		15 May 1834	Schoeckingen	Leon.	Jan 1852	N.-Amer	837964
Ziegler, Caroline		30 Jun 1835	Malmsheim	Leon.	Aug 1854	N.-Amer	837958
Ziegler, Catharina			Malmsheim	Leon.	May 1853	N.-Amer	837958
Ziegler, Catharina (wife)			Leonberg	Leon.	Sep 1854	N.-Amer	835786
Ziegler, Christian		16 yrs.	Leonberg	Leon.	Sep 1854	N.-Amer	835786
Ziegler, Christian & F			Leonberg	Leon.	Sep 1854	N.-Amer	835786
Ziegler, Daniel David		16 Jan 1861	Ennahofen	Krch.	1886	N.-Amer	835943
Ziegler, Emma Bertha		1 Jan 1878	Dettingen	Krch.	Jul 1882	N.-Amer	835944
Ziegler, Ernst Gottlieb		1 Apr 1871	Leonberg	Leon.	Mar 1888	N.-Amer	835787
Ziegler, Eva & C		11 Jun 1827	Kuchen	Gsl.	Feb 1854	N.-Amer	572042
Ziegler, Friederike Pauline			Leonberg	Leon.	Oct 1853	Worms	835786
Ziegler, Friedrich		12 yrs.	Leonberg	Leon.	Sep 1854	N.-Amer	835786
Ziegler, Georg		7 Feb 1838	Kuchen	Gsl.	Feb 1854	N.-Amer	572042
Ziegler, Georg & F		6 Nov 1802	Kuchen	Gsl.	Feb 1854	N.-Amer	572042
Ziegler, Georg Michael		17 Nov 1815	Renningen	Leon.	bef 1846	N.-Amer	837963
Ziegler, Gottlieb			Friolzheim	Leon.	bef 1850	N.-Amer	835791
Ziegler, Gottlob		9 yrs.	Leonberg	Leon.	Sep 1854	N.-Amer	835786
Ziegler, Gottlob & W		29 Sep 1824	Eltingen	Leon.	Jan 1862	N.-Amer	835789

Ziegler, Gottlob Michael	26 Jun 1850	Sulpach	Krch.	Sep 1865	N.-Amer 835949
Ziegler, Jakob	42 yrs.	Gingen	Gsl.	Dec 1853	N.-Amer 572042
Ziegler, Jakob	2 Jul 1839	Renningen	Leon.	Feb 1857	N.-Amer 837963
Ziegler, Johann Georg	10 Apr 1851	Eltingen	Leon.	Apr 1870	N.-Amer 835789
Ziegler, Johann Konrad Diet.	31 Aug 1866	Ochsenwang	Krch.	May 1888	N.-Amer 835947
Ziegler, Johannes		Kuchen	Gsl.	Feb 1853	N.-Amer 572041
Ziegler, Johannes	1 Jul 1840	Bissingen	Krch.	Feb 1870	N.-Amer 835943
Ziegler, Johannes & F	25 Nov 1842	Dettingen	Krch.	Jul 1882	N.-Amer 548403
Ziegler, Josef		Oberndorf	Obd.	bef 1854	N.-Amer 838635
Ziegler, Josef		Eltingen	Leon.	Dec 1851	N.-Amer 835789
Ziegler, Josephine		Oberndorf	Obd.	Sep 1854	N.-Amer 838635
Ziegler, Julie	9 Apr 1873	Dettingen	Krch.	Jul 1882	N.-Amer 835944
Ziegler, Karl Friedrich	24 Jun 1868	Dettingen	Krch.	Jul 1882	N.-Amer 835944
Ziegler, Louise		Oberndorf	Obd.	Sep 1854	N.-Amer 838635
Ziegler, Magdalena	20 yrs.	Friolzheim	Leon.	May 1852	N.-Amer 835791
Ziegler, Margaretha	25 Jun 1850	Kuchen	Gsl.	Feb 1854	N.-Amer 572042
Ziegler, Margaretha (wife)	30 Jan 1806	Kuchen	Gsl.	Feb 1854	N.-Amer 572042
Ziegler, Maria Barbara	6 Nov 1865	Dettingen	Krch.	Jul 1882	N.-Amer 835944
Ziegler, Maria Barbara (wife)	2 Mar 1843	Dettingen	Krch.	Jul 1882	N.-Amer 835944
Ziegler, Peter	21 Feb 1834	Kuchen	Gsl.	May 1872	N.-Amer 572047
Ziegler, Regine (wife)	28 Nov 1822	Eltingen	Leon.	Jan 1862	N.-Amer 835789
Ziegler, Reinhold Ewald Wilh.	2 Oct 1856	Leonberg	Leon.	Sep 1873	N.-Amer 835787
Ziegler, Severin	21 yrs.	Oberndorf	Obd.	Nov 1852	N.-Amer 838635
Ziegler, Stephan		Oberndorf	Obd.	1854	N.-Amer 838635
Ziegler, Theresia		Oberndorf	Obd.	Sep 1854	N.-Amer 838635
Ziller, Joseph	15 Feb 1865	Weissenstein	Gsl.	May 1883	N.-Amer 572049
Zimmer, Thomas	19 yrs.	Oberhausen	Rtl.	Feb 1880	N.-Amer 841051
Zimmerer, Johannes	29 Jan 1846	Unterhausen	Rtl.	Apr 1864	N.-Amer 841058
Zimmermann, Andreas	7 yrs.	Westerheim	Gsl.	May 1853	N.-Amer 572041
Zimmermann, Christof Gottlieb	6 Apr 1838	Gerlingen	Leon.	Aug 1856	Africa 837953
Zimmermann, Elisabetha	2 yrs.	Westerheim	Gsl.	May 1853	N.-Amer 572041
Zimmermann, Friederike		Nabern	Krch.	1853	N.-Amer 835940
Zimmermann, Georg	25 May 1833	Grosssuessen	Gsl.	Aug 1853	N.-Amer 572041
Zimmermann, Jakob		Pfullingen	Rtl.	May 1832	N.-Amer 841051
Zimmermann, Johann Gottlieb	29 Aug 1830	Gerlingen	Leon.	1854	N.-Amer 837953
Zimmermann, Johann Jacob	5 Dec 1846	Gerlingen	Leon.	Jul 1863	N.-Amer 837953
Zimmermann, Johann Ludwig	17 Aug 1837	Weilheim	Krch.	bef 1853	N.-Amer 835949
Zimmermann, Johannes	23 Jan 1850	Treffelhausen	Gsl.	Jun 1869	N.-Amer 572047
Zimmermann, Johannes	22 Feb 1845	Jesingen	Krch.	Jul 1866	N.-Amer 835946
Zimmermann, Johannes & F		Westerheim	Gsl.	May 1853	N.-Amer 572041
Zimmermann, Louise Regine	15 Oct 1837	Gerlingen	Leon.	Sep 1862	Bavaria 837953
Zimmermann, Marie Barb. (wid.)	7 Oct 1818	Kirchheim	Krch.	bef 1883	N.-Amer 548403
Zimmermann, Max		Wiesensteig	Gsl.	bef 1865	N.-Amer 572045
Zimmermann, Rosina (wife)		Westerheim	Gsl.	May 1853	N.-Amer 572041
Zimmermann, Simon	9 mon.	Westerheim	Gsl.	May 1853	N.-Amer 572041
Zimmermann, Wilhelm Friedrich	3 Oct 1822	Ditzingen	Leon.	bef 1859	N.-Amer 835788
Zimmermannn, Johannes	5 Sep 1834	Grosssuessen	Gsl.	Feb 1854	N.-Amer 572042
Zink, Johannes & F		Eltingen	Leon.	Apr 1830	N.-Amer 835789
Zinser, Ernst Johannes	11 Jul 1893	Herrenberg	Herr.	Jul 1896	N.-Amer 834629
Zinser, Karl	4 Nov 1844	Herrenberg	Herr.	Jul 1896	N.-Amer 834629

Name		Birth		Emigration			Film
Last	First	Date	Place	O'amt	Appl. Date	Dest.	Number
Zinser, Karl Gottlob		28 Jul 1888	Herrenberg	Herr.	Jul 1896	N.-Amer	834629
Zinser, Maria Barbara (wife)		23 Dec 1858	Bondorf	Herr.	Jul 1896	N.-Amer	834629
Zinzer, Johann Georg		27 Nov 1863	Gaertringen	Herr.	Apr 1882	N.-Amer	834630
Zinzer, Johann Heinrich		29 Apr 1891	Gaertringen	Herr.	Oct 1907	N.-Amer	834630
Zipperer, Georg		27 Jan 1812	Hemmingen	Leon.	Mar 1831	N.-Amer	837956
Zipperle, Gabriel		17 Feb 1846	Malmsheim	Leon.	1867	N.-Amer	837958
Zipperle, Johann Jakob		6 Feb 1842	Malmsheim	Leon.	1867	N.-Amer	837958
Zipperle, Johann Michael & F			Malmsheim	Leon.	Jan 1817	N.-Amer	837958
Zipperle, Wilhelm Gottfried		4 Mar 1866	Malmsheim	Leon.	Apr 1882	N.-Amer	837958
Zirn, Jacobine Friederike		20 Aug 1829	Kirchheim	Krch.	Jan 1860	Antwerp	835940
Zirn, Maria Anna		8 Nov 1829	Oberndorf	Obd.	May 1867	France	838635
Zonder, Adolf		10 Dec 1844	Hochdorf	Krch.	Jul 1864	N.-Amer	835945
Zonder, Ernst		4 Sep 1843	Hochdorf	Krch.	Dec 1865	N.-Amer	835945
Zonder, Maria Pauline			Kirchheim	Krch.	Apr 1886	Switz.	835945
Zonder, Paul Hermann		2 Jul 1872	Kirchheim	Krch.	Apr 1886	Switz.	835945
Zuber, Aegidius		19 Aug 1837	Epfendorf	Obd.	May 1847	N.-Amer	838632
Zuber, Anna Maria		21 Sep 1804	Epfendorf	Obd.	Aug 1817	N.-Amer	838629
Zuber, Anna Maria			Epfendorf	Obd.	Mar 1841	France	838632
Zuber, Balbina		25 Mar 1841	Epfendorf	Obd.	May 1847	N.-Amer	838632
Zuber, Balthasar		4 Jan 1836	Epfendorf	Obd.	May 1847	N.-Amer	838632
Zuber, Bernhard		5 Nov 1839	Epfendorf	Obd.	May 1847	N.-Amer	838632
Zuber, Christian		10 Nov 1809	Epfendorf	Obd.	Aug 1817	N.-Amer	838629
Zuber, Christian		18 Dec 1835	Epfendorf	Obd.	May 1847	N.-Amer	838632
Zuber, Christian (wid.) & F		10 Nov 1809	Epfendorf	Obd.	May 1847	N.-Amer	838632
Zuber, Crescenzia		6 Jun 1802	Epfendorf	Obd.	Aug 1817	N.-Amer	838629
Zuber, Dorothea		6 Feb 1834	Epfendorf	Obd.	May 1847	N.-Amer	838632
Zuber, Edeltraud		23 Jun 1827	Epfendorf	Obd.	May 1847	N.-Amer	838632
Zuber, Eduard		17 Apr 1840	Epfendorf	Obd.	May 1847	N.-Amer	838632
Zuber, Josepha		25 Jun 1812	Epfendorf	Obd.	Aug 1817	N.-Amer	838629
Zuber, Konrad		24 Nov 1844	Epfendorf	Obd.	May 1847	N.-Amer	838632
Zuber, Kreszentia & C		6 Jun 1802	Epfendorf	Obd.	May 1847	N.-Amer	838632
Zuber, Rudolph		15 Apr 1829	Epfendorf	Obd.	May 1847	N.-Amer	838632
Zuber, Stephan & F			Epfendorf	Obd.	Aug 1817	N.-Amer	838629
Zuber, Theresia & C		4 Sep 1815	Epfendorf	Obd.	May 1847	N.-Amer	838632
Zuber, Theresia (wife)			Epfendorf	Obd.	Aug 1817	N.-Amer	838629
Zuschnitt, Barbara		23 Sep 1829	Ditzingen	Leon.	Apr 1862	N.-Amer	835788
Zuschnitt, Caroline			Ditzingen	Leon.	1858	N.-Amer	835788
Zuschnitt, Christof		30 Jan 1834	Ditzingen	Leon.	bef 1859	N.-Amer	835788
Zuschnitt, Friederike		15 yrs.	Ditzingen	Leon.	Sep 1864	N.-Amer	835788
Zuschnitt, Friederike		37 yrs.	Ditzingen	Leon.	1858	N.-Amer	835788
Zuschnitt, Friedrich		17 Dec 1840	Ditzingen	Leon.	Sep 1859	N.-Amer	835788
Zuschnitt, Gottlieb & F			Ditzingen	Leon.	Jul 1853	N.-Amer	835788
Zuschnitt, Gottlob		9 yrs.	Ditzingen	Leon.	Sep 1864	N.-Amer	835788
Zuschnitt, Jakob		8 yrs.	Ditzingen	Leon.	Sep 1864	N.-Amer	835788
Zuschnitt, Jakob			Ditzingen	Leon.	1858	N.-Amer	835788
Zuschnitt, Johann Georg		27 Feb 1831	Ditzingen	Leon.	Sep 1859	N.-Amer	835788
Zuschnitt, Johannes		8 Jul 1845	Ditzingen	Leon.	Jul 1862	N.-Amer	835788
Zuschnitt, Johannes		13 Nov 1839	Ditzingen	Leon.	Jun 1860	N.-Amer	835788
Zuschnitt, Johannes (wid.) & F			Ditzingen	Leon.	Sep 1864	N.-Amer	835788
Zuschnitt, Karl Gottfried		17 Jul 1841	Ditzingen	Leon.	Jun 1862	N.-Amer	835788